CADOGAN GUIDES

"Cadogan Guides really need no introduction and are mini-encyclopaedic on the countries covered ... they give the explorer, the intellectual or cultural buff – indeed any visitor – all they need to know to get the very best from their visit ... it makes a good read too by the many inveterate armchair travellers."

—*The Book Journal*

"Rochelle Jaffe, owner and manager of Travel Books Unlimited in Bethesda, Maryland, attributes [Cadogan Guides'] popularity to both their good, clean-looking format and the fact that they include 'information about everything for everyone' .... These guides are one of the most exciting series available on European travel."

—*American Bookseller* magazine

"The Cadogan Guide to Italy is the most massive, literate, and helpful guide to Italy in years."

—*International Travel News*, USA

"*Italy*, by Dana Facaros and Michael Pauls is an absolute gem of a travel book, humorous, informed, sympathetic, as irresistible as that land itself."

—Anthony Clare, Books of the Year, *The Sunday Times*, 1988–89

Other titles in the Cadogan Guide series:

AUSTRALIA
BALI
THE CARIBBEAN
GREEK ISLANDS
INDIA
IRELAND
ITALIAN ISLANDS
ITALY
NORTHEAST ITALY
NORTHWEST ITALY
MOROCCO
PORTUGAL
ROME
SCOTLAND
SPAIN

THAILAND & BURMA
TURKEY
TUSCANY & UMBRIA

Forthcoming:

ECUADOR,
   THE GALAPAGOS
   & COLOMBIA
MEXICO
NEW YORK
NEW ORLEANS
TUNISIA
VENICE

ABOUT THE AUTHORS

From their base in a tiny Umbrian village, travel writers DANA FACAROS and MICHAEL PAULS have researched and written a string of *Cadogan Guides* to Italy: a big fat tome on the whole country, *Italy*; regional guides to *Northwest Italy*, *Northeast Italy*, *South Italy* and *Tuscany and Umbria*; a city guide to *Rome*; and an update to their successful guide to the *Italian Islands*.

They have also written a highly acclaimed series for *The Observer* magazine on 'Hidden Italy'.

They have finally torn themselves and their two children away from the pasta and have moved on to foie gras and a tiny French village in the Lot.

Dear Readers,

Please, please help us to keep this book up to date. We would be delighted to receive any additional information or suggestions. Please write to us or fill in the form on the last page of this book. Writers of the best letters will be acknowledged in future editions, and will receive a free copy of the Cadogan Guide of their choice.

The Publisher

CADOGAN GUIDES

SOUTH ITALY

DANA FACAROS and MICHAEL PAULS

Illustrations by Pauline Pears

CADOGAN BOOKS
London

THE GLOBE PEQUOT PRESS
Chester, Connecticut

Cadogan Books Ltd
16 Lower Marsh, London SE1

The Globe Pequot Press
138 West Main Street, Chester, Connecticut 06412

Cover design by Keith Pointing
Cover illustration by Povl Webb
Maps © Cadogan Books Ltd,
drawn by Thames Cartographic Services Ltd

Series Editors: Rachel Fielding and Paula Levey

First published in 1990

British Library Cataloguing in Publication Data
Facaros, Dana
South Italy: Rome & Lazio, Abruzzo, Molise, Campania,
Apulia, Basilicata & Calabria. (Cadogan guides).
1. Italy: Southern Italy – Visitors' guides.
I. Title   II. Pauls, Michael
914.5704929
ISBN 0–947754–14–8

Library of Congress Cataloging-in-Publication Data
Facaros, Dana
South Italy / Dana Facaros and Michael Pauls.
p.   cm.   – (Cadogan guides)
ISBN 0–87106–350–6
1. Italy, Southern – Description and travel – 1981 – Guide-books.
2. Rome (Italy) – Description – 1975 – Guide-books.
I. Pauls, Michael. II. Title. III. Series.
DG416.F35   1990   914.5'704928–dc20   90–3309 CIP

Photoset in Ehrhardt on a Linotron 202
Printed and bound in Great Britain by Redwood Press Limited,
Melksham, Wiltshire

CONTENTS

CONTENTS

Part VIII: Apulia *Pages 313–55*

Architectural, Artistic and Historical Terms *Pages 356–8*

Chronology *Pages 359–64*

Language *Pages 365–77*

Further Reading *Pages 378–9*

General Index *Pages 380–94*

Index of Artists and Craftsmen *Pages 394–6*

LIST OF MAPS

ACKNOWLEDGEMENTS

We would particularly like to thank Michael Davidson and Brian Walsh, whose unfailing good humour helped us through the darkest corners of Italy, and who have contributed substantially to this book by updating all the practical information. We would like to thank the Italian National Tourist Office, and all the local and municipal tourist boards who so kindly answered all our questions that had answers and loaded us down with enough information to write several more volumes about Italy. Special thanks go to Paola Greco, in London, and the Terni tourist office for their kind help to Michael and Brian. Also we would like to extend our warmest gratitude to Mario, Fiorella, Alessandra and Sara who never minded having a couple of extra children in their happy home; to Anna and Tito Illuminati, who guided us through the intricacies of life in Rosciano and always let us use their phone; to Bruce Johnston, for his innumerable suggestions and his Deux Chevaux; to longtime residents Clare Pedrick, Anne, and Santino, for their invaluable insights into the Italian miasma; to Carolyn Steiner and Chris Malumphy, who crossed the Atlantic to cheer us up; and especially to Rachel Fielding, who like Hercules in the Augean stables, makes us printable.

The publishers would particularly like to thank Dorothy Groves and Stephen and Meg Davies for respectively copy-editing, proof-reading and indexing.

PLEASE NOTE

INTRODUCTION

The *Mezzogiorno*, the Noonday. The Italian south is one of the extremities of Europe, poised in a calm sea between the Balkans and the Sahara. And extremities are what this book is all about. On one hand the south is the true home of many Italian stereotypes—pizza, piety and emigration; on the other, its history is so crowded with Greeks, Lombards, Byzantines, Saracens, Normans, Spaniards and such that there hardly seems any room for the Italians. The Spaniards must have felt most at home. Like Spain much of the south is a land of harshness and clarity—merciless sun and strong castles, false starts, ruined cities and bare eroded mountains. Unlike the rest of Italy, it has shown little interest in embellishing itself with polished country landscapes and serene art towns. Its attractions are equally compelling, but they always carry a touch of the exotic: the palm trees and whitewashed villages on the long Apulian shore, mirages and bergamots on the Straits of Messina, bears and wolves, Greek temples, Albanian villages, crusader ports.

Some of the Mezzogiorno lies under the volcano, the rest is regularly smashed to bits in invasions and epic earthquakes. Nothing is permanent, and an outrageous nature obliges the ancient sun-bleached towns to play a grim round of Russian roulette across the centuries. Southerners live on the edge. They like hot peppers and strong wine; they collect in crowds on streetcorners, and sometimes they start revolts. Unlike their northern cousins, they can't paint, but they are good at flashy architecture, sculpture and music. They have given Italy most of her philosophers since the days when the Pythagoreans ruled at Croton. Where history is such a forceful teacher, people understandably become philosophical.

Guide to the Guide

We have included Rome and its region of Lazio in this book, perhaps a controversial point—Africa begins at Rome, say the Milanese, but the Romans say it begins at Naples, and so on down the coast. But Rome has more in common with the south; it has usually been the strongest force pulling on the Mezzogiorno, and the source of many of its problems. The book begins with Rome, followed by its region of Lazio, extending along the coast and into the Apennines. From there we have organized it in what we hope is the most logical manner, down the Tyrrhenian coast through Campania (Naples and its bay and hinterlands), then around the toe of Calabria and along the shore of the Ionian sea. After that we take you down the opposite coast, along the Adriatic, through the regions of Abruzzo, Molise and Apulia.

Despite being right at the centre of things the attractions of **Lazio** (ancient Latium) are not well known. Northern Lazio, an area of large lakes and hills, was the homeland of the ancient Etruscans, containing fascinating archaeological sites such as those at Tarquinia and Cervéteri. There is a lot to see in towns like Viterbo and Anagni, two

ix

places that contributed much to the history of the popes in the Middle Ages, important Renaissance villas and gardens (as at Caprarola, Tivoli and Bomarzo), major Roman ruins at Ostia Antica and Tivoli—not to mention Rome itself—and a pretty stretch of coast between Cape Circeo and Formia.

The regions of Italy's deep south often seem an entirely different country from the green and tidy north. Not many visitors ever make it further south than **Campania**, where Naples and its famous bay make up the south's prime attraction—including Pompeii, Vesuvius, Capri, Sorrento, the infernal volcanic Phlegraean fields, dozens of Roman ruins and much more. The wonderful Amalfi Drive between Sorrento and Salerno covers the most spectacular bit of coastline in Italy, passing the heavenly towns of Positano, Amalfi and Ravello. Naples itself, famous for pizza and animated *Italianità*, is also the south's art capital, with many surprises from the Middle Ages and Baroque. The rest of Campania includes venerable and interesting towns like Benevento, with its Egyptian idols and the magnificent Arch of Trajan, Salerno, Caserta, and Capua, the well-preserved Greek temples at Paestum, and the pleasant, unspoiled Cilento coast.

Lovers of fine Italian art and cuisine will not find them in **Calabria** and the **Basilicata**, once the most backward corners of the nation and now struggling gamely to catch up. The west coast from Maratea to Règgio Calabria, the 'Calabrian Riviera', offers some clean beaches and beautiful scenery (especially around Maratea and Cape Vaticano) and the heavily forested mountain plateau west of Cosenza called the Sila attracts hikers and nature-lovers. Of the once-mighty Greek cities of the Ionian coast, there's little left but the great museum at Règgio and some scanty ruins at Metaponto. The bare, eroded hills of the inland Basilicata are not particularly inviting, unless you want to see the famous *sassi* (cave-dwellers' quarters) of Matera.

East of Lazio lie two less familiar regions, **Abruzzo** and **Molise**. Abruzzo, containing the loftiest peaks in the Apennines, is Rome's mountain playground, with winter sports at the Gran Sasso and summertime exploring in the National Park of the Abruzzo, the home of the Abruzzo bear and other fauna. The coast is fairly nondescript, lined with family resorts; inland there's the interesting capital of L'Aquila and a fascinating collection of unspoiled medieval villages and churches. With the highest villages in the Apennines, Molise is a small mountain-bound region tucked in south of Abruzzo, utterly obscure, quiet, and for a number of reasons well beyond the pale of tourism.

Apulia for many will be the real find in the south. The flat *tavoliere*, covered with fields of corn, covers most of the region, but the rugged limestone Gargano Peninsula offers scenery unique in Italy, along with growing but still enjoyable resorts like Vieste. Apulia was doing quite well in the Middle Ages, as can be seen in the fine Apulian Romanesque cathedrals in so many towns on the *tavoliere*, including that of Bari, the south's prosperous second city and the second burial place of Santa Claus. This plain also grows some of Italy's most robust wines; on it Hannibal whipped the Roman legions and Emperor Frederick II built his mysterious Castel del Monte. Tàranto, founded by the ancient Greeks, has a museum full of Greek vases, great seafood and a wonderful maritime atmosphere. You won't see anything in Italy like the *trulli*, the whitewashed houses with conical stone roofs that turn the areas around Alberobello into a fairytale landscape; if you press on further south into Italy's 'heel', the Salentine Peninsula, you can visit Baroque Lecce, the south's most beautiful city.

Best of the South

Abbeys and Convents: Montecassino; **Subiaco**; **Farfa**; **Fossanova**; S. Martino, Naples; Certosa di San Lorenzo, **Padula**.

Amphitheatres and Theatres: besides **Rome's** Colosseum and Theatre of Marcellus, there are well-preserved theatres at Ferento, near **Viterbo**; tufa amphitheatre, **Sutri**; **Cassino**; **Ostia Antica**; **Pompeii**; **Pozzuoli** and **Benevento**; **Capua**, famous for its gladiator school, has an enormous amphitheatre.

Aqueducts: These stretch out like tentacles from **Rome**; and in the city are best seen around Piazza Maggiore—a pope-a-duct links St Peter's to Castel Sant'Angelo. **Sulmona** has a Gothic aqueduct. The biggest one ever built is the modern Apulian Aqueduct, fertilizing much of the Fóggia *tavoliere*.

Beaches: Chiaia di Luna, **Ponza**; **Sperlonga**; **San Felice Circeo**; Gargano coast near **Vieste**.

Byzantine Relics: Museo di Palazzo Venezia, Sant'Agnese, Santa Prassede,**Rome**; cathedral crypt, **Anagni**; church at **Stilo**; cave churches around **Matera** and **Massafra**; Sant'Angelo in Formis, **Capua**; Pinacoteca, **Bari** .

Castles: Frederick II's Castel del Monte, **Lagopésole**, **Melfi** and **Lucera** in Apulia; Castel Sant'Angelo, **Rome**; Castello degli Orsini, by **Lake Bracciano**; Rocca Sinibalda, near **Rieti**; Julius II's castle at **Ostia**; Castel Nuovo and Egg Castle in **Naples**; odd castle at **Civitella del Tronto**.

Caves: Blue Grotto, **Capri**; Grotto di Pastena, near **Ceprano**; Grotto del Cavallone, **Taranta Peligna**, near Sulmona; **Pertosa**, south of Eboli; Grotta Smeralda, near **Praiano**; Cave of the Cumaean Sibyl, **Cuma**, entire cave neighbourhoods (*Sassi*) in **Matera**, and lots of cave churches nearby.

Ceramics: Majolica is still a thriving craft in many towns, notably **Castelli** (Abruzzo) and **Grottaglie** (Apulia).

Elephants: besides the frisky inmates of **Rome's** Villa Borghese zoo, there are some fine marble ones on the zoo gate and a Renaissance one under the obelisk in front of Santa Maria sopra Minerva. **Bomarzo's** monster park has the most ferocious, while at **Ostia Antica** there are elephant mosaics; the National Museum at **L'Aquila** has the bones of one which used to live in the Abruzzo.

Fountains: **Rome** is one of the best cities anywhere for fountains, most famously the Trevi fountain, and Bernini's fountains in Piazza Navona and Piazza Barberini; **Viterbo**, too, has at least a score. Late Renaissance garden fountains are the delight of the Villa d'Este, **Tivoli** and Villa Lante, near **Viterbo**; the Villa Aldobrandini at **Frascati** has a curious 'theatre of waters'; there's a good Mannerist fountain, the Fontana Papacqua at **Soriano nel Cimino**. In L'Aquila, there's one with 99 spouts; in **Caserta**, the Fontana di Diana.

Gardens: Villa d'Este, **Tivoli**; Villa Lante, near **Viterbo**; secret garden of Villa Farnese, **Caprarola**; Caetani Botanical Gardens, **Ninfa**; Villa Floridiana,**Naples**; Villa Cimbrone and Villa Rùfolo, **Ravello**; Gardens of Augustus, **Capri**.

Ghost towns: **Civita di Bagnoregio**, near Lake Bolsena; **Ninfa**; **Craco** in the Basilicata—and a hundred other mountain villages in Calabria and the Basilicata in various stages of abandonment.

Lakes: Lazio's volcanic lakes, especially **Nemi, Albano** and **Vico**; **Lago del Matese**, in the Molise; at Cape Misenum, **Lakes Avernus, Fusaro** and **Miseno**.

Landscapes: besides the spectacular fireworks of the **Amalfi coast** and **Gargano peninsula**, the South has the **Matese**, an unspoiled mountain region between Campania and Molise; the great, forested mountain plateau called the **Sila** in Calabria; the **Gran Sasso** and the **Maiella** in the Abruzzo; the **Abruzzo National Park**; and Campania's **Cilento coast**.

Manmade Curiosities: **Rome** is full of them, including its amazing Aurelian walls, catacombs that descend down six floors, a 1st-century pyramid, and Monte Testaccio, a hill made entirely of potsherds. In **Naples** there's the Crypta Napoletana, an impressive road tunnel built by Augustus, and the canals and lagoons of the naval base at Misenum. Matera's *Sassi* have already been mentioned, and there's the *trullo* landscapes around **Alberobello**.

Megalithic walls: startling defences of massive polygonal blocks made when Rome was still a twinkle in Romulus' eye survive in many towns in southern Lazio, especially **Alatri, Cori, Ferentino**, and **Arpino**; also the Messapian capital of **Manduria**.

Mithraeums: underground temples of Christianity's chief rival in the early days: in **Rome**, at San Clemente and Santa Prisca; others in **Ostia Antica**, and a great one with frescoes at **Capua**.

Natural Curiosities: Phlegraean Fields, baby volcanoes; Sasso Menicante (rocking rock), at **Soriano nel Cimino**; 'floating island' in the lake at **Posta Fibreno**; Pozzo Santullo, a sinkhole wood near **Alatri**; eroded rocks and infernal pits, **Atri** (Abruzzo) and **Aliano** (Basilicata); Furore Gorge, near **Praiano**; *Fata Morgana*, **Straits of Messina**.

Obelisks and similar tall virile symbols abound in the South: **Rome** has more obelisks than Egypt—the world's tallest, by the Lateran, and some endearing midgets in Piranesi's Piazza dei Cavalieri di Malta, and one Mussolini stole from Ethiopia, in front of FAO headquarters. **Naples** has its *Guglie*—tall Rococo obelisks; there's another one in **Nardò**. **Tagliacozzo** has a Renaissance obelisk, **Pescara** a concrete one from the 1960s, and **Capri** a natural one, the Pizzolungo. Then there are the portable models: the *Macchine di S. Rosa* of **Viterbo** and the 'Lilies' of **Nola**.

Off-Beat Attractions: Fish Museum and D'Annunzio's birthplace, **Pescara**; romantic mementoes in the Keats-Shelley Memorial House and EUR scale model of ancient Rome, in **Rome**; incredible sculpture in the Sansevero Chapel, **Naples**; Museum of Ex-Votos, S. Maria della Quercia, near **Viterbo**; Paper Museum, **Amalfi**; giant Jesus, **Maratea**; memorial to Rudolph Valentino, **Castellaneta**. Two of the occult wonders of the world are **Monte Sant'Angelo** and Frederick II's **Castel del Monte**, and nearby is the famed Colossus of **Barletta**.

Opera: Teatro San Carlo in **Naples** is one of the premier houses in Italy; the Teatro dell'Opera, **Rome** has excellent winter productions in the theatre and summer performances in the Baths of Caracalla; other important houses are in **Bari** and **Fóggia**.

Parks: National Park of the **Abruzzo**, **Monte Circeo** National Park.

Presepi: According to tradition, St Francis made the first Christmas crib in **Greccio**. Since then the art has become a speciality of the south, especially in **Naples**, which has a *presepi* market, and a few roomfuls at the museum of San Martino. Other notable cribs are at S. Maria Maggiore and SS. Cosma e Damiano, **Rome**; **Leonessa**, from the

1500s; a vast one at the Abbazia de Valvisciolo (near **Sermoneta**); a beautiful ceramic one at **Castelli**.

Spas: nearly the entire island of **Ischia**; also Terme di Bulicame, near **Viterbo**; **Fiuggi** in the Ciociaria.

Spooky Stuff: Most of this is in **Rome**, beginning with the Hallowe'en Cappuccini catacombs on Via Veneto, the canopic jars of papal guts in the crypt of SS. Vicenzo ed Anastasio, the dungeons of Castel Sant'Angelo, the eyeball chapel in S. Maria Trastevere, and the Bocca della Verità. In **Naples**, there's the Baroque nightmare Chiostro Grande of San Martino. **Benevento** is Italy's witch capital; **Cocullo** has a procession of serpents; while in **Bominaco**'s church of San Pellegrino you can hear the saint's heart beat. The sentimental favourite: **Bomarzo**'s Monster Park.

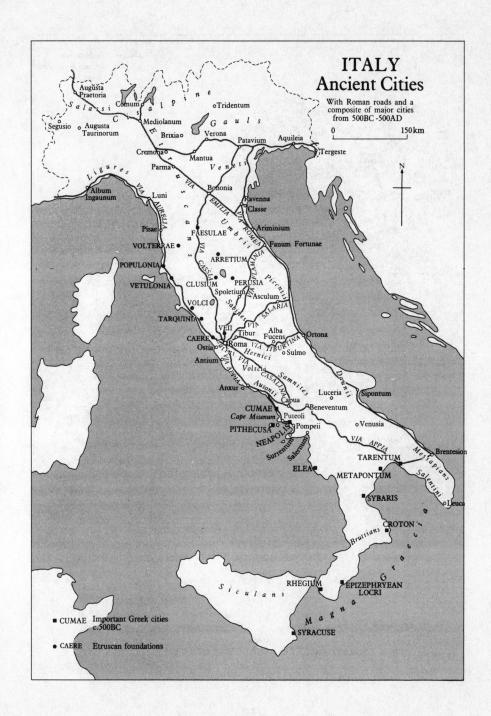

ITALY
Ancient Cities

With Roman roads and a
composite of major cities
from 500BC -500AD

0   150km

N

Augusta
Praetoria

Salassi

Comum

Segusio   Augusta
Taurinorum

Mediolanum

Tridentum

C l p i n e

Ci

Gauls

Brixia

Verona

Patavium

Aquileia

Cremona

Mantua

Veneti

Tergeste

Parma

Ligures

V I A

Bononia

E t r u s c a n s

Album
Ingaunum

Luni

A U R E L I A

VIA

Ravenna

Classe

Umbri

Ariminium

Pisae

FAESULAE

VIA FLAMINIA

VIA AEMILIA

Fanum Fortunae

VOLTERRAE

ARRETIUM

VIA ROMEA

POPULONIA

VIA CASSIA

CLUSIUM

PERUSIA

Picenini

VETULONIA

Spoletium

Asculum

VOLCI

Sabines

VIA SALARIA

TARQUINIA

VEII

VIA

Alba
Fucens

Ortona

CAERE

Roma

Tibur

VIA TIBURTINA

Ostia

Latini

VIA

Hernici

Sulmo

Antium

Daunii

CASALINA

Volsci

Samnites

Ausoni

Capua

Luceria

Sipontum

Anxur

Beneventum

CUMAE

Cape Misenum

Puteoli

Venusia

PITHECUSA

Pompeii

NEAPOLIS

Surrentum

VIA   *APPIA*

Salernum

Messapians

TARENTUM

Brentesion

ELEA

METAPONTUM

Salentini

Leuca

SYBARIS

CROTON

Bruttians

Magna

Siculans

RHEGIUM

EPIZEPHRYEAN
LOCRI

Graecia

■ CUMAE   Important Greek cities
          c.500BC

● CAERE   Etruscan foundations

SYRACUSE

XV

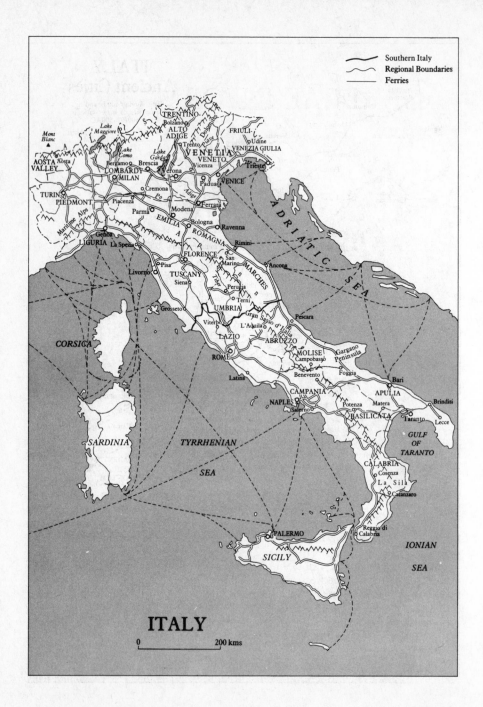

Southern Italy
Regional Boundaries
Ferries

Mont Blanc

Lake Maggiore
TRENTINO-
Bolzano
ALTO
ADIGE
Dolomites
FRIULI-
Udine
VENEZIA GIULIA
Trento
Piave
Lake Como
Lake Garda
VENETIA
Trieste
AOSTA
VALLEY
Aosta
Bergamo
Brescia
Verona
VENETO
Vicenza
TURIN
LOMBARDY
MILAN
Padua
VENICE
Cremona
Adige
PIEDMONT
Piacenza
Po
Ferrara
Maritime Alps
Parma
Modena
EMILIA
Bologna
Ravenna
Genoa
LIGURIA
La Spezia
ROMAGNA
Rimini
FLORENCE
Ancona
Pisa
San
Marino
Livorno
MARCHES
TUSCANY
Siena
Tiber
Perugia
CORSICA
Grosseto
UMBRIA
Terni
Gran Sasso d'Italia
Pescara
Viterbo
L'Aquila
LAZIO
ABRUZZO
Gargano
MOLISE
Peninsula
ROME
Campobasso
Foggia
Latina
Benevento
Bari
CAMPANIA
APULIA
Brindisi
NAPLES
Potenza
Matera
Salerno
BASILICATA
Taranto
Lecce
SARDINIA
TYRRHENIAN
GULF
OF
TARANTO
SEA
CALABRIA
Cosenza
La Sila
Catanzaro
IONIAN
Reggio di
Calabria
PALERMO
SEA
SICILY

ITALY

0   200 kms

ADRIATIC SEA

Part I

GENERAL INFORMATION

Fruit and Vegetables

Before You Go

There's simply too much to see and do in Southern Italy to wander about hoping you'll stumble across Da Vinci's *Last Supper* somewhere in Rome—and yet it's amazing how many travellers do exactly that. A little preparation can make your trip many times more enjoyable (or at least less frustrating). Although this book was designed to be especially useful to frequent visitors who are ready to poke into some of Italy's nooks and crannies, it will also get you around the major sights if this is your first trip; study the Guide to the Guide (p. ix) and the list of festivals (p. 22) to get some idea of where you want to be and when. There are several tour operators who specialize in holidays to Italy. In the UK Citalia (tel (081) 686 5533 or (071) 434 3844) probably has the widest range. (See also p. 32 for Self-Catering Holidays and p. 21 for Special Interest Holidays). You can pick up free hints, brochures, maps, and information from the Italian National Tourist Offices, at the following addresses; an especially useful booklet to request is the annually updated *Travellers' Handbook*, which has loads of good information and current prices.

UK: 1 Princes Street, London W1R 8AY (tel (071) 408 1254; telex 22402).
Eire: 47 Merrion Square, Dublin 2, Eire (tel (001) 766397; telex 31682).
USA: 630 Fifth Avenue, Suite 1565, New York, NY 10111 (tel (212) 245 4961; telex 236024).
500 N. Michigan Avenue, Chicago, Ill. 60611 (tel (312) 644 0990/1; telex 0255160).
360 Post Street, Suite 801, San Francisco, California 94108 (tel (415) 392 6206; telex 67623).

Canada: Store 56, Plaza 3, Place Ville Marie, Montreal, Quebec (tel (514) 866 7667; telex 525607).

Once you know where you want to go, you can pick up more detailed information by writing directly to any of the city or provincial tourist offices. These are usually very helpful in sending out lists of flats, villas, or farmhouses to hire, or at least lists of agents who handle the properties.

Getting to South Italy

By Air

By Regular Scheduled Flights
The main international airports serving the region are at Rome and Naples; connecting flights can drop you at Bari, Brindisi, Fòggia, Lamezia Terme (near Catanzaro) and Règgio Calabria. Alitalia and British Airways will take you non-stop to Naples, and a score of other airlines will fly you to Rome, where cheap flights are readily available, especially on the more outlandish airlines, as it takes most Mediterranean stopovers between London and Timbuktu, and everywhere in between. The real challenge is finding a discount in the high season (Easter and mid-May–mid-September); start hunting around a few months in advance, or if you're a gambler, at the last minute.

There are advantages in paying out for a normal fare, mainly that it does not impose any restrictions on when you go or return; most are valid for a year. To sweeten the deal, Alitalia in particular often has promotional perks like rental cars (Jetdrive), or discounts on domestic flights within Italy, on hotels, or on tours. Ask your travel agent. Children under the age of two travel for 10 per cent of the adult fare on British Airways flights; Alitalia has a nominal charge of £20. Children between 2 and 12 travel for half fare, and bona fide students with proof of age and school attendance between the ages of 12 and 25 receive a 25 per cent discount on British Airways flights, and a 20 per cent discount on Alitalia.

The carriers listed above have a variety of discounts for those who book in advance or are able to decide their departure and return dates in advance. If you're travelling from Europe, you can save quite a tidy sum by paying for your ticket when you make your reservations (Eurobudget); an extra advantage is that the return date is left open. Travellers from anywhere can save money by downing a little alphabet soup—PEX, APEX, and SUPERPEX, which like Eurobudget require reservations and payment at the same time on return-only flights. PEX (or APEX) fares have fixed arrival and departure dates, and the stay in Italy must include at least one Saturday night; from North America the restrictions are at least a week's stay but not more than 90 days. SUPERPEX, the cheapest normal fares available, have the same requirements as PEX, but must be purchased at least 14 days (or sometimes 21 days in North America) in advance. Disadvantages of PEXing are that there are penalty fees if you change your flight dates. At the time of writing, the lowest APEX fare between London and Rome in the off season is £188; the lowest mid-week SUPERPEX between New York and Rome in the off-season is $780.

2

Other advantages of taking a regular flight over a charter are an increase in reliability in dates and in punctuality, and you're not out of a wad of cash if you miss your flight. Also, if you live in neither London nor New York, they will often offer big discounts to get you from your home airport to the international one. If you live in the US boondocks, you can dial some '800' numbers to check out prices on your own: Alitalia's number is 800 223 5730.

From the USA, you almost always have to go through New York, and can fly directly only to Rome and Milan. Fares from Canada are often much higher than they are from the States. Also, it's worth while checking on budget fares to London (especially if Virgin Atlantic stays around), Brussels, Paris, Frankfurt, or Amsterdam; these routes are more competitive than the Italian ones, and you may save money by either flying or riding the rails to Italy from there.

Charter Flights

These aren't as much of a bargain to Italy as they are to other Mediterranean destinations, though they're certainly worth looking into—check ads in the travel section of your newspaper (*Sunday Times* and *Time Out* are especially good) and your travel agent. From London, Pilgrim Air (44 Goodge St, tel (071) 637 5333) has regularly scheduled charters to Rome; from the US, CIEE has regular charters from New York to Rome (tel 800 223 7402). Other charter flights are usually booked by the big holiday companies. To find out about extra seats on these and on commercial flights, visit your local bucket shop (in the USA, call Access (tel 800 333 7280) or Air Hitch for similar services—check listings in the *Sunday New York Times*). Pickings are fairly easy in the off season, and tight in the summer months, but not impossible. You take your chances, but you can save some of your hard-earned dough. The cheapest charter fare at the time of writing from London to Rome is £140, from New York $700.

The problem with charters is they are delayed more often than not, and since the same plane is usually commuting back and forth it can mean arriving at Rome's Ciampino airport at 3 am, which must be one of the lower rings in Dante's *Inferno*. Another disadvantage is that you have to accept the given dates, and if you miss your flight (bus and train strikes in Italy do make this a distinct possibility) there's no refund. Most travel agencies, however, offer traveller's insurance that includes at least a partial refund of your charter fare if strikes or illness keep you from the airport.

Students

Besides saving 25 per cent on regular flights, students under 26 have the choice of flying on special discount charters. From the US, CIEE (see above) is a good place to start looking. From Canada, contact Canadian Universities Travel Services, 44 St George St, Toronto, Ontario M55 2E4, tel (416) 979 2406. From London, check out STA Travel, 117 Euston Road, NW1 or 86 Old Brompton Rd, SW7, for telephone enquiries for European destinations ring (071) 937 9921; WST, 6 Wrights Lane W8 tel (071) 938 4362 or USIT, 52 Grosvenor Gardens, SW1, tel (071) 730 8518.

By Train

At the time of writing approximate single, second class fares to Southern Italy from London are: Bari £112 (33 hours); Brindisi £115 (35 hours); Naples £100 (30 hours);

Pescara £105 (30 hours); Règgio Calabria £114 (39 hours); Rome £97 (29 hours). Prices do vary according to the route you go take, i.e. whether you via Belgium, via Switzerland or simply through France into Italy.

These trains require reservations and a couchette, and are a fairly painless way of getting there. Discounts are available for families travelling together, for children—free under age 4 and 40 per cent discount between the ages of 4 and 8. Under 26-ers, students or not, can save up to 40 per cent and over on second-class seats by purchasing Eurotrain tickets available in the UK from any student travel office in the UK, many high street travel agents or direct from Eurotrain tel (071) 730 3402. Eurotrain also has a kiosk at Victoria Station which is open from 8 am to 8 pm seven days a week. Eurotrain tickets are also available throughout Europe at student travel offices (CTS in Italy) in main railway stations. Any rail tickets purchased in Britain for Italy are valid for two months and allow any stopovers you care to make on the way.

Rail travel to Italy becomes an even more attractive option if you intend to purchase an Inter-Rail pass (in Europe), or a EurRail pass (from North America). Inter-Rail cards (about £155) are sold by British Rail to people under 26 and offer discounts of over 30 per cent in Britain and 30 or 50 per cent on Channel Ferries, and free rail passage on the Continent, and are valid for a month. Inter-Rail Senior cards offer similar discounts to people over 60. EurRail passes must be purchased before leaving for Europe, and are valid for from 15 days to 3 months of unlimited first-class travel. These passes are a good deal if you plan to do lots and lots of rail travel and can't be bothered to buy tickets, etc. They seem rather less rosy if your travelling is limited to Italy, where domestic rail tickets are one of the few bargains available. Within Italy itself there are several discount tickets available (see below, travelling within Italy), which you can inquire about at CIT Italian State railways offices before you leave home:

UK: 50 Conduit St, London, W1, tel (071) 434 3844
also at Wasteels Travel, 121 Wilton Rd, London SW1, tel (071) 834 7066 or at any branch of Thomas Cook Ltd
USA: 666 Fifth Ave, New York NY 10103, tel (212) 223 0230. There's also an 800 number you can call from anywhere: (800) 223 0230
Canada: 2055 Peel St, Suite 102, Montreal, Quebec H3A 1VA, tel (514) 845 9101

By Coach

Not really to be recommended. Eurolines will take you from London Victoria's Coach Station to Rome (£83 single, £133 return from 1 July to 30 September; £79 single, £126 return the rest of the year). Contact National Express, Victoria Coach Station, London SW1, tel (071) 730 0202 for times and bookings.

By Car

Driving to Southern Italy from London is a rather lengthy and expensive proposition, and if you're only staying for a short period figure your costs against Alitalia's or other airlines' fly-drive scheme. Depending on how you cross the Channel, it is a good two-day trip—about 1800 km from Calais to Rome. Ferry information is available from the Continental Car Ferry Centre, 52 Grosvenor Gardens, London SW1. You can avoid many of the costly motorway tolls by going from Dover to Calais, through France, to

Basle, Switzerland, and then through the Gotthard Tunnel over the Alps; in the summer you can save the steep tunnel tolls by taking one of the passes. You can avoid some of the driving by putting your car on the train (although again balance the sizeable expense against the price of hiring a car for the period of your stay): Express Sleeper Cars run to Milan from Paris or Boulogne, and to Bologna from Boulogne, and from either you can continue to Bari, Brindisi, or Villa San Giovanni, one of the bunions on Italy's toe. If you're aiming for Naples, though, you have to go through Milan. Services are drastically cut outside the summer months, however. For more information, contact the CIT offices listed above.

To bring your car into Italy, you need your car registration (log book), valid driving licence, and valid insurance (a Green Card is not necessary, but you'll need one if you go through Switzerland). Make sure everything is in excellent working order or your slightly bald tyre may enrich the coffers of the Swiss or Italian police—it's not uncommon to be stopped for no reason and have your car searched until the police find something to stick a fine on. Also beware that spare parts for non-Italian cars are difficult to come by, almost impossible for pre-1988 Japanese models. If you're coming to live in Italy, remember that cars with foreign plates are obliged to leave the country every six months for a hazily defined period of time.

One advantage of taking your own car to Southern Italy (Basilicata, Calabria, Campania, Molise, Apulia, Sardinia and Sicily) is that your are eligible to pick up the most **Petrol Coupons**, saving 15 per cent on motorway tolls and Europe's most expensive petrol; if you're going as far as Basilicata, Calabria, Sicily or Sardinia, you can pick up even more. Coupons are issued to owners of GB-registered vehicles by London's CIT office (see above), at Wasteels Travel, 121 Wilton Rd, London SW1, tel (071) 834 7066, or at your local AA or RAC office (though ring them first to make sure they have the coupons in stock) or at the frontier from Italian Auto Club offices. Coupons are sold only in person to the car-owner with his or her passport and car registration, and cannot be paid for in Italian lire—prices are tagged to current exchange rates, and unused coupons may be refunded on your return. Along with the coupons and motorway vouchers, you get a *Carta Carburante* which entitles you to breakdown services provided by the Italian Auto Club (ACI) (offices in Southern Italy, p. 13). At the time of writing motorway tunnel tolls are:

Mont Blanc Tunnel, from Chamonix (France) to Courmayeur: small car or motorcycle L15 000 single, L19 000 return. Medium-sized car (axle distance 2.31–2.63 m) L23 000 single, L29 000 return. Large cars (axle distance 2.64–3.30) or cars with caravans L31,000 single or 38,000 return.

Fréjus Tunnel, from Modane (France) to Bardonécchia: same as above except for large cars or cars with caravans (trailers) L28 000 single, L36 000 return.

Gran San Bernardo, from Bourg St Pierre (Switzerland) to Aosta: small car or motorcycle: L13 500 single, L19 000 return. Medium car L20 000 single, L28 000 return. Large car or car with caravan L27 000 single, L38 000 return.

Traveller's Insurance and Health

You can insure yourself for almost any possible mishap—cancelled flights, stolen or lost baggage, and health. While national health coverage in the UK and Canada takes care of their citizens while travelling, the US doesn't. Check your current policies to see if they cover you while abroad, and under what circumstances, and judge whether you need a special traveller's insurance policy. Travel agents sell them, as well as insurance companies; they are not cheap.

Minor illnesses and problems that crop up in Italy can usually be handled free of charge in a public hospital clinic or *ambulatorio*. If you need minor aid, Italian pharmacists are highly trained and can probably diagnose your problem; look for a *Farmacia* (they all have a list in the window detailing which ones are open during the night and on holidays). Extreme cases should head for the *Pronto Soccorso* (First Aid services). The emergency number from anywhere in Italy is 113.

Most Italian doctors speak at least rudimentary English, but if you can't find one, contact your embassy or consulate for a list of English-speaking doctors.

What to Pack

You simply cannot overdress in Italy; whatever grand strides Italian designers have made on the international fashion merry-go-round, most of their clothes are purchased domestically, prices be damned. Now whether or not you want to try to keep up with the natives is your own affair and your own heavy suitcase—you may do well to compromise and just bring a couple of smart outfits for big nights out. It's not that the Italians are very formal; they simply like to dress up with a gorgeousness that adorns their cities just as much as those old Renaissance churches and palaces. The few places with dress codes are the major churches, abbeys, and basilicas (no shorts or sleeveless shirts), and some of the smarter restaurants.

After agonizing over fashion, remember to pack small and light: trans-Atlantic airlines limit baggage by size (two pieces are free, up to 62 inches in height and width; in second-class you're allowed one of 62 inches and another up to 44 inches). Within Europe limits are by weight: 23 kilos (59 lbs) in second-class, 30 kilos (66 lbs) in first. You may well be penalized for anything bigger. If you're travelling mainly by train, you'll especially want to keep bags to a minimum: jamming big suitcases in overhead racks in a crowded compartment isn't much fun for anyone. Never take more than you can carry, but do bring the following: any prescription medicine you need, an extra pair of glasses or contact lenses if you need them, a pocket knife and corkscrew (for picnics), a flashlight (for dark frescoed churches and hotel corridors), a travel alarm (for those early trains) and a pocket Italian-English dictionary (for flirting and other emergencies; outside the main tourist centres you may well have trouble finding someone who speaks English). If you're a light sleeper, you may want to invest in ear plugs. Your electric appliances will work in Italy if you adapt and convert them to run on 220 AC with two round prongs on the plug. Of course, what you bring depends on when and where you go...

Climate

O Sole Mio notwithstanding, all of Italy isn't always sunny; it rains just as much in Rome every year as in London. **Summer** comes on dry and hot in the south; the high Apennines stay fairly cool, while the coasts are often refreshed by breezes. You can probably get by without an umbrella, but take a light jacket for cool evenings. For average touring, August is probably the worst month to stump through southern Italy. Transport facilities are jammed to capacity, prices are at their highest, Rome and Naples are abandoned to hordes of tourists while the locals take to the beach. Drier regions, such as most of Apulia, will be brown and uninviting from July until the rains return in October or November.

Spring and **autumn** are perhaps the loveliest times to go: spring for the infinity of wild flowers in Italy's countryside, autumn for the colour of the trees in the hills and the vineyards. The weather is mild, places aren't crowded, and you won't need your umbrella too much, at least until November. From **December to March** you can enjoy blissful solitude at reasonable temperatures anywhere close to the coasts, though it will probably be too cold for swimming. Just stay out of the mountains—places like Benevento and Potenza have fiercer winters than Scotland. Anywhere, especially in Rome and in the mountains, it can rain and rain, and mountain valleys will lie for days under banks of fog and mist.

Average Temperatures in °C (°F)

	January	April	July	October
Amalfi	12.5 (54)	15.0 (59)	26.1 (79)	17.9 (63)
Bari	8.4 (46)	13.9 (56)	24.5 (76)	18.2 (64)
Capri	11.3 (52)	13.4 (55)	23.7 (74)	17.4 (63)
Fóggia	6.3 (43)	12.6 (54)	26.5 (79)	17.9 (63)
Naples	8.7 (47)	14.3 (57)	24.8 (76)	18.1 (64)
Règgio Calabria	11.1 (52)	15.4 (59)	25.9 (78)	19.3 (67)
Rome	7.4 (44)	14.4 (57)	25.7 (78)	17.7 (63)

Average monthly rainfall in millimetres (inches)

	January	April	July	October
Amalfi	135 (5)	193 (7)	10 (½)	194 (7)
Bari	39 (2)	35 (2)	19 (1)	111 (4)
Capri	57 (2)	67 (3)	06 (0)	34 (2)
Fóggia	35 (2)	32 (1)	21 (1)	39 (2)
Naples	87 (3)	55 (2)	14 (1)	102 (4)
Règgio Calabria	74 (3)	52 (2)	06 (0)	53 (2)
Rome	74 (3)	62 (3)	06 (0)	123 (4)

Passports and Customs Formalities

To get into Italy you need a valid passport or a British Visitor's Card. Nationals of the UK, Ireland, USA, Canada, and Australia do not need visas for stays of up to three months. If you mean to stay longer than three months in Italy, get a visa from your Italian consulate or face the prospect of having to get a *Visa di Soggiorno* at the end of three months—possible only if you can prove a source of income and are willing to spend a couple of exasperating days at some provincial Questura office filling out forms.

According to Italian law, you must register with the police within three days of your arrival. If you check into a hotel this is done automatically. If you come to grief in the mesh of rules and forms, you can at least get someone to explain it to you in English by calling the Rome Police Office for visitors, tel (06) 4686, ext. 2858.

Italian Customs are usually benign, though how the frontier police manage to recruit such ugly, mean-looking characters to hold the submachine guns and drug-sniffing dogs from such a good-looking population is a mystery, but they'll let you be if you don't look suspicious and haven't brought along more than 150 cigarettes or 75 cigars, or not more than a litre of hard drink or three bottles of wine, a couple of cameras, a movie camera, 10 rolls of film for each, a tape-recorder, radio, phonograph, one canoe less than 5.5 m, sports equipment for personal use, and one TV (though you'll have to pay for a licence for it at Customs). Pets must be accompanied by a bilingual Certificate of Health from your local Veterinary Inspector. You can take the same items listed above home with you without hassle—except of course your British pet. US citizens may return with $400 worth of merchandise—keep your receipts. British subjects are permitted £200 worth of dutiable merchandise.

There are no limits to how much money you bring into Italy, although legally you may not transport more than L400 000 in Italian banknotes, though they rarely check.

On Arrival

Money

It's a good idea to bring some Italian lire with you when you arrive; unforeseen delays and unexpected public holidays may foul up your plans to change at a bank when you arrive. Traveller's cheques or Eurocheques remain the most secure way of financing your holiday in Italy; they are easy to change and insurance against unpleasant surprises. Credit cards (American Express, Diners Club, Mastercard, Access, Eurocard, Barclaycard, Visa) are usually only accepted in hotels, restaurants, and shops (but never at any petrol stations) frequented by foreign tourists—Italians themselves rarely use them— and it is not unknown for establishments to fiddle with the exchange rates and numbers on your bill once you've left. Use them with discretion. Lately there has been a rebellion of sorts against credit cards on the part of many Italian shops and restaurants; they're tired of the inconvenience and added expense.

There's been a lot of loose talk about knocking three noughts off the Italian lira, but it never seems to happen; as it is, everybody can be a 'millionaire'. It is also confusing to the visitor unaccustomed to dealing with rows of zeros, and more than once you'll think you're getting a great deal until you realize you've simply miscounted the zeros on the price tag. Some unscrupulous operators may try to take advantage of the confusion when you're changing money, so do be careful. Notes come in denominations of L100 000, L50 000, L10 000, L5000, L2000, and L1000; coins are L500, L200, L100, L50, L20, all the way down to the ridiculous and practically worthless aluminium coinage of L10, L5 and L1. Telephone tokens (*gettoni*) may be used as coins as well and are worth L200.

The easiest way to have money sent to you in Italy is for someone from home to get a bank to telex the amount to an Italian bank, and for you to go and pick it up. Technically—and if you're really lucky—it shouldn't take more than a couple of days to arrive, but make sure the telex includes the number of your passport, ID card, or driver's licence, or the Italians may not give you your money. Save all the receipts of your currency exchanges.

Getting Around Within Italy

Italy has an excellent network of airports, railways, highways, and byways and you'll find getting around fairly easy—until one union or another takes it into its head to go on strike (to be fair, they rarely do it during the high holiday season). There's plenty of talk about passing a law to regulate strikes, but it won't happen soon, if ever. Instead, learn to recognize the word in Italian: *sciopero* (SHOW-per-o) and be prepared to do as the Romans do when you hear it—quiver with resignation. There's always a day or two's notice, and strikes usually last only 12 or 24 hours—just long enough to throw a spanner in the works if you have to catch a plane. Keep your ears open and watch for notices posted in the stations.

By Air

Domestic flights are handled by Alitalia, Itavia, and ATI, and come in most handy when you want to hop from north to south. There are certain flights, such as from Rome to Naples, where, if you count the time it takes to get to and from the airports, check in, etc., as well as the flight itself, you may find a *Rapido* train only slightly slower and much less expensive.

Domestic flight prices are comparable to other continental countries, but there are discounts available for night flights of up to 30 per cent, youth fares (12–26, 25 per cent discount), while younger children pay half the adult fare. Travelling by air becomes especially attractive if you're travelling as a family (husband, wife, children) when you can get a discount of up to 50 per cent. Each airport has a bus terminal in the city; ask about timetables when you purchase your ticket or face a hefty taxi fare.

By Train

A recent newspaper poll on government services found the Italians disgusted with their railways, and relatively happy with the postal system. You figure it out; the post, as everyone knows, is a national scandal, while Italy's national railway, the FS (*Ferrovie dello Stato*) is well run, efficient, inexpensive, (though prices have recently risen, it is still cheap by British standards) and often a pleasure to ride. In addition to it, there are several private rail lines around cities and in country districts. We have tried to list them all in this book. Some, you may find, won't accept Inter-Rail or EurRail passes. On the FS, some of the trains are sleek and high-tech, but much of the rolling stock hasn't been changed for 50 years; the most beautiful is the swank Mussolini-era *Rapido* rocket ship between Rome and Ancona, the *Settebello*. Possible FS unpleasantnesses you may encounter, besides a strike, are delays, crowding (especially at weekends and in the summer), and crime on overnight trains, where someone rifles your bags while you sleep. The crowding, at least, becomes much less of a problem if you reserve a seat in advance at the *Prenotazione* counter. The fee is small and can save you hours standing in some train

9

corridor. On the upper echelon trains, reservations are mandatory. Do check when you purchase your ticket in advance that the date is correct; unlike in some countries, tickets are only valid the day they're purchased unless you specify otherwise. If you're coming back the same way in three days or less, save money with a *ritorno* (a one-way ticket is an *andata*). A number on your reservation slip will indicate in which car your seat is—find it before you board rather than after. The same goes for sleepers and couchettes on overnight trains, which must also be reserved in advance.

Tickets may be purchased not only in the stations, but at many travel agents in the city centres. The system is computerized and runs smoothly, at least until you try to get a reimbursement for an unused ticket (usually not worth the trouble). Be sure you ask which platform (*binario*) your train arrives at; the big permanent boards posted in the stations are not always correct. If you get on a train without a ticket you can buy one from the conductor, with an added 20 per cent penalty. You can also pay a conductor to move up to first class or get a couchette, if there are places available.

There is a fairly straightforward hierarchy of trains. At the bottom of the pyramid is the humble *Locale* (euphemistically known sometimes as an *Accelerato*), which often stops even where there's no station in sight; it can be excruciatingly slow. When you're checking the timetables, beware of what may look like the first train to your destination—if it's a *Locale*, it will be the last to arrive. A *Diretto* stops far less, an *Expresso* just at the main towns. *Rapido* trains whoosh between the big cities and rarely deign to stop. On some of these reservations are necessary, and on some there are only first-class coaches. On all of them, however, you'll be asked to pay a supplement—some 30 per cent more than a regular fare. The real lords of the rails are the TEE (Trans-Europe Express) *Super-Rapido Italiano* trains, kilometre-eaters that will speed you to your destination as fast as trains can go. Italy has three lines all to itself: the *Vesuvio* (Milan, Bologna, Florence, Rome, Naples), the *Adriatico* (Milan, Rimini, Pésaro, Ancona, Pescara, Fóggia, Bari), and the *Colosseum/Ambrosiano* (Milan, Bologna, Florence, Rome). For these there is a more costly supplement and only first-class luxury cars. Of course there are others travelling between Italy and northern Europe; ask at any travel agent for details.

The FS offers several passes. One which you should ideally arrange at a CIT office before arriving in Italy, is the 'Travel-at-Will' ticket (*Biglietto turistico libera circolazione*), available only to foreigners. This is a good deal only if you mean to do some very serious train riding on consecutive days; it does, however, allow you to ride the *Rapidos* without paying the supplement. Tickets are sold for 8, 15, 21, or 30-day periods, first or second class, with 50 per cent reduction for children under 12. At the time of writing an eight-day second-class ticket is around £65, first-class £102. A more flexible option is the 'Flexi Card' which allows unlimited travel for either 4 days within a 9-day period (second class £48, first class £70), 8 days within 21 (second class £66, first class £100) or 12 days within 30 (second class £86, first class £128) and you don't have to pay any supplements. Another ticket, the *Kilometrico* gives you 3000 kilometres of travel, made on a maximum of 20 journeys and is valid for two months; one advantage is that it can be used by up to five people at the same time. However, supplements are payable on Intercity trains. Second-class tickets are currently £68, first-class £116. Other discounts, available only once you're in Italy, are 15 per cent on same-day return tickets and three-day returns (depending on the distance involved), and discounts for families of at least four travelling together. Senior citizens (men 65 and over, women 60) can also get a *Carta d'Argento* ('silver card') for L10 000 entitling them to a 30 per cent reduction in fares. For young people under 26 a *Carta Verde* entitles one to a 30 per cent discount (20 per cent in peak season—Easter and Christmas holidays and 25 June to 31 August).

Refreshments on routes of any great distance are provided by bar cars or trolleys; you can usually get sandwiches and coffee from vendors along the tracks at intermediate stops. Station bars often have a good variety of take-away travellers' fare; consider at least investing in a plastic bottle of mineral water, since there's no drinking water on the trains.

Besides trains and bars, Italy's stations offer other facilities. All have a *Deposito*, where you can leave your bags for hours or days for a small fee. The larger ones have porters (who charge L800–1000 per piece) and some even have luggage trolleys; major stations have an *Albergo Diurno* ('Day Hotel', where you can take a shower, get a shave and haircut, etc.), information offices, currency exchanges open at weekends (not at the most advantageous rates, however), hotel-finding and reservation services, kiosks with foreign papers, restaurants, etc. You can also arrange to have a rental car awaiting you at your destination—Avis, Hertz, Eurotrans, and Autoservizi Maggiore are the firms that provide this service.

Beyond that, some words need to be said about riding the rails on the most serendipitous national line in Europe. The FS may have its strikes and delays, its petty crime and bureaucratic inconveniences, but when you catch it on its better side it will treat you to a dose of the real Italy before you even reach your destination. If there's a choice, try for one of the older cars, depressingly grey outside but fitted with comfortably upholstered seats, Art Deco lamps, and old pictures of the towns and villages of the country. The washrooms are invariably clean and pleasant. Best of all, the FS is relatively reliable, and even if there has been some delay, you'll have an amenable station full of clocks to wait in; some of the station bars have astonishingly good food (some do not), but at any of them you may accept a well-brewed *cappuccino* and look blasé until the train comes in. Try to avoid travel on Friday evenings, when the major lines out of the big cities are packed. The FS is an honest crap shoot; you may have a train uncomfortably full of Italians (in which case stand by the doors, or impose on the salesmen and other parasites in first class, where the conductor will be happy to change your ticket). Now and then, you and your beloved will have a beautiful 1920s compartment all to yourselves for the night.

By Coach and Bus

Intercity bus travel is often quicker than train travel, but also a bit more expensive. The Italians aren't dumb; you will find regular bus connections only where there is no train to offer competition. Buses almost always depart from the vicinity of the train station, and tickets usually need to be purchased before you get on. In many regions they are the only means of public transport and are well used, with frequent timetables. If you can't get a ticket before the bus leaves, get on anyway and pretend you can't speak a word of Italian; the worst that can happen is that someone will make you pay for a ticket. Understand clearly that the base for all country bus lines will be the provincial capitals, even if they're dinky towns like Frosinone or Avellino; we've done our best to explain the connections even for the most out-of-the-way routes.

11

City buses are the traveller's friend. Most cities label routes well; all charge flat fees for rides within the city limits and immediate suburbs, at the time of writing around L1000. Bus tickets must always be purchased before you get on, at a tobacconist's, a newspaper kiosk, in many bars, or from ticket machines near the main stops. Once you get on, you must punch your ticket in the machines in the front or back of the bus (or as the Italian signs say: *Arm yourself with a ticket on the ground, and obliterate it when on board!*). Fines for cheaters are about L20 000, and the odds (in Rome) are about 18 to 1 against a random check by the controllers, so you may take your chances against how lucky you feel. If you're good-hearted, you'll buy a ticket and help some overburdened municipal transit line meet its annual deficit.

By Taxi

Taxis are about the same price as in London. The average meter starts at L2500, and adds L600 per kilometre. There's an extra charge for luggage and for trips to the airport; and rates go up after 10 pm and on holidays. Forget about meters in and around Naples, and negotiate as best you can before you get in; anywhere else, when they have meters you may politely request that they use them.

By Car

The advantages of driving in Italy generally outweigh the disadvantages. Before you bring your own car or hire one, consider the kind of holiday you're planning. If it's a tour of Rome, Naples, and other large cities, you'd be best off not driving at all: parking is impossible, traffic impossible, deciphering one-way streets, signals, and signs impossible. Take public transport. In nearly every other case, however, a car gives you the freedom and possibility of making your way through Italy's lovely countryside. Purchase the excellently drawn and accurate green-cover **maps** issued by the Italian Touring Club (obtainable in good Italian bookshops, or from Stanfords, 12 Long Acre, London WC2; or Rizzoli International Bookstore, 712 Fifth Avenue, New York).

Be prepared, however, to face not only the highest fuel costs in Europe (when everyone else lowered theirs with slumping international prices, Italy raised them) but also the Italians themselves behind the wheel, many of whom, from 21-year-old madcaps to elderly nuns, drive like idiots, taking particular delight in overtaking at blind curves on mountainous roads. No matter how fast you're going on the *autostrade* (Italy's toll motorways, official speed limit 130 km per hour) someone will pass you going twice as fast. Americans in particular should be wary about driving in Italy. If you're accustomed to the generally civilized rules of motoring that obtain in North America, Italy will be a big surprise. Italians, and their northern visitors, do not seem to care if someone kills them or not. Especially in the cities, rules do not exist, and if you expect them to stop riding on your tail you'll have a long time to wait. Even the most cultured Italians become aggressive, murderous humanoids behind the wheel, and if you value your peace of mind you'll stick with public transport.

If you've purchased petrol coupons (see 'Getting to Italy'), you'll find the petrol stations that accept them put out signs. Many stations close for lunch in the afternoon, and few stay open late at night, though you may find a 'self-service' where you feed a machine nice smooth L10 000 notes. Petrol stations in the cities also sell the discs you

12

can put on your windscreen to park in the *Zona Disco* areas of a city. Autostrada tolls are high—to drive on the A1 from Milan to Rome, for example, will cost you around L40 000. The rest stops and petrol stations along the motorways are open 24 hours. Other roads—*superstrada* on down through the Italian grading system—are free of charge. The Italians are very good about signposting, and roads are almost all excellently maintained—some highways seem to be built of sheer bravura, suspended on cliffs, crossing valleys on enormous piers—feats of engineering that will remind you, more than almost anything else, that this is the land of the ancient Romans. Beware that you may be fined on the spot for speeding, a burnt-out headlamp, etc.; if you're especially unlucky you may be slapped with a *Super Multa*, a superfine, of L100 000 or more. You may even be fined for not having a portable triangle danger signal (pick one up at the frontier or from an ACI office for L1500).

The ACI (Automobile Club of Italy) is a good friend to the foreign motorist. Assistance number 116; English-speaking operators are on duty 24 hours to answer your questions—also use this number if you have an accident, need an ambulance, or simply have to find the nearest service station. If you need major repairs, the ACI can make sure the prices charged are according to their guidelines; if you have a Fuel Card (given when you purchase petrol coupons) you will be given a car to use while your car is being repaired. If you need a tow, your car will be taken to the nearest ACI garage. ACI provincial offices are:

Avellino: Viale Italia 271, tel (0852) 36 459
Bari: Via O. Serena 26, tel (080) 331 354
Benevento: Via S. Rosa 24–26, tel (0824) 21 582
Brindisi: Via B. Buozzi, tel (0831) 83 053
Campobasso: Via Cavour 10, tel (0874) 92 941
Caserta: Via N. Sauro 10, tel (0823) 321 442
Catanzaro: Viale dei Normanni 99, tel (0961) 74 131
Chieti: Piazza Garibaldi 3, tel (0871) 32 307
Cosenza: Via Tocci 2a, tel (0984) 74 381
Fóggia: Via Mastelloni, tel (0881) 36 833
Frosinone: Via Firenze 49, tel (0775) 850 006
Isernia: SS 17, Palazzo Valerio, tel (0865) 50 732
L'Aquila: Via Bone Novelle, tel (0862) 26 028
Latina: Via A. Saffi 23, tel (0773) 29 481
Lecce: Via G. Candido 2, tel (0832) 29 481
Matera: Viale delle Nazioni Unite 47, tel (0835) 213 963
Naples: Piazzale Tecchino 49d, tel (081) 614 511
Pescara: Viale del Circuito 49, tel (085) 32 841
Potenza: Viale del Basento, tel (0971) 56 466
Règgio Calabria: Via de Nava 43, tel (0965) 97 901
Rieti: Via Lucandri 26, tel (0746) 43 339
Rome: Viale C. Colombo 261, tel (06) 5106
Salerno: Via G. Vicinanza 11, tel (089) 226 677
Tàranto: Viale Magna Grecia 108, tel (099) 335 911
Teramo: Corso Cerulli 81, tel (0861) 53 244
Viterbo: Via A. Marini 16/a, tel (0761) 224 806

13

If driving your own car, your ordinary licence is valid in Italy if it is accompanied by a translation, although an International Driving Licence is more convenient to carry (and necessary for those who hire cars). Insurance is mandatory in Italy. A 'Green Card' will be sufficient for 40 to 45 days (you can also purchase 'Frontier Insurance' when you enter), but for longer stays an Italian insurance policy is required. If you are caught breaking the Italian highway code (note that the size of your car determines your speed limit), it is advisable to pay the fine for your *infrazione* to the policeman writing your ticket.

Hiring a Car

Hiring a car is fairly simple if not particularly cheap. Italian car rental firms are called *Autonoleggi*. There are both large international firms through which you can reserve a car in advance, and local agencies, which often have lower prices. Air or train travellers should check out possible discount packages.

Most companies will require a deposit amounting to the estimated cost of the hire, and there is 18 per cent VAT added to the final cost. At the time of writing, a 5-seat Fiat Panda costs around L64 000 a day. Petrol is generally twice as expensive as in the UK. Rates become more advantageous if you take the car for a week with unlimited mileage. If you need a car for more than three weeks, leasing is a more economic alternative. The National Tourist Office has a list of firms in Italy that hire caravans (trailers) and campers.

Hitch-hiking

It's legal to thumb a ride anywhere in Italy except on the *autostrade*. The problem is that in most rural places there isn't that much traffic, and you may have a long wait. Increase your chances by looking respectable and carrying a small suitcase instead of a huge backpack.

By Motorbike or Bicycle

The means of transport of choice for many Italians, motorbikes, mopeds, and Vespas can be a delightful way to see the country. You should only consider it, however, if you've ridden them before—Italy's hills and aggravating traffic make it no place to learn. Italians are keen cyclists as well, racing drivers up the steepest hills; if you're not training for the Tour de France, consider Italy's mountains and hills well before planning a bicycling tour—especially in the hot summer months. Bikes can be transported by train in Italy, either with you or within a couple of days—apply at the baggage office (*ufficio bagagli*). Renting either a motorbike or bicycle is difficult. Depending on how long you're staying, you may find it sensible (especially if you're coming from North America) to buy a second-hand bike in Italy when you arrive, either in a bike shop or through the classified ad papers put out in nearly every city and region. Alternatively, if you bring your own bike, you'll have to check the airlines to see what their policies are on transporting them.

Embassies and Consulates

UK
Rome: Via XX Settembre 80a, tel (06) 475 5441
Naples: Via Francesco Crispi 122, tel (081) 663 320

14

USA
Rome: Via Vittorio Veneto 121, tel (06) 4674
Naples: Piazza della Repubblica, tel (081) 660 966

Eire
Rome: Largo Nazareno 3, tel (06) 678 2541

Canada
Rome: Via Zara 30, tel (06) 854 825

Official Holidays

The Italians have cut down somewhat on their official national holidays, but note that every town has one or two local holidays of its own—usually the feast day of its patron saint. Official holidays, on timetables for transport and museum opening hours, etc. are treated the same as Sundays.

1 January (New Year's Day—*Capodanno*)
6 January (Epiphany, better known to Italians as the day of *La Befana*—a kindly witch who brings the bambini the toys Santa Claus or *Babbo Natale* somehow forgot)
Easter Monday (picnics, but usually pretty dull)
25 April (Liberation Day—even duller)
1 May (Labour Day—lots of parades, speeches, picnics, music and drinking)
15 August (Assumption, or *Ferragosta*—the biggest of them all—woe to the innocent traveller on the road or train!)
1 November (All Saints, or *Tutti Santi*—liveliest at the cemeteries)
8 December (Immaculate Conception of the Virgin Mary—a dull one).
Christmas Day
Boxing Day (*Santo Stefano*)

Time

Italy is one hour ahead of Greenwich Mean Time. From the last weekend of March to the end of September, Italian Summer Time (daylight saving time) puts the country ahead another hour, though moves are afoot to standardize time in Europe for 1992.

Opening Hours

Although it varies from region to region, most of Italy closes down at 1 pm until 3 or 4 pm to eat and properly digest the main meal of the day. Afternoon hours are from 4–7, often from 5–8 in the hot summer months. Bars are often the only places open during the early afternoon. Shops of all kinds are usually closed on Saturday afternoons, through Sunday, and Monday mornings as well—although grocery stores and supermarkets do open on Monday mornings. Banking hours in Italy are Monday to Friday 8:35–1:35 and 3–4, those these vary slightly from place to place.

Italy's **churches** have always been a prime target for art thieves and as a consequence are usually locked when there isn't a sacristan or caretaker to keep an eye on things. All churches, except for the really important cathedrals and basilicas, close in the afternoon at the same hours as the shops, and the little ones tend to stay closed. Always have a pocketful of coins to batten the light machines in churches, or what you came to see is bound to be hidden in ecclesiastical shadows. Don't do your visiting during services, and don't come to see paintings and statues in churches the week preceding Easter—you will probably find them covered with mourning shrouds.

Many of Italy's **museums** are magnificent, many are run with shameful neglect, and many have been closed for years for 'restoration' with slim prospects of re-opening in the near future. With two works of art per inhabitant, Italy has a hard time financing the preservation of its national heritage; in the big cities you would do well to inquire at the tourist office to find out exactly what is open and what is 'temporarily' closed before setting out on a wild goose chase across town.

We have listed the hours of the important sights and museums. In general, Sunday afternoons and Mondays are dead periods for the sightseer—you may want to make them your travelling days. Places without hours usually open on request—but it is best to go before 1 pm. We have also designated which attractions charge admission; unless labelled 'expensive' you'll have to pay between L500 and L4000 to get in. Expensive ones are more, usually L5000 but up to L8000 for the Vatican Museums. Citizens of Common Market countries under 18 and over 60 get free admission to state museums, at least on principle.

Post Offices

The postal service in Italy is the least efficient and most expensive in Europe; if you're sending postcards back home you can count on arriving there before they do. If it's important that it arrive in a week or so, send your letter *Expresso* (Swift Air Mail) or *Raccomandata* (registered delivery), for a L2000 supplement fee. Stamps (*francobolli*) may also be purchased at tobacconists (look for a big black T on the sign), but you're bound to get differing opinions on your exact postage. Mail to the UK goes at the same rate as domestic Italian mail, but it's still twice as much to send a letter from Italy to Britain as vice versa. Air-mail letters to and from North America quite often take three or four weeks. This can be a nightmare if you're making hotel reservations and are sending a deposit—telex or telephoning in advance is far more secure if time is short.

Ask for mail to be sent to you in Italy either care of your hotel or addressed *Fermo Posta* (poste restante: general delivery) to a post office, or, if you're a card-holder, to an American Express Office. When you pick up your mail at the *Fermo Posta* window, bring your passport for identification. Make sure, in large cities, that your mail is sent to the proper post office, easiest is to the **Posta Centrale**.

The Italian postal code is most inscrutable in dealing with packages sent overseas. Packages have to be of a certain size, and under a certain weight to be sent in certain ways, and must have a flap open for inspection or be sealed with string and lead. You're best off taking it to a stationer's shop (*cartolibreria*) and paying L500 for them to wrap it—they usually know what the postal people are going to require.

Telegrams (sent from post offices) are expensive but the surest way to get your message out of Italy. You can save money by sending it as a night letter (22 words or less).

16

Telephones

Like many things in Italy, telephoning can be unduly complicated. In many places you'll still find the old token *gettoni* telephones, in which you must insert a token (or better yet, several) before dialling. *Gettoni* cost L200 and are often available in machines next to the telephones, or from bars, news-stands, or *tabacchi*. If more *gettoni* are required while you are speaking, you'll hear a beep, which means put in more *gettoni* quickly or you'll be cut off. For long-distance calls (anyone in Italy with a different telephone code), put in as many as the telephone will take (about 10) and be ready to feed in more as you go along. Any unused *gettoni* will be refunded after your call if you push the return button. Other public phones will take either coins, phone cards, or *gettoni*.

For international calls, head either for a telephone office with booths (usually only in the larger cities and major train stations, operated by either SIP or ASST) or a bar with a telephone meter. If you want to reverse the charges (call collect) you must do it from an office (tell them you want to telephone *a erre* and fill out the little card). Rates are lower if you call at a weekend (after 2:30 pm on Saturday until 8 am Monday morning—unfortunately just when many provincial telephone offices are closed). Phoning long-distance from your hotel can mean big surcharges.

Direct-dial codes are: USA and Canada 001, UK 0044 (leaving out the '0' before the British area code). If you're calling Italy from abroad, the country code is 39, followed by the area prefix—omitting the first '0'.

Police Business

There is a fair amount of petty crime in Italy, especially in Rome and Naples—purse snatchings, pickpocketing, minor thievery of the white collar kind (always check your change) and car break-ins and theft—but violent crime is rare. Nearly all mishaps can be avoided with adequate precautions. Scooter-born purse-snatchers can be foiled if you stay on the inside of the pavement and keep a firm hold on your property. Pickpockets most often strike in crowded street cars and gatherings; don't carry too much cash or keep some of it in another place. Be extra careful in train stations, don't leave valuables in hotel rooms, and always park your car in garages, guarded lots, or on well-lit streets, with temptations like radios, cassettes, etc. out of sight. Don't take your car into Naples at all. Purchasing small quantities of reefer, hashish, cocaine, and LSD is rarely dangerous, although what a small quantity might be exactly is unspecified, so if the police don't like you to begin with, it will probably be enough to get you into big trouble.

Once the scourge of Italy, political terrorism has declined drastically in recent years, mainly thanks to special squads of the *Carabinieri*, the black-uniformed national police, technically part of the Italian army. Local matters are usually in the hands of the *Polizia Urbana*; the nattily dressed *Vigili Urbani* concern themselves with directing traffic, and handing out parking fines. If you need to summon any of them, dial 113.

Photography

Film and developing are much more expensive than they are in the US or UK. You are not allowed to take pictures in most museums and in some churches.

Lavatories

Frequent travellers have noted a steady improvement over the years in the cleanliness of Italy's public conveniences, although as ever you will only find them in places like train and bus stations and bars. Ask for the *bagno*, *toilette*, or *gabinetto*; in stations and the smarter bars and cafés, there are washroom attendants who expect a few hundred lire for keeping the place decent. You'll probably have to ask them for paper (*carta*). Don't confuse the Italian plurals: *Signori* (gents), *Signore* (ladies).

Women and Children

Italian men, with the heritage of Casanova, Don Giovanni, and Rudolph Valentino as their birthright, are very confident in their role as great Latin lovers, but the old horror stories of gangs following the innocent tourist maiden and pinching her behind are out of date. Most Italian men these days are exquisitely polite and flirt on a much more sophisticated level, still, women travelling alone may frequently receive undesired company, 'assistance', or whatever, from local swains (usually of the balding, middle-age-crisis variety): a firm 'no!' or '*Vai via!*' (Scram!), repeated as often as necessary, will generally solve the problem, which can be greatly reduced if you avoid lonely streets and train stations after dark. Travelling with a companion of either sex will buffer you considerably from such nuisances.

Even though a declining birthrate and the legalization of abortion may hint otherwise, children are still the royalty of Italy, and are pampered, often obscenely spoiled, probably more fashionably dressed than you are, and never allowed to get dirty. Yet with all those points against them, most of them somehow manage to be well-mannered little charmers. If you're bringing your own bambini to Italy, they'll receive a warm welcome everywhere. Many hotels offer advantageous rates for children and have play areas, and most of the larger cities have permanent **Luna Parks**, or fun fairs; the one in Rome's EUR is huge and charmingly old-fashioned (and a great trade-off for a day in the Vatican Museum).

Most of the other kids' stuff in the south is around Rome, too, where they are most useful in negotiating for a grown-up's day of culture. There's the Villa Borghese zoo, the **Bomarzo Monster Park** in northern Lazio, **Edenlandia** near Naples. In Apulia, there is a small zoo at Oria and a safari-zoo at Fasano, both near Brindisi. If your kids know some Italian, there are **puppet theatres** in Rome. If a **circus** visits the town you're in, you're in for a treat; it will either be a sparkling showcase of daredevil skill or a poignant, family-run, modern version of Fellini's *La Strada*.

Sports and Activities

Italians are sports fiends; the newspaper enjoying the widest circulation in the country is the pink-tinted *Gazzetto dello Sport*, and it is mainly concerned with *calcio*, or **football**, not surprisingly the country's most popular sport—both for the thrills and the Sunday results that may make anyone an instant billionaire in the Lotteria Sportiva. Although modern football was introduced by English visitors, there was a football-rugby type game in the Renaissance, re-enacted in costume in Florence on the second Sunday in

September. Modern Italian teams are known for their grace, precision, and teamwork; rivalries are intense, scandals, especially bribery and cheating, are rife. Probably nowhere in Europe is big-time sport more plagued by big money; recently a first-division club owner was caught fixing matches, and got off with a slap on the wrist. On the other hand, crowd violence is minimal compared with other countries. The recent successes of Naples on the field (league champions for the first time ever in 1986) have earned the city more respect and legitimacy than any of the billions of lire spent on its more substantial problems.

Rugby and **baseball** are growing sports, with teams in some cities, attracting enough support to make the national TV, although it will be a decade before play reaches international levels. **American football** is a few steps behind, an exotic, trendy sport that mystifies most Italians. **Cycling** is uncannily popular, and squads of aficionados in colour-coordinated outfits will sooner or later make you slam on the brakes on some winding mountain road. The springtime, seemingly endless *Tour d'Italia* is the big event on the calendar. In the summer there are numerous **rowing** events—once every four years Amalfi hosts the annual race between the four Old Maritime Republics (Genoa, Pisa, Amalfi, and Venice), which alternates between cities. The real centre for rowing is pretty Lake Piediluco, in the mountains near Rieti; the nearby plain of Rieti enjoys the kind of perfect updraughts that makes it Italy's capital of **gliding**. **Horse racing** is popular, with tracks in Rome and Naples. Old men play **bocce** (boules) and rapid-fire card games in the backrooms of bars, the rules of which are known only to them (though Luigi Barzini, in his excellent book, *The Italians*, cites the basic principle as 'Try to see your opponent's cards').

The most controversial sport in Italy is **hunting**, pitting avid enthusiasts against a burgeoning number of environmentalists, who have recently elected the first Greens to parliament; anti-hunting petitions garner thousands of signatures, and the opening day of the season is marked by huge protests. It is, indeed, rather painful to run into some macho Italian hunter returning from the field with a string of tiny birds around his belt; in many places they have been hunted so thoroughly that it's rare to hear a bird sing. Without their natural predators, pesky insects and poisonous snakes have become a problem in many rural areas. Boar hunting is also extremely popular. **Fishing** is managed better; many freshwater lakes and streams are stocked, and if you're more interested in fresh fish than the sport of it, there are innumerable trout farms where you can practically pick the fish up out of the water with your hands. Sea fishing, from the shore, from boats, or underwater (though not with an aqualung) is possible almost everywhere without a permit; to fish in fresh water you need to purchase a year's membership card for L5000 from the Federazione Italiana della Pesca Sportiva, which has an office in every province; they will inform you about local conditions and restrictions.

If you were considering an Italian beach holiday, it will be reassuring to know that pollution is less serious than in the north, even along the Adriatic, though most of the southern shores are disappointingly flat and dull, and they haven't been improved by endless neat rows of parasols and lounge chairs full of people scientifically perfecting their tans. Few venture into the water around the Bay of Naples or Rome's nightmarish Lido di Ostia, though in general the southernmost beaches—the mile upon mile of sand along the sea in Calabria, Basilicata, and Apulia—are very clean and much less developed than the ones further north. The clear turquoise sea of the south is excellent for **diving**, most spectacularly around the Gargano peninsula, and the Tremiti and Pontine islands.

You can bring your boat to Italy for six months without any paperwork if you bring it by car; if you arrive by sea you must report to the Port Authority of your first port to show passports and receive your 'Costituto' which identifies you and allows you to purchase fuel tax free. Boats with engines require a number plate, and if they're over 3 horsepower you need insurance. If you want to leave your boat in Italy for an extended period, you must have a Navigation Licence; after a year you have to start paying taxes on it. All yachts must pay a daily berthing fee in Italian ports. For a list of ports which charter yachts, write to the National Tourist Office. **Yacht Charters** in the south include: ALTO MARE, Via Crispi 22, 74100 **Tàranto**, tel (099) 96 426; MED, Via Piave 52, 00187 **Roma**, tel (06) 462 729; SAIL ITALIA, Via Roma 63, **Procida** (Naples), tel (081) 896 9962.

Many regions(especially Lazio and the Abruzzo) now offer **riding holidays**, as well as stables where you can hire a horse for a few hours; write to the provincial tourist offices for details. **Golfers** will find about 60 courses in Italy where they may try their skill and luck; for particulars on visitors to the clubs, their locations, opening seasons, etc., write directly to the clubs:

Oligiata (27 holes), Largo dell'Oligiata 15, 00123 **Roma**, tel (06) 378 9141
Rome (18 holes), Via Appia Nuova 716/a, 00178 **Roma**, tel (06) 783 407
Marina Velca (9 holes), 01016 **Tarquinia**, tel (0766) 812 109
Fiuggi (9 holes) 03015 **Fiuggi** (Frosinone) tel (0775) 55 250
Fioranello (9 holes), 00040 **Santa Maria della Mole** (near Rome), tel (06) 608 291
Naples-Afsouth Golf Club (9 holes), 80078 **Pozzuoli**, tel (081) 426 207
Riva dei Tessali (18 holes), 74025 **Marina di Ginosa** (Tàranto), tel (099) 643 071
Porta d'Orra (9 holes), 88063 **Catanzaro Lido**, tel (0961) 34 045

The **skiing** is excellent in Italy, but not in the sunny south; there are a few small resorts, the most important of which is Monte Terminillo near Rieti, a favourite of the Romans. There are also some challenging runs on the Gran Sasso d'Italia, the highest peak of the Apennines, in the Abruzzo; the southernmost skiing on the peninsula can be had at Gambarie, near Règgio Calabria, though only a week or two each year. There are high and low ski seasons—prices are highest during the Christmas and New Year holidays, in part of February, and at Easter. Most resorts offer *Settimane Bianche* (White Weeks) packages, which include room and board and ski passes for surprisingly economical rates; the National Tourist office can supply particulars on other special ski holidays.

Hiking and mountaineering become more and more popular among the Italians themselves every year, and the country has a good system of marked trails and alpine refuges. Many of the trails and refuges are kept up by local offices of the Italian Alpine Club (CAI), located in every province (even the flat ones, where they organize excursions into the hills). If you're taking some of the most popular trails in the summer (especially in Abruzzo National Park), you would do well to write in advance to reserve beds in the refuges. The local tourist offices can put you in touch with the right people and organizations. Walking in the high Apennines is generally practicable between May and October, after most of the snows have melted; all the necessary gear—boots, packs, tents, etc. are readily available in Italy but for more money than you'd pay at home. The CAI can put you in touch with Alpine guides or climbing groups if you're up to some real adventures, or write to the National Tourist organization for operators offering mountaineering holidays.

Courses for Foreigners and Special Interest Holidays

The Italian Institute, 39 Belgrave Square, London SW1X 8NX, tel (071) 235 1461 or 686 Park Avenue, New York NY 10021, tel (212) 397 9300, is the main source of information on courses for foreigners in Italy. Graduate students should also contact their nearest Italian consulate to find out about scholarships—apparently many go unused each year because no one knows about them.

Among the possiblities are: summer language and culture courses run by the Centro Relazioni e Scambi Culturali of Naples (Via Mezzocannone 119); Feb-June, master classes for instrumentalists and conductors at Rome's celebrated Accademia Nazionale di Santa Cecilia, Via Vittoria 6; archaeology courses at Herculaneum (July–August), run by Europa, Via Mezzocannone 119, Naples; and in April at Rome, run by the Fondazione Lerici, Via Vittorio Veneto 108, Rome. In Lecce, art restoration workshops are held at the Istituto per l'Arte e il Restauro, Palazzo Spinelli, Borgo Santa Croce 10.
Special Interest holidays are an increasingly popular way to see Southern Italy. UK operators include:
ACROSS TRUST (handicapped tours of Rome), Crown House, Morden, Surrey, tel (081) 540 3897
ART IN EUROPE (art and architecture, language and music in Rome) 78 Shaftesbury Way, Twickenham, Middx, tel (081) 898 9888
BROMPTON TRAVEL (opera at Naples), 204 Walton St, London SW3, tel (071) 584 6143
C.H.A. (walking and mountaineering in Abruzzo National Park), Birch Heys, Cromwell Range, Manchester, tel (061) 225 1000
LEAHY'S TRAVEL (singles and pilgrimage tours to Rome, Monte Cassino, and Assisi) 116 Harpenden Rd, St Albans, Herts, tel (0727) 52 394
MAGIC OF ITALY (art and archaeology in Apulia, Campania, and Basilicata), 47 Shepherds Bush Green, London, W12, tel (081) 743 9555
MAGNUM (senior citizens in Rome), 7 Westleigh Park, Blaby, Leicester, tel (0533) 777 123
MAJOR AND MRS HOLT'S BATTLEFIELD TOURS (art and archaeology tours of Pompeii, Herculaneum, Vesuvius, Paestum, and Naples; also battlefield tours of Salerno and Cassino), Golden Key Building, 15 Market St, Sandwich, Kent, tel (0304) 612 248
THE PLANTAGENET TOURS (Frederick II tour), 85 The Grove, Moordown, Bournemouth, tel (0202) 521 895
RAMBLERS HOLIDAYS (walks and mountaineering at Amalfi and Vico Equense) Box 43, Welwyn Garden City, Herts, tel (0707) 331 133
SAGA HOLIDAYS (senior citizens at Rome, Sorrento, Paestum, and Capri), The Saga Building, Middelburg Square, Folkestone, Kent, tel (0303) 40 000

SERENISSIMA AND HERITAGE TRAVEL (art and architecture from Tuscany to Campania), 21 Dorset Square, London, NW1 tel (071) 703 9841

SJA (language and culture in Rome), 48 Cavendish Rd, London SW12, tel (081) 673 4849

SOLO'S (single tours of Positano and Sorrento), 41 Watford Way, Hendon, London NW4, tel (081) 202 0855

SWAN HELLENIC (art and archaeology tour of Southern Italy) 77 New Oxford St, London, SW1, tel (071) 831 1515

TAVEL WITH FRIENDS (opera at Rome and Naples), 117 Regent's Park Rd, London NW1, tel (071) 483 2297

WAYMARK HOLIDAYS (walks and mountaineering at Amalfi), 295 Lillie Rd, London SW6, tel (071) 385 5015

VOYAGES JULES VERNE (Botany and wild flowers in the Gargano peninsula and Paestum) 21 Dorset Square, London NW1, tel (071) 724 6624

Festivals

There are literally thousands of festivals answering to every description in Italy. Every *comune* has at least one or two, not only celebrating a patron saint; others are sponsored by the political parties (especially the Communists and Socialists), where everyone goes to meet their friends and enjoy the masses of cheap food. No matter where you are, look at the posters; Italy is swamped with culture, and most refreshingly unsnobbish or elitist about it all. On the other hand, do not expect anything approaching uninhibited gaiety. Italy is a rather staid place these days, and festivals are largely occasions to dress up and have a pleasant outdoor supper. If, at a festival, you should ever happen to notice Italians laughing too loudly, drinking too much, or singing extemporaneously, drop us a line; we would love to see it.

Below is a calendar of the some of the most popular annual events; some of particular interest will be mentioned in the text. For many you'll have to check at the tourist office for precise dates, which change from year to year.

Calendar of Events

January

1	Lively New Year's celebration, **Capri**, with musicians playing the *putipù*, a local folk instrument.
6	Climax of the Epiphany toy fair in Piazza Navona, **Rome**; live Christmas tableau at **Rivisondoli** in Abruzzo; re-enactment of the Magi's visit to Bethlehem, in **Lizzano** (Tàranto).
Jan–April	Chamber music at the Teatro delle Palme, **Naples**.
Jan–June	Opera at Teatro dell'Opera, **Rome**.
Jan–June	Symphony and chamber music concerts of the Accademia Nazionale di Santa Cecilia, **Rome**.

Jan–mid-July	Opera at the San Carlo, **Naples**.
15	*Fritella* festival, **Tuscania** (Viterbo), with cauliflower fritters and Maremma cowboy rodeo.
Mid-month	*Zampogna* festival—bagpipe competitions at **Acquafondata** in Lazio.
16–17	Sant'Antonio, **Collelongo** (L'Aquila), where cooking pots are blessed and a prize given to the most beautiful; at **Sutri** (Viterbo), a parade of caparisoned horses are paraded and blessed; in **Velletri** (Rome) the saint is celebrated with horsemen trying to lance a ring; bonfires and games at **Novoli** (Lecce).
20	San Sebastiano, when a metal framework covered with fireworks is ignited, at **Ortona** (Chieti).
24	Festival of the salatielli (lupins), at **Casale di Carinola** (Caserta).

February

1–3	San Biagio, celebrated by special hand-shaped rolls and a parade at **Taranta Peligna** (Chieti).
2–3	The *stuzze*, with great bonfires fo S. Biagio, at **Fiuggi** (Frosinone).
3	Feast of San Biagio, at **Monte San Biagio** (Latina).
First week	Wine and liquor show, **Naples**.
Thurs before Ash Wednesday	Feast of the Incappucciati, at **Gradoli** (Viterbo), in which members of the Confraternity of Purgatory in hooded robes collect food for communal banquet on Ash Wednesday.
Carnival	Not as big as in the north, though you'll find traditional carnivals at **Putignano** (Bari), which starts on December 16th, making it Italy's longest; also **Ronciglione** (Viterbo), with riderless horse races, parades, and floats.
Ash Wedneday	*Palio del viccio*, at **Palo del Colle** (Bari), a contest of donkey riders who try to pierce a bladder suspended over the street.
Last Sun	S. Silverio, **Ponza**.

March

Mid-month	Art and antique print shows, **Bari**.
19	San Giuseppe, bonfires at **Fara San Martino** (Chieti); stewed beans at **Rocca Pia** (L'Aquila).
28	Blessing of the quadrupeds, **Montoro Superiore** (Avellino), recalling the day Mary saved the town from a maddened bull; Festival of the *talami*, allegorical floats on which children act out Bible scenes, at **Orsogna** (Chieti).

April

10	Country Festival of Santa Lucia, **Montemitro** (Campobasso), with a procession and handicrafts, etc. relating to the village's Slavic origins.

Palm Sunday	Re-enactment of Christ's entry into Jerusalem, at **Maenza** (Latina).
Holy Week	In the south Holy Week celebrations have a definite Spanish flavour, many featuring processions of floats carried by robed and hooded members of local confraternities, most impressively in Tàranto.

Tuesday, Passion Play at **Agnone** (Isernia); Wednesday, Passion Play of Christ and the emigrant at **Gessopalena** (Chieti); Thursday and Friday, solemn processions and floats of scenes from Christ's Passion (*misteri*) in **Tàranto**; Friday and Saturday, Passion Play at **Ginosa** (Tàranto); on Friday, torchlight Way of the Cross in **Nemoli** (Potenza), followed by omelette feast on Easter; Friday, traditional confraternity procession at **Calitri** (Avellino); very ancient processions at **Chieti**, also at **Civitavecchia** (Rome); Friday Passion tableaux and processions at **L'Aquila**, **Mirabella Eclano** and **Lapio** (both in Avellino), **Sessa Aurunca** (Caserta) and **Sorrento**; in **Rome** the Pope leads midnight procession in the Colosseum. Holy Saturday procession of Spanish origin at **Caulonia** (Règgio Calabria), called the *caracolo* (snail) because of its pace; at **Nocera Ticinese** (Calabria), Procession of the Flagellants.

Easter	Procession of figures at **Lanciano** (Chieti); **La Madonna chi scappa** (the fleeing Madonna) at **Sulmona** (L'Aquila).
Orthodox Easter	Albanian Easter celebrations, at **Lungro** in Calabria.

May

4	Procession of the serpents and snake handlers, at **Cocullo** (L'Aquila), with the image of the town's patron saint San Domenico (often evoked against snake bites) wrapped in serpents as well; Festival of torches, at **Sonnino** (Latina), an ancient rite that traces the periphery of the town in torchlight.
6–7	San Nicola, **Bari**, nighttime re-enactment in Norman costumes of the 'pious theft' of St Nicholas' relics from Myra by the merchants of Bari; next day, holy procession by boat; Feast of pardon, at **Ortona** (Chieti), with another procession by sea.
7	Another snake procession in honour of San Domenico, at **Pretono** (Chieti), along with a pantomine of the wolf tamed by the saint.
8–10	San Cataldo, at **Tàranto**, with sea-borne processions.
14	Exhibition of the *pugnaloni*, in honour of the Madonna of Flowers, at **Acquapendente** (Viterbo), displays of flowering panels recalling the miraculous flowering branch that served as a good omen in the revolt against Frederick Barbarossa in 1176.

Mid-month	Sagra di S. Pardo, with ox carts, **Larino** (Molise).
Last half	International Music festival in **Naples**.
14–21	Feast of Madonna di Capocolonna, **Crotone** (Catanzaro), festival with sea-borne processions and fish fry.
21	Festival of the *Banderesi*, in honour of St Urban, with an historical pageant, at **Bucchianico** (Chieti); *Barabbata*, feast of ancient guilds, at **Marta** (Viterbo).
Corpus Domini	Magnificent floral carpets, or *Infiorata*, at **Genzano** (Rome) and **Bolsena** (Viterbo); at **Campobasso**, the Procession of the *Misteri*— tableaux featuring children suspended in mid-air; in **Brindisi** a magnificently caparisoned white horse carries the holy Tabernacle through the town.
3rd week	Comic strip and illustration show, **Naples**.
28–29	Parade of the Turks, in **Potenza**, for San Gerardo.

June

Second Sat	Gypsy Festival at **Isernia**.
Mid-June–July 22	Baroque music festival, **Viterbo**; festival of American musicians at **Sulmona** (L'Aquila).
27	Sant'Andrea, with fireworks, costumes, and processions at **Amalfi**.
4th Sun	*Festa dei Gigli* in **Nola**, near Naples— procession of enormous 'lilies' (wooden tower floats), recalling the homecoming of Bishop Paolino after his imprisonment in Africa in 394; Challenge of the Trombonieri, arquebus shooting contest in period costume, recalling a defeat over the Angevins, at **Cava de' Tirreni** (Salerno).
27–29	Fair of San Pietro of the Onions, **Isernia**, traditional fair, since 1254, celebrating the local speciality.

July

July-Aug	Grand opera in the Baths of Caracalla, **Rome**.
First week	Wagner music festival, **Ravello**.
2	Palio Madame Margherita, **Castel Madama** (Rome), parade in 16th-century costumes and races; Festa of the Madonna della Bruna, **Matera**, religious procession with allegorical float, torn apart by the crowd at the end of the day.
2–9	Festival of the *renie*, **Minturno** (Latina), folklore and harvest festival.
9	Dance of the *fantàsima* at **Castel di Tora** (Rieti), featuring a 10-foot tall 'ghost' who scares everyone before being burned on a bonfire.
16	Feast of the Madonna del Carmine, at **Agnone** (Isernia), procession and major fireworks show.
16–24	*Festa de Noiantri*, in **Rome's** Trastevere.

23-24	Misteri of Santa Cristina, with children in costumes in tableaux representing the saint's martyrdom, **Bolsena** (Viterbo).
26	Wheat festival, **Jelsi** (Campobasso), parade of wheel-less carts called *traglie*, decorated with wheat; Festival of the horsemen of Sant'Anna, at **San Magno sul Calore** (Avellino), with a gallop along the river; Feast of the Madonna del Carmine, **Palmoli** (Chieti), harvest festival with displays of corn and children in costume.
End of July	Bagpipe festival in **Scapoli** (Isernia); second hand fair, **Lanciano** (Chieti).

August

1–5	Wine festival, at **Montefiascone** (Viterbo), with a pageant re-enacting the tale of Est! Est!! Est!!!
First weekend	Grape and wine festival, **Pollutri** (Chieti) with floats, folk songs, and a competition of dialect poetry; Lamb festival at **Collelongo** (L'Aquila).
6–8	Feast of San Nicola Pellegrino, **Trani** (Bari), waterfront festival.
2nd Sun	Pezzata, at **Capracotta** (Isernia), with mutton dishes, folk songs, and dances.
14–16	Madonna della Madia, **Monópoli** (Bari), water festival celebrating an icon of the Madonna that floated ashore.
15	Wheat festival, **Foglianise** (Benevento), procession of decorated tractors, with a light pageant in the evening; Festival of the Straw Obelisk, **Fontanarosa** (Avellino), harvest festival centred around a 100-foot straw obelisk; Feast of San Rocco, **Roccanova** (Potenza), patron saint folk festival; Festival of the sea, **Termoli** (Campobasso), greased pole fun and a simulated burning of the local Swabian castle; feast of mutton chops, **Longone** (Rieti); gliding (sail plane) races in **Rieti**.
22	Fishermen's Procession on the Sea, fireworks, etc. at **Porto Cesareo** (Lecce).
Last Sun	Fish festival and fireworks at **Termoli** (Campobasso).
28–29	Perdonanza, **L'Aquila**, recalling the coronation of local hermit as Celestine V in 1294 at S. Maria di Collemaggio; a major festival with plenty of concerts and other activities.
Last week	*Panatenee Pompeiane*, opera, dance and symphonies in the ruins of **Pompeii**.

September

| First 10 days | Neapolitan song contest, fireworks, etc. at **Piedigrotta** (Naples). |
| 3 | Procession of the enormous *Macchina di Santa Rosa* in **Viterbo**. |

8	Procession of the *donativi*, **Lanciano** (Chieti), where the Madonna del Ponte is celebrated by women carrying decorated local produce in copper pots on their heads.
3rd Sun	Festival of the straw cart, **Mirabella Eclano** (Avellino), where a tall straw obelisk is drawn into town on a cart.
19	Feast of San Gennaro, **Naples**, where the faithful gather to watch the liquefaction of the saint's blood
26–28	Feast of SS. Cosma e Damiano, **Longone** (Rieti).
End Sept–first week Oct	Apulian handicrafts show, **Fóggia**.

October

1st Sun	Porchetta festival, **Poggio Bustone** (Rieti).
2nd Sun	Wine festival in **Tivoli**.

November

10	Feast of San Trifone, **Adelfia** (Bari), calvacade of children dressed as angels riding caparisoned horses.
16	Feast of San Rocco, **Roccanova** (Potenza) with wine, food, and folklore.
21	*Pastorale*, a religious celebration in **Agnone** (Isernia).

December

Throughout	Christmas Fair, selling figures and decorations for the *presepi*, **Naples**.
6	Feast of San Nicola, **Bari** and **Pullutri** (Chieti), the latter featuring a fava bean feast.
8	Immaculate Conception sausage and polenta festival, **San Bartolomeo in Galdo** (Benevento).
2nd week	Christmas gift show, **Fóggia**.
13	Feast of Santa Lucia, **Belpasso** (Chieti), parade, floats, and an antique Christmas crib; also a fair and events at **Lecce nei Marsi** (L'Aquila).
24	Nocturnal Procession of the *'ndocciata*, at **Agnone** (Isernia), with great fir torches and a bonfire at the end; Christmas crib in the Zinzalusa grotto, at **Castro** (Lecce), until Epiphany; Franciscan crib at **Greccio** (Rieti), celebrating the first one set up by St Francis in Greccio in 1223; Midnight mass and Christmas tableaux in caves at **Grottaglie** (Tàranto) and **Nardò** (Lecce).
25–26	Festa del maio, **Baiano** (Avellino), celebration centred around a large chestnut tree set up in front of the church of Santo Stefano.
26	*Ballo della pupa*, **Lama dei Peligni** (Chieti), festivities centred around the *pupa*, a large papier mâché figure.

Shopping

'Made in Italy' of late has become a byword for style and quality, especially in fashion and leather, but also in home design, ceramics, kitchenware, jewellery, lace and linens, glassware and crystal, chocolates, bells, Christmas decorations (especially *presepi*, figures for Christmas cribs), hats, straw work, art books, engravings, handmade stationery, gold and silverware, bicycles, sports cars, woodworking (especially in the Alps), a hundred kinds of liqueurs, wine, aperitifs, coffee machines, gastronomic specialities, antique reproductions, as well as the antiques themselves. If you are looking for the latter and are spending a lot of money, be sure to demand a certificate of authenticity—reproductions can be very, very good. To get your antique or modern art purchases home, you will have to apply to the Export Department of the Italian Ministry of Education—a possible hassle. You will have to pay an export tax as well; your seller should know the details.

You'll find the best variety of goods in Rome and some of the lowest prices in Naples, especially in its various markets (see the shopping sections following each city). Italians don't like department stores, but there are a few chains—the classiest is the oldest, *Rinascente*, while *COIN* stores often have good buys in almost the latest fashions. *Standa* and *UPIM* are more like Woolworth's; they have good clothes selections, housewares, etc., and often supermarkets in their basements. A few stay open throughout the day, but most take the same break as other Italian shops—from 1 pm to 3 or 4 pm. Be sure to save your receipts for Customs on the way home. Shipping goods is a risky business unless you do it through a very reputable shop. Note well that the attraction of shopping in Italy is strictly limited to luxury items; for less expensive clothes and household items you'll always, always do better in Britain or America. Prices for clothes, even in street markets, are often ridiculously high. Bargains of any kind are rare, and the cheaper goods are often very poor quality.

Italian clothes are lovely, but if you have a large-boned Anglo-American build, you may find it hard to get a good fit, especially on trousers or skirts (Italians are a long-waisted, slim-hipped bunch). Shoes are often narrower than the sizes at home.

Sizes

Women's Shirts/Dresses

UK	10	12	14	16	18
US	8	10	12	14	16
Italy	40	42	44	46	48

Sweaters

10	12	14	16
8	10	12	14
46	48	50	52

Women's Shoes

3	4	5	6	7	8
4	5	6	7	8	9
36	37	38	39	40	41

Men's Shirts

UK/US	14	14½	15	15½	16	16½	17	17½
Italy	36	37	38	39	40	41	42	43

Men's Suits

UK/US	36	38	40	42	44	46
Italy	46	48	50	52	54	56

Men's Shoes

UK	2	3	4	5		6	7	8	9		10	11	12
US	5	6	7	7½		8	9	10	10½		11	12	13
Italy	34	36	37	38		39	40	41	42		43	44	45

Weights and Measures

1 kilogramme (1000 g)—2.2 lb
1 etto (100 g)—¼ lb (approx)
1 litre—1.76 pints

1 metre—39.37 inches
1 kilometre—0.621 miles

1 lb—0.45 kg

1 pint—0.568 litres
1 quart—1.136 litres
1 Imperial gallon—4.546 litres
1 US gallon—3.785 litres
1 foot—0.3048 metres
1 mile—1.161 kilometres

Where to Stay

Hotels

Italy is endowed with hotels (*alberghi*) of every description, from the spectacular to the humble. These are rated by the government's tourism bureaucracy, from five stars at the luxurious top to one star at the bottom. The ratings take into account such things as a restaurant on the premises, plumbing, air conditioning, etc., but not character, style, or charm. Use the stars, which we include in this book, as a quick reference for prices and general amenities only. Another thing to remember about government ratings is that a hotel can stay at a lower rating than it has earned, so you may find a three-star hotel as comfortable as a four.

There's no inflation in Italy, if you believe the government; the prices simply keep increasing. With the vacation business booming, this curious paradox is well expressed in the prices of the country's hotels; every year costs rise by 6–8 per cent across the board, and are quickly catching up with northern Europe. **The prices listed in this book are for double rooms only.** For a single, count on paying two-thirds of a double; to add an extra bed in a double will add 35 per cent to the bill. Taxes and service charges are included in the given rate. Some establishments charge L10–25 000 for air conditioning. Also note that if rooms are listed without bath, it simply means the shower and lavatory are in the corridor. Prices are by law listed on the door of each room; any discrepancies could be reported to the local tourist office. Most rooms have two or three different rates, depending on the season. Costs are sometimes a third less if you travel in the district's low season. Some hotels, especially in resorts, close down altogether for several months of the year. Reservations are indispensable in summer. The Italian Tourist Office publishes annually lists of hotels and pensions with their most recent rates and amenities, which are very helpful (although note that the Tourist Boards do not make reservations).

Breakfast is optional in most hotels, although in pensions it is mandatory. And you may as well expect to face half-board (breakfast and lunch or dinner) or full-board requirements in the hotels that can get away with it—seaside, lake, or mountain resorts in season, spas and country villa hotels. Otherwise, meal arrangements are optional. Although eating in the hotel restaurant can be a genuine gourmet experience, in the majority of cases hotel food is mass-produced and bland, just as it is anywhere else. As a general rule, expect to pay (in lire) in 1990:

Category	Double With bath
Luxury (*****)	L300–700 000
Class I (****)	L200–400 000
Class II (***)	L100–200 000
Class III (**)	L60–100 000
Class IV (*)	L40–60 000
Pension	L30–40 000

For rooms without bath, subtract 20–30 per cent. Many resort hotels in particular offer discounts for children and children's meals. A *camera matrimoniale* is a room with a double bed, a *camera doppia* has twin beds, a single is a *camera singola*. There are several hotel chains in Italy. CIGA (*Compagnia Grandi Alberghi*) has many of the most luxurious, many of them grand, turn-of-the-century establishments that have been exquisitely restored. Another plush chain, *Chateaux et Relais* specializes in equally comfortable, but more intimate accommodation, often in historic buildings. Both chains pride themselves on their gourmet restaurants. Even the once fairly standard *Jolly Hotels*, Italy's oldest chain, are quickly upgrading. The petrol company AGIP operates most of the motels along the major motorways, and usually makes a decent effort to give them good restaurants; you can book AGIP motels at Quo Vadis Ltd, 243 Euston Road, London NW1 (tel (071) 388 7512). The National Tourist office has a complete list of these and booking information for both motels and five- and four-star hotels and chains. If you want to stay in a different kind of accommodation, you'll have to book ahead on your own. Outside the high season this is generally unnecessary; otherwise, and especially if you have a certain place in mind, it is essential to book several months in advance or even earlier if possible, considering the sorry state of the Italian post (while you're at it, remember to request a room with a view). If your Italian is non-existent, the National Tourist Office's *Travellers' Handbook* has a sample letter and list of useful terms. Under Italian law, a booking is valid once a deposit has been paid. If you have to cancel your reservation, the hotel will keep the deposit unless another agreement has been reached. If you arrive in the summer without reservations, start ringing round for a place in the morning.

Facilities for the Handicapped
Hotel listings sometimes make a note of which establishments are suitable for the physically handicapped. There are also a number of tours that can make a holiday much smoother—a list is available from the National Tourist Office. RADAR publishes an extremely useful book, *Holidays and Travel Abroad— A Guide for Disabled People*, available for £3.00 from their offices at 25 Mortimer St, London W1M 8AB, tel (071) 637 5400. Another useful book, *Access to the World: a Travel Guide for the Handicapped* by Louise Weiss covers a wide range of topics with listings for individual countries. It's available for $14.95 from Facts on File, 460 Park Ave South, New York, NY 10016.

Inexpensive Accommodation

Bargains are few and far between in Italy. The cheapest kind of hotel is called an inn, or *locanda*; some provinces treat these as one-star hotels or list them separately (or not at all). The majority of inexpensive places will always be around the railway station, though in the large cities you'll often find it worth your while to seek out a more pleasant location in the historic centre. You're likely to find anything in a one-star Italian hotel. Often they will be practically perfect, sometimes almost luxurious; memorably bad experiences will be few, and largely limited to the major cities (around the train stations!).

Besides the youth hostels (see below), there are several city-run hostels, with dormitory-style rooms open to all. In Rome, and other pilgrimage towns, religious institutions often rent out extra rooms. Monasteries in the country sometimes take guests as well; if you seek that kind of quiet experience, bring a letter of introduction from your local priest, pastor, etc. Women can make arrangements through the *Protezione della Giovane*, an organization dedicated to finding inexpensive and virtuous lodgings in convents, hostels, etc. They have desks in major railway stations, or you can contact them at their headquarters at Via Urbana 158, Rome, tel 460 056.

Youth and Student Hostels

Italy isn't exceptionally well endowed with Youth Hostels (*Albergo per la Gioventù*), but they are usually pleasant and often in historic buildings. Hostels in the south are: Beata Solitudo, at **Agerola-S. Lazzaro** (Naples); Dei Levante, **Bari-Palese**; Adriatico, at **Lecce-San Cataldo**; **Brindisi**; Mergellina at **Naples**; Le Torri, at **Pescocostanzo** (L'Aquila); dei Galli, at **Praiano Vettica** (Salerno); Delle Neve, **Rieti-Terminillo**; del Foro Italico, **Rome**; Irno, in **Salerno**; Principessa Paola del Belgio, at **Scilla** (Règgio Calabria); Surriento, at **Sorrento**; Marina degli Ulivia, at **Sperlonga** (Latina).

Anyone can stay in a youth hostel, and senior citizens are often given added discounts. Many youth hostels sell cards or you can pick up one in advance from:

US: American Youth Hostels, 1332 Eye St NW, Suite 800, Washington, DC, 20005
Canada: Canadian Hostelling Association, Place Vanier, Tower A, 333 River Rd, Ottawa, Ontario, K11 8H9
UK: Youth Hostels Association, 14 Southampton St, London WC2

Accommodation—a bunk bed in single-sex room and breakfast—costs around L10 000 per day. There is often a curfew, and you usually can't check in before 5 or 6 pm. You can book in advance by sending your arrival and departure dates along with the number of guests (by sex) to the individual hostel, including international postal coupons for the return reply. The worst time to use the hostels is the spring, when noisy Italian school groups use them for field trips.

There are two other organizations to help students find lodgings in Italy—the Centro Turistico Studentesco e Giovanile (CTS), which has offices in every Italian city of any size and can book cheap accommodation for you, in their own town or at your next stop. The Associazione Italiana per il Turismo e gli Scambi Universitari can obtain rooms for foreign university students all year round in Rome, Bari, and Salerno. Write to them at Via Palestro 11, Rome 00185, tel 475 5265.

Alpine Refuges

The Club Alpino Italiano operates a large percentage of the *Rifugi Alpini*, or mountain huts in both the Alps and the Apennines. Facilities range from the basic to the grand; some are exclusively for hikers and mountain-climbers, while others may be reached by funivias, and are used by skiers in the winter and holidaymakers in the summer. Rates average L10 000 a night, but rise by 20 per cent between December and April. Write to the Club at Via Foscolo 3, Milan, tel (02) 802 554 for a list of huts, their opening dates, and booking information.

Self-Catering Holidays: Villas, Flats, and Farmhouses

Self-catering holiday accommodation is *the* way to beat the high costs of Italy, especially if you're travelling with the family or with a group of friends. Most of the options available from the UK in the south are along the coast or in the hill towns in Lazio. Look for ads in major Sunday papers, or if you have your heart set on a particular region, write to its tourist office for a list of local agencies and individuals. These ought to provide photos of the accommodation to give you an idea of what to expect. Maid service is included in the more glamorous villas, while for others be sure to inquire about sheets and towels. Prices vary widely: you can spend L2 000 000 a week, or L100 000. In general minimum lets are for two weeks. Rental prices usually include insurance, water, and electricity. For a genuine country experience, contact Agriturist, located in every province (offices listed below).

Don't be surprised if upon arrival the owner 'denounces' (*denunziare*) you to the police; according to Italian law, all visitors must be registered upon arrival. Common problems are water shortages, unruly insects and low kilowatts (often you can't have your hot water heater and oven on at the same time). Many of the companies listed below offer, in addition to homes, savings on charter flights, ferry crossings or fly-drive schemes to sweeten the deal. Try to book as far in advance as possible for the summer season.

Villa and Flat Agencies

ALLEGRO HOLIDAYS (**Maiori, Minori**, in Campania), 15a Church St, Reigate, Surrey, tel (0737) 221 323

AT HOME IN ITALY (**Formia, Gaeta, Sperlonga**) 87 Heathless Rd, Blackheath, London SE3, tel (081) 318 7579

BEACH VILLAS (**Capo Vaticano, Tropea**), 8 Market Passage, Cambridge, tel (0223) 311 113

CHAPTER (**Rome, Cervéteri, Grottaferrata, Tarquinia, Positano, Lake Bracciano, Lake Bolsena**), 126 St John's Wood High Street, London NW8, tel (071) 586 9451

CITALIA (**Ischia**) Marco Polo House 3-5, Lansdowne Road, Dover, Kent, tel (0304) 204 515

DAVID NEWMAN'S EUROPEAN COLLECTION (**Rome, Cervéteri, Grottaferrata, Lake Bracciano, Lake Bolsena**) P.O. Box 733, 40 Upperton Rd, Eastbourne, Sussex, tel (0323) 410 347

INTERHOME (**Rome, Genzano, Amalfi, Ischia**) 383 Richmond Rd, Twickenham, tel (081) 891 1294

ITALIAN JEWELS (**Amalfi, Positano, Sorrento**), 18 Hammet St, Taunton, Somerset, tel (0305) 62 831
MAGIC OF ITALY (**Atrani, S. Maria di Castellabate**), 47 Shepherds Bush Green, London W12, tel (081) 743 9555
PEGASUS (**Capo Palinuro, Paestum, Soverato**), River House, Restmor Way, Hackbridge Rd, Wallington, Surrey, tel (081) 773 2323
PERRYMEAD (**Capo Palinuro, Conca dei Marini, Positano, Ravello, Sorrento; Rodi Garganico and Villanova di Ostuni (Apulia); Belvedere Marittimo, Capo Vaticano, Diamante, Maratea, Sibari, Tropea, Capri, Ischia**), 54 Perrymead St, London SW6, tel (071) 736 4592
TOURAUTO HOLIDAYS (**Gaeta**) Bridge House, Ware, Herts, tel (0920) 30 50
VACANZE IN ITALIA (**S. Vito dei Normanni (Apulia), Genzano, Campana Romana, Soriano**), Bignor, Nr. Pulborough, W. Sussex, tel (079) 87 426
VILLAS ITALIA (**Cervéteri. Amalfi, Baia Domizia, Positano**) 227 Shepherds Bush Rd, London W6, tel (081) 748 8668.
Alternatively, Agriturist accommodation is often extremely reasonably priced, and often includes extras like chickens, rabbits, horses, and cheap homegrown produce and wine. Write directly to the provincial offices for listings.

Provincial Agriturist Addresses, for rural accommodation and farmhouses
LAZIO
Via Firenze 80, 03100 **Frosinone**, tel (0775) 850 035
Via Don Minzoni 1, 04100 **Latina**, tel (0773) 493 056
Via Moisé di Gaio 16, 02100, **Rieti**, tel (0746) 43 264
Via Giulia 4, 00186 **Roma**, tel (06) 687 2441
Corso Italia 91, 01100 **Viterbo**, tel (0761) 221 306–7
ABRUZZO
Via Vezzia 38, 67100 **Avezzano** (L'Aquila), tel (0863) 23 202
Corso Marrucino 39, 66100 **Chieti**, tel (0871) 65 951
Via Catullo 39, 65100 **Pescara**, tel (085) 61 544
Via G. d'Annunzio 12, 64100 **Teramo**, tel (0861) 30 919
MOLISE
Via Cavour 18, 86100 **Campobasso**, tel (0874) 92 912
Via Roma 85, 86170 **Isernia**, tel (0865) 29 193
CAMPANIA
Via Circumvallazione 42, 83100 **Avellino**, tel (0825) 35 447
Viale dei Rettori 40, 82100 **Benevento**, tel (0824) 21 910
Via Nazario Sauro 22, 81100 **Caserta**, tel (0823) 327 181
Via S. Lucia 90, 80132 **Napoli**, tel (081) 425 238
Via Piacenza 76, Piazza Arbostella, 84100 **Salerno**, tel (089) 331 729
BASILICATA
Via XX Settembre 39, 75100 **Matera**, tel (0835) 214 565
Via XXV Aprile 20, 85100 **Potenza**, tel (0971) 21 035
CALABRIA
Via XX Settembre 42, 88100 **Catanzaro**, tel (0961) 45 084
Via Ganale Doria, Palazzo CAP, 87100 **Cosenza**, tel (0984) 26 133
Via Cardinale Tripepi 7, 89100 **Règgio Calabria**, tel (0965) 91 822

APULIA
Via G. Petroni 23, 70124 **Bari**, tel (080) 365 025
Via F. Consiglio 4, 72100 **Brindisi**, tel (0831) 222 042
Via G. Matteotti 86, 71100 **Fóggia**, tel (0881) 78 128
Via Cicolella 3, 73100 **Lecce**, tel (0832) 648 686
Via XX Settembre 2/C, 74100 **Tàranto**, tel (099) 24 032

Camping

Most of the official camp sites are near the sea, but there are also quite a few in the mountains and near the lakes, and usually one within commuting distance of major tourist centres. A complete list with full details for all of Italy is published annually in the Italian Touring Club's *Campeggi e Villaggi Turistici*, available in Italian bookshops for L22 000, or you can obtain an abbreviated list free from the Centro Internazionale Prenotazioni Federcampeggio, Casella Postale 23, 50042, Calenzano (Firenze); request their booking forms as well to reserve a place—essential in the summer months when the tents and caravans (campers) are packed cheek to cheek. Camping fees vary according to the camp ground's facilities, roughly L5000 per person (less for children); L5000–15 000 per tent or caravan; and L4000 per car. Camping outside official sites is kosher if you ask the landowner's permission first.

Hiring tents and similar equipment is generally impossible, but you can rent a fully equipped caravan or camper; you can arrange to have one waiting upon your arrival in Italy through one of the following **Camper and Caravan Hire** firms:

CAMPER SI, Via Pontina, km 14.5, 00100 **Rome**, tel (06) 648 1504
CARAVAN TRAVEL, Via Germanie 15, 00040 Tor Vaianica **Rome**, tel (06) 915 7945
FREEDOM HOLIDAY, Via C. Colombo, km 23.5, 00100 **Rome**, tel (06) 609 4212
SAFARILAND, Via del Banco di Santo Spirito 42, 00186 **Rome**, tel (06) 654 8941
CARAVAN CAMPER CAMPANIA CLUB, Via Terracina 169, **Naples**, tel (081) 616 226
EDEN CARAVAN, Via del Mare, Lecce, tel (0832) 56 000
MAREMONTI, Via Lucrezia della Valle (loc. Serena), **Catanzaro**, tel (0961) 72 654

Buying a House

Rural real estate is one of Italy's great buys, and the recommended way to do it is to buy a run-down property and restore it to your own needs and taste. But beware the pitfalls.

One estate agent is constantly amazed that his English clients invariably express two major concerns about a property: drainage and the presence of a bidet in the bathroom, as if it were a tool of the devil! What they should be asking are questions about water supply, electricity, and road access—often big problems for that isolated, romantic farmhouse that has caught your eye. Another thing to remember before purchasing a home or land is that you need permission from the local *comune* to make any changes or improvements, and it's no good buying anything unless you're pretty sure the *comune* will consent (for a sizeable fee, of course) to let you convert the old cellar or stable into a spare bedroom. Another thing to remember is that though there are no annual rates (property tax) to pay, there's a 10 per cent IVA (VAT) to be paid on the purchase price for a house and 17 per cent on land, as well as a hefty Capital Gains Tax on selling price and profit to be paid by the seller. Italians tend to get round this by selling at one price and writing down another on the contract. But remember if you sell you'll be in the same bind.

Once you've agreed to buy, you pay a deposit (usually 25–30 per cent) and sign a *compromesso*, a document that states that if you back out, you lose your deposit, and if the seller changes his mind, he forfeits double the deposit to you (be sure your *compromesso* includes this feature, called *caparra confirmatoria*). Always transfer payment from home through a bank, taking care to get and save a certificate of the transaction so you can take the sum back out of Italy when you sell. After the *compromesso*, your affairs will be handled by a *notaio*, the public servant in charge of registering documents and taxes who works for both buyer and seller. If you want to make sure your interests are not overlooked, you can hire a *commercialista* (lawyer-accountant) who will handle your affairs with the *notaio*, including the final transfer deed (*rogito*), which completes the purchase at the local Land Registry. Upon signing, the balance of the purchase price generally becomes payable within a year. The next stage for most buyers, restoration, can be a nightmare if you aren't careful. Make sure the crew you hire is experienced and that you're pleased with their work elsewhere—don't hesitate to ask as many other people in your area as possible for advice. One book that offers some clues on the ins and outs of taxes, inheritance law, residency, gardening etc., is *Living in Italy*, published by Robert Hale, London 1987.

Eating Out

There are those who eat to live and those who live to eat, and then there are the Italians, for whom food has an almost religious significance, unfathomably linked with love, La Mamma, and tradition. In this singular country, where millions of otherwise sane people spend much of their waking hours worrying about their digestion, standards both at home and in the restaurants are understandably high. Few Italians are gluttons, but all are experts on what is what in the kitchen; to serve a meal that is not properly prepared and more than a little complex is tantamount to an insult. To test the true feelings of an Italian lover, ask him or her to cook something for you—the more painstaking the result, the more powerful the passion.

For the visitor this national culinary obsession comes as an extra bonus to the senses—along with Italy's remarkable sights, music, and the warm sun on your back, you can enjoy some of the best tastes and smells the world can offer, prepared daily in Italy's kitchens and fermented in its countless wine cellars. Eating *all'Italiana* is not only delicious and wholesome, but in recent years it has become undeniably trendy. Foreigners flock here to learn the secrets of Italian cuisine and the even more elusive secret of how the Italians can live surrounded by such delights and still fit into their sleek Armani trousers.

Breakfast (*colazione*) in Italy is no lingering affair, but an early morning wake-up shot to the brain: a *cappuccino* (espresso with hot foamy milk, often sprinkled with chocolate), a *caffè latte* (white coffee), or a *caffè lungo* (a generous portion of espresso), accompanied by a croissant-type roll, called a *cornetto* or *briosce*, or else a *sfogliatella* or one of the other fancy pastries that are a special talent of Naples. This can be consumed in nearly any bar, and repeated during the morning as often as necessary, which is why breakfast in most Italian hotels is no big deal and seldom worth the price charged.

35

Lunch or *pranzo*, generally served around 1 pm, is the most important meal of the day for the Italians, with a minimum of a first course (*Primo piatto*—any kind of pasta dish, broth or soup, or rice dish or pizza), a second course (*Secondo piatto*—a meat dish, accompanied by a *contorno* or side dish—a vegetable, salad, or potatoes usually), followed by fruit or dessert and coffee. You can, however, begin with a platter of *antipasti*—the appetizers Italians do so brilliantly, ranging from warm seafood delicacies, to raw ham (*prosciutto crudo*), salami in a hundred varieties, lovely vegetables, savoury toasts, olives, paté, and many, many more. There are restaurants that specialize in antipasti, and they usually don't take it amiss if you decide to forget the pasta and meat and just nibble on these scrumptious hors d'oeuvres (though in the end it will probably cost more than a full meal). Most Italians accompany their meal with wine and mineral water—*acqua minerale*, with or without bubbles (*con* or *senza gas*), which supposedly aids digestion—concluding their meals with a *digestivo* liqueur.

Cena, the evening meal, is usually eaten at around 8 pm. This is much the same as pranzo although lighter, without the pasta; a pizza and beer, eggs, or a fish dish. In restaurants, however, they offer all the courses, so if you have only a sandwich for lunch you have a full meal in the evening.

In Italy the various types of restaurants—*ristorante, trattoria*, or *osteria*—have been confused. A trattoria or osteria can be just as elaborate as a restaurant, though rarely is a ristorante as informal as a traditional trattoria. Unfortunately the old habit of posting menus and prices in the windows has fallen from fashion, so it's often difficult to judge variety or prices. Invariably the least expensive restaurant-type place is the *vino e cucina*, simple places serving simple cuisine for simple everyday prices. It is essential to remember that the fancier the fittings, the fancier the bill, though neither of these points has anything at all to do with the quality of the food. If you're uncertain, do as you would at home—look for lots of locals. When you eat out, mentally add to the bill (*conto*) the bread and cover charge (*pane e coperto*, between L1500–2000), and a 15 per cent service charge. This is often included in the bill (*servizio compreso*); if not, it will say *servizio non compreso*, and you'll have to do your own arithmetic. Additional tipping is at your own discretion, but never do it in family-owned and -run places.

People who haven't visited Italy for years and have fond memories of eating full meals for under a pound will be amazed at how much prices have risen; though in some respects eating out in Italy is still a bargain, especially when you figure out how much all that wine would have cost you at home. In many places you'll often find restaurants offering a *menù turistico* —full, set meals of usually meagre inspiration for L15–20 000. Good, imaginative chefs often offer a *menù degustazione*—a set-price gourmet meal that allows you to taste their daily specialities and seasonal dishes. Both of these are cheaper than if you had ordered the same food à la carte. When you leave a restaurant you will be given a receipt (*ricevuto fiscale*) which according to Italian law you must take with you out of the door and carry for at least 60 metres. If you aren't given one, it means the restaurant is probably fudging on its taxes and thus offering you lower prices. There is a slim chance the tax police may have their eye on you and the restaurant, and if you don't have a receipt they could slap you with a heavy fine.

There are several alternatives to sit-down meals. The 'hot table' (*tavola calda*) is a stand-up buffet, where you can choose a simple prepared dish or a whole meal, depending on your appetite. The food in these can be truly impressive (especially in the centre of Naples, where the sign out front may read *Degustazione*; some of these offer the best gourmet delights to be had in the south, and are always crowded); many offer only a few hot dishes, pizza and sandwiches, though in every fair-sized town there will be at least one *tavola calda* with seats where you can contrive a complete dinner outside the usual hours. Little shops that sell pizza by the slice are common in city centres. At any grocer's (*alimentari*) or market (*mercato*) you can buy the materials for countryside or hotel-room picnics; some places in the smaller towns will make the sandwiches for you. For really elegant picnics, have a *tavola calda* pack up something nice for you. And if everywhere else is closed, there's always the railway station bars—these will at least have sandwiches and drinks, and perhaps (usually in unlikely locations in the south) some surprisingly good snacks you've never heard of before. Some of the station bars also prepare *cestini di viaggio*, full-course meals in a basket to help you through long train trips. Common snacks you'll encounter include *panini* of prosciutto, cheese and tomatoes, or other meats; *tramezzini*, little sandwiches on plain, square white bread that are always much better than they look; pizza, of course, or regional variations like the Apulian *focaccia*; or fried, breaded balls of rice with cheese or meat fillings called *supplì* around Rome and *arancini* further south (because they look like little oranges).

Many Italian dishes need no introduction—pizza, spaghetti, lasagne, and minestrone are familiar to all. What is perhaps less well known is the tremendous regional diversity at the table. Every corner of Italy prides itself on its own specialities, the shape of its pasta, its soups and sauces, its wines and desserts. This makes travelling around a constant adventure, pleasure, and confusion, especially when menus list dishes by their local names or in dialect. You'll find many of these described and listed in the 'Eating Out' sections in the text, and in the menu vocabulary at the back of this book, but even so, expect to be overwhelmed, especially since many Italian chefs have wholeheartedly embraced the concept of nouvelle cuisine, or rather *cucina nuova*, and are constantly inventing dishes with even more names.

Rome, the meeting place of north and south, has a style of cooking all its own, with specialities like *saltimbocca*, thin slices of veal with ham and cheese on top, fried artichokes (*carciofi alla giudea*), stewed tripe, and *baccalà*—dried codfish, which can be fried or boiled in a stew. Many of Rome's cooks come from the Abruzzo or Rieti province, and many of the city's favourites really began up in the mountains: pasta *all'Amatriciana*, with bacon or salt pork, from Amatrice; grilled lamb *al scottadito* ('burn-the-fingers'); and *penne all'arrabbiata*, pasta 'quills' with lots of chilli peppers. Rome also has Italy's biggest collection of regional and foreign restaurants—any night you may choose any cuisine from Emilia's to Ethiopia's.

Everywhere in central and southern Italy, factory spaghetti gives way to the real monarch of pasta—nothing more than thick, homemade spaghetti, really, though the difference is unmistakable. It goes by a million aliases—*cirioli, troccoli, pici* or whatever you like; here it is usually called *spaghetti alla chitarra* from the guitar-like gadget used to cut it. One of the best ways to have it is with wild boletus mushrooms, *porcini*, abundant everywhere in the southern Apennines. Game dishes, hare and boar especially, are common, and up in the mountains the roast and grilled meats, scented with rosemary, make up for the scarcity of fresh seafood. The Abruzzo makes excellent ricotta and sheep cheese—*pecorino*—not as sheepy as you might expect, and you will find both white and black truffles in various spots around the Abruzzo and Molise. Molisano cooking, humble even in restaurants, can be pure mountain soul food: beans and polenta, less desirable parts of swine and sheep, and plenty of hot peppers.

Naples, of course, invented both pizza and spaghetti, and what more needs to be said? Campania tends to be overly modest about its cuisine. Its biggest favourites are simple enough: *pasta e fagioli* (pasta and beans), *spaghetti alle vongole* (with baby clams); the seafood, as everywhere else along the southern coasts, is exceptional (and as far as we've heard, quite safe everywhere except for perhaps the northern Adriatic). In Campania, as elsewhere around the south, specialities are often seasoned with condiments like capers, anchovies, lemon juice, oregano, olives, and fennel.

Apulia, perhaps, has the most interesting regional cuisine of the south. It has its own pasta speciality: *orecchiete*, 'little ears', a practical and unquestionably aesthetic form that is lately becoming popular far beyond the confines of the region—in the trattorias it is often served with greens, a seafood concoction called *ciambotta*, or even turnips instead of tomato sauces. Pasta in the oven, various sorts of lasagne and macaroni casseroles, are also very popular.

The Apulian *Murge*, as you will notice, is fairly solidly packed with sheep, and lamb is a natural favourite. Apulians are proud of their sheep cheese, mozzarella, and a thousand types of salamis and sausages. Many dishes are baked in special clay dishes called *tielle* (*tiane* in the Molise); one of the best is a mixture of mussels, potatoes, rice and onions. Seafood is excellent throughout the region, and especially in Tàranto, a city renowned throughout Italy for it. They'll show you every sort of fish you've ever heard of, and a few you haven't; favourites range from the luxurious—the langoustes, prawns and scampi, as well as the fish stews that can be the ultimate southern treat if you pick the right restaurant—to the 'poor' fish, the various small creatures lumped together as *pesce azzurro*. Tàranto's maritime exotica extend to such uncommon things as sea urchins, *datteri* (razor clams) and *mitili* (special black mussels farmed in the city's lagoons).

As for Calabria and the Basilicata, expect little more than variations on the above, along with plenty of hot peppers and intriguing hints at the area's Greek heritage—stuffed aubergines being the most obvious. Few Calabrians, even, know that their region can take credit for introducing pasta into Italy. In ancient Croton and Sybaris, among other cities of the Ionian sea, a small, cylindrical form of pasta called *makaria* was a ritual food eaten at funeral banquets. By 600 BC the Sybarites, always on the hunt for new culinary experiences, had invented the rolling pin and were turning out *tagliatelle* and even *lasagna*.

NB: Prices quoted for restaurants indicate the cost of a complete meal per person.

Wine

This is a country where everyday wine is cheaper than Coca-Cola or milk, and where nearly every family owns some vineyards or has some relatives who supply most of their daily needs—which are not great. Even though they live in one of the world's largest wine-growing countries, Italians imbibe relatively little, and only at meals.

If Italy has an infinite variety of regional dishes, there is an equally bewildering array of regional wines, many of which are rarely exported because they are best drunk young. Unless you're dining at a restaurant with an exceptional cellar, do as the Italians do and order a carafe of the local wine (*vino locale* or *vino della casa*). You won't often be wrong.

Most Italian wines are named after the grape and the district they come from. If the label says D.O.C. (*Denominazione di Origine Controllata*) it means that the wine comes from a specially defined area and was produced according to a certain traditional method.

Italians are fond of postprandial brandies (to aid digestion)—the famous *Stock* or *Vecchia Romagna* labels are always good. **Grappa** (acquavitae) is usually rougher, and often drunk in black coffee after a meal (a *caffè corretto*). Other members of any Italian bar include *Campari*, the famous red bitter, drunk on its own or in cocktails; *Vermouth*, *Fernet Branca*, *Cynar* and *Averno*, popular aperitif/digestives; and liqueurs like *Strega*, the witch potion from Benevento, apricot-flavoured *Amaretto*, cherry *Maraschino*, aniseed *Sambuca*, the Roman favourite with three 'flies' or coffee beans, as well as any number of locally brewed elixirs, often made by monks. Apulia has some select local poisons, including styles of *amaro* in chocolate and almond flavours, and a sweet *amarella* from Fóggia.

When discussing southern wines, throw the opinions of the experts out the window. The stronger, richer, non-subtle (what word would an indiscreet wine authority use—*blatant?*) and non-travelling vintages of the Mezzogiorno are an entirely different world, one that suffers a good bit of prejudice at the hands of the France-Piedmont-Tuscany-orientated oenophile. But many of those renowned northern labels carry a dark secret—the powerful wines of Apulia or Sicily blended in to give them character. You'll find character enough in the wine that stays behind. Apulia alone puts out some 22 D.O.C. varieties, and you can drink yourself silly trying to do justice to all the wines produced in this ever-surprising region.

If that is precisely what you mean to do, a good one *not* to start with is the redoubtable elixir called *primitivo*: all genuine primitive grapes, and alcoholically running as high as 18 per cent. Before the evening deteriorates, try some of the more distinguished varieties: really excellent reds like Cacc'e Mitte, Cerignola or Rosso di Canosa, all from around Fóggia, or the dry and delicate white wines from Martina Franca, Castel del Monte or Locorotondo.

Apulia's is the south's best. Campania, which was known for wine in Roman times, produces surprisingly little now, and not all of it very good; for a white, ask for Greco di Tufo, and for a red, Taurasi. Calabrian hillsides are always either too hot or too acidic to make anything special; the label called Ciro (both red and white) is ubiquitous in the region, and as honest and likeable a plonk as you'll ever find; there are also pleasant and golden-coloured wines like Greco di Gerace. The Abruzzo too will offer its modest vintages. Serious winemaking is a relatively recent phenomenon in these parts, with the transplanting of Montepulciano and Trebbiano grapes from Tuscany, but Trebbiano white, red Montepulciano d'Abruzzo and a more refined version of the latter called Cerasuolo have become legitimate D.O.C. wines, and promise to get better in the future. In Rome you can usually get anything you want, but if you order the house wine it will be a fruity white from Frascati or somewhere else in the Castelli Romani—and that in itself will be one of your best memories of a trip to Rome.

Part III

HISTORY AND ART

Detail of Bronze Warrior found at Riace, Règgio Calabria museum

History

The First Italians

Some 50,000 years ago, when the Alps were covered by an ice cap and the low level of the Mediterranean made Italy a much wider peninsula than it is now, Neanderthal man was gracing Italy with his low-browed presence. But even that is not the beginning of the story. Recently, scientists have become excited over the discovery of a new type, *Homo Aeserniensis*, perhaps the first inhabitant of Europe, living in caves around Isernia a million years ago. Italy makes a convenient bridge from Africa to Europe, and it seems there was a lot of traffic all through prehistory. Nevertheless, none of the earliest inhabitants of Italy have much to show for themselves in terms of art or culture. For whatever reason, Neanderthal man turned out to be an evolutionary dead end. His successors, the much more talented and debonaire Cro-Magnon Italians, appeared about 18,000 BC; they knew something about keeping animals and fishing, and also created genuine art: female statuettes carved from bone, and other bones incised with tidy geometric patterns. They were fond of molluscs, and used the shells for decoration.

The transition from the Paleolithic (old stone age) to Mesolithic (middle stone age) can be placed in the ninth millennium BC. The age of the nomadic hunters had passed; Mesolithic men had more advanced weapons, and true settled agricultural economy comes with the **Neolithic era**, perhaps reaching Italy in the 7th millennium. The first Neolithic Italians may have come in an invasion or migration from the Balkans. These peoples installed themselves first on the plains around Fóggia, in Apulia; by 4000 BC they had spread across the peninsula. Never great builders, these apparently peaceful folk proved easy marks for the first **Indo-Europeans**, who arrived about 3000.

About 2000 BC the skill of alloying copper and tin into bronze reached Italy, along with a host of disruptions—including invasions, about which we know little. When the dust cleared, a new, largely pastoral culture, using horses and practising cremation burials, dominated most of central and southern Italy, the **Protoapennine**; within this broad grouping we can discern the origins of perhaps the original Italic peoples, including the Ausonians of Campania, the Siculans and the **Latins**.

By the 8th century BC, most of the population is lumped together as 'Italics', a number of powerful, distinct tribes with related languages. Among them were the **Samnites**, who occupied much of Campania and the south, the **Daunii** and dolmen-building **Messapii** in Apulia, the **Picentes** along the northern Adriatic coast, and a boiling kettle of contentious peoples in the centre: **Sabines, Aequi, Volsci** and the Latins. The mighty Cyclopean walls of their cities can still be seen today around southern Lazio. Two of Italy's most culturally sophisticated peoples lived on the islands: the **Siculi** of Sicily and the castle-building, bronze-working **Sards** of the Nuraghe culture.

750–509 BC: Greeks and Etruscans

The most interesting nations of the time, however, were two relative newcomers who contributed much towards bringing Italy out of its ancient isolation, the **Etruscans** and **Greeks**. With their shadowy past and as yet undeciphered language, the Etruscans are one of the puzzles of ancient history. According to their own traditions, they arrived from somewhere in western Anatolia about 900 BC (Etruscan inscriptions have been found on the Greek island of Lemnos), probably as a sort of warrior-aristocracy that imposed itself on the existing populations of Tuscany and north Lazio. By the 8th century BC they were the strongest people in Italy, grouped in a loose confederation of 12 city states called the **Dodecapolis**. At the same time, the Greeks, whose trading routes had long covered Italy's southern coasts, began to look upon that 'underdeveloped' country as a New World for exploration and colonization. All over the south, there are tantalizing archaeological clues that the Greeks had begun settlements even earlier, in the Mycenaean age before the fall of Troy, but about these little is known.

In 775, Greeks founded a settlement at Pithecusa, on the island of Ischia, squarely in the middle of the important trade route that carried Tuscany's iron to the east. Among the first planned urban colonies were Cumae, in 750, and Syracuse, in 734, both on good natural harbours. Others followed, as each of the contentious Greek states struggled to get a foothold in their New World: Neapolis (Naples), Elea, Taras (Tàranto), Metapontum, Sybaris, Croton, Rhegium (Règgio Calabria), Akragas (Agrigento), Gela, Zancle (Messina) and many others. All of these were carefully planned enterprises, laid out in rigid grids of streets as meticulous as those of Manhattan or Chicago. Except in eastern Sicily and Apulia, the Greeks had a generally easy time with the natives, pushing them into the interior and tutoring them in a slow, gradual process of cultural Hellenization.

From the beginning, the Greek cities prospered beyond their wildest dreams. The fertile coastal plains, never before ploughed, provided two or three abundant crops a year with little effort. Timber from the mountains, the most important resource, built fleets of ships and provided a very profitable export back to Greece. Trade became increasingly important, and the new cities developed some specialities of their own: the sheep of Apulia, for example, which produced the finest and most expensive wool in the Mediterranean, and which wore little overcoats to protect it. By the 6th century, the opulence of Magna Graecia, as Greek southern Italy had come to be called, was legendary. Greeks at home joked about the famous sentries of Akragas, in Sicily, who were said to have gone on strike for softer pillows. Sybaris, the city on the Ionian Sea that gave us our word *sybarite*, once sent heralds to every shore promising a fantastic reward for the chef who could create the perfect sauce for seafood.

Greek Italy's painters and sculptors took their places among the greatest of Greece's golden age, but its most memorable contributions were in philosophy. The famous Elean School included some of the most important pre-Socratics: Parmenides, who invented the concept of atoms, and Zeno, with his famous paradoxes. Empedocles came from Akragas. Pythagoras visited about 535, and had a remarkable influence—his followers often dabbled in politics, and once turned Croton into a mystic-philosophical state until a popular revolution threw them out. But from the first, there was more passion and wrath than philosophy in the affairs of Magna Graecia. The city states, much like those back in Greece, dissipated their energies by engaging in constant wars with each other. Some, like Sybaris, were completely destroyed, and by *c.* 400 BC, the failure of the rest to work together sent them into a slow but irreversible economic decline.

The Etruscan story is much the same. Repeated defeats at the hands of the wild Gauls weakened their confederation, but the economic decline that led to Etruria's virtual evaporation in the 4th century BC is harder to account for. Rome, a border city between the Etruscans and Latins, threw out its Etruscan king and established the **Republic** in 509 BC (see 'Rome': History p. 75). Somehow this relatively new city managed to grow to perhaps 100,000 people, ranking it with Taras and Capua, an Etruscan colony in the growing region of Campania, as the largest on the peninsula.

509–268 BC: The Rise of Rome

After expelling its Etruscan kings, Rome spent a hundred years at war with the various cities of Etruria, while at the same time gradually subjugating the rest of the Latins and neighbouring tribes. The little republic with the military camp ethic was successful on all fronts, and a sack by marauding Gauls in 390 BC proved only a brief interruption in Rome's march to conquest. Southern Etruria and Latium were swallowed up by 358 BC, and Rome next turned its attention to the only power in Italy capable of competing with her on an equal basis: the Samnites. These rugged highlanders of the southern Apennines, with their capital at Benevento, had begun to seize parts of coastal Campania. The Romans drove them out in 343–41 BC, but in the **Second Samnite War** the Samnites dealt them a severe defeat (Battle of the Caudine Forks, 321 BC). In the third war, feeling themselves surrounded by Roman allies, the Samnites formed an alliance with the Northern Etruscans and Celts, leading to a general Italian commotion where the Romans beat everybody, annexing almost all of Italy by 283 BC.

A strange interlude, delaying Rome's complete flattening of Italy, came with the arrival of **Pyrrhus of Epirus**, an adventurer with a big army who was invited in by the cities of Magna Graecia as a protector. From him we get the term Pyrrhic victories, for he outmatched the Romans in one battle after another, but never followed up his advantage. After finally losing one in 275 BC, at Benevento, he quit and returned to Epirus, while the Romans leisurely took the deserted Greek cities one by one. Now the conquest was complete. All along the Romans had been diabolically clever in managing their new demesne, maintaining most of the tribes and cities as nominally independent states, while planting Latin colonies everywhere (re-founded cities like Paestum, Pozzuoli, Venosa and Benevento were such colonies, along with new ones in the north like Florence). The great network of roads centred on Rome was carried on with speed, and a truly united Italy seemed close to becoming a reality.

268–91 BC: Empire Abroad, Disarray at Home

After all this, Rome deserved a shot at the Mediterranean heavyweight title. The current champ, the powerful merchant thalassocracy of Carthage, was alarmed enough at the successes of its precocious neighbour, and proved happy to oblige. Rome won the first bout, beating Carthage and her ally Syracuse in the **First Punic War** (264–241 BC), and gained Sicily, Sardinia, and Corsica. For the rematch, the **Second Punic War** (219–202 BC), Carthage sent **Hannibal** and his elephants over the Alps to bring the war into the Romans' backyard. Undeterred by the brilliant African general's victory at Cannae (Apulia) in 216 BC, where four legions were destroyed, the Romans hung on tenaciously even when Hannibal appeared at the gates of Rome. In Hannibal's absence, they took Spain and much of Africa, and after **Scipio Africanus'** victory at Zama in 202 BC, Carthage surrendered. The **Third Punic War** was a sorry affair. Rome only waited long enough for Carthage to put a foot wrong in its treaty obligations before razing the city to the ground. The west conquered, Rome looked east. Already by 200 BC she had been interfering in Greek affairs. The disunited Greeks and successor states of Alexander's empire offered little resistance, and by 64 BC the legions were camped on the Cataracts of the Nile, in Jerusalem, and half-way across Asia Minor.

Nothing corrupts a state like easy conquests, and all this time things in Italy were going very wrong. Taxation ceased for Roman citizens, as booty provided the state with all the revenues it needed, and tens of thousands of slaves were imported. Thus Italy became a parasite nation. Vast amounts of cheap grain brought from Africa and Egypt ruined the Italian farmer, who had the choice of selling his freehold and becoming a share-cropper, joining the army, or moving to Rome as part of the burgeoning lumpenproletariat. The men who profited most from the wars bought up tremendous amounts of land, turning Italy into a country of huge estates (*latifundia*), and becoming a new aristocracy powerful enough to stifle any attempts at reform. Only Rome, of course, and a few other cities prospered. In this period many of the Greek and Etruscan towns withered and died. Many country districts were abandoned, and rural Italy knew constant famine and plagues, while in Rome the new rich were learning the delights of orgies, gladiatorial combats, and being carried about the streets by slaves.

Not that degeneracy and social disintegration had proceeded far enough for Italy to fail to resist. Rome, and indeed all Italy was divided into extremist factions, the reactionary 'Senatorial Party' and the radical 'Popular Party'. (The Senate, and the senatorial class, were not yet a nobility *per se*. A hefty fortune was all that was needed for entry. Their populist opponents included not only the poor, but most of the businessmen and the hard-pressed middle class.) In 133 BC, a remarkable reformer named **Tiberius Gracchus** was elected tribune, but his plans for land reforms earned him assassination the following year. His brother **Gaius Gracchus** went even further, attempting to turn Rome into a genuine democracy when he gained the tribunate in 123 BC, but he, too, was murdered after the Senate declared martial law that same year. By this time Rome's Constitution was reduced to a travesty, and both sides realized that the only real power lay with the legions. The populists staked their hopes on **Gaius Marius**, an illiterate but good-hearted general who saved Italy from the last surprise Celtic raid in 113 BC. Marius' ascent to power proved a disappointment, and a whole new generation of populist statesmen was assassinated one by one.

91–31 BC: Sixty Years of Civil War

Italy had had enough; the year 91 saw a coordinated revolt among the southern peoples called the **Social Wars**, which was defeated by the campaigns of Marius and **Sulla** (the Senate's darling in the army), and by an offer to extend Roman citizenship to all Italians. A military coup by Sulla followed, with the backing of the Senate; it was the first time armed Roman soldiers ever actually entered Rome, a religious and constitutional taboo. But when Sulla's army left for conquest and booty on the Black Sea, a populist counter-coup ruled Rome for three years. Sulla's triumphal return threw them out, and the haughty general unleashed a bloody reign of terror unlike anything Italy had ever seen. An effective autocracy was created, and all opponents either murdered or exiled. Italy careered into anarchy, with many rural districts reverting to bandit-ridden waste-lands, a setting for the remarkable revolt in 73 BC of **Spartacus**, an escaped gladiator of Capua who led a motley army of dispossessed farmers and runaway slaves—some 70,000 of them— back and forth across the south until the legions finally defeated him in 71 BC.

All this had exhausted both sides, and finally discredited the senators. After Sulla's death, no one minded when the consulship and real power passed to **Pompey**, another successful general but one who cared little for politics. Like Sulla before him, Pompey soon set out for the east, where the glory and booty were to be gained, and his departure left the stage in Rome open to 33-year-old **Julius Caesar**, a tremendously clever soldier-politician, but a good man anyhow. With his two surpassing talents, one for rhetoric and the other for attracting money, he took up the popular cause in better style than anyone had done it before. A taint of connection to the **Catiline conspiracy** of 68 BC, a revolt of adventurers, disaffected nobles, and other loose ends, proved a temporary setback, just as it advanced the fortunes of **Marcus Tullius Cicero**, the great orator, writer, and statesman who still dreamed of founding a real republic with a real consti-tution, opposing both extreme parties and pinning his hopes on the still-surviving Italian middle class. Few people in Rome cared for such high principles, however, and after Pompey returned from bashing the Pontic Kingdom and the Cilician pirates, he, Caesar, and a wealthy building contractor named Licinius Crassus sliced up the republic between them, forming the **First Triumvirate** in 59 BC.

What Caesar really wanted, of course, was a military command. He managed to buy himself one in the north, and marched on Transalpine Gaul with well-known results. When Pompey grew jealous and turned against him, he turned back, 'crossed the

Rubicon', and became unchallenged master of Rome while not even holding public office (Pompey and most of the Senate fled to Greece, where Caesar caught up with them three years later). In his four years as ruler of Rome, Caesar surprised everyone, even his enemies; everything received a good dose of reform, even the calendar, and a beginning was made towards sorting out the economic mess and getting Italy back on its feet. His assassination by a clique of senatorial bitter-enders in 44 BC plunged Italy into civil war again, and left historians to ponder the grand question of whether Caesar had really intended to make himself a king and finally put the now senile republic to sleep. A **Second Triumvirate** was formed, of Caesar's adopted son Octavian, a senatorial figurehead named Lepidus, and Caesar's old friend and right-hand man, a talented, dissipated fellow named Marcus Antonius (Mark Antony), who according to one historian spent the equivalent of $3 billion (of other people's money) in his brief lifetime. While he dallied in the east with Cleopatra, Octavian was consolidating his power in Italy. The inevitable battle came in 31 BC, at Actium, and it was a complete victory for Octavian.

31 BC–AD 251: The Empire

With unchallenged authority through all the Roman lands, Octavian (soon to rename himself **Augustus**) was free to complete the reforms initiated by Caesar. Avoiding a complete break with the past, he maintained the forms of the republic while accumulating enough titles and offices for himself to justify his absolute rule constitutionally. The title he chose for public use was 'first citizen', while behind the scenes the machinery was being perfected for the deification of the Caesars (practical policy for the eastern half of the empire, where such things were common practice), and for a stable, constitutional monarchy after his death. It all worked brilliantly; peace was restored, a professional civil service created, and Italy in particular was able to recover from its time of troubles with the help of Augustus' reforms and huge programmes of public works.

For his career, and those of his successors, you may read the gossipy, shocking, and wonderfully unreliable *Lives of the Caesars* of Suetonius. All Rome tittered at the scandals of the later Julian Emperors, but everyday reality was usually much more prosaic. **Tiberius** (AD14–37) may have been a monster to his girlfriends and boyfriends, but he proved an intelligent and just ruler otherwise; his criminally insane successor **Caligula**, or 'Bootkin', lasted only four years (37–41) while the bureaucracy kept things going. **Claudius** (41–54) governed well and conquered southern Britain, while his stepson **Nero** (54–68) generally made a nuisance of himself in Rome but did little to disturb the system. Nevertheless, a commmander in Spain (Galba) declared him unfit to be emperor and marched on Rome to take his place; Nero just managed to commit suicide before they caught him. Now the genie was out of the bottle again, as the soldiers once more realized that the real power lay with them. Another general, Otho of the Praetorian Guard, toppled Galba, and soon lost out in turn to Vitellius, commander on the Rhine. The fourth Emperor of the fateful years AD 68–69 was **Vespasian**, leader of the eastern armies. He had the strongest legions and so got to keep the job; his reign (69–79) and those of his sons **Titus** (79–81) and **Domitian** (81–96), the three Flavian Emperors, were remembered as a period of prosperity. Vespasian began the Colosseum; whether intentionally or not, this incomparable new charnel house made a perfect symbol for the reviving decadence and militarization of the state.

For the moment, however, things looked rosy. After the assassination of Domitian, another bad boy but not an especially calamitous ruler, Rome had the good fortune to be ruled by a series of high-minded and intelligent military men, carefully choosing their successors beforehand to avoid civil war. They presided over the greatest age of prosperity the Mediterranean world ever knew; in Italy they ran an enlightened and surprisingly modern state that would seem familiar to us today: public libraries, and public water boards to maintain the aqueducts, rent control, agricultural price supports, low-cost loans for starting new businesses and many other such innovations. The first of this enlightened group was **Nerva** (96–98), followed by **Trajan** (98–117) and **Hadrian** (117–138), both great soldiers and builders on a monumental scale, especially in Rome; next come the two Antonines, **Antoninus Pius** (138–61), little known only because his reign was so peaceful, and **Marcus Aurelius** (161–80), soldier, statesman, and Stoic philosopher. His choice of successor was his useless son **Commodus** (180–93) and the string of good emperors was broken.

The 2nd-century prosperity was not without its darker side. The arts were in serious decline, as if the imagination of the Greco-Roman Mediterranean were somehow failing. Education was in poor shape at all levels, and every sort of fatuous mysticism imported from the East permeated the minds of the people. Economically, this period saw the emergence of the well-known north-south split in Italy. The rural south, impoverished by the Roman Republic, now sank deeper into decline, while even the commerce of wealthy Campania began to fail, ruined by foreign competition. In the north, especially in Cisalpine Gaul, a sounder, more stable economy led to the growth of new centres—Milan, Padua, Verona, and Ravenna the most prominent—beginning the economic divide that continues even today. On balance, though, both politically and economically Italy was becoming an increasingly less significant part of the empire. Of the 2nd-century emperors, fewer came from Italy than from Spain, Illyria, and Africa.

251–475: Decline and Fall

For all it cost to maintain them, the legions were no longer the formidable military machine of Augustus' day. Bureaucratic and a little tired, their tactics and equipment were also falling behind those of the Persians and even some of the cleverer German barbarians. The Goths were the first to demonstrate this, in 251, when they overran the Balkans, Greece, and Asia Minor. Five years later Franks and Alemanni invaded Gaul, and in 268 much of the east detached itself from the empire under the leadership of Odenathus of Palmyra. Somehow the empire recovered and prevailed, under dour soldier-emperors like **Aurelian** (270–75), who built Rome's walls, and **Diocletian** (284–305) who completely revamped the structure of the state and economy. His fiscal reforms, for example, fixing prices and decreeing that every son must follow the trade of his father, ossified the economy and made the creeping decline of Italy and all western Europe harder to arrest. A gigantic bureaucracy was created, taxes reached new heights as people's ability to pay them declined, and society became increasingly militarized in every respect; the emperors themselves began to assume the trappings of an oriental despot. The biggest change was the division of the empire into halves, each ruled by a co-emperor called 'Augustus'; the western emperors after Diocletian usually kept their court at army headquarters in Mediolanum (Milan), and Rome itself became a marble-veneered backwater.

More than ever, the empire had become an outright military dictatorship, in a society whose waning energies were entirely devoted to supporting a bloated, all-devouring army and bureaucracy. Medieval feudalism actually had its origins in this period, as the remaining freehold farmers sold their lands and liberty to the local gentry—for protection's sake, but also to get off the tax rolls. In the cities, the high taxes and uncertain times ruined business and trade; throughout Italy and the West towns both large and small began their fatal declines. Diocletian reduced Italy to the status of a mere province, and the peninsula had little to do with imperial events thereafter. The confused politics of the 4th century are dominated by **Constantine** (306–337), who ruled both halves of the empire, defeated various other contenders (Battle of the Milvian Bridge, outside Rome, in 312), and adroitly moved to increase his and the empire's political support by favouring Christianity, by now the majority religion in the East but largely identified with the ruling classes and urban populations in Italy and the West.

The disasters began in 406, with Visigoths, Franks, Vandals, Alans, and Suevi overrunning Gaul and Spain. Italy's turn came in 408, when Western Emperor Honorius, ruling from the new capital of Ravenna, had his brilliant general Stilicho (who himself happened to be a Vandal) murdered. A Visigothic invasion followed, including Alaric's sack of Rome in 410. St Augustine, probably echoing the thoughts of most Romans, wrote that it seemed the end of the world must be near. Rome should have been so lucky; judgement was postponed long enough for **Attila the Hun** to pass through Italy in 451. Then Genseric the Vandal, who had set up a pirate kingdom in Africa and learned to sail, raided Italy and sacked Rome again in 455.

So completely had things changed, it was scarcely possible to tell the Romans from the barbarians. By the 470s, the real ruler in Italy was a Gothic general named **Odoacer**, who led a half-Romanized Germanic army and probably thought of himself as the genuine heir of the Caesars. In 476, he decided to dispense with the lingering charade of the Western Empire. The last emperor, young, silly Romulus Augustulus, was packed off to premature retirement in Naples, and Odoacer had himself crowned King of Italy at Pavia.

476–1000: The Dark Ages

At the beginning, the new Gothic-Latin state showed some promise; certainly the average man was no worse off than he had been under the last emperors. In 493, Odoacer was replaced (and murdered) by a rival Ostrogoth, **Theodoric**, nominally working on behalf of the Eastern Emperor at Constantinople. Theodoric proved a strong and able, though somewhat paranoid ruler; his court at Ravenna witnessed a minor rebirth of Latin letters with Cassiodorus, Symmachus, and the great Christian philosopher Boethius. Nevertheless, stability was compromised by religious quarrels between the Arian Christian Goths and the Orthodox Catholic populations in the cities.

A disaster as serious as those of the 5th century began in 536, with the invasion of Italy by the Eastern Empire, part of the relentlessly expansionist policy of the great **Justinian**. The historical irony was profound; in the ancient homeland of the Roman Empire,

Roman troops now came not as liberators, but as foreign, largely Greek-speaking conquerors. Justinian's brilliant generals, Belisarius and Narses, ultimately prevailed over the Goths in a series of terrible wars that lasted until 563, but the damage to an already stricken society and economy was incalculable. Italy's total exhaustion was exposed only five years later, when the **Lombards**, a Germanic tribe who worked hard to earn the title of barbarians, overran northern Italy and parts of the south, establishing a kingdom at Pavia and the separate duchies of Benevento and Spoleto. A new pattern of power appeared, with semi-independent Byzantine dukes defending many coastal areas, the Exarchs of Ravenna controlling considerable territory on the Adriatic and in Calabria, and Lombard chiefs ruling most of the interior. The popes in Rome, occasionally allied with the Lombards against Byzantium, became a force during this period, especially after the papacy of the clever, determined **Gregory the Great** (590–604).

With trade and culture at their lowest ebb, the 7th century marks the rock bottom of Italian history. The 8th showed some improvement; while most of the peninsula lay in feudal darkness, Venice was beginning its remarkable career as a trading city, and independent **Amalfi** and **Naples** emulated its success on the Tyrrhenian coast. The popes, typical of the urban bishops who had taken advantage of the confused times to become temporal powers, intrigued everywhere to increase their influence; they finally cashed in with a Frankish alliance in the 750s. At the time the Lombard kings were doing well, finally conquering Ravenna (751) and considerable territories formerly under the dominion of the popes, who invited in **Charlemagne** to protect them. He eliminated the last Lombard king, Desiderius (his father-in-law, incidentally), and tucked all Italy as far south as Rome (with the exception of Venice) into his patchwork empire.

A Lombard Duchy of Benevento survived until 846 up in the mountains, and the Byzantines kept a tenuous hold on the heel and toe; the Greek villages and relics of troglodyte Greek monasticism in Calabria and Apulia date from this period. At the same time, Arabs from Tunisia were beginning a gradual conquest of Sicily, and with permanent bases on the coast and in the mountains, their raiders menaced the entire peninsula. The Arabs established an **Emirate of Bari**, controlling much of Apulia, and they sacked Rome itself in 846.

Charlemagne's conquests, though short-lived, changed the political face of Italy for ever, beginning the contorted *pas de deux* of pope and emperor that was to be the mainspring of Italian history throughout the Middle Ages. Meanwhile, Italy reverted to a finely balanced anarchy. Altogether the 9th century was a bad time, with Italy caught between the Arab raiders and the endless wars of petty nobles and bishops in the north. The 10th century proved somewhat better—perhaps much better than the scanty chronicles of the time attest. Even in the worst times, Italy's cities never entirely disappeared. Sailing, and trading over the sea, always lead to better technologies, new ideas, and economic growth, and in these respects the maritime cities of Italy had become the most advanced in Europe.

A big break for the cities, and for Italy, came in 961 with the invasion of the German **Otto the Great**. He deposed the last feeble King of Italy, Berengar II of Ivrea, and was crowned Holy Roman Emperor in Rome the following year. Not that any of the Italians were happy to see him, but the strong government of Otto and his successors beat down the great nobles and allowed the growing cities to expand their power and influence. A new pattern was established; the Germanic Emperors would be meddling in Italian affairs for centuries, not powerful enough to establish total control, but at least usually able to keep out important rivals.

1000–1194: The Normans and the Papal Revival

On the eve of the new millennium, most Christians were convinced that the turn of the calendar was bringing with it the end of the world. On the contrary, if there had been economists and social scientists around, they would have had ample evidence to reassure everyone that things were looking up. Especially in the towns, business was very good, and the political prospects even brighter. Northern cities, acquiring the wealth that would make them the economic and cultural leaders of medieval Europe, were beginning to organize themselves as free *comuni*, asserting their independence against both popes and emperors.

Southern Italy knew a far different fate. The first **Normans** arrived in the 8th or 9th century, as mercenaries or pilgrims to Monte Sant'Angelo in the Gargano. They liked the opportunities they saw for booty and conquest, and from about 1020 younger sons of Norman feudal families were moving into the south, first as mercenaries but gradually gaining large tracts of land for themselves in exchange for their services. Often allied with the popes, they soon controlled most of Apulia and Calabria. One of their greatest chiefs, **Roger de Hauteville**, began the conquest of Sicily from the Arabs in 1060, six years before William the Conqueror sailed for England. Roger's brother, Robert Guiscard, was travelling in the opposite direction. In 1084, he descended on Rome for a grisly sack that put the best efforts of the Goths and Vandals to shame.

Roger eventually united all of the south into the 'Kingdom of Sicily', and by the 1140s, under Roger II, this strange Norman-Arab-Jewish-Italian state, with its glittering, half-oriental capital of Palermo, had become the cultural centre of the Mediterranean, a refuge of religious tolerance and serious scholarship. Under Roger and his successors (William the Bad and William the Good), it was also one of the strongest and best-organized states in Europe.

Throughout this period the papacy had declined greatly in power and prestige, a political football kicked between the emperors and the piratical Roman nobles. Beginning in the 1050s, a remarkable Tuscan monk named Hildebrand controlled papal policy, working behind the scenes to reassert the influence of the Church. When he became pope himself, in 1073, **Gregory VII** immediately set himself in conflict with the emperors over the issue of investiture—whether the church or the secular powers would name church officials. The various Italian (and European) powers chose sides, and fifty years of intermittent war followed, including the famous penance in the snow of Emperor Henry IV in Canossa (1077).

1194–1300: Hohenstaufens and Angevins

One of the most important designs of the new militant papacy was the First Crusade (1097–1130). For Italy, and especially for the trading cities, with plenty of boats to help ship Crusaders, the affair meant nothing but pure profit. Culture and science, already flourishing, gained a big boost from contact with the Byzantines and the Muslims of Spain and Africa.

By the 12th century, far in advance of most of Europe, Italy had attained a prosperity unknown since Roman times. The classical past had never been forgotten—witness the attempt of Arnold of Brescia (1154) to recreate the Roman Republic. Free *comuni* in the north called their elected leaders 'consuls', and artists and architects turned ancient Roman styles into the Romanesque. Even Italian names were changing, an interesting sign of the beginnings of national consciousness; quite suddenly the public records (such as they were) show a marked shift from Germanic to classical and Biblical surnames: fewer Ugos, Othos, and Astolfos, more Giuseppes, Giovannis, Giulios, and Flavios.

No doubt every schoolboy wonders why the Austrians were so beastly to Richard Lionheart, locking him up on the way back from the Crusades and extorting such a big ransom. In fact, the entire affair was a sideshow to a momentous event in Italian politics. Richard had already passed through Italy twice, staking his claim to some lands left him by distant cousin William the Good. **Henry VI**, the Hohenstaufen Holy Roman Emperor, also had a claim on those properties, and the rest of southern Italy too. He used the English ransom money to finance a bloody campaign in 1194, conquering almost the entire south and murdering the last Norman heir. His son, **Frederick II** inherited not only the Empire, but also the Kingdom of Sicily, thus giving him a strong power base in Italy itself.

Frederick's career dominated Italian politics for 30 years (1220–50). With his brilliant court, in which Italian was used for the first time (alongside Arabic and Latin), his half-Muslim army, his incredible processions of dancing girls, eunuchs, and elephants, he provided Europe with a spectacle the like of which it had never seen. Frederick founded universities (as at Naples), gave Sicily a written constitution (perhaps the world's first), wrote elegant poetry and built geometrically arcane castles and towers all over the south. The popes excommunicated him at least twice. Now the battle had become serious. All Italy divided into factions: the **Guelphs**, under the leadership of the popes, supported religious orthodoxy, the liberty of the *comuni*, and the interests of their emerging wealthy merchant class. The **Ghibellines** stood for the emperor, statist economic control, the interests of the rural nobles, and religious and intellectual tolerance. Frederick's campaigns and diplomacy in the north met with very limited success, and his death in 1250 left the outcome very much in doubt.

His son **Manfred**, not emperor but merely King of Sicily, took up the battle with better luck; Siena's defeat of Florence in 1260 gained that city and most of Tuscany for the Ghibellines. The next year, however, Pope Urban IV began an ultimately disastrous precedent by inviting in **Charles of Anjou**, a powerful, ambitious leader and brother of the King of France. As protector of the Guelphs, Charles defeated Manfred (1266) and murdered the last of the Hohenstaufens, Conradin (1268). He held unchallenged sway over Italy until 1282, when the famous revolt of the Sicilian Vespers chased the hated French from Sicily and started the party wars up again. The Angevins held on in the south of the peninsula, though to do it they had to increase the power of the southern barons, and effectively ruin the prosperous economies of the Apulian and Campanian trading cities. Apulia in particular, a region strongly attached to the Hohenstaufens, raised frequent revolts against the French; their repression, combined with high taxes to support Angevin ambitions elsewhere, was a fatal blow to the richest and most cultured part of the south.

1300–1493: The Beginnings of Spanish Rule

By now, it was clear that Italy's north and south were following quite different destinies. North of Rome, the trading cities had grown into strong states: Venice, Milan, Florence, Genoa, and the rest, either maintaining their republican institutions (like Florence), or coming under the personal rule of powerful families (like Milan). Though the 14th century was not the most prosperous of times, none of them suffered excessively. With no serious threats from the emperors or any other foreign power, these states were able to menace each other joyfully without outside interference, leaving the fighting to bands of paid mercenaries led by a *condottiere*. The arrangement suited everyone well. The cities were usually free from grand ambitions; everyone was making too much money to want to go and wreck the system. Without heavy artillery, walled towns and castles were nearly impossible to take, making the incentives to try hard even less. Best of all, the worst schemers and troublemakers on the Italian stage were fortuitously removed from the scene. Holy Roman Emperors no longer crossed the Alps, and with the election of the French Pope Clement V in 1303, the papacy moved to Avignon, a puppet of the French king and temporarily without influence in Italian affairs.

The South, despite its nominal unity, was falling behind both politically and economically. The Normans may have ruled their domains fairly and intelligently, but they also deserve the blame for introducing feudalism into a country that had never known it—just as the mercantile states of the north were breaking loose from the feudal arrangements brought down by the Goths and Lombards. Now the 'Kingdom of Naples', as the southern state had become known, was a tapestry of battling barons, each busily building or improving his castle and increasingly less inclined to listen to kings or popes or anyone. The trading cities—Naples, Gaeta, Amalfi and the towns of the Apulian coast—saw their woes increase with strong competition from the Venetians and Genoese. With little encouragement from king or barons, they could only continue to decline.

Robert the Wise (1309–43) was a good king, and patron of Giotto, Petrarch and Bocaccio. For a successor, he left only a granddaughter, **Joan I**, and under her unsteady hand the barons mightily increased both their power and their contentiousness. Her reign witnessed the **Black Death** (1347–48), in which Italy lost one third of its population, and also the beginnings of civil war between Angevin factions, something that would continue fitfully through a century of confusing intrigues and insurrections. It ended in the hands of yet another foreign intriguer, **Alfonso the Magnanimous**, King of Aragon, who conquered Naples and tossed out the last Angevins in 1435. Once more the Kingdom was reunited with Sicily, part of the Aragonese crown since the Sicilian Vespers. Spain had its foothold in Italy, and after the union of Aragon and Castile in 1492, under Ferdinand and Isabella, Spain would be the strongest player on the Italian chessboard.

1494–1529: The Wars of Italy

The Italians brought the trouble down on themselves, when Duke Lodovico of Milan invited the French King **Charles VIII** to cross the Alps and assert his claim to the throne of Milan's enemy, Naples. Charles did just that, and the failure of the combined Italian states to stop him (at the inconclusive Battle of Fornovo, 1494) showed just how helpless

51

Italy was at the hands of emerging new nation-states like France or Spain. The Spaniards sent a strong army under *El Gran Capitan*, Gonsalvo di Córdoba, and he restored Naples to its Spanish king the following year. Before long, the German emperor and even the Swiss entered this new market for Italian real estate. The popes did as much as anyone to keep the pot boiling. Alexander VI and his son Cesare Borgia carried the war across central Italy in an attempt to found a new state for the Borgia family, and Julius II's madcap policy led him to egg on the Swiss, French and Spaniards in turn, before finally crying, 'Out with the barbarians!' when it was already too late.

By 1516, with the French ruling Milan and the Spanish in control of the south, it seemed as if a settlement would be possible. The worst possible luck for Italy, however, came with the accession of the insatiable megalomaniac **Charles V** to the throne of Spain in that year; in 1519 he bought himself the crown of the Holy Roman Empire, making him the most powerful ruler in Europe since Charlemagne. Charles felt he needed Milan as a base for communications between his Spanish, German and Flemish possessions, and as soon as he had emptied Spain's treasury, driven her to revolt, and plunged Germany into civil war, he turned his attentions to Italy. The wars began anew, bloodier than anything Italy had seen for centuries, climaxing with the defeat of the French at Pavia in 1525, and the sack of Rome by an out-of-control imperial army in 1527. The French invaded once more, in 1529, and were defeated this time at Naples by the treachery of their Genoese allies. All Italy, save only Venice, was now at the mercy of Charles and the Spaniards.

1529–1796: Italy in Chains

The broader context of these events, of course, was the bitter struggles of the Reformation and Counter-Reformation. In Italy, the Spaniards found a pefect ally in the papacy. One had the difficult job of breaking the spirit of a nation that, though conquered, was still wealthy, culturally sophisticated and ready to resist; the other saw an opportunity to recapture by force the hearts and minds it had lost long before. With the majority of the peninsula still nominally controlled by local rulers, and an economy that continued to be sound, both the Spanish and the popes realized that the only real threat would come not from men, but ideas. Under the banner of combating Protestantism, they commenced a reign of terror across Italy, beginning in Naples under Giovanni Carafa, later to become pope as **Paul IV**. In the 1550s, the revived Inquisition began its manhunt for free-thinkers of every variety; the Index of Prohibited Books followed in 1559 (some works of Dante included), accompanied by public book-burnings in Rome and elsewhere. A long line of Italian intellectuals trudged to the stake, while many more buried their convictions or left for exile in Germany or England. The job of re-educating Italy was put in the hands of the new Jesuit order; their schools and propaganda campaigns bored the pope's message deeply into the Italian mind, while their sumptuous new churches, spectacles and dramatic sermons helped re-define Catholicism.

Despite the oppression, the average Italian at first had little to complain about. Spanish rule brought peace and order to a country that had long been a madhouse of conflicting ambitions. Renaissance artists attained a brilliance and virtuosity never seen before, just in time to embellish the scores of new churches, palaces, and villas of the mid-16th-century building boom. The combined Christian forces had turned back the Turkish threat at Malta (1566) and Lepanto (1571), and the southern coasts were finally spared the ravages of Muslim corsairs.

After 1600 nearly everything started to go wrong for the Italians. The textiles and banking of the north, long the engines of the economy, both withered in the face of foreign competition, and the old port towns began to look half-empty as the English and Dutch took control of the declining Mediterranean trade. Worst-off of all was the south, under direct Spanish or papal rule. Combining incompetence and brutality with outrageously high taxes (the Spaniards' went to finance foreign wars, the popes' to build up Rome), they rapidly turned the already poor south into a nightmare of anarchic depravity, haunted by legions of bandits and beggars, and controlled more tightly than ever by its violent feudal barons. To everyone's surprise, the south rose up and staged an epic rebellion. Beginning in Naples (Masaniello's Revolt, 1647), the disturbances soon spread all over the south and Sicily. For over a year peasant militias ruled some areas, and makeshift revolutionary councils defended the cities. But when the Spanish finally defeated them, they massacred some 18,000, and tightened the screws more then ever.

Bullied, humiliated and increasingly impoverished, 17th-century Italy at least tried hard to keep up its ancient prominence in the arts and sciences. Galileo looked through telescopes, Monteverdi wrote the first operas, and hundreds of talented though uninspired artists cranked out pretty pictures to meet the continuing high demand. Bernini and Borromini turned Rome into the capital of Baroque—the florid, expensive coloratura style that serves as a perfect symbol for the age itself, an age of political repression and thought control where art itself became a political tool. Baroque's heavenly grandeur and symmetry helped to impress everyone with the majesty of Church and State. At the same time, Baroque scholars wrote books that went on for hundreds of pages without saying anything, but avoided offending the government and the Inquisition. Baroque impresarios managed the wonderful pageantry of Church holidays, state occasions and carnivals that kept the ragged crowds amused. Manners and clothing became decorously berserk, and a race for easily bought noble titles occurred that would have made a medieval Italian laugh out loud. Italy was being rocked to sleep in a Baroque cradle.

By the 18th century, there were very few painters or scholars or scientists. There were no more heroic revolts either. Italy in this period hardly has any history at all; with Spain's increasing decadence, the great powers decided the futures of Italy's major states, and used the minor ones as a kind of overflow tank to hold surplus princes and those dispossessed by wars elsewhere (Napoleon on Elba was the last and most famous of these). In 1713, after the War of the Spanish Succession, the **Habsburgs of Austria** came into control of Milan and Lombardy, Mantua and the Kingdom of Naples.

Naples' hard luck continued when the Austrians were forced to transfer it to a branch of the **House of Bourbon** (1734); under them the kingdom was independent, but just as poorly governed as before. An exception was the reign of **Charles III** (1734–59) who introduced many long overdue reforms. Naples had taken advantage of the free-spending Spanish and Bourbon rule (as well as the despair and unemployment of the countryside) to become the biggest city in Europe; in this period the city acquired much of its spirit, and its landmarks. Charles built the San Carlo Opera, and the palaces at Capodimonte and Caserta.

53

1796–1848: Napoleon and Reaction

Napoleon, that greatest of Italian generals, arrived in 1796 on behalf of the French revolutionary Directorate, sweeping away the Piedmontese and Austrians and setting up republics in Lombardy (the 'Cisalpine Republic'), Liguria, and Naples (the 'Parthenopean Republic'). Italy woke up with a start from its Baroque slumbers, and local patriots gaily joined the French cause. In 1799, however, while Napoleon was off in Egypt, the advance through Italy by an Austro-Russian army, aided by Nelson's fleet, restored the status quo. This was often accompanied by bloody reprisals, as peasant mobs led by clerics like the 'Army of the Holy Faith' marched across the south massacring liberals and French sympathizers.

In 1800 Napoleon returned in a campaign that saw the great victory at Marengo, giving him the opportunity once more to reorganize Italian affairs. Napoleon crowned himself King of Italy; Joseph Bonaparte, and later Joachim Murat, ruled at Naples. Rome was annexed to France, and the pope was carted off to Fontainebleau. Napoleonic rule lasted only until 1814, but in that time important public works were begun and laws, education and everything else reformed on the French model; immense Church properties were expropriated, and medieval relics everywhere put to rest. The French, however, soon wore out their welcome. Besides hauling much of Italy's artistic heritage off to the Louvre, implementing high war taxes and conscription (some 25,000 Italians died on the Russian front), and brutally repressing a number of local revolts, they systematically exploited Italy for the benefit of the Napoleonic elite and the crowds of speculators who came flocking over the Alps. When the Austrians and English came to chase all the little Napoleons out, no one was sad to see them go.

But the experience had given Italians a taste of the opportunities offered by the modern world, as well as a sense of national feeling that had been suppressed for centuries. The 1815 Congress of Vienna put the clock back to 1796; indeed the Habsburgs and Bourbons seemed to think they could pretend the Napoleonic upheavals had never happened, and the political reaction in their territories was fierce.

Almost immediately, revolutionary agitators and secret societies like the famous *Carbonari* kept Italy convulsed in plots and intrigues. A big revolt in Naples forced the reactionary King Ferdinand to grant a constitution (1821) but when Austrian troops came down to crush the rebels he took it back. The French July Revolution of 1830 also spread to Italy, encouraged by the liberal King **Carlo Alberto** in Piedmont-Savoy, but once more the by now universally hated Austrians intervened.

1848–1900: The Risorgimento and United Italy

Conspirators of every colour and shape, including the legendary **Giuseppe Mazzini**, had to wait another 18 years for their next chance. The big change came in the revolutionary year of 1848, when risings in Palermo and Naples (in January) anticipated even those in Paris itself. Soon all Italy was in the streets. Piedmont and Tuscany won constitutions from their rulers, and the people of Milan chased the Austrians out after a month of extremely bloody fighting; at the same time the Venetian Republic was restored. Carlo Alberto, the hope of most Italians for a war of liberation, marched against the Austrians, but his two badly bungled campaigns allowed the enemy to re-establish control over the peninsula. By June 1849, only Venice, under Austrian blockade, and the recently declared Roman Republic were left. Rome, led by Mazzini, and with a small army under **Giuseppe Garibaldi**, a former sailor who had fought in the wars of independence in Latin America, beat off several attacks from foreign troops invited in by the pope. The republic finally succumbed to a large force sent by, of all people, the revolutionary republican government in France.

Despite failure on a grand scale, at least the Italians knew they would get another chance. Unification was inevitable, but there were two irreconcilable contenders for the honour of accomplishing it. On one side, the democrats and radicals dreamed of a truly reborn, revolutionary Italy, and looked to the popular hero Garibaldi to deliver it; on the other, moderates wanted the Piedmontese to do the job, ensuring a stable future by making **Vittorio Emanuele II** King of Italy. Vittorio Emanuele's minister, the polished, clever **Count Camillo Cavour**, spent the 1850s getting Piedmont in shape for the struggle, building its economy and army, participating in the Crimean War to earn diplomatic support, and plotting with the French for an alliance against Austria.

War came in 1859, and French armies did most of the work in conquering Lombardy. Tuscany and Emilia revolted, and Piedmont was able to annex all three. In May of that year, Garibaldi and his red-shirted 'Thousand' sailed from Genoa—Cavour almost stopped them at the last minute—and landed in Sicily, electrifying Europe by repeatedly beating the Bourbon forces in a quick march across the island. The Thousand had become 20,000, and when they crossed the straits bound for Naples it was clear that the affair was reaching its climax.

Meeting little resistance across the south, Garibaldi entered Naples on 7 September, and though he proclaimed himself temporary dictator on Vittorio Emanuele's behalf, the Piedmontese were alarmed enough to occupy Umbria, the Marches, and most of the Papal States. The last King of Naples, Francesco II, took refuge in Gaeta, while a force of Bourbon bitter-enders made a last stand at Civitella del Tronto in the Abruzzo. The King met Garibaldi on 27 October, near Teano, and after finding out what little regard the Piedmontese had for him, the greatest and least self-interested leader modern Italy has known went off to a quiet retirement on the island of Caprera.

Just as the French had made all this possible, more unexpected help from outside allowed the new Italy to add two missing pieces and complete its unification. When the Prussians defeated Austria in the war of 1866, Italy was able to seize the Veneto. Only Rome was left, defended by a French garrison, and when the Prussians beat France at Sedan in 1870, the Italian army marched into Rome almost without opposition.

The first decades of the Italian Kingdom were just as unimpressive as its wars of independence. A liberal constitutional monarchy was established, but the parliament almost immediately decomposed into cliques and political cartels representing various interests. Finances started in disorder and stayed that way, and corruption became widespread.

In the south, agents of the displaced Bourbons, and of the pope, contributed to the continuing unrest, though conditions were such that most of the troubles began spontaneously. Through the 1860s over a hundred thousand troops were tied down pursuing the 'bandits' of the south. The guerrilla bands concentrated on killing landowners and officials of the new government, raiding town halls to burn the tax and property records; the army responded in kind, with the brutality of an occupying power. The woes of the south found scant sympathy in the more developed regions of Italy. For its part, the government found it more convenient to favour the old aristocracy—enrolling Bourbon officers wholesale into the new Italian army, for example, while refusing to accept the more capable, better educated patriots who had held commissions under Garibaldi.

Ironically, southerners came to hold a disproportionate share of power and positions in the new regime. The *galantuomini*, the useless and backward class of local bosses and landlords, soon learned the possibilities offered them by Italy's limited democracy, and found it as easy to manipulate as the Bourbon kingdom had been. Their influence has contributed much to Italy's political troubles in all the years since. Thus was the new Italy born with the 'problem of the south' as the first item on its agenda—and with a regime determined to do little or nothing about it.

After 1900, with the rise of a strong socialist movement, strikes, riots, and police repression often occupied centre stage in Italian politics. Even so, important signs of progress, such as the big new industries in Turin and Milan, showed that at least the northern half of Italy was becoming a fully integral part of the European economy. The southern half was packing its suitcases. Some two and a half million Italians emigrated for the Americas and elsewhere between 1880 and 1914, well over three quarters of them from the south. The severe agricultural depression that began in the 1880s, combined with an upsurge in malaria and the other chronic diseases of the south, were a fitting complement to the disappointments of unification.

1900–1945: War, Fascism, and War

Italy could have stayed out of World War I, but let the opportunity slip for the usual reasons—a hope of gaining some new territory, especially Austrian Trieste. Irredentists, the radical right, and bored intellectuals like Gabriele d'Annunzio helped Italy leap blindly into the conflict in 1915. Italian armies fought with their accustomed flair, masterminding an utter catastrophe at Caporetto (October 1917) that any other nation but Austria would have parlayed into a total victory. No thanks to their generals, the poorly armed and equipped Italians somehow held firm for another year, until the total exhaustion of Austria allowed them to prevail (the *Vittorio Veneto* you see so many streets named after), capturing some 600,000 prisoners in November 1918.

In return for 650,000 dead, a million casualties, severe privation on the home front, and a war debt higher than anyone could count, Italy received Trieste, Gorizia, the South Tyrol, and a few other scraps. Italians felt they had been cheated. The economy was in shambles and, at least in the north, revolution was in the air; workers in Turin raised the Red Flag over the Fiat plants and organized themselves into soviets. The troubles had encouraged extremists of both right and left, and many Italians became convinced that the liberal state was finished.

Enter **Benito Mussolini**, a professional intriguer in the Mazzini tradition with bad manners and no fixed principles. Before the War he had found his real talent as editor of the Socialist Party paper *Avanti!*—the best it ever had, tripling the circulation in a year. When he decided that what Italy really needed was war, he left to found a new paper, and contributed mightily to the jingoist agitation of 1915. In the post-War confusion, he found his opportunity. A little bit at a time, he developed the idea of **fascism**, at first less a philosophy than an astute use of mass propaganda and a sense of design. (The *fasces*, from which the name comes, were bundles of rods carried before ancient Roman officials, a symbol of authority. *Fasci* also referred to organized bands of rebellious peasants in 19th-century Sicily.)

With a little discreet money supplied by frightened industrialists, Mussolini had no trouble in finding recruits for his black-shirted gangs, sending them against trade unionists, Slavic minorities and leftist politicians. Mussolini's accession to power came as the result of an improbable gamble. In the particularly anarchic month of October 1922, he announced that his followers would march on Rome. King Vittorio Emanuele III refused to sign a decree of martial law to disperse them, and there was nothing to do but offer Mussolini the post of prime minister. At first, he governed Italy with undeniable competence. Order was restored, and the economy and foreign policy handled intelligently by non-fascist professionals. Mussolini increased his popularity by singling out especially obnoxious unions and corrupt leftist local governments for punishment. In the 1924 elections, despite the flagrant rigging and intimidation, the Fascists only won a slight majority. One brave politician who was not intimidated was Giacomo Matteotti, and when some of Mussolini's close associates took him for a ride and murdered him, a major scandal erupted. Mussolini survived it, and during 1925 and 1926 the Fascists used parliamentary methods to convert Italy into a permanent fascist dictatorship.

Compared with the governments that preceded him, Mussolini looked quite impressive. Industry advanced, great public works were undertaken, with special care towards the backward south, and the Mafia took some heavy blows at the hands of a determined Sicilian prefect named Mori. The most lasting achievement was the Concordat of 1929 with the pope, founding the Vatican State and ending the Church's isolation from Italian affairs. The regime evolved a new economic philosophy, the 'corporate state', where labour and capital were supposed to live in harmony under syndicalist government control. But the longer fascism lasted, the more unreal it seemed, a patchwork government of Mussolini and his ageing cronies, magnified and rendered heroic by cinematic technique—stirring rhetoric before oceanic crowds, colourful pageantry, magnificent, larger-than-life post offices and railway stations built of travertine and marble, dashing aviators and winsome gymnasts from the fascist youth groups on parade. In a way it was the Baroque all over again, and Italians tried not to think about the consequences. In the words of one of Mussolini's favourite slogans, painted on walls all over Italy, 'Whoever stops is lost'.

Mussolini couldn't stop, and the only possibility for new diversions lay with the chance of conquest and empire. His invasion of Ethiopia and his meddling in the Spanish Civil War, both in 1936, compromised Italy into a close alliance with Nazi Germany. Mussolini's confidence and rhetoric never faltered as he led an entirely unprepared nation into the biggest war ever. Once more, Italian ineptitude at warfare produced embarrassing defeats on all fronts, and only German intervention in Greece and North Africa saved Italy from being knocked out of the War as early as 1941. The Allies invaded Sicily in July 1943, and the Italians began to look for a clever way out. They seized Mussolini during a meeting of the Grand Council, packed him into an ambulance and sent him off first to Ponza, then to a little ski hotel up in the Apennines. The new government under Marshal Badoglio didn't know what to do, and confusion reigned supreme.

While British and American forces slogged northwards, in this ghetto of the European theatre, with the help of the Free French, Brazilians, Costa Ricans, Poles, Czechs, New Zealanders and Norwegians, the Germans poured in divisions to defend the peninsula. They rescued Mussolini, in a spectacular exploit with a small plane, and made him set up a puppet state called the Italian Social Republic in the north. In September, the Badoglio government finally signed an armistice with the Allies, too late to keep the War from dragging on another year and a half, as the Germans made good use of Italy's difficult terrain to slow the Allied advance. Meanwhile Italy finally gave itself something to be proud of, a determined, resourceful Resistance that established free zones in many areas, and harassed the Germans with sabotage and strikes. The *partigiani* caught Mussolini in April 1945, while he was trying to escape to Switzerland; after shooting him and his mistress, they hung him by the toes from the roof of a petrol station in Milan.

1945–the Present

Post-War Italy *cinema-verità*—Rossellini's *Open City*, or de Sica's *Bicycle Thieves*—captures the atmosphere better than words ever could. In a period of serious hardships that older Italians still remember, the nation slowly picked itself up and returned things to normal. A referendum in June 1946 made Italy a Republic, but only by a narrow margin. The first governments fell to the new Christian Democrat Party under Alcide di Gasperi, which has run the show ever since in coalitions with a preposterous band of smaller parties. The main opposition has been provided by the Communists.

The economic miracle that began in the 1950s continues today, and it has propelled the Italians into fifth place among the world's national economies. The south has not caught up with the rest of the country, despite sincere efforts of the government and its special planning fund, the *Cassa per il Mezzogiorno*. Indeed, recent statistics suggest that some parts of the south are beginning to fall further behind, though the extreme poverty and despair of the pre-War years no longer exist. Some changes have been profound. Perhaps the most striking symbol of this is the *sassi*, the bleak neighbourhoods of Matera in the Basilicata, where until recently thousands of people lived in caves—now nearly abandoned, and becoming a tourist attraction. Land reform in the late '40s and '50s, though not entirely successful, eradicated the last vestiges of feudalism, education was improved, and new roads built into regions that badly needed them. Tàranto, Naples and Bari became important industrial cities, while tens of thousands of southerners migrated to Turin, Milan or Germany looking for work, leaving half-abandoned villages across the region, especially in Calabria.

Some things do not change. Instead of extortionate barons, there are the crime syndicates: not just the Mafia, largely limited to Sicily until its drug-financed expansion of the last two decades, but the *Camorra* of Naples and the *'Ndrangheta* of Calabria. They cut their own slice from the local economy, discourage new investment and political reform, and the result is just the same. Natural disasters keep their accustomed southern rhythm; the earthquake of 1980, largely ignored in the press, caused tremendous damage and suffering in rural Campania, the Basilicata and the Molise. Southerners do not complain. Though it has the least reason to be so, the Mezzogiorno politically is the least troublesome corner of a complacent nation. Haunted by their pitiless history, its people build and save, plant new vines as they always have done, and hope for the best.

Art and Architecture, and where to find it
Prehistoric, Greek and Etruscan

Some of the first art of Europe was produced in Italy—the stubby Paleolithic fertility Venuses of the Italian Riviera, and the rock incisions in the Val Camonica, near the Dolomites—but Italy's south has yielded very little. From the Neolithic era to the threshold of Greek colonization, the most ambitious builders lived in Apulia; the Messapians and related peoples left behind some dolmens (around **Fasano**, Bari and a few near the tip of the Salentine peninsula), ambiguous small stone buildings, and the little towers called *specchie* (around **Cèglie Messapico**) and also the remains of their cities, such as **Manduria**. Nearly all the native cultures produced pottery with geometric decoration, some of it quite elegant (museums in **Manfredonia, Brindisi** and **Lecce**). The most surprising production of indigenous art is the 'Warrior of Capestrano' (6th century), glaring out from under his sombrero in the museum at **Chieti**.

With the arrival of the Greeks and Etruscans in the middle of the 8th century BC, Italy finally joined the wider Mediterranean world, artistically as well as politically. The wealthy cities of Magna Graecia imported classical Greek art and artists wholesale, and even though the cities themselves have disappeared, the south's museums have a huge store of ceramics, architectural decoration, figurines and lovely terracotta ex-votos (the best collections at **Naples, Tàranto** and best of all **Règgio Calabria**, which has the spectacular *Warriors of Riace*; also smaller collections at **Locri** and **Policoro**. For architecture, there is of course the great Doric temple at **Paestum** (which also has an extremely rare Greek fresco in a tomb), and little else—fragmentary temples at Tàranto and **Metapontum**.

From the beginning, Greek culture had a strong influence on the rapidly developing native peoples of the south. Apulian and Campanian artists made endless copies of painted Greek ceramics, many of them excellent; proper Greek theatres can be seen not only at Pompeii, but in country backwaters like **Pietrabbondante** in the Molise. To the end of the empire, Romanization was only superficial outside the big cities and the colonies Rome planted for Latins and army veterans; Greek and the various Italic tongues remained the local languages in most places, with Latin used only for business.

The Etruscans, in their art, managed the trick of being at once strikingly original and blatantly imitative. For centuries, every advance and stylistic innovation imported from Athens or Corinth soon had to suffer comparison with the clever copies of Etruria's artistic magpies—black and red painted ceramics, Archaic-style sculpture, followed in the 5th century by naturalistic bronze statues, and burial urns with relief scenes from Greek mythology. Their most creative work was in jewellery, with fantastically intricate gold and silver work that could scarcely be duplicated today, and especially in portrait sculpture. Here they excelled even the Greeks in depth and expressiveness; the hundreds of bronze and terracotta figures in Italy's museums—the gods, noble families, statesmen, comic caricatures and laughing children—are part of the Etruscan legend, an art that could only have been produced by a people that truly enjoyed life, and understood it well.

Etruscan customs devoted so much care to burials and the afterlife that tombs came to be built more solidly than the cities of the living, most notably the acres of bizarre domed tombs at **Cervéteri**. Every Etruscan city is surrounded by such necropolises, with tombs painted and sculpted in lively scenes of sport or battle, and articles of everyday life to help the deceased enjoy the symbolic feasting of the world beyond death. They are our greatest source of knowledge of this lost culture. The two exceptional collections of Etruscan art are in **Rome**'s Villa Giulia museum, and at **Tarquinia**.

Roman Architecture

The Romans were the greatest builders of antiquity, no less—though even in late imperial times, when it was a question of aesthetics they would usually hire a Greek. In architecture, ancient Roman practicality found its greatest expression. They did not invent the arch, or concrete, or the aqueduct; they learned how to build roads and bridges from the Etruscans. Nevertheless, they perfected all these serviceable things to build works never dreamed of before, combining beauty and utility for their most significant contribution to western culture. Speaking strictly of design, the salient feature of Roman building was its conservatism. Under the Republic, Rome rejected its Etruscan traditions, in favour of pure Greek architecture, with a predilection for the more delicate Corinthian order. When the money started rolling in, the Romans began to build in marble (the 2nd century BC Temple of Portunus, still standing by the Tiber, was one of the first), but for 400 years, until the height of empire under Trajan and Hadrian, very little changed (outside Rome, the best-preserved temples are at **Cori, Tivoli** and **Palestrina**).

As Rome became the capital of the Mediterranean world, its rulers introduced new building types to embellish it: the series of *imperial fora*, variations on the Greek agora, the first of which was begun by Julius Caesar; *public baths*, a custom imported from Campania; *colonnaded streets*, as in Syria and Asia Minor; and *theatres*. Unlike Greek theatres, these were enclosed (though not covered), with a semicircular orchestra and columned stage buildings. Rome's own contribution was the *basilica*, a large rectangular hall supported on columns, impossibly noisy as a courtroom but still the perfect stage for the Romans in their togas to act out their boisterous public life. Eventually the form would be copied all over the Roman world. In an urban society, some advances in planning and design were to be expected. Rome's Forum of Trajan (AD 100–12 by **Apollodorus of Damascus**) makes the work of most modern planners look primitive. Besides providing noble buildings, and open space in the crowded city centre, the Forum skilfully combines widely divergent land uses—temples, libraries, government, and a big market—to create the first and finest of large-scale civic centres.

Concrete may not seem a very romantic subject, but in the hands of imperial architects it opened up entirely new possibilities. Roman concrete, made with volcanic sand from Pozzuoli, lasts almost for ever. First in the palaces (such as Nero's Golden House), and later in the Pantheon, with its giant concrete dome (AD 128), and in the huge public baths (those of Caracalla and Diocletian were the largest and most elaborate), an increasingly sophisticated use of arches and vaults created a genuine revolution in architecture. Concrete seating made the Colosseum and the vast theatres possible (and you may visit the second and third largest amphitheatres of the Roman world, both well preserved, at **Capua** and **Pozzuoli**), and allowed *insulae*—Roman apartment blocks—to climb six storeys and occasionally more; the best examples of these are at Rome's Capitoline Hill and at **Ostia**. Remains of Roman engineering can be seen all over Lazio and Campania:

the long arcades of the aqueducts outside Rome, the reservoirs and canals of the great naval base at **Cape Misenum**, and the long road tunnel, unique in the ancient world, at **Naples**.

Near the end of the empire, the tendency towards gigantism seems a symptom of Roman decadence; the clumsy forms of late monsters like Diocletian's Baths (298–306) and the Basilica of Maxentius (306–10) do show a technology far outstripping art, and the nascent Christian Church never did find an original architectural inspiration for its worship. When Constantine, the last of the big builders, financed Christian foundations around Rome, they all took the form of the basilica—an interesting comment on the early Roman church, that it would choose not a contemplative temple for its gatherings, but a form that to any Roman mind signified temporal authority.

Roman Sculpture, Painting and Mosaics

As in architecture, the other arts were dependent for centuries on the Greeks, either importing artists or copying classical works. Portrait sculpture, inherited from the Etruscans, is the notable exception, with a tradition of almost photographic, warts-and-all busts and funeral reliefs extending well into the imperial centuries. Augustus, who did so much else to decorate Rome, first exploited the possibilities of sculpture as a propaganda tool; the relief scenes of his reign on the Ara Pacis (AD 13) exemplify the clarity and classical restraint Romans preferred. Neither state policy nor private tastes encouraged experimentation, and Rome's sculptors continued to churn out endless copies of celebrated Greek works, even when their originals were on display in the emperor's gardens and temples.

As in architecture, sculptors began to consider new departures only in the confident, self-assured age of the Flavian and Antonine emperors. Some scholars have called the new style in reliefs 'impressionism' (as on the Arch of Titus or Trajan's Column in **Rome**, or Trajan's arch in **Benevento**). More than any other form of art, sculpture provides a compelling psychological record of Rome's history. In the troubled 3rd century, sculpture veers slowly but irreversibly towards the introverted and strange. Already under the Antonines, the tendency has begun, with the grim, realistic battle scenes on Marcus Aurelius' column, or the troubled portraits of that emperor himself. Later portraits become even more unsettling, with rigid features and staring eyes, more concerned with psychological depth than outward appearances, while 3rd-century reliefs can be either vigorous and queerly contorted, tending towards the abstract, or awkward and stiff, as in the many imperial propaganda pieces—a precursor of the Byzantine style.

In any case, after about 250 there was little art at all. In its brief revival under Constantine, we see how far the process had gone. No work better evokes the Rome of the unbalanced, totalitarian late empire than the weird, immense head of Constantine in the Capitoline museum.

Painting and mosaic work were never exposed to the same storm and stress as sculpture. Though both present from at least the 1st century BC Romans always considered them as little more than decoration, and only rarely entrusted to them any serious subjects. Both are a legacy from the Greeks, and both found their way to Rome by way of talented, half-Greek Campania to the south. Painting, in the days of Caesar and

Augustus, usually meant wall frescoes in the homes of the wealthy, with large scenes of gardens in the form of window views, making small Roman rooms look brighter and bigger; also mythological scenes and paintings of battles. (The best, courtesy of Vesuvius, are at **Pompeii** and **Herculaneum**, also in the museum of **Naples** and Diocletian's Baths in **Rome**, and in the little-known Mithraeum in **Capua**.) Like the Etruscans, Romans liked to paint the walls of their tombs, though less ambitiously (you can see some in the excavations under St Peter's).

No important advances ever came to Roman painting, though skill and grace seemed gradually to deteriorate over the centuries—few of the paintings in the Christian catacombs are anything more than primitive. Mosaics, another import that had its greatest centre at Antioch, in Hellenized Syria, only became a significant medium at Rome in the 2nd century AD just as painting was declining. As with the other arts, mosaics were done better in civilized Campania. If Rome too, had been buried under volcanic lava, at whatever period, it is unlikely that much would be found to surpass the 2nd- and 1st-century paintings and mosaics discovered at **Pompeii**. More fine mosaics can be seen at Diocletian's Baths in Rome, and at the museum in **Palestrina**.

Rome (the ruins, and the Capitoline and EUR museums), Pompeii, Herculaneum and the Naples museum are of course the most important sites for getting to know Roman civilization. But just as good in their way, and well worth a stop if you are anywhere in the neighbourhood, are **Ostia**, Rome's port, well preserved by the sands, Hadrian's colossal villa at **Tivoli**, **Saepinum** in the Molise and **Alba Fucens** in the Abruzzo. The museums in many cities have interesting collections of Roman antiquities; in addition to those mentioned above, there are good ones at **L'Aquila** and **Sperlonga**.

Early Christian Art and the Dark Ages

Almost from the beginning, Christians sought to express their faith in art. The catacombs' primitive paintings are no indication of the sophistication they often reached (besides Rome's there are also extensive catacombs at **Naples**). On dozens of finely carved sarcophagi and statues from the third century onwards (many to be seen in the Vatican Museums) the figure of Christ is usually represented as the 'Good Shepherd', a beardless youth with a lamb slung over his shoulder. Occasionally he wears a proper Roman toga. Familiar New Testament scenes are common, along with figures of the early martyrs. The fourth-century building programme financed by Constantine filled **Rome** with imposing Christian basilicas, though little of the original work remains. The Lateran Baptistry, begun in 315, is the oldest in Christendom; its octagonal shape was copied for baptistries all over Italy for over a thousand years. Sculpture and architecture may have been in decline, but 4th-century mosaic artists were still able to create graceful syntheses of antique art and Christian symbolism, as in the church of Santa Pudenziana, or the imperial family mausoleum on the Via Nomentana that is now Santa Costanza.

Through the 5th and early 6th centuries, Christian art—now the only art there was—changed little in style but broadened its subject matter, including scenes from the Old Testament (as in the Santa Maria Maggiore mosaics,and Naples cathedral), and the Passion of Christ. The new symbolism included the representation of Christ as the Lamb (as in SS. Cosma e Damiano), the animal symbols of the four Evangelists, and the four rivers, both the 'four rivers of Paradise' and the four Gospels. There was little money, and few artists, to continue after the destructive Greek-Gothic Wars, but San Lorenzo (579), and Sant'Agnese (638, with exquisite mosaics) show how the Romans could build even in the worst of times.

Ravenna, not Rome, was now the artistic centre of Italy, and through it came the stiff, mystical art ('hieratic', the Italians call it) of Byzantium. Greek dominance increased in the next three centuries, with an influx of artists fleeing Antioch and Alexandria after the Arab conquests, and from Constantinople itself during the persecutions of the Iconoclast emperors. An impressive revival of Roman building came in the late 8th century, with peace, relative prosperity, and the enlightened reigns of popes like Hadrian, Leo III and Paschal I. New churches went up—Santa Maria in Cosmedin, Santa Prassede, Santa Maria in Domnica—all decorated with mosaics by Greek artists. The return of hard times after the collapse of the Carolingian Empire put an end to this little Renaissance, and very little was done in Rome until the 1100s. Until about 1000, poverty and backwardness prevented the regions south of Rome from contributing much of anything. Earthquakes in the mountains and abandonment along the coasts have wiped out almost all of what was built, and even the most rudimentary structure from the Dark Ages is a rarity. Two that survived are the small 5th-century church of S. Maria Maggiore, near **Nocera Inferiore**, and the 8th-century Santa Sofia, at **Benevento**.

The Middle Ages

Recovery came through a number of factors: the trade and overseas contacts of Amalfi, Naples and the Apulian towns; the arrival of the Normans, bringing political stability and fresh influences from France; and especially the work of Abbot Desiderius at **Montecassino**, importing artists and architects from Constantinople, and helping to spread their advanced styles and techniques across the south—one good example being finely incised bronze church doors, a Greek speciality. Nearly a score of southern towns have them, beginning with the sets made for **Amalfi**(1066) and **Monte Sant'Angelo**(1076). The fashion spread to many other cities, and it was not long before Italian artists were producing their own, notably those of Barisano da Trani at the cathedrals of **Trani** and **Ravello**.

Reintroducing art into southern Italy, in this age, was indeed largely a matter of importing styles and artists from Greece, and Byzantine art, so unfairly disparaged by the Renaissance, would continue to influence all of Italy, not only the south, until the fall of Constantinople. Byzantium's own medieval 'renaissance' shows up clearly here, in the exceptional 11th-century frescoes at S. Angelo in Formis at **Capua**, and those of Santa Maria Maggiore at **Monte Sant'Angelo**, a century later. Romanesque buildings like **Molfetta** cathedral (1150) still can show a plan derived from the Greeks, and as late as the mid-14th century there are very Byzantine frescoes at S. Maria del Casale at **Brindisi**.

Because of religious and cultural prejudices, the role of Muslim influence in Italian medieval art has never been satisfactorily examined. In Campania it is often obvious, in the interlaced arches of **Amalfi** cathedral, and the arabesque decoration in the churches of **Salerno** and **Caserta Vecchia**, and perhaps in the domes of some Apulian churches. Another Muslim contribution is the decoration of pavements, pulpits, paschal candlesticks and tombs with geometric patterns in chips of coloured stone or glass, an art that reached a plateau of excellence at Amalfi, Ravello, and Salerno, spreading to dozens of other towns and reaching as far north as Tuscany; this exotically precise work became the prime inspiration for the decorative style of the Roman Cosmatesque.

The emerging Romanesque found its way to south Italy by the most unlikely route—by sea, with the Normans from faraway France. Early works influenced by the Normans begin with **Gerace** cathedral in 1045, one of the largest in the south, and La Trinitá at **Venosa**, the ambitious, unfinished project in the wilds of the Basilicata that holds the tombs of the Hauteville brothers (1046). **Salerno** cathedral, mentioned above, was begun by Robert Guiscard in 1085. The Crusades touched the south profoundly, especially Apulia, astride the most important routes to the Holy Land. In art the first reflections of this were the Templar church of S. Giovanni Sepolcro in **Brindisi**, a circular work based on the Holy Sepulchre in Jerusalem, and the peculiar and evocative Tomb of Bohemond at **Canosa di Puglia** (1111). In the long run, this Apulia suddenly at the crossroads of world history would draw on influences from every direction to create a major artistic movement all its own.

Four imported styles contributed to the **Apulian Romanesque**: the austere Lombard manner (as elsewhere in Italy, many of the masons at work in the south were probably from Lombardy); the Pisan, with its play of blind arcades and lozenge-shaped decoration (**Troia**, and S. Maria di Siponto, near **Manfredonia**); the Norman French, contributing the fashion for carved tympana and other details, and the Greek—many of these new churches were built on central Greek plans (Greek influence was even stronger in Calabria, where entirely Byzantine building styles, on a modest scale, were still common through the 13th century, as in the famous five-domed church at **Stilo**). The work that inaugurated the new style was definitely San Nicola at **Bari**, begun in 1087.

As the Apulian Romanesque, and later, Gothic, developed over the next two centuries, it retained a simplicity that gave its architects plenty of room for fancy. Common elements remained: a largely blank façade, with decoration concentrated on the ornate portals; blind arcades; an uncluttered, strongly defined roofline; small rose windows, set high up; sometimes small loggias on the sides; a strange, and perhaps religiously motivated aversion to right angles in the ground plan. Important cathedrals, besides those already mentioned, are at **Barletta, Trani, Bisceglie, Molfetta, Bari** and **Bitonto**; later ones, in a more Gothic vein, can be seen at **Altamura** and **Ruvo di Puglia**. Apart from Tuscany, no region of Italy has such an impressive collection of cathedrals, a remarkable achievement. To decorate them, a distinctive school of sculpture appeared, again taking its inspiration from such varied sources as northern Europe, Byzantium and the Arab world. Some of its greatest productions are bishops' thrones, as at **Bari, Monte Sant'Angelo** and **Canosa di Puglia**. Other works include the exterior decoration at **Trani** and **Bitonto** and the unique rose window at **Troia**.

To the north, the Abruzzo also has its share of fine Romanesque buildings. Often originating as abbey churches in isolated locations, they are consequently little known. Some show the clear influence of neighbouring Apulia (**S. Liberatore di Maiella**, c. 1080), while others are closer to Tuscan and northern styles. The best, including **Atri** cathedral, **Sant'Angelo in Pianella, San Clemente in Casauria** and **San Giovanni in Venere**, do not fit easily into any category. With stylistic innovations of their own, and some first-rate sculpture, they mark the beginning of the Abruzzo's particular contribution to medieval art, a subject that has been unfairly neglected. The effort would continue through the Middle Ages, reaching a climax in the magnificent polychrome façade of Santa Maria di Collemaggio at **L'Aquila** (1280), and the roughly contemporary frescoes at **Bominaco**. Medieval Abruzzo painting, more influenced by neighbouring Umbria and Tuscany than points further south, can best be seen at the museum in L'Aquila.

Gothic and Cosmatesque

The city of **L'Aquila** was a foundation of Emperor Frederick II; its monuments, especially its famous 99-headed fountain, can be taken as steps in what French art historian André Chastel has called the 'Ghibelline Renaissance'. With Frederick and his accomplished court, the most learned south Italy ever knew, came an impulse to see what the rest of Europe was up to, and also to recapture the classical past, fragments of which lay close at hand in every town. Frederick built castles all over the south as strongholds of imperial authority, often strangely abstract works of art as at **Lagopésole** and **Melfi**, or buildings for arcane purposes, as the octagonal **Castel del Monte** near Andria. Castel del Monte's gate, and the more elaborate Porta Romana at **Capua** are the most significant attempts at recapturing antiquity in art before the 1400s. Traces of the sculpture inspired by this movement can be seen in many of the Apulian and Abruzzese churches, and in many places in northern Italy and in Rome. Frederican art is a tendency, a matter of style, rather than a pronounced movement; with all of its greater works destroyed by the Angevins or by time, it requires an effort of the imagination to catch its dry, exact lines in fragments of southern sculpture. By way of Nicola Pisano, it was to be a crucial influence on northern Italy, though perhaps just another false start in the south.

Another feature of Frederick's time was the introduction of the Gothic into Italy. The first buildings came in Lazio, via cultural missionaries from France in a territory that never was anything but cordially hostile: **Fossanova** in 1208, nearby **Casamari** soon after, and **Cosenza** cathedral in 1227. The Angevins encouraged Gothic building in **Naples**: San Lorenzo Maggiore and Santa Chiara after 1300, about the same time as the popes were finishing their Gothic papal palace in **Viterbo**. Even Rome got into the act, with the Florentine Gothic Santa Maria sopra Minerva in 1280. But the movement, easily becoming the 'international style' everywhere else in Europe, never really took hold. Experiments, however, would continue: the Annunziata at **Sulmona** in 1320, and the Sienese S. Maria della Consolazione at **Altomonte** in Calabria (1380), and sculptural imports in the Gothic mode, such as the works by Tuscan Tino di Camaino in many churches in **Naples**.

When Rome began building again, it was largely with native artists, and stylistically there was almost a clean break with the past. The **Cosmati**, perhaps originally a single family of artisans, but eventually a name for a whole school, ground up fragments of precious stone from Rome's ruins (sometimes coloured glass) and turned them into intricate pavements, altars, paschal candlesticks, pulpits and other decoration, geometrically patterned in styles derived from Campania. Some of the Cosmati school eventually became accomplished sculptors, architects and mosaicists, such as Pietro Vassalletto, who built the cloisters at the Lateran and St Paul's (late 12th century), and Iacopo Torriti (mosaic of the Coronation of the Virgin at S. Maria Maggiore; late 13th c.). One of the Cosmati artists, Pietro Oderisi, even made it to London, to design Henry III's tomb in Westminster Abbey. Other Cosmatesque artists stayed closer to home; their work can be seen in many southern towns, as at **Sessa Aurunca, Anagni** and **Tuscania**.

Southern precursors of the Renaissance are few. Arnolfo di Cambio visited Rome, as did Giotto, who worked at St Peter's and at Naples, where he did a lost set of frescoes for the Castel dell'Ovo. But perhaps equal to Giotto as an artistic revolutionary was a native Roman, Pietro Cavallini (c. 1250–1330). In both paintings and mosaics (**Rome**, S. Maria in Trastevere, S. Cecilia, and **Naples**, Santa Maria Donnaregina), he introduced a new freedom in composition and a brilliant talent for expressive portraiture.

A Renaissance Almost Missed

The 'Babylonian Captivity', when the popes moved to Avignon in 1307, may have been a mixed blessing for the faith, but as patronage ceased almost completely in Rome it proved an unmitigated disaster for art. For over a century, nothing important was built or commissioned in the city, and the brilliant head start achieved by Cavallini and the Cosmati sculptors died on the vine. The Kingdom of Naples had its troubles too. The continuing factional disputes among the Angevins, and the economic decline of the southern trading cities—especially in Apulia—created an atmosphere in which there was little opportunity for artistic advance. Northern artists, especially Tuscans, still came to Naples in the 1400s, but like the Gothic masons and sculptors of 200 years before they must have found themselves acting as cultural missionaries. They left some fine works behind, but for reasons that are difficult to see clearly they never seemed to make a strong impression on the southern sensibility (notable visitors at **Naples** include Donatello and Michelozzo, tomb in S. Angelo a Nilo; Antonio Rossellino, tombs at Monteoliveto; Giuliano da Maiano, the Capua Gate; almost all the important early Renaissance painters are represented at the Capodimonte museum).

There are a few exceptions, unexpected little candles in the prevailing gloom. Giovanni da Nola, a first-rate sculptor though little known, decorated many churches in **Naples**. That city also contributed some fine though often idiosyncratic buildings, such as Romolo Balsimelli's Santa Caterina a Formiello. In the Abruzzo, Cola d'Amatrice built an impeccable Renaissance façade for San Bernardino in **L'Aquila** (1472), and a local artist named Andrea Delitio painted gaily colourful frescoes in **Atri** Cathedral; Antonio Lombardo left a perfect Renaissance portal in **Tossicia**, in the most obscure corner of the Abruzzo an artist was ever asked to decorate. The most promising starts came in Naples: the Triumphal Arch at the Castel Nuovo (1454–67), built for Alfonso I, was a Renaissance landmark, a mythological rendering of statesmanlike virtue entirely equal to the arches and columns of antiquity. Local talent, such as Tommaso Malvito's Cappella Carafa at the Duomo, seemed to carry the trend onwards, but in Naples the ideals of the Renaissance would never really take hold.

With the return and revival of the papacy, **Rome** was to have the last word in the Renaissance. Almost every Tuscan master is represented by something in Rome (minor works of Donatello at St Peter's and the Aracoeli, Botticelli, Ghirlandaio and Perugino in the Sistine Chapel, Masolino at San Clemente, Pinturicchio in the Vatican, Aracoeli, and S. Maria del Popolo, Melozzo da Forli in the Vatican and S. Croce, among others);

they came, however, as instructors to a city that had been a backwater since 1308. Pius II, the most artistically inclined of the early Renaissance popes, preferred to expend most of his patronage on his native Tuscany. Paul II (1464–71), a Venetian, commissioned many works, including Rome's first proper Renaissance palace, the Palazzo Venezia, and Alexander VI (1492–1503) commissioned the Pinturicchio frescoes in his Vatican apartments.

Rome's high Renaissance, though, begins with Julius II (1503 –13). Michelangelo Buonarroti (1475–1564) had already arrived, to amaze the world of art with his *Pietà* in St. Peter's (1499), but the true inauguration of Rome's greatest artistic period comes with Julius and the work of Donato Bramante (1444–1514), an architect who had already made a name for himself in Milan. In Rome, where the example of the ancients impressed him deeply, he immediately left off the busy, somewhat ecccentric style of his youth and began creating a refined classicism that seemed to exemplify the aspirations of the Renaissance more completely than anything that had gone before. This new marriage of the Renaissance and ancient Rome can best be seen at Bramante's *Tempietto* at S. Pietro in Montorio (1503), or at his cloister at **Montecassino**. The round Tempietto, the first modern building to depend entirely on the proportions of the classical orders (the Doric, in this case), was the most sophisticated attempt at creating the perfect temple, fusing the highest conceptions of faith and art, an idea captured in the architectural fantasies of many Renaissance paintings (for example, in Perugino's *Donation of the Keys* in the Sistine Chapel).

For painting and sculpture, the High Renaissance meant a greater expressiveness and dynamic movement, along with a virtuosity never seen before. Rome had the same effect on Raphael—Raffaello Sanzio of Urbino (1483–1520)—who arrived from Florence in 1508, learned the grand manner from antique sculpture, and ancient decorative patterns from the paintings in Nero's recently unearthed Golden House. He applied these lessons in the frescoes of the Vatican Stanze (begun 1511), one of the definitive achievements of the age. A versatile artist, Raphael excelled at portraiture, painted mythological frescoes (as in the Villa Farnesina), and was at times capable of almost visionary religious work (the *Liberation of St. Peter* in the Vatican Stanze). He was the most influential painter of his time, though he would have been mortified to know that his weakness for sweet Madonnas, clouds, putti and floating holy celebrities was introducing a kitsch element that would plague European sensibilities for the next three centuries.

Michelangelo, unwashed and overworked as ever, spent much of his time sulking over the successes of these two men, who he claimed stole all their ideas from him. Pope Julius kept him busy enough with the gargantuan project for his papal tomb that was to bother the artist for much of his life, and which was finally scaled down to the small ensemble, including the famous *Moses*, at S. Pietro in Vincoli. Michelangelo tried to flee his terrible patron in 1506, but Julius snatched him back and put him up on the ceiling of the Sistine Chapel two years later. The artist responded to the unusual commission (ceilings are not exactly the best place for great art, though this one started a fad that would last for centuries) with the most profound and imaginative synthesis of art and faith Rome would ever see.

After Julius came the Medici pope, Leo X, open-handed to artists though greatly overrated as a patron—thanks largely to Voltaire, who wrote of the 'Age of Leo X' as an unsurpassed golden age of culture. Raphael and Michelangelo kept at their work (at least until 1520, when the former died and the latter returned to Florence), and poetry and humanist scholarship were still fostered at the papal court, but through his reign and that of the other Medici, Clement VII, nothing in art appeared that was as revolutionary as the works done under Julius.

Rome in the 16th Century: the Counter-Reformation

The Sack of Rome in 1527 brought a rude interruption to artistic endeavours of all kinds. Many artists left Rome for ever, and the creative intensity of the years before 1527 was never attained again. Among the artists who returned to Rome, there was of course Michelangelo, who began the Last Judgement in the Sistine Chapel in 1536. Its sombre tones, and of course its subject matter, illustrate more clearly than any other work the change in mood that had come over Roman art. In his later years, Michelangelo produced little sculpture or painting. Pope Paul III, one of the more serious patrons ever to occupy the papal throne, appointed him architect of St Peter's in 1547—when he was 72. Other late works include the civic centre on the Campidoglio (1547) and Santa Maria degli Angeli (1563).

Tuscan Mannerism, the often eccentric, avant-garde tendency that rebelled against the Olympian high art of the Renaissance, found a place in Rome only for its less shocking exponents: painters such as Francesco Salviati and Baldassare Peruzzi (1510–63), who besides his paintings contributed original architectural creations like the Palazzo Farnesina and Palazzo Massimo alle Colonne on Corso Vittorio Emanuele (1537). In architecture, Giacomo della Porta (most of the Sapienza) and Antonio da Sangallo the Younger (Farnese Palace 1546) carried on Renaissance traditions to the bitter end. Two distinctive architects who did their best work in and around Rome in this period, fanciful buildings with a touch of Mannerist restlessness, were Iacopo da Vignola (Villa Giulia, Palazzo Farnese at **Caprarola**) and Pirro Ligorio (Casino of Pius IV in the Vatican Gardens, 1558; Villa d'Este at **Tivoli**, 1560). Their works, some of the most delightful and challenging buildings of the Roman Cinquecento, found no one to follow their example in the tough years that followed.

The decades of the rampant Counter-Reformation and the advent of the Inquisition put a chill on the Italian imagination that would never really be dispelled. In 1563, the final documents of the Council of Trent decreed the new order for art; it was to be conformist and naturalistic, a propaganda tool entirely in the service of the new totalitarian Church, with a touch of Spanish discipline and emotionalism to remind everyone where the real power lay. Largely under the direction of the Jesuits, a large building programme was undertaken, with large, extravagant churches meant to overawe the faithful and provide an opulent background for the pageantry and bombastic sermons of the new Catholicism: the Gesù Church (1568), Santa Maria in Vallicella (1575), and Sant'Andrea della Valle (1591), all on Corso Vittorio Emanuele, remain the chief works of the transitional order past centuries called the 'Jesuit Style'.

Rome itself was ordained to become the urban symbol of the Church resurgent, the most modern, most beautiful city in the world. Under the papacy of Sixtus V (1585–90), Domenico Fontana and other architects designed an epochal planning scheme, uniting the sprawling medieval city with a network of long, straight avenues sighted on obelisks in the major piazzas. Fontana's attempts at architecture, such as the drab Lateran Palace

(1607), were less fortunate, but other architects were pointing the way towards the dawning Baroque. Carlo Maderno's façade for Santa Susanna (1603) was one of the first symptoms, though the more conventional façade he designed for St Peter's ten years later has been universally condemned ever since as one of the missed opportunities of Roman art.

The times were right for a change. The militant, intolerant atmosphere of the early Counter-Reformation could never last too long among the worldly aristocrats of Rome (no matter how much mischief they were causing to the rest of Europe), and hedonism and artistic innovation resurfaced under a very thin veneer of piety and propriety. Many of the first challenges came from the painters: first Annibale Carracci, who reintroduced mythological subjects, taboo in the early Counter-Reformation terror, along with an intense, dynamic style of presenting them that harks back to Michelangelo's Sistine ceiling (Palazzo Farnese gallery, begun 1597); his greatest follower, a figure whose dramatic altarpieces and ceilings contributed much to the birth of the Baroque, was Guercino (Casino Ludovisi frescoes, 1621).

Carracci's artistic antagonist, Michelangelo Merisi da Caravaggio, worked in Rome at roughly the same time (1590–1603) before leaving town over the little matter of a homicide. Rome's first certified bohemian (whom modern Italy has suavely coopted by putting his face on the L100 000 note) was the last person you would have wanted to argue with at the tavern, but he was all business at painting. His impeccable drafts-manship, combined with a revolutionary, *tenebroso* use of light and shadow, and a new, naturalistic manner of portraying biblical subjects (S. Luigi dei Francesi, S. Maria del Popolo), made him many followers, and inspired many others to find their own new approaches for breaking out of the High Renaissance straitjacket.

To Roman opinion, however, the dry, academic painting of the expiring Renaissance was a pinnacle of artistic achievement. And to many later critics, especially in the 1700s, Guido Reni (in Rome about 1604–14) and Domenichino (1613–31, also worked in Naples) ranked with Raphael and Michelangelo as the greatest of all time; today the former's brilliantly coloured but often lifeless art, and the latter's vapid classicism hardly ever get a second glance from visitors to Rome's museums.

The Age of Baroque

No one is really sure where the word 'Baroque' originated. One possibility, according to Luigi Barzini in *The Italians*, is the irregular, oversized pearls still called *perle barocche* in Italy. Barzini goes on to explain how 'the term came to be used metaphorically to describe anything pointlessly complicated, otiose, capricious and eccentric...' Such is the reputation Baroque has acquired in our time. The opprobrium is entirely deserved for an age when Italy was subjected to reactionary priests and despotic tyrants, and art was reduced to mere decoration, forbidden to entertain any thoughts that might be politically dangerous or subversive to Church dogma. But in this captive art there was still talent and will enough for new advances to be made, particularly in architecture.

Plenty of churches, fountains and palaces were still going up in Rome, and there was every opportunity for experimentation. A second landmark, after Maderno's Santa Susanna, was the fountain of the Acqua Paola, built by Flaminio Ponzio in 1610. The real breakthrough came in the 1630s, with three great masters who between them inaugurated the Roman High Baroque and determined the course of European architecture for the next century: first Pietro da Cortona, with his intricate, flowing façade and dome for SS. Martina e Luca; then Francesco Borromini, with his earliest and most memorable works, S. Carlo alle Quattro Fontane (1638) and Sant' Ivo (1642), and finally Gianlorenzo Bernini, who began the famous colonnades in front of St Peter's in 1656, and the church of Sant'Andrea al Quirinale two years later.

These three men came to architecture from diverse backgrounds, between them exposing something of the diverse talents and ambitions of the Baroque movement. Cortona, from the town of Cortona and steeped in the tradition of Florentine Mannerism, began as a painter and designer, already famed for his ceiling frescoes in the Palazzo Barberini (1633–39). Borromini, a profound architect and the son of an architect, came from Lombardy, and brought to Rome the centuries-old tradition of Lombard building skills. The exotic geometry behind his two great churches, mentioned above, was a medieval throwback, repudiating the classical Vitruvian architecture of the Renaissance, but he used it to create amazingly sophisticated forms and spaces. Few architects were able to match this tortured soul's grasp of the art, or the sincere piety that informed it—Borromini himself, in his later career, created nothing as interesting as those two churches—but everyone who followed did his best to conjure up even more striking and unusual combinations of shapes.

Among the first to catch the fever was Bernini. Neapolitan by birth, with some experience as a playwright and stage designer, Bernini always thought of himself as a sculptor first, and in fact his best known and most original works are decorations, occupying the vague ground between sculpture and architecture: the St Peter's colonnades, the essential statement of Baroque flourish and grandiosity, and the Fountain of the Four Rivers in Piazza Navona (1648). As architect of St Peter's from 1629 on, and the most popular artist in Rome for decades thereafter, Bernini had an opportunity to transform the face of the city afforded to no other man before or since; his churches, palaces and fountains can be seen all over Rome. Other distinctive contributions to the High Baroque came from Martino Longhi (SS. Vincenzo ed Anastasio, 1646) and Carlo Rainaldi (S. Maria in Campitelli, 1662).

In sculpture, the Baroque meant a new emphasis on cascading drapery and exaggerated poses, typecasting emotion or saintliness or virtue in a way Renaissance artists would have found slightly trashy. Here Bernini led the way, with such works as his early *David* in the Galleria Borghese (1623), the florid papal tombs, equestrian statue of Constantine, and bronze baldachin, all at St Peter's, and the incredible *Ecstasy of St Teresa* in S. Maria della Vittoria (1652). His careful, eloquent portrait sculptures seem hardly to come from the same hand—for this self-assured and somewhat arrogant artist, apparently the less he was able to follow his fancy, the better. Bernini proved a hard act to follow; the only other Roman Baroque sculptors worthy of mention are the more sober Alessandro Algardi, and Francesco Duquesnoy, from Brussels, whose modest works, scattered around Rome's museums, often recall something of the freshness and lack of affectation of the early Renaissance.

Painting was on a definite downward spiral, though one usually had to look up to see it. Decorative ceiling frescoes, such as those of Pietro da Cortona, were all the rage, though few artists could bring anything like Cortona's talent to the job. Andrea Sacchi's *Divina Sapienza* fresco (1633) in the Palazzo Barberini was a notable exception. After this, preciosity and tricky illusionism rapidly gained the upper hand, most flagrantly in G. B. Gaulli's ceiling for the Gesù Church (1679) and the Jesuit Andrea Pozzo's *trompe l'oeil* spectacular in Sant'Ignazio (1691). Serious painting was breathing its last, though while in Rome's galleries keep a look out for the works of Pier Francesco Mola (1612–68) and two of the more endearing genre painters: the scenes of Roman life and ruins by Michelangelo Cerquozzi (1620–60), and the landscapes of the Neapolitan Salvator Rosa (1615–73).

But if the Baroque began in Rome, it soon found a warm welcome throughout the south. With its escapism, emotionalism and excess, the new style proved an inspiration to a troubled and long somnolent region; even though the south's poverty and backwardness increased with each year of Spanish and Bourbon misgovernment, the concentration of wealth in the hands of the court and the Church ensured a lavish patronage. **Naples**, the centre of Spanish power, led the way; its greatest exponent of the Baroque was a brilliant, tortured soul named Cosimo Fanzago (1591–1678), sculptor, architect and decorative artist who designed the great cloister of San Martino, the *guglia* at the Cathedral and a little masterpiece of a church, Santa Maria Egiziaca at Pizzofalcone. His speciality, exquisite floral patterns in brightly coloured marble inlay (S. Domenico Maggiore), set the trend for the lush interiors of Neapolitan churches over the next century. Another Neapolitan worthy of mention is Ferdinando Sanfelice, a light-hearted pastry chef of churches (the Nunziatella) and palaces, popular in the first half of the 18th century.

In sculpture, the best Neapolitan works are the most eccentric—the spectacular virtuosity of Francesco Queirolo, Antonio Corradini and Giuseppe Sammartino in the Sansevero Chapel. Almost all the Neapolitan sculptors devoted much effort to figures for *presepi*—Christmas cribs; the San Martino museum has a delightful collection. In painting, Naples and the south began the Baroque era under the spell of Caravaggio, who arrived in Naples in 1607 (paintings at Capodimonte). Among his followers, adapting the dark and dramatic realism of the master to different ends, were the Spaniard José Ribera (San Martino) and the Calabrian Mattia Preti, one of the most talented of all southern artists, who did much of his best work for the Knights of Malta in Valletta (also Capodimonte, S. Pietro a Maiella, and works in his home town, **Taverna**).

Later Neapolitan painting, facetious and colourful, with little to challenge the intellect or the imagination, was just right for the times and enjoyed a widespread influence. Luca Giordano, the mercurial and speedy 'Luca fa presto'(1634–1705), painted all over Italy, spent ten years at the court in Madrid, and still found time to cover acres of Neapolitan ceilings with clouds and putti, tumbling horses and pastel-robed floating maidens (as at San Martino). His greatest follower, in his time perhaps the most popular painter in Italy, was Francesco Solimena (1657–1747; S. Paolo Maggiore).

The Baroque architecture of **Lecce**, at Apulia's southern tip, deserves something more than a postscript. It was a remarkable achievement—an obscure provincial city, only a little more prosperous than its neighbours, and doing its best to uphold a threadbare but ardent heritage of cultural distinction, it created and advanced its own brand of architecture for almost two centuries. It begins in the 1500s, with the surprisingly sophisticated Renaissance folly called the *Sedile* on the central piazza, and reached its height with architects Giuseppe and Antonio Zimbalo and sculptor Cesare Penna in the mid-17th century (all three collaborated on Lecce's masterpiece, Santa Croce).

Exotic, ornate decoration, more than any advances in building forms, is the hallmark of the Leccese style, and upon close examination this proves to be more influenced by the Renaissance and even the Apulian Romanesque than anything from contemporary Naples or Rome. Echoes of Lecce's architecture can be seen in the churches and palaces of many towns in southern Apulia, notably **Ostuni, Manduria, Maglie** and **Nardò**.

Baroque Twilight, Followed by a Void

From Rome, the art of the High Baroque reached out to all Europe—just as the last traces of inspiration were dying out in the city itself. The death of Pope Alexander VII (1667) is often mentioned as a convenient turning-point, after whom there was less money, and less intelligent patronage. But as the Baroque trudged slowly off to its grave, bad paintings and sculptures were still being cranked out by the hundreds. Ironically, at the time when Rome's artistic powers were reaching their lowest ebb, the popes chose to restore dozens of churches to the degraded tastes of the age, destroying much of Rome's early Christian and medieval artistic patrimony in the process.

At the tail end of the Baroque, Rome's most popular architect was Carlo Fontana (S. Marcello in Corso, 1683, plenty of undistinguished palaces, and unrealized plans for extending Piazza San Pietro even worse than the one finally built by Mussolini). After him, though, Roman architecture bounced back for a brief flurry of surprisingly creative work, beginning with Francesco de Sanctis' Spanish Steps of 1726, and Filippo Raguzzini's lovely, arch-Rococo San Gallicano hospital in Trastevere (1724). Raguzzini also designed the intimate, stage-set ensemble in Piazza Sant'Ignazio (1728). Another accomplished architect to embellish Rome in the 18th century was Fernando Fuga, who designed the Palazzo della Consulta (1737) and rebuilt Santa Maria Maggiore (1743). Some things had not changed; all these works continued the Baroque love of the grand gesture—and a hint of stage decoration, nowhere more so than in Nicola Salvi's endearing and utterly Roman Trevi Fountain of 1762.

Fuga also worked in **Naples**, where he was for a time court architect to the Bourbons (the 'Albergo dei Poveri'), but in that city the 18th century belonged to Luigi Vanvitelli (1700–73), son of the Italianized Dutch painter Gaspar van Wittel and favourite architect of Charles III, the most assiduous builder among the Bourbon kings. Most of Vanvitelli's energies were expended on the huge Royal Palace at **Caserta**, fully in line with the international Neoclassicism of the time with its tastefully unimaginative façades, grand stairways and axis-planned gardens. Neoclassicism in Naples, a surprising reaction against the city's longstanding love affair with the Baroque and the bizarre, dominated the 1700s and indeed the remainder of the Bourbon period, as seen in such buildings as the Capodimonte palace and the San Carlo opera house (both by G. A. Medrano, in the 1730s) and the grandiose domed San Francesco di Paola (1817).

And that is the end of the story. In all the years since, neither Rome nor the Mezzogiorno has contributed much of anything in painting, sculpture or architecture. There have been opportunities: Italian unification resulted in a great surge of building in Rome, resulting in such bloated monstrosities as the Altar of the Nation, the Palace of Fine Arts and the Ministry of Justice along the Tiber, but nothing of merit. Mussolini initiated public works projects on a grand scale, and visitors to courthouses and post offices in scores of southern cities can still be properly awed by the majesty of the

Corporate State. (Though for the apotheosis of fascist building, see Rome's EUR or the Foro Mussolini.) Cities destroyed by earthquakes (Règgio Calabria) or bombing (Benevento) were rebuilt, though shabbily, and ambitious modern projects, such as Naples' *Centro Direzionale* or the *Baricentro* in Bari, are content to be architecturally thirty years behind the times. Sadly, despite the advances the south has made, there is as yet no clue that the region is even beginning to recover any of its long-lost confidence or its cultural identity.

Part III

ROME

Colosseum

To know what Rome is, you might pay a visit to the little church of San Clemente, unobtrusively hidden away on the back streets behind the Colosseum. The Baroque façade conceals a 12th-century basilica with a beautiful marble choir screen 600 years older. Underneath the church, a cardinal from Boston in 1857 discovered the original church of 313, one of the first great Christian basilicas. And under that they have recently found a few houses and a Temple of Mithras from the time of Augustus; from it you can walk out into a Roman alley that looks exactly as it did 2000 years ago, now some 9 m below ground level. There are commemorative plaques in San Clemente, placed there for various reasons by a Medici duke, a bishop of New York, and the former chairman of the Bulgarian Communist Party.

You are not going to get to the bottom of this city, or even begin to understand it, whether your stay is for three days or a month. We are not going to write a hundredth part of what could be written about its sights and its legends; no one has ever really done it justice. With its legions of headless statues, acres of paintings, 913 churches, and megatons of artistic sediment, this metropolis of aching feet will wear down even the most resolute of travellers (and travel writers). The name Rome passed out of the plane of reality into legend some 2200 years ago, when princes as far away as China first began to hear of the faraway city and its invincible armies building an empire in the west. At the same time, the Romans were cooking up a personified goddess, the Divine Rome, and beginning the strange myth of their city's destiny to conquer and pacify the world. Over a thousand years after that, the ghost of Rome still haunted Europe, while Mongol Khans and Turkish chieftains found themselves magnetically drawn westward, seeking the conquest of the fabled empire that they still believed existed.

In our prosaic times, though, you may find it requires a considerable effort of the imagination to break through to the past Romes of the Caesars and popes. All of them may be found if sought, but first you will need to peel away the increasingly thick veneer of the 'Third Rome', the burgeoning, thoroughly up-to-date creation of post-Reunification Italy. Ancient Rome at the height of its glory had perhaps a million and a half people; today there are four million, and at any given time at least half of them will be pushing their way into the underground train while you are trying to get off. The popes, for all their centuries of experience in spectacle and ceremony, cannot often steal the show in this new Rome, sharing the stage with the Colosseum and the rest of the ruins, with a deplorable superabundance of preposterous politicians, with *Cinecittà* and the rest of the cultural apparatus of a great nation, and of course with the tourists, who sometimes put on the best show in town.

This glittering new Rome, struggling manfully to keep up with Milan in influence, in creativity, and in trendiness, does not always have time to appreciate its past. The old guard Romani, now a minority in a city swollen with new arrivals, often bewail the loss of old Rome's slow and easy pace, its vintage brand of *dolce vita* that once impressed other Italians, let alone foreigners. Lots of money, lots of traffic, and an endless caravan of tour buses have a way of compromising even the most beautiful cities. Don't concern yourself; the present is only one snapshot from a 2600-year history, and no one has ever left Rome disappointed.

History

The beginnings of Rome are obscure enough. Historians believe the settlement of the Tiber Valley began sometime about 1000 BC, when an outbreak of volcanic eruptions in the Alban hills to the south forced the Latin tribes down into the lowlands. Beyond that there are not many clues for the archaeologists to follow. But remembering that every ancient legend conceals a kernel of truth— perhaps more a poetic than a scientific truth—it would be best to follow the accounts of Virgil, the poet of empire, and Livy, the great 1st-century BC Roman chronicler and mythographer.

When Virgil wrote, in the reign of Augustus, Greek culture was an irresistible force in all the recently civilized lands of the Mediterranean. For Rome, Virgil concocted the story of **Aeneas**, fleeing from Troy after the Homeric sack and finding his way over the sea to Latium. Descent from the Trojans, however specious, connected Rome to the Greek world and made it seem less of an upstart in its Imperial Age. As Virgil tells it, Aeneas' son **Ascanius** founded Alba Longa, a city that by the 800s was leader of the Latin Confederation. Livy takes up the tale with **Numitor**, a descendant of Ascanius and rightful king of Alba Longa, tossed off the throne by his usurping brother **Amulius**. In order that Numitor should have no heirs, Amulius forced Numitor's daughter **Rhea Silvia** into service as a Vestal Virgin. Here Rome's destiny begins, with an appearance in the Vestals' chambers of the god Mars, staying just long enough to leave Rhea Silvia pregnant with the precocious twins **Romulus and Remus**.

When Amulius found out, of course he packed them away in a little boat, which the gods directed up the Tiber to a spot somewhere near today's Piazza Bocca della Verità. The famous she-wolf looked after them for a while until they were found by a shepherd, who brought them up. When Mars revealed to the grown twins their origin, they returned to Alba Longa to sort out Amulius, then returned home (753 BC, traditionally) to found the city the gods had ordained. Romulus soon found himself constrained to kill Remus, who would not believe the auguries that declared his brother should be king, a fratricide that set the pattern for the bloody millennium of Rome's history to come. The legends portray early Rome as a glorified pirates' camp, and the historians are only too glad to agree. Finding themselves short of women, the Romans stole some from the Sabines. Not especially interested in farming or learning a trade, they adopted the hobby of subjugating their neighbours and soon polished it to an art.

Seven Kings of Rome

Romulus was the first, followed by **Numa Pompilius**, who by divine inspiration laid down the forms for Rome's cults and priesthoods, its auguries and its College of Vestals. **Tullus Hostilius**, the next, made Rome ruler of all Latium, and **Ancus Martius** founded the port of Ostia. The next king, **Tarquinius Priscus**, was an Etruscan, and probably gained his throne by a conquest from one of the great Etruscan city-states. Tarquin made a city of Rome, building the first real temples, the Cloaca Maxima, and the first Circus Maximus. His successor, **Servius Tullius**, restored Latin rule, inaugurated the division of the citizens into Patricians (the Senatorial class) and Plebeians, and built a great wall to keep the Etruscans out. It apparently did not work, for as next king we find **Tarquinius Superbus** (Tarquin the Proud, about 534 BC), another great builder. His misfortune was to have a hot-headed son like **Tarquinius Sextus**, who imposed himself on a noble and virtuous Roman maiden named **Lucretia** (cf. Shakespeare's *Rape of Lucrece*). She committed public suicide next morning, and the enraged Roman Patricians, under the leadership of **Lucius Junius Brutus** (later to be the first consul), chased out proud Tarquin and the Etruscans and established the Roman Republic before the day was out.

The Invincible Republic

Taking an oath never to allow another king in Rome, the Patricians designed a novel form of government, a republic (*res publica*—public thing) governed by the two consuls elected by the Senate, the assembly of the patricians themselves; later innovations in the Roman constitution would include a *tribune*, an official with inviolable powers elected by the plebeians to protect their interests. The two classes fought like cats and dogs at home, but combined with impressive resolve in the eternal wars. Etruscans, Aequi, Hernici, Volsci, Samnites, and Sabines, all powerful nations, were defeated by Rome's citizen armies. Some of Livy's best stories come from this period: old **Cincinnatus** coming out of retirement to accept the title of Dictator (the constitution provided for such an office in emergencies) in a tight situation during the wars against the Aequians, then returning quietly to his farm after a brilliant victory; the taking of Rome by marauding Gauls in 390, when the cackling of geese awakened the Romans and saved the citadel on the Capitoline Hill.

By 270 BC, Rome had eliminated all its rivals to become master of Italy. It had taken about two hundred years, and in the next two hundred Roman rule would be established from Spain to Egypt. The first stage proved more difficult. In Rome's final victory over the other Italians, the city digested its rivals; whole cities and tribes simply disappeared, their peoples joining the mushrooming population of Rome. After 270 it was much the same story, but on a wider scale. In the Punic Wars against Carthage (264–41 and 219–202 BC), Rome gained almost all the western Mediterranean; Greece, Africa, and Asia Minor disappeared in small bites over the next hundred years. Rome's history was now the history of the world.

Imperial Rome

The old pirates' nest had never really changed its ways. Rome, like old Assyria, is a fine example of that species of carnivore that can only live by continuous conquest. When the Romans took Greece, they first met Culture, and it had the effect on them that puberty has on little boys. After some bizarre behaviour, evidenced in the continuous civil wars (Sulla, Marius, Pompey, Julius Caesar), the Romans began tarting up their city in the worst way, vacuuming all the gold, paintings, statues, cooks, poets, and architects out of the civilized East. Beginning perhaps with **Pompey**, every contender for control of the now constitutionally deranged republic added some great work to the city centre: Pompey's theatre, the Julian Basilica, and something from almost every emperor up to Constantine. **Julius Caesar** and **Augustus** were perhaps Rome's greatest benefactors, initiating every sort of progressive legislation, turning dirt lanes into paved streets, erecting new forums, temples, and the vast network of aqueducts. In their time Rome's population probably reached the million mark, surpassing Antioch and Alexandria as the largest city in the western world.

After Augustus, Rome's position as administrative and judicial centre of the empire kept it growing, creating a new cosmopolitan population as provincials from throughout the empire—from Britain to Mesopotamia—crowded in. The city also became the unquestioned capital of banking and the financial markets—and also of religion; Rome's policy was always to induct everyone's local god as an honorary Roman, and every important cult image and relic was carried off to the Capitoline Temple. The emperor himself was *Pontifex Maximus*, Head Priest of Rome, whose title derives from the early Roman veneration of bridges (*pontifex* means keeper of bridges; crossing running water for many ancient religions was a slightly sacred business). Of course, **St Peter** arrived and was martyred in AD 67. His successor, **Linus**, became the first pope—or *pontiff*—first in the long line of hierophants who would inherit Rome's longstanding religious tradition.

For all its glitter, Rome was still the complete economic predator, producing nothing and consuming everything. No one with any spare *denarii* would be foolish enough to go into business with them, when the only real money was to be made from government, speculation or real estate. At times almost half the population was on the dole. Naturally, when things went sour they really went sour. Uncertain times made **Aurelian** give Rome a wall in 275. By 330 the necessity of staying near the armies at the Front led the western emperors to spend most of their time at army headquarters in Milan. Rome became a bloated backwater, and after three sacks of the city (**Alaric the Goth** in 410, **Genseric the Vandal** in 455, and **Odoacer the Goth** in 476), there was no reason to stay. The sources disagree: perhaps 100,000 inhabitants were left by the year 500, perhaps 10,000.

Rome in the Shadows

Contrary to what most people think, Rome did not ever quite go down the drain in the Dark Ages. Its lowest point in population and prestige undoubtedly came in the early

1300s, when the popes were at Avignon. The Dark Ages were never entirely dark; the number of important churches built (most, unfortunately, 'Baroqued' later) and the mosaics that embellished them, testify to the city's continuing importance. There was certainly enough to attract a few more sacks (Goths and Greeks in the 6th-century wars, Saracens from Africa in 746). As in many other western cities, the bishops of Rome—the popes—picked up some of the pieces when civil administration disintegrated, and extended their power to temporal offices. Chroniclers report fights between them and the local barons, self-proclaimed heirs of the Roman Senate, as early as 741. It must have been a fascinating place, much too big for its population though still, thanks to the popes, thinking of itself as the centre of the western world. The Forum was mostly abandoned, as were the gigantic baths, rendered useless as the aqueducts decayed and no one had the means to repair them. Almost all of the temples and basilicas survived, converted to Christian churches. Hadrian's massive tomb on the banks of the Tiber was converted into a fortress, the Castel Sant'Angelo, an impregnable haven of safety for the popes in times of trouble.

The popes deserve credit for keeping Rome alive, but the tithe money trickling in from across Europe confirmed the city in its parasitical behaviour. With two outrageous forgeries, the 'Donation of Constantine' and the 'Donation of Pepin', the popes staked their claim to temporal power in Italy. **Charlemagne** visited the city after driving the Lombards out in 800; during a prayer vigil in St Peter's on Christmas Eve, **Pope Leo III** sneaked up behind the Frankish king and set an imperial crown on his head. The surprise coronation, which the outraged Charlemagne could not or would not undo, established the precedent of Holy Roman Emperors having to cross over the Alps to receive their crown from the pope; for centuries to come Rome was able to keep its fingers in the political struggles of all Europe.

Arnold of Brescia and Cola di Rienzo

Not that Rome ever spoke with one voice; over the next 500 years it was only the idea of Rome, the spiritual centre of the universal Christian community, that kept the actual city of Rome from disappearing altogether. Down to some 30–40,000 people in this era, Rome evolved a sort of stable anarchy in which the major contenders for power were the popes and various noble families; first among these were the **Orsini** and **Colonna**, racketeer clans who built fortresses for themselves among the ancient ruins and fought over the city like gangs in 1920s Chicago. Very often, outsiders would get into the game. A remarkable woman of obscure birth named **Theodora** was able to seize the Castel Sant'Angelo in the 880s; with the title of Senatrix she and her daughter **Marozia** ruled Rome for decades. Various German emperors seized the city, but were never able to hold it. In the 10th century, things got even more complicated as the Roman people began to assert themselves. Caught between the people and the barons, nine of the 24 popes in that century managed to get themselves murdered. The 1140s was a characteristic period of this convoluted history. A Jewish family, the Pierleoni, held power, and a Jewish antipope sat enthroned in St Peter's. Mighty Rome occupied itself with a series of wars against its neighbouring village of Tivoli, and usually lost. A sincere monkish reformer appeared, the Christian and democrat **Arnold of Brescia**; he recreated the Senate and almost succeeded in establishing Rome as a free *comune*; somehow in 1155 he fell into the hands of a German emperor, **Frederick Barbarossa**, who sold him to the English pope (Adrian IV) for hanging.

Too many centuries of this made Rome uncomfortable for the popes, who removed themselves to Avignon in 1305. Pulling strings from a distance, they only made life more complicated for the Romans left behind. Into the vacuum they created stepped one of the noblest Romans of them all, later to be the subject of Wagner's first opera. **Cola di Rienzo** was the son of an innkeeper, but he got a good enough education to read the Latin inscriptions that lay on ruins all around him, and the works of Livy, Cicero, and Tacitus wherever he could find them. Obsessed by the idea of re-establishing Roman glory, he talked and talked at the bewildered inhabitants until they caught the fever too. With Rienzo as Tribune of the People, the Roman Republic was reborn in May of 1347. Power does corrupt, however, in Rome more than any spot on the globe, and an increasingly fat and ridiculous Rienzo was hustled out of Rome by the united nobles before the year was out. His return to power, in 1354, ended with his murder by a mob after only two months. Rome was now at its lowest ebb, with only some 15,000 people, and prosperity and influence were not to be completely restored until the reign of **Pope Nicholas V** in 1447.

The New Rome
The old papacy, before Avignon, had largely been a tool of the Roman nobles; periods when it was able to achieve real independence were the exception rather than the rule. In the more settled conditions of the 1400s, a new papacy emerged, richer and more sophisticated. Political power, as a guarantee of stability, was always its goal, and a series of talented Renaissance popes saw their best hopes of achieving this in rebuilding Rome. By the 1500s this process was in full swing. Under **Julius II** (1503–13), the papal domains for the first time were run like a modern state; Julius also laid plans for the rebuilding of St Peter's, beginning the great building programme that was to transform the city. New streets were laid out, especially the Via Giulia and the grand avenues radiating from the Piazza del Popolo; Julius' chief architect, **Bramante**, knocked down medieval Rome with such gay abandon that Raphael nicknamed him 'Ruinante'.

Over the next two centuries, the work continued at a frenetic pace. Besides St Peter's, hundreds of churches were either built or rebuilt, and cardinals and noble families lined the streets with new palaces, imposing if not always beautiful. A new departure in urban design was developed in the 1580s, under **Sixtus V**, recreating some of the monumentality of ancient Rome. Piazzas were cleared in front of the major religious sites, each with its Egyptian obelisk, linked by a network of straight boulevards. The New Rome, however, symbol of the Counter-Reformation and the majesty of the popes, was bought at a terrible price. Besides the destruction by Bramante, buildings that had survived substantially intact for 1500 years were cannibalized for their marble; the popes wantonly destroyed more of ancient Rome than Goths or Saracens had ever managed. To pay for their programme, they taxed the economy of the Papal States out of existence. Areas of Lazio that had been relatively prosperous even in the Dark Ages turned into wastelands as exasperated farmers simply abandoned them, and the other cities of Lazio and Umbria were set back centuries in their development. The New Rome was proving as voracious a predator as the old.

Worst of all, the new papacy in the 1500s inaugurated terror as an instrument of public policy. Through the previous century the last vestiges of Roman liberty had been gradually extinguished. The popes allied themselves with Spain and **Emperor Charles V** to extend their power, but reaped a bitter harvest in the 1527 Sack of Rome. An out-of-control imperial army occupied the city for almost a year, causing tremendous destruction, while the calamitous **Pope Clement VII** looked on helplessly from the Castel Sant'Angelo. Afterwards, the popes were happy to become part of the Imperial-Spanish system. Political repression was fiercer than anywhere else in Italy; the Inquisition was refounded in 1542 by **Paul III**, and book burnings, torture of freethinkers, and executions became even more common than in Spain itself.

The end of Papal Rule

By about 1610, there was no Roman foolish enough to get burned at the stake; at the same time workmen were adding the last stones to the cupola of St Peter's. It was the end of an era, but the building continued. A thick accretion of Baroque, like coral, collected over Rome. **Bernini** unveiled his Piazza Navona fountain in 1650, and the Colonnade for St Peter's 15 years later. The political importance of the popes, however, disappeared with surprising finality. As Joseph Stalin was later to note, the popes had plenty of Bulls but few army divisions, and they drifted into irrelevance in the power politics of modern Europe during the Thirty Years War and after. Rome was left to enjoy a decadent but rather pleasant twilight. A brief interruption came when revolutionaries in 1798 once more proclaimed the Roman Republic, and sent the pope packing. Rome later became part of **Napoleon's** empire, but papal rule was restored in 1815. Another republic appeared in February 1849, at the crest of the 1848 revolutionary wave, but a French army besieged the city and had the pope propped back on his throne by July. **Garibaldi**, the republic's commander, barely escaped with his life.

Napoleon III maintained a garrison to look after the pope, and consequently Rome became the last part of Italy to join the new Italian kingdom. After the French defeat in the war of 1870, Italian troops blew a hole in the old Aurelian wall near the Porta Pia and marched in. **Pius IX**, who ironically had decreed Papal Infallibility just the year before, locked himself in the Vatican and pouted; the popes were to be 'prisoners' until the Concordat of 1929. As capital of the new state, Rome underwent another building boom; new streets like Via del Tritone, Via Vittorio Veneto, and Via Nazionale made circulation a little easier around the seven hills; villas and gardens disappeared under endless blocks of speculative building (everything around Termini Station, for example), and the kingdom strove mightily to impress the world with gigantic, absurd public buildings and monuments, such as the Altar of the Nation and the Finance Ministry on Via XX Settembre, as big as two Colosseums. Historical events are few since 1879, but growth has been steady. From some 200,000 people in that year, Rome has increased twenty-fold.

A Little Orientation

'There's three things I want to see in Rome:
the Colosseum, St Peter's and the Acropolis.'

A big-time tourist from Texas

Two Walls: Of Rome's earliest wall, built by King Servius Tullius before the republic was founded, little remains; you can see one of the last surviving bits right outside Termini Station. The second, built by Aurelian in 275, is one of the wonders of Rome, though taken for granted. With its 19-km length and 383 towers, it is one of the largest ever built in Europe—and certainly the best-preserved of antiquity. In several places you can see almost perfectly preserved bastions and monumental gates.

Three Romes: Historians and Romans often think of the city in this way. Classical Rome began on the Palatine Hill, and all through its history its business and administrative centre stayed nearby, in the original Forum and the great Imperial Fora built around it. Many of the busiest parts of the city lay to the south, where now you see only green on the tourist office's map. After Rome's fall, these areas were never really rebuilt, and even now substantial ruins like Trajan's Baths remain unexcavated. The second Rome, that of the popes, had its centre in the Campus Martius, the plain west and north of the Capitoline Hill, later expanding to include the 'Leonine City' around St Peter's, and the new Baroque district around Piazza del Popolo and the Spanish Steps. The Third Rome, capital of United Italy, has expanded in all directions; the closest it has to a centre is the long, straight Via del Corso.

Seven Hills: Originally they were much higher; centuries of building and rebuilding have made the ground level in the valleys much higher, and at various times emperors and popes shaved bits off their tops in building programmes. The **Capitoline Hill**, smallest but most important, now has Rome's City Hall, the Campidoglio, roughly on the site of ancient Rome's greatest temple, that of Jupiter Greatest and Best. The **Palatine**, adjacent to it, was originally the most fashionable district, and eventually was entirely covered by the palaces of the emperors—the heart of the Roman Empire; the usually plebeian **Aventine** lies to the south of it, across from the Circus Maximus. Between the Colosseum and the Termini Station, the **Esquiline** (Colle Oppio), the **Viminal** and the **Quirinal** stand three in a row. The Quirinal was long the residence of the popes, and the later Italian kings. Finally, there is the **Caelian Hill** south of the Colosseum, now a charming oasis of parkland and ancient churches in the centre of Rome. Rome has, of course, other hills not included in the canonical seven: **Monte Vaticano**, from which the Vatican takes its name, **Monte Pincio**, including the Villa Borghese, Rome's biggest park, and the Gianicolo, the long ridge above Trastevere the ancients called the **Janiculum**.

Fourteen Regions: Ancient Rome had neither street lights nor street signs; drunks trying to find their way home had a job on their hands. Modern Rome has plenty of both. This being Rome, the street signs are, of course, marble. In the corner, you will notice a small number in Roman numerals; this refers to the *rione*, or ward. In the Middle Ages, there were 14 of these, descendants of the 14 *regiones* of the ancient city; even after the fall of Rome they maintained their organization and offered some protection to their people in the worst of times. With the growth of the city in the last 100 years, there are now many more *rioni*, but on a few of the older buildings you will still see the heraldic devices of the originals at the *rione* boundaries.

Street Furniture: Some of Rome's is unique. As a symbol of endurance, the emperors brought home a dozen Egyptian **obelisks**. The tallest, at 31.7 m, stands in front of St John Lateran. Many of them were in the Circus Maximus, but the Renaissance popes shifted them about to provide reference points for their grand planning scheme. The most recent is in the Porta Capena south of the Colosseum, looted by Mussolini from the Ethiopian city of Axum in 1937. **Fountains** are everywhere, often silly, frilly Baroque works, but some like the famous Trevi Fountain, near Piazza Colonna, are among the most grandiose anywhere. There are also street fountains on hundreds of corners; the water is drinkable. Of **ruins** there are quite a few. All that is left of most of them is the honest Roman brick, eroded into strange forms. The first you'll see, if you arrive by train, are near the tracks coming into Termini station; a length of the Aurelian wall, carrying an aqueduct on the right, and the round Temple of Minerva on the left. **Marble plaques** average two per block in some old quarters; to anyone who can read Latin they will provide some entertainment, and an insight into the strangeness and Mandarin abstraction of papal rule. Finally there is the ubiquitous device **SPQR** ('the Senate and the People of Rome'), still on the city's coat-of-arms, and still decorating all the buses, notice-boards, breakdown trucks and sewer lids.

A Day in Ancient Rome

Recreating some of the atmosphere of the old days is not hard; a score of books have been written on the subject, of which one of the best is *Daily Life in Ancient Rome* by Jerome Carcopino (available in Penguin). Roman poets such as Horace, Martial, and especially Juvenal also have plenty to say about it. Life in Rome at the height of empire was an imperial pain: ridiculously high rents, high taxes, street crime, noise around the clock, and neighbours from Baetica or Rhaetia with peculiar habits—but naturally everyone in the empire dreamed of moving there some day. The most significant difference between the way they lived then and our times was the sharp contrast between the quality of life in public versus private places. The average Roman, usually unemployed or under-employed, could loll about magnificent baths and forums all day; only with reluctance did he drag himself home to his nasty fourth-floor flat at night.

Public Rome: The Roman *forum*, developed from the Greek *agora*, usually took the form of an open space surrounded by temples, basilicas, and colonnades. In the centre, the original Roman Forum and the Fora of Augustus and Trajan made up a single vast complex, the public stage of Roman life. A typical Roman citizen would be there in the morning, to transact business, meet friends, watch the cosmopolitan crowd go by, or indulge in the favourite pastime of watching court proceedings in the basilica. Often they would have their own actions running; the Romans were easily the most litigious nation in all history. Always, surrounding the fora would be the market-places of the city, some of them imposing buildings like the five-storey Market of Trajan (this can be visited today, but to get a good idea of what one was like, see the Covered Market in Istanbul).

For all their skill at plumbing, the Romans never managed to bring running water into many of their homes. The baths, therefore, were a daily item on any respectable Roman's agenda. He could have stayed all day, for these great establishments were a stage for public life as much as the forum. Every neighbourhood had some, and counting the big ones built by the emperors they covered almost 10 per cent of Rome. The biggest ones, with bathing halls bigger than the present St Peter's, also included parks, museums, libraries, lunch counters, and, of course, the *palaestrae*—athletic grounds for the Romans' favourite ball games and wrestling. No civilization, perhaps, ever conceived a more useful institution for its citizens to spend their leisure time. The baths were cheap and accessible to even the poorest Roman; many of the emperors frequented them, too. There were other places to pursue the classical *dolce vita*—the emperors' extensive gardens, usually open to the public, the temples, which in an irreligious age were really glorified art museums, the taverns—one on every block, usually with a few prostitutes upstairs and gambling in the back room. Romans were terrible gamblers; even the virtuous Augustus would regularly present his children, slaves, and dinner guests with bags of *sestertii* to wager against him. Finally, there were the races and games, something on the average of 90–100 days a year. These were free, though you needed a ticket just to remind you of the Imperial largesse that made it all possible. You also needed a toga, unless you were in the plebeian cheap seats, for these were among this informal city's few dressing-up occasions.

Private Rome: Over 90 per cent of Romans lived in flats, in pretty but generally poorly built *insulae* up to 10 storeys in height. From the outside, they looked much the same as some of the older Roman palazzi today, but with more imaginative façades of brick, stucco, and patterned timbers. Many had balconies, and every part of these balconies and windows that received any sun would be full of climbing vines and flowers. Unfortunately, most of the streets were less than 4 m across. Rich and poor Romans lived mixed together in every *regio*; the very rich in walled houses of their own (like those at Pompeii), set perhaps next to a four-storey block with wine and oil shops, taverns, and ironmongers on the ground floor, middle-class bureaucrats and clients of the rich on the first (with perhaps three or four slaves in the household), and the very poor above them. These would have the furthest to climb, and they could sleep at night dreaming of their certain doom in case of fire or collapse. Both of these were constant worries. Crassus, who ruled Rome in the second Triumvirate with Caesar and Pompey, got his start as a weaselling building contractor, following the fire squads.

People who lived in flats did not use them much for entertaining, or even for cooking. Flats may have had paid water-carriers, but no heating except braziers, no glass windows, and little furniture. The shops that filled the ground floors of almost every building always spilled out into the narrow streets, occupying them along with the market barrows and the grammar school classes, which rented space under shop awnings or in porticoes—learning to live with distractions was a part of any Roman's education. Traffic was probably Rome's biggest headache after the 2nd century BC; Julius Caesar decreed an end to chariots and carriages (the rich had to get by with slave-borne litters) and banished wagons during daylight hours.

GETTING IN AND OUT

Airports

It's a little confusing; the big airport, **Leonardo da Vinci**, will often be referred to as **Fiumicino**. Officially the first name (tel 60 121) means the part of this sprawling complex that handles international flights, and Fiumicino (tel 5456) is the domestic terminal (most Romans don't know this, either). Taking a taxi there will prove financially ruinous, no matter how many people in your party; the only way to go will be by the new Metropolitana line which is being built for the 1990 World Cup (though it is unlikely it will be finished in time), linking the airport to Termini Station. In the meantime the ACOTRAL bus runs every 15 minutes from Via Giolitti 36 (coming out of Termini Station, that is the street on your left). Buses cost L5 000. **Allow two hours** to catch your flight.

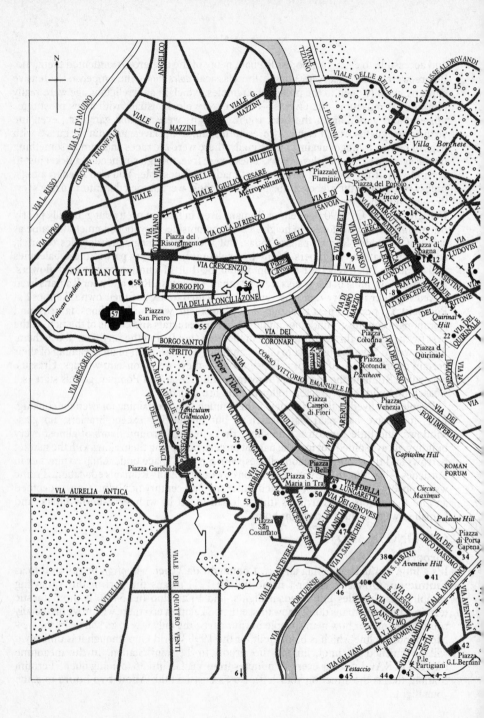

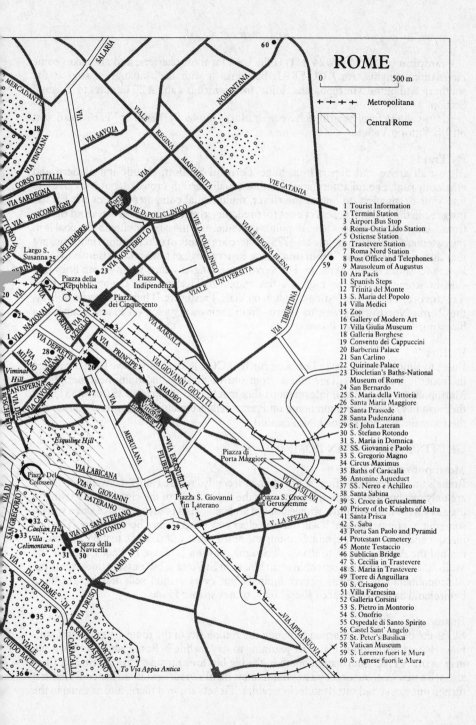

ROME

0   500 m

✛ ✛ ✛ ✛   Metropolitana

        Central Rome

1 Tourist Information
2 Termini Station
3 Airport Bus Stop
4 Roma-Ostia Lido Station
5 Ostiense Station
6 Trastevere Station
7 Roma Nord Station
8 Post Office and Telephones
9 Mausoleum of Augustus
10 Ara Pacis
11 Spanish Steps
12 Trinità del Monte
13 S. Maria del Popolo
14 Villa Medici
15 Zoo
16 Gallery of Modern Art
17 Villa Giulia Museum
18 Galleria Borghese
19 Convento dei Cappuccini
20 Barberini Palace
21 San Carlino
22 Quirinale Palace
23 Diocletian's Baths-National
   Museum of Rome
24 San Bernardo
25 S. Maria della Vittoria
26 Santa Maria Maggiore
27 Santa Prassede
28 Santa Pudenziana
29 St. John Lateran
30 S. Stefano Rotondo
31 S. Maria in Domnica
32 SS. Giovanni e Paolo
33 S. Gregorio Magno
34 Circus Maximus
35 Baths of Caracalla
36 Antonine Aqueduct
37 SS. Nereo e Achilleo
38 Santa Sabina
39 S. Croce in Gerusalemme
40 Priory of the Knights of Malta
41 Santa Prisca
42 S. Saba
43 Porta San Paolo and Pyramid
44 Protestant Cemetery
45 Monte Testaccio
46 Sublician Bridge
47 S. Cecilia in Trastevere
48 S. Maria in Trastevere
49 Torre di Anguillara
50 S. Crisogono
51 Villa Farnesina
52 Galleria Corsini
53 S. Pietro in Montorio
54 S. Onofrio
55 Ospedale di Santo Spirito
56 Castel Sant' Angelo
57 St. Peter's Basilica
58 Vatican Museum
59 S. Lorenzo fuori le Mura
60 S. Agnese fuori le Mura

Ciampino (tel 4694 or 724 241) is the base for most charters, and also takes some international flights. An ACOTRAL bus links it with the Subaugusta stop at the southern end of the Metropolitana A line, from which it's about 20 minutes to Termini Station.

Almost all the foreign airlines have their offices on Via Barberini or Via Bissolati, just off Via Vittorio Veneto.

By Train

Almost all arrive and depart from huge **Termini Station**, chaotic but modern and efficiently run. The rail information booth is usually terribly crowded, but you can try to find your destination on one of the clever, multilingual computer screens the FS has installed in the lobby. Keep an eye out for predatory gypsies. There is a taxi stand right in front, along with city buses to most points in Rome, and the Metropolitana terminal is in the basement (rail information: tel 4775). There are plenty of other stations in Rome, but they do not see much use: **Tiburtina** on the eastern edge of town and **Ostiense** (Metro: Piramide) south of the Aventine Hill serve some long-distance north–south lines that stop in Rome during the night. A few trains to Tuscany and Umbria start from **Trastevere**, close to the Ostiense station on Viale Trastevere. There is a private railway, the **Roma Nord**, with trains to Viterbo from their own station on Piazza Flaminia, a block north of Piazza del Popolo.

By Bus

Buses to almost every town in Lazio are run by ACOTRAL. Many leave from the piazza in front of Termini Station, others from out-of-the-way locations near peripheral Metropolitana stops. Their information office is at Via di Portonaccio 25 (tel 57 531), but they also have an information booth on Piazza della Repubblica (the round piazza with the fountain two blocks north of Termini).

GETTING AROUND IN ROME

Metropolitana

Rome's underground is efficient but often indecently crowded and inconvenient. There are only two lines, and very few stops near the oldest parts of the city; imagine trying to dig any sort of hole in Rome, with legions of archaeologists ready to pounce when you hit something interesting, and it will become clear why progress has been so slow. The two lines, A and B, cross at Termini Station; one or the other will take you to the Colosseum, around the Aventine Hill, to Piazza di Spagna, St John Lateran, St Paul's Outside the Walls, Piazza del Popolo, or within eight blocks of St Peter's, but outside these areas the Metropolitana's usefulness is very limited. Not every station sells tickets; get them beforehand at nearby tobacco shops, bars, or newspaper kiosks.

Buses

By far the best way to get around, though the complexity of the route system intimidates most visitors. First thing, if you are planning to stay a while in Rome, study the *old* route map at the ATAC information booth in the big bus area outside Termini Station (they also sell a new one, but don't waste your money: thanks to some million-lire consultants it turned out glossy and utterly indecipherable). Tickets are sold there, and as usual in the news-stands, bars, etc. There are bargains for full-day, half-day and weekly tickets for tourists. Most routes run quite frequently, and are, of course, often crowded. One of Rome's minor delights is the cute, rickety Route 30 tram, which makes almost a circle around the city centre, taking in many of the sights along the way. Some useful routes:

23: Vatican Museums–Castel Sant'Angelo–along the Tiber–Porta San Paolo–St Paul's Basilica (very convenient, but one of ATAC's worst meatwagons, with a clientele prone to sticking their hands where they oughtn't).

27: Termini–Via Cavour–Colosseum–Porta San Paolo.

30: Piazza Risorgimento (near the Vatican)–Viale delle Milizie–Villa Borghese (passes the Villa Giulia museum and zoo)–Viale Regina Margherita–Porta Maggiore–St John Lateran–Colosseum–Viale Aventino–Porta San Paolo–Viale Trastevere.

36: Termini–Via Nomentana (Sant'Agnese Church).

46: Piazza Venezia–Corso Vittorio Emanuele–Vatican.

56: Piazza Sonnino (in Trastevere)–Argentina–Via del Corso–Via Tritone–Via del Vittorio Veneto.

64: Termini–Via Nazionale–Corso Vittorio Emanuele–Vatican (but even more unpleasant than no. 23)

115: Piazza del Popolo–Villa Borghese–Via Vittorio Veneto–Via del Tritone–Augustus' Mausoleum–Piazza del Popolo.

118: St John Lateran–Colosseum–Caracalla's Baths–Via Appia Antica (passing all the catacombs and tombs).

119: Electric Minibus that tours the medieval lanes between the Pantheon and Piazza del Popolo.

Another line of interest to visitors is the **Circuito turistico ATAC** (bus 110, special ticket L6000) which leaves daily from in front of Termini at 3:30 pm (in winter, Sat and Sun only at 2:30) for a three-hour overview of the principal sights of the city.

Taxis cruise everywhere; they are expensive, with plenty of mysterious surcharges. Don't expect to find one when it's raining.

Walking

Looking at the map, Rome seems to be a city made for getting around on foot. It's deceptive—city blocks in the newer areas are huge, and it will always take you longer than you think to walk anywhere. The hills, the outsize scale, and the traffic and noise make Rome a very tiring place, but there is some pleasant strolling to be had in the old districts west of the Corso, around the Tiber Island, and in the old parts of Trastevere.

Driving

Absolutely not recommended! Rome isn't as chaotic as Naples, but nearly so. Parking is expensive, street parking impossible to find; so many areas in the centre are closed to traffic (and the signs for them so hard to spot) you can easily make a mistake that will earn you a ticket. Recently a judge has ordered the city to close off even more areas, or he will do so himself; Rome and its cars are mortal enemies; sooner or later one or the other will have to succumb.

TOURIST INFORMATION

The big main office is at **Via Parigi 11** (tel 461 851), just behind Diocletian's Baths, three blocks north of Termini Station; they have plenty of interesting things in English to

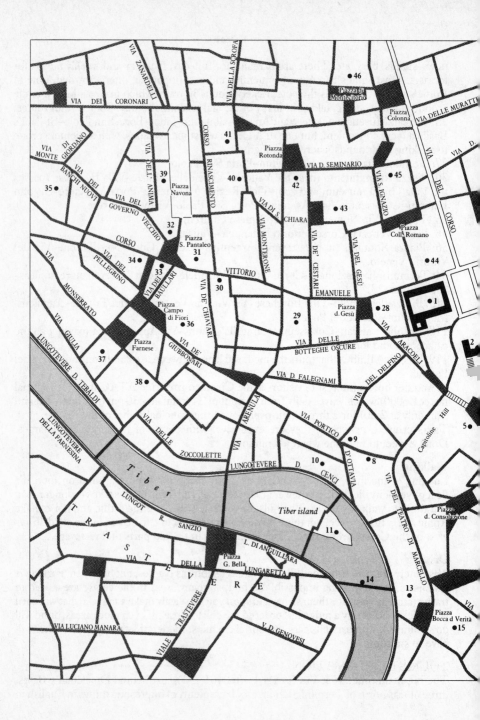

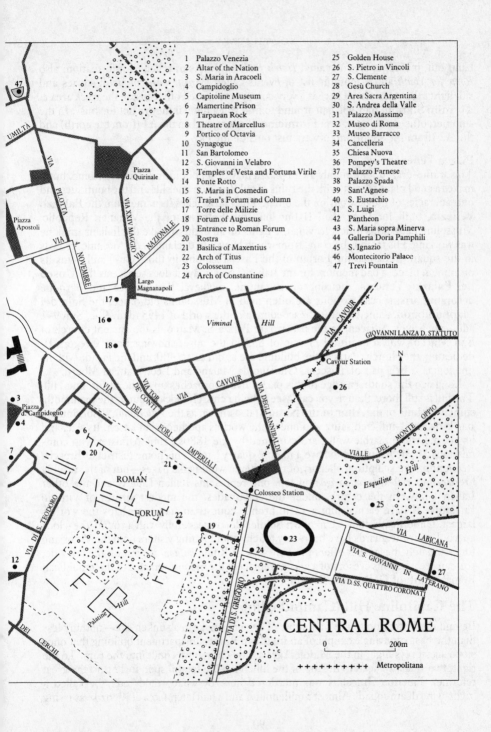

1 Palazzo Venezia	25 Golden House
2 Altar of the Nation	26 S. Pietro in Vincoli
3 S. Maria in Aracoeli	27 S. Clemente
4 Campidoglio	28 Gesù Church
5 Capitoline Museum	29 Area Sacra Argentina
6 Mamertine Prison	30 S. Andrea della Valle
7 Tarpaean Rock	31 Palazzo Massimo
8 Theatre of Marcellus	32 Museo di Roma
9 Portico of Octavia	33 Museo Barracco
10 Synagogue	34 Cancelleria
11 San Bartolomeo	35 Chiesa Nuova
12 S. Giovanni in Velabro	36 Pompey's Theatre
13 Temples of Vesta and Fortuna Virile	37 Palazzo Farnese
14 Ponte Rotto	38 Palazzo Spada
15 S. Maria in Cosmedin	39 Sant'Agnese
16 Trajan's Forum and Column	40 S. Eustachio
17 Torre delle Milizie	41 S. Luigi
18 Forum of Augustus	42 Pantheon
19 Entrance to Roman Forum	43 S. Maria sopra Minerva
20 Rostra	44 Galleria Doria Pamphili
21 Basilica of Maxentius	45 S. Ignazio
22 Arch of Titus	46 Montecitorio Palace
23 Colosseum	47 Trevi Fountain
24 Arch of Constantine	

47

UMILTA

VIA PILOTTA

Piazza Apostoli

VIA 4 NOVEMBRE

Piazza d. Quirinale

VIA XXIV MAGGIO

VIA NAZIONALE

Largo Magnanapoli

17

16

18

Viminal   Hill

VIA CAVOUR

GIOVANNI LANZA D. STATUTO

Cavour Station

N

3
Piazza d. Campidoglio
4

6

20

7

VIA TOR DE' CONTI

VIA DEI FORI

VIA CAVOUR

VIA DEGLI ANNIBALDI

VIALE DEL MONTE OPPIO

26

21

IMPERIALI

ROMAN

FORUM   22

19

Colosseo Station

Esquiline   Hill

25

VIA DI S. TEODORO

24

23

VIA LABICANA

12

VIA DI S. GREGORIO

VIA S. GIOVANNI IN LATERANO

27

VIA D. SS. QUATTRO CORONATI

Palatine   Hill

DEI CERCHI

CENTRAL ROME

0   200m

+ + + + + + + + + Metropolitana

hand out, including a book called *Here's Rome* with lots of practical information; also *Rome for Youth* and a monthly list of events called *Carnet*, with colourful stories and sidelights about the city. There is a very competent branch office inside the track area at **Termini Station**; they will call around to find you a hotel if they're not too busy. In the summer, offices also operate at **Fiumicino Airport**, and on the **A1** (from the north) and the **A2** (from the south) motorways just outside the city.

Piazza Venezia

This traffic-crazed, thoroughly awful piazza may be a poor introduction to Rome, but it makes a good place to start, with the ruins of old Rome on one side and the boutiques and bureaucracies of the new city on the other. The piazza takes its name from the **Palazzo Venezia**, built for Pope Paul II but long the Embassy of the Venetian Republic. Mussolini made it his office, leaving the lights on all night to make the Italians think he was working. His famous balcony, from which he would declaim to the 'oceanic' crowds in the square (renamed the Forum of the Fascist Empire in those days) still holds its prominent place, a bad memory for the Italians. Nowadays it does service as the **Museo del Palazzo Venezia**, focusing on Byzantine, medieval Renaissance and Baroque decorative arts; special exhibits are often held in Mussolini's old office, the **Sala del Mappamondo**, named after its frescoed map of the world of 1495 (daily 9–2, Sun 9–1 adm expensive). Adjacent to the palazzo, in Piazza S. Marco, is the ancient church of **San Marco**, with a beautiful mosaic of 833 in the apse, showing Pope Gregory IV dedicating the church. Parts of the building are as old as AD 400, and the façade with its fine loggia is by a pair of Tuscans, Giuliano da Maiano and Leon Battista Alberti.

Long ago the southern edge of this piazza had approaches up to the Capitoline Hill. The hill is still there, though you can't see it, being entirely blocked out by the mammoth, stupefying bulk of the **Altar of the Nation** (also known as the *Vittoriano*), Risorgimento Italy's own self-inflicted satire and one of the world's apotheoses of kitsch. Its size, and its glaring white marble walls, are explained by the 1880s Prime Minister who commissioned it; he happened to have a marble quarry back in his home district of Brescia. Recounting the sculptural allegory of the scheme would take pages—but of the two big bronze imperial-style *quadrigae* on top, one represents Italian Liberty and the other Italian Unity. In the centre, under the colonnades, the modest virtues of Vittorio Emanuele II have earned him a 12-m bronze equestrian statue, perhaps the world's largest. Underneath, Italy's Unknown Soldier sleeps peacefully with a round-the-clock guard. Lately the guards have been very touchy about letting visitors onto the Vittoriano (unfortunately, because it offers the only view of Rome *without* it), but on the left side, you can see what this eyesore of a glacier replaced: the modest remains of the republican Roman **tomb of C. Publius Bibulus**.

The Capitoline Hill (Campidoglio)

Behind the Vittoriano, there's a jumble of ancient bricks in a sunken site—nothing less than the best surviving example of an **insula** in Rome, an apartment building that once stood six storeys high; in the Middle Ages a little church was built into the ruin. To the right, two stairways lead to the top of the hill. This is a fateful spot; in 121 BC the great reformer Tiberius Gracchus was murdered here by what would today be called a 'right-wing death squad'. Almost a millennium and a half later, Cola di Rienzo was trying to escape Rome in disguise when the enraged mob recognized him by the rings on his fingers and tore him to pieces. Rienzo built the steep left-hand staircase, and was the first to climb it. It leads to the church of **Santa Maria in Aracoeli**, begun in the 7th century over the temple of Juno Moneta—the ancient Roman Mint was adjacent to it. The Aracoeli, which in Rienzo's time served as a sort of council hall for the Romans, is one of the most revered Roman churches; legend has it that one of the ancient Sibyls, that of Tivoli, prophesied the coming of Jesus and told Augustus to build a temple here to the 'first-born of God'. In its interior, hung with ballroom chandeliers, seek out frescoes by Pinturicchio (*St Bernard of Siena*, first chapel on the right), and in the next, the *Santo Bambino*, Rome's busiest miracle-working icon (it even makes house calls), and the nearby *Tomb of Luca Savelli* (early 1300s), built around an ancient sarcophagus by Arnolfo di Cambio, architect of Florence Cathedral. The *Tomb of Matteo di Acquasparta* in the right transept, has a painting by Pietro Cavallini; in the first chapel on the left, there's an unusual allegory of the Virgin from the Book of the Apocalypse (1500s).

The second stairway takes you to the real heart of Rome, Michelangelo's **Piazza del Campidoglio**, passing on the left a rather flattering statue of Rienzo set on a bronze pedestal. At the top, among a formidable cast of statues and Roman odds and ends, stand colossal figures of Castor and Pollux in their eggshell caps. You may or may not see the Campidoglio's centrepiece, **Marcus Aurelius**, the great bronze equestrian statue of the benign and philosophical emperor; although he is now restored and re-gilded (fortunately, since it was an old Roman saying that the world would end when all the original gold flaked off), the Romans can't decide whether to put him back, where traffic fumes will unrestore him, or replace him with a copy. But he has already been through a lot; the Christians of old only refrained from melting him down for cash because they believed he was not Marcus Aurelius, but Constantine.

Michelangelo's original plans for the square may have been adapted and tinkered with by later architects, but nevertheless his plan for the Campidoglio has come out as one of the triumphs of Renaissance design. His refined **Palazzo Senatorio**, with its distinctive stairway and bell tower, is built over the ruins of the Roman *tabularium*, the state archive. At the base of the stair note the statue of Minerva, in her aspect of the allegorical goddess Roma. Rome's City Council holds its meetings in this building; a stairway behind offers a fine view of the Roman Forum (see below).

The Capitoline Museum

Flanking the Senate, Michelangelo's **Palazzo dei Conservatori** has been incorporated into the **Capitoline Museum** with its opposite number, the 1655 **Palazzo Nuovo**. One of the most interesting of Roman museums, its exhibits display both the heights and depths of ancient society and culture (daily 9–2, Sun 9–1:30, closed Mon; also open Tues and Sat afternoons 5–8 pm, and—the most magical time to visit—Sat 8:30–11 pm; adm). For the heights, there are the *reliefs from the triumphal arch of Marcus Aurelius*—first-class work in scenes of the emperor's clemency and piety, and his triumphal receptions in Rome. Marcus always looks a little worried in these, perhaps considering his good-for-nothing son Commodus and the empire he would inherit, sinking into corruption and excess. What was to come is well illustrated by the degenerate art of the 4th century, like the colossal bronze head of Constantine, and the giant foot and pointing hand in the courtyard of the Conservatori, looking like lost props from a Fellini movie.

In between these extremes come roomfuls of statuary, including the famous *Capitoline Wolf*, symbol of Rome; statues of most of the emperors, busts of Homer, Sophocles, Pythagoras and other leading lights; the voluptuous *Capitoline Venus*; *The Dying Gaul*; the *Muse Polyhymnia*, one of the most delightful and beautiful statues of antiquity. Later works include a statue of Charles of Anjou by Florence's Arnolfo di Cambio; the **Pinacoteca**, with a dignified Velazquez gentleman looking aloof in the company of two Caravaggios, a room of Venetian masters, a *Witch* by Salvator Rosa, and some lovely, though at times silly, 18th-century porcelains—orchestras of monkeys in powdered wigs, and such. Reclining by a pool in the Palazzo Nuovo courtyard, is a statue of *Marforio*, a river god once employed as one of the 'talking statues' of Rome, decorated with graffiti and placards commenting on current events.

At the southern end of the Capitol, one of the quietest corners of Rome, lie a few bits of cornice that mark the golden roofed Temple of Jupiter Greatest and Best, built originally by the Etruscan kings. At the time it was the largest in Italy, testimony to Rome's importance as far back as 450 BC. Along the southern edge of the hill, the cliffs you see are the supposed location of the **Tarpeian Rock**, from which traitors and other malefactors were thrown in Rome's early days.

Along the Tiber

The early emperors did their best to import classical Greek drama to Rome, and for a while, with the poets of the Latin New Comedy it seemed the Romans would carry on the tradition. Great theatres were built in Rome, like the **Theatre of Marcellus** at the foot of the Capitoline (along Via del Teatro di Marcello) begun by Caesar and completed by Augustus. By the second century, however, theatre had already begun to degenerate into music hall shows, lewd performances with naked actresses and grisly murders (condemned prisoners were sometimes butchered on stage), and shows by celebrity actors probably much like some unseemly spectacles of our own time. Marcellus' theatre (Augustus named it after one of his nephews) survived into the Middle Ages, when the Orsini family converted it into their palace-fortress, the strongest in Rome after the Castel Sant'Angelo. Today it presents one of Rome's more curious sights, the tall arches of the circumference surmounted by the rough medieval walls of the Orsini. Behind it, the **Portico of Octavia** stands battered but erect; Augustus built it as a decoration and place of rest for the shops and markets that once covered this area.

The streets to the west mix some of Rome's oldest houses with new buildings; the latter replacing the old walled **ghetto** demolished only a century ago. The Jews had a sizeable community in Rome since Pompey and Titus brought them as slaves. They helped finance the career of Julius Caesar, who would prove to be their greatest benefactor. For centuries they lived near this bend in the river and in Trastevere. The worst pope, Paul IV, took time off from burning books and heretics to wall them into the tiny ghetto in 1555; at the same time he forced them to wear orange hats, attend Mass on Sunday, and limited them to the rag and old iron trades. Tearing down the ghetto walls was one of the first acts of the Italian kingdom after the entry into Rome in 1870. The exotic, eclectic main **Synagogue** was built after the last of the ghetto was demolished. Inside, there is a small museum, the **Permanent Exhibition of the Jewish Community in Rome** (daily except Sat 10–2, Sun 10–12; adm).

Opposite the synagogue, the ship-shaped **Tiber Island** is joined to both sides of the river by surviving ancient bridges. In imperial times, the island was sacred to Aesculapius, god of healing; a legend records how some serpents brought from the god's shrine in Greece escaped and swam to the spot, choosing the site by divine guidance. Now, as in ancient times, most of the lovely island is taken up by a hospital, the Ospedale Fatebenefratelli; in place of the Temple of Aesculapius, there is the church of **San Bartolomeo**, most recently rebuilt in the 1690s. Rahere, King Henry II's jester, was cured here of malaria, and in thanksgiving founded London's St Bartholomew the Great.

The Velabrum, the area east of the Tiber island, was in the earliest days of Rome, a cattle market (interestingly, when Rome reverted to a small town in the Middle Ages, the Roman Forum itself was used for the same purpose). On Via Velabro, **San Giorgio** in **Velabro** is in parts as old as the 7th century; there is a good Cosmatesque altar and canopy, and a fresco in the apse by Pietro Cavallini; of the two ancient arches outside, the **Arch of the Argentarii** was erected by the moneychangers in honour of Septimius Severus (AD 204). The larger, the unfinished **Janus Quadrifons**, dates from the time of Constantine.

Piazza Bocca della Verità

Tourists almost always overlook this beautiful corner along the Tiber, at the south end of Via del Teatro di Marcello, but here you can see the only complete Roman temples. Both are probably misnamed: the round **Temple of Vesta**, used as an Armenian church in the Middle Ages, and the **Temple of Fortuna Virile**. Some bits of an exotic, ornate Roman cornice are built into the brick building opposite, part of the **Palace of the Crescenzi**, a powerful family in the 1000s, descended from Theodora Senatrix. Look over the side of the Tiber embankment here, and you can see the mouth of the **Cloaca Maxima**, the great ancient sewer begun by King Tarquin. Big enough to drive two carriages through, it is still in use today. Just upstream, past the Palatine Bridge, a single arch decorated with dragons in the middle of the river is all that remains of the ancient *Pons Aemilius* (2nd century BC), vandalized by the Renaissance popes for building-stone and now familiarly known as the 'broken bridge', or **Ponte Rotto**.

Across from the temples, the handsome medieval church with the lofty campanile is **Santa Maria in Cosmedin**, built over an altar of Hercules by Byzantine Greeks escaping from the heretic Iconoclast emperors in the 8th century. The name (like 'cosmetic') means decorated, but little of the original art has survived; most of what you see is from the 12th century, including some fine Cosmatesque work inside. In the portico, an ancient, ghostly image in stone built into the walls has come down in legend as the Bocca della Verità—the Mouth of Truth. Medieval Romans would swear oaths and close business deals here; if you tell a lie with your hand in the image's mouth, he will most assuredly bite your fingers off. Try it.

West of the Capitol: the Imperial Fora

In the thirties, Mussolini built a grand boulevard between the Vittoriano and Colosseum to ease traffic congestion, the **Via dei Fori Imperiali**. It covers part of ancient Rome's heart, the great, completely ruined forums built by Caesar, Augustus, Trajan, Vespasian, and Nerva, to relieve pedestrian congestion in the original Roman Forum. **Trajan's**

Forum, giving on to Piazza Venezia, was built from the spoils of his conquest of Dacia (modern Romania). The grandest architectural and planning conception ever built in Rome, it had a broad square surrounded by colonnades, with a huge basilica flanked by two libraries and a covered market outside. All that remains of the great square is its centrepiece, **Trajan's Column**. The spiralling bands of sculptural reliefs, illustrating the Dacian Wars, reach to the top, some 30 m high. They rank with the greatest works of Roman art, but there are plenty of Romans today who have never seen them all; even now it is partly encased in scaffolding and green plastic, to keep the reliefs and inscriptions from being totally dissolved by traffic fumes.

Next to the column, the church of **Santa Maria di Loreto** is a somewhat garish High Renaissance bauble, begun by Antonio da Sangallo the Younger in 1501. The Romans liked it so much they built another one just like it next door, the **Santissimo Nome di Maria**, from the 1730s. Take the stair beyond them up to the entrance to the **Market of Trajan's Forum** (10–5, Sun 9–1, closed Mon; adm), a great five-storey hemicycle that was the Harrods of its day, with over 150 shops (a second hemicycle facing it has completely vanished). Behind it, you can see Rome's own leaning tower, the 12th-century fortress called the **Torre delle Milizie**. Of the adjacent **Forum of Augustus**, only the mighty fire wall and the steps of a temple remain, best seen along Via dei Fori Imperiali. The mighty stump of the striped, medieval **Torre de' Conti** covers most of Vespasian's Forum; the **Forum of Nerva** has a beautiful pair of Corinthian columns. Across Via dei Fori Imperiali, in the shadow of the Vittoriano, 12 columns still stand in the **Forum of Caesar**, the first annexe to *the* Forum, the entrance of which is just down the street.

Next to Caesar's Forum, under the church of San Giuseppe dei Falegnami, you can visit the **Mamertine Prison**, the tiny calaboose used by the ancient Romans for their most important prisoners—the Catiline conspirators, Vercingetorix (the Gaulish chief captured by Caesar), and finally St Peter. For that, the prison is now a shrine to the saint (9–12:30 and 2–6:30, donation). Next to it, overlooking the Forum, is the good Baroque church of **SS. Luca e Martina** (with a beautifully moulded interior) built by Pietro da Cortona in the 1660s.

The Roman Forum

For a place that once was the centre of the Mediterranean world, there is surprisingly little to see; centuries of use as a quarry have seen to that. The word *forum* originally meant 'outside' (like the Italian *fuori*), a market-place outside the original Rome that became the centre of both government and business as the city expanded around it (daily 9–4; Sun and Thurs 9–1, adm expensive).

The path from the entrance follows the course of the **Via Sacra**, where the religious processions and triumphs of ancient Rome took place. To the left is the **Temple of Antoninus Pius and Faustina**, converted into the church of San Lorenzo in Miranda in the 6th century; most of the columns survive and the porch, with a fine sculptural frieze of griffons on top (the height of the door marks the ground level of the Forum before its excavation). To the right lie the scant remains of the **Basilica Aemilia**, the Forum's oldest basilica—note the fine Republican era reliefs in the back. Standing on the other side is the **Curia**, the Senate House, last rebuilt by the Gothic King Theodoric and found intact (but minus its rare marble façade) under a 7th-century church (if you're lucky enough to find it open, you can see the lively reliefs called the *Plutei of Trajan*). In front of the Curia are the remains of a raised stone area which was the **Rostra**, the speakers' platform in public assemblies under the republic, decorated with ships' prows (*rostra*) taken in a sea battle about 338 BC.

Just under the capitol stands the recently restored **Arch of Septimius Severus**, of AD 203, with reliefs of some rather trivial victories over the Arabs and Parthians; conservative Romans of the time must have strongly resented this upstart African Emperor planting his monument in such an important spot. The arch also commemorated Septimius' two sons, Geta and Caracalla; when the nasty Caracalla did his brother in, he had his name effaced from it—you can see where the bronze letters once were. In front of the arch, the **Lapis Niger** is the Forum's most ancient relic, a mysterious slab of black marble with an underground chamber beneath it—the legendary tomb of Romulus. The 6th-century BC inscription down below, a threat against the profaning of this sacred spot, is the oldest ever found in the Latin language. The famous Golden Milestone also stood nearby, the 'umbilicus' of Rome and the point from which all distances in the Empire were measured. Of the great temples on the Capitol slope, only a few columns remain; from left to right, the **Temple of Saturn** (479 BC) which, with its associations of a mythical 'Golden Age' became Rome's Treasury; the **Temple of Vespasian** (three columns standing); and the **Temple of Concord**, built by Tiberius to honour the peace—so to speak—that the emperors had enforced between the patricians and plebeians.

Behind the Rostra, in the open area once decorated with scores of statues and monuments, the simple standing **column** was placed by the Romans in honour of Phocas, Byzantine Emperor in 608—the last monument ever erected in the Forum (and they had to steal the column from a ruined building). Just behind this and the replanted Sacred Olive, Fig, and Vine, an irregularly-shaped pavement marks the spot of the **Lacus Curtius**, scene of one of ancient Rome's favourite legends. In 362 BC, according to Livy, an abyss suddenly opened across the Forum and the Sibyls predicted that it would not close unless the 'things that Rome held most precious' were thrown in. A Consul, Marcus Curtius, took this as meaning a Roman citizen and soldier. He leapt in fully armed, horse and all, and the crack closed over him.

Basilica Julia to the south, was built by Caesar with the spoils of the Gallic Wars; although only the foundations remain, it was once, as the seat of the civil law courts, the noisiest place in the Forum. The **Temple of Caesar** closes the east end, built by Augustus as a visual symbol of the new imperial mythology. The adjacent **Temple of the Dioscuri** is a good example of how temples were used in ancient times. This one was a meeting hall for men of the equestrian class (the knights, though they were really more likely to be businessmen); they had safe deposit boxes in the basement, where the standard weights and measures of the empire were kept. The pretty little round temple is a reconstruction of the **Temple of Vesta**, where the sacred hearth fire was kept burning by the six Vestal Virgins. Next to the temple are the rose-planted ruins of the Vestals' apartments, which resembled cloisters, with two ponds in the centre; the long dress and veil you can see on the Vestals' statues may well have been the prototype for habits adopted by the first nuns.

Across from the Vestals are some walls of the **Regia**, the oldest cult building of the Forum (7th century BC) and home of the Pontifex Maximus, high priest and the only man

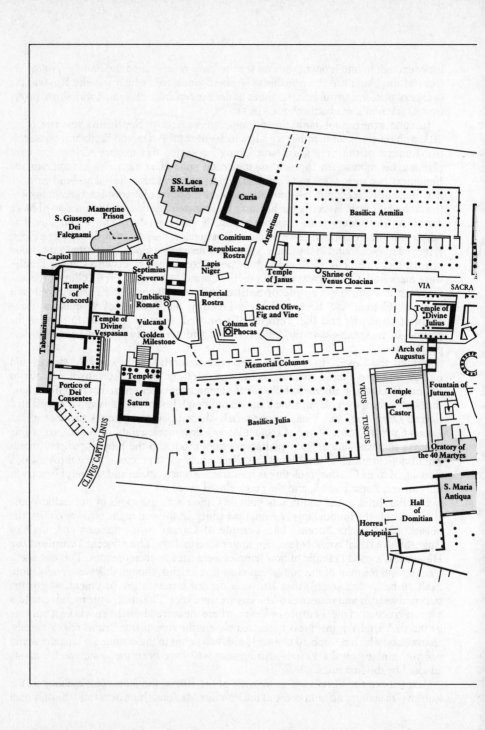

SS. Luca
E Martina

Curia

Mamertine
Prison

S. Giuseppe
Dei
Falegnami

Comitium

Republican
Rostra

Basilica Aemilia

Argiletum

← Capitol

Arch
of
Septimius
Severus

Lapis
Niger

Temple
of Janus

Shrine of
Venus Cloacina

VIA   SACRA

Temple
of
Concord

Umbilicus
Romae

Imperial
Rostra

Sacred Olive,
Fig and Vine

Temple of
Divine
Julius

Tabularium

Temple of
Divine
Vespasian

Vulcanal

Column of
Phocas

Arch of
Augustus

Golden
Milestone

Memorial Columns

Fountain of
Juturna

Temple
of
Saturn

Temple
of
Castor

VICUS

Portico of
Dei
Consentes

TUSCUS

Basilica Julia

Oratory of
the 40 Martyrs

CLIVUS CAPITOLINUS

S. Maria
Antiqua

Hall
of
Domitian

Horrea
Agrippina

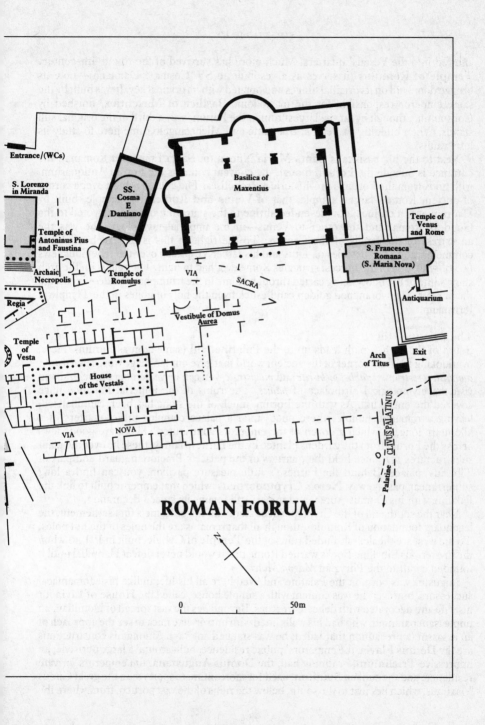

Entrance/(WCs)

S. Lorenzo
in Miranda

Temple of
Antoninus Pius
and Faustina

Archaic
Necropolis

Regia

Temple
of
Vesta

SS.
Cosma
E
Damiano

Temple of
Romulus

House
of the Vestals

VIA   NOVA

VIA

SACRA

Basilica of
Maxentius

Temple of
Venus
and Rome

S. Francesca
Romana
(S. Maria Nova)

Antiquarium

Vestibule of Domus
Aurea

Arch
of Titus

Exit
→

Palatine   CLIVUS PALATINUS

ROMAN FORUM

N

0   50m

allowed into the Vestals' quarters. Much more has survived of the round 4th-century **Temple of Romulus** (it serves as a vestibule to SS. Cosma e Damiano)—note its bronze door, still on its original hinges and opened with its original key. It was built by the same emperor responsible for the mastodonic **Basilica of Maxentius**, finished by Constantine; though by far the largest ruin in the Forum, only a third of the original still stands. When building St Peter's, Bramante and Michelangelo came here to study its lofty vaults.

Next to the big basilica is **Santa Maria Nuova** (or Santa Francesca Romana); the entrance is outside the Forum, though the convent contains the Forum Antiquarium, with finds from the Forum's pre-historic necropolises. The church is built over a corner of ancient Rome's largest temple, that of **Venus and Rome**. The temple, built by Hadrian, was a curious, double-ended shrine to the state cult; one side devoted to the Goddess Roma, and the other to Venus—in the imperial mythology, she was the ancestress of the family of the Caesars. To the right of this is the **Arch of Titus** commemorating the victories of Titus and his father Vespasian over the rebellious Jews (AD 60–80), one of the fiercest struggles Rome ever had to fight. The reliefs on the arch show some of the booty being carted through Rome in the triumphal parade—including the famous seven-branched golden candlestick from the holy of holies in the Temple at Jerusalem.

The Palatine Hill

South of the arch, a path leads up to the **Palatine Hill** (same adm as Forum). Here, overlooking the little corner of the ancient world that gave our language words like *senate, committee, rostrum, republic, plebiscite* and *magistrate*, you can leave democracy behind and visit the etymological birthplace of *palace*. The ruins of the imperial *Palatium* once covered the entire hill. As with the Forum, much of the stone has been cannibalized, leaving a romantic jumble where once stood a palace complex three-quarters of a kilometre long, to which a dozen of the emperors contributed. There are good views across the Forum from the gardens planted by the Farnese family; these lie over the giant substructures that once held the quarters of the palace's Praetorian guard and part of Tiberius' palace. Behind the Farnese's little pleasure pavilion, you can find a long subterranean passageway, **Nero's Cryptoporticus**, which that emperor built to link the Palatine with his Domus Aurea, and in part still retains its stucco decoration.

Near the south end of the Cryptoporticus stood the site of Rome's first settlement, the legendary foundation of Romulus, though all that remains are the holes of the hut poles. To the west are the ilex-shrouded ruins of the **Temple of Cybele**, built in 191 BC when the mysterious Sibylline Books warned Rome that it would never defeat Hannibal until it founded a cult to the Phrygian *Magna Mater*.

Augustus was born on the Palatine and lived here all his life; unlike his egomaniacal successors, however, he was content with a simple house, called the **House of Livia** for his wife and decorated with delicate frescoes. Beyond lies the vast spread of Domitian, an unpleasant paranoid, who had his walls lined with mirror-like mica to see the approach of an assassin (a precaution that failed; he was stabbed anyway). Among his constructions are the **Domus Flavia**, the emperors' public residence, built around a large peristyle; an impressive **Triclinium**, or dining hall; the **Domus Augustana**, the emperors' private residence; and the sunken **Stadium**, used for more intimate sports than the great Circus Maximus, which lies just to the south, below the ruins of the vast portico, from where the emperor could watch the races. Nor did his slaves have far to carry him to see the sport in the Colosseum, located just to the left of the Forum's rear exit.

The Colosseum

Its real name was the Flavian Amphitheatre, after the family of emperors who built it, beginning with Vespasian in AD 72; Colosseum refers to the *Colossus*, a huge gilded statue of Nero (erected by himself, of course) that stood in the square in front. There doesn't seem to be much evidence that Christians were ever thrown to lions here—there were other places for that—but what did go on was perhaps the grossest and best-organized perversity in all history. Gladiatorial contests, either Etruscan or Samnite in origin, became an institution in the late days of the republic, designed to make Romans better soldiers by rendering them indifferent to the sight of death. Later emperors introduced new displays to relieve the monotony—men versus animals, lions versus elephants, women versus dwarfs, sea battles (the arena could be flooded at a moment's notice), public tortures of condemned criminals, even genuine athletics, a Greek import the Romans never much cared for. In one memorable day of games, 5000 animals were slaughtered, about one every 10 seconds. The native elephant and lion of North Africa and Arabia are extinct thanks to such shenanigans.

However hideous its purpose, the Colosseum ranks with the greatest works of Roman architecture and engineering; all modern stadiums have copied most of its general plan. One surprising feature was a removable awning that covered the stands. A detachment of sailors from Cape Misenum was kept to operate it; they also manned the galleys in the mock sea battles. Originally there were statues in all of the arches, and a ring of bronze shields all around the cornice. The concrete stands have been eroded, showing the brick structure underneath. Renaissance popes hauled away half the travertine exterior—enough to build the Palazzo Venezia, the Palazzo Barberini, a few other palaces and bridges and part of St Peter's. Almost all of the construction work, under Vespasian and Titus, was performed by Jewish slaves, brought here for the purpose after the suppression of their revolt (open 9am–7:30pm, winter 9–4; Sun 9–1; free, but adm to the upper levels and to excavations underneath, 9–12).

Just outside the Colosseum, the **Arch of Constantine** (AD 315) marks the end of the ancient Triumphal Way (now Via San Gregorio) where victorious emperors and their troops would parade their captives and booty before turning up the Via Sacra. The arch, with a coy inscription mentioning Constantine's 'divine inspiration' (the Romans weren't sure whether it was yet respectable to mention Christianity), is covered with reliefs stolen from older arches and public buildings—a sad commentary of the state of art in Constantine's day.

Before leaving the neighbourhood, you may want to take in the Forum's two ancient churches, entered from Via dei Fori Imperiali: **Santa Maria Nuova** (Santa Francesca Romana), built into the portico of the Temple of Venus and Rome, with a fine 12th-century mosaic of the Madonna in the apse and three important relics: the knee prints of SS. Peter and Paul, whose weighty prayers in the Forum succeeded in making their airborne nemesis, the sorcerer Simon Magus, plummet to earth, the **tomb of Pope Gregory XI** (d. 1378) who brought the papacy back to Rome from Avignon (both in the right transept), and in the crypt, the patron saint of motorists, S. Francesca Romana. On the other side of Mussolini's wall maps showing the conquests of Rome, is

SS. Cosma e Damiano, preserving its fine golden mosaics of the 520s in its triumphal arch and apse; you may also want to illuminate its charming 18th-century Neapolitan *presepio*.

The Esquiline Hill: the Domus Aurea and *Moses*

When Nero decided he needed a new palace, money was no object. Taking advantage of the great fire of AD 64 (which he apparently did *not* start), he had a quarter of Rome's total area (temporarily renamed Neropolis) cleared to make himself a rural estate right in the middle of town. The **Golden House** was the most sumptuous palace ever built in Rome, decorated in an age when Roman art was at its height—accounts say it even had a revolving dining room, with a ceiling that opened to shower guests with flower petals. Nero never lived to see it finished. He committed suicide during an army coup by Spanish legions. When the dust settled, the new Emperor Vespasian realized that this flagrant symbol of imperial decadence had to go. He demolished it, and Titus and Trajan later erected great bath complexes on its foundations; Nero's gardens and fishponds became the site of the Colosseum. In the 1500s, some beautifully decorated rooms of the Domus Aurea were discovered underground, saved for use as the basement of Titus' baths. Raphael and other artists studied them closely, and incorporated some of the spirit of the fresco decoration into the grand manner of the High Renaissance (our word 'grotesque', originally referring to the leering faces and floral designs of this time, comes from the finds in this 'grotto'). The rooms are at present closed for restoration, which may take years.

The Domus Aurea is on the **Esquiline Hill**, so named because it was the home of the Roman knights (the class ranking below the patricians), but better known today as the *Colle Oppio*. Much of it is covered with a park; beside the Domus Aurea are very substantial ruins of the **Baths of Trajan**, still unexcavated. On the northern slope of the hill, at the west end of Via delle Sette Sale, **San Pietro in Vincoli** takes its name from the chains that King Agrippa I used to bind Peter in Jerusalem, and which miraculously separated to free him. These are kept in the Confessio, in front of the main altar, but the real attraction of this church is the famous, ill-fated **Tomb of Julius II** which tortured Michelangelo for so many years. Of the original project, planned as a sort of tabernacle with 40 individual statues, the artist completed only the powerful figure of Moses, perhaps the closest anyone has ever come to capturing prophetic vision in stone. It has irreverently been claimed that this Moses bears a resemblance to Charlton Heston, and it does. Michelangelo also worked on the figures of Rachel and Leah, but the rest of the tomb was completed by his students; the one who carved the effigy of Julius must have been the class clown.

San Clemente

Not many visitors find their way to this church, three blocks east of the Colosseum on Via San Giovanni in Laterano, but here are a few more fascinating remnants of Rome's many-layered history. One of the first substantial building projects of the Christians in Rome, the original basilica of *c.* 375 burned along with the rest of the quarter during the Norman sack of 1084. It was rebuilt soon after with a new Cosmatesque pavement and the 7th-century choir screen—a rare example of sculpture from that ungifted time— saved from the original church. The 12th-century mosaic in the apse represents the

Triumph of the Cross, and the chapel in the left aisle by the side entrance contains a beautiful series of frescoes on the *Life of St Catherine* (1420s) by the Florentine master Masolino, currently under restoration. From a vestibule, nuns sell tickets to the **Lower Church** (9–12, 3:30–6:30, Sun 10–12, 3:30–6:30; adm). This is the lower half of the original San Clemente, and on some of its walls are remarkable, though deteriorated, frescoes from the 900s, some of the oldest medieval painting to have survived anywhere in Italy. The plaque from Bulgaria, mentioned in the introduction, commemorates SS. Cyril and Methodius, who came from this church to spread the Gospel among the Slavs; they translated the Bible into Old Slavonic, and invented the first Slavic alphabet (Cyrillic) to do it.

From here, steps lead down to the lowest stratum, an alley and a block of houses dating from the 1st century AD; this includes the **Mithraeum**, the best-preserved such temple after the one in Capua. Apparently the older buildings were filled with rubble to serve as a foundation for the basilica; Father Mulhooly of Boston cleared out tons of it in the 1860s to uncover the well-preserved complex, which includes a Mithraic school with a fine stuccoed ceiling and the temple proper, a small cavern-like hall with benches for the initiates to share a ritual supper. Mithraism was a mystery religion, full of secrets closely held by the initiates (all male, largely soldiers) and it is difficult to say what else went on down here. Two altars were found, each with the usual image of the Persian import god Mithras despatching a white bull, with plenty of snakes and astrological symbolism in the decorative scheme. Underneath all this, there is yet a fourth building level, foundations from the republican era. At the end of the 1st century alley you can look down into an ancient sewer or underground stream, one of a thousand entrances to the surreal sub-Roma of endless subterranean caves, buildings, rivers and lakes, mostly unexplored and unexplorable. A century ago a schoolboy fell in the water here; they found him, barely alive, in open country several kilometres from the city.

Along Corso Vittorio Emanuele

This street, chopped through the medieval centre of Rome by the Renaissance popes, still hasn't quite been assimilated into its surroundings; nevertheless, this ragged, smoky traffic tunnel will come in handy when you find yourself lost in the tortuous, meandering streets of Rome's oldest quarter. Starting west from Piazza Venezia, the **Gesù Church** (1568–84) was a landmark for a new era and the new aesthetic of cinquecento Rome. When Baroque was new, it was often referred to as the 'Jesuit style', and here in the Jesuits' head church architects Vignola and Giacomo della Porta first laid down Baroque's cardinal principle: an intimation of paradise for the impressionable through decorative excess. It hasn't aged well. The stone frippery and writhing bodies pasted to the vertiginous *trompe l'oeil* ceiling look faded and foolish, but at the time it must have seemed to most Romans a perfect marriage of Renaissance art and a reformed, revitalized faith. St Ignatius, the Jesuits' founder, is buried in the left transept right under the altar, Spanish-style; the globe incorporated in the sculpted Trinity overhead is the biggest piece of lapis lazuli in the world.

Two blocks down, the street opens into Largo Argentina, a ghastly square full of buses and ruins. Remains of several **republican-era temples**, unearthed far below ground level, can be seen in the square's centre. Next comes another grand Baroque church,

Sant' Andrea della Valle, with the city's second-tallest dome. Maderno, one of the architects of St Peter's, did most of the work. The curving façade across the street belongs to the **Palazzo Massimo**, the masterpiece of the Renaissance architect Baldassare Peruzzi: he transplanted something of the Florentine style of monumental palaces, adding some light-hearted proto-Baroque decoration. The curve follows the outline of a theatre built on this spot by the Emperor Domitian. The neighbouring Palazzo Braschi houses the small **Museo di Roma**, with old views and pictures of the city, though the only part you're likely to ever find open is that housing changing art exhibitions.

One of the earliest and best of the palaces on Corso Vittorio Emanuele, the delicate **Piccola Farnesina** by Antonio da Sangallo the Younger, has another little museum, a collection of ancient sculpture called the **Museo Barracco** (daily, except Mon, 9–1, Tues and Thurs evenings 5–8, Sun 9–2; adm). A third museum—not a well known one—is just around the corner from Sant Andrea on Via Sudario. The **Burcardo Theatre Museum** is a collection of fascinating old relics from the Roman theatrical tradition—plenty of puppets and marionettes, too (but at the time of writing closed, too).

The biggest palace on the street, attributed to Bramante, is the **Cancelleria**, once the seat of the Papal Municipal Government. St Philip Neri, the gifted, irascible holy man who is Patron Saint of Rome, built the **Chiesa Nuova** near the eastern end of the Corso (1584). Philip was quite a character, with something of the Zen Buddhist in him. He forbade his followers any sort of philosophical speculation or dialectic, but made them sing and recite poetry; two of his favourite pastimes were insulting popes and embarrassing new initiates—making them walk through Rome with a foxtail sewn to the back of their coat to learn humility. As was common in those times, sincere faith and humility were eventually translated into flagrant Baroque. The Chiesa Nuova is one of the larger and fancier of the species. Its altarpiece is a *Madonna with Angels* by Rubens. Even more flagrant, outside the church you can see the curved arch-Baroque façade of the **Philippine Oratory** by Borromini. The form of music called the *oratorio* takes its name from this chapel, a tribute to St Philip's role in promoting sacred music.

South of Corso Vittorio Emanuele: the Campo dei Fiori

Few cities anywhere can put on such a variety of faces to beguile the visitor; depending on where you spend your time in Rome, you may come away with the impression of a city that is one great Baroque stage set, or all grimy early 1900s palazzi and bad traffic, or a city full of nothing but ruins and parks. Around **Campo dei Fiori**, one of the spots dearest to the hearts of the Romans, you may think yourself in the middle of some scruffy south Italian village. Rome's market square, disorderly, cramped and chaotic, is easily the liveliest corner of the city, full of market barrows, buskers, teenage Bohemians, and the folkloresque types who have lived here all their lives—the least decorous and worst-dressed crowd in Rome. During papal rule, the old square was also used for executions—most notoriously the burning of Giordano Bruno in 1600. This well-travelled philosopher was the first to take Copernican astronomy to its logical extremes—an infinite universe with no centre, no room for Heaven, and nothing eternal but change. The Church had few enemies more dangerous. Italy never forgot him; the statue of Bruno in Campo dei Fiori went up only a few years after the end of papal rule.

Just east of the square, the heap of buildings around Piazzetta di Grottapinta is built over the cavea of **Pompey's Theatre**, ancient Rome's biggest. The complex included a *curia*, where Julius Caesar was assassinated in 44 BC. Walk one block south of Campo dei Fiori, and you will be thrown back from cosy medievality into the High Renaissance with the **Palazzo Farnese**, one of the definitive works of that Olympian style. Giuliano da Sangallo began it in 1514, but much of the upper storey is Michelangelo's. The building now serves as the French Embassy, and it isn't easy to get in to see it (tours Sun. mornings at 10; rear entrance). Most of the palaces that fill up this neighbourhood have one thing in common—they were made possible by someone's accession to the papacy, the biggest jackpot available to any aspiring Italian family. Built on the pennies of the faithful, they provided the most outrageous illustration of Church corruption at the dawn of the Reformation. Alessandro Farnese, who as Pope Paul III was a clever and effective pope though perhaps the greatest nepotist ever to decorate St Peter's throne (see Caprarola, p. 169), managed to build this palace 20 years before his election—with the income from his 16 absentee bishoprics.

Palazzo Spada, a block east, was the home of a mere cardinal, but its florid stucco façade (1540) almost upstages the Farnese. Inside, the **Galleria Spada** is one of Rome's great collections of 16th- and 17th-century painting. Guido Reni, Guercino, and the other favourites of the age are well represented (daily 9–2, Sun 9–1; adm). To the south, close to the Tiber, **Via Giulia** was laid out by Pope Julius II, a famous and pretty thoroughfare lined with churches and palazzi from that time. Many artists (successful ones) have lived here, including Raphael.

Piazza Navona

In 1477, the area now covered by Rome's most beautiful piazza was a half-forgotten field full of huts and vineyards, tucked inside the still-imposing ruins of the Stadium of Domitian. A redevelopment of the area covered the long grandstands with new houses, but the decoration had to wait for the age of Baroque. In 1644, with the election of Innocent X, it was the Pamphili family that won the papal sweepstakes. Innocent, a great grafter and such a villainous pope that when he died no one—not even his newly wealthy relatives—would pay for a proper burial, built the ornate **Palazzo Pamphili** (now the Brazilian Embassy) and hired Borromini to construct the gaudy **Church of Sant'Agnese**.

Borromini's nemesis, Bernini, got the commission for the piazza's famous fountains; the Romans still tell stories of how the two artists carried on. All the figures in Bernini's great **Fountain of the Four Rivers** seem to be expressing shock at the church across the street—one even has his head veiled. Supposedly, Borromini started a rumour that the tall obelisk atop the fountain was about to topple; when the alarmed papal commissioners arrived to confront Bernini with the news, he tied a piece of twine around it, secured the other end to a lamppost, and laughed all the way home. The fountain is Bernini's masterpiece, Baroque at its flashiest and most likeable. Among the travertine grottoes and fantastical flora and fauna under the obelisk, the four colossal figures represent the Ganges, Danube, Rio de la Plata, and Nile (with the veiled head because its source was unknown). Bernini also contributed the two smaller fountains, the *Calderari* and the 'Moor' (who is really the god Neptune). Off the southern end of the piazza, on the back of Palazzo Braschi, a lumpish torso and head are all there is of **Pasquino**, the original 'talking statue', embellished with placards and graffiti 'pasquinades' since the 1500s—one of his favourite subjects in those days was the insatiable pigginess of families like the Farnese; serious religious issues were usually too hot to touch, even for a statue.

Piazza Navona seems mildly schizoid these days, unable to become entirely part of high-fashion, tourist-itinerary Rome, yet no longer as comfortable and unpretentious as the rest of the neighbourhood. One symptom will be readily apparent should you step into any of the old cosy-looking cafés and restaurants around the piazza; they're as expensive as any part of Rome. The best time to come to Piazza Navona is at night, when the fountain is illuminated—or if you can, for the noisy, traditional toy fair of the Befana in the days just before Epiphany (6 January). Some of the churches in the neighbourhood are interesting. For example, **Santa Maria della Pace**, with Raphael's famous series of *Sibyls and Prophets* on the vaulting and a cloister by Bramante, his first work in Rome. **San Luigi dei Francesi**, the French church in Rome, is worth a stop for the great paintings on the *Life of St Matthew* by Caravaggio, in a chapel in the left aisle. Towards the Pantheon, **Sant'Ivo** was part of Rome's old university. Borromini made it one of his most singular buildings (1660), with its dome and spiralling cupola.

The Pantheon

When we consider the fate of so many other great buildings of ancient Rome, we begin to understand what a slim chance it was that allowed this one to come down to us. Built in 27 BC by Agrippa, Emperor Augustus' son-in-law and right-hand man, the monument's history has been precarious ever since. Several emperors had to effect repairs; Hadrian, a dabbler in architecture, rebuilt it, perhaps even contributing the unique design. In 609 the empty Pantheon was consecrated as 'St Mary of the Martyrs'. Becoming a church is probably what saved it, though the Byzantines hauled away the gilded bronze roof tiles soon after, and for a while in the Middle Ages the portico saw use as a fish market. The Pantheon's greatest enemy, however, was Gianlorenzo Bernini. He not only 'improved' it with a pair of Baroque belfries over the porch (demolished in 1887), but he had Pope Urban XIII take down the bronze covering on the inside of the dome, to use the metal for his baldachin over the altar at St Peter's. Supposedly there was enough left over to make the pope 60 cannons. (Urban was of the Barberini family, and Pasquino's comment about this act was, 'What the barbarians didn't do, the Barberini did.')

Looking at the outside, you may notice the building seems perilously unsound. There is no way a simple vertical wall can support such a heavy, shallow dome (steep domes push downwards, shallow ones outwards). Obviously the walls will tumble at any moment. That is a little joke the Roman architects are playing on us, for here they are showing off their engineering virtuosity as shamelessly as in the Colosseum, or the aqueduct with four storeys of arches that used to run up to the Palatine Hill. The wall that looks so fragile is really 7.6 m thick, and the dome on top isn't a dome at all; the real, hemispherical dome lies underneath, resting easily on the walls inside. The ridges you see on the upper dome are courses of cantilevered bricks, effectively almost weightless.

The real surprise, however, lies behind the enormous, original bronze doors, an interior of precious marbles and finely sculpted details, the grandest and best-preserved building to have survived from the ancient world. The movie directors who made all those Roman epics in the 1950s and '60s certainly took much of their settings from this High Imperial creation of Hadrian's time, just as architects from the early Middle Ages onwards have tried to equal it. Brunelleschi learned enough from it to build his dome in Florence, and a visit here will show you at a glance what Michelangelo and his contemporaries were trying so hard to outdo. The coffered dome, the biggest cast concrete construction ever made before the 20th century, is the crowning audacity, even without its bronze plate. At 42.6 m in diameter, it is probably the largest in the world (a little-known fact—but St Peter's dome is almost 2 m less, though much taller). Standing in the centre and looking at the clouds through the 9 m oculus at the top is an odd sensation you can experience nowhere else; sudden thunderstorms are a thrill.

Inside, the niches and recesses around the perimeter were devoted to statues of the Pantheon's 12 gods, plus those of Augustus and Hadrian; in the centre, illuminated by a direct sunbeam at mid-summer noon, stood Jove Ultor—the Avenging Jupiter, patron of Augustus' protracted revenge on his adoptive father, Caesar. All these are gone, of course, and the interior decoration is limited to an *Annunciation*, right of the door, attributed to Melozzo da Forli, and the tombs of Vittorio Emanuele II and Umberto I, as well as that of Raphael and other artists. Hardly ever used for church services, the Pantheon simply stands open, with no admission charges (daily, except Mon, 9–1, 2–5, Sun 9–1) probably fulfilling the same purpose as in Hadrian's day—no purpose at all, save that of an unequalled monument to art and the builder's skill. The Cult of the Twelve Gods, a Greek import from Augustus' time, never attracted many followers in Rome—even though many of the individual gods were present in Roman religion from the earliest times.

Just behind the Pantheon, the big church of **Santa Maria Sopra Minerva** is interesting for being one of the few important medieval churches of Rome (*c.* 1280) to escape the Baroque treatment; its Gothic look owes much to restoration work in the 1840s. Two Medici Popes, Leo X and Clement VII, are buried here, as is Fra Angelico. Santa Maria's Florentine connection began with the Dominican monks who designed it; they also did Florence's Santa Maria Novella. A work of Michelangelo, *Christ with the Cross*, can be seen near the high altar; the Carafa Chapel off the right aisle, where you can pay your respects to Pope Paul IV, has an earlier (1489) series of frescoes on the *Life of St Thomas* by Filippino Lippi, his best work outside Florence.

Via del Corso

The Campus Martius, the open plain between Rome's hills and the Tiber, was the training ground for soldiers in the early days of the republic. Eventually the city swallowed it up, and the old path towards the Via Flaminia became one of the most important thoroughfares, *Via Lata* (Broad Street). Not entirely by coincidence, the popes of the 14th and 15th centuries laid out a new grand boulevard almost in the same place. **Via del Corso**, or simply the Corso, has been the axis of Roman society ever since. Goethe recorded a fascinating account of the Carnival festivities held here in Rome's benignly decadent 18th century; the horse races that were the climax of it give the street its name. Most of its length is taken up by the overdone palaces of the age, such as the Palazzo Doria (1780), where the **Galleria Doria Pamphili** has some fine paintings, though in the old spirit of Pamphili greed, you have to fork out another L5000 for the guide to identify them. But the best works are unmistakable: Velazquez's *Portrait of Innocent X*, Caravaggio's *Flight into Egypt* and *Maddalena*, and works by Raphael, Parmigianino, Rubens, Titian, Pieter and Jan Brueghel. To see Filippo Lippi's lovely *Annunciation* or Lotto's *Portrait of a Gentleman*, you'll have to pay another fee to take the palace tour; included is a rare taste of Roman upper crustiness—the family still uses the rooms (open Tues, Fri, Sat, Sun 10–1; adm).

Continuing northwards, the palaces have come down in the world somewhat, tired-looking blocks that now house banks and offices. Look on the side-streets for some hidden attractions: **Sant'Ignazio**, on Via del Seminario and its own delightful piazza, another spectacular Jesuit church with very tricky *trompe l'oeil* frescoes on the ceiling; the church faces a cute Rococo piazza of 1728, designed by the free spirit of 18th-century architects, Filippo Raguzzini. A block north, columns of the ancient **Temple of Hadrian** are incorporated into the north side of the Roman Exchange. **Piazza Colonna** takes its name from the column of Marcus Aurelius, erected by his son Commodus and modelled after Trajan's, though here the scenes on the spiralling bands are more violent and realistic; without the gold statues of the emperor and his wife on top, it looks forlorn and dingy. The obelisk in adjacent Piazza di Montecitorio once marked the hours on a gigantic sundial in Emperor Augustus' garden; the **Montecitorio Palace**, built by Bernini, now houses the Italian Chamber of Deputies. Ask at the back of the building, at no 24, about permission to see a parliamentary session—not to listen to Italian oratory, but to see the remarkable Art Nouveau frescoes by Aristide Sartorio around the chamber.

Trevi Fountain and Augustus' Altar of Peace

Two blocks east of Piazza Colonna, you can throw your coins into the **Trevi Fountain** to guarantee your return trip to Rome. You may also scoop everyone else's coins out to help pay for it; there is no law against it (but just try explaining that to a Roman cop). The fountain, completed in 1732, commemorates the building of a new aqueduct that brought a famous spring called the *Acqua Vergine* into Rome (still the best tasting water in the city). It makes a grand sight—enough to make you want to come back, especially after dark, when the hordes are gone and it's beautifully lit; not many fountains have an entire palace for a stage backdrop (the Palazzo Poli). The big fellow in the centre is Oceanus, drawn by horses and tritons through cascades of travertine and blue water. Across from the fountain, the little church of **SS. Vincenzo and Anastasio** has the distinction of caring for the hearts and entrails of two dozen popes, an odd custom. They're down in the crypt.

To the right of the fountain, on Via della Stamperia, you can contemplate Guercino's *Venus*, the most sensuous in Rome, among the fine portraits, classical Roman landscapes, and other works by Raphael, Titian, Salvator Rosa, and Rome's unique 19th-century Aristide Sartorio in the **Accademia di San Luca** (Mon, Wed, Fri, and the last Sun of each month; adm).

Further north, the Corso reaches close to the Tiber and the pathetically sad **Mausoleum of Augustus**, a cylinder of shabby brick once covered in marble and golden statues. All the Julian emperors except Nero were interred here, in the middle of what were Augustus' enormous gardens. After the centuries despoiled the tomb of its riches, the Colonna family turned the hulk into one of its fortresses. Further indignities were in store. Until 1823, when the pope forbade them, bullfights were extremely popular in Rome; a certain Spanish entrepreneur found the circular enclosure perfect for the torreros. After that, the tomb was used as a theatre and a circus; now no one knows what to do with it, and it sits locked and empty. Across the street, Augustus' **Ara Pacis** (Altar of Peace) has had a better fate. Bits and pieces of the beautiful sculpted reliefs, dug up in 1937, were joined with casts of others from museums around Europe to recreate the small building almost in its entirety. One of antiquity's noblest (and least pretentious) conceptions now sits protected under an attractive glass pavilion; among the mythological reliefs, note the side facing the mausoleum, with the emperor and his family dedicating a sacrifice (daily, except Mon, 10–4, Sun 9–1; adm).

Piazza di Spagna

The shuffling crowds of tourists who congregate here at all hours of the day are not a recent phenomenon; this irregular but supremely sophisticated piazza has been a favourite with foreigners ever since it was laid out in the early 16th century. The Spaniards came first; their embassy to the popes has occupied the same spot since 1646. Later, the English Romantic poets made it their headquarters in Italy; typical Romantic mementoes—locks of hair, fond remembrances, mortal remains, death masks—are awaiting your inspired contemplation at the **Keats-Shelley Memorial House**, at no 26, where the 25-year-old Keats died of consumption in February 1821 (Mon–Fri 9–1, 3:30–5:30; adm). Almost every artist, writer or musician of the last century spent some time in the neigbourhood, but today the piazza often finds itself bursting at the seams with refreshingly philistine gawkers and wayward youth from all over Europe, America and Japan, caught between the charms of the gargantuan, controversial 700-seat Mc-Donald's and the fancy shops on and around nearby Via Condotti.

All these visitors need somewhere to sit, and the French obliged them in 1725 by paying Francesco de Sanctis to build the **Spanish Steps**, or more correctly, the *scalinata di Trinità dei Monti*, an exceptionally beautiful and exceptionally Baroque ornament about which it is hard to be cynical. The youth of today who loll about here are taking the place of the hopeful artists' models of the more picturesque centuries, who once crowded the steps, striking poses of antique heroes and Madonnas, waiting for some easy money. At the top of the stairs, the simple but equally effective 16th-century church of **Trinità dei Monti**, with a façade by Domemico Fontana was paid for by the King of France (open 9:30–12:30, when you can see the damaged but dynamic *Descent from the Cross* by Michelangelo's star pupil, Daniele da Volterra, in the left aisle). At the southern end of Piazza di Spagna, a rare joint effort by Bernini (the piazza façade) and Borromini (the claustrophobic Via di Propaganda façade) resulted in the **Collegio di Propaganda Fide**, whose job was just what the name implies. The column out front (1856) celebrates the proclamation of the Dogma of the Immaculate Conception of the Virgin Mary, one of their hardest tasks.

Via del Babuino, a street named after a Silenus on a fountain so ugly that Romans called him the 'baboon', connects Piazza di Spagna with the Piazza del Popolo. Besides its very impressive and equally expensive antique shops, the street carries on the English connection, with All Saints' Church, a sleepy neo-pub or two, and an English bookshop. The Greeks check in as well with their church Sant'Atanasio at the corner of Via dei Greci; the 'Baboon', long hidden in disgrace, has resurfaced in front of it in all its hideous glory.

Piazza del Popolo

If you have a choice of how you enter Rome, this is the way to do it, through the gate in the old Aurelian wall and into one of the most successful of all Baroque designs. No city has a better introduction, and the three diverging boulevards direct you with thoughtful efficiency towards your destination. Valadier, Rome's chief architect after the Napoleonic occupation, gave the piazza the form it has today, but the big obelisk of Pharaoh Ramses II punctuating the view down the boulevards arrived in the 1580s. It is 3200 years old, but like all obelisks it looks mysteriously brand new; Augustus brought it to Rome from Heliopolis and planted it in the Circus Maximus. The two domed churches, set like bookends at the entrance to the three boulevards, are from the 1670s, part of the original plan for the piazza to which Bernini, Fontana, and many of the other Baroque architects may have contributed.

Emperor Nero's ashes were interred in a mausoleum here, at the foot of the Pincio Hill. The site was planted with walnut trees, and soon everyone in Rome knew the stories of how Nero's ghost haunted the grove, sending out demons—in the forms of flocks of ravens that nested there—to perform deeds of evil. In 1099, Pope Paschal II destroyed the grove and scattered the ashes; to complete the exorcism he built a church on the site, **Santa Maria del Popolo**. Rebuilt in the 1470s, it contains some of the best painting in Rome: Caravaggio's stunning *Crucifixion of St Peter* and *Paul on the Road to Damascus* (in the left transept). Pinturicchio frescoed the first chapel to the right and painted the odalisque-like Sibyls in the ceiling of Bramante's barrel-vaulted Tribune behind the altar—a scaled-down version of his original plan for St Peter's. Raphael designed the Chigi Chapel, off the left aisle, as a miniature pantheon to his banker patron, Agostino Chigi, though both artist and patron died before its completion, and Bernini, Sebastiano del Piombo, and others finished it to Raphael's classic design.

Villa Borghese

From the Piazza, a winding ramp leads up to central Rome's biggest and prettiest park. Just by coincidence, this was mostly parkland in ancient times. The hill of the **Pincio** formed part of Augustus' Imperial gardens, and the adjacent **Villa Medici** occupies the site of the Villa of Lucullus, the 2nd-century BC philosopher and general who conquered northern Anatolia and first brought cherries to Europe. Now the home of the French Academy, the Villa Medici was a posh jail of sorts for Galileo during his Inquisitorial trials. The Pincio, a fine formal garden designed by Valadier, offers rare views over Rome, especially at sunset. It is separated from the **Villa Borghese** proper by the Aurelian wall and the modern sunken highway that borders it; its name, Viale del Muro Torto, comes from the old days under papal rule when the area was a cemetery for prostitutes, thieves, and actors.

Villa Borghese has its charms, lessened somewhat by the ubiquitous squads of Carabinieri trying gamely to keep the place respectable. Exploring its vast spaces, you will come across charming vales, woods, and lagoons (rowing boats for rent), an imitation Roman temple or two, Rococo avenues where the bewigged dandies and powdered tarts of the 1700s came to promenade, bits of ancient aqueduct, and the pleasant **Zoological Garden** (daily 8:30–one hour before sunset; adm). On the northern edge, late 19th-century Rome created a ponderous boulevard called **Viale delle Belle Arti** as a setting for new museums and foreign 'academies', where, for example, really jaded visitors can assault their senses with exhibits of post-Modernist art from Romania. The **National Gallery of Modern Art** makes its home in one of Rome's biggest and most inexcusable buildings (1913), but the collection includes representative works of the Futurists, De Chirico and the Metaphysical school as well as a fair sampling of the 19th- and 20th-century artists from the rest of Europe (daily, except Mon, 9–2, Sun 9–1; adm expensive). From there, gingerly skirting the aforementioned Romanian Academy, you come to the **Villa Giulia Museum**.

If you cannot make it to Tarquinia, this is the best place to get to know the Etruscans. Some of their best art has been collected here, as well as laboriously reconstructed terracotta façades to give you some idea of how an Etruscan temple looked. As usual, the compelling attraction of the art here is the Etruscans' effortless, endearing talent for portraiture: expressive faces that help bridge the gap between the centuries can be seen in terracotta ex-votos (some of children), sarcophagi, and even architectural decoration. Serious art is often more stylized; fine examples are the charming couple on the *Sarcofago dei Sposi* from Cervéteri and the roof statues of *Apollo and Hercules* from the Temple of Portonaccio at Veii—these by Vulca, the only Etruscan artist whose name has survived along with his work. The museum building and its garden are attractions in themselves; Julius III had Vignola and Ammannati build this quirky Mannerist villa with its semi-circular portico and sunken Nymphaeum in 1553, with Vasari and Michelangelo as consultants (daily 9–7, Sun 9–1, closed Mon; adm expensive).

The Borghese family, a minor ecclesiastical dynasty of the 17th century, collected an impressive hoard of ancient and modern art, which ended up in their Mannerist garden pleasure palace—at least the items not shipped off to the Louvre in the 1800s, when the head of the family made a gift of it to please his brother-in-law, Napoleon. What remains was purchased by the Italian state and is kept in the **Galleria Borghese**; today offers an intriguing mix of great art and Roman preciosity. Often the two go hand in hand, as with the sensuously charged showpieces of Bernini: *Apollo and Daphne, The Rape of Proserpina*, and especially his *David*, which the artist modestly chiselled in his own image. Canova, the hot item among sculptors in Napoleon's day, contributes a titillating languorous statue of Mme Borghese (Napoleon's ardent sister, Pauline) as the *Conquering Venus*. Even the ancient world joins in the fun, with such works as the famous Hellenistic *Sleeping Hermaphrodite*.

Upstairs, the sensuous theme is continued by three of Rome's most provocative paintings: Titian's *Sacred and Profane Love*, Dosso Dossi's *Circe* and Correggio's erotic *Danaë*. Also here is Raphael's *Deposition* and *Lady and the Unicorn*, beautiful works by Caravaggio, Antonello da Messina, Giovanni Bellini, and many other Italian household names; also Rubens' *Deposition*, one of the weakest paintings of all time with its pink, chubby Jesus and a crowd of bored-looking attendants (how much, if any, of the Galleria is open when you get there is debatable—the restoration of the palace has been an off-and-on affair since 1986—ask at the tourist office if any parts are temporarily open).

Via Vittorio Veneto and the Quirinal

Once, the chain of gardens including the Villa Borghese was much bigger; at the end of the last century, many of the old villas that hemmed in Rome were lost to the inevitable expansion of the city. Perhaps the greatest loss was the Villa Ludovisi, praised by many as

Bernini's Fontana del Tritone, Rome

the most beautiful of all Rome's parks. Now the choice 'Ludovisi' quarter, it has given the city one of its most famous streets, Via Vittorio Veneto, the long winding boulevard of grand hotels, cafés, and embassies that stretches down from Villa Borghese to the Piazza Barberini. A promenade for the smart set in the '50s, now that fashion has moved on the street wears the forlorn air of a jilted beau. Forget the passing show on the boulevard, and take in the unique spectacle provided by the **Convento dei Cappuccini** at the southern end of the street, around the corner from Piazza Barberini. Unique, that is, outside Palermo, for, much like the Capuchin convent there, the Roman monks have created a loving tribute to our friend Death. In the cellars, 4000 dead monks team up for an unforgettable *Danse Macabre* of bones and grinning skulls, carefully arranged by serious-minded Capuchins long ago to remind us of something we know only too well (entrance to the right of Santa Maria della Concezione church; daily 9–12 and 3–6; donation).

On the other side of Piazza Barberini, down a gloomy Baroque avenue called Via delle Quattro Fontane, you'll find the Barberini's palace, one of the showier places in Rome, decorated everywhere with the bees from the family arms. Maderno, Borromini, and Bernini all worked on it, with financing made possible by the election of a Barberini as Pope Urban VIII in 1623. Currently it houses the **National Museum of Ancient Art**—a misleading title, since this is a gallery devoted to Italian works of the 15th–18th centuries. Often the original decoration steals the show from the pictures: Pietro da Cortona's magnificent ceiling fresco in the Great Hall on *The Triumph of Divine Providence* (complete with Barberini bees flying in formation) or the ceiling in Room 7, with a fresco by Andrea Sacchi called the *Triumph of Divine Knowledge,* where the enthroned Virgin looking down on the round earth seems a Baroque attempt to create a new Catholic astronomy. Works present include some celebrated works by Raphael (his mistress, *La Fornarina,* or baker's girl, who loved him to death), Caravaggio's *Narcissus* and *Judith and Holofernes,* Holbein's *Henry VIII,* Quentin Metsys' *Erasmus,* an *Annunciation* by Filippo Lippi, a Guido Reni long presumed to be a portrait of the ill-fated Beatrice Cenci, and two rather sedate pictures by El Greco, among the few by that artist ever to stay in Italy, where he lived before moving to Spain (daily 9:15–7, closed Mon; adm).

San Carlino, just a block away on the corner of Via delle Quattro Fontane and Via Quirinale, is one of Borromini's best works—and his first one (1638), a purposefully eccentric little flight of fancy built exactly the size of one of the four massive pillars that hold up the dome in St Peter's; its undulating shapes and ellipses make it geometrically the most complex building in Rome. Follow **Via Quirinale** and you'll reach the summit of that hill, covered with villas and gardens in ancient times, and totally abandoned in the Middle Ages. Then even the name Quirinale had been forgotten, and the Romans called the place 'Montecavallo' because of the two big horses' heads projecting above the ground. During the reign of Sixtus V, they were excavated to reveal monumental Roman statues of the **Dioscuri** (Castor and Pollux), probably copied from Phidias or Praxiteles. Together with a huge basin found in the Forum, they make a centrepiece for Piazza Quirinale. Behind it, stretching for a dreary half-kilometre along the street (but only two rooms wide) is the **Quirinale Palace,** built in 1574 to symbolize the political domination of the popes, later occupied by the kings of Italy, and now by the presidents.

On the right side of Via Quirinale, dreariness gives way to architectural fireworks in the form of Bernini's **Sant'Andrea al Quirinale** (1658–70); behind the elegant classical portico lies a masterful, unique play of elliptical forms. Commissioned by the Jesuits, its opulence expresses their philosophy that the glory of heaven may best be imparted to the faithful by the glory of worldly richness—an effect contributed by the expensive stone, the theatrical light that falls on the high altar, and the beautiful stucco angels in the dome.

Around Termini Station: Diocletian's Baths

Even though the big station truly is the terminus for all Italy, its name in fact comes from the *thermae* or **Baths of Diocletian** on the other side of Piazza Cinquecento. Until the popes dismantled it for building stone, this was by far Rome's biggest ruin; its outer wall followed the present-day lines of Via XX Settembre, Via Volturno, and Piazza Cinquecento; while the big semi-circular **Piazza della Repubblica,** with its mouldering, grandiose 1890s palazzi and huge fountain of buxom nymphs, occupies the site of the baths' exercise ground, or *exedra.* Altogether the complex covered some 11 hectares. The surviving portions were converted into a monastery in the 1560s. Michelangelo, not on one of his better days, gave it a broad new cloister and converted a section of the lofty, vaulted central bathhouse into the church of **S. Maria degli Angeli,** conserving some of the building's original form. The cloister and adjacent buildings now house the **National Museum of Rome** (9–4:30, Mon and holidays 9–1; adm), the greatest Italian collection of antiquities after the museum in Naples—and like Naples' it is very badly run and usually half-closed; you'll be lucky if they let you see more than a few of the treasures inside. These include a unique, incredible collection of the finest Greek and Hellenistic-era sculpture, much of it in the rooms of the Ludovisi Collection: the famous **Ludovisi Throne,** with reliefs of the *Birth of Venus,* and statues of Hermes and the *Resting Ares.* Some of the Roman works are here, too—skilful copies like the *Discus Thrower* after Myron, and an unusual image of the pope's great predecessor, Emperor Augustus, in the dress of a Pontifex Maximus. Hundreds of other statues fill up several halls and all four sides of Michelangelo's cloister. Upstairs there are more rooms of mosaics and fragmentary frescoes, including an entire room moved here from the Villa of Livia on the Palatine, painted to look like an open courtyard.

A block north of the baths, Piazza San Bernardo marks the beginning of Via Barberini, a repulsive modern street with most of Rome's travel and airline offices. The Piazza itself has two interesting churches—**San Bernardo**, built out of a circular library that once occupied a corner of the baths' walls, and **Santa Maria della Vittoria**, home to one of the essential works of Baroque sculpture, the titillating *St Teresa in Ecstasy* by Bernini, the star of the sculptor's amazing stage set of a chapel in the left aisle.

The Patriarchal Basilicas: Santa Maria Maggiore

Besides St Peter's, there are three Patriarchal Basilicas, ancient and revered churches under the care of the pope that have always been a part of the Roman Pilgrimage. Santa Maria Maggiore, St Paul's, and St John Lateran are all on the edges of the city, where the earliest Christian communities lived; by the Middle Ages they stood in open countryside, and only recently has the city grown outwards to swallow them once more.

Santa Maria Maggiore, at the end of the Esquiline Hill, was probably begun about 352, when a rich Christian saw a vision of the Virgin Mary directing him to build a church; Pope Liberius had received the same vision at the same time, and the two found the site marked out for them by a miraculous August snowfall. With various rebuildings over the centuries, the church took its current form in the 1740s, with a perfectly elegant façade by Fernando Fuga and an equally impressive rear elevation in Piazza dell'Esquilino, by other architects; the obelisk here came from the Mausoleum of Augustus. Above everything rises the tallest and fairest **campanile** in Rome, an incongruous survival from the 1380s. Despite the changes on the outside, Santa Maria Maggiore preserves its 5th-century basilican form, though crowned by a coffered ceiling by Renaissance architect Giuliano da Sangallo, gilded with the first gold brought back from the New World by Columbus, a gift from King Ferdinand of Spain. In the apse, there are splendid but faded mosaics from 1295 of the *Coronation of the Virgin*. Mosaic panels from the 5th century run along the upper nave and in the 'triumphal arch' in front of the apse. Santa Maria has a prize relic—nothing less than the genuine manger from Bethlehem, preserved in a sunken shrine in front of the altar; in front, kneeling in prayer, is a colossal, rather grotesque statue of Pope Pius IX. Pope Sixtus V built himself Rome's other 'Sistine Chapel' on the right, encased in sumptuous marbles cannibalized from the ancient Septizonium, a mysterious edifice that once stood where the Palatine hill faced the Appian Way. Its temple-baldachin shelters Arnolfo di Cambio's 13th-century figures of Joseph, the Magi and animals—all that survives of Santa Maria Maggiore's Christmas Crib, where the popes for nearly ten centuries came to say Christmas Eve mass; when Sixtus V tried to move it into his chapel it broke into bits.

Two little churches in the streets around Santa Maria Maggiore commemorate two sisters, early Christian martyrs of the 1st century; both of them have fascinating mosaic decorations, among the oldest and best in Rome. In **Santa Pudenziana**, in Via Urbana, there is a mosaic of *Christ and the Apostles* from the 300s, a thoroughly classical work from the very beginnings of Christian art. At **Santa Prassede**, on Via Santa Prassede, the mosaics reveal a different world; the shadowy Rome of the not-entirely-Dark Ages. In

822, two decades after Charlemagne visited the city, Pope Paschal I found the money and the talent to build works he hoped would be compared to the magnificent ruins that lay on every side. The churches he had rebuilt were not large, but they were a start, and to embellish them he imported Byzantine artists who created a rebirth of mosaic work and painting in Rome. The jewel of Santa Prassede is the small **San Zeno Chapel**, which Paschal intended as a mausoleum for his mother. The square vaulted chamber is entirely covered with gold-ground mosaics of Christ Pantocrator, saints, and some very digni-fied, classical angels who look as if they had never heard anything about the fall of Rome. The 9th-century mosaics around the altar are even better, though not as lavishly gilded.

St John Lateran

Where is Rome's cathedral? It isn't St Peter's, and never has been. The true seat of the Bishop of Rome, the end of a Roman Pilgrimage, the 'Mother and Head Church of Rome and the World' is here in the shadow of the Aurelian wall, a church believed to have been established by Constantine himself. The family of Plautus Lateranus, accord-ing to ancient records, had their property here confiscated after a failed coup against Nero in AD 66. It eventually became part of imperial real estate, and Constantine and his wife Fausta (whom he later executed) once kept house in the Lateran Palace. Later he donated it to Pope Miltiades as a cult centre for the Christians of Rome. Almost nothing remains of the original basilica; the sacks of the Vandals and Normans, two earthquakes and several fires have resulted in a building with some bits and pieces left from each of the last sixteen centuries.

Like Santa Maria Maggiore, this church has an 18th-century exterior that is almost miraculously good, considering other Italian buildings from that age, a west front by Alessandro Galilei (1736) that confidently and competently restates the High Renais-sance architectural vernacular. In the narthex stands an ancient statue of Constantine, found at the baths he built on the Quirinal; the bronze doors in the central portal once graced the entrance to the Curia in the Forum. Inside, the nave is dominated by giant, impressive statues of the Apostles (*c*. 1720), glaring down like Roman emperors of old. There is some carefree and glorious Baroque work in the side chapels—also remains of a fresco by Giotto (*Boniface VIII's Jubilee*) behind the first pier on the right. Near the apse, decorated with 13th-century mosaics (reindeer worshipping the cross, an odd conceit probably adapted from older mosaics in Ravenna), the Papal Altar, decorated with a bright Gothic baldacchino, supposedly contains the heads of Peter and Paul. Below floor level is the tomb of Pope Martin V; for some reason the Romans drop flowers and telephone tokens on him for good luck.

Rome in the later Middle Ages had evolved an architectural style entirely its own, strangely uninterested in Gothic or reviving classicism, or, for that matter, anything else that was going on in the rest of Italy. Sadly, almost all of it disappeared in the Renaissance and Baroque rebuildings. The towers of Santa Maria in Cosmedin and Santa Maria Maggiore are good examples of it, as well as the expressive mosaics of Pietro Cavallini and his school and the intricate, geometrical Cosmatesque pavements in this church and so many others. Perhaps the most striking survival of this lost chapter in art is the Lateran **Cloister**, with its pairs of spiral columns and 13th-century Cosmatesque mosaics; it completely upstages everything else in the church. All around the cloister walls, frag-ments from the earlier incarnations of St John's have been assembled, a hoard of broken pretty things that includes an interesting tomb of a 13th-century bishop, maybe the work of Arnolfo di Cambio.

If you leave the Lateran by the right transept, you can see the equally fine north façade, designed by Domenico Fontana in 1586, incorporating two earlier twin medieval bell towers into the design. Just to the right is the **Lateran Palace**, rebuilt in 1588 after a fire destroyed the original building that served as home of the popes for a thousand years (4th–14th centuries). It overlooks Piazza San Giovanni, with the obligatory **obelisk**, though this 100-ft pinnacle of red granite from the Temple of Ammon at Thebes (15th century BC) is nothing short of the world's tallest. To the left is the **Baptistry**—nothing less than the first one in Christendom, converted from an older temple by Constantine; its octagonal form has been copied in other baptistries all over Italy. Inside there are unusual pairs of bronze doors on either side: one from 1196 with scenes of how the Lateran basilica appeared at that time, and the other from the Baths of Caracalla, 'singing' doors that make a low, harmonic sound when you open them slowly. Built around the baptistry are three venerable chapels, two with delicate floral mosaics from the 5th century, and the third, San Venanzio, with mosaics of Dalmatian saints from the 640s. Across the piazza is the **Scala Santa**, supposedly the stairs of Pilate's palace in Jerusalem, descended by Christ after his Judgement and brought to Rome by Constantine's mother, St Helen. The central stair may only be ascended on the knees; Martin Luther, on his pilgrimage, made it halfway up when he had a sudden revelation—he got off his knees and walked back down, went back to Germany and started the Reformation. At the top, the **Sancta Sanctorum** or Chapel of San Lorenzo survives from the medieval Papal Palace and contains a miraculous portrait of Jesus, painted by angels, which you can see through the gate.

While you're here, you have a good opportunity to explore the Aurelian wall. The stretch of it behind the Lateran looks much as it did in Aurelian's time, and its **Porta Asinara** is one of the best-preserved monumental ancient gateways. The adjacent **Porta di San Giovanni** was rebuilt in 1564.

The Caelian Hill

South of the Colosseum you can see nothing but trees, but on every inch of this vast tract of parkland, almost 2.5 square kilometres in extent, the ruins of ancient neighbourhoods wait just a few feet beneath the surface. Modern Rome never expanded in this direction, and the whole of it has been preserved as open space. It's a fascinating place to walk around, if you can avoid the traffic thundering down the big boulevards towards the southern suburbs. The Caelian Hill is only a small part of it, but it is one of the least known and most delightful corners of Rome. Have a picnic in the big park called the **Villa Celimontana**, and you may find some genuine squirrels, imported from the United States, to keep you company (we never saw one; they may have had some problems with the ferocious Roman cats).

Some of Rome's most ancient churches repose in quiet settings here, all worth a look inside if they are open: **Santo Stefano Rotondo**, the oldest circular church in Italy, was built around 470 over the ruins of a market-place of Nero's time and decorated in the 1580s with Rome's most perverse frescoes of martyrdoms. Across the street, more mosaics from the age of Paschal I (*c.* 820) can be seen in **Santa Maria in Domnica** in

114

Piazza Navicella, with an ancient fountain in the form of a Roman ship. From here Via S. Paolo della Croce leads up to the Caelian's summit, with the entrance to the Villa Celimontana and **SS. Giovanni e Paolo**, built over a Roman house in the 4th century, as seen by the original mosaic on the floor and the bits of 2nd-century frescoes in the crypt. Down the western slope, the Clivo di Scauro, you pass **San Gregorio Magno**, once the villa of Pope Gregory the Great, which he converted to a monastery in 590. St Augustine lived here before being sent by Gregory to convert the Angles and Saxons of Britain, but in the 1620s it was completely rebuilt, with a fine proto-Baroque façade by G. B. Soria.

Circus Maximus and Caracalla's Baths

Piazza Porta Capena, at the foot of the Caelian hill, has an odd decoration, an obelisk erected by Mussolini to commemorate his conquest of Ethiopia—he stole it from the Ethiopian city of Axum. The piazza itself is a vortex of Mussolini pretensions; the dictator built himself a new Triumphal Way (now Via San Gregorio) along the route of the original one, to celebrate his piddling triumphs in proper Roman style. Behind the obelisk an unfinished building that was to be the Ministry of Africa found a more agreeable use after the War—now it is the home of the United Nations Food and Agricultural Organisation. To the west, a broad green lawn is all that's left of the great **Circus Maximus**. Archaeologists have estimated that as many as 300,000 Romans could squeeze in and place their bets for the chariot races. Founded by King Tarquin and completed in its final form by Trajan, the stadium proved simply too convenient a quarry; the banked, horseshoe-shaped depression follows the line of the ancient grandstands.

The **Baths of Caracalla** (AD 206–220), in a large park south of Porta Capena, rank with those of Diocletian as the largest and most lavish of the type (daily 9–one hour before sunset, Sun and Mon 9–1; adm). Roughly 305 m square, with excellent libraries and spacious exercise courts, the baths probably boasted more gold, marble, and precious works of art than any building complex in Rome; here the Farnese family dug up such masterpieces as the *Hercules* and the *Farnese Bull*, now in the Naples museum. In the 1700s these baths were one of the obligatory sights of the Grand Tour; their lofty, broken arches and vaults appealed to the Romantic love of ruins like no others. Much of the central building survives, with its hot and cold rooms, great hall and swimming pool, all decorated with colourful mosaics. Someone may be around to take you down to the extensive halls and corridors underground. A large tunnel connects the baths with the area around Palazzo Venezia, over a kilometre away; its purpose was to transport the vast amounts of wood needed to keep the baths hot. Mussolini initiated the custom of holding summer concerts and opera here; he liked to drive his roadster through the tunnel and pop out dramatically on stage at the beginning of the festivities.

Behind the baths a stretch of the **Antonine Aqueduct** that supplied it can still be seen. On the other side, facing Via Terme di Caracalla, **SS. Nereo e Achilleo** has more mosaics from the time of Leo III (*c.* 800) and a Cosmatesque altar. A bit further south, on the other side of the traffic-laden Piazzale Numa Pompilio, a short stroll down Via di Porta Latina will take you to one of Rome's most serene churches, the 12th-century **San Giovanni a Porta Latina**, its frescoes illuminated by the glow of selenite windows. The little octagonal chapel across the street, **San Giovanni in Oleo**, marks the site where the Romans unsuccessfully tried to deep-fry St John (he walked away 'refreshed'). If you cut through the little public garden next to the chapel, you'll find yourself at the entrance of the **Sepolcro degli Scipioni**, the forsaken family tomb of the charismatic Scipios, built in 290 BC (9–2, Tues, Thurs, and Sat also 4–7, guided tours; adm). The tomb was discovered under a house in 1780; but the most striking part of the tour is the 1st-century AD **Columbarium of Pomponius Hylas**. A columbarium is a communal tomb, with dovecote-like niches for urns of ashes; this one, with its mosaics and stuccoes, is the most luxurious ever found. The Tomb of the Scipios is just before Porta San Sebastiano and the Appian Way.

The Appian Way: Rome's Catacombs

Rome's 'Queen of Roads', the path of trade and conquest to Campania, Brindisi, and the East, was begun in 312 BC by Consul Appius Claudius. Like most of the consular roads outside Rome, over the centuries it became lined with cemeteries and the elaborate mausoleums of the wealthy; ancient Roman practice, inherited from the Etruscans, prohibited any burials within the *pomerium*, the sacred ground of the city itself. Later, the early Christian community built some of its most extensive catacombs here—the word itself comes from the location, *ad catacumbas*, referring to the dip in the Appian Way near the suburban Circus of Maxentius. The road, now Via Appia Antica to distinguish it from the new Via Appia in Rome's southeast surburbs, makes a pleasant excursion outside the city; the No 118 bus from the Colosseum goes as far as the Tomb of Cecilia Metella—from where you can walk back to the catacombs, or walk south along the most beautiful stretch of the road.

Via Appia Antica passes under the Aurelian wall at **Porta San Sebastiano**, one of the best preserved of the old gates and entrance to the **Museo delle Mura**, with exhibits on the walls and your best chance to walk along them (9–1:30, Thurs also 4–7, closed Mon; adm). After about 1 km, with some ruins of tombs along the way, there is the famous church of **Domine Quo Vadis?**, on the spot where Peter, fleeing from the dangers of Rome, met Christ coming the other way. 'Whither goest thou, Lord?' Peter asked. 'I am going to be crucified once more,' was the reply. As the vision departed the shamed Apostle turned back, soon to face his own crucifixion in Rome.

Another kilometre or so takes you to the **Catacombs of St Calixtus**, off a well signposted side road to the right (but if you're riding the bus, wait for the next stop; open daily, except Wed, 8:30–12, 2:30–5, 6 pm in the summer; guided tours; adm). Here the biggest attraction is the 'Crypt of the Popes', burial places of 3rd- and 4th-century pontiffs with some well-executed frescoes and inscriptions. A word about catacombs: popular romance and modern cinema notwithstanding, these were never places of refuge from persecution or anything else, but simply burial grounds. The word catacombs was only used after the 5th century; before that the Christians preferred simply to call them 'cemeteries'. The burrowing instinct is harder to explain. Few other Mediterranean cities have catacombs (Naples, Syracuse, Malta, and the Greek island of Milos are among them). One of the requirements for catacombs seems to be tufa, or some other stone that can be easily excavated. Even so, the work involved was tremendous, and not explainable by any reasons of necessity. Christians were still digging them after they had become a power in Rome, in Constantine's time. No one knows for certain what sort of funeral rites were celebrated in them, just as no one knows much about any of the prayers or rituals of the early Christians; we can only suspect that a Christian of the 4th century and one of the 16th would have had considerable difficulty recognizing each other as brothers in the faith.

Most catacombs began small, as private family cemeteries; over generations some grew into enormous termitaries extending for miles beneath the surface. Inside, most of the tombs you will see will be empty *loculi*, niches with only a symbol or short inscription scratched in to identify the deceased. Others, especially the tombs of popes or the wealthy, may have paintings of scriptural scenes, usually very poor work that reflects more on the dire state of late Roman imagination than on the Christians.

You can detour from here, another kilometre west to the **Catacombs of Domitilla** (guided tours 8:30–12 and 2:30–5, closed Tues; adm). Domitilla was a member of a senatorial family, and interestingly the catacombs seem to incorporate parts of earlier pagan *hypogea*, including a cemetery of the Imperial Flavian family, besides the paintings, which include an unusual *Last Supper* scene, portraying a young and beardless Jesus and Apostles in Roman dress. There is an adjacent basilica, built about the tombs of SS. Nereus and Achilleus, on Via delle Sette Chiese. Not far away is a monument to martyrs of a very different sort, the **Mausoleum of the Fosse Ardeatine**, dedicated to the hundreds of Romans massacred on this spot in 1944 after a Resistance uprising.

Back on the Via Appia Antica, there are several catacombs near the corner of Via Appia Pignatelli, including a Jewish one (tel ahead to visit, 735 824) but the largest, and the only ones normally open to the public are the **Catacombs of San Sebastiano** (guided tours 8:30–12 and 2:30–5, closed Thurs; adm). This complex, too, began as a pagan cemetery. It is one of the largest, with intriguing paintings and incised symbols throughout. The place had some special significance for the early Christians, and it has been conjectured that Peter and Paul were originally buried here, before their removal to the city basilicas in Constantine's time. The **Basilica of San Sebastiano** was built over the holy site in the 4th century, but had to be completely rebuilt in 1612; in the left aisle, a languorous statue of *St Sebastian*, completed after a design of Bernini, is the closest male equivalent to the same sculptor's St Teresa in Ecstasy.

A bit further south, the Via Appia Antica passes the **Circus of Maxentius**, built in the early 4th century and the best preserved of Rome's many race tracks; adjacent, through the mighty walls, is the round **Tomb of Romulus**, Maxentius' son, under an old farmhouse (Tues–Sat 9–1:30 and Sun 9–12:30; adm). Further up is the Via Appia Antica's most famous landmark, the imposing, cylindrical **Tomb of Cecilia Metella**, from the time of Augustus (open 9–1:30, closed Mon; adm). In the Middle Ages the Caetani family turned the tomb into a family fortress, charging such extravagant tolls that Via Appia Antica was abandoned for centuries in favour of other routes like the Via Appia Nuova; at other times, before and since, it was a famous rendezvous for *banditti*. Its lovely ox-head frieze gave the entire district its name: Capo di Bove. Tombs—mostly strangely eroded brick forms—continue as far as 16 km from the walls of Rome, where you can see a long stretch of the original Via Appia still in use. The most classical section is another half-kilometre from the Tomb of Cecilia Metella, just beyond Via Tor di Carbone, where the road passes under the lonely parasol pines and cypresses of the Roman campagna.

The Aventine Hill

Every now and then, when the left-wing parties walk out on a government coalition, the Italian newspapers may call it an 'Aventine Secession', an offhand reference to events in Rome 2500 years ago. Under the Roman Republic, the Aventine Hill was the most solidly plebeian quarter of the city. On several occasions, when legislation proposed by the Senate and consuls seriously threatened the rights or interests of the people, they retired *en masse* to the Aventine and stayed there until the plan was dropped. Rome's unionists today often keep the city tied up in knots, but most are probably unaware that their ancestors had the honour of inventing the general strike.

The Aventine had another distinction in those times. In its uninhabited regions, the steep, cave-ridden slopes and parks towards the south, Greek immigrants and returning soldiers introduced the midnight rituals of Dionysos and Bacchus. Though secret, such goings-on soon came to the attention of the Senate, which saw the orgies quite rightly as a danger to the state and banned them in 146 BC. They must not have died out completely, however; in the Middle Ages the Aventine had a reputation as a haunt of witches. The early Christian community also prospered here, and some of their churches are the oldest relics on the Aventine today. Coming up from the Circus Maximus along Via Santa Sabina, you'll find the **Parco Savello**, a walled garden of orange trees, affording one of Rome's most memorable views. Its neighbour, **Santa Sabina** (6:30–12:45 and 3:30–7), perhaps Rome's most serendipitous church, is a simple, rare example of a 5th-century basilica, with an atrium at its entrance and an original 5th-century door of cypress carved with scriptural scenes; within, it is lined with Corinthian columns, and softly lit by selenite windows. Some of the original mosaics survive by the door, and on the floor of the nave is Rome's only mosaic tomb (c. 1300). This has been the head church of the Dominicans ever since a 13th-century pope gave it to St Dominic. The church of **Sant'Alessio** down the street has good Cosmatesque cloisters.

At the end of the street is one of the oddities only Rome can offer: the quirky **Piazza dei Cavalieri di Malta**, designed by the great engraver Giambattista Piranesi. Decorated with reliefs and baby obelisks, it has a monumental gate to the **Priory of the Sovereign Order of Malta** and **Santa Maria del Priorato**, a fancy Rococo church, the only one Piranesi ever designed (to enter, apply at the Order's headquarters in Via Condotti 68). The Knights of Malta—or more properly, the Knights Hospitallers of St John—no longer wait for the popes to unleash them against Saracen and Turk. Mostly this social club for old nobles bestirs itself to assist hospitals, its original job during the Crusades. Even if you can't get through the gate, peep through the keyhole for the famous view of St Peter's at the end of a tree-lined path.

Elsewhere on the Aventine, **Santa Prisca** has beginnings typical of an early Roman church; its crypt, the original church, was converted from the house of the martyr Prisca, host to St Peter; the Apostle must often have presided over Mass here. A Mithraeum, vandalized by the Christians in the year 400, was discovered under the church in 1958 and pieced together (open Mon, Wed, and Fri 10–12). Via S. Prisca crosses Viale Aventino to the 'Little Aventine' and **San Saba**, built by Syrian monks fleeing the Arab invasions of the 7th century. Most of this beautiful church comes from a 1205 rebuilding, including a Cosmatesque door and floor, the baldacchino, and frescoes on the life of

St Nicolaus. The loggia is from the 1400s, though the relief of a knight and falcon may date from the first monks.

Rome's Pyramid

Porta San Paolo stands in one of the most perfectly preserved sections of the Aurelian wall. The gate itself looks just as it did 1700 years ago, when it was the *Porta Ostiense*; its change of name came about because Paul passed through it on the way to his execution. Built into the wall near the gate is a unique site: the **Pyramid of Gaius Cestius Poplicius** may seem a strange self-tribute for a Roman, but Cestius, an official who had served in Egypt, at least paid for it himself. The tomb was built in 12 BC, and it is 28 m tall. Behind it, following the inside of the walls, the lovely **Protestant Cemetery** was a popular Romantic pilgrimage in the last century. The graves of Shelley and Keats are there, as is that of Antonio Gramsci, philosopher and founder of the Italian Communist Party (entrance at Via Caio Cestio 6, open 8–11:30 and 2:30–4:30, later in the summer; donation). They have recently been joined across the street, in Via Zabaglia's Rome War Cemetery, by 400 British soldiers who died during the march on Rome in 1944.

Just to the west, you can climb the youngest and certainly the oddest of Rome's hills. **Monte Testaccio** is made entirely of potsherds. In ancient times, wine, oil, olives, grain, and nearly everything else was shipped in big *amphorae*; here, in part of what was Rome's warehouse district, all the broken ones were collected in one place—no one knows why. The hill is 35 m at its highest point and covers about seven city blocks—the world's greatest monument to the butter-fingered. The vast cellars the Romans left beneath it are now used for storing wine; some are car repair shops.

St Paul's Outside the Walls

Paul was beheaded on a spot near the Ostia road; according to an embarrassing old legend, the head bounced three times, and at each place where it hit the ground a fountain sprang up. The Abbazia delle Tre Fontane (in EUR) occupies the site today. Later, Constantine would build a basilica down the road as a fitting resting-place for the saint. Of the four patriarchal basilicas, this one has had the worst luck. Today it sits in an unpleasant neighbourhood of factories, gasworks and concrete flats. Once it was the grandest of them all; 9th-century chroniclers speak of the separate walled city of 'Giovannipoli' that had grown up around St Paul's, connected to the Aurelian wall by a 1½ km-long colonnade built by Pope John VIII in the 870s. The Norman sack of 1084, a few good earthquakes, and finally a catastrophic fire in 1823 wiped Giovannipoli off the map and left us with a St Paul's that for the most part is barely more than a century old. Palm trees take some of the bright chill off the façade of golden mosaics and sturdy Corinthian columns. The 11th-century bronze Holy Door is one of the older features to survive—others are a Gothic baldachin over Paul's tomb by Arnolfo di Cambio, a beautiful 13th-century Cosmatesque cloister, almost a double of the one in the Lateran, and especially the strange, inexplicable 5th-century mosaics over the 'Triumphal Arch' in front of the apse, contributed by Empress Galla Placidia. Art Deco is not what you would expect from those times, but Americans at least will have a hard time believing these frescoes were not done by President Roosevelt's WPA. The apse itself has some more conventional mosaics from the 13th-century Venetian school. The right transept has a huge carved Paschal candlestick of the 12th century. Along the top of the nave runs a frieze with mosaic portraits of all the 265 popes down to John Paul II; the first 40 survived the fire, while the others are replacements.

EUR

By the late '30s, Mussolini was proud enough of his accomplishments to plan a great world's fair. Its theme was to be the Progress of Civilization, measured no doubt from the invention of the wheel up to the invention of the Corporate State. A vast area south of Rome was cleared and transformed into a grid of wide boulevards broken by parks and lagoons. Huge Mussolini-style pavilions and colonnades were begun, and a design was accepted for a tremendous aluminium arch—like the famous one in St Louis but many times bigger—that would overspread the entire site. War intervening, the arch never appeared, and the Esposizione Universale di Roma never came off. After 1945 the Italians tried to make the best of it, turning EUR into a model satellite city and trade centre on the lines of La Défense in Paris. The result will derange your senses as much as it does the average Roman's, a chilly nightmare of modernism with street names like the Boulevard of Humanism, Boulevard of Electronics, and the Boulevard of Social Security. All these are immensely wide speedways where the few foolish pedestrians are mowed down like ducks in a shooting gallery—some are desolately empty, while all are lined with glass skyscrapers that make the crumbling old Mussolini buildings look positively cosy and cheerful.

Still, for those who can appreciate the well-landscaped macabre, EUR can be fun (and Metro B will take you right there). Some of the older corners reveal giant fascist mosaics of heroic miners, soldiers, assembly-line workers, and mothers, and at the end of the Boulevard of Civilization of Labour you can have a look at the modest masterpiece of Mussolini architecture, a small, elegantly proportioned building called the **Palazzo di Civiltà e di Concordia**. Liberal, post-War Italy has rarely, if ever, been able to conceive anything with such a sure sense of design and a feeling for history (of course some Roman malcontents call it the 'Square Colosseum'). The only serious reason to come to EUR is for museums, especially the **Museo della Civiltà Romana** (at the eastern end of EUR on Piazza G. Agnelli; open 9–1:30, Thurs also 4–7, Sun 9–1, closed Mon; adm expensive), with scale models of Roman buildings, a collection of casts from every aspect of Roman life, and a huge 1:250 scale model of ancient Rome in the 4th century with every building present, a great place to feed your imagination with visions of the old city's splendour. One long skinny room holds a complete collection of plaster casts from Trajan's Column.

Other EUR museums include the **Prehistorical and Ethnographic Museum** nearby on Viale Lincoln, covering civilizations before classical Rome (daily 9–2, Sun 9–1; adm) and the **Museum of the Early Middle Ages** in the same building (9–2, Sun 9–1; free). A kilometre east of EUR on Via delle Tre Fontane is the **Abbazia delle Tre Fontane,** founded by refugee monks from Syria in the 650s, on the site of St Paul's martyrdom. Once plagued by malaria, the abbey's Trappist residents have sucked the swamps dry with eucalyptus. The abbey has three old churches to visit: **SS. Vincenzo ed Anastasio**, rebuilt in 1221, **S. Maria Scala Coeli**, with a Cosmatesque altar, and **San Paolo alle Tre Fontane**, with two mosaic pavements from Ostia Antica.

Trastevere

So often, just being on the wrong side of the river encourages a city district to cultivate its differences and its eccentricities. Trastevere isn't really a Left Bank—more of a pocket-sized Brooklyn, and as in Brooklyn those differences and eccentricities often turn out to be the old habits of the whole city, distilled and preserved in an out-of-the-way corner. The people of Trastevere are more Roman than the Romans. Indeed, they claim to be the real descendants of the Romans of old; one story traces their ancestry back to the sailors who worked the great awning and choreographed the mock sea battles at the Colosseum. Such places have a hard time surviving these days, especially when they are as trendy and popular as Trastevere is right now. But even though such things as Trastevere's famous school of dialect poets may be mostly a memory, the quarter remains the liveliest and most entertaining in Rome. The young crowd that Trastevere attracts now provides much of the local colour, dressed in various styles of Roman Punk that somehow seem a perfect match for the medieval alleys and jumbles of flats.

If you cross over on the **Sublician Bridge** under the Aventine Hill, the successor to Rome's first bridge (the one Horatio defended), you'll be at Porta Portese, on Sunday mornings home to Rome's big **flea market**. From there, Via Anicia takes you to the church of **Santa Cecilia in Trastevere**, founded over the house of the 2nd-century martyr whom centuries of hagiography have turned into one of the most agreeable of saints, the inventor of the organ and patroness of music. Cecilia was disinterred in 1599, apparently out of curiosity, and her body was found entirely uncorrupted. Clement VIII commissioned Stefano Maderno to sculpt an exact copy before they put her back; this charming work can be seen near the high altar, graced by a Gothic baldacchino by Arnolfo di Cambio similar to the one in St Paul's, and a Ravenna-style 9th-century mosaic in the apse. The church has any number of other treasures: some Renaissance tombs, including one of a 14th-century cardinal from Hertford named Adam Easton; a crypt with mosaics from Cecilia's home; ancient frescoes from the church that succeeded it; and a 13th-century cloister (open on request) with fragments of Pietro Cavallini's *Last Judgement* (1295), his masterpiece that was destroyed in Santa Cecilia's 18th-century rebuilding.

Across Viale Trastevere, an intrusive modern boulevard that slices the district in two, lies the heart of old Trastevere, around **Piazza Santa Maria in Trastevere** and the church of the same name. Most of this building dates from the 1140s, though the original church, begun perhaps in 222, may be the first anywhere dedicated to the Virgin Mary. The medieval building is a treasure-house of Roman mosaics, starting with the frieze of saints on the façade and continuing with the remarkable series from the *Life of Mary* by Cavallini, a bit of the early Renaissance one hundred years ahead of schedule (c. 1290). These adorn the arch in front of the apse, under earlier, more glittering mosaics from the 1140s. On the left side, the entrance to the sacristy has a wonderful small ancient mosaic displayed; the 1680s Chapel of San Girolamo is a theatrical Baroque work with its own natural lighting. On the right, watch out for the chapel with the painted staring eyes—it's haunted.

The piazza, and the streets around it, have been for decades one of the most popular spots in Rome for restaurants; tables are spread out wherever there's room, and there will always be a crowd in the evening hours. Just around the corner from the church, on

Via della Paglia, see a greener, fairer Rome than the one you're visiting at the **Folklore Museum**: old paintings of street scenes, papal festivals and ruins, a reconstructed block of 19th century shops and much more—an excellent place to begin a visit to the city (weekdays 9–1:30, and Thurs also 5–7:30; Sun 9–1; closed Mon; adm).

Down Via della Lungaretta, Piazza Sidney Sonnino faces Ponte Garibaldi, Trastevere's front door. The **Torre di Anguillara** is an uncommon survival of the defence towers that loomed threateningly over medieval Rome, and the 12th-century church of **San Crisogono** has mosaics by followers of Cavallini. Near the bridge, the dapper statue in the top hat is Giuseppe Gioacchino Belli, Trastevere's famous 19th-century dialect poet; the charming relief on the back of the pedestal shows old Romans enjoying a *pasquinade* of Pasquino.

Two Roads to St Peter's

One is broad and straight, the route of the many; the other is tortuous and narrow, and after it but few inquire. **Via della Lungara**, the route of the slothful, takes you past the **Villa Farnesina**, an early 1500s palace built for the Chigi family, that is now the home of the distinguished old Accademia dei Lincei (open daily 9–1, closed Sun; free) where you will have a chance to see some of the best fresco painting in Rome: the *Galatea* and *Cupid and Psyche* of Raphael; a prospect of the constellations by Baldassare Peruzzi, who also designed the building; and works of Sodoma. Across the street, the **Galleria Corsini** contains an exceptional collection of 16th- and 17th-century art, including works of Caravaggio, Murillo, Rubens, Mattia Preti, and Salvator Rosa, whose *Prometheus* wins the blood and gore prize, with its keen, hungry eagle (daily 9–7, Mon 9–2, Sun 9–1; adm).

The other road may be more difficult to find, but repays the effort with lovely gardens and some of the best views over Rome from Monte Gianicolo, the ancient *Janiculum*. First find Via Garibaldi, in the back streets behind Santa Maria Trastevere, and it will carry you up to the Renaissance church of **San Pietro in Montorio**, once erroneously believed to be the spot of St Peter's upside-down crucifixion. The chief painting inside is Sebastiano del Piombo's *Flagellation of Christ* in the first chapel on the right, but the true reason for stopping is in the adjacent courtyard, the now half-forgotten **Tempietto** of Bramante. In so many Renaissance paintings—Perugino's *Donation of the Keys* in the Sistine Chapel, or Raphael's well-known *Betrothal of the Virgin* in Milan—the characters in the foreground take second place in interest to an ethereal, round temple centred at the perspectival vanishing point. These constructions, seemingly built not of vulgar stone but of pure intelligence and light, could stand as a symbol for the aspirations of the Renaissance. Bramante was the first to try to actually build one; his perfect little Tempietto (1502), the first building to re-use the ancient Doric order in all of its proportions, probably inspired Raphael's painting two years later.

Further up the Janiculum, you'll come to the Garibaldi Monument, overlooking the Botanical Gardens. An even better monument nearby commemorates Mrs. Garibaldi, the remarkable Anita; she is shown here with a pistol in one hand, and a baby in the other. From here one street, the Viale delle Mura Aurelie, follows the outside of the wall as far as St Peter's. The other, the Passeggiata del Gianicolo, curves downwards into the Janiculum gardens, passing the Renaissance church of **Sant'Onofrio**, with frescoes by

Annibale Carracci and Antoniazzo Romano. After the descent, you'll pass out of Trastevere and into the Borgo district; the Passeggiata ends at the venerable hospital of Santo Spirito and its church of **Santo Spirito in Sassia**. Both these names may ring a bell for antiquarians. 'Sassia' refers to the Saxons of England, who immediately upon their conversion became among the most devoted servants of the Church. King Ina of Wessex founded this hospital sometime around 717—astounding enough when you think about it. The Angles and Saxons who settled in Rome made up almost a small village unto themselves at this bend of the Tiber, and their 'burgh' gave its name to the big neighbourhood called the Borgo today.

Castel Sant'Angelo

Though intended as a resting-place for a most serene emperor, this building has seen more blood, treachery, and turmoil than any in Rome. Hadrian, it seems, designed his own mausoleum three years before his death in 138, an eccentric plan consisting of a huge marble cylinder, surmounted by a conical hill planted with cypresses. The marble, the obelisks, the gold and bronze decorations did not survive the 6th-century sacks, but in about 590, during a plague, Pope Gregory the Great saw a vision of St Michael over the mausoleum, ostensibly announcing the end of the plague, but perhaps also mentioning discreetly that here, if anyone cared to use it, was the most valuable fortress in Europe.

There would be no papacy, perhaps, without this castle—at least not in its present form. Hadrian's great cylinder is high, steep, and almost solid—impregnable even after the invention of artillery. With rebellions of some sort occurring on average every two years before 1400, the popes often had recourse to this place of safety. It last saw action in the Sack of 1527, when the miserable Clement VII withstood a siege of several months while his city went up in flames around him. The popes also used Castel Sant'Angelo as a prison; famous inmates included Giordano Bruno, and Beatrice Cenci (better known to the English than to the Italians, thanks to Shelley's verse). In the castle today, you can study models of the castle's previous incarnations, then proceed up the original spiral ramp inside the stone cylinder to a small museum of arms and armour and the **Papal Apartments**, decorated as lavishly by 16th-century artists as anything in the Vatican. The most interesting rooms, like Clement VII's bathroom by Giulio Romano, are almost entirely done in grotesques and stucco, attempts to reproduce the decoration of a room in an ancient palace like Nero's Golden House. Just a floor below lie the dreadful **Historical Prisons**, where skeletons found just under the floor seem to confirm tales of prisoners murdered in the cells. Above everything, fans of Puccini's *Tosca* will at once recognize the mighty statue of Michael sheathing his sword, commemorating Pope Gregory's vision (open 9–1, Sun 9–12, Mon 2–6:30; adm).

Hadrian also built the **Ponte Sant'Angelo** (*Pons Aelius*) to link his tomb to the city, though two arches had to be added in the 19th century with the construction of the Tiber Embankment. For centuries it was decorated with gallows, until 1688, when Bernini's students carved its angels to his design. Whipped by a perpetual Baroque hurricane, they were at once dubbed 'Bernini's Breezy Maniacs'.

St Peter's Basilica

Along Borgo Sant'Angelo, leading towards the Vatican, you can see the famous **covered passageway**, used by the popes since 1277 to escape to the castle when things became dangerous. The customary route, however, leads up **Via della Conciliazione**, a broad boulevard laid out under Mussolini over a tangled web of medieval streets. Critics have said it spoils the surprise, but no arrangement of streets and buildings could really prepare you for Bernini's Brobdingnagian **Piazza San Pietro**. Someone has calculated there is room for about 300,000 people in the piazza, with no crowding. Few have ever noticed Bernini's little joke on antiquity; the open space almost exactly meets the size and dimensions of the Colosseum. Bernini's **Colonnade** (1656), with 284 massive columns and statues of 140 saints, stretches around it like 'the arms of the Church embracing the world'—perhaps the biggest cliché in Christendom by now, but exactly what Bernini had in mind. Stand on either of the two dark stones at the foci of the elliptical piazza, and you will see Bernini's forest of columns resolve into neat rows, a subtly impressive optical effect like the hole in the top of the Pantheon. Flanked by two lovely fountains (the one on the right by Carlo Maderno, the other a copy) the Vatican **obelisk** seems nothing special as obelisks go, but it is one of the most fantastical relics in all Rome. This obelisk comes from Heliopolis, the Egyptian city founded as a capital and cult centre by Ikhnaton, the half-legendary Pharaoh and religious reformer who, according to Sigmund Freud and others, founded the first monotheistic religion, influencing Moses and all that came after. It arrived here apparently by divine coincidence. Sixtus V brought it from the now-disappeared Circus Vaticanus built by Nero, where it overlooked Peter's martyrdom.

The original St Peter's, begun over the Apostle's tomb by Constantine in 324, may well have been a more interesting building, a richly decorated basilica full of gold and mosaics with a vast porch of marble and bronze in front and a lofty campanile, topped by the famous golden cockerel that everyone believed would some day crow to announce the end of the world. This St Peter's, where Charlemagne and Frederick II received their imperial crowns, was falling to pieces by the 1400s, conveniently in time for the popes and artists of the Renaissance to plan a replacement. Nicholas V, in about 1450, conceived an almost Neronian building programme for the Vatican, ten times as large as anything his ancestors could have contemplated. Still, nothing happened until Julius II, who owned perhaps the biggest papal ego of them all, realized that there was no room in old St Peter's for the tomb he commissioned from Michelangelo; Bramante was duly commissioned to demolish the old church and begin the new. His original plan called for a great dome over a centralized Greek cross. Michelangelo, who took over the work in 1546, basically agreed, and if he had had his way St Peter's might indeed have become the crowning achievement of Renaissance art that everyone hoped it would be.

Unfortunately, over the nearly 200 years of construction too many popes and too many artists got their hand in—Rossellino, Giuliano da Sangallo, Raphael, Antonio da Sangallo, Vignola, Ligorio, della Porta, Fontana, Bernini, and Maderno all contributed something to the tremendous hotchpotch we see today. The most substantial tinkering came in the early 1600s, when a committee of cardinals decided that a Latin cross was desired, a decision which resulted in the huge extension of the nave that blocks the view of Michelangelo's dome from the piazza. Baroque architects, mistaking size and virtuosity for art, found perfect patrons in the Baroque popes, less interested in faith than in the power and majesty of the papacy. Passing though Maderno's gigantic façade seems like entering a Grand Central Station full of stone saints and angels, keeping an eye on the big clocks overhead as they wait for trains to Paradise. Pause, though, in the portico, which contains some of St Peter's finest art—the doors, especially the central ones by Tuscan sculptor Antonio Filarete (1439–45), depicting the ecumenical council of 1441, which attempted to unite the Eastern and Western churches; the doors to the left, by Giacomo Manzù (1963) feature harrowing scenes of martyrdoms, though on the back he refers to his friend Pope John XXIII's Second Ecumenical Council. Opposite, in the tympanum over the main entrance, is Giotto's much restored mosaic of the *Navicella*; on the right is Bernini's dramatic equestrian statue of *Constantine*, showing the emperor starting at a vision of the cross.

Inside, all along the nave, markers showing the length of other proud cathedrals prove how each fails miserably to measure up to the Biggest Church in the World—though this being Rome, they aren't very accurate. The best work of art is right in front, to the right; Michelangelo's *Pietà*, now restored and kept behind glass to protect it from future madmen. The work, done when he was only twenty-five, helped make Michelangelo's reputation. Its smooth and elegant figures, with the realities of death and grief sublimated onto some ethereal plane known only to saints and artists, made a turning point in religious art. From here the beautiful, unreal art of the religious Baroque was the logical next step. Note how Michelangelo has carved his name in small letters on the band around the Virgin's garment; he added this after overhearing a group of tourists from Milan who thought the *Pietà* the work of a fellow Milanese.

Not much else in St Peter's stands out. In its vast spaces scores of popes and saints are remembered in assembly-line Baroque, and the paintings over most of the altars have been replaced by mosaic copies. Stealing the show, just as he knew it would, is Bernini's great, garish **baldachin** over the high altar, cast out of bronze looted from the Pantheon roof (though some scholars today doubt this). From the moment you enter the basilica, it draws your attention back to the radiant **Tribune**, also by Bernini, which encases St Peter's chair in hyper-Baroque theatrics. The Confessio in front of the baldachin is perpetually lit by 95 lamps; just below it is the ancient necropolis holding the presumed relics of St Peter (see below). The four mighty piers supporting the dome are adorned with mastodonic saints; seated by the pier of St Longinus (also by Bernini) is a much venerated bronze, seated statue of St Peter (perhaps from the 5th century, or the 13th), its foot worn away by the kisses of the faithful.

Many visitors head straight for Michelangelo's **dome** (entrance just before the right transept, daily Oct–April 8–4:45, until 6 in the summer; adm and additional fare for the elevator halfway to the top). To be in the middle of such a spectacular construction is worth the climb itself. You can walk out on the roof for a view over Rome, but even more startling is the chance to look down from the interior balcony over the vast church 53 m below; an even loftier balcony is closed to the public. In the left aisle, the Sacristy, built in the 18th century, contains **St Peter's Treasure** (9–5:45; adm), at least the treasure that the Saracens, the imperial soldiers of 1527, and Napoleon couldn't steal. The ancient bronze cockerel from the old St Peter's is kept here, along with relics like a cross donated by Justin II in 578 and the twisted Colonna Santa, a Baroque extravaganza, and a gown that may have belonged to Charlemagne. Perhaps the greatest work of art here is the bronze tomb of Sixtus IV, a definitive Renaissance confection by Antonio Pollaiuolo (1493).

Do not pass up a visit to the crypt, or **Sacred Grottoes,** the foundation of the earlier St Peter's converted into a crypt. Dozens of popes are buried here, along with distinguished friends of the Church like Queen Christina of Sweden and James III, the Stuart Pretender, though the most visited is undoubtedly the simple monument to John XXIII. Underneath the Grottoes lies the **ancient Roman necropolis,** secretly excavated during World War II; this road of remarkably well-preserved tombs of AD 150–300, was used by both pagans and Christians, the latter buried as close to St Peter as possible. Decorated with paintings or mosaics—including one representing Christ as the sun god, the fragile condition of the tombs dictates that only 15 people at a time can visit the necropolis (see 'Vatican Practicalities', below).

The Vatican Museums

The admission (currently L8000) may be the most expensive in Italy, but for that you get about ten museums in one, with the Sistine Chapel and the Raphael rooms thrown in free. Altogether almost 7 km of exhibits fill the halls of the Vatican Palace, and unfortunately for you there isn't much dull museum clutter that can be passed over lightly. Seeing this infinite, exasperating hoard properly would be the work of a lifetime. On the bright side, the pope sees to it that his museum is managed more intelligently and thoughtfully than anything run by the Italian state (the contrast with the shabby National Museum in Diocletian's Baths is striking). A choice of colour-coded itineraries, which you may follow according to the amount of time you have to spend, will get you through the labyrinth in 90 minutes or five hours.

Near the entrance (with a Vatican Post Office branch), the first big challenge is the large **Egyptian Museum,** with authentic Egyptian items and Roman imitations made for Hadrian's villa at Tivoli, followed by the **Chiaramonti Museum,** full of Roman statuary and reliefs and endless rows of busts of Caesar, Mark Antony, and Augustus and seemingly every Roman before and after. The **Pio Clementino Museum** contains some of the best-known statues of antiquity; the dramatic *Laocoön,* dug up in Nero's Golden House, and mentioned in the works of many classical authors, and the *Apollo Belvedere.* No other ancient works recovered during the Renaissance had a greater influence on sculptors than these two. A 'room of animals' captures the more fanciful side of antiquity and the 18th-century taste of Pope Pius VI. The plaster and bronze papal fig leaves that protect the modesty of hundreds of nude statues are a good joke at first—later you'll see the Damned in Michelangelo's *Last Judgement,* wearing the britches ordered by Pius IV the year Michelangelo died.

The best things in the **Etruscan Museum** are Greek, a truly excellent collection of vases imported by discriminating Etruscan nobles that includes the famous, often reproduced picture of *Oedipus and the Sphinx.* Beyond that, there is a hall hung with tapestries designed by Raphael's 'New School' (16th century), and the long, long **Map Room,** lined with carefully painted town views and maps of every corner of Italy; note the long scene of the 1566 Great Siege of Malta at the entrance. Anywhere else, with no Michelangelos to offer competition, Raphael's celebrated frescoes in the **Stanze di Raffaello** would have been the prime destination on anyone's itinerary. The *School of Athens* in the Stanza della Segnatura is too well known to require much of an introduction, but here is a guide to some of the figures: on Aristotle's side, Archimedes and

Euclid surrounded by their disciples (Euclid, drawing plane figures on a slate, is supposedly a portrait of Bramante); off to the right, Ptolemy and Zoroaster hold the terrestrial and celestial globes. Raphael includes himself among the Aristotelians, standing between Zoroaster and the painter Il Sodoma. Behind Plato stand Socrates and Alcibiades, among others, and to the left, Zeno and Epicurus. In the foreground, a crouching Pythagoras writes while Empedocles and the Arab Averroes look on. Diogenes sprawls philosophically on the steps, while isolated near the front is Heraclitus—really Michelangelo, according to legend; Raphael put him in at the last minute after seeing the work in progress on the Sistine Chapel.

Across from this apotheosis of philosophy, Raphael painted a Triumph of Theology to keep the clerics happy, the *Dispute of the Holy Sacrament*. The other frescoes include the *Parnassus*, a vision of the ancient Greek and Latin poets; the *Miracle of Bolsena*; the *Chastisement of Heliodorus*, an allegory of the triumphs of the Counter-Reformation papacy; the *Meeting of Leo I and Attila*; and best of all, the solemn, spectacular *Liberation of St Peter*. Nearby, scholars with prior permission can visit the so-called **Loggie of Raphael**, designed by Bramante and decorated with designs and grotesques by Raphael (but executed by other artists). You can compare the Stanze with the efforts of earlier artists: the **Chapel of Nicholas V**, covered with charming, ethereal frescoes (*Lives of SS. Stephen and Lawrence*) by Fra Angelico, and just downstairs, the luxurious **Borgia Apartment**, built for Pope Alexander VI, with frescoes with saints, myths and sibyls by Pinturicchio (1492–95). These run into the **Gallery of Modern Religious Art**, a game attempt by the Vatican to prove that such a thing really exists (and perhaps it does, most convincingly in Charles Burchfield's *Eye of God in the Woods*, the most spiritual work by the master from Buffalo, considered by many to be the greatest American painter).

The Sistine Chapel

To the sophisticated Sixtus IV, building this ungainly barn of a chapel may have seemed a mistake in the first place. When the pushy, despotic Julius II sent Michelangelo, against his will, up to paint the vast ceiling, it might have turned out to be a project as hopeless as the tomb Julius had already commissioned. Michelangelo spent four years (1508–12) on his back to get it done. No one can say, though, what drove him to turn his surly patron's whim into a masterpiece: the fear of wasting those years, the challenge of an impossible task, or maybe just to spite Julius—he exasperated the pope by making him wait, and refused all demands that he hire some assistants. Everywhere on the Sistine ceilings you will note the austere blankness of the backgrounds. Michelangelo always eschewed stage props; one of the tenets of his art was that complex ideas could be expressed in the portrayal of the human body alone. With sculpture, that takes time. Perhaps the inspiration that kept Michelangelo on the ceiling so long was the chance of distilling out of the Book of Genesis and his own genius an entirely new vocabulary of images, Christian and intellectual. Like most Renaissance patrons, Julius asked for nothing more than virtuoso interior decoration. What he got was nothing like simple illustrations from scripture; this is the way the Old Testament looks in the deepest recesses of the imagination.

The fascination of the Sistine ceiling, and the equally compelling **Last Judgement** on the rear wall, done much later (1534–41), is that while we may recognize the individual figures we still have not captured their secret meanings. Hordes of tourists stare up at the heroic Adam, the mysterious *ignudi* in the corners, the Russian masseuse sibyls with their longshoremen's arms, the six-toed prophets, the strange vision of Noah's deluge. They wonder what they're looking at, a question that would take years of inspired wondering to answer. Mostly they direct their attention to the all too famous scene of the Creation, with perhaps the only representation of God the Father ever painted that escapes being merely ridiculous. One might suspect that the figure is really some ageing Florentine artist, and that Michelangelo only forgot to paint the brush in his hand.

At the time of writing, the controversial restorations on the ceiling have been finished and work has begun on the Last Judgement. Despite a recent chorus of protest from some fashionable artists, there seems to be a consensus that the work is accurately revealing Michelangelo's true colours—jarring, surprise colours that no interior decorator would ever choose, plenty of sea-green, with splashes of yellow and purple and dramatic shadows. No new paint is being applied, only solvents to clear off the grime. They hope to be finished by 1992. Most visitors overlook the earlier frescoes on the lower walls, great works of art that would make the Sistine Chapel famous by themselves: scenes from the *Exodus* by Botticelli, Perugino's *Donation of the Keys*, and Signorelli's *Moses Consigning his Staff to Joshua*.

More Miles in the Big Museum
There's still more: the **Museum of Christian Art**, with art from the catacombs, including the oldest known portrait of SS. Peter and Paul, up to the Byzantine era. Here, too, are pagan Roman frescoes, from Ostia and the famous 1st-century AD *Aldobrandini Marriage*, found on the Esquiline. Beyond is the vast **Vatican Library**, with its endless halls and precious manuscripts tucked neatly away in cabinets. The brightly painted rooms contain every sort of oddity; thousands of reliquaries and an entire wall of monstrances, a memorable collection of medieval ivories, gold-glass medallions from the catacombs, every sort of globe, orrery and astronomical instrument. If you survive this, the next hurdle is the **Braccio Nuovo** (a disjointed arm of the Chiaramonti Gallery), with more classical sculpture: here is the finest imperial statue of them all, *Augustus of the Prima Porta*, while the 2nd century Roman Baroque tendency comes out clearly in a giant group called *The Nile*, complete with sphinxes and crocodiles—it came from a Roman temple of Isis. Near the Vatican cafeteria is the new and beautifully laid out **Museo Gregoriano**, with a hoard of excellent classical statuary, mosaics, and inscriptions collected by Pope Gregory XVI. Then comes a **Carriage Museum**, the **Pio Cristiano Museum** of early Christian art, finally one of the most interesting of all, though no one has time for it: the **Ethnological Museum** with wonderful art from peoples of every continent, brought home by Catholic missionaries over the centuries.

By itself, the Vatican **Pinacoteca** would be by far the finest picture gallery in Rome, a representive sampling of Renaissance art from its beginnings, with works by Giotto (*Stefaneschi Triptych*) and contemporary Sienese painters, as well as Gentile da Fabriano, Daddi, and Filippo Lippi. Don't overlook the tiny but electrically surreal masterpiece of Fra Angelico, the *Story of St Nicolas at Bari*, or the *Angelic Musicians* fresco fragments of Melozzo da Forli set next to Melozzo's famous painting of Platina being nominated by Sixtus IV to head the Vatican Library—a rare snapshot of Renaissance humanism. From the same period, Leonardo da Vinci's *St Jerome* is that artist's only work in Rome. Venetian artists are not well represented, but there's a pair of Titians, a lovely *Pietà* by

128

Giovanni Bellini and another by the fastidious Carlo Crivelli. Perhaps one of the best-known paintings is the recently restored *Transfiguration of Christ*, Raphael's last work, laid in grief over his funeral bier.

Vatican Practicalities

The **museums** are open daily from 9–2 pm (last admission at 1 pm) and from 9–5 during Holy Week and in the months of July, August, and September. They are closed on Sundays, except the last Sunday of each month (9–2) when admission is free (and the crowds the worst). Note that the entrance is rather far from St Peter's Square, to the north on Viale Vaticano, close to the Metro A: Ottaviano station. St Peter's is open 7–7 pm; there may be a Mass going on somewhere in the vast church, but visitors are never excluded. The papal gendarmes, however, will certainly give you the bum's rush if you don't meet the dress code—no shorts, short skirts, or sleeveless dresses.

The **Vatican Information Office** in St Peter's Square is very helpful, and is the place to sign up for three-hour-long morning tours of the extensive **Vatican Gardens**, easily Rome's most beautiful park, with a remarkable Renaissance jewel of a villa inside, the **Casina of Pius IV** by Pirro Ligorio and Peruzzi (1558–62). For tours (in English) of the **Roman Necropolis**, sign up at the Uffizi degli Scavi, entered through the gateway just to the left of the basilica; if you're coming in the busy spring or summer, write to them to book a place (stating the date, number of your party, etc—and confirm your reservation). The rest of the Vatican is strictly off limits, patrolled by genuine Swiss Guards (still recruited from the three Catholic Swiss Cantons, though now usually lacking the fancy uniforms Michelangelo—or some say Raphael—designed for them).

Michelangelo also designed the **defensive wall** that since 1929 has marked the Vatican boundaries. Behind them are things most of us will never see: a train station, several small old churches, a printing press, the headquarters of *L'Osservatore Romano* and Vatican Radio (run, of course, by the Jesuits), a motor garage, a 'Palazzo di Giustizia' and prison, even a big shop—everything the world's smallest nation could ever need. Modern popes, in glaring contrast to their predecessors, do not take up much space. The current Papal Apartments are in a corner of the Vatican Palace overlooking Piazza San Pietro; John Paul II usually appears to say a few electrically amplified words from his window at noon on Sundays. For tickets to the 11 am Wednesday **papal audiences**, apply at the Papal Prefecture—through the Bronze Door in the right-hand colonnade of Piazza San Pietro (open Tues–Wed 9–1), or write no more than a month ahead (Prefettura della Casa Pontificia, 00120, Città del Vaticano), with your address in Rome. These large affairs are relatively easy to get into; private audiences are of course much harder.

Peripheral Attractions of Rome

There are plenty of interesting things on the city's outskirts; here is a brief review, tracing a clockwise circle around Rome from the north. Near the Tiber, the **Foro Italico** was certainly Mussolini's most blatant monument to himself; he left his mark everywhere, on a giant obelisk, in the paving stones, and around the kitschy grandiose **Marble Stadium**, chiselled too deep ever to be worn away. The adjacent sports complex housed the 1960 Olympics. Across the Tiber, on Via Salario, **Villa Ada** once served as the hunting reserve of Vittorio Emanuele III; now a huge city park (though one section serves as the Egyptian Embassy), it contains the entrance to the **Catacombs of Priscilla** with 2nd-century frescoes and the tombs of many early Popes and martyrs (daily, except Mon, 8:30–12 and 2:30–5; in summer until 6; adm).

Via XX Settembre, the important thoroughfare coming off the Quirinal Hill, passes the Aurelian Wall at **Porta Pia**, redesigned by Michelangelo. Here it changes its name to Via Nomentana, a chic boulevard where many of the old villas have not yet been swallowed by creeping urbanization (take bus 36 from Termini station). A kilometre or so east, you can make a stop at the thoroughly charming complex of **Sant'Agnese Outside the Walls**, including a 4th-century church with a beautiful early mosaic of St Agnes in the apse and 15 ancient marble columns. All around the rear of the church and sacristy, early Christian reliefs and inscriptions have been arranged as in a museum; nearby is the entrance to the small, aristocratic **catacombs** (3rd century), absorbing parts of earlier pagan catacombs (same hours as Catacombs of Priscilla). Around the back, through gardens where the neighbourhood children play, stands one of Rome's least known but most remarkable churches. **Santa Costanza** was built as a mausoleum for Constantia, daughter of Emperor Constantine. In this domed, circular building, one of the finest late Roman works, more than anywhere else you can see the great religious turning-point of the 4th century come alive; among the exquisite mosaics (regrettably not all have survived) are scenes of Christ and the Apostles, as well as scenes of a grape harvest and motifs that would be familiar to any ancient devotee of Dionysos or Bacchus.

At the end of Viale Regina Elena, tucked between the University City and the enormous Verano Cemetery, **San Lorenzo** is another of the Seven Churches on a Roman pilgrim's itinerary. The original basilica, begun under Constantine, was so popular that in the early 13th century it was linked to a neighbouring church, which accounts for its unique interior, containing some fine work of the Cosmati family around the altar and a 6th-century mosaic in the Triumphal Arch. From here you can re-enter the city through the impressive **Porta Maggiore**, built under Emperor Claudius; note how this section of the wall carries one of the ancient aqueducts on top. The real attraction, however, lies almost directly under the tracks going into Termini Station. The **Underground Basilica**, discovered only in 1916 near Porta Maggiore, was not covered up by the centuries like so many other Roman relics—it was built that way for a secret, possibly illegal, religious sect in the 1st century AD. Its stucco reliefs are fascinating and strange; scholars can't guess anything about the cult's beliefs, but venture to call it 'neo-Pythagorean' (under restoration at least until 1991, but you can call the Soprintendenza Archeologica di Roma, Piazza delle Finanze 1, tel 475 0181–2 and they *might* let you in). Up the tracks towards the station you can see the **Temple of Minerva Medica** on Via Giolitti, a ten-sided brick ruin from the 4th century AD, actually believed to be the nymphaeum in a patrician's garden. From Piazza Maggiore, Via Eleniana leads to **Santa Croce in Gerusalemme**, another of the 'Seven Churches', founded by Constantine's mother, St Helena, though given a striking convex Rococo façade and mostly Baroque interior; head down to the **Chapel of St Helen** (steps in the right aisle), to see the mosaics by Melozzo da Forli and a statue of St Helena, derived from a figure of Juno found in Ostia.

Jumping all the way over to the western edge of Rome, behind the Janiculum, **Villa Doria Pamphili** is an enormous old estate, recently bought by the city, and its beautiful parks opened to the public.

ACTIVITIES

The best entertainment in Rome is often in the passing cosmopolitan spectacle of its streets; as nightlife goes, the capital can be a real snoozer. Even if you pinpoint the current 'in' spots of the hour you may not have much of a good time; lots of ultra-chic posturing by glamorous Romans is about all. If you're determined, prowl the alleys and back-streets around Piazza Navona or the funkier Campo dei Fiori and see what's cooking. Two favourite places are the **Bar della Pace**, in Via della Pace near Piazza Navona, or the jovial and often crowded wine bar in Campo dei Fiori. During your wanderings you can judge who serves the best *cappuccino* in town, at Sant'Eustachio, Piazza Sant'Eustachio or **Tazza d'Oro**, Via degli Orfani 84; at both, ask for it *amaro* (no sugar) if you don't want it with three spoons of sugar, like the Italians do. Or try a famous Roman/Jewish cheesecake, *torta di ricotta*, at **La Deliziosa**, Vicolo Savelli 48/50.

Buy a copy of *La Repubblica*, especially on Saturdays, for the weekly supplement *Trovaroma*, to hunt up some music or a film. The tourist offices put out a monthly four-language calendar as well, called the *Carnet di Roma*; watch for posters. Another source of listings is the English-language classifieds paper *Wanted in Rome*, available at the English bookshops.

One activity Rome is usually good for is music in all forms, although the city has become notoriously lax in getting it together for special events in the summer. One of Mussolini's most enduring legacies is the Cecil B. De Millesque **summer opera** performances in the Terme di Caracalla, in July and August, put on by Rome's Opera Theatre. Ticket prices are reasonable (around L25 000), and you can pick them up at the opera box office on Piazza Beniamino Gigli, near Via Nazionale, tel 575 8300 for information. For other summer music, you may want to do as the Romans do and head out to Umbria for the Spoleto Festival or the Umbrian Jazz Festival, or fight it out for a ticket to one of the big-name rock concerts at Stadio Flaminio or PalaEUR (EUR's Palazzo dello Sport), neither of which wins any blue ribbons. Even more cacophonous is the **Festa dei Noantri** in Trastevere (16–31 July), where you may well find a gust of old Roman spontaneity along with music from across the spectrum, acrobats, dancing, etc., spread out all over the quarter's piazzas.

From November until May you can take in a performance at the excellent **Teatro dell'Opera di Roma** (Via del Viminale, tel 463 641; tickets on sale two days before each performance). Classical music, John Cage, ballet, Sunday concerts, etc. are on tap at the **Teatro dell'Opera al Brancaccio**. Other serious concerts and chamber music are performed at and by the **Accademia Nazionale di Santa Cecilia** in the auditorium on Via della Conciliazione 4 (tel 654 1044); and by the **Filarmonica Romana** at the Teatro Olimpico, Piazza Gentile da Fabriano (tel 360 1752). There are Sunday 'Aperitivo' concerts at 10:30 am sponsored by Italcable in the Teatro Sistina (Via Sistina 129, tel 4770 4664), concerts performed by the RAI Orchestra at the Auditorium in the Foro Italico every Saturday in season at 9 pm (tel 368 65625). Medieval music, Baroque music, chamber music and choral music are frequently performed at the **Oratorio del Gonfalone**, Vicolo della Scimmia, near Via del Gonfalone (tel 687 5952). If you want to go to any concerts in Rome, try to get tickets as soon as possible to avoid disappointment.

Rome also has several clubs, with music almost every night—listings are available daily in *La Repubblica* for places like Trastevere's **Folkstudio**, Via Gaetano Sacchi 3, tel 589

2374 (closed in the summer); **Music Inn**, Lungotevere dei Fiorentini 3, tel 654 4934; **Big Mama**, Vicolo San Francesca a Ripa 18, tel 582 551; or **Alexanderplatz**, Via Ostia 9, tel 359 9398, all of which have foreign as well as Italian performers. Romans of late have evolved a made-in-Rome swing cult—to hear what it's all about, check out **Saint Louis Music City**, Via del Cardello 13a, tel 474 5076.

Rome is not the best place to find films in English. **Pasquino**, on Vicolo del Piede near Piazza Santa Maria in Trastevere (tel 580 3622), shows a different English-language film every few days. **Cinema clubs** also frequently show films in the original; it will say so in the listings.

Much of monumental Rome is illuminated at night, and strolling through the city then is a unique pleasure (though mugging statistics suggest you don't wander too far from the crowds. For even bigger, brightly lit thrills, head out to the **LunEur Park**, with its rickety old-fashioned roller-coaster, huge Ferris wheel and over 100 attractions. More bright lights attract visiting moths in the fountains and gardens of Tivoli's Villa d'Este, lit four nights a week 8:30–11:30 pm, May–Sept.

SHOPPING

Rome on the whole isn't as exciting for big-game shoppers as Milan, though the Roman shops are as well designed, just as enticing, and quite expensive. Rome is also the capital of Italian *haute couture*, made-to-order clothes designed for a tiny proportion of the buying public. It is also a good city for antiques, and it's easy enough to have a look at what's available because all the shops are clustered together between the Tiber and Piazza Navona; look especially off Via Monserrato, Via dei Coronari, and Via dell'Anima—for antique clothes try **Perchè No?**, Via Piscinula 27; for antique jewellery (from the '20s), **Oximoron**, Via Monserrato 122a; for art nouveau, **1900 Art Nouveau**, Via Vittoria 37 or **L'Art Nouveau**, Via dei Coronari 221. High-calibre antique shops line Via del Babuino; funkier antiques also occasionally show up in Rome's large and celebrated Sunday **Flea Market** at Porta Portese, as well as anything else you can imagine, all lumped together in often surreal displays. It lasts from dawn and closes abruptly at 1 pm; beware! pickpockets are not unknown here. For clothes, most Romans head out to the Monday through Saturday morning **market in Via Sannio**, just outside the gate of Piazza S. Giovanni in Laterano; this is also the address of **COIN**, the best department store for clothes, or peruse the rather more staid offerings on the six floors of **La Rinascente**, in Piazza Colonna.

The most **fashionable shopping** is in the old 'English ghetto', around Piazza di Spagna. In spring and autumn there are outdoor art exhibitions along Via Margutta, and a daily print, book, and postcard market in Largo Fontanella Borghese. You'll find the chic and elegant boutiques of Italy's traditional and trendy designers (Gucci, Fendi, Missoni, Armani, Krizia, Versace, etc.) along Vie Condotti, Frattini, Vite, Bocca di Leone, Borgognona, and della Croce, and up at the top of the steps around Via Sistina. Some special items: handtailored shirts and suits, at **Battistoni**, Via Condotti 61; handmade shawls and clocks, at **Miranda**, Via Bocca di Leone 28; candles and imaginative kitchen gear at **Spazio Sette**, Via dei Barbieri 7; or visit the dressmakers of the stars since the 1930s, the **Sorelle Fontana**, Via San Sebastianello, just off Piazza di Spagna; or Italy's most palatial jewellery shop, **Bulgari**, Via Condotti 11; for art supplies, paper, stationery, **Vertecchi**, Via della Croce 70a; for Hollywood glamour on your feet,

Beltrami, Via Condotti 19; or stop at Rome's most dignified wineshop, **Enoteca Isabelli**, Via della Croce 76, for a bottle or glass of wine. When you're tired of window-shopping, you can rest your dogs at Rome's oldest and most beautiful café, the **Antico Caffè Greco**, founded in the early 1700s at Via Condotti 86, and fantasize that you are sitting in Keats' favourite corner.

Elsewhere in Rome—for the world's best hats, **Borsalino**, Via IV Novembre 157b. For costumes for your next film or carnival, there's **Tirelli**, Visconti's favourite, at Via Alessandro Farnese 14a; or **Ferroni**, used by Rossellini and many other directors, at Via Arco della Pace 6. For toys, the most imaginative, for all ages, may be found at **Città del Sole** (two addresses: Via della Scrofa at Largo Toniolo or on the Corso, next to the Chiesa Nuova); for homemade chocolates, **Confetteria Moriondo e Garaglio**, Via della Pilotta 2; for a wide range of products from Italy's monasteries, **Ai Monasteri**, on the north end of Corso del Rinascimento; for prints of Rome, **Casali**, Piazza Firenze.

If you need a good read in Rome, try the **Anglo-American Bookshop**, Via della Vite 57; or the **Lion Bookshop**, Via del Babuino 181; or **Economy Bookshop**, Via Torino 136, near Via Nazionale.

WHERE TO STAY (tel prefix 06)

For a city that has been entertaining crowds of visitors for the last 2000 years, Rome does not seem to have acquired any special flair for accommodating them. Hotels here are neither better nor worse than anywhere else in Italy; from Belle Epoque palaces on Via Vittorio Veneto to grimy hovels on the wrong side of Termini Station, there will be something for you to come home to after a hard day's sightseeing. Rome is short on anything really distinctive: places with a history, a famous view, or quiet gardens to shut out the city noise. Exceptions have been found, of course, but all things considered this is not the place to make the big splurge. Check into some modest, comfortable spot in the area that suits your fancy, and save your hotel money for the Amalfi Drive.

Any of the city tourist offices will help you find a place, but in the summer months, when tourists are queued up to the door and beyond, you may prefer to try your own luck. The further you get from Termini station the happier you'll be; old Rome, around Piazza Navona and Campo dei Fiori is the cosiest and least bedevilled by traffic noise.

Around the Spanish Steps: This area has been a favoured spot since the 1700s, especially with the British. Two of Rome's best hotels share a fine location at the top of the stairs, with a view over the city for the fortunate ones who book far enough in advance: the *******Villa Medici-Hassler**, around for over a century, seems to have regained its position as the elite hotel of Rome; it offers a garage and a beautiful garden courtyard, deferential service, and large wood-panelled rooms. Of course it is also one of the city's most expensive: L450–510 000 for a double room. (Piazza Trinità dei Monti 6, tel 678 2651.) If you don't have that kind of money to throw around, you can do just as well down the block at the *****Gregoriana**, a small, tasteful and gratifyingly friendly place that has accumulated a devoted regular clientele—there are only 19 rooms, so book early. Air-conditioned doubles go for L65–115 000 (Via Gregoriana 18, tel 679 4269).

A third favourite in this area, convenient for the deluxe shopping around Via Condotti, is the ******D'Inghilterra**, Via Bocca di Leone 14, tel 672 161. Parts of this building date from the 15th century, when it served as a prince's guest house; in its career as a hotel, since 1850, it has played host to most of the literati and artists of Europe and America.

Recent restorations have left it looking more palatial than ever (L320–350 000). Around the corner, almost at the foot of the Spanish Steps, the ***Carriage at Via delle Carrozze 36, tel 679 3152, is a quiet but well-run place; L135 000, air conditioning available. The ***Fontana would be a good hotel anywhere, but its unique amenity is a location right across the street from the Trevi Fountain—something to look at out of your window at night that will guarantee nice dreams (Piazza di Trevi 96, tel 678 6113; L100 000). More modest choices in the neighbourhood are also in high demand and need to be booked early: **Forte, Via Margutta 61, tel 678 6109, is one of the quietest, around the corner from the Steps (L40–68 000 without bath, L50–90 000 with). *Erdarelli, Via Due Macelli 28, tel 679 1265, is very comfortable for a one-star-hotel (L35–65 000 without bath, L42–75 000 with); also try *Fiorella, Via del Babuino 196, tel 361 0597, simple, with only 8 rooms, so book very early (L32–38 000, all without bath).

Around Via Vittorio Veneto: This, too, is a choice area, though lacking the aura of glamour it had in the '50s. Nowadays the marble-frosted façades of the 1900s conceal packs of well-heeled package tourists and businessmen on expense accounts. Still, if you can spare L340–620 000 for a good night's sleep, the *****Excelsior, vintage 1911, will prove an experience. The reception areas have thicker carpets, bigger chandeliers and more gilded plaster than anywhere in Italy, and most of the rooms are just as good—don't let them give you one of the modernized ones. There are saunas, boutiques, a famous bar, and as much personal attention as you could ask for (Via Veneto 125, tel 47 08; L340–620 000). There are quite a few other Grand Hotels in the area, with slightly lower prices and smaller chandeliers. More modest places can be found on the sidestreets; among them the ***La Residenza stands out (Via Emilia 22, tel 460 789), a very pleasant base for a visit to Rome, with beautifully appointed rooms in an old town house and some luxuries more common in the most expensive hotels (L120–130 000; some cheaper without bath).

In Old Rome: Anyone serious about experiencing this city at its best should consider spending some time in its oldest and most convivial neighbourhoods; unfortunately, there is not a wide choice of hotels. The only real luxury establishment near the ancient Forum is called, not surprisingly, the ****Forum, a dignified and somewhat old-fashioned hotel, with a unique view over the ruins from the rooftop bar and restaurant (Via Tor de' Conti 25, tel 679 2446; L250–320 000 for discreetly elegant rooms with air conditioning and TV). The **Nerva, just down the street, has plain but comfortable rooms for L72 000, L85 000 with bath (Via Tor de' Conti 3, tel 679 3764).

Hotels around Piazza Navona and the Pantheon tend to be less expensive; an exception is the ****Cardinal, at Via Giulia 62, tel 654 2719, perhaps the best place to experience Renaissance Rome in style—in a building attributed to Bramante, though completely restored inside (air-conditioning does not really spoil the atmosphere; L170 000). Another charming choice, ****Raphael, Largo di Febo 2, tel 650 881, is very close to Piazza Navona, covered with vines and filled with antiques (and often politicians); beautiful air conditioned rooms for L220–250 000. For some peace and quiet, in comfortable middle-range lodgings in the middle of Rome, the **Due Torre is a rare find—at Vicolo del Leonetto 23, an old alley north of Piazza Navona close to the Tiber (tel 654 0956). Doubles go for L70–77 000 with bath (it even has a garage). The next choice in this range is the **Rinascimento, Via del Pellegrino 122, just west of

134

Campo dei Fiori, tel 654 1886 (some very nice rooms; L89 000, all with bath). Campo dei Fiori is also the area to look for inexpensive rooms if you want to escape staying around Termini Station. The large, old *Sole, built on the foundations of Pompey's theatre, has lots of character, as it should, just off the market-place at Via del Biscione 76, tel 654 0873 (L56–60 000 with bath, L40–47 000 without; it also has a garage). Also near Campo dei Fiori, there's the *Piccolo on Via dei Chiavari, tel 654 2560 (L38 000 without bath), and near Piazza Navona, the *Navona, Via dei Sediari 8, tel 654 3802 (L40 000 without bath, L50 000 with). The **Abruzzi is a little more expensive, at L50–60 000 for rooms without bath, but compensates with a view of the Pantheon right across the square (Piazza della Rotonda 69, tel 679 2021).

Around Termini Station: In the 1890s, when this district was the newest and choicest part of Rome, the streets around the station spawned hundreds of hotels, some quite elegant. Today the majority of the city's accommodation is still here. Unfortunately, it has gone the way of all such 19th-century toadstool neighbourhoods: overbuilt, dingy and down-at-heel, not at all the place to savour the real Rome. It's also inconvenient for most of the sights.

This area is good for the really inexpensive hotels; there is such a wide choice you'll be able to find a place even when the city is at its most crowded. These range from plain, family-run establishments, often quite comfortable and friendly, to bizarre dives with exposed plumbing run by Sudanese and Sri Lankans for the benefit of visiting countrymen. A couple of places do their best to ignore their surroundings: ****Massimo D'Azeglio, Via Cavour 18, tel 460 646, a grand hotel in the old mould, built in 1875 (L130–260 000) and the ***Villa delle Rose, Via Vicenza 5, tel 495 1788, with 29 rooms in a former villa (L75 000 without bath, L100 000 with). Via Principe Amedeo is a good place to look, particularly at No 76, a big building with a pretty courtyard that houses about eight old pensioni. Try the *Licia (tel 475 5293; L36 000 without bath), though any of the others will be acceptable. Other blocks with a choice of places are Nos 62, 82, and 79, this last including the *Tony, tel 736 994 (L35–45 000 without bath, L45–58 000 with).

Near the Vatican: Surprisingly, there isn't a wide choice around the Vatican. The most modern and comfortable, with a great roof garden, is the ****Atlante Star, Via Vitelleschi 34, tel 687 9558, where air-conditioned rooms are L240–350 000. The ***Columbus at Via della Conciliazione 33, tel 656 5435, is a somewhat staid but reliable place frequented by visiting cardinals, with nice rooms and views over St Peter's from some of them (a little expensive at L78–88 000 without bath, L130–140 000 with). *Alimandi, near the Vatican Museums at Via Tunisi 8, tel 679 9343, is perhaps the most convenient bargain (L45 000, L55 000 with bath).

Elsewhere in Rome: If you don't mind long trips to the city centre, there are some good hotels in outlying districts, some in old villas with gardens and some room to stretch out. Near the Porta Pia and the British Embassy, the ***Villa Florence at Via Nomentana 28 is one of these, a 19th-century estate thoroughly restored inside. Very well run and friendly (tel 844 2841; L85–150 000; only a few of the less expensive rooms). Much the same, only a better bargain, the ***Villa del Parco, Via Nomentana 110, tel 864 115 (L94 000; most rooms air-conditioned). The quiet villa hotels on the Aventine are closer to the action, and parking usually isn't a problem: try ***Sant'Anselmo, Piazza Sant'Anselmo 2, tel 574 3547, with a garden (L77–95 000 without bath, L98–135 000) or **Aventino, Via S. Domenico 10, tel 575 5231 (L50–70 000, all with bath). Rome's youth hostel, **Ostello del Foro Italico**, is inconveniently located in one of Mussolini's dreamlands, at Viale delle Olimpiadi 61, tel 396 4709; from Termini station, take bus 492 to Piazza del Risorgimento, and then bus 32 to the Foro Italico; L14 000 a night with breakfast.

EATING OUT

Unlike many other Italians, the Romans aren't afraid to try something new. Lately, for example, Chinese restaurants have been appearing in numbers that culinary conservatives find alarming, not to mention Arab, Korean and macrobiotic places and the occasional hamburger stand. This should not be taken as a reflection on local cooking. Rome attracts talented chefs from all over Italy, and every region is represented by a typical restaurant somewhere in town, a microcosm of Italian cuisine you'll find nowhere else.

Of course, there is also a grand old tradition of Roman cooking, on the whole featuring dishes prepared with ingredients fresh from the Roman campagna; many dishes, especially in the pastry department, were adopted from the Jews. Among the specialities are *saltimbocca alla romana* (literally, 'jump in the mouth'), tender veal escalopes with ham and sage, cooked in butter and white wine; *bucatini all'amatriciana* (thin tubes of pasta with a sauce of salt pork, tomatoes, chilli peppers and grated *pecorino*—sharp Roman sheep cheese); *stracciatella* (a soup with eggs, parmesan cheese and parsley); fried artichokes called *carciofi alla giudea; involtini al sugo* (ham and cheese rolled in veal); *coda alla vaccinara* (stewed ox tail); *baccalà* (salt cod); *spaghetti alla carbonara* (with egg and bacon); *trippa alla romana* (tripe stewed with onions and white wine), and *gnocchi di patate* (potato dumplings, served with tomato sauce). Unless you ask for something different, the wine will probably come from the Castelli Romani—light, fruity whites of which the best come from Frascati and Velletri.

Though you can drop as much as L120 000 in a Roman restaurant if you follow the politicians and the TV crowd, prices somehow manage to keep not too far above the Italian average. Unfortunately, the humble, very cheap, but satisfying beaneries called *vini e cucina*, once the mainstay of old Rome, are an endangered species. Watch out for tourist traps—most places near a major sight with a 'tourist menu', for example. Rome also has some quite expensive joints that could best be described as parodies of old, famous establishments; they advertise heavily, and aren't hard to smell out. Hotel restaurants, those in the deluxe class, can often be quite good but ridiculously expensive.

In Old Rome (see also Around the Forum, p. 138): At the top of the list, perhaps, **Papà Giovanni** at Via dei Sediari 4, just east of the Piazza Navona, tel 686 5308 (do reserve). This old favourite, now under the control of one of Rome's most imaginative master chefs, is full of surprises—a constantly changing menu for the adventurous diner. The collection of lesser-known fine Italian wines is excellent. Altogether a complete experience that will set you back L70 000 or more. Many have acclaimed **Chez Albert**, Vicolo della Vaccarella, off Via della Scrofa, tel 686 5549, as Rome's best French restaurant; most dishes come from the south, like the famous *bouillabaisse Marseillaise*, but the cook's talent extends to specialities from around the Western Mediterranean—even to paella and couscous for around L60 000. For something just a little bit different, you can come to terms with *mallorredus* (perhaps the weirdest shape ever invented for pasta) and *carta di musica* (country-style crisp, very thin bread) at **Il Drappo**, featuring the delights of one of

136

Italy's least known and most distinctive regional cuisines, that of Sardinia. Fish are a speciality on the impressive menu (Vicolo del Malpasso, off the middle of Via Giulia, tel 687 7365; L60 000).

Notice how the best places are always hardest to find, tucked away on alleys where you can build up an appetite searching for them. For an aromatic Genoese feast, hunt for **Girone VI**, Vicolo Sinibaldi (near Piazza Argentina), tel 654 2831 (L50 000). There's no better place to try *carciofi alla giudea* than right on the edge of the old ghetto. **Piperno**, Via Monte de' Cenci 9, tel 654 0629, is famous for traditional Jewish variations on Roman cooking—simple dishes on the whole, but prepared and served with refinement (L50 000, maybe more.) Only in Rome would you find a good French restaurant run by a Catholic lay missionary society—*sole meunière* and onion soup in the well-scrubbed and righteous atmosphere of **L'Eau Vive**. Don't be put off; besides offering a serendipitous experience this is also one of the best and trendiest places in Rome (L40 000 average; Via Monterone 85, between Piazza Navona and the Pantheon, tel 654 1095).

Less expensive places are not hard to find, especially if you're hungry for pizza, everybody's favourite economical standby. **L'Orso 80**, Via dell'Orso 33, tel 656 4904, has both Roman and Abruzzese dishes in the L30 000 range, or try one of the last surviving **Vino e Cucina** restaurants at Via Pavone, off Via Banchi (L15 000). Some other delights: **ice cream parlours** flourish in Rome, and you can try some of the best in this area: **Giolitti**, elegant and old-fashioned, on Via degli Uffici (near the Chamber of Deputies), and **Tre Scalini** on Piazza Navona. In the ghetto, you can sample some unusual sweets at the no-name Jewish bakery at the west end of Via del Portico (note the incredible building it's in, a recycled ancient structure covered with reliefs and inscriptions). Every night until midnight, an artsy crowd collects in the **Cul de Sac**, a wine bar that also offers cheese, soups, sandwiches, and other snacks in Piazza Pasquino.

Around Piazza di Spagna: Not as promising for restaurants as it is for hotels, but there are a few. For the most haute of *haute cuisine* in Rome, reserve a place at the refined **Relais le Jardin**, Via G. Notaris 5, north of the Villa Giulia, tel 360 9541 (L100 000 and up), or go for the elegant Old World atmosphere at **Ranieri**, Via Mario de' Fiori 26, tel 679 1592, founded by Queen Victoria's chef and unchanged since; L100 000. All this seems a world away if you stop in at Via della Croce 21, at the **Birreria Viennese**, a venerable, unchangeable place where you can forget all about the Baroque while hoisting a few with your plate of kraut and wurst—about L20 000 (tel 679 5569). Down the street at No 39, you can re-cross the Italian border for dinner at **Beltramme**, a simple but excellent *vini e cucina* that will let you go for L25 000 at the most (no phone). You can sink your teeth in a *bistecca alla fiorentina* and other Tuscan dishes at **Mario**, Via della Vite 55, tel 678 3818 (L40 000). **Margutta** at Via Margutta 119, tel 678 6033, is an airy and delightful vegetarian place (L12–20 000). Vegetarian cooking raised to Italian standards could prove a revelation to you.

Cafe Rosati, in Piazza del Popolo, is an old place popular with a literary and artistic crowd, no doubt attracted by its extravagant ice cream as well as its Liberty-style elegance; there's a restaurant upstairs, too (L50 000). Other cafés in the area can be dignified, historic, or crazily expensive—for example, the 150-year-old **Babington's Tea Rooms** on Piazza di Spagna, for scones and tea in the proper atmosphere; and the even older **Caffé Greco**, Via Condotti 86, headquarters for visiting poets in the

Romantic era and now the average tourist's cheapest chance of a 20-minute dose of *ancien régime* luxury in Rome.

In Trastevere: This has long been one of the most popular corners of the city for dining—an outdoor table at one of the neighbourhood's many quiet piazzas seems idyllic to refugees from across the Tiber. Many of the places specialize in fish, most notably **Alberto Ciarla**, at Piazza San Cosimato 40, tel 581 8668, a long block south of S. Maria in Trastevere. The French-trained owner, proud enough to put his name on the sign, sees to it that everything is delicately and perfectly done, and graciously served: oysters, seafood ravioli, and quite a few adventurous styles of *pesce crudo* (raw fish) are among the most asked for, though you will find the lamb and game dishes may tempt you away from the seafood; eve only, L110 000, less for the *menu degustazione*. On Piazza S. Maria, **Sabatini**, tel 582 026, has been a Roman tradition for many long years, as much for the cuisine (again, lots of seafood) as the tables outside, which face the lovely piazza and its church (strolling musicians may sound trite, but it's always fun at the time; L60 000 and up). At **Le Cabanon**, you get better entertainment: cabaret numbers, Greek or Latin American tunes, more often than not performed by the irrepressible owner himself. The food is similarly eclectic, with French dishes, North African, Spanish—maybe even Italian—but somehow it always comes off well (on Vicolo della Luce, between Via della Lungaretta and the Tiber, tel 581 8106; about L55 000).

Less expensively, say about L35 000 or so, there's fresh fish, a serve-yourself antipasti table, and according to one moderately reliable source 'the best *spaghetti alla carbonara* in the world', all at **La Canonica**, on Vicolo del Piede, behind S. Maria in Trastevere, tel 580 3845. Truly cheap places in the L15–20 000 range abound on the back streets; the authentic **Osteria dell'Aquila**, Via Natale del Grande 4, tel 581 0924; **Al Drago**, a neighbourhood joint in Piazza del Drago and **Mario's**, Via del Moro, famous as the cheapest restaurant in Rome; get there early, and expect to stay most of the evening waiting to be served.

Around Termini Station: The hotel restaurant of the **Massimo D'Azeglio** was the place to find statesmen and diplomats in the early days of United Italy. Power and fashion may have left the neighbourhood, but the same family still runs this establishment, and they keep up standards very well. Good wines and exceptional antipasti, and portraits of old Italian premiers staring down from the walls wishing they could still be there to enjoy it (Via Cavour 14, tel 481 4101; L50–60 000 on average). One of Rome's newest addresses for seafood is **Bonne Nouvelle**, a smart little place in Via del Boschetto 73, tel 486 781 (L40 000). Every street around the station has a few little trattorias, pizzerias and tavola caldas. None seem to be especially good or especially awful—at least they give you a chance to avoid the depressing Termini Station self-service. Visitors with more adventure than finances can try the Ethiopian fare at **Africa**, Via Gaeta 26, tel 494 1077 (L10 000); or pay a bit more for a foretaste of Apulia at **Vecchia Puglia**, Via Principe Amedeo 325, tel 731 6919.

Around the Forum and Piazza Venezia, there isn't much choice, but **La Giada**, at Via IV Novembre 137, tel 679 8334, may well be the best Chinese restaurant in Italy—dinners L45 000 or so. Nearby, at Piazza del Grillo, **Mario's Hostaria** has decent Italian food out in a little piazza far from the tourist buses (L25–35 000, tel 679 3725). By the Colosseum, don't let the name of **Il Gladiatore** keep you away; after all, the gladiators were always served a feast before a fight, in case it was their last (Piazza del Colosseo 15, tel 736 276, L25 000).

The Vatican area has plenty of restaurants, most of the mediocre variety, though none is as awful as the Vatican Museums' cafeteria. Les Etoiles of the Atlante Star hotel, Via Vitelleschi 32, tel 687 9558, has excellent pasta to match the views from the rooftop garden (L50 000). Taverna Negma, Borgo Vittorio 92, tel 656 5143, has Rome's best North Arican menu (L25 000), or try your luck among the cheap tratts and pizzerias around Borgo Pio; Federico has the best 1950s atmosphere (L20 000).

Elsewhere in Rome: Porta Pia, and the quarters just outside the Aurelian wall and behind the Villa Borghese, are good places to look for restaurants. At Via Busento 56 (between Via Solana and Viale Regina Margherita), Club 56, tel 844 0196, may be the most beautiful restaurant in Rome, done in an Art Nouveau lavishness that makes the unusual combination of French and Neapolitan cooking seem even better (L55–80 000). If you find yourself anywhere around Porta San Paolo at dinnertime, don't pass up a chance to dine at the acknowledged temple of old Roman cooking; Checchino dal 1887, tel 574 6318, has been owned by the same family for over a century—the longest family record in Rome. Both the fancy and humble sides of Roman food are well represented, and the setting is unique—hollowed into the side of Monte Testaccio, Via di Monte Testaccio 30 (soul-satisfying *menu degustazione* for L75 000). For half that price you can dine at Cannavota, across the piazza from St John Lateran, tel 775 007, another thoroughly Roman trattoria with especially good seafood antipasti and pasta dishes.

Day Trips from Rome: Ostia

According to the archaeologists, Rome's port was founded only in the 4th century BC, 400 years after Rome itself. But in the centuries of conquest, Ostia grew into a major city in its own right, with a population of perhaps 100,000 and nearly 2 km of *horrea* (warehouses) near the mouth (the *Ostium*) of the Tiber. In the 4th century AD, when the flow of trade and tribute slowed, and even the grain supply from Africa was diverted to Constantinople, Ostia lost its reason for existing. The Tiber's silt relocated the coast a few miles to the west; malaria increased, and by 800 the site was totally abandoned, but preserved remarkably intact by mud and neglect. Beginning in the 19th century, excavations have recovered an ancient attraction that many visitors overlook. It's easy to reach: several B-line Metropolitana trains go all the way, or you may have to change at the Piramide/Ostia Lido station by Porta San Paolo; get off at the Ostia Antica stop. The excavations are open 9 to one hour before sunset, closed Mon; adm expensive.

Ostia, made lovely by its romantic park of parasol pines and wild flowers, is the best place in the world to see what ancient Rome once looked like, with its temples, baths, and *insulae* (apartment buildings) an interesting contrast to Pompeii or Herculaneum. Like these cities, it's easy to walk along the streets and imagine what life was like; so far two thirds of the city have been excavated. From the entrance follow the main road from Rome, the Via Ostiense, its flagstones deeply grooved by ancient cart wheels, which leads up to the Porta Romana, Ostia's main gate. Once in town, Via Ostiense becomes the main street, the Decumanus Maximus. On the right it passes the first horrea, or warehouses, and the Baths of the Cisiarii, with a mosaic of the first Roman buses. The fancier Baths of Neptune, still on the right side of the Decumanus have elaborate

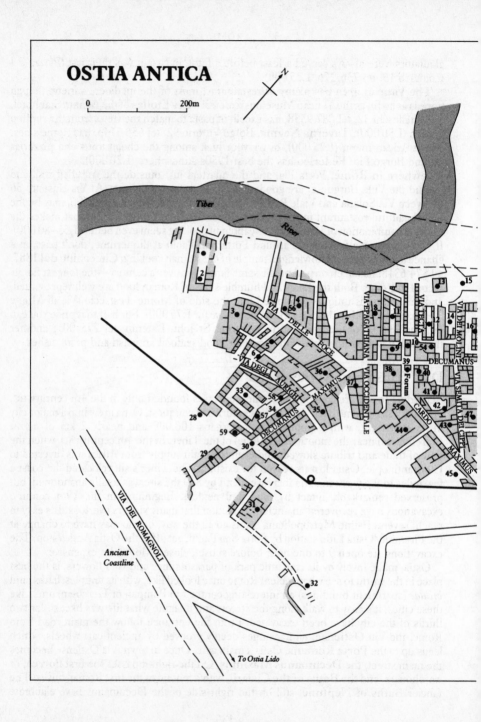

OSTIA ANTICA

0   200m

N

Tiber River

Ancient Coastline

VIA DELLE FOCE

VIA DEGLI AURIGHI

VIA EPAGATHANA

VIA OCCIDENTALE

VIA DEI MOLINI

VIA DELLA FOCE

DECUMANUS MAXIMUS

VIA DEI ROMAGNOLI

VIA SEMITA DEI CIPPI

DECUMANUS

CARDO MAXIMUS

Forum

To Ostia Lido

1. Baths of the Imperial Palace
2. Mithraeum
3. House of Bacchus/Serapis
4. Baths of Mithras
5. Terme delle Sette Sapienti
6. Insula degli Aurighi
7. House of Cupid and Psyche
8. Horrea Epagathiana
9. Curia
10. Capitolium
11. Piccolo Mercato
12. Casa dei Dipinti
13. Museum
14. Casa di Diana
15. Car Park

16. Horrea
17. Casa d'Apuleius
18. Mithraeum
19. Theatre
20. Piazzale delle Corporazioni
21. Temple of Ceres
22. Insulae
23. Firemen's Barracks
24. Baths of Neptune
25. Horrea/Baths of the Cisiarii
26. Porta Romana
27. Car Park
28. Maritime Baths
29. Domus Fulminata
30. Porta Marina

31. Baths of the Marciana
32. Synagogue
33. Casa a Giardino
34. Casa delle Muse
35. Scola di Traiano
36. Christian Basilica
37. Macellum
38. Basilica Tempio
39. Temple of Rome and Augustus
40. Casa Triclini
41. Forum Baths
42. Terme del Faro
43. Mills
44. Domus delle Colonne
45. Campo della Magna Mater

46. Edificio degli Augustali
47. House of Fortuna Annonaria
48. Porta Laurentina
49. Horrea
50. Cinta Sillana
51. Necropolis of Via Ostiense
52. Entrance
53. Stazione Ostia Antica
54. Thermopolium
55. Casa di Giove Fulminatore
56. Hall of the Wheat Measurers
57. Domus of the Dioscuri
58. Insula of the Painted Vaults
59. Tomb of Cartilius Popicola

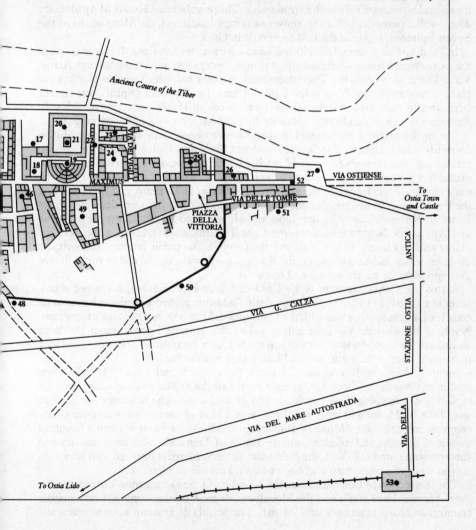

mosaics of frolicking sea gods. From here Via dei Vigili leads back to the *Mosaic of the Winds* and the **Police and Firemen's Barracks**, marked by a steeply inclined ramp (an early version of a firemen's pole?). The mosaic here, of men leading a bull to sacrifice, was part of a shrine to the deified emperors, or *Augusteum*. Further along the Decumanus was the **Tavern of Fortunatus**, its mosaic one of the world's first examples of advertising: 'Fortunatus says: if you're thirsty, drink a bowl of wine.'

Beyond it stands the **Theatre**, its arcades now supporting a souvenir shop, bar, and WC. In front of the theatre is the fascinating **Forum of the Corporations**, a quadrangle where Ostia's 61 maritime concerns had their offices. Black and white mosaics indicate the special business of each with its trademark. The neighbouring **House of Apuleius**, a *domus* with a peristyle, is like the houses of Pompeii; adjacent, the **Mithraeum of the Seven Spheres**, is one of the best preserved in Ostia.

In Via dei Molini, named after its mills and olive presses, the **Casa di Diana** is one of the more elegant *insulae*—originally four storeys, with its own private mithraeum. Across Via di Diana, don't miss the **Thermopolium**, or snack bar, which wouldn't look out of place in modern Rome. Next to the Casa di Diana, the **Casa dei Dipinti**, was equally large, and the most luxurious *insula* ever found, once entirely covered on the outside with festoons and paintings; climb the stair to the top floor for a view of the excavations.

Just to the north, a converted 15th-century salt deposit now contains the **Museo Ostiense**'s fine deposit of antiquities found in Ostia and Portus; among the statues, sarcophagi, and mosaics is a pair of marble footprints, facing in opposite directions, probably a soldier's votive offering of thanks for returning safely from war. From the museum, Via Tecta leads past the well-preserved **Piccolo Mercato**, and continues into the **Forum**, with its two temples: the **Capitolium**, with the broad stair, dedicated to the Etruscan/Roman trinity of Jupiter, Juno, and Minerva, and the older **Temple of Rome and Augustus**. Next to the latter is the **Casa Triclini**, which takes its name from the dining couches found within; built into the corner is the public lavatory, or **Forica**, a 20-holer which lacked only paper; the Romans used swabs on the end of sticks (hence the expression 'to get the wrong end of the stick').

Across the Cardo Maximus is the **Casa di Giove Fulminatore**, decorated with a relief of a foot-long willy. The **Domus delle Colonne**, named after the columns in its courtyard, is just south, along with the **Caupona del Pavone**, one of Ostia's nicer inns. North of the Forum, Via Epagathiana passes the **Horrea Epagathiana**; the large swastika in the mosaic was an ancient sun symbol, later degraded to a charm—good luck if the arms bent to the right, and bad luck if they went to the left.

South of here the Decumanus Maximus forks; the branch called Via della Foce continues towards the Tiber. On the right are the **Baths of Mithras**, especially good for exploring its plumbing if it's not flooded by ground water. The buildings on the right were built by Hadrian in what may have been a kind of ancient self-sufficient estate complex, including the **House of Bacchus**, the **House of Serapis** (with a beautiful mosaic of Bacchus and Ariadne), and the **Baths of Trinacria**, with more mosaics and subterranean plumbing. Next, the **Baths dei Sette Sapienti** is frescoed with advice on how to wash your rude parts and has a beautiful mosaic of a hunt scene.

The last section of Ostia lies along the extension of the Decumanus Maximus to the Porta Marina. Here you'll find the **Macellum**, or meat market, complete with marble counters and basins that once held live fish. The **Schola di Traiano** was a monumental complex with a long niched pool. Further along the Decumanus stands the **Insula of the Painted Vaults**, an apartment house later converted into a bordello, as the traces of fresco and graffiti bear witness. Next are more sophisticated *insulae*, the **Casa delle Muse** and the **Casa dei Giardini**, the Garden Homes, which looked onto their private garden like a Bloomsbury square; and the **Domus of the Dioscuri**, embellished with beautiful polychrome mosaics of 4th-century AD mermaids. The Decumanus leaves Ostia by the **Marine Gate**; one of its towers was converted into an inn, the **Caupona of Alexander Helix** with mosaics of Egyptian contortionist-dancers and wrestlers. Four tall columns with composite capitals are all that remains of the **Synagogue** (1st century AD), which stood right on the beach.

From the excavations it's a 10-minute walk to the sleepy hamlet of **Ostia**, founded to protect Rome after the Saracens captured Sicily in 831. It failed, but in 1483 Pope Julius II, then only Ostia's cardinal, built the huge brick **Castello** (open 9–12 and 3–6, closed Mon), a landmark of Renaissance fortifications which lost its purpose when the river shifted course; it now holds a a humble historical collection. Ostia's inhabitants worked the papal salt pans; their small Renaissance church of **Sant'Aurea** was built over the 5th-century basilica of Ostia's first martyr. Ask if the **Episcopio**, or bishop's palace, is open to see the unusual decorations done by Baldassare Peruzzi 1511–13, recently discovered under layers of whitewash. At the time Julius was trying to kick the French out of Italy, and the 15 grisaille frescoes, adaptations of scenes from Trajan's Column, are pure Renaissance flattery, comparing the wars of the Pope to the conquests of that emperor.

Ancient Ostia began its decline when Claudius planned a larger port just north at *Portus Ostiae*, later simply called **Porto**, which in turn succumbed in the Middle Ages to malaria; remains were found during the construction of Fiumicino Airport. Trajan later added a canal linking the port to the Tiber, creating an island known as the **Isola Sacra** (from Ostia Antica, follow the sign to Fiumicino on SS296 across the Tiber). Isola Sacra was the necropolis of ancient Portus until the 4th century, discovered excellently preserved under layers of sand (open 9–12:30 and 3:30–5, closed Mon). Trajan also added hexagonal docks that have survived as the little lake, **Lago Traiano**, on Via Portuensis; you can pick it out when flying into Fiumicino airport. The **Museo delle Navi Romane** near the airport (open 9–1 and 2–5, closed Mon; free) contains seven ships uncovered during the construction of the airport in 1961.

From the seaside town of **Fiumicino** you can take bus 020 north to the relatively benign pine-shaded beach of **Fregene**, or 02 back past Ostia Antica to Rome's own beach, the nightmarish **Lido di Ostia**. A monument near the mouth of the Tiber marks the spot where film director Pier Paolo Pasolini was murdered in 1975; if you swim here the pollution will do the same to you. Better, slightly less crowded beaches are further south, in the pine forests of **Castel Fusano** and beyond.

EATING OUT (tel prefix 06)

If it's a nice day in Ostia, buy picnic supplies and lunch among the ruins, with cool drinks from the theatre bar—or try the unabashedly touristy **Allo Sbarco di Enea**, with a Ben Hur chariot under the pergola, located between the station and the archaeological zone (average Roman food, L35 000). Fiumicino is well-known for its seafood restaurants along the seaside Via Torre Clementina, especially the large and popular **Bastianelli al**

Molo, at no. 312, tel 644 0118, where the price depends very much on what kind of fish you order (L40–80 000, closed Mon) and **Il Pescatore da Alberto**, at no. 154, tel 644 0189, which specializes in fried oysters and other fishy delights (around L40 000, closed Thurs).

Tivoli and Hadrian's Villa

Tivoli, or ancient *Tibur* is set in a cliff with a beautiful view over the Roman Campagna, a view that made it a garden retreat for the Senatorial class in the early days of the empire. But a town with a view is also usually easily defensible, and by the early Middle Ages, despite all the dirty work of Goths and Huns, Tibur had changed its name to Tivoli and managed a successful transition from posh resort to feisty, independent hill town. Today it is mainly visited for two amazing villas—the Renaissance Villa d'Este and Hadrian's city-sized country retreat.

Hadrian's Villa

GETTING AROUND
ACOTRAL buses leave for Tivoli every half hour from Via Gaeta, just to the left as you leave Termini Station. The ACOTRAL bus from Rome can leave you a 20-min walk away from Hadrian's villa at the Bivio Villa Adriana; local buses from Tivoli will take you much nearer the entrance.

TOURIST INFORMATION
Piazza Nazioni Unite, tel (0744) 21 249

Villa d'Este
Once, in Tivoli's frequent struggles with Rome, it defeated its big bossy neighbour in battle and captured a pope. But pachydermic Rome never forgets a grudge, and in the

1460s Pope Pius II built a castle, the **Rocca Pia**, at the town's door to keep Tivoli in line. Wealth returned in the late Renaissance in the form of moneybags cardinals; one in particular, Ippolito d'Este, son of Lucrezia Borgia and Duke Ercole I of Ferrara, created in 1550 perhaps the most fantastically worldly villa and gardens Italy had seen since antiquity. That is no small statement, but the **Villa d'Este** still has charms enough to attract hordes of day-trippers from Rome all year round (open 9:30–one hour before sunset; from May–early Oct the gardens are illuminated nightly except Mon from 9–12 pm; adm expensive). The musty villa itself, designed by Pirro Ligorio and heavily decorated with Mannerist frescoes, was rented by Franz Liszt and the inspiration for his *Fountains of the Villa d'Este*. But the house is entirely upstaged by the symmetrical Italian gardens, set on a series of terraces on the slopes below the town centre. Among the palms and cypresses, flowers and lawns, every corner turned will expose some incredible hydraulic confection of woven water: the *Fountain of Glass* by Bernini, the stuccoed *Grotto of Diana*, the *Fountain of Dragons*, the *Fountain of the Owl and Birds*, a favourite water trick that no longer warbles or moves; nor has the cardinal's *Water Organ* worked for donkey's years. One of the most curious features is 'Little Rome', a pint-sized replica of the Tiber Island in Rome, with models of ancient buildings.

Tivoli has an interesting Romanesque church with early medieval frescoes, **San Silvestro** located on steep and narrow Via del Colle (just north of the Villa d'Este); at the bottom, just beyond the gate are the remains of the vast **Sanctuary of Hercules** (2nd century BC), once the office of the sibyl of Tivoli. Like Cumae near Naples, Tibur had a college of sibyls (pictured so memorably on the Sistine Chapel ceiling); their Christian connection is derived from the story that they prophesied the birth of Christ. The presence of these oracular ladies, cousins to the oracle at Delphi, show the influence of Greek thought and religion in Latium from the earliest times. The stiff climb up Via del Colle leads eventually to Tivoli's gaudy 17th-century **Cathedral** at the corner of Via del Duomo, containing a moving 13th-century wooden sculpture of the *Deposition*.

Villa Gregoriana

The centre of Tivoli makes a sudden drop to form a nearly vertical natural park called the **Villa Gregoriana** in honour of Pope Gregory XVI, who put an end to the periodical flooding of the Aniene (the ancient Anio) in 1831 with the construction of a vast double tunnel through Mt Catillo (open 9–one hour before sunset; adm). The park was laid out in a natural chasm around the 120 m waterfall, or **Grande Cascata**, created where the Aniene dramatically shoots through the Pope's tunnel in a pluming mist of rainbows. The shady paths wind down past various viewpoints; if you can put off thinking about the awful climb back up, descend to the artificial **Cascata Bernini** and the limestone cavern called the **Grotta della Sirena**, where the waters are squeezed into an abyss. From the bottom a path leads up the other lip of the chasm, the acropolis of *Tibur*, where stand two remarkably well-preserved Roman temples, the famous circular **Temple of Vesta** and the rectangular **Temple of the Sibyl** as fancy has named them (they can also be reached from above, on Via della Sibilla). Both date from the Republican era; the Temple of Vesta, in particular, with its beautiful frieze and Corinthian columns was a favourite of romantic tourists, and has been reproduced in many a Hyperborean's park.

Lining the Via Tiburtina towards Rome you'll see the strange, sheer-sided travertine quarries that have helped Tivoli to make a living since ancient times. Almost all of Rome is built of it; one solemn grey variety went into the Colosseum, the city gates, and most of the other ruins. The other, streaked with beige and black, is the material Mussolini used for scores of railway stations all over Italy. Nowadays demand is still great, and Tivoli ships travertine all over the world.

Hadrian's Villa

Just outside Tivoli, signs direct you to the quiet residential neighbourhood that has grown up around **Hadrian's Villa**, a 180-acre spread that was nothing less than one man's personal World's Fair and the largest villa ever built in the entire Roman Empire; the Villa d'Este is a mere anthill in comparison (open daily except Mon, 9–sunset; adm expensive). To get some idea of the scale on which a 2nd-century emperor could build, stop first at the room-sized model of the villa near the entrance. Built entirely of marble and travertine, and about the same size as the monumental centre of Rome—the Imperial Fora included—Hadrian's dream 'house' clearly shows the excess that even the most intelligent and useful emperors were capable of. Archaeologists have found features that would surprise even a Californian—a heated beach, for example, with steam pipes under the sand and a network of subterranean service passages for horses and carts (a private Underground!). Other emperors used the villa until Constantine initiated the usual plundering, in this case to embellish Constantinople; invaders, builders, and lime burners gnawed at it until Pope Alexander VI began the first excavations. Yet despite the depredations many of the finest Roman statues in Europe's museums were discovered here.

Hadrian fancied himself an architect (he was at least partly responsible for the Pantheon, the Temple of Venus and Rome, and the urban redevelopment of Ostia Antica), but no other student of architecture has ever had the resources of the Roman empire at its peak at his disposal. He especially wanted to remember famous buildings he had seen on his travels and helped design reproductions: the **Stoa Poikile** of Athens, near the entrance, a rectangular peristyle with a massive fish pond in the centre; the **Canopus**, or Temple of Serapis near Alexandria, complete with a canal reproducing the Nile and decorated with Egyptian statues (now mostly restored; a nearby **Museum** contains finds from the most recent excavations); the **Platonic Academy** in an ancient olive grove, with an Odeon, a round Temple of Apollo, and just beyond, the entrance to an underground rectilinear hell, or **Hades**. Baths, libraries, an imperial palace, nymphaeums, temples, Praetorian barracks, and a reproduction of the Valle di Tempe with a Greek theatre are among the other buildings discovered in the ongoing excavations. But the most charming corner of the complex is the so-called **Naval Theatre**, actually a little circular palace on an island in an artificial lagoon, attainable only by a retractable bridge on rollers; it may have been Hadrian's private retreat, where he would come to write poetry and paint.

WHERE TO STAY AND EATING OUT $\qquad$ (tel prefix 0771)

In Tivoli, a good place to stay is the ******Torre Sant'Angelo**, tel 23 292, a bargain at L45 000 for a double with bath; or, less expensively, the ***Eden Sirene**, Piazza Massimo, tel 21 352, a simple place but with great views over the temples and the Villa Gregoriana—also a nice restaurant, where dinners usually go for under L30 000 (L32 000 with bath, L25 000 without). The **Sibilla**, Via della Sibilla, tel 20 281, restaurant is famous above all else for its location, incorporating the famous 'Temple of the Sibyls' right in its building. The place makes a living off tourists, but the food is still good (grilled trout, for example) and the price is right—about L40 000. **Del Falcone**, Via del Trevi 34, tel 22 358, has a good menu of Roman dishes, and pizza, too (L25 000, much less for pizza).

The Aniene Valley, Subiaco, and Palestrina

East of Tivoli, which can turn into a real Roman circus in the summer, lies the lovely and wooded Aniene valley, where few tourists ever venture. Horace and Nero once had villas here; the hill towns are reminiscent of some in Umbria. And like Umbria, these hills have attracted earthly expressions of the divine—the Latin tribes' oracular temple of Fortuna Primigenia and St Benedict's first monasteries, in Subiaco.

GETTING AROUND
A car comes in handy to explore the valley and its towns. Otherwise, ACOTRAL buses depart from Rome's Viale Castro Pretorio to Vicovaro, Licenza, Antícoli Corrado, Saracinesco, and Subiaco on average every other hour. For Zagarolo and Palestrina, buses from Via Gaeta by Termini Station every 45 min, which offer the advantage over driving—you can doze through Rome's vast and gruesome suburbs along Via Casilina.

TOURIST INFORMATION
Subiaco: Via Cadorna 59, tel (0774) 85 397
Palestrina: Piazza Santa Maria degli Angeli

Between Tivoli and Subiaco
The first town of interest after Tivoli is **Vicovaro** (46 km from Rome), worth a stop for the little octagonal Renaissance **Tempietto di San Giacomo** (1450), a work by two Dalmatian architects, Domenico da Capodistria and Giovanni Dalmata, who designed the charming porch. Just beyond Vicovaro, a road turns left up a lovely valley towards Licenza for **Horace's Sabine farm** (bus riders should ask the driver to stop at the unpaved lane leading to the *Villa d'Orazio*; always open; tip the custodian). No farm has ever enjoyed so many poetic musings as the country estate the fabulously wealthy Maecenas gave to Horace in 33 BC. The spring still flows; the lovely mosaic pavements, garden swimming-pool, and some of the lead pipes and the pretty surroundings survive to give substance to Horace's raptures. The custodian of the site has a roomful of small finds from the excavations; the more interesting items are in the little Antiquarium (open 9–4) 8 km up the road in the castle of **Licenza**, one of Lazio's handsomest villages.

Among the other little hilltowns in the Aniene valley which have escaped the worst of modern tourism, there's lovely **Antícoli Corrado** on its steep cliff, famous for producing Rome's most beautiful artists' models. The town has had an art colony of its own for almost two hundred years, some of whose works may be seen in the local pinacoteca. Recently discovered frescoes by their predecessors in the 1100s may be seen in the well-preserved church of **San Pietro**, in the piazza with a fountain of Noah's Ark. Another striking town, **Saracinesco** was founded on a nearly inaccessible crag by Saracen raiders in the 9th century; the present townspeople are their direct descendants.

Subiaco

Few towns can claim as glorious a past as **Subiaco**, up at the head of the Aniene valley where St Benedict retired in the troubled late 5th century to write his *Rule* and set Christian monasticism on its way. All through the dark centuries his monasteries provided a haven for learning and piety, and were still important enough in the 1460s for the first printing press in Italy to be brought here by two monks from Germany.

Originally Subiaco had 12 monasteries; those not destroyed by the Lombards fell to earthquakes and the worldly ambition of the monks. Today there are but two, 2.5 km above town, reached by road or footpath, both passing by way of the dismal remains of Nero's once grand Sublaqueum villa and his now dried-out artificial lake. The first, the **Convento di Santa Scholastica** (Benedict's twin sister) is shown daily 9–12 and 4–6, except during Sun mass (10–11:30). A feudal abbey in the Middle Ages, and later ruled by princely abbots of Rome's noblest families, S. Scholastica is still enormous, a holy bulwark of the faith, guarded by a stout Romanesque campanile. It has three cloisters, the first built in 1580, incorporating columns from Nero's villa; the second an early Gothic cloister of 1052; the third beautifully decorated in the 13th century by the Cosmatis. The library contains the first two books printed in Italy. Apparently the Germans and their newfangled contraption upset the monastery's scribes, and after printing these two tomes they went off in a huff to Rome.

Further up is the **Convento di San Benedetto**, or Sacro Speco, named after the cavern to which St Benedict retired as a hermit and attracted his first disciples (same hours as S. Scholastica). Partly natural, and partly built into the mountain side, the monastery includes a 14th-century **Upper Church** with fine Sienese frescoes and a 13th-century **Lower Church**, built on several levels to incorporate St Benedict's Holy Grotto, now lined with marble from Nero's villa. The frescoes illustrating the saint's life are by Master Consulus, a 13th-century painter. In 1210, an anonymous monk painted the *portrait of St Francis* upstairs in the Chapel of St Gregory, believed to be the first live portrait done in Italy since Roman times. Don't miss the quattrocento frescoes of deathly Death along the Scala Santa, leading to the Shepherd's Grotto, this containing a rare fresco from the 700s. From here you can see what had been an ancient bramble where Benedict had lain to mortify his flesh, but which turned into a rose tree at the gentler touch of St Francis.

Nearby, at the bottom of the gorge of the Aniene, there's a beautiful little lake with a waterfall; it may have been one of the three mentioned by Tacitus in connection with Nero's villa. Just outside of Subiaco town, the church of **San Francesco** contains frescoes attributed to Pinturicchio, Sodoma, and Sebastiano del Piombo, and on the altar a triptych undoubtedly by Antoniazzo Romano, who knew enough to sign his work.

Zagarolo and Palestrina

As soon as the Via Casilina leaves Greater Rome, the scenery perks up, especially near **Zagarolo**. Famous for its wine, Zagarolo is a pretty half-medieval, half-Baroque town of churches, theatrical squares and palaces, and a thoroughly strange gate, the **Porta di S. Martino** decorated with reliefs of armour in curling ribbons. The 13th–18th-century **Palazzo Rospigliosi**, with frescoes by the Zuccari and period furnishings, is open for tours on request (tel 475 4344).

Another 5 km leads up to **Palestrina**, ancient Praeneste and birthplace of the composer Giovanni Pierluigi da Palestrina (1524–94) who invented the polyphonic mass when the chips were down—the Council of Trent was about to ban church music altogether, with its melodies straight from popular love songs and the tavern. But Praeneste was on the map long before there was such a thing as a church; one of the oldest Latin towns, traditionally founded by Telegonus, son of Odysseus and Circe, it predates Rome and long battled with the upstart on the Tiber before making an alliance, rebelling, submitting, etc. But it had something even Rome couldn't match—the greatest Hellenistic temple in Italy, dedicated to Fortune, the mother of gods: the **Sanctuary of Fortuna Primigenia**. When Palestrina was bombed in the war, it uncovered ruins of the sanctuary as large as the town itself. Like many ancient temples, it was built into the side of a hill, neatly combining nature with architecture—though here on a scale previously unheard of. No one is sure when it was built, but in 80 BC it was partially burned during the Social Wars, and rebuilt by Sulla; it was revolutionary in its use of the Roman's special, high-silica concrete that would later top the Pantheon and vault a hundred baths.

Remains of the ancient sanctuary stretch from the bottom to the top of Palestrina in a series of wide, artificial terraces. Along Via degli Arconi, you can see the first level of arches that supported the town core; from the ACOTRAL bus stop, near the top of Via degli Arconi, a road curves up to the 17th-century **Porta del Sole** and remains of Praeneste's Cyclopean polygonal walls. Continue up to Via Anicia and turn left for Piazza Regina Margherita, the terrace of the ancient Forum now occupied by a statue of Giovanni Pierluigi, a section of the ancient road and steps, and the unique, brick collage façade of the **cathedral**, built in the 5th century over an ancient temple, perhaps dedicated to Jupiter. The nave is lined with a frieze of portraits of Palestrina's cardinals and in the left aisle is a copy of the *Palestrina Pietà*, sometimes attributed to Michelangelo (the original was carted off to Florence).

Adjacent to the cathedral are columns embedded like fossils in the flank of the ex-Seminary. This was built around Praeneste's sacred area and at the time of writing is closed to the public (though check at the tourist office). Within is the so-called **Apsidal Hall** (perhaps a temple of Isis) where the famous Barberini mosaic was discovered (see below); the **Aerarium**, or treasury, containing the remains of an obelisk, busts, and votive offerings; and the **Antro delle Sorti**, formerly believed to be the home of the oracle, and now thought to be the temple of Serapis, decorated with a beautiful mosaic of Alexandria.

Above rise the great steps of terraces leading into the main sanctuary of Fortune; zigzag up the steep streets and stairways to Piazza della Cortina. This, the highest terrace, was once the courtyard of the sanctuary's theatre; the cavea of seats was restored in 1640 to form the steps of the Palazzo Colonna-Barberini, built around the highest temple in the sanctuary. It now houses the **Museo Nazionale Archeologico Prenestino** (daily 9–6; adm includes the excavations), containing a model of the sanctuary, sculptural fragments, *cistae*, or bronze vanity cases with etched pictures (a local speciality) and most splendiferous of all, on the top floor, the exquisite **Barberini mosaic of the Nile**, a brilliantly coloured Hellenistic masterpiece of the 2nd century BC, showing the Nile in flood, with islands of Egypt's flora and fauna, a banquet of lovers, a religious procession, the Canopus of Alexandria, obelisks, a towered city, etc.

Opposite the museum is the excavated area of the sanctuary; from the courtyard steps descend to a colonnaded terrace, and then down again to the **Terrazza degli Emicicli**, or hemicycles, with the famous oracle of Fortune in the centre. This was the heart of the sanctuary, where the Sibyl of Palestrina responded to queries with *sorti*, or small wooden lots with letters carved in them, some of which were discovered in a well. There is a splendid view reaching to the sea from here, and it is said that in ancient times—until the temple was disbanded in the 4th century—that two fires would be lit every night from here as beacons for sailors.

To the left of the museum is the pretty church of **Santa Rosalia** (1660), and beyond it, the road up to Palestrina's citadel, the ruined **Castel S. Pietro** (3.5 km), once property of the Colonna. Pietro da Cortona made the altarpiece in its little church, but the magnificent view steals the show.

EATING OUT   (tel prefix 06)
In Palestrina lunch can be anything from a slice of pizza or picnic in the city park, to a plate of homemade fettuccine etc. at the **Stella**, an old favourite (Piazza della Liberazione 3, tel 955 172; L30 000). One advantage of driving, however, is that you can detour south 9 km to Làbico for lunch in one of Italy's top restaurants: **Antonello Colonna Vecchia Osteria**, Via Casilina km 38.3, where regional specialities become sublime (reserve: tel 951 0032, L60–75 000; closed Mon).

The Castelli Romani

'Extinction' may be one of the dirtiest words of the 20th century, but with volcanoes it usually translates into lovely scenery, romantic lakes, and fertile soil for vines. Such are the charms of the Alban Hills, the ruins of a horseshoe-shaped crater 60 km round just south of Rome. But Rome was still a twinkle in Mars' eye when the ancient Latins found these hills a convivial place to settle, and their towns grew to become some of the strongest members of the Latin League. Since being pounded into submission 2200 years ago, their role has been reduced to that of providing the capital with wine, flowers, and a pleasant place to spend summer weekends. Heavy bombing in 1944 during the battle for Rome wrecked many fine old churches, villas, and works of art in the Castelli, as the hilltowns are called. The damage has been repaired, although much is new; some of the nearer Castelli are becoming strangled in Rome's suburban tentacles. Still, the countryside, especially around Lake Nemi, is beautiful. Another attraction is the numerous old-fashioned wine cellars; so old that one in Marino, along the lake road, was formerly used as an underground mithraeum, and has a fine fresco of Mithras inside.

GETTING AROUND
All the Castelli and Cori can be reached by ACOTRAL bus, from the depot at the Anagnina Metropolitana A station; there's also a little train to Frascati departing from Termini station. While connections between the towns are frequent, the links are not always very convenient; with a car you can easily see the highlights in a day.

TOURIST INFORMATION
Frascati: Piazza G. Marconi 1, tel (06) 942 0331
Albano Laziale: Via Olivella 2, tel (06) 932 1323

Castel Gandolfo: Piazza Libertà 10, tel (06) 936 0340
Velletri: Via dei Volsci, tel (06) 963 0896

Frascati

The nearest of the Castelli (21 km, on Via Tuscolana) and one of the most visited, Frascati was a medieval replacement for the ancient Etruscan and Latin city of Tusculum, which whipped the Romans in 1167, and was destroyed in a vendetta in 1191. In ancient times Tusculum was famous for its magnificent villas, including Cicero's, and it was a tradition inherited by Frascati on its refreshing hillside. Unfortunately Field Marshal Kesselring made it his headquarters, and 80 per cent of the town was destroyed in the bombing to squeeze him out. Still famous for its white wine, it is mostly visited for its two parks: the **Villa Aldobrandini** (open 9–12, tickets from the tourist office). Built by Clemente VIII's Cardinal-nephew Pietro Aldobrandini in the 1590s, the villa has a fine park behind it, with a perfectly mossy elliptical Renaissance nymphaeum, or **Theatre of Waters**, begun by Giacomo della Porta and finished by Giovanni Fontana and Carlo Maderno. The water that feeds it cascades between the 'Pillars of Hercules'—a pair of tall, spiralling mosaic columns; the mythological figures in the theatre's niches, with typical papal *chutzpah*, are an allegory of Clement VII's papacy—the Pope is 'Atlas' in the centre, holding up the world's cares; his cardinal nephew is the figure of 'Hercules' in the next niche, offering a helping hand, while on the other side are the Hesperides, whose garden is the paragon of the villa; elsewhere the cardinal associates himself with Apollo, and Frascati with Parnassus. Although the hydraulic trickery that once made the theatre come to life with movements and sound no longer works, it is still a fine fancy, and one that nearly bankrupted the Curia.

The adjacent **Villa Torlonia** is now Frascati's pubic park, though its own more modest theatre of waters stands derelict. In the centre of Frascati, Piazza San Pietro has a pretty fountain and cathedral, much restored after the bombing; beyond the fountain, the church of the **Gesù** was designed by Pietro da Cortona and decorated with frescoed 'perspectives' by Antonio Colli. Other famous 16th-century villas in Frascati (visible only from the road) include the **Villa Falconieri**, designed by Borromini, with a lakelet in a ring of cypresses, and the **Villa Lancellotti**, built over the 1st-century BC farm of Lucullus, once a residence of the Savoys, and visited by George Sand. **Tusculum** (5 km east, on a minor road from Villa Aldobrandini) was flattened by the vengeful Romans in the 12th century but you can still pick out the ruins of the 'Villa of Cicero' and have a picnic in the well-preserved theatre. Climb up to the former citadel (760 m) for one of the finest views over the Alban Hills; the villa here, **Villa Tuscolana** (1580), was rebuilt by Vanvitelli in 1741 and once belonged to Lucien Bonaparte and Queen Christina of Sweden.

Grottaferrata and Marino

Grottaferrata, only 3 km south of Frascati, was built around an 11th-century abbey, the well-fortified Basilian **Abbazia di Grottaferrata**, founded by SS. Nilus and Bartholomew and still home to a congregation of Greek Catholic monks (daily except Mon, 9–12 and 4–7, and shown by a monk; offering). The monastery has a small museum with some beautiful classical sculpture, as well as frescoes, vestments, and icons, all with a Greek touch. The abbey church of **Santa Maria**, consecrated in 1025, has a pretty 12th-century campanile in the colourful Roman party-favour style, and a wonderfully carved marble portal of the same period, topped by a Byzantine mosaic. In the **Chapel of St Nilus,** Domenichino painted what his fans claim are his best frescoes, on the lives of the abbey's founders.

Another 6 km will take you to **Marino**, like Frascati a famous wine town that suffered seriously during the war. The best time to visit is on the first Sunday in October, when the town's fountains flow with last year's vintage in its merry *Sagra dell'Uva*. One of these, the **Fountain of the Four Moors** in Piazza Lepanto commemorates the many natives who fought in the Battle of Lepanto—a Turkish shield taken as a trophy still hangs in the church of San Barnaba.

Around Lake Albano

From Marino you can continue along the panoramic **Via dei Laghi** (SS217) which overlooks the elliptical **Lake Albano**. Romans, whose taste for vicarious battles followed them even on holiday, used to come to watch mock sea fights from their lakeside villas; now they prefer trout fishing. Beyond the lake there's a turn-off for **Rocca di Papa**, a dramatically sited town with a picturesque medieval citadel called the *Quartiere dei Bavaresi*, from the Bavarian troops of Emperor Ludwig stationed here in the 1320s.

A private toll road leads up from Rocca di Papa to the second highest of the Alban Hills, **Monte Cavo** (948 m; or you can walk up from town). Monte Cavo or *Mons Albanus*, was the sacred mountain of the Latin tribes. Aeneas' son Anchises founded Alba Longa, their most ancient city and political centre nearby at Castel Gandolfo (see below), while at the summit was the sanctuary of Latian Jupiter, the cult centre of all Latium. James Frazer writes how one of the ancient kings of Alba Longa considered himself the equal of Jupiter, and sought to prove it by inventing machines that mimicked thunder and lightning, banging and sparking enough to drown out the real storm. Jupiter did not take kindly to the competition and blasted the impudent king with a tremendous thunderbolt, followed by a cloudburst that drowned his very palace under the waters of Lake Albano, traces of which, they say, you can still see when the water is low.

Despite this setback, Mons Albanus remained the political and religious centre of the Latin League until the Romans *did* steal Jupiter's thunder by building him a superior temple on the Capitol. But the importance of his first sanctuary was never forgotten, and it became the practice for any conquering hero whose victories weren't grand enough for the Forum to be given a second-class triumph here, along Mt Cavo's Via Triumphalis. The footpath from the upper reaches of Rocca di Papa follows its route beyond the **Campi d'Annibale**, the hollow of an ancient crater, where Hannibal and his elephants are said to have camped, to the top where there are fabulous views in all directions. No trace of the temple of Jupiter Latius has ever been discovered here; as god of sky, thunder, and oaks he was apparently worshipped outdoors in a sacred grove. Tarquin the Proud built a wall to define the sacred precinct, and when Cardinal Henry, Duke of York built a Passionist monastery here (since converted into a hotel) he re-used some of its blocks, which you can still see. And where the ancient pagans and not so ancient Christian monks worshipped, there is now a television transmitter.

The Mirror of Diana

Next along the Via dei Laghi is **Nemi**, a picturesque little village wrapped around its 9th-century castle and famous for its June strawberry festival. From here, (or from **Genzano**; see below) you can descend to the magical 'Mirror of Diana', the round, deep, blue **Lake Nemi**, its still waters encompassed by dripping forests and plastic-coated strawberry farms. On the way down, the road passes the meagre ruins of the **Temple of Diana Nemorensis**, the celebrated sanctuary of Diana of the woodlands, in whose forest, known as the grove of Aricia, were held the barbaric rites that inspired Sir James Frazer's monumental *The Golden Bough*, the foundation of modern anthropology. Within this sanctuary grew an oak wood, guarded by a priest known as King of the Wood, a former runaway slave who had become Diana's priest by plucking a sprig of mistletoe from the trees, which gave him the right to fight and slay the former king. And so, even into the days of Hadrian, would the next king be made by slaying the former. Ancient authorities linked the mistletoe to the golden bough plucked by Aeneas before his descent into the underworld.

Caligula took a special interest in the cult, and had two magnificent ships constructed to ferry visitors across the lake to the temple (and entertain with his notorious perversities on the way). These ships were sunk during the time of Claudius, and although they were discovered in 1446 by Leon Battista Alberti, they remained at the bottom of the lake until 1932, when they were brought up in a remarkable state of preservation. It's a shame that they didn't stay there a little longer, for as a last act of gratuitous chagrin the retreating Germans set fire to the lakeshore **Nemi Museum of Roman Ships** and burnt them to bits. The museum has since been reconstructed, with bronze figurines and bits salvaged from the fire, and models one fifth the size of the originals; ask in the village if it's been reopened.

Across Lake Nemi from Nemi is the larger town of **Genzano di Roma**, overlooking the Via Appia; it is best known for the *Infiorita* on the Sunday after Corpus Domini (June), when the streets are covered with patterns made from over 8000 lbs of flower petals. From here the Via Appia crosses a series of viaducts on its way to Rome, passing by way of **Aríccia**, a pretty village immersed in trees that boasts several minor works by Bernini: the unexciting **S. Maria di Galloro** on the edge of the town, the medievalesque **Palazzo Chigi**, set in a gorgeous park, and **Santa Maria dell'Assunzione** whose round dome resembles the nipple of a baby's bottle.

The biggest viaduct of all, the three-tiered Ponte di Aríccia, passes on the left the striking truncated cones of the so-called **Tomb of the Horatii and Curiatii**, built in the Etruscan style. Roman legend has it that three Roman Horatii and three Latin Curiatii fought in single combat to end the war between Alba Longa (see above) and Rome during the reign of Tullus Hostilius, but Alba Longa's tyrant proved deceitful, and the result was its total destruction by the Romans.

Albano Laziale and Castel Gandolfo

Alba Longa's name lingers, however, in **Albano Laziale**, the next important town up the Via Appia, although spoilsport historians say it wasn't founded until Septimius Severus created a large permanent camp for the 2nd Legion here, called *Castra Albano*, ostensibly to defend the Via Appia but perhaps more to impress travellers and get the imperious troops out of Rome. The modern town, shaped like a wedge on the slope of Monte

Cavo's crater, just about fills the space of the legion's huge camp. Along the main Corso Matteotti, the church of **San Pietro** was built over the camp's baths in the 6th century and has a fine Romanesque campanile. On the next street up, Via Don Minzoni, you can see the mighty ruins of the **Porta Praetoria**, the camp's principal gate, rediscovered after a bomb fell on the surrounding buildings. Via Saffi continues up, past **S. Maria della Rotonda** (on the left), an unusual circular medieval church built over a nymphaeum of Domitian; inside there's a pulpit of Cosmati work on an ancient column. At Via Saffi 100 is a perfectly preserved underground reservoir, or **Cisternone**, carved into the living rock to supply the troops, and still used today to hold Albano's water. Ruins of the **Amphitheatre** lie behind the church in genteelly dilapidated Piazza San Paolo. From the very top of the hill, you can look down on Lake Albano shimmering far below.

The prettiest route from Albano to **Castel Gandolfo** is the upper of Urban VIII's two roads, called the **Galleria di Sopra**, or upper tunnel, because of its roof of interwoven ilex branches—the lower 'tunnel', the **Galleria di Sotto** is the busy main road. The Upper Road begins above Albano's Piazza San Paolo and follows the rim of Mt Cavo's crater, with views of lake and the surrounding country. Castel Gandolfo itself is a happy little village, perched 1400 ft above Lake Albano, and famous as the Vatican enclave where the pope spends the dog days of summer. The discovery of an Iron Age necropolis used from the 9th–7th centuries BC strengthens Castel Gandolfo's claim that it was the site of Alba Longa. Interestingly, the graves were found coated with a thin layer of lava, supporting the old legend that volcanic eruptions forced the early inhabitants down from these hills to Rome.

Castel Gandolfo is named for the Gandolfi family of Genoa, who built a castle here in the 12th century. The **Papal Palace** was constructed on its ruins by Carlo Maderno in 1624, but was much remodelled by Pius IX. To attend the Pope's general audience on Wednesdays at 11 am you need to have tickets from the Vatican (see p. 129), though on Sundays at noon John Paul II appears to give a homily to the crowd in the palace courtyard. The other thing to do in Castel Gandolfo is walk down the track below the rail station to the cave entrance of the **Emissarium**, a tunnel nearly $1^{1}/_{2}$ km long, carved in the living rock by the Romans in 397 BC. At the time the war with Veii seemed endless, and they asked an oracle what it took to win. 'Drain the lake,' came the reply, and so they did in their direct, literal Roman way. They did the job well; the Emissarium is still used to control the level of the lake.

Velletri

If you really want to escape Rome and its bedroom townlets, continue south instead of north along the Via Appia from Genzano to **Velletri**, an ancient Volscian town that has grown to become the largest of the Castelli (40 km from Rome, the last ACOTRAL stop). Although bombed almost to smithereens in the war, its landmark **Torre del Trivio**, a leaning 45-m needle-like campanile from 1353, has been restored. The town museum contains a collection of Volscian sarcophagi, while the crazy quilt of a **cathedral**, built over a Roman basilica, has art from the Cosmati to the smarmy 1950s, with nearly every style in between. Under the portico is the entrance to a small **museum**, with Madonnas by Gentile da Fabriano and Antoniazzo Romano and a fairy tale Byzantine reliquary from the 12th century.

WHERE TO STAY AND EATING OUT

Frascati makes a good place to stop for dinner, with restaurants like **Cacciani**, Via Armando Diaz 13, tel (06) 942 0378, small price to pay for inventive dishes like fettucine with artichokes, chicken breasts with porcini mushrooms and cream, good Frascati D.O.C. wine, too (L40 000). **La Nuova Tavernetta**, high up in Rocca Priora (Via Roma 37, tel (06) 947 0369), has beautiful pasta and beautiful views (closed Mon; L25 000). **La Torre** in Marino (Via M. Montecchi, tasty home cooking; closed Mon; L30 000). **Al Fico Nuovo**, one of a score of eateries in Grottaferrata, is owned by Claudio Ciocca, whose face you may recognize from a score of Fellini films; good fish and other dishes from other corners of Italy (outdoors in summer, Via Anagnina 86, tel (06) 945 9290, closed Wed; L40 000).

If you have a car, the area around Nemi and the lakes is a relaxing place to stay: at the ****Al Rifugio** just outside Nemi (tel 937 8075; L49 000) or the ****Culla del Lago** in Castel Gandolfo, on the shore of Lake Albano (tel 936 0407; L46 000). In Genzano di Roma, **Il Castagnone**, Via Nemorense 13, tel (06) 937 8051, has a pretty setting and is well known for its many tasty, and many varied pasta dishes (L30 000; closed Tues). And in Velletri, **Benito** is one of the few places in the area to get good fresh seafood (Via Lata 71, tel 963 2220; L40 000, or less).

Part IV
LAZIO

Monteleone Sabino

On a Saturday night variety show, the television host discusses the founding of Rome with two comedians dressed up as Romulus and Remus; turning to Remus, the sillier-looking of the pair, he asks: 'What did you ever do?' Remus gets a big laugh from the audience by proudly claiming, 'Well, I founded Lazio.' Despite being the location of the capital city, Lazio does not get much respect from the average Italian, who thinks of it as a sort of vacuum, half swamps and half poor mountain villages that need to be crossed to get to Rome. Northerners often lump it in with Campania and Calabria as part of the backward south. To an extent it is, though great changes have come in the last 50 years with land reclamation and new industry. Lazio's problem is a simple one: Rome, that most parasitic of all cities. Before there was a Rome, this was probably the wealthiest and most densely populated part of non-Greek Italy, the homeland of the Etruscans as well as the rapidly civilizing nations of Sabines, Aequi, Hernici, Volsci, and the Latins themselves, from whom Lazio (*Latium*) takes its name.

After the Roman triumph, the Etruscan and the Italic cities shrivelled and died; those Romans who proved such good governors elsewhere meant utter ruin to their own backyard. A revival came in the Middle Ages, when Rome was only one of a score of squabbling feudal towns, but once again, when the popes restored Rome, Lazio's fortunes declined. To finance their grandiose building projects, Renaissance popes literally taxed Lazio into extinction; whole villages and large stretches of countryside became abandoned, given over to bandits, and land drained in medieval times reverted to malarial swamps. Modern Rome, at least since Mussolini's day, has begun to mend its ways; the government still considers Lazio a development area, and pumps a lot of money into it.

156

WHAT TO SEE
Many of Lazio's attractions are easily seen as day trips from Rome—Tivoli, Ostia, and a garland of interesting hill towns. These are detailed in a special section following that on 'Rome'. Northern Lazio contains no fewer than 28 excavated **Etruscan sites**, and if these ancient charmers interest you, there will be plenty of opportunities for Etruscan detours whether you approach Rome from Tuscany on the Via Cassia (N. 2) or A12 along the coast—including the spectacular painted tombs of **Cervéteri**. Northern Lazio also offers the fine old city of **Viterbo**, and a string of large **lakes** in a pretty landscape of jumbled hills.

In Southern Lazio, you'll see new land and new towns: the reclaimed Pontine Marshes, with Mussolini-founded towns like Aprília and Latina, and others with a completely modern look only because they had to be rebuilt from the bottom up after the last War. Others, like **Alatri** and **Cori** with their impressive Cyclopean walls, are among the oldest towns in Europe. Early monastic centres make up most of the religious sights, with **Montecassino** first among them. The coast is generally plain and empty, with some noteworthy exceptions: the old walled port of **Gaeta**, some of the Tyrrhenian's nicest beaches around **Sperlonga** and **Terracina**, and the wetlands wilderness of the **Monte Circeo** national park.

Itineraries

A motorist's itinerary for seeing the major sites of Lazio (omitting Rome which deserves at least a week) might look like this. Make Viterbo your first base (days 1–2), one day for the city and one for Caprarola, the Bomarzo Monster Park, and a look at Lakes Bolsena and Vico. The next day (day 3) you may stop at the Etruscan necropolis at Tarquinia and Cervetéri on the way to Rome. After Rome, resume with day trips to Tivoli or Ostia (day 4) and a tour of Lake Nemi and the Castelli Romani (day 5). There are two good routes to Naples and the south, each of about equal interest. One, generally following the ancient Via Appia, will take you near the villages of Cori and Norba and the Abbey of Fossanova (day 6); then along the coast for a look at Cape Circeo, Terracina and Gaeta (and maybe some beach lolling around San Felice Circeo, day 7). Along the northern route, the Autostrada del Sole, you can detour for Anagni and Alatri (alternative day 6) and the next day stop at Montecassino before continuing on to Naples (alternative day 7).

The North Coast: Etruscan Towns and Tombs

It seems hard to believe, but this empty quarter of northern Lazio, often used for the live sets of Cinecittà's spaghetti westerns, was the richest and most heavily populated part of ancient Etruria, including the only two sites really worth visiting for those not enchanted with archaeology: the museums and necropolis at Cervéteri and Tarquinia. Of the cities themselves, little remains. Living Etruscans preferred ephemeral homes and temples of wood and clay, but when it came to the afterlife they built for eternity. Their cities of the dead, tombs made of stone and carved in the rock, reproduced within many of their luxuries and favourite things, 'a pleasant continuance of life, with jewels and wine and flutes playing for the dance', as D. H. Lawrence wrote.

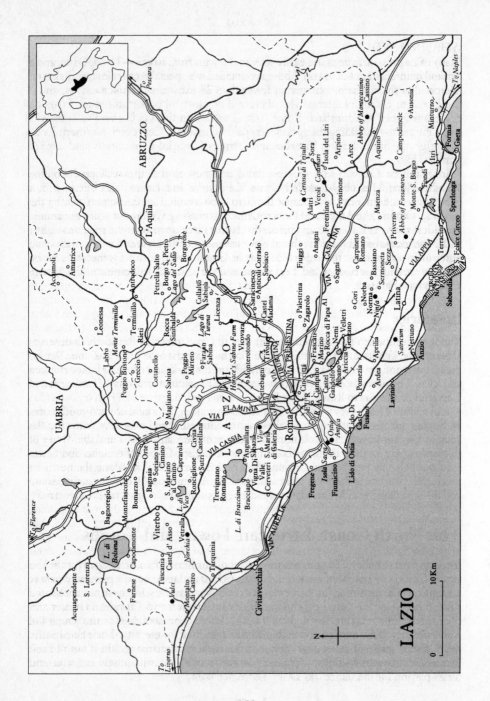

GETTING AROUND
ACOTRAL buses from Via Lepanto (Metro A) go to Cervéteri (46 km), Tarquinia (96 km), and Tuscania (130 km); both towns may also be reached by train from Termini, and then by catching a bus from the local station. By car, take the Via Aurelia (SS1).

TOURIST INFORMATION
Tarquinia: Piazza Cavour 1, tel (0766) 856 384

Cervéteri

One of the best of the necropolises and the closest to Rome is at **Cervéteri**, the abandoned medieval citadel of *Caere Vetere* 'Old Caere' in memory of the richest, if not the strongest, Etruscan city. Among the Etruscans towns, Caere, called *Agylla* by the Greeks, had the closest cultural ties with Greece; according to Herodotus, it was the only non-Greek city with a sanctuary at Delphi. It had three seaports (a total population of 25,000) and mined the Tolfa mountains for the metals it exchanged for Attic vases and other luxury goods; it later imported not only Greek art but Greeks, who founded the local fine arts industry. Decline began when the Greek cities in Southern Italy utterly defeated the Etruscan fleet in 474 BC, ending their sea supremacy. Caere then turned to agriculture and became a close ally of Rome, offering a safe refuge to the Vestal Virgins when the Gauls sacked Rome in 390 BC. A falling-out came a century later, when Caere rebelled and was put in its place, minus the rights of full Roman citizenship. In the early Middle Ages the city was abandoned, then had a brief rerun in the 13th century; the Orsini later added a small castle in the piazza, which now serves as the **Museo Nazionale di Cervéteri** (open 9–4, summer 9–2 and 4–7; adm), with a well-arranged display of tomb finds from the 8th–1st centuries BC, including a magnificent collection of Greek and Greek-style vases.

It's a 2-km drive or walk up from here to the round tufa mound of the **Banditaccia Necropolis** (turn right from the piazza, and then another right on the narrow branch lane; open daily except Mon, 9–one hour before sunset; L4000). This is only one of Cervéteri's four cemeteries (which cover three times as much ground as the city for the living!), but it's the most interesting, in a park setting of cypresses and parasol pines. The tombs were laid out in the form of a town, with streets and squares, and almost like some Etruscan Model Tumulus Show you can see every style available, from the early grave trenches carved in the tufa to 'cube' tombs resembling the houses, to the round mounds with hypogea carved into the rock below—heavy stone domes, set low to the ground, that look more like some sort of defence bunkers than tombs. The largest measure over 40 m in diameter, and in them you can see the forerunners of all the Mausolea of Augustus and Hadrian. The tombs of men are marked at the entrance with a phallic symbol, while women get a little house. Not all of the tombs are lit; the site is quite large, and you may want to buy the map on sale at the entrance to find your way. For serious explorations, ask about a guide to unlock and light the more distant tombs for you, though in winter and early spring these may well be flooded. Don't miss the **Tomb of the Capitals** near the entrance, carved from tufa to resemble Etruscan houses, or the **Tomb of the Shields and Chairs**, with unusual military decoration; another, even stranger, the **Tomb of the Stuccoes** is covered with painted stone reliefs of cooking utensils and other household objects.

Between Cervéteri and Tarquinia, you'll pass the not-so-old-looking city of **Civitavecchia**, a port for Rome and the gateway for ferries to Sardinia. The big fortress overlooking the harbour was designed by Michelangelo for the popes, but there's little else to detain you. Unless, that is, you feel a sudden desire to bolt for the island of *nuraghi* and *mallorredus*, in which case repair to the offices of the Tirrenia Line or the FS ferries, both at the harbour near the docks.

Tarquinia

Unlike Cervéteri, **Tarquinia** is a large, modern town, of interest in its own right, with a 12th-century Cosmatesque church and a Roman aqueduct, rebuilt in the Middle Ages and still in use. In the 15th-century Palazzo Vitelleschi, many of the finest discoveries from the Etruscan city and its necropolis have been assembled for the **Museo Nazionale Tarquinia** (open daily except Mon, 9–2, Sun 9–1; adm). Undoubtedly, the stars of the collection are the famous **Winged Horses** from the 'Altar of the Queen' temple on the acropolis; beautiful beasts, but made of clay like most Etruscan temple decorations, which explains why so few have survived. Well-carved sarcophagi are present in abundance, and there is a collection of Greek vases by some of the greatest 6th–5th-century Attic painters. The Etruscans were talented at ceramics, too, as evidenced by the fine samples of *bucchero* ware, or black pottery incised or painted with the usual puzzling Etruscan images. Some of the paintings from the tombs have been relocated here for their protection, including scenes of chariot riding and athletics—almost any subject is likely to turn up on Etruscan tomb walls; the **Tomb of the Triclinium** with its dancers is one of the most beautiful.

There aren't enough staff to keep open the hundreds of tombs at Tarquinia's **Necropolis**, all that remains standing of the city 100,000 strong that dominated southern Etruria for centuries and enforced on Rome its early dynasty of Etruscan kings (open daily except Mon, 9–7; the tombs are a 15-minute walk from the museum). The few you can see on any given day, however, rank among the finest productions of Etruscan painting, rare in Cervéteri where stucco was the decoration of preference. Tombs like that of the 'Augurs' and the 'Lionesses' with their beautiful 'Ionic'-style paintings, seem remarkably close to the art of the ancient Minoans of Crete. These began to appear in the 6th century BC, and only in the tombs of the richest Etruscans; more typical of the rest is the 'Tomb of the Warrior', carved simply out of the tufa and hung with arms and trophies. The 'Tomb of the Leopards' is decorated with fascinating scenes of an Etruscan feast.

Vulci and Tuscania

To the north, at Montalto di Castro, truly dedicated Etruscophiles may wish to detour into the hills to **Vulci**, an important town in the 9th–1st centuries BC and a renowned centre of bronze-working and art. There are scanty ruins of the city, a small museum in modern Vulci's 13th-century **Castello dell'Abbadia**, and a possibly interesting necropolis, closed at present while excavations are under way.

Further inland, **Tuscania** stands alone in one of the emptiest, eeriest corners of Italy, a region of low green hills where you will find Etruscan ruins, old castles, and religious shrines but no people. Tuscania was a leading Etruscan city after the 4th century BC, and regained its importance for a short while in the early Middle Ages. Today the city is still recovering from a bad earthquake in 1971. Etruscan sarcophagi from several nearby necropolises are on display in the **Museo Archeologico** in the former S. Maria del Riposo (daily except Mon 9–2, 2:30–6; adm); best among them are the complacent bonvivants of the Curunas family reclining lazily on their urns and a mysterious Etruscan rebus from the 6th-century BC tomb of the 'Dado' in Pescheria.

But enough Etruscans: Tuscania is most worth a stop for its two unique churches east of town. **San Pietro** and **Santa Maria Maggiore** were both begun in the 700s, with additions in the 11th and 12th centuries. Besides their carved altars, pulpits, and bits of painting from the 8th–14th centuries, both churches' best features are their unusual sculpted façades—San Pietro's especially, with colourful Cosmati work, fragments of ancient sculpture, and outlandish carved grotesques. Perhaps some of the churches in Rome looked like this before their Renaissance and Baroque rebuildings.

A minor road south of Tuscania leads to **Vetralla**, with the pretty Romanesque church of **San Francesco**. Another 12 km from here, on the road to Monte Romano, a track leads back the isolated, unenclosed **Necropolis of Norchia**, a collection of Etruscan rock-cut tombs with carved, temple-like façades (4th–2nd century BC) cut into the wall of a ravine. Steep winding paths lead down amongst the terraces, where you can visit the two 'Temple tombs' decorated with a Doric frieze, the 'Tomb of three heads'. In **Monte Romano** itself, the 18th-century prison has been converted to an **Antiquarium**, with not only Etruscan but Roman finds (open Thurs and Fri 4–7 pm and Sun 9–1).

WHERE TO STAY AND EATING OUT
Near Cervéteri at Ceri you can eat well and cheaply at **Sora Lella**, in Piazza Alessandrina 1 (actually Ceri is so small it's hard to miss), tel (06) 991 7051, closed Wed and in Sept; L20 000. Montalto di Castro makes a good stopover between Tarquinia and Vulci; for a quiet bed off the main highway, there's **Montebello*, Via Aurelia Vecchia 1, tel (0766) 89 014 (L37 000, all with bath, meals L20 000). Alternatively, in central Tarquinia, ****San Marco**, Piazza Cavour 18, tel (0766) 857 190, has comfortable, air-conditioned rooms and a garden (L65 000). In Tuscania, choices are limited to **Al Gallo*, Via del Gallo 24, tel (0761) 435 028, with a little restaurant (L35 000 without bath, L45 000 with; meals L15–20 000).

Viterbo

Viterbo ought to be visited. Where else in Italy can one rest a while in a café on Death Square, or stroll over to the Piazza of the Fallen to pay one's respects to Our Lady of the Plague? Surrounded by grey, forbidding walls and the ghastly modern districts beyond them, the city is actually rather cute inside, full of grand churches and palaces, and well-preserved medieval streets brightened everywhere with fountains and flowers. The population seems evenly divided between teenagers on scooters, as bejewelled and trendy as their counterparts in Rome, and blasé young soldiers from Italy's biggest army base.

Like the rest of Lazio, Viterbo has had more than its share of troubles, most of them traceable to the proximity of Rome. That geographical necessity, however, also gave Viterbo its greatest period of glory. For much of the 13th century, Viterbo, and not Rome, was the seat of the popes.

History

Although a small city in both Etruscan and Roman times, Viterbo's modern history begins with a fortification of the Lombards in the 8th century. By 1100, it was a free *comune*, one of the few cities in this part of Italy strong and energetic enough to manage it. Viterbo was usually an enemy of Rome, and when Arnold of Brescia's revolution made Pope Eugenius III a refugee in 1145, he sought refuge here. Emperor Frederick Barbarossa soon restored the popes to Rome, but again in 1257, Martin V found Viterban hospitality gratifying when the Guelph-Ghibelline wars made Rome too hot for him. In this most confusing period of Italian history, over a dozen popes were crowned, died, or at least spent time here, in short stays on their way to or from France, Tivoli—sometimes even Rome. In 1309, when the 'Babylonian Captivity' began and the pope was carted off to Avignon, Viterbo could only decline, and when the popes came back to Rome once more, the city that once was Rome's strongest rival found itself a mere provincial town of the Papal States.

GETTING AROUND

There are three railway stations, all just outside the city walls. Regular FS trains to Orvieto and Florence leave from Stazione Porta Fiorentina, north of the walls on Viale Trento. Trains for Rome usually begin here too, also stopping at Stazione Porta Romana, on Viale Raniero Capocci, the big boulevard east of the walls. In addition there is a private line, the tortoise-slow Ferrovie Roma-Nord, which rattles along a separate route, via Bagnaia, Soriano del Cimino, and Civita Castellana to Rome's Piazzale Flaminio station. Buses for Rome, also Tarquinia, Bolsena, Civitavecchia, and other provincial towns leave from Piazza Martiri d'Ungheria, next to Piazza dei Caduti in the town centre. If you're driving, there's a convenient car park in Piazza Martiri d'Ungheria.

TOURIST INFORMATION

Piazza dei Caduti 14, tel (0761) 234 795; Piazza della Morte (summer only), tel 345 229; Piazza Verdi 4/a, tel 226 666.

Palazzo del Plebiscito

In Viterbo's centre, two not-so-fierce lions, the city's ancient symbols, gaze out over the 13th-century **Palazzo del Podestà** with its clock tower, and the elegant **Palazzo dei Priori** (or Comunale) of the 1460s, the typical pair of buildings representing the often conflicting imperial and local powers. The politicians won't mind if you look around the Palazzo dei Priori and its fine Renaissance courtyard, with a 16th-century fountain; if you ask, they'll let you see the Council Chamber, the **Sala Regia** done in fanciful Mannerist frescoes on the history of Viterbo from Etruscan times. In the chapel, the pride of place goes to Sebastiano del Piombo's *Pietà* and a *Visitation* by a follower of Caravaggio. Across the square, the Roman sarcophagus built into the façade of **Sant'Angelo** contains the body of a medieval lady of incomparable virtue and beauty named Galiena, whose fatal charm caused a war between Rome and Viterbo.

There's any number of directions you can take from here. Via Ascenzi, under the arch, leads to Piazza dei Caduti and the **Madonna della Peste**, an octagonal Renaissance church next to the tourist office. Beyond that, Piazza della Rocca contains a pretty fountain by Raffaele da Montelupo and the austere **Rocca**, a citadel built by Cardinal Albornoz in 1354 to keep watch on the Viterbans when the pope returned to Rome. This squat palace-fortress has been restored to hold the Etruscan collection of the **Museo Nazionale Archeologico**, only recently reopened (daily except Mon 9–1; adm). Two of Viterbo's 13th-century popes, Adrian V and Clement IV, are buried in the 13th-century **San Francesco** church, near Porta Murata at the northern end of the walls. Nearby, off Piazza Verdi stands the late 19th-century church of **Santa Rosa**, housing the considerable remains of Viterbo's 13th-century patroness, too holy to decompose and usually on display for all to see. Santa Rosa's preaching helped the Viterbans defeat a siege by the heretical Emperor Frederick II in 1243. To commemorate her, each year on 3 September the men of the town carry a 30-m wooden steeple called the *macchina* through the streets, surmounted by an image of the saint. Local artists create a new *macchina* every four years (see the museum below).

East of Piazza del Plebiscito, Via Cavour takes you to the **Casa Poscia**, an interesting 13th-century house on a stairway to the left, and then the 1206 **Fontana Grande**, the best and biggest of Viterbo's many fountains. Via Garibaldi leads east to the Roman Gate and **San Sisto**, a church in parts as old as the 800s, with an altar made of sculptural fragments. Outside the walls and across Viale Capocci, **Santa Maria della Verità** from the 13th century suffered terrible vandalism at the hands of the 18th-century redecorators. The frills and plaster frosting are gone now, but only a few bits survived of the Renaissance frescoes by Melozzo da Forli. The 15th-century **Cappella Mazzatosta**, behind an iron grille, has good frescoes of the *Marriage of the Virgin* by a local Renaissance artist named Lorenzo of Viterbo. In the adjacent cloisters, a fine work from the 1300s, Viterbo keeps its **Museo Civico** (daily 9–1:30; adm) with a small archaeological section and a picture gallery; in the former, note the marble sphinx, its nose missing just like the larger model in Egypt; among the paintings are works by another Viterban painter, Giovan Francesco Romanelli.

The Pope's Palace
From Piazza del Plebiscito, Via S. Lorenzo leads into the heart of Viterbo's oldest quarter. Three blocks down and off to the left, **Santa Maria Nuova** is the best preserved of the city's medieval churches. On the façade there is an ancient image of Jupiter set into the portal and a small outdoor pulpit where St Thomas Aquinas once preached. On the other side of Via S. Lorenzo, Viterbo's old market square faces the **Gesù Church** (11th century), a medieval tower-fortress, one of the several left in the city, and a palazzo that long ago was the town hall. To the south, the aforementioned **Piazza della Morte** (ironically one of the lovelier squares in Viterbo) has a pretty little fountain and the 13th-century **Palazzetto of San Tommaso**, where a shop sells baskets and other local handicrafts on the ground floor, while upstairs the **Museo delle Confraternite**, with a collection of artefacts related to the Tuscia Viterbese confraternity (open June–Sept, 9am–7pm; free). Trailing off Piazza della Morte, the **San Pellegrino** quarter hangs its web of alleys, arches, and stairs along Via San Pellegrino with a romantic and thoroughly medieval air, though in fact few of the buildings are quite that old. In Via San Pellegrino 60, the **Museo della Macchina di Santa Rosa** has a fascinating display of previous *macchina* models, artefacts, and other souvenirs of the annual festival (open Sat and Sun, 10–12 and 4–7; free).

In the opposite direction from San Pellegrino, a bridge on Roman and Etruscan foundations called the **Ponte del Duomo**, carries you over to Piazza San Lorenzo and the **Papal Palace**, begun in the 1260s by Alexander IV. Moving the papacy to Viterbo (then pop. 60,000) from Rome (pop. 18,000, mostly bullies and layabouts) seemed like a good idea at the time, and this squarish, battlemented building, very much in the style of a medieval city hall, is a finer building than the pope's present address in Rome, though admittedly much smaller. On the best part, the open Gothic loggia, you will see in the decoration lions (for Viterbo) interspersed with the striped coat-of-arms of the French pope Clement V, who completed the building. But fate conspired against the move from the start: Alexander IV died 17 days after moving into the palace. Five popes were afterwards elected in Conclaves held in the Great Hall, among them Urban IV, who was chased out by the Imperial army of Manfred, and Clement IV, who died two weeks after his coronation. In the selection of his successor, arguments between the French and Italian factions led to a two-year deadlock among the cardinals. The exasperated people of Viterbo finally tried to speed up the Conclave, first by locking the cardinals in the palace, and then by tearing off the roof; somehow, according to the story, the churchmen got around this by making tents in the Great Hall. Finally the Viterbans decided to starve them out, and before too long the Church was blessed with the rather undistinguished compromise of Gregory X. He had the roof fixed, but maybe skimped on the materials, for the whole thing came down six years later on the head of his successor, John XXI. He is buried next door in Viterbo's plain Romanesque **cathedral**. Not surprisingly, the cardinals finally got the hint and high-tailed it back to Rome.

East of Viterbo
East of Viterbo, the road for Orte enters the old suburb of La Quercia, passing in front of a landmark of Renaissance architecture: **Santa Maria della Quercia**, built in the late 1470s. The distinctive 1509 façade has a carved oak tree (*quercia*) and lions, and lunettes by Andrea della Robbia over the doors. Inside, the beautiful marble tabernacle by Antonio Bregno of Verona contains a miraculous painting of the Virgin, and there is also a fine Gothic cloister. Ask someone to let you into the **Ex-Voto Museum**, a collection of some 200 devotional plaques brought to this shrine over the centuries, painted with fascinating scenes of miracles attributed to the Madonna.

Six km further east is **Bagnaia**, an old hill village expanded by wealthy Viterban bishops into a residence town. In the 1570s they commissioned Vignola to create the **Villa Lante**, with one of the most striking of all Renaissance gardens (open May–Aug 9–7:30; until 6:30 in spring and autumn; until 4 in the winter; closed Mon. Guided tours of the garden every half hour; adm). Besides the two villas (decorated with Mannerist frescoes, open mornings only by request) there is a large park and a classic Italian garden, geometrically arranged and full of groves and statuary; water shoots up from the fountains, then cascades down decorative stairs and terraces—an impressive sight, especially when they feel like turning it on.

This road continues through the beech forests of the Cimini hills, meeting the town of **Soriano nel Cimino** with a medieval castle and an extinct volcano, **Monte Cimino** (1054 m), for a neighbour, its summit reached by a road from Soriano; don't miss the unusual rocking rock called the **Sasso Menicante**. Soriano has a fine 16th-century palace of its own, Vignola's 1562 **Palazzo Chigi Albani**, built around a magnificent

Mannerist fountain called the *Fontana Papacqua*, with masks and figures carved into the rock (to visit, ring the Comune, tel (0761) 728 178). South of Viterbo, towards Lake Vico, is the lovely town of **San Martino al Cimino**, built around a fine 13th-century Cistercian abbey in the French Gothic style, with a window of fine tracery in the façade; the town itself is an unusual example of Baroque planning, full of trees and half-surrounded by a single curving lane of terraced houses.

WHERE TO STAY   (tel prefix 0761)
Viterbo doesn't have a lot of choices, but for a good place to stay you need look no further than Via della Cava, where there is one in each category: the ***Leon d'Oro**, at No 36, quiet and a little staid, with rooms for L95 000 with bath (tel 344 444). Almost next door at No 26, is the **Roma** (tel 227 274; L60 000 with bath). Both of these have garages. The *Milano, at No 54, has doubles with bath for L47 000—some of them with TV—and rooms without bath for L35 000 (tel 340 705). Alternatively, wallow in the lap of Viterban luxury at the air-conditioned ****Balletti Park**, at Via Umbria 2/a, tel 379 777, in nearby San Martino al Cimino, where furnishings are modern and there's a pool, tennis courts, and plenty of peace and quiet (L130 000, or L85–95 000 in the annexe). Near the woods of Soriano nel Cimino, the ***La Bastia Residence** has attractive terrace-style apartments with air conditioning (on Via Giovanni XXIII, tel 729 062; L90 000, some cheaper without bath).

EATING OUT
Restaurants in these parts are often very good, with a determined adherence to traditional Viterbese dishes: slender fettucine called *fieno*, roast baby lamb, eels and fish from the lakes: *lattarini*, *coregone* (whitefish) or *persico* (perch). In Viterbo, by all means do not miss a dinner at **Il Richiastro**, occupying the well-restored courtyard and cellars of a medieval palace. At bargain rates—about L25–30 000—you can dine on smoked trout, roast lamb, polenta, and some unusual homemade desserts, everything fresh according to the season, and prepared with pride and care (open Thurs–Sat only; tel 223 609; at Via della Marrocca 18 near Piazza Dante). The **Scaletta**, at Via Marconi 45, tel 340 003, is another old favourite, with traditional cooking for about L35 000 and also pizza if you don't feel like a big dinner; and the **Tre Re** on Via Marcel Gattesco (a few blocks north of Piazza del Plebiscito; tel 234 619) has a very good tourist menu for L15 000, and more elaborate dinners for up to L25 000. If you make it out to Bagnaia and the Villa Lante, try a meal at **Checcarello**, Piazza XX Settembre 26, tel 288 255, another solid old establishment and another good bargain—roast lamb or rabbit for L25 000.

Around Viterbo: Hot Mud and Tombs

West of the city, some of the Etruscans' and Romans' favourite thermal springs carry on, doing whatever it is they do that makes the Italians so happy. At the ancient **Terme of Bulicame** you can stop by the roadside for a dip in a sulphurous pool, check into a hotel spa, or visit the municipally-run baths for an aerosol inhalation to help your sinuses, and a frosting with hot mineral mud to calm your nerves. The city also runs a naturally heated outdoor pool where swimming in January is quite fashionable. Further along the road is a diversion to **Castel d'Asso**, a dense clutch of Etruscan tombs just under the ancient acropolis.

Another road north of Viterbo—this one an 8 km dead end—leads to the site of **Ferento** (*Ferentium*), a rival city that Viterbo destroyed in 1172, because one of its artists painted a Crucifixion, depicting Christ with open eyes—signifying support for a heretical belief that Christ only pretended to die on the Cross. Little of Ferento is left, really, save a very well-preserved **Roman Theatre**, where concerts are sometimes held in the summer (daily except Mon, 9–1:30).

The Monster Park

Some of the same sculptors who worked on St Peter's in Rome made this shabby little nightmare, hidden away in the Lazio hills. The two works seem somehow related, opposite sides of the coin that may help to explain the tragic, neurotic atmosphere of late 16th-century Italy. One of the Orsini, that ancient and powerful Roman family, commissioned this collection of huge, strange sculptures; he called it his *Sacro Bosco*—Sacred Wood—and in its present state it is impossible to tell whether it was the complex allegory it pretends to be, or just a joke.

The **Parco dei Mostri** lies just outside **Bomarzo**, one of the most woebegone little towns in this part of Italy. The setting adds to its charm, as does the habit of the present owners of running it like some Alabama roadside attraction, complete with tame deer for your children to pet, an albino peacock, miniature goats, and plenty of souvenirs. Near the entrance, you come upon the impressive though dilapidated **Tempietto**, a domed temple of unknown purpose attributed to Vignola. From there, you wander the ill-kept grounds, encountering at every turn colossal monuments and eroded illegible inscriptions: a 6-m screaming face, where you can walk inside the mouth, under an inscription that reads 'every thought flees', and find a small table and benches, apparently waiting for a dinner party; a life-sized elephant, perhaps one of Hannibal's, crushing a terrified Roman soldier in its trunk; a giant wrestler, in the act of ripping a defeated opponent in two from the legs; a leaning tower, just for fun. In every corner decayed Madonnas, mermaids, sphinxes, nymphs, and harpies wait to spook you. All are done in a distorted, almost primitive style. It would be almost too easy to read too much into these images; a cry of pain from the degraded, humiliated Italy of the 1560s, half-pretending madness as the only way to be safe from the Spanish and the Inquisition—or perhaps merely a symbol for the loss of mental balance that followed too many centuries of high culture and over-stimulation. Whatever, the Monster Park will make you feel that you are an archaeologist, discovering some peculiar lost civilization. Perhaps the Italians understand it too well; it may be the only important monument of the 16th century that neither the government nor anyone else is interested in preserving (open daily 9–sunset; adm expensive).

Orte and Magliano Sabino

Orte, known to most travellers as the main rail junction between Rome and Florence, is an old hill town; its Etruscan name, *Horta*, honours the goddess of gardens. Orte has a better than par **Museo Diocesano** in the Romanesque church of San Silvestro, open on request; star exhibits include a 1420 Madonna by Taddeo di Bartolo, a 15th-century *polyptych of Sant'Egidio*, a 1282 painting of St Francis and his life, and more. **Magliano Sabino**, spread over its hilltop, has a number of venerable buildings, beginning with the **Cathedral of San Liberatore**, Baroqued in the 18th century, with paintings by Jacobetti da Calvi, and the 12th-century church of **San Pietro**.

Three Lakes

All of these, surrounded by circular ranges of hills, are the craters of long-dead volcanoes; long ago they must have been like the famous Phlegraean Fields outside Naples. They are also the most gratifying features in the Lazio landscape, with a few sleepy beaches here and there; not exactly off the main tourist tracks, and popular enough with the Romans.

GETTING AROUND
From Rome, ATAC bus 201 from Piazzale Ponte Milvio for Isola Farnese and Veio; ACOTRAL bus from Via Lepanto (Metro A) or train from Termini for Lake Bracciano. If you're driving, take Via Cassia (N. 2), and near Veio, turn left on the Via Braccianese Claudia. ACOTRAL buses from Via Lepanto (Metro A) go to Lake Vico and Caprarola. Lake Vico and Lake Bolsena can also be reached by bus from Viterbo; Ronciglione, Sutri, and Civita Castellana are on the Roma Nord railway between Viterbo and Rome.

TOURIST INFORMATION
Bracciano: Via Claudia 72, tel (06) 902 3665

Veio and Lake Bracciano

For Veio, head 17 km up the Via Cassia (the ancient road linking Etruria to Rome) to La Storta; after another kilometre you'll see the sign for Isola Farnese (no island, but a wee medieval townlet and castle) and **Veio**, ancient *Veii*, from the 8th–6th centuries BC the largest city in the Etruscan Federation, and a bitter rival of Rome (excavations open daily except Mon, winter 10–2, Sat and Sun 9–one hour before sunset; summer 9–one hour before sunset; adm). The rather sparse, widely extended remains (Veii's walls were 11 km long) make this the most difficult Etruscan site to visit, although the striking location, on a sheer tufa plateau over a moat of two streams invites a vigorous country ramble. Unlike its Etruscan neighbour and rival Cervéteri, Veii had no port, and in the 8th century it tried to establish one on the Tiber. It had to be heavily fortified, since Cervéteri claimed the west bank and the Latin League under Alba Longa claimed the east. In 753 BC the Latins under the leadership of Romulus and with the help of Caere, ousted Veii from its Tiber port, in its place founding *Rumon*, which any Etruscan will tell you really means 'city on the river'. The Veiians, left without a port and the salt pans of Ostia, held a mighty grudge against Rome. When the Republic's Fabii clan took it upon themselves to guard and harass Veii, the Etruscans ambushed and massacred all but one (475 BC). Some 25 years later each city could no longer tolerate the other, and a fight to the finish became inevitable; of all Rome's wars, this was the most crucial, for its very existence was at stake. Veii called upon its fellow Etruscan cities for aid (none came) and the Romans under M. Furius Camillus began a siege that ended only when the Romans unblocked one of the city's marvellous irrigation tunnels that led under the walls. Veii was thus surprised, captured and thoroughly destroyed; its chief deity, Juno, was carted off to a new temple on the Aventine. Julius Caesar and Augustus tried to plant a colony on the site, but it never prospered.

Nowadays, you can see the ruins of the Temple of Apollo (where the Villa Giulia's beautiful Apollo of Veio was found), cisterns, a tunnel in the rock (where Camillus led the Romans?), and most interestingly, the 7th-century BC **Tomba Campana**, though you'll have to ask the custodian to open it for you. Inside are some of the oldest Etruscan paintings ever discovered, of strange Etruscan animals and Mercury escorting the dead to the next world. Further up the path is the **Ponte Sodo**, an Etruscan bridge and a truly lovely spot for a picnic.

Equally picturesque are the ruins of the **Castle of Galéria**, 7 km up Via Claudia Braccianese from Veio; below is its pretty little offshoot hamlet, Santa Maria di Galéria. Another 16 km will bring you to the shores of **Lake Bracciano**. There is little of great interest around this broad sheet of water, sloshing about in the round volcanic crater of Mt Sabatini. You've probably already seen some of it in the Fontana Paola or the fountains in St Peter's Square (where apparently the lake's baby eels sometimes end up and clog the pipes). From June–Sept you can take boat tours from the town of **Bracciano**, but the best view of it is from the ramparts of the grim, five-towered **Castello degli Orsini**, stronghold of the bearish clan from 1470 to 1696, when they ceded castle and town of Bracciano to the Odescalchi (open daily except Mon, 10–12 and 3–5, guided tours only; adm expensive). Although the Orsini were usually supporters of the papacy against their nemesis, the Colonna, they knew the Roman pot could boil over at any time, and built this castle as a private bunker close to Rome—not exactly in the style of the day, but when did the Orsini ever care to be progressive? But it served them in good stead, fending off the attack of the entire papal army of Alexander VI who didn't think much of their fraternizing with the French invader, Charles VIII. Frescoes and painted ceilings by Antoniazzo Romano in the 1490s, and later frescoes by the two Zuccari, busts of the Orsini by Bernini, and suits of armour are the artistic highlights within.

During World War I, Lake Bracciano was Italy's dirigible- and seaplane-testing area. Two old hangars in **Vigna di Valle**, 6 km east of Bracciano, were converted in the 1970s to hold the **Historical Museum of the Italian Air Force** (open daily except Mon, 9–6 in summer, 9–4 winter; free). Exhibits begin with a model of Leonardo da Vinci's wing-flapping machine and include fighter planes, racers, seaplanes, planes that went to the North Pole and the plane that D'Annunzio flew over Vienna in 1918. Most curious of all is a hot air balloon launched from Paris in 1804 in honour of Napoleon's coronation, bearing instead of a basket a large glass replica of the emperor's crown. Considering Napoleon's later troubles with the watery element, from island exiles to Waterloo and Well-ington, it was no small omen that the whole thing fell into Lake Bracciano before reaching Rome.

A scenic road (especially between Bracciano and Trevignano on the north shore) encircles the lake. Although only ruins remain of the Orsini castle in pretty **Trevignano Romano**, do the walk up to see the church of the **Assunta**, for its views over the lake and beautiful fresco of the Assumption by the school of Raphael.

Lake Vico and Caprarola

The smallest and perhaps loveliest of the lakes, Vico is ringed by rugged hills; parts of the shore are unspoiled marshes, a favourite stop for migratory birds now protected as a wildlife reserve. At the northern edge, this ancient crater has a younger volcano (also extinct) poking up inside it: **Monte Venere**. Just over the hills from the lake, you should definitely not pass up a chance to see one of Italy's most arrogantly ambitious late Renaissance palaces, the **Villa Farnese** in Caprarola.

When Alessandro Farnese, member of an obscure Lazio noble family, set his sister Giulia up as mistress to Pope Alexander VI, his fortune was made; Alessandro later became Pope Paul III, a great pope who called the Council of Trent, rebuilt Rome, and kept Michelangelo busy—also a rotten pope, who oppressed his people, refounded the Inquisition, and became the most successful grafter in papal history. Before long the Farnese family ruled Parma, Piacenza, and most of northern Lazio. With the fantastic wealth Alessandro accumulated, his grandson, also named Alessandro, built this family headquarters; Vignola, the family architect, turned the entire town of Caprarola into a setting for the palace, ploughing a new avenue through the town as an axis that led to a grand stairway, then a set of gardens (now disappeared), then another stairway up to the huge pentagonal villa, built over the the massive foundations of an earlier, uncompleted fortress. The palace is empty today; the Farnese lost everything in later papal intrigues, and someone, sometime, probably had to sell the furniture.

Nevertheless, it is still an impressive place; some of the highlights of the guided tour include Vignola's elegant central courtyard, a room with uncanny acoustical tricks that the guides love to demonstrate, frescoes of the *Labours of Hercules*, another room with a wonderful ceiling painted with the figures of the constellations, and an incredible **spiral staircase** of stone columns and Neoclassical frescoes, Vignola's decorative masterpiece. The best part, however, is the '**Secret garden**' in the rear, an extensive park full of azaleas and rhododendrons leading up to a sculpture garden of grotesques and fantastical telamones that recall the Monster Park (there's a connection; one of the Orsinis of Bomarzo was Alessandro Farnese's secretary), and finally a delightful, smaller villa, the **Palazzina del Piacere** (daily, except Mon, 9–4, until 6 in the summer; adm).

South of Lake Vico

Near the south shore of Vico, **Ronciglione**, a village famous for its carnival, was once more exalted as a duchy of the Farnese family; it has a pretty little medieval quarter and, by the cathedral, a fountain from the 1500s decorated with unicorns. Further south **Sutri**, is the site of ancient *Sutrium*, the 'Gate of Etruria', captured by the Romans back in 389 BC. Sutri later became the beginning of another, less brilliant empire—the Papal States—when the Lombards donated it to Pope Gregory II in 730. The archaeological zone around the Via Cassia encompasses a 6th–4th century BC cemetery with Etruscan tombs, one converted in the Middle Ages to the church of the Madonna del Parto ('of birth'), with fragments of Etruscan votive frescoes. A singular elliptical **amphitheatre** carved in the tufa is a bit further along the road (all of the above may be visited by asking at Sutri's Comune (tel (0761) 68 012) or Pro Loco, tel (0761) 68 330. Some of Sutri's later history is incorporated into its **Duomo**—a Lombard crypt, a partial Cosmatesque pavement and Byzantine painting on the left, a campanile built in 1207, and much later Baroqueing.

The most important town in the region is **Civita Castellana**, set on a tufa hill surrounded by sharply cut ravines; in ancient times this was *Falerii Veteres*, the capital of a tribe called the Falisci, who though not Etruscan, belonged to their Confederation. Destroyed by the Romans in 241 BC, a new town called Falerii Novi was founded, leaving the old site uninhabited for a thousand years, when Dark Age conditions encouraged its resettlement. The **Duomo** is one of the gems of Lazio, its portico and façade beautifully sculpted by the Cosmati family in 1210. Although the interior was redone in the 18th century, a large section of the Cosmati's pavement survives, while a lovely pair of plutei (marble altar parapets) by the same family of artists are displayed in the sacristy. Near the Duomo, in Via Roma, is the entrance to the pentagonal **Rocca**, a citadel designed by Antonio da Sangallo and until recently used as a prison. Nowadays, as the **Museo Archeologico** (open 9–1, closed Mon) its inmates are Greek vases (including some beautiful Attic works), bronzes, mirrors, terracottas and other artefacts of the Falisci, Etruscans, and Romans of the region.

The ruins of Civita Castellana's two predecessors are along the road leading west towards Fabrica di Roma: first **Falerii Veteres**, with ruined temples, tombs, and an aqueduct, while in another 5 km further lie the more interesting remains of Falerii Veteres' Roman replacement, **Falerii Novi**; a lovely setting wrapped in walls, stretching over two kilometres in the form of an immense triangle, still guarded by 50 towers. Almost as impressive is the fact that so little survives within these bulwarks—only a long-abandoned abbey made of ancient fragments, and a 12th-century church that has lost its roof.

From Civita, buses go southwest to **Nepi**, with the mighty ruins of its castle and Etruscan walls. The highlight of the neighbourhood, however, is another three km east, in the town of **Castel Sant'Elia**: the **Santuario di Maria Santissima ad Rupes**, located under a tufa cliff in a little cemetery, a church almost entirely made of Roman odds and ends pieced together by 11th-century Benedictines, and painted with bright Byzantine frescoes from the 11th or 12th century (open winter 8:15–5, summer 8:15–7).

Lake Bolsena

Lazio's northernmost lake, and the fifth largest in Italy, Lake Bolsena is best known for a rather convenient miracle, of such importance that Raphael painted it in his Vatican *Stanze*: in the 13th century the popes were having trouble putting over the dogma of transubstantiation, an archaic, genuinely pagan survival that many of the Church's mystics and reformers secretly found repugnant. In 1263, while Urban IV was visiting nearby Orvieto the necessary miracle occurred. A Bohemian priest named Peter, while on his way to Rome, was asked to celebrate mass in the town of Bolsena. Father Peter had long been sceptical about the doctrine of the Host becoming in truth the body of Christ, but during this mass the Host itself answered his doubts by dripping blood on the altar linen. Marvelling, Peter took the linen to the Pope in Orvieto, who declared it a miracle and instituted the feast of Corpus Christi. Thomas Aquinas, also in Orvieto at the time, was asked to compose a suitable office for the new holy day, while Urban IV promised Orvieto (and not poor Bolsena!) a magnificent new cathedral to enshrine the blood-stained relic.

Instead of a cathedral, the town of **Bolsena** on the lake's north shore has the medieval **Castle Mondaleschi**, with a small archaeological collection and fine views of the lake from its tower (open April–Sept 9–1 and 4–8, closed Mon; adm; Oct–Mar open only by request). The 15th-century church of **Santa Cristina**, was before its last rebuilding the site of the Miracle of Bolsena; it preserves a small Christian catacomb underneath with traces of paintings and a decorative 'Grotta della Santa' (open 9–12:30 and 3–7; adm). A kilometre up the Orvieto road is Bolsena's **Zona Archeologico** (open 9–1, closed Mon) where parts of the Roman walls and amphitheatre are currently being uncovered. There are a number of narrow beaches nearby, though unfortunately pollution makes swimming a risky business.

Instead, head east to **Civita di Bagnoregio**, 'the dying city', or more properly, 'half a city'. Medieval Civita, romantically piled on a hill, was once easily reached from Bagnoregio by bridge. The bridge was damaged in the war, and because of crumbling, rough terrain below, was impossible to repair, abandoning Civita's silent lanes and striking views to a handful of refugees from the 20th century. Other towns near Bolsena include **San Lorenzo Nuovo**, an 18th-century century town rather ambitiously modelled on the plan of Copenhagen, and **Acquapendente**, with an ancient church crypt under its cathedral, built as a copy of the Holy Sepulchre in Jerusalem; and a nature reserve on nearby Monte Rufeno.

On the southern shore of Lake Bolsena, **Capodimonte** on its small promontory offers more beaches and small boat excursions (tel 98 213) to the lake's two islands: the pretty rock of **Martana**, with steep granite cliffs and woods above, and the **Isola Bisentina**. This was a favoured retreat of the Farnese in the 1500s, when the family was just beginning its spectacular career. They commissioned Antonio da Sangallo the Younger to build them a palace and a large domed church, **SS. Giacomo e Cristoforo**, now in decay. The island's hill also has a string of Calvary Chapels. The church, however, survived better than Castro, the town the Farnese had Sangallo build from scratch just to the west of Lake Bolsena. Castro and Ronciglione was the title of the dukedom created by Paul III for his son, Pier Luigi Farnese, and Castro was designed as a perfect 16th-century city. But don't look for it on the map: the Farnese later picked a quarrel with Innocent X, who punished their pride by flattening Castro to the ground.

Montefiascone has been famous for its 'Est! Est!! Est!!!' wine since a German bishop named Giovanni Defuc did himself in by drinking too much of it in 1113. His tomb is in the 12th-century church of **S. Flaviano**, just outside town. Montefiascone makes a living from its wine and the embroidered legend that goes with it (but wine critics do not rate it very highly today). There are, however, suitably high views from the belvedere, by the papal fortress.

WHERE TO STAY AND EATING OUT   (tel prefix 0761)

Getting in and out of Viterbo can be a little hectic, and if you're just passing through on the way to or from Rome, you might consider stopping at one of the smaller towns in the region instead. At Lago di Vico, the ****Bella Venere** is a rare find, a lovely small hotel on the lake with gardens, a beach and tennis (L65 000 for one of the 14 double rooms with bath; tel 646 453; the address is Loc. Lago di Vico, and you'll find it on the eastern shore towards Caprarola). Another choice around Lake Vico is the *****Sans Soucis**, at Punta del Lago near the road to Ronciglione, also with a beach and garden, and views over the lake from a roof terrace (tel 612 052; L95 000). A less costly place to sleep and eat is **Il Cardinale**, again on the Ronciglione side of the lake at Via Cassia Cimina 12, tel 625 188; rooms are L65 000, all with bath; meals can be either surf or turf—in autumn try roasted porcini mushrooms for a special treat—L35 000.

Towards Caprarola, you can sample mushrooms in every conceivable form, and also big Florentine steaks, at the **Rifugio del Parco Cimino**, on the Via Cassia Cimino near Caprarola, tel 646 121; about L30–35 000 at the most and well worth it. In Civita Castellana, near the Duomo, **L'Altra Bottiglia**, Via delle Palme 14-18, tel 517 403, is a first-class little restaurant that incorporates local ingredients, from Lake Bolsena's eels (which in Dante's *Purgatorio* were the chief cause of Pope Martin IV's gluttony) and pheasant to pecorino cheese and asparagus, in a parade of gourmet delights; *menu degustazione* L45 000, closed Wed.

Up by Lake Bolsena, there's the bright modern ***Columbus Hotel Del Lago**, Via del Lago, tel 799 009, with a beach and tennis courts (L66 000 without bath, L85 000 with). On the lake but outside Bolsena, *Eden**, Via Cassia km 114.4, tel 799 015, has ten rooms, a beach, garden, and restaurant, all you need for a simple, restful holiday (L28 000 without bath, L38 000 with). Just outside Montefiascone, the **Caminetto**, Via Cassia km 102, tel 826 486, has lovely views over the lake and a fairly good restaurant (rooms L64 000, all with bath). *Dante**, also in Montefiascone, has four simple rooms, all with bath, for L30 000, and even better, one of the finest restaurants in the area—a good place to try Bolsena's eels, or fish from the sea for prices Romans drive miles for: L25–30 000.

Rieti Province: the Land of the Sabines

This comes as something of a digression, but this strip of land reaching over the Apennines to touch the borders of the Marches is also a part of Lazio. It was the land of the Sabines, an uncouth hill tribe that was sometimes an ally but often the fierce enemy of Rome. In the earliest days they were near neighbours around the Forum—when the Roman bachelors stole their women—but in historical times they were confined to these hills, though not without a struggle. The Romans pushed their Via Salaria (the main route of the salt trade) through here on its way to the Adriatic; to their dismay the Sabines used it as an easy route to march down into the plains and Rome itself. In 460 BC they even occupied the Capitol. The Sabines kept their independence until 290 BC when the Romans defeated them, putting the province into the orbit of the urbs for ever after.

Unless you're a keen student of Italy, none of the discreet charms of this Sabine country will sound familiar. Yet much of it resembles its increasingly popular northern neighbour, Umbria; green mountains, medieval hill towns, and Romanesque churches—a quiet, unassuming land that St Francis of Assisi found perfect for his retreats from the world.

GETTING AROUND

Trains are scarce here; the only line in the province links Rieti to Terni in Umbria and to Antrodoco en route to L'Aquila and Sulmona in the Abruzzo (in Rieti, tel 43 143 for information). ACOTRAL buses link Rieti with the rest of the province and Rome; tel 41 113.

TOURIST INFORMATION
Rieti: Piazza Vittorio Emanuele 17, tel (0746) 43 220
Terminillo: Pian de' Valli, tel (0746) 61 121

Into the Monti Sabini

From Rome it's 40 km up the Via Salaria to the Monti Sabini. Medieval **Fara in Sabina**, 12 km north of the road, has in its church of **Sant'Antonio** a curious tabernacle by Vignola, in the form of an ideal Renaissance temple. A 5-km by-road leads from here leads to the **Abbazia di Santa Maria di Farfa**, founded in the 6th century by San Lorenzo Siro but soon after destroyed by the Lombards. In the 7th century, St Thomas of Maurienne on pilgrimage in Jerusalem had a vision of the Virgin Mary instructing him to rebuild the abbey, and it soon became one of the stars in the Benedictine constellation, inheriting vast tracts of land, holding celebrated fairs, declared an 'Imperial Abbey' by Emperor Henry IV. The whole was rebuilt in the 15th and 16th centuries, including the **Abbey Church**, with a fine Romanesque portal, coffered ceiling, frescoes—especially a *Last Judgement* (1561) by Hendrick van der Broek—remains of a Cosmatesque pavement, and a Carolingian altar. The semi-circular crypt dates from the 7th century; at its entrance is a 3rd-century AD Roman sarcophagus with a battle scene, while the campanile, first built in the 9th century, has in a room at its base rare bits of fresco of the same period.

Northeast of Farfa, **Poggio Mirteto** is one of many towns that once belonged to the abbey; its 13th-century church **San Paolo** shelters a primitive *Triumph of Death* fresco from the 1300s, complete with dialect captions; in the apse and arch are frescoes painted in 1521 by Lorenzo Torresani. Aldo Moro, assassinated by the Red Brigade in 1978, is buried in nearby **Torrita Tiberina**. **Roccantica**, a tiny village perched over some of the lushest scenery in the Monti Sabini, is crowned by an Orsini castle, while below are two churches worth a look: **Santa Caterina d'Alessandria**, just below the castle, with colourful late Gothic frescoes on the life of St Catherine, and **Santa Maria Assunta**, with an elaborate 16th-century altarpiece by Bartolomeo Torresani.

Further north, **Torri in Sabina** was long an Orsini fief, and is still well fortified with its medieval walls. Within, the **Collegiata di S. Giovanni Battista** boasts a rare 7th-century baptismal font. The main attraction is just outside of town: the 11th-century **Santa Maria in Vescovio**, set in a grove of cypresses among the ruins of the Roman town of *Forum Novum*. The courtyard has fragments of Roman sculptures. The apse and crypt are decorated with a series of early 14th-century frescoes by the school of Rome's master, Pietro Cavallini.

East of the modern Via Salaria, **Scandriglia** is where St Barbara had her head lopped off by her exasperated father in the year 290. Dad's sudden demise by thunderbolt aided Barbara's posthumous career as the patroness of others who provoke abrupt endings: artillerymen and bombardiers. The site of her martyrdom is marked by a little rural church on the Contrada di S. Barbara, a picturesque stair, and a relief of a shepherd miraculously turned into a dog. **Monteleone Sabino**, built over the Sabine capital of *Trebula Mutuesca*, was the birthplace of Consul Lucius Mummius, who in 146 BC scandalized the civilized world by razing the city of Corinth. Much of the ancient city lies unexcavated under the sports facilities, but beyond these lies the 11th–12th-century

Romanesque **Santa Vittoria**. Columns from Trebula Mutuesca sprout like mushrooms on the lawn, and one of the stone lions that gave Monteleone its name is embedded in the façade, next to the lovely marble portal carved with curling animal motifs. The 10th-century campanile, made of Roman funerary stones, has one of the oldest bells in Italy, dated 1223. Inside is a Roman sarcophagus that once contained the remains of St Vittoria, and a cistern in the middle of the nave, filled by a spring that gushed forth at her death.

Rocca Sinibalda, further north, has one of the country's premier castles, perched on a rocky spur over a little hamlet, its crenellated towers now planted with cypresses and hanging gardens. Designed in the 1540s by Baldassare Peruzzi, its unusual scorpion-shaped plan fits in hundreds of rooms, some of which have good Mannerist frescoes and were restored in the 1920s (open Sat and Sun, 9–1 and 3–5; adm).

Rocca Sinibalda

The road to Rocca Sinibalda continues to **Longone**, a hill village that from 26 to 28 September celebrates a primitive bonfire festival in honour of the medical saints Cosma and Damian—a fine 15th-century painting of them with their instruments, stolen from the church (a common fate for art in this remote area) has been replaced by a copy. Longone is a few kilometres from the ruins of the **Abbey of San Salvatore**, built over a Roman villa in 733, desolate and roofless in some of Italy's loneliest countryside. South of Rocca Sinibalda lies long, artificial **Lake Turano**, and beyond it, **Collalto Sabino**, dominated by a massive, well-preserved 15th-century castle, entered by way of a drawbridge and restored with a fairytale touch in 1895 (open by request, tel (0765) 98 260); from its towers the view takes in 30 villages.

Rieti

Rieti, the provincial capital, was built over the Sabine capital *Reate*, captured by Curius Dentatus in 290 BC. Unlike most conquerors, he decided that, instead of humbling his conquest, he would do it a favour and with Roman know-how drain the surrounding swamps, creating the Marmore Falls in Terni and a fertile plain for Rieti, protected by some of the highest peaks of the Apennines. Nowadays it uses its plain not only for agriculture, but for gliding; the first Italian world championship was held there in 1985.

Central **Piazza Vittorio Emanuele** is dominated by the 18th-century **Palazzo Comunale**, home of Rieti's **Museo Civico** (open Tues–Thurs 10–12 and Sat and Sun 4–6; free). Contents include a rare Iron Age urn, Roman sculptures, and some good paintings: the only signed work of a Gothic Venetian painter named Zannino di Pietro; a 13th-century polyptych by the Sienese Luca di Tomè; a 1464 *Madonna* by Antoniazzo Romano; a Piero della Francesca-inspired *Resurrection* (1511) by Marcantonio di Antonazzo; *San Leonardo visiting a prisoner* (1698) by Gherardi, and a plaster cast of Hebe by Canova. Nearby, Piazza Cesare Battisti's little garden lies between a charming loggia and Rieti's 12th-century **Cathedral of Santa Maria Assunta**, with its formidable bell tower and original central doorway. Although Baroqued inside, note the fourth chapel on the left, dedicated to St Barbara, with a statue of the saint designed by Bernini, while the second last chapel on the right has Andrea Sacchi's *Guardian Angel*. There are good examples of Renaissance gold-work—as in the Abruzzo, a local speciality—in the sacristy and its adjacent reliquary chapel. Across Piazza Mariano Vittori is the **Palazzo Vescovile**, with high Gothic vaulting over its lower, Via Cintia entrance. A plaque in the loggia records the palace's most famous wedding, the 1185 banns of Emperor Henry IV of Hohenstaufen and Constance of Hauteville, daughter of King Roger of Sicily, parents of Frederick II—who came to this palace in 1234 to meet Pope Gregory IX.

On Via Roma, the main street descending to the river Velino, is Carlo Maderno's monumental **Palazzo Vecchiarelli**, and in Via San Francesco, just before the bridge, the church of **San Francesco** has a series of colourful 1245 frescoes on the life of St Francis, inspired by the Giottoesque frescoes in Assisi. On the north side of Rieti stretches a kilometre of well-preserved and very medieval-looking walls.

St Francis slept here, and here, and here

The wooded hills around the lovely plain of Rieti and the rivers Turano and Velino were a favourite retreat of St Francis, and so many convents and chapels sprang up in his wake that the region is called the Valle Santa. Outside Rieti's Porta Romana, the 15th-century **Convento di Fonte Colombo** is on a hill of venerable ilexes, called the 'Franciscan Sinai' for a vision of Christ Francis had here in 1223, inspiring the Rule of his order. The river road continues to **Contigliano**, dominated by the tall **Collegiata di San Michele Archangelo**; almost as tall are the romantically desolate and ivy-wreathed ruins of the 13th-century **Abbey of St Pastore** (2 km), architecturally superior to the surrounding Franciscan efforts, but so morally inferior it was closed in the 1500s.

To the northwest, the convent at **Greccio** clings dramatically to the side of the cliff. Francis spent part of 1217 in a humble retreat on top of this mountain, and he returned on Christmas Eve 1223, to make the first Christmas crib, or *presepio*, in the Chapel of Santa Lucia carved into the side of the mountain. Umbrian frescoes record the event in the convent's Cappella del Presepio. You can also visit the old dormitory where Francis slept on the bare rocks, and the 13th-century **Chiesina**, its ceiling spangled with stars, while below are the original rough choir stalls, lectern, and lantern holder. There are panoramic views from the convent terrace, and even more vertiginous ones from the loggia by the Hermitage of Giovanni da Parma, reached by a path through the woods.

Directly north of Rieti is the **Convento La Foresta**, where Francis helped a local priest out with a miraculous grape harvest; the convent's best feature is a rustic cloister in warm stone, built in the 1400s and sheltering a lush garden. To the north at **Poggio Bustone**, the lofty **Convento di San Giacomo** was built near 'Lo Speco', a hermitage where Francis had a number of visions—serious ones that left imprints all over the rocks—of his breviary, his body (after a wrestling match with the devil), feet, and knees—all marked with shrines along the path to Lo Speco. From Poggio Bustone, it's a short drive to Lazio's 'Little Belgium' or **Labro**, a pale village perched aloofly above zigzaggy Lake Piediluco, beautifully restored by a Belgian entrepreneur.

The biggest hill in these parts, visible from many a Franciscan cell, is **Monte Terminillo** 'Rome's Mountain', with the nearest skiing to the capital on the slopes of its 2132-m peak. In the summer, there's a host of roads and trails into the mountains, a few ending up in **Leonessa**, an attractive medieval town that is one of the quietest, most out-of-the-way places in Italy. There are several attractive churches in its low, porticoed lanes; one, **San Francesco** (1446) has a *presepio* with painted terracotta figures from the early 1500s.

Via Salaria, from Rieti to Amatrice

From Rieti, Via Salaria continues to **Cittaducale**, founded as a Neapolitan outpost in 1309 by Charles II of Anjou, and named after his son, Robert, then Duke of Calabria. It minted its own coins, and spent much of its time brawling with the papal loyalists in Rieti. The town has preserved its original rectangular plan and a smooth, ship-shaped white Angevin tower nicknamed San Magno's Quarter Deck. **Cotilia**, further up the road, was the favourite spa of Emperor Vespasian, whose Flavian clan were from the region. He came here to die in AD 79 and his last words were a joke on the habit of deifying emperors: 'My goodness, I think I'm about to become a god'. The three valleys that merge at **Antrodoco** were important even in Strabo's day, when the town was called *Vicus Interocrea*. Historically, it always seemed to side with the underdog, earning itself a siege by Frederick II, destruction from L'Aquila and Cittaducale, and devastation in 1455 and 1485 from the Aragonese. At the entrance of Antrodoco (from Rieti) stands the ancient church of **Santa Maria Extra Moenia** and its hexagonal **Baptistry**, both dating from the 5th century though later enlarged.

From Antrodoco the N. 17 leads to L'Aquila (p. 295) while the Via Salaria continues towards the Adriatic, increasingly hemmed in by hills as far as **Posta**, where the road runs through a green plain, then past another artificial lake, to the crossroads for **Amatrice**, a name that makes Italians think of spaghetti sauce 'all'amatriciana'. When it supported Francis I of France in 1528, it was flattened by his rival Emperor Charles V and rebuilt on a rectangular plan. Amatrice has two lovely churches: **San Francesco** (mid-14th century), decorated with a fine Gothic portal, with doll-like stone statues of the Virgin and angels in the lunette; inside are Renaissance frescoes by an anonymous painter from the Marches, a curious *Last Judgement* fresco (1330s) over the altar and a magnificent reliquary in the form of a Gothic temple (1472). On the northeast extreme of town, the late Gothic church of **Sant'Agostino** (1420s) has another remarkable sculpted Gothic portal, with funny little figures of monks, while above is a splendid marble rose window.

WHERE TO STAY AND EATING OUT

This is the land of chestnuts and homemade pasta, especially fettucine, raggedy, uneven *stracci*, and *strengozzu*, cut in thick leaves and served with ham and peas. Also try a soft cheese from Leonessa called *fiore molle*, flavoured with saffron.

If you're letting the ACOTRAL bus company do the driving, Rieti is the best base for seeing the province. Right in the centre of town, near the cathedral, ***Quattro Stagioni**, Piazza C. Battisti 14, tel (0746) 497 705 is a discreet but comfortable hotel (rooms with bath, L68 000). An older hotel, in the centre, **Europa**, Via San Rufo 49, tel 495 149, has bathless rooms for L28 000, with for L34 000. Rieti is blessed with an exceptional restaurant: **Checco al Calice d'Oro**, Via Marchetti 10 (near Piazza Vittorio Emanuele), tel (0746) 44 271; try its famous, unique *lesso misto* (L35–60 000, closed Mon and mid July). Less expensive, **Il Grottino**, Piazza C. Battisti 4, tel (0746) 45 146 specializes in *strengozzu* (L22 000). There are several smart hotels up at Terminillo: ***La Lucciola**, tel (0746) 61 138 at Pian de' Valli is one of the few open all year (rooms with bath and TV, L65 000) as is **Regina**, Via dei Villini, tel (0746) 61 375 (L44 000, with bath). In Albaneto, near Leonessa, **Da Tonino**, tel (0746) 932 284 is very small and very quiet; L39–45 000, all with bath.

In Greccio **Delle Fonte**, tel (0746) 753 110, enjoys a pretty setting and has rooms for L32 000 without bath, L44 000 with. For a special meal, aspire to Greccio's 'Crow's Nest', **Il Nido del Corvo**, which hangs on the cliffs near the convent and is built on various levels, all with views that match the excellent meals—plenty of game dishes, innovative risotti, and much more for L35 000 (tel (0746) 753 181). If you make it as far as Antrodoco, you're sure to have worked up an appetite. The hefty portions at **Dionisio**, Via Marmorale 70, are the answer; if you feel a bit adventurous, try the salt cod with chestnuts (L25–30 000). For a genuine *spaghetti all amatriciana* in Amatrice, head for the **Roma**, Via dei Bastiani, tel (0746) 85 035; add antipasti, a meat course, dessert, and wine and the bill will be around L25–30 000.

Southern Lazio

> . . . nowhere else has the creative power of Fascism left
> a deeper mark. The immense works can be summed
> up in the lapidary phrase of Il Duce:
> 'You redeem the land, you found some cities.'
> *From a 1939 Italian guidebook*

You wouldn't be travelling this way 60 years ago, when the broad plain of the **Pontine Marshes** or *Agro Pontino* was the biggest no man's land in Italy, racked by malaria and healthy only for the water buffalo. Julius Caesar was the first to plan its drainage, but the design died with him. Augustus later dug a ditch along the Via Appia to reclaim the swamps, and canal barges helped to make the soles on many a traveller's *caligae* last a bit longer. In the Dark Ages the canals became blocked up when no one had the money to keep them cleared. Once again, during the 13th century, some of the marshes were drained, but a few centuries of papal rule had the area back to its pristine emptiness when Mussolini decided to make it one of the showpieces of his regime. Today, except for the small corner preserved as a park and wildlife refuge, the Pontine Marshes no longer exist, and brand-new towns like Aprília, Pomezia, Pontinia, and Sabaudia sit amidst miles of prosperous farms as curious monuments to the brighter side of fascism.

If you plan to be in the area on the first weekend of a month between April and October, you can visit one of Italy's prettiest botanical gardens and bird sanctuaries at the ghost town of Ninfa, though make sure you get a ticket before you set off (see below).

GETTING AROUND
This area is served by hourly ACOTRAL buses from Rome, departing the Metro B station EUR Fermi; the trip takes a bit more than an hour; trains from Termini make the trip to Anzio and Nettuno in the same time. Both Latina and Priverno-Fossanova stations are on the main Rome-Naples line; from the latter a spur descends to Terracina. Local buses will get from the stations to the surrounding towns.

TOURIST INFORMATION
Anzio: Riviera Zanardelli 105, tel (06) 984 8135
Latina: Via Duca del Mare 19, tel (0773) 498 711
Norma: Via Passeggiata S. Giovanni, tel (0773) 34 705
Priverno: Piazza Vittorio Emanuele, tel (0773) 96 230
Sabaudia: Piazza del Comune, tel (0773) 55 046
San Felice Circeo: Via De Gaspari, tel (0773) 527 770

Pomezia and Lavinium
Along N. 148, the new town of **Pomezia** lies just east of the site of ancient **Lavinium**, which readers of Virgil will recognize as the town founded by Aeneas and named after Lavinia, daughter of the local king Latinus who becomes the hero's wife at the end of the Aeneid. It was the custom of elected officials in Rome to make a sacrifice in Lavinium. Beyond that, nothing was known until the 1950s, when archaeologists studying aerial photos taken during the war noticed that the flora growing near the village of Prática di Mare had a different shade from its surroundings, a telltale sign of ancient ruins. Excavations over the past 30 years have revealed a row of 13 stone altars from the 6th–4th centuries BC and an even earlier monumental tomb that may have been worshipped as that of Aeneas. In 1977 some 100 life-sized terracotta votive statues from the 5th–4th centuries BC were discovered under the wall of a temple of Minerva, apparently deposited in a pit in the 2nd century BC when a new temple was constructed. Many of the statues are of children carrying toys and pets, believed to have been left with the goddess while the real child passed on to adulthood. Others are of Minerva, and one that has especially interested scholars, a 4th-century BC terracotta copy of the wooden Palladium, the statue of Athena that Aeneas was said to have brought from Troy. This later ended up as one of the Vestal Virgins' holy of holies and its discovery in Lavinium suggests not only an early link between Greek and Latin cultures, but a mythic tradition much older than Virgil.

Between Pomezia and Aprília is **Ardea**, the capital of King Turnus, Aeneas' rival for the hand of Lavinia. It is also a pilgrimage destination for admirers of one of Italy's best contemporary sculptors, Giacomo Manzù, who lives in a villa in town; the **Raccoltà Amici di Manzù** (a branch of the National Museum of Modern Art) in the village displays over 400 works, including portraits of the sculptor's friend Pope John XXIII, his Swedish wife Inge, and his children, as well as sketches and jewellery (open daily 9 am–7 pm, Sun 9–1:30, closed Mon; free).

Anzio and Nettuno

If you drive along the coast you'll find many a boring beach, and **Anzio**, the *Antium* of the ancient Volscians. *Antium* was one of the more uppity cities from Rome's point of view—here Coriolanus took refuge when banished from Rome in 491 BC; shortly afterwards *Antium* was captured, then rebelled again, and in 338 BC was recaptured and humiliated by having all of its ships stripped of their beaks, or *rostra*, which were carted off to become the rostrums of the Roman Forum. Caligula and Nero are believed to have been born here, and the latter built a large seaside villa, traces of which may still be seen at the promontory of Arco Muto (where the Apollo Belvedere was discovered in 1510).

After that the town then fell out of history until January 1944, when British, American, and Polish troops found its beaches an ideal spot for a landing; that bloody but successful end run forced the Germans to abandon their Gustav Line and opened the way for the liberation of Rome. Not surprisingly, much of Anzio had to be rebuilt after the war, and British and Polish military cemeteries stretch from Anzio up to an ominously named crossroads called Campo di Carne (Field of Flesh); the largest American military cemetery in Italy is near **Nettuno**, with 7862 graves near the beach-head. A nearly solid 3 km of beach umbrellas and pizzerias link Anzio to Nettuno, though above the beach-arama Nettuno has retained its moated **Castello**, built for Alexander VI, and a pretty medieval quarter, the **Borgo**. Anzio goes one better with summer hydrofoils to the Pontine Islands (see below).

From Nettuno, it's 11 km north to Borgo Montello, near the ruins of **Satricum**, a city founded in the 9th century BC and once famous for its temple to the Mater Matuta, the goddess of dawn. It was the northernmost of 24 Volscian cities cited by Pliny, and the first to fall to the expanding power of the Latins and the Romans in the 4th century BC.

Inland: Latina and its hilltowns

Latina, largest of the Pontine towns and Italy's youngest provincial capital, was founded in 1932, a bright and busy place built on a radial plan with plenty of trees and chunky Mussolini palazzi. It lies to the south of the Via Appia, the old road cutting straight from Velletri in the Castelli Romani to Terracina, avoiding most of the once pestilent marshes. East of the Via Appia rise the **Monti Lepini** and some charming old hill towns well off the beaten track. **Cori**, like Rome and so many other Latin towns, likes to trace its founding to Trojan refugees. It may well be 3000 years old; that, at least, is the date archaeologists assign to its Cyclopean walls, built of huge, neatly fitted polygonal chunks of rock, still visible in many places. There are also many Roman ruins, including an intact bridge outside the Porta Ninfina and at the highest point, with views over the sea, the **Temple of Hercules** (really a temple of Jupiter), a small Doric building complete except for its roof. Further down, in Via Papa Giovanni XXIII, the pretty cloister of the medieval/Renaissance church of **Sant'Oliva** has a small archaeological collection.

Three interesting towns beginning with 'N' are even closer to Latina (15 km), especially **Ninfa** a 'Medieval Pompeii', abandoned in the 17th century because of malaria. A great many of the buildings survive in an exceptionally romantic setting of small streams and lakes, overgrown with wild flowers and trees that now form part of the Caetani Botanical Gardens (open 9–12 and 2:30–6 on the first Sat and Sun of each month, from April to Oct. You have to get a ticket in advance, from the Latina tourist office or in Rome at the Portineria di Palazzo Caetani, Via Botteghe Oscure 32, tel (06) 654 3231; or the WWF, Via Mercadante 10, tel (06) 844 0108).

Norma, built on the edges of a steep, curving cliff, seems almost like a city hanging in the air. Nearby are more Cyclopean walls around the ruins of **Norba**, once capital of Rome's bitter enemies, the Volscians. It was besieged and destroyed by the legions in the Social Wars in 89 BC, never to be rebuilt. **Sermoneta**, the odd man out amongst the Ns, is a well-preserved medieval hilltown, guarded by the intact glowering triple-walled **Castello Caetani** (13th century) which you can poke around in daily 10:30–11:30 and 3–6; in winter 2–4. In the centre of Sermoneta, the **Collegiata dell'Assunta** preserves part of its Cistercian-Gothic origins, and a *Madonna in Glory with Sermoneta in her lap* by Tuscan painter Benozzo Gozzoli.

Cistercian Gothic bloomed and drooped in southern Lazio without leaving much of an impression elsewhere in Italy—the Italians, it seems, just didn't take to it; when they labelled it 'Gothic' they meant 'Barbarian'. The **Abbazia di Valvisciolo**, between Sermoneta and Norma, is one of the few buildings to go up in the 13th century while the style was still popular, inspired by Fossanova (see below); and it's hard to imagine a more generic example; even the rose window is simple, with a quadrifoil heart, a popular motif of the Templars, who briefly held sway in the region. The pale marble cloister, with its paired columns, is elegant and contemplative, and still used by the resident Cistercians. You can purchase monkish chocolates and honey, or take in their amazing 49-square-metre *presepio*, or Christmas crib, where the sun rises and sets, the water trickles in the fountains, and church bells ring.

Southeast of Sermoneta the geography is occupied by the bulk of Monte Acquapuzza ('Mt Smelly Water'). North of it is **Bassiano**, a little hill town encircled by a medieval wall with nine towers; it has a shrine to the Madonna della Bufala ('Our Lady of the Female Buffalo'). To the south, **Sezze**, an ancient Volscian town famous for artichokes, has polygonal walls from the 4th century BC, a 14th-century half-Romanesque, half-Gothic **Cathedral** (unlike most, entered through the apse) and an **Antiquarium**, containing Paleolithic and Mesolithic artefacts from the area's caves, as well as Roman coins, mosaics and ceramics (Tues-Sun 9–12 and 4–6). To the east are two little medieval hamlets floating above their valleys, both dominated by baronial palaces: **Roccagorga** and **Maenza**.

Fossanova and Priverno

In 1135 French Cistercians came down to Fossanova to show the Italians how to make a proper Gothic building; the Italians weren't interested, of course, and Fossanova survives along with San Galgano in Tuscany, Sant'Andrea in Vercelli, and San Martino nel Cimino near Viterbo as the most notable examples of the northern style on this side of the Alps. Fossanova was a great centre of learning in its day (St Thomas Aquinas died here in 1274), but after the 1400s both wealth and talent deserted it. After centuries of decadence, the monastery was suppressed in 1811 and its treasures sold in an auction; in 1873 it was declared a national monument.

The **Abbey Church**, of cathedral proportions, is a fine, sedate Burgundian Gothic work with a beautiful rose window; although its façade was never finished, the few details around the central portal and the beautiful Cosmati mosaic in the tympanum seem especially lovely for the warm colour of the stone. The interior, with its stately rows of piers and pointed arches has been stripped of all decoration to become a work of medieval abstract. The **Cloister** is a fine compromise between the Romanesque and Gothic; from here you can visit the chapter house, sacristy, kitchen, refectory, and upstairs, the monks' cells. In the detached Foresteria (guest house), the room where Thomas Aquinas died was made into a chapel.

Priverno, 5 km up the road from Fossanova, replaces another ancient Volscian town, *Privernum*. In its heart is one of those perfect little theatrical squares that only the Italians seem to know how to design, a stage set with a triple stair, a charming Romanesque-Gothic **Cathedral** (1280s) and a Gothic **Palazzo Comunale**.

Circeo National Park

Between Anzio and Cape Circeo, the coast is almost a solid stretch of beaches and dunes; the Romans had the damnedest time keeping the Via Appia cleared of sand and swamp. These are now concentrated into a series of coastal lakes, the same which Nero planned to convert into a canal called the Fossa Augusta, which, if it had ever been finished, would have let the fleets sail from Lake Averno to Ostia, avoiding the stormy coast altogether (by the Torre Paola at Lake Sabaudia you can see how the work progressed). To the south the promontory of **Monte Circeo** (541 m) was an island in ancient times, one of many candidates around the Mediterranean for Homer's Isle of Circe from the *Odyssey*. A few ruins of a temple of Venus survive on its summit. **San Felice Circeo** on its slopes is a growing resort, offering boat trips around the big rock and its many caves; in 1939 a 60,000-year-old Neanderthal skull was discovered in one of them.

'The woods inspire fear and disgust... a green area which is both putrid and nauseous, where thousands of horrible swamp plants live.' Thus wrote an Italian botanist in the 1880s of a region now included in the **Circeo National Park**, Italy's smallest, founded in 1934 as the Pontine marshes were being drained. But what seemed putrid and nauseous now seems a marvel—a beautiful, unspoiled expanse of watery landscape, dunes, forests, and flowers. Migratory birds of all kinds stop here twice a year, and besides a wealth of wild flowers and primeval forests you may see woodpeckers, buzzards, peregrine falcons, and herons—maybe even that most overdressed of sea birds, the *Cavaliere d'Italia*. The park's information office is in Sabaudia, Via Carlo Alberto 107, tel (0773) 57 251, open Mon–Sat 8–2; they can tell you where to hire a bicycle, a canoe, or a horse to explore the park properly. There are three main paths for walkers: **Quarto Freddo**, a 4-hour trek around the promontory, **Laghi costieri e dune**, an easy 4-hour walk through the main nesting areas, and the **Cerasella**, a 2^1/2-hour walk into the forests and verdant pools, ending at the dreamy Piscina della Verdesca.

WHERE TO STAY AND EATING OUT

Coast in Italian may as well translate as seafood, but this is wine country as well, especially around Aprília, which produces its own D.O.C. Merlot, Sangiovese, and

181

Trebbiano vintages. In Anzio two of the best places to study the subject at fork range are both in Piazza Sant'Antonio: **All'Antica Darsena**, tel (06)984 5146, or **Da Alceste**, tel (06) 984 6744, both offering the day's catch for around L45 000. In Nettuno, you'll find the same speciality and price range, at **Gambero Secondo**, Via della Liberazione 50, tel (06) 980 0871.

Latina province still produces its excellent true mozzarella with buffalo milk, but the restaurants also do some inspired chemistry with pasta, herbs, and seafood. In Latina, a visit to **Cantina Ludi**, Via Parini 5, tel (0773) 499 783, will provide an excellent introduction with a choice of two fixed price menus, with meat (L40 000) or seafood (L45 000); closed Sun. Up at Cori, the **Pergolato La Vedova** enjoys a delightful Baroque setting with stairs and terraces at Via della Gradinata 2, tel (06) 967 8204, and serves delightful fettuccine and grilled meats (L15–22 000, closed Mon).

The coast by Monte Circeo is one of the most serendipitous places for a seaside holiday. For idle seaside luxury you can't do better than San Felice Circeo's ******Maga Circe**, Via A. Bergamini 1, tel (0773) 527 821, with its own beach, pool, air-conditioned rooms, and discotheque, if you feel like a light fantastic (L120–130 000); its restaurant is the best in the region; try the divine oyster and prawn antipasto (L40–50 000). Further out on the promontory at Quarto Caldo, there's ****Da Alfonso al Faro**, tel (0773) 528 019, where a seaside room with bath is L50–55 000. Alternatively, little ***Vittoria**, with its garden on Lungomare Circe, tel (0773) 528 048, has rooms for L27 000 without bath, L34 000 with.

Southern Lazio: Terracina to Formia

After Monte Circeo, the Tyrrhenian coast begins to come into its own, a kind of rough preview to the magnificent Bay of Naples. Most visitors fly by on the train to the bigger attractions; it is also a rather long haul for daytripping Romans; the sea is fairly clean, especially around the Pontine islands.

GETTING AROUND
One train an hour races between Rome and Naples, though do check the timetables to make sure they stop where you want to. Buses run inland from Latina, Terracina, Gaeta, Sperlonga, and Formia.

TOURIST INFORMATION
Terracina: Via Leopardi, tel (0773) 727 759
Sperlonga: Corso S. Leone 22, tel (0771) 54 796
Fondi: Via S. Francesco 8, tel (0771) 503 477
Gaeta: Piazza Traniello, tel (0771) 462 767 and Piazza XIX Maggio, tel 461 165
Formia: Viale Unità d'Italia 30–34, tel (0771) 21 490

Terracina

Halfway between Rome and Naples, the Ausonian Mountains crowd against the sea at **Terracina**, once the Volscian port of *Anxur*; stop here for a look at the lovely hotchpotch of a **cathedral**, with Baroque and Neoclassical elements on the façade and a Moorish-looking 14th-century campanile. Inside, besides the remains of the Temple of Roma and

Augustus that the cathedral replaced, there are medieval mosaics in the apse and on the floor. Bombs dropped across from the cathedral in the last war uncovered the ruins of a 1st-century BC **Capitolium**, dedicated to Jove, Juno, and Minerva. To the east, Emperor Trajan cut a deep passage through the mountains called the **Pisco Montano**, to allow the Appian Way to continue along the coast; along the side, the proud engineers marked how far down they cut: CXX Roman feet. If you can stay a while, take the Strada Panoramica up to the top of Monte Sant'Angelo, with ruins of the 1st-century AD **Temple of Jupiter Anxurus**, built on a mighty stone platform that survives intact, some of Terracina's medieval walls, and a wonderful view for miles along the coast. At **Campo Soriano**, 7 km north on a white road, the rock formations create an uncanny landscape recently declared a 'natural monument'.

From Terracina there are some possible detours into the mountains by way of the Via Appia (N. 7). Near the Lago di Fondi it passes a large Roman tomb, the **Torre dell'Epitaffio**, marking the frontier of the Papal States, and then, a mile further on, the **Portella**, where the Kingdom of the Two Sicilies began. It continues to **Monte San Biagio**, a hill town immersed in orange and cork groves, and to **Fondi**, an old town that has stuck to its rectilinear Roman street plan almost without change, with gates at the four cardinal points. It has seen some strange doings; legend has it that it was built over a Hellenistic town called Amyclae, whose residents founded Gaeta and Formia. Total believers in the philosophy of Pythagoras, they refrained from killing any living creature—and were soon annihilated by poisonous vipers. Fondi's **Castello** once belonged to Onorato Caetani II, a typical Roman baron and enemy of Pope Urban VI, who in 1378 offered it to dissident French cardinals for an enclave electing anti-pope Clement VII, beginning the Great Schism after the 'Babylonian exile' in Avignon. Clement was crowned in the church of **San Pietro**, which retains a pulpit and throne from the 1200s. Fondi also received a surprise visit from the noxious Turkish pirate Barbarossa, who came to abduct the legendary beauty Giulia Colonna. But warned in time, the damsel had fled, and Barbarossa was left to pillage and massacre in frustration.

Sperlonga and Gaeta

Continuing south along the scenic coastal road N. 213 (replacing the ancient Via Flacca), **Sperlonga** is one of the most pleasant small resorts on the Tyrrhenian coast, with a medieval quarter on its steep promontory and miles of fine beaches to either side. About 3 km beyond it, you may inspect the pretty sea cave called the **Grotto of Tiberius**, once fitted out as a sort of pleasure dome for that thoroughly hedonistic emperor. Some excellent statues in the 2nd century AD Roman 'Baroque' style have been excavated here, included one large composition of *Scylla and Ulysses*, perhaps by the same sculptors as the *Laocoön* in the Vatican. A small **museum** further down the road has been built for them (both open daily 9–5, till 6:30 in the summer, closed Mon; adm).

At the end of this scenic stretch of coast, **Gaeta** stands behind its medieval walls on a narrow, sand-swept headland, the grandest sight between Monte Argentario and the Bay of Naples. For a while in the early Middle Ages, this town was an important Mediterranean trading centre, a rival to Amalfi and Pisa. Its naturally defensible site made it a valued stronghold for centuries after; in 1861, it was briefly the last redoubt of the House of Bourbon, when the King of Naples and his palace guard withstood a siege from the army of the new Italy, hoping for help from France that never came. The town has a quiet medieval atmosphere, with a much rebuilt **Cathedral of Sant'Erasmus** with a 12th-century campanile made from a collage of Roman buildings; the adjacent **Museo Diocesano** has other sculptural fragments (May–Sept, daily 9–10 and 5–7, otherwise Sun only, 3:30–4:30). Further out is a 13th-century castle built by the Angevins, and evocative, crumbling old streets and alleys around the harbour and little **San Giovanni a Mare**, built in the 900s. On Monte Orlando, above Gaeta, you can make the difficult climb to see the rich and well-preserved tomb of Caesar's ablest general, Munatius Plancus, the founder of *Lugdunum* (Lyon) and *Augusta Raurica* (Basel), decorated with a frieze of battle scenes. Be sure to look down the Montagna Spaccata, the sheer vertical cliff face on the southwest of the hill.

Between Gaeta and Formia, near the crossroads of the Appian Way, stands a Roman sepulchre known as the **Tomb of Cicero**. The town of **Itri**, just inland from here, has preserved a large tract of the original Via Appia at the **Gole di S. Andrea**. Guarded by an impressive if ruined castle, Itri was the birthplace of the awful Fra Diavolo, the Bourbons' one-man reign of terror. Further inland on N. 82, **Campodimele** ('Apple field') is a miniature hill town wrapped in orchards, as round as an apple and surrounded by a wall with 11 towers.

Formia

Around the curve of the bay is Formia, the major base for ferries to the Pontine islands, which enjoyed a blessed past as one of the gilded resorts of Imperial Rome, like Capri or Baiae. Mark Antony's men caught up with the virtuous but capitally tedious orator Cicero here, after the assassination of Caesar, and knifed him in the baths of his villa. Little of ancient Formia survived through the Dark Ages, and the city that replaced it suffered grievously in 1944. Today Formia is entirely new, a happy and growing place that seems to have a bright future ahead of it. Some ancient bits salvaged from the Roman town may be seen in the **Antiquarium** in Piazza della Vittoria, in the centre of town. One of the best, or at least most panoramic things to do is take the road behind Formia up Monte Altino to **Punta del Redentore** (1250 m), from where on a clear day you can see as far as Vesuvius.

Before you reach Campania, the last town along the coast is **Minturno**, a medieval replacement for ancient Ausonian *Minturnae*, a town closer to the coast, along the Via Appia that reached its peak in the age of Augustus. Only the town skeleton remains today, covered with flowers in the spring: a bath complex, slight remains of temples, and an aqueduct, and a restored theatre.

WHERE TO STAY AND EATING OUT (tel prefix 0771)
The stretch of coast between Terracina and Formia makes a great place to rest if you are passing along the coast between Rome and Naples. Sperlonga has some nice spots around the beaches: ***La Playa**, outside town at Località Fiorella, modern, with pool, tennis, and a bit of beach (tel 54 106; L53–66 000); or the less expensive ***Parkotel Fiorelle** very close by (tel 54 092; L46 000). There are plenty of relatively inexpensive fish restaurants around the beaches; try **Fortino** on the main route, Via Flacca (tel 54 337; L30–35 000). Near Gaeta, on the same, coastal Via Flacca, the ***Summit** is a fine modern hotel in a good location, but a bit large and only open from April–Sept (L55–78 000; tel 463 087; TV and pool).

184

But if you want to splurge on this part of the coast, the best place may well be the ****Grande Albergo Miramare in Formia, a beautiful old villa with extensive gardens on the shore, with beach and pool, and modernized but nice rooms for L60–95 000, also an elegant restaurant in a little pavilion (tel 267 181; Via Appia on the southern edge of Formia). Another good restaurant in town, in fact an excellent one, is Italo, on the central Viale Unità d'Italia. More seafood, like fish cooked in *cartoccio* (in paper!), and a surprisingly large choice of what comes out of this part of the Tyrrhenian, but also memorable *primo piatti* (tel 21 529; L40 000).

The Pontine Islands

Scattered across the Gulf of Gaeta, there are five Pontine islands. All are volcanic in origin, fertile, dramatically beautiful, and until recently almost unknown to the flood of tourists which swept down on the nearby Bay of Naples. This changed noticeably in the 1980s, when Ponza enjoyed (or endured) a veritable stampede of visitors, fleeing the crowds on Capri and Ischia. Outside the high season, however, you'll find an island as peaceful, charming and unspoiled as Capri was 50 years ago.

GETTING AROUND
The main all-year-round port for Ponza and Ventotene is Formia. CAREMAR, tel (0771) 22 710, runs ferries and hydrofoils to both; other hydrofoils are run by Basso Lazio, tel (0771) 770 614. There is also a daily boat (Mazzella Line, tel (0773) 723 979) from Terracina. In the summer Aliscafi SNAV, tel (06) 984 5085, offers a hydrofoil service from Anzio to Ponza (4 a day), continuing to Ischia and Naples. CAREMAR also operates a summer ferry from Anzio to Ponza and Ventotene (tel (06) 983 1231). Every Wednesday at 8 am a guided excursion boat for Zannone leaves from Porto di S. Felice Circeo.

TOURIST INFORMATION
Ponza: Piazza Roma 3, tel (0771) 80 031
Ventotene: Via Piazzetta, tel (0771) 85 132

Ponza

Inhabited in the Paleolithic era, Ponza became an exporter of that most valuable Stone Age commodity, obsidian, used to make tools. Rome forced its rivals off the island in 313 BC; at first favouring the island, Tiberius and Caligula later made Ponza a place of political exile. Later abandoned, it eventually came under the Farnese family, who occasionally sent expeditions to see what they could exploit. In 1731 the island passed to the Bourbons of Naples, who set up the first colonies. But under the Fascists, Ponza once more became an island of exile, first for anti-Fascists and, after the liberation, for Il Duce himself, for six days. More recently, Fellini filmed the last weird scenes of his classic *Satyricon* on Ponza's beaches.

The principal town and port, called Ponza or simply Porto, is an archetypal Tyrrhenian town of pastel houses arranged around the amphitheatre of the busy fishing port, overlooking the sea and its stately assortment of monolithic rocks. One side of the town is dominated by the **Torre dei Borboni**, now a hotel, and the lighthouse at Punta Madonna. Tunnels link the port with its suburbs, **Santa Maria**, where a sea cave known as the **Grotto di Circe** nearby may be visited by boat.

A Roman tunnel leads from the port area to the loveliest of Ponza's bays, **Chiaia di Luna** ('moonlight bay'), a luminescent crescent of beach beneath a steep, pale 300-ft cliff that amply deserves its romantic name. Although on the other side of the island, it's within easy walking distance—Ponza is a long, thin sickle, following the shape of an ancient crater.

Outside the port, the island's single road twists and turns through the vineyards with frequent panoramas of cliff and sea. The only other real settlement is **Le Forna**, named after the kilns that line the bottom of Capo Bosco hill. From here the houses and farms extend to **Punta Forte Papa**, many of them built in the North African style, their low domes coated with whitewash. What are particularly impressive at Le Forna, however, are the *case di tufa*—cisterns dug in the rock to collect the maximum amount of precious rainwater. A narrow lane from Le Forna descends to the **Piscina Naturale**, a volcanically-created swimming-pool separated from the sea by a narrow strip of land. Other beaches near Le Forna are **Cala Feola** and **Cala Fontana**, marked by the jetty of the company that mines the Ponza's unique white bentonite. On the promontory of Forte Papa to the northwest is a 16th-century watchtower of the Farnese family, so named because of their contribution to the *sedia gestatoria*, Pope Paul III. **Cala Inferno**, on the other side of the island (within easy walking distance), derives its name from the 'infernal' whiteness of its cliffs.

Many of the island's wonders are accessible only (or at least most easily) by sea, including the **Grotte di Pilato**, not far from the port, a natural grotto containing a rock-cut pool, with something resembling an apse carved in the back. Volscian augurs used this cave to dissect the entrails not of birds or goats but of sea eels. A hole bored in the wall opens up towards the constellations of the Great Bear and Draco, thought to have had some significance in auguries. Near the cave are two fine beaches, **Frontone** and **Core**, with the magnificent cliffs of Punta Bianca in between. From Core you can take a small boat into the **Grotta degli Smeralda**, where the water lives up to its emerald name. Passing the small islet of **Sant'Evangelista**, the enormous **Natural Arch** comes into view.

Ventotene and the Pontine Archipelago

Tiny Ventotene resembles a billiards table from many angles, supported on a platform of tufa carved into curious shapes by the wind. With no hills or forests to shelter it, Ventotene deserves its name, and it has acquired two interesting scientific phenomena: the highest part of the island, Montagnozzo (452 ft), is covered with sand carried there from Africa. The sand is particularly deep around Cala Nave and Parata Grande, where roots of ancient trees have chemically petrified in its fine, loose layers.

Called Pandataria by the Romans, little Ventotene saw a disproportionate number of Imperial celebrities come and go—on holiday, in disgrace, or in pieces. The first to come was Julia, only child of Augustus and the most famous adulteress of her day. In 25 BC she built a grand summer villa, far from the wagging tongues of Rome, and introduced the island to the cult of Venus-Isis. But when Augustus heard of the scandal, he exiled Julia in her pleasure dome, although he eventually sent her to more comfortable surroundings at Règgio Calabria.

The presence of Julia's villa on tiny Ventotene, close to yet so far from Rome, made it an ideal place for exiles of noble blood, beginning with Julia's daughter Agrippina, unjustly accused of conspiring against Tiberius (she got back at him by starving herself to death). Agrippina's grandson Nero perpetuated the cruelties when he had his young wife Octavia exiled to Ventotene to pacify his new mistress, Poppaea Sabina. When even that failed to satisfy Poppaea, Nero sent his henchmen to the villa, where they slew the young Empress in a hot bath.

Over the centuries Ventotene was practically abandoned, until 1768, when the Bourbons tried an experiment à la Rousseau. Some 300 thieves, prostitutes and other evil-doers from Naples were taken to the island to demonstrate that, once removed from the evils of society, they would become models of virtue. Unfortunately it wasn't long before Ventotene became the Sodom and Gomorrah of the Tyrrhenian Sea. Armed forces had forcibly to evict the wild islanders, and an honest colony from Torre del Greco near Naples replaced them in 1772. Mussolini used the island to deposit 800 political prisoners, two of whom, Rossi and Spinelli, wrote the 'Manifesto di Ventotene' (1942) formulating the ideas that were to be the basis of the modern European parliament.

Ventotene, the only town, is piled over the old Porto Romano, carved out of the tufa by Julia's second husband, Agrippa. Its neat dark basin, measuring 7,980 square yards, is filled with the island's modest fishing fleet. The town's landmark, the Baroque church of **Santa Candida** has recently been restored inside with bright colours; on the altar, the statue of the saint is an ex-voto donated by two woodcutters saved from Algerian pirates; notice the little figures of woodsmen beside her.

Beyond the rocky beach at Cala Rossano, Punta d'Eolo has the meagre, windswept ruins of **Julia's villa** scattered across the promontory: ruined walls, sections of mosaic floor, archways and steps. You can stroll around the rest of the island in less than an hour; though the jagged coastline is best visited by sea. Another excursion is to the nearby **islet of Santo Stefano**. The Bourbons managed to squeeze a curious circular penitentiary called **La Citadella** on it in 1795 to house their political enemies. The most famous was Luigi Settembrini, founder of the 'Sons of Young Italy' and father of a character in Thomas Mann's *The Magic Mountain*.

Palmarola and Zannone

West of Ponza and most easily reached from that island is the small mountainous islet of **Palmarola**, surrounded by picturesque volcanic debris, most spectacularly a rock known as 'The Cathedral' on the west side of the island. The main beach is located beneath a rugged cliff of white and gold, and the deserted terraced farms of the old inhabitants are now the site of new summer houses. Northeast of Ponza lies **Zannone**. Unlike Palmarola, it was never cultivated and retains its original Mediterranean flora. Now part of the National Park of Circeo, the island is the natural reserve of the curved-horn *mouflons* (wild sheep), and over a hundred species of birds and rare plants.

WHERE TO STAY   (tel prefix 0771)

The most picturesque place to stay on Ponza is the ***La Torre dei Borboni** in the port (Via Madonna; tel 80 109), with a third of its rooms and apartments in the 18th-century castle, affording wonderful views over the town and port. Steps lead down to a small private beach, and the restaurant is one of Ponza's finest. Prices begin at L80 000, though they drop to nearly half that outside July and Aug. In the same price range is the ***Bellavista**, Via Parata, tel 80 036, which sits at the top of its own little secluded cove. For something less pricey and right on the sea, try **Gennarino a Mare** on the Via Dante; tel 80 071, with balconies overlooking the sea, and a restaurant (L40–60 000, with bath). There are also many rooms to let in private homes; inquire at the Pro Loco for a list.

On Ventotene, the choice is somewhat narrower, between **Lo Smeraldo**, Via Olivi 4, tel 85 130; L54–70 000, much less in the off season and **Calabattaglia**, Via Olivi, tel 85 195, provides the most luxury, if you can call it that (L58 000 with bath). The three pensions are *Il Cacciatore, Loc. Montagnozzo, tel 85 055, *Isolabella, Via Calarossano 2, tel 85 027, and *La Vela, Via Olivi 37, tel 85 185, all of which cost about L33 000 for a bathless room.

EATING OUT
Island specialities include *lenticchie alla ponzese* (lentil soup), *coniglio alla cacciatore* (rabbit with onions, tomatoes etc.) and lobster. The best wines of Ponza are Forna Grande, del Fieno and delle Grottelle. Of the restaurants along the waterfront, **L'Ancora** may well be the best (L30 000), or try **La Lanterna**, above the port at Via C. Pisacane, tel 809 826, a straightforward family-run trattoria with straightforward good food—L20 000. Outside the port area there's **Alle Piscine**, Via Forna Grande, tel 808 786, with lentils, rabbit, fish, and a fine view of the sea (L25 000) and in Le Forna, on Via Forna Chiesa, **Zi Arcangelo** has a similar cuisine and views over Palmarola (tel 808 921; L30 000).

On Ventotene, try the lentil soup and fresh fish at **Zi Amalia** in Piazza Castello (around L25 000 for fish). Down at Porto Nuovo, **L'Aragosta** serves, naturally, lobster amongst its other fish dishes (L35 000). Palmarola has two little seaside trattorias in the summer—**O'Francese** and **La Marina**, both offering fresh fish for around L30 000.

The Ciociaria

If you're in a hurry to get to Naples, the quickest route is the *Autostrada del Sole*, following the route of the Roman Via Casilina behind the coastal mountains. This humble corner of Lazio is known as the **Ciociaria**, after the *ciocie*, or bark and sheepskin sandals, worn by the countrymen not so long ago, when this was one of the backwaters of Italy. As they were the first outsiders who came into Rome seeking work, Romans picked up the habit of calling all new arrivals *Ciociari*—and rarely in a flattering vein. But don't let Roman snobbery get in the way of a few detours in this charming but seldom visited region of lakes, venerable hill towns, and medieval abbeys, culminating in Italy's most famous monastery—Monte Cassino.

GETTING AROUND
Parallel with the mighty A2 is the Roman Via Casilina (N. 6), from which you can explore the Ciociaria at leisure. Trains between Rome and Caserta/Naples stop at Frosinone and Cassino, from where buses run to Monte Cassino. Other buses run from Frosinone, the provincial capital, not always very conveniently.

TOURIST INFORMATION
Fiuggi: Piazza Frascara 4, tel (0775) 55 019
Frosinone: Piazzale De Matthaeis, tel (0775) 872 526
Atina: Via Ponte Melfa, tel (0776) 60 379
Cassino: Via Condotti 6, tel (0776) 21 292

Anagni, 'The City of Popes'

In ancient times Anagni was an important town of the Hernici, one of the more obscure of the many Italic tribes the Romans tested their mettle on before moving up to big league conquests. As small as it is, Anagni held centre stage in European politics on several occasions during the Middle Ages. Four 14th-century popes were born here, and several others made it their summer home. Greatest among them was Boniface VIII, a nasty intriguer who initiated the first Jubilee Year in 1300 to raise some money and then had the poor timing to proclaim loudly the temporal supremacy of the popes long after anyone else took the idea seriously. Captured in Anagni by the Colonna family and the forces of the King of France, Boniface expected to be executed. Resolving to face death with dignity, he sat himself on the papal throne in his residence, tensely waiting as Sciarra Colonna strode in with his henchmen. Stern and silent, the prince walked up to the Pope—and dealt him a resounding slap across the face, the celebrated 'Slap of Anagni' that put a temporary end to papal dreams of world domination.

Boniface VIII's palace can still be seen, along with the complex, stout and squarish **cathedral**, one of the finest in central Italy, sharing a little of the genius of the Tuscan and Apulian churches of the same period. Outside, it is 11th-century Romanesque; a rebuilding in the 1300s left it tentatively Gothic within. There is a Cosmatesque pavement and a wonderful 13th-century stone baldachin over the altar. Be sure to see the crypt, with blue and gold Byzantine frescoes from the 1200s that are among the best of their kind in Italy, attributed to Master Consulus, who also painted Subiaco's Sacro Speco. Take some time for a walk around Anagni, a medieval time capsule with its walls, towers, and palaces like the charmingly eccentric **Palazzo Comunale** (1200) and **Casa Barnekow**, from the same period, in Via Vittorio Emanuele.

Up in the mountains above Anagni, **Fiuggi** has been a popular spa for centuries; Michelangelo came here to take the waters after the strain of working on the Sistine Chapel; one of the two springs is named after Boniface VIII, who came here to cure the humiliation of his slap. The town is divided in two: Fiuggi Fonte, with the spa, has a grand Teatro Comunale from the turn of the century, a golf course, and the church of San Pietro, with a bright 20th-century interior; Fiuggi Città is an old medieval town of steep stone lanes. West of Anagni, flamingoes seem to rule the roost in **La Selva Natural Park**, while to the north, **Piglio** produces the Ciociaria's most potable wines—red *Cesanese* and white *Passerina*.

The Cities of Saturn: Ferentino and Alatri

From here the Via Casilina passes near two cities traditionally founded by Saturn, the chief god of the misty Golden Age—a code for their extreme antiquity. The first is **Ferentino**, dominating the Valle del Sacco, once encompassed by Cyclopean walls of great polygonal blocks, most prominently by the **Porta Sanguinaria**, the 4th-century BC

Gate of Blood. Nearby, in Piazza dell'Ospizio, is another fine Cistercian Gothic church, the 1150 **Santa Maria Maggiore**, as lofty, austere, and unadorned as all the others. In Via Sabina you can see some remains of the Roman **theatre**; in Via Morosini, and nearly perfectly intact, is a vaulted building that may have been a **Roman Market** (1st century BC); and the **Testamento di Aulo Quintilio** by Porta Maggiore, a tomb inscribed with the will of a civic-minded magistrate in the time of Trajan, who left all he had to the city. The terrace of the ancient acropolis, supported by a mighty stone substructure, no longer has any temples beyond the little Romanesque **Duomo**.

From Ferentino it's 12 km through the olive groves to **Alatri** (ancient *Aletrium*), 2400 years ago the capital of the Hernici and different from its neighbours in that it managed to be spared the destruction that befell many of the other ancient cities of Lazio. Consequently, Alatri remains the best example we have of a pre-Roman Italian town, with almost a complete double circuit of **Cyclopean walls** (6th century BC): the defending wall and another set, with five gates, that marked the boundaries of the ancient acropolis. Most powerful of these is the **Porta Maggiore** (or Porta Civita) where stairs ascend under a prodigious monolithic architrave. The contrast between the building blocks of giants and the puny pebbles piled on top by the Romans and others is staggering; a marble plaque quotes the German historian Gregorovius: 'When I found myself before this dark titanic construction, it aroused in me an admiration for human strength even greater than that inspired by the sight of the Colosseum.'

At the summit, Alatri's trapezoidal acropolis is now known as the **Civita**, where trees, the 17th-century cathedral and the Bishop's Palace stand over the temples of the long-forgotten Hernici. Under the Civita, in the ancient Forum, the 12th–13th century church of **Santa Maria Maggiore** with its beautiful rose window was built over a temple of Jupiter; inside is a 15th-century triptych by local artist Antonio da Alatri and a carved wood and painted panel from the 1200s. In Via S. Francesco, the 13th-century fortress-palace Gottifredi has recently been restored as Alatri's **Museo Civico**. Just outside the town SS155 leads to **Collepardo**, where you can look down into the **Pozzo Santullo**, an iridescent karstic sinkhole 60 metres deep, with a sunken emerald forest at the bottom. Beyond this, set in the mountains and oak forests, the **Certosa di Trisulti** was founded by the Benedictines in 999, and rebuilt by the Carthusians in 1208, and occupied by Cistercians since 1946. Although mostly remodelled in the dire 17th century, the rooms you can visit—especially the wonderfully ornate rooms of the **Pharmacy**—are decorated with Pompeii-inspired motifs and grotesques; the monks are famous for their herbal elixirs, liqueurs and medicines. Another room, called the 19th-century Salottino dei Balbi, has a *trompe l'oeil* monk entering the room through an imaginary doorway and also a richly decorated ceiling. **Vico nel Lazio**, just west of the Certosa, is nicknamed the 'Carcassonne of the Ciociaria' for its mighty medieval walls, guarded by 24 crenellated towers, their lines still amazingly pristine.

Casamari and the Valley of the Liri

Little **Frosinone**, the provincial capital for the Ciociaria, was all but totally destroyed in the last war; the Romanesque campanile of its cathedral has the dogged air of a last surviving veteran in a memorial parade. Unless you revel in the anonymity of Italy's post-War urban design, take the side road from here (SS216) for a delightful detour to the **Abbey of Casamari**, a little-known French Cistercian complex with a Fossanova-style church, consecrated in 1217 by Pope Honorius III. Unlike other abbeys in south Lazio, Casamari was never abandoned, and is today inhabited by some fifty monks. The whole complex, from the cloister to the Chapter house, is infused with a quiet, eloquent simplicity. All of the abbey's things of this world are concentrated in its museum: tusks from a primeval pachyderm, folksy ex-votos from the 3rd-century-BC Roman shrine at nearby *Cereatae Marianae*, and Baroque paintings by Annibale Carracci, Guercino, and Sassoferrato. Near Casamari, the little town of **Veroli** is most famous for its marble Roman calendar, the *Fasti Verulani*. Although the 14th-century cathedral was destroyed by an earthquake, its delightful rose window survives, as does the treasure in the last chapel on the right, with reliquaries and ivory caskets made in Arab Sicily. Even more off the beaten track are the quiet towns to the south, partaking of the bucolic charms of the Liri valley: **Boville Ernica**, an ancient town of the Hernici with a triple medieval wall, **Monte S. Giovanni Campano** with its baronial castle, and the hamlet of **Strangolagalli** ('chicken chokers'), which threatening as it is to pullets, otherwise enjoys an especially healthy climate.

East of Casamari, **Isola del Liri** is no island but rather a pretty paper-making town sliced down the middle by a dramatic 100-foot waterfall, with the beautiful fountain-filled gardens of the Parco Boncompagni around it. Up the valley of the Liri is the much older Volscian town of **Sora** which was devastated by an earthquake in 1915; though now a bustling paper-manufacturing centre, memories of its pre-earthquake days survive in the 11th-century crypt of San Domenico, built of Roman columns and capitals, and in the weedy bastions of its Castello di San Casto.

A road curls east of Isola to **Arpino**, another Volscian town almost as old as the hills around it. Anciently *Arpinum*, its Cylopean walls are unique for the pointed, parabolic arch of their gate. The nearest civilization that produced the like were the Hittites in Hattusa (modern Turkey), nor do parabolic arches reappear until Antoni Gaudí made them one of the keystones of his architecture in Barcelona. Arpino was a fertile ground for famous Romans—Marius, Agrippa, and Cicero were born here, as was the Cavaliere d'Arpino, who is responsible for the soupy frescoes in St Peter's dome. Besides the arch and walls, Arpino has a fine Roman bridge and medieval watchtowers. Further down the Via Casilina, **Aquino** is full of Roman-era ruins, including a small decorative arch near the village church; St Thomas Aquinas was born in nearby Roccasecca castle, son of Count Landolfo d'Aquino. **Monte Cairo**, just north of Aquino, was the northern point of the Germans' double string of defences erected in 1943: the Hitler Line stretching down to Terracina and the Gustav Line, which met the sea at Minturno.

For something really out of the way, you might venture up into the highest and least-visited corner of Lazio, the **Valle di Comino** on the borders of the Abruzzo National Park. In this mountainous region, there are beautiful springfed lakes, especially at **Posta Fibreno** (unusual for its floating islet, or *isola galleggiante*, mentioned by Pliny the Elder) and **Biagio Saracinesco**, and ruins of a 12th-century castle at **Vicalvi**. **Atina** is the most important town in this district, and has been since the days of the Samnites; Virgil rated it as one of the top five before the advent of Rome. Besides its Cyclopean walls, relics from its past are preserved in the Municipal Museum.

Halfway between Frosinone and Montecassino, **Ceprano** has of late been the scene of some enlightening excavations, especially at Casale Madonna del Piano, where a Roman villa with beautiful mosaic pavements was discovered, and to the southeast at

Volscian *Fregellae*, founded in 328 BC, a city that in its heyday was a third larger than Pompeii. To the south, the **Grotto di Pastena** is the most beautiful in this part of Italy, with an underground river, waterfalls, and dripping draperies of stalactites; illuminated and provided with walkways, it can be visited on request from the Pastena municipio.

Montecassino

Montecassino is reached from the modern town of **Cassino**, the Volscian *Casinum*, rebuilt after it was flattened in the fighting of 1944. Halfway up to the monastery, part of ancient Casinum has been enclosed in an archaeological zone, with the remains of the amphitheatre and **tomb of Ummidia Quadratilla**, a wealthy patroness of the arts, which was converted into a church. In 1980 the **National Archaeological Museum of Cassino** was opened here, with a large collection of pre-Roman and Roman artefacts. A short walk away, the well-preserved **Roman Theatre**, was carved into the hillside during the reign of Augustus. From here the road passes the silent tiers of the **Polish Military Cemetery**, where the graves look towards the bright white walls of **Montecassino**.

If divine guidance led St Benedict from Subiaco to found a monastery on Casinum's former acropolis, as the old legend states, perhaps God just wasn't thinking clearly that day. Montecassino may be the most famous monastery in Italy, and it certainly owns the most dramatic site, high on a mountaintop over the Garigliano valley, but that very location has caused the honest monks nothing but trouble over the centuries. They were essential in keeping alive the traditions of letters and scholarship through the Dark Ages, all the more remarkable when you consider that Montecassino has been utterly destroyed five times. Benedict came in 529, but the Lombards wrecked the place only 60 years later. The Saracens and the Normans repeated the scene in the 9th and 11th centuries, and an earthquake finished off what must have been one of Italy's treasures of medieval architecture in 1348. Each time the place has been rebuilt, but the reason why Montecassino attracts so much strife was demonstrated again during the Italian Campaign of 1944. The rock happens to be the most strategically important spot in central Italy, the key to either Rome or Naples, depending on which way your army is walking.

In 1944, the Germans made it the western bastion of their Gustav Line, and it held up the Allied advance for four months. Enough bombs were dropped to destroy the monastery once more, without seriously disconcerting the defenders, and typically for the polyglot Italian Front, New Zealanders, Indians, Brazilians, and French participated in unsuccessful attacks between January and May. It was the Poles who finally beat their way in, losing over 1000 men on the way up. The Benedictines began the rebuilding within months of the battle, and have replicated the previous incarnation as closely as possible. Although not the art treasure it once was, it's still a popular place to visit (daily, 9:30–12, 3:30–sunset). The entrance to the church lies beyond four cloisters; the third one, with its Loggia del Paradiso, affords a tremendous view over most of southern Lazio. The **Church** was rebuilt as it appeared in the 17th century, designed by Cosimo Fanzago, and covered with a veritable carapace of gilded stuccoes. Unable to reproduce Luca Giordano's rich Baroque frescoes, the Benedictines commissioned Pietro Annigoni to paint the scenes in the dome and drum. In the crypt (the only part of the church to survive the tons of bombs) are the tombs of St Benedict and his twin sister, St Scholastica (like all of Monte Cassino's treasures, their relics were packed away in crates and taken to a safe place before the fighting broke out). On the left side of the apse you can see another pre-War survivor, the **Tomb of Pietro de' Medici** by Antonio and Francesco da Sangallo. Exhibits from the abbey's rich library and archives may be seen in the long ambulatory flanking the church; perhaps the most famous item is the *Placito of Monte Cassino*, the first known document written in 'vulgar' Italian.

WHERE TO STAY AND EATING OUT

In the Ciociaria, carbohydrates are the happy food for all seasons—in fettucine, polenta, and gnocchi productions that tend to eclipse the grilled meats of the *secondi*. The best local wines are the Cesanese del Piglio, though you may also want to give a tumbler to a Cabernet di Atina or Selva di Paliano.

In the centre of Anagni, you can both sleep and eat well at ***Del Gallo**, Via Vittorio Emanuele 164, tel (0775) 727 309, where the rooms are medievally simple (L22 000, without bath) and the speciality of the kitchen is a *timballo di Bonifacio VIII* (fettucine baked with meatballs); full meals around L40 000. Fiuggi has the most hotels in the region, beginning with the grand old ******Silva Splendid**, Corso Nuova Italia, tel (0775) 55 791, with a swimming-pool and tennis courts in its park and comfortable, air-conditioned rooms (open May–Oct, L43–75 000 without bath, L74–135 000 with bath, depending on when you come). Another, smaller hotel with a pool *****Mondial Park**, Via S. Emiliano, tel (0775) 55 848 (open April–Nov, L64 000 in season, L44 000 out, all rooms with bath). Among the bargains, there's ****Villa Taormina**, Via S. Emiliano, tel (0775) 55 179, open April–Oct, all rooms with bath for L36 000. The Ciociaria's best restaurant is in Fiuggi as well: **Hernicus**, Via Villa Comunale 1, tel (0775) 55 2545, where you can indulge in ravioli filled with ricotta and radicchio, seafood or beef in pastry, and delicious fruit desserts for L40–50 000 (closed Jan).

In Ferentino, on the Via Casilina (km 74.6) the modern *****Bassetto** is the most comfortable place to sleep for miles around with 72 air-conditioned rooms and an excellent restaurant (L69–74 000, all with bath). In central Alatri, ***La Rosetta**, Via Duomo 31, tel (0775) 450 068 may be simple but seems downright cosy next to all those megalithic walls (L28 000, all with bath). You probably won't want to spend a night in Frosinone, but if it's time to eat, **Il Quadrato**, Via De Matheis 53, tel (0775) 874 474 will take care of you with pasta and risotto dishes that change according to season, followed by fish or meat courses (L30 000, L40 000 with seafood; closed Sun).

At Civitavecchia, near Arpino, *****Sunrise Crest**, tel (0776) 848 901, is a pleasant 16-room resort hotel, with a pool, garden, and restaurant (L37 000, all with bath). Near Sora, in a pretty mountain setting at Gallinaro, *****Tramp's**, despite a name that someone found in an English–Italian dictionary, is actually a stylish little resort hotel, with two pools, tennis courts, sauna, garden, and a fairly good restaurant (Via Vico 81, tel (0775) 85 135; L38–43 000, all with bath). Cassino is well endowed with hotels: two that offer gardens, pools, TVs, etc. are *****La Rocca**, Via Sferracavalli 105, tel (0776) 25 427 (L43 000, all with bath) and *****Silva Park**, Via Ausonia 47, tel (0776) 300 021 (L41–46 000, all with bath). Among the bargains, try ***Stella**, Via Carducci 3, tel (0776) 22 308 (L16 000, without bath). Cassino offers few thrills in the kitchen, though you'll dine well enough at **Gaetanella**, Via Abruzzi 8, tel (0776) 22 288 (L25 000).

Part V

CAMPANIA

Sansevero Chapel, Naples

In Roman times, to distinguish the *Campania* around Naples from parts further north (the present Roman *Campagna*), the southern region acquired the nickname of *Campania Felix*. A happy land it was, the richest and most civilized province in Italy, with a mix of Greek and Etruscan culture superimposed on the native Samnites and Ausonians, not to mention the merry Oscans and their perfumed city of Capua. Campania's charm, then as now, starts with one of the most captivating stretches of coastline in Italy—the Amalfi Drive—and includes Capri and Ischia, Sorrento, Vesuvius, the Phlegraean Fields around Pozzuoli, and the beautiful but lesser-known Cilento coast at the southern tip of the region. Roman emperors and senators spent as much time here as business would allow, and even today it is said that the dream of every Italian is to have a villa at Capri or Sorrento overlooking the sea.

In the middle of all this, of course, sprawls Italy's third-largest city, Naples—a place that may well be either your favourite, or least favourite, Italian city—or both at the same time.

History simply has not been very kind to Campania. After a wonderful head start in classical times, the decline began under Rome. The region had grown wealthy largely from the manufacture of ceramics; business went bad when competitors out in Spain and Gaul started making cheaper lamps and pots. In the Middle Ages, there were difficult Lombards and Normans; later came even more useless rulers like the Bourbons. Today, Campania shares fully in all the complexes and problems of the Italian south. It has large new industries, ambitious planning schemes to attract still more, and substantial difficulties with pollution, poverty, corruption and crime. Though the potential certainly exists, there is a long way to go before the region can reclaim the position it had in the days of the Caesars.

Campanian Itineraries

A tour of less than two weeks should get you through the major sights of the region—almost all of them are along the coast. Begin with Naples (days 1–4), and if you like it enough, you can make the city a base for day trips to Pompeii and Herculaneum (day 5), the Phlegraean Fields or Vesuvius (day 6), and the islands (days 7–8). Otherwise, Sorrento or any of the islands can provide a more pleasant base. The Amalfi Drive is certainly worth two days (9 and 10; seeing Positano, Amalfi, Ravello, and having a look at old Salerno when you finish) though you may never want to leave. Paestum and its Greek temples come next (day 11), and, if you're heading further south, you can continue from here along the Cilento coast (day 12), or else return to Naples through inland Campania, stopping at Benevento (alternative day 12) then visiting Capua and Caserta (day 13).

A **seven-day excursion through classical antiquity**: for ancient sites and museums, Campania is the equal of Sicily and even Rome itself. Again, start with Naples and its great Archaeological Museum, and a walk through the Spaccanapoli district (day 1). Pompeii and Herculaneum will each require a day if you wish to see them in detail (days 2 and 3), and another day can be spent exploring the sites west of Naples: Cumae, Baiae, Cape Misenum, Pozzuoli etc. (day 4). Be sure to make at least a day trip to Benevento to see the Arch of Trajan and the odd Egyptian relics around town (day 5). Capua, with its unique *mithraeum* and amphitheatre, comes next (day 6). Depending on what direction your travels are taking, you may either begin or end this itinerary with mainland Italy's best-preserved Greek temples, plus an interesting museum, at Paestum (day 7).

NAPLES

For many, Naples is the true homeland of a particular Italian fantasy, the last bastion of singing waiters and red checked tablecloths, operatic passion and colourful poverty, balanced precariously between Love's own coastline and the menace of Vesuvius. But mention Naples or the Neapolitans to any modern, respectable North Italian, and as they gesticulate and roll their eyes to heaven you will get a first-hand lesson in the dynamics of Italy's 'Problem of the South'. Many Italians simply cannot accept that such an outlandish place can be in the same country as they are, a sentiment that probably contains as much envy as contempt. Naples, the city that has given the world Enrico Caruso, Sophia Loren, pizza, and syphilis (the disease appeared here in 1495, and was immediately blamed on the French garrison) may also be the first city to make social disorder into an art form.

Degradation, Italian Style

On Naples' Piazza Garibaldi you can buy a boiled pig organ on a stick, served with a slice of lemon, and watch eight-year-old *scugnizzi*—street children—puff on contraband

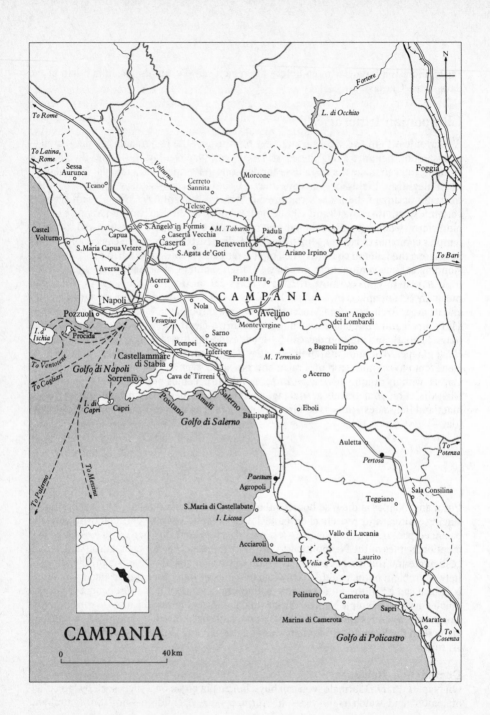

To Rome

To Latina,
Rome

Sessa
Aurunca

Tcano

Volturno

Cerreto
Sannita

Morcone

Fortore

L. di Occhito

Foggia

Castel
Volturno

Capua

S.Maria Capua Vetere

Aversa

Napoli

Pozzuoli

I.d'
Ischia

Procida

To Ventotene

To Cagliari

Golfo di Napoli

Sorrento

Castellammare
di Stabia

I. di
Capri

Capri

Positano

Amalfi

To Palermo

To Messina

Golfo di Salerno

S.Angelo in Formis

Caserta Vecchia

Caserta

S.Agata de'Goti

M. Taburno

Paduli

Benevento

Ariano Irpino

To Bari

Acerra

Prata Ultra

C A M P A N I A

Nola

Vesuvius

Avellino

Montevergine

Sant' Angelo
dei Lombardi

Sarno

Nocera
Inferiore

Pompei

M. Terminio

Bagnoli Irpino

Cava de' Tirreni

Acerno

Salerno

Battipaglia

Eboli

Auletta

To
Potenza

Pertosa

Paestum

Agropoli

Sala Consilina

Teggiano

S.Maria di Castellabate

I. Licosa

Vallo di Lucania

Acciaroli

Ascea Marina

Velia

Cilento

Laurito

Polinuro

Camerota

Marina di Camerota

Sapri

Maratea

To
Cosenza

Golfo di Policastro

N

CAMPANIA

0   40km

Marlboros while casually tossing firecrackers into traffic. Fireworks, along with slamming doors, impromptu arias, screams, ambulance sirens and howling cats, are an essential part of the Neapolitan ambience. This anarchic symphony is harder to catch these days, unfortunately, drowned as it is under the roar of Italy's worst traffic problem. In central Naples, half a million rude drivers chase each other around a street plan that hasn't changed much since Roman times. The car crisis is all Naples talks about; at one point, the Communists and the radical right were united, against nearly everyone else, in a proposal for a car-free centre that never got off the ground. Meanwhile, the nation's worst air pollution keeps the hospitals full, and every few weeks some old lady on a back street burns to a crisp while the firemen, just down the block, gamely push illegally parked cars out of their way.

Another chronic problem is housing, enough of a nightmare even before the earthquake of 1980; on the outskirts of the city, you may see Napoletani living in stolen ship cargo containers, with windows cut in the sides, in shacks made of sheet metal and old doors, or in abandoned buses. In the city centre, thousands of earthquake refugees are still camping in hotels.

No hope for reform seems yet in sight. Even if Naples' notorious city government should some day miraculously turn competent and honest, it would still first have to deal with the spectre of the *Camorra*, a loose term for the crime syndicates that keep Naples as securely strung up as any mountain village in Sicily. Crime is so well organized here, to give one example, that seagoing smugglers have formed a trade union to protect their interests against the police.

In the 18th century, when the city and its spectacular setting were a highlight of the Grand Tour, the saying was 'See Naples and die...' Nowadays you usually can't see much of anything through the smog, and you'll probably survive if you're careful crossing streets. Don't let Naples' current degradation spoil your visit, though; you haven't seen Italy—no, you haven't seen the Mediterranean—until you have spent some time in this fascinating metropolis. The only thing subtle about Naples is its charm, and the city will probably win your heart at the same time as it is deranging your senses.

On the Other Hand...

If Naples immediately repels you, however, it means you are probably a sticky sort, and will miss all the fun. In spite of everything, after the first shock wears off, Naples has a way of making us partisans in her not yet hopeless cause. The incomparable setting, and the admitted beauty of much of the city, are part of it, but Naples' real attraction is a priceless insight into humanity, at the hands of a population of 2.2 million dangerous anarchists. The Napoletani may be numbered among the very few peoples of Europe who realize they are alive, and try to enjoy it as best they can. Their history being what it is, this manifests itself in diverse ways. The Napoletani do not stand in lines, or fill out forms, or stop for traffic signals; they will talk your ears off, run you over in their ancient Fiats, criticize the way you dress, whisper alarming propositions, give you candy, try to pick your pockets with engaging artlessness, offer surprising kindnesses, and with a reassuring smile they will always, always give you the wrong directions. In an official capacity, they will either break the rules for you or invent new ones; in shops and restaurants, they will either charge you too much or too little. The former is much more common, though whichever it is they will do it with a flourish.

If the accounts of long-ago travellers are to be believed, Naples has always been like this. Too much sunshine, and living under such a large and ill-mannered volcano, must contribute much to the effect. It would be harder to explain some of Naples' ancient distinctions. First and foremost, Naples is Italy's city of philosophers. Her greatest, Giambattista Vico, was a son of the Spaccanapoli, and others, such as St Thomas Aquinas and Benedetto Croce, spent much of their time here. (On a recent visit to the city, a huge banner was seen hanging in front of the Royal Palace, announcing a week of celebrations in honour of 'the Hegelians of Naples and their contributions to the national state'.) Naples can also claim to be first in music. Among native composers are Gesualdo, Scarlatti, and Leoncavallo, and the conservatory is claimed to be the oldest in Europe. Even today, members of the opera company at San Carlo look down on their colleagues at Milan's La Scala as a band of promising upstarts who could take their jobs a little more seriously. Neapolitan popular song, expressive and intense, is an unchained Italian stereotype, performed in the impenetrable Neapolitan dialect. While perusing the displays of bootleg tapes on the pavement *bancarelle* (stalls), look for anything by Bruno Venturini, long the foremost exponent of the art. Some of the songs are about familiar subjects, love and life and such—but most of them seem to be just about Naples.

History

Naples' rise to become the metropolis of Campania was largely the result of the lucky elimination of her rivals over the centuries. Capua, Cumae, Benevento rose and fell, and Pompeii and Herculaneum disappeared under volcanic ash, but fortune has always seemed to protect Naples from the really big disasters. As a Greek colony founded by Cumae in 750 BC, the city began with the name Neapolis, and prospered moderately throughout the periods of Greek, Samnite, and Roman rule. Belisarius, Justinian's famous general, seized the region for Byzantium in 536, after invasions of the Goths and Vandals, but a Duke of Naples declared the city independent in 763, acknowledging only the authority of the pope.

The chronicles are understandably slim for this period; early medieval Naples offers us more fairytales than facts. Many of its early legends deal with none other than the poet Virgil; somehow, folklore in the dark ages had transformed the greatest Latin poet into Master Virgil, a mighty magician who was given credit for many of the unexplainable engineering feats of the ancient Romans. Naples claimed him for its founder, and its legends told of how he built the Castel dell'Ovo, balancing it on an egg at the bottom of the harbour. Master Virgil also built a talking statue that warned the city of enemies, earthquakes, or plagues, and medieval chroniclers mention the bronze horses and bronze fly he built over two of the city's gates, still to be seen in those days, and said to be magical charms on which the fortune of the city depended.

Naples lost its independence to the Normans in 1139, one of the last cities in the south to fall—its long resistance cost it the chance of becoming the Norman capital, an honour that fell on Palermo instead. Later, it passed under the rule of the Hohenstaufen emperors along with the rest of southern Italy. Charles of Anjou took over in 1266, and lopped off the head of the last Hohenstaufen, Conradin, in what is now Naples's Piazza del Mercato. Under the Angevins, Naples for the first time assumed the status and architectural embellishments of a capital. The Angevin Kings of Naples, however, did little to develop their new realm, expending most of their energy in futile attempts to recapture Sicily, lost to them after the Sicilian Vespers revolution of 1282. When their line expired in 1435 with the death of Giovanno II, the kingdom fell to Alfonso V of Aragon—a fateful event, marking Spain's first foothold on the Italian mainland.

Habsburgs and Bourbons
Spanish rule seemed promising at first, under the enlightened Alfonso. Very soon, though, it became clear that the Spaniards were mainly interested in milking Italy for taxes with which to finance further conquests. The city itself, as the seat of the viceregal court, prospered greatly; by 1600 its population of 280,000 made it perhaps the largest city in Europe. The long period of Spanish control did much to give Naples its distinct character, especially during the 17th and 18th centuries, when the city participated almost joyfully in the decadence and decay of the Spanish Empire. This period saw the construction of the scores of frilly, gloomy Baroque churches—now half-abandoned, with bushes growing out of the cornices—that add so much to the Neapolitan scene. In manners especially, the Imperial Spanish influence was felt; 'nothing', in the words of one observer, 'is cheaper here than human life'.

In 1707, after the War of the Spanish Succession, Naples passed under the rule of Archduke Charles of Austria. Prince Charles of Bourbon, however, snatched it away from him in 1734, and mouldering, picturesque Naples for the next century and a half made the perfect backdrop for the Rococo shenanigans of the new Bourbon kingdom. The new rulers were little improvement on the Spaniards, but immigrants from all over the South poured into the city, chasing the thousands of ducats dropped by a free-spending court. Naples became not only the largest, but the most densely populated city in Europe, a distinction it still holds today; crime and epidemics were widespread.

Nevertheless, this was the Naples that became the main event for thousands of northern aesthetes doing the Grand Tour in the 18th and 19th centuries. Goethe flirted with contessas here, while the English poets were flirting with dread diseases and Lord Nelson was making eyes at Lady Hamilton. The Neapolitans are frank about it; Naples owed its prominence on the Grand Tour less to Vesuvius and the ruins of Pompeii than to good old-fashioned sex. Naples at the time was incontestably the easiest place in Europe to find some, and everyone knew it—saving Goethe and the rest the trouble of ever mentioning the subject in their travel accounts and letters home.

Garibaldi's army entered Naples in February, 1861 (Garibaldi had arrived the day before—in style, on Italy's first railroad, one of the few constructive achievements of the last Bourbons). As the new Italy's biggest basket case, the city has since received considerable assistance with its planning and social problems— though not nearly enough to make up for the centuries of neglect. World War II didn't help; in late September, 1944, the city staged a heroic though unsuccessful revolt against the Germans. Even more damage was done by Allied bombing, and in the destruction of the city's port and utilities by the retreating Nazis.

While the post-War period saw considerable rebuilding, it also brought new calamities. Illegal and speculative building projects grabbed most of the already crowded city's open space (you'll notice the almost total absence of parks), and turned the fringe areas and much of the once-beautiful Bay of Naples shore into a nightmare of human detritus, one of the eeriest industrial wastelands of Europe. At the moment, there seems to be a common realization that Naples has reached a point of no return, and it will soon have to either clean itself up or perish; discussions of the city's problems in the press are often conducted in alarmingly apocalyptic tones. Leave some room for exaggeration—the Napoletani probably couldn't enjoy life properly without a permanent state of crisis. Naples has marked one genuine accomplishment in the books, though not one that will have much effect on the most serious problems—the *Centro Direzionale*, a huge modernistic development built over the wastelands around Corso Malta, north of the Central Station. Currently nearing completion, the district is meant to provide a new centre for the regional economy.

GETTING AROUND

Orientation is a little difficult. If you arrive by sea—the only proper way to do it—you'll get a good idea of the layout. Naples' dominant landmarks, visible from almost anywhere in town, are Castel San Elmo and the huge, fortress-like Monastery of San Martino. They are neighbours on the steep hill that slopes down to the sea near the port, neatly dividing the city into its old and new quarters. Modern Naples is on the western side, the busy, pleasant districts of Mergellina, Vomero and Fuorigrotta, to which middle-class Napoletani escape from the city centre each night on their creaking old funicular railways. To the east, towards Vesuvius, lies the centre, along Via Toledo, and beyond it the oldest neighbourhoods, tall tenements jammed into a grid of narrow streets, reaching a climax in the oriental bazaar atmosphere of the Piazza Mercato and the Piazza Garibaldi.

If you are coming by air, there is a regular bus service from **Capodichino Airport** to the Stazione Centrale. At present there will be at least one daily flight to and from Alghero, Bologna, Cagliari, Genoa, Milan, Palermo, Pisa, Rome, Turin, Trieste, Venice, and Verona, as well as the islands of Pantelleria and Lampedusa in the summer, and many foreign cities. The airport information number is 789 6111.

Most visitors arrive by train, at the modern **Stazione Centrale** (info. tel 553 4188 or 266 817) on Piazza Garibaldi, convenient since this is also a node for city buses and the Circumvesuviana train. Trains along the west coast towards Rome or Règgio Calabria pass through every half hour on the average. In addition, many trains also stop at *Naples Mergellina* and *Naples Campi Flegrei* on the western side of the city. Naples' **port** has more steamship connections than anywhere in the Mediterranean, and if you find a sudden desire to get away, regularly scheduled lines can take you to Sicily, the Aeolian Islands, Malta, Tripoli, Tunis or Sardinia, not to mention all the islands in the Bay of Naples (see below, p. 240).

Travelling **around the city** is a fascinating subject. First of all, let's get this straight: *Leave your car elsewhere*. Cars do disappear with alarming frequency, and foreign number plates are especially prized. Even if you manage to keep your car, you'll be sorry. Driving in Naples is a unique experience. Motorists studiously disregard all traffic signals and warnings, and the city has given up trying to coerce them. There are no rules, except to get there first, and fatalities are common. Even if this sounds exciting, note that the novelty soon wears off even for the most boorish motorhead. For scant sympathy about stolen cars, call the police at 794 1435; for emergencies tel 112. If you get into trouble on the motorway, call the Auto Club assistance 116; if you still need help, beyond what Naples can give, ring the ACI central assistance for English speaking sympathy: (06)

4212. Taxis are uniformly dishonest; if you want to ride in one, always agree on the fare in advance, whether there is a meter or not.

That leaves you with the **buses**, which is small cheer, since Naples indisputably has the worst bus system in Italy. Buses will be slow and usually indecently crowded. There are no schedules, no maps, and nowhere you can get accurate information; even the drivers usually do not have the faintest idea what is happening. The ultimate Neapolitan experience is waiting an hour for a bus after being misinformed by line employees, and then finding out the right bus is the one marked 'out of service'. Most lines start at either Piazza Garibaldi or Piazza del Plebiscito. Some that might be useful:

Nos. 1 and 4 trolleys: from Piazza Garibaldi to Corso Umberto, Piazza Plebiscito, Riviera di Chiaia, Mergellina.

No. 24, from Piazza Plebiscito up Via Roma to Capodimonte.

Nos. 120, 127, from Piazza Garibaldi to Piazza Cavour, Capodimonte.

No. 150, 152, to Pozzuoli.

Naples also has a sort of Underground. The **Metropolitana,** a single line from Piazza Garibaldi to Fuorigrotta (basement of the Stazione Centrale), is really a part of the state railway, and uses the same underground tracks. The FS runs it as anarchically as the buses, but it will be helpful for reaching the station, the archaeological museum, and points in Vomero and Fuorigrotta. As on the buses, few ever buy tickets. A much more agreeable way to travel, though you can't go very far, is the three **funicolari,** or inclined railroads, up to Vomero. The longest—one of the longest in the world, in fact—is the **Funicolare Centrale,** from Via Toledo, just behind the Galleria, up to Via Cimarosa. The **Funicolare di Chiaia** also reaches that street, starting from Via Crispi in Chiaia. Finally, the **Funicolare di Montesanto** travels up to Via Morghen from Montesanto Station, the start of the suburban Circumflegraean and Cumaean Railway. All three funicolari will take you near the San Martino Museum. All run until about 7 pm.

(For inter-city travel around the Bay of Naples and Campania, by train and bus, see below, p. 220)

TOURIST INFORMATION

The best place to go is the well-run and friendly information booth run by the city's **Azienda Autonima di Soggiorno,** on Piazza Gesù Nuovo in the old town (open Tues–Sat, 9–6; Sun, Mon, 9–3; tel 552 3328). Their main office is in the Royal Palace (551 2701). In the summer they also open offices in the Castel dell'Ovo, in the harbour at Mergellina, and in a trailer in the Piazza Garibaldi. Do not expect much from the notoriously bad **EPT** (Via Partenope 10; tel 406 289), though if anyone is around at their office in the Stazione Centrale, they may be some help in finding a hotel.

Castel Nuovo

The port of Naples has been protected by this odd, beautiful castle for some 700 years. Charles of Anjou built it in 1279; many Napoletani still call it by the curious name of *Maschio Angioino.* Most of what you see today, however, including the eccentric, ponderous round towers, is the work of Guillermo Sagrera, the great Catalan architect who built the famous Exchange in Palma de Mallorca. Between two of these towers at the entrance, the conquering Aragonese hired the finest sculptors from all over Italy to build

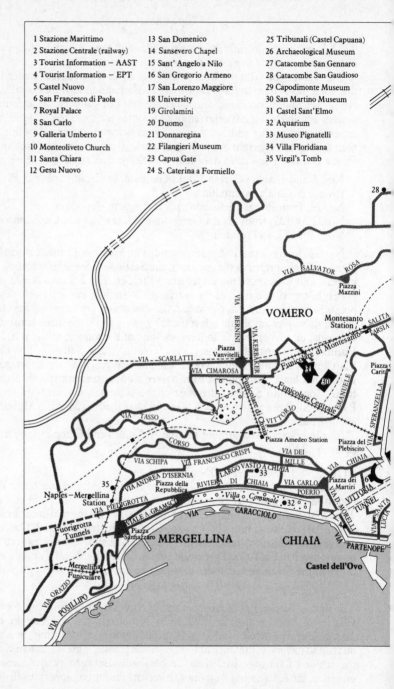

1 Stazione Marittimo
2 Stazione Centrale (railway)
3 Tourist Information – AAST
4 Tourist Information – EPT
5 Castel Nuovo
6 San Francesco di Paola
7 Royal Palace
8 San Carlo
9 Galleria Umberto I
10 Monteoliveto Church
11 Santa Chiara
12 Gesu Nuovo
13 San Domenico
14 Sansevero Chapel
15 Sant' Angelo a Nilo
16 San Gregorio Armeno
17 San Lorenzo Maggiore
18 University
19 Girolamini
20 Duomo
21 Donnaregina
22 Filangieri Museum
23 Capua Gate
24 S. Caterina a Formiello
25 Tribunali (Castel Capuana)
26 Archaeological Museum
27 Catacombe San Gennaro
28 Catacombe San Gaudioso
29 Capodimonte Museum
30 San Martino Museum
31 Castel Sant'Elmo
32 Aquarium
33 Museo Pignatelli
34 Villa Floridiana
35 Virgil's Tomb

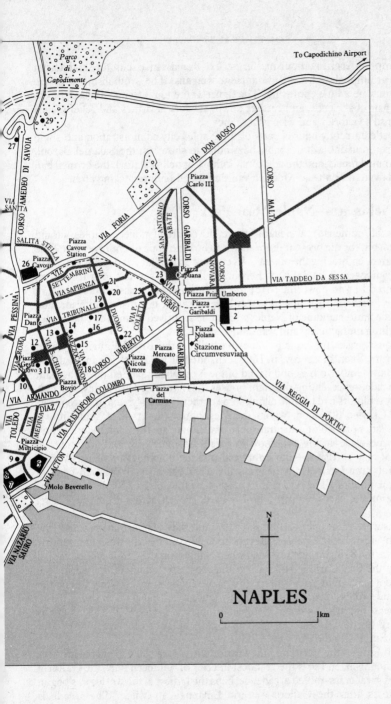

To Capodichino Airport

Parco di Capodimonte

VIA DON BOSCO

Piazza Carlo III

CORSO MALTA

VIA SANTA

CORSO AMEDEO DI SAVOIA

VIA FORIA

CORSO GARIBALDI

VIA SAN ANTONIO ABATE

SALITA STELLA

Piazza Cavour Station

CORSO NOVARA

VIA TADDEO DA SESSA

Piazza Cavour

VIA SETTEMBRINI

VIA SAPIENZA

Piazza Capuana

Piazza Prim Umberto

VIA PESSINA

VIA TRIBUNALI

VIA DUOMO

VIA POERIO

VIA P. COLLETTA

Piazza Garibaldi

Piazza Dante

Piazza Nolana

VIA ROMA

VIA S. CHIARA

VIA MEZZOCANNONE

CORSO UMBERTO

Piazza Mercato

CORSO GARIBALDI

Stazione Circumvesuviana

Piazza Gesù Nuovo

Piazza Nicola Amore

VIA ARMANDO

Piazza Bovio

VIA REGGIA DI PORTICI

VIA TOLEDO

VIA MEDINA

DIAZ

Piazza del Carmine

VIA CRISTOFORO COLOMBO

Piazza Municipio

VIA ACTON

Molo Beverello

VIA NAZARIO SAURO

N

NAPLES

0   1km

Alfonso's **Triumphal Arch**, a unique masterpiece of Renaissance sculpture and design inspired by the triumphal arches of the ancient Romans. The symbolism, as in the Roman arches, may be a little confusing. The figure at the top is Saint Michael; below him a matched pair of sea gods, and further down, allegorical virtues and relief panels portraying Alfonso's victories and wise governance.

Inside, the castle currently houses parts of the Naples city administration and some cultural societies. Someone will probably be around to show you the Sala dei Baroni, where the city council meets, and the adjacent Gothic Cappella Palatina; the council hall features a cupola with an unusual Moorish vaulting based on interlocking arches.

Piazza del Plebiscito—Naples' Car Park

It's a shame that this immense and elegant square, the centre of modern Naples, should suffer such a fate, but for the present there seems to be little hope of improvement. The huge domed church, embracing the piazza in its curving colonnades as does St Peter's in Rome, is **San Francesco di Paola**. King Ferdinand IV made a vow to construct it when the British restored him to power in 1815; the great dome and classical portico were modelled on the Pantheon in Rome. There's little to see in the austere interior, and anyone with a little understanding of Naples will not be surprised to find the colonnades given over to light manufacturing and warehouse space.

Across the square rises the equally imposing bulk of the **Royal Palace** (Palazzo Reale), begun by the Spanish viceroys in 1600, expanded by the Bourbons and finished by the kings of Italy. Umberto I, a good friend of the Neapolitans, added the eight giant figures on the façade, representing the eight houses that have ruled at Naples. It seems the 19th-century sculptors had trouble taking some of them seriously; note the preposterous figures of Charles of Anjou, whom the Neapolitans never liked, and Vittorio Emanuele II, the latter probably an accurate portrayal. There are Ruritanian stone sentry boxes and stone peacocks in the courtyard to recall the Bourbons, and a number of rooms inside that may be visited—those that escaped the bombings in World War II, including a suitably grand staircase, a theatre, and several chambers in the 18th-century style (open irregular hours). The rear of the palace, now the home of Naples' important **Biblioteca Nazionale**, faces a pretty, little-visited garden across from the Castel Nuovo.

The Bourbons were great opera buffs, and they built Italy's largest opera house, the **San Carlo**, right next to their palace. Begun in 1737, the theatre was sumptuously restored after a fire in 1816, during the period when Naples was the unquestioned capital of opera. Today the San Carlo is still among the most prestigious in the world (the Neapolitans, of course, would place it first), and its productions are certainly among the most polished and professional, and occasionally among the most adventurous. Also, each season at least one lesser-known Neapolitan opera is performed. Tickets are as dear as anywhere (up to L150 00 on opening night), but you can take a brief tour (weekdays, 9–2; Sun 9–1; adm) for only L2000.

Naples' Grand Cafés—the **Verdi** and the **Gambrinus**—are conveniently nearby for post-opera exhibitionism, and so is the grandest interior of Southern Italy, the **Galleria Umberto I**. This great glass-roofed arcade, perhaps the largest in the world, was begun in 1887, nine years after the Galleria Vittorio Emanuele in Milan. The arcade is cross-shaped, with a mosaic of the zodiac on the floor at the centre, and its dome is 56 m tall; surprisingly, the Neapolitans do not seem to like it as much as they once did; even at high noon, you are likely to find its vast spaces deserted but for a few small clouds of grey-suited men arguing politics around the entrances.

Via Toledo and Via Medina
Outside the Galleria, **Via Toledo** commemorates its builder, Don Pedro de Toledo, the Spanish viceroy at the beginning of the 1500s, and a great benefactor of Naples. This is the city's main business and shopping street, eventually changing its name to Via Roma on its way to Capodimonte and the northern suburbs. Don Pedro's elegant Renaissance tomb, among others, can be seen in the little 18th century church of **San Giacomo degli Spagnuoli**, now swallowed up by the 19th-century Palazzo Municipale complex, originally a home for the Bourbon royal bureaucracy.

On its eastern side, the Palazzo Municipale faces a Neapolitan rarity, a well-kept park called the **Piazza del Municipio**, leading toward the Castel Nuovo and the harbour. Some out-of-the-way sights in the area: S. **Maria Incoronata**, a church built by the formidable Neapolitan Queen Joan I in the 1350s, with some excellent frescoes of the same period; the artist is believed to be a certain Oderisi, though Vasari's *Lives of the Artists* attributes them to Giotto. **Santa Maria la Nova**, a few blocks north across Via Sanfelice, is a Renaissance church that belonged to the Franciscans.

Back on Via Toledo, continuing north, on the left is a dense, very typical old Neapolitan neighbourhood, a grid of narrow streets laid out under Spanish rule and now called the *Tavoliere*, or chessboard, sloping up towards San Martino; to the right, the confusion of Naples' half-crumbling, half-modern business centre conceals a few buildings worth a look. **Palazzo Gravina**, on Via Monteoliveto, is a fine palace in the northern Renaissance style, built between 1513 and 1549. Almost directly across the street, the church of **Monteoliveto** is a little treasure-house of late Renaissance sculpture and painting, with tombs and altars in the various chapels by southern artists like Giovanni da Nola (tomb of Alfonso II in the apse, among others) and also a number of famous Tuscans. Antonio Rossellino did the *Nativity* in the Piccolomini Chapel, and began the tomb beneath it, of Mary of Aragon; Benedetto da Maiano finished it, and also contributed a lovely *Annunciation* in the first chapel of the right aisle.

Spaccanapoli

The street's familiar name means 'Split-Naples', and that is exactly what it has done for the last 2000 years. On the map, it changes its name with alarming frequency—Via Benedetto Croce and Via San Biagio dei Librai are two of the most prominent—but in Roman times you would have found it by asking for the *decumanus inferior*, the name for the second east–west street in any planned Roman city. No large city in all the lands conquered by Rome has maintained its ancient street plan as completely as Naples. It is easier here to imagine the atmosphere of a big ancient city than in Rome itself, or even in Pompeii. The narrow, straight streets and tall *insulae* cannot have changed much; only the forum and temples are missing.

This is the heart of old Naples—and what a street it is, lined with grocery barrows and scholarly bookshops, shops that sell old violins, plaster saints, pizza, or used clothes pegs.

Drama is supplied by the arch-Neapolitan characters who live here, haunting the street corners and dodging the manic motorists; the colour comes from the district's laundry—down any of the long alleys of impossibly tall tenements you may see as many as a hundred full clothes-lines, swelling bravely in the breeze and hoping for a glint of southern sun.

This has always been a poor neighbourhood, though even now it is not a desperate one. As always, its people live much of their life on the streets, carrying on whatever is their business from makeshift benches on the kerbs. The visitor will probably find that claustrophobia is right around the corner, but anyone born and raised here would never feel at home anywhere else.

Santa Chiara and the Gesù Nuovo

Your introduction to this world, just off Via Roma, is the cramped, disorderly, most characteristic of Neapolitan squares: the **Piazza Gesù Nuovo**, decorated by the gaudiest and most random of Neapolitan decorations, the **Guglia dell' Immacolata**. A *guglia* (pinnacle), in Naples, is a kind of Rococo obelisk, dripping with frills, saints and putti; there are three, all in this area. The unsightly, unfinished façade behind this guglia, covered with pyramidal extrusions in dark basalt, belongs to the church of **Gesù Nuovo**. As strange as it is, the façade has become one of the landmarks of Naples, originally part of a late 15th-century palace. The interior is typical lavish Neapolitan Baroque, gloriously overdone in acres of coloured marbles and frescoes, some by the Spanish artist Ribera.

Santa Chiara, just across the piazza, was begun in the early 14th century, though it later gained a Baroque interior as good as the Gesù; Allied bombers remodelled it to suit modern tastes in 1943, and only a few of the original Angevin tombs have survived. To get some idea of what the interior must have been like, step in and see the adjacent **Cloister of the Clarisse**, nothing less than the loveliest and most peaceful spot in Naples—especially in contrast with the neighbourhood outside. So much in Naples shows the Spanish influence—like the façade of the Gesù, or the use of the title 'Don', now unfortunately rare—and here someone in the 1740s transplanted the Andalusian love of pictures done in painted *azulejo* tiles, turning a simple monkish cloister into a little fairyland of gaily coloured arbours, benches and columns, shaded by the only trees in the whole district.

Just recently, during the restoration of a vestibule off the cloister, it was discovered that underneath the indifferent 18th-century frescoes were some earlier, highly original paintings of the Last Judgement. These have been uncovered and restored, revealing an inspired 16th-century vision of the event, in a style utterly unlike the slick virtuosity of the time, with plenty of novel tortures for the damned and angels welcoming some cute naked nuns among the elect.

San Domenico Maggiore and the Sansevero Chapel

Just a few blocks down Via Benedetto Croce, tiny Piazza San Domenico has monuments of Naples' three most creative periods. **San Domenico Maggiore**, an enormous Gothic church begun in 1289, became a favourite church of the Aragonese and Spanish and contains some interesting Renaissance funerary monuments: two of the chapels in the left aisle have sculptures by Giovanni di Nola, and painting by Mattia Preti.

Across the Piazza, the church of **Sant'Angelo a Nilo** contains a rare jewel—the tomb of Cardinal Brancaccio, designed by Michelozzo with a relief of the *Assumption of the Virgin* by Donatello. The second of the Baroque pinnacles decorates the Piazza, the **Guglia di San Domenico**. Best of all, just around the corner on Via F. De Sanctis, you can inspect Neapolitan Rococo at its very queerest in the **Sansevero Chapel**.

Prince Raimondo di Sangro (b. 1701), who was responsible for the present form of this, his family's private chapel, was a strange bird, a sort of aristocratic dilettante mystic. Supposedly there is a grand allegorical scheme behind the arrangement of the sculptures and frescoes he commissioned, but a work like this, only 200 years old, seems as foreign to our sensibilities and understanding as a Mayan temple. The sculptures, by little-known Neapolitan artists like Giuseppe Sammartino and Antonio Corradini, are inscrutable allegories in themselves, often executed with a breathtakingly showy virtuosity. Francesco Queirolo's *Il Disenganno* (disillusion) is an extreme case; nobody else, perhaps, has ever tried to carve a fishing-net, or the turning pages of a book out of marble. Others, such as Sammartino's *Cristo Velato*, display a remarkable illusion of figures under transparent veils. There are a dozen or so of these large sculptural groups, all under a crazy heavenly vortex in the ceiling fresco by Francesco Mario Russo (daily 10–1:30; Sun 11–1:30; adm).

Also just off the Spacca, on Vico Sansevero, you may make a short detour to **SS. Severino e Sosio**. The Baroque decoration inside is as forgettable as any in Naples, but while admiring it you can muse over the fate of the painter, Baldassare Corenzio. After finishing the year-long job in 1643, Corenzio climbed back up the scaffolding to touch up just one small bit—and fell off. He's buried in the crypt.

Around Via dei Tribunali

Continuing down the Spaccanapoli (now Via San Biagio ai Librai), just around the corner on Via San Gregorio the **San Gregorio Armeno** church has another gaudy Baroque interior. In December, this street and others around it become Naples' famous Christmas Market, where everyone comes to buy figurines of the Holy Family and Three Kings for their Christmas *presepi*, or manger scenes—as well as little trees, sheep, donkeys, amphorae, cooking pots, Turks, salamis, ruined Roman columns, dogs, chickens, angels, cheese wheels, and all the other items without which no Neapolitan *presepio* would be complete. (If you doubt just how seriously the Neapolitans take these things, wait until you see the ones in the San Martino museum.) The Christmas Market is quite an affair, with several hundred stands filling up most of the neighbourhood's narrow streets.

A little further up Via San Gregorio, **San Lorenzo Maggiore** (*c.* 1330) is one of Naples' finest medieval churches; Petrarch lived for a while in the adjacent monastery. **San Paolo**, across the street, isn't much to see now, but before an earthquake wrecked it in the 17th century, its façade was the portico of an ancient Roman temple to Castor and Pollux. Andrea Palladio studied it closely, and it provided much of the inspiration for his classical palaces in the Veneto. Only two of its columns survived the earthquake.

After Spaccanapoli, **Via dei Tribunali** (*decumanus major*) is the busiest street of old

Naples. The arcades that line the street in places, a sort of continuous covered market, are a thousand years old or more. Here, the gaudy **Girolamini Church** was the last proper Baroque church built in Naples, with a marble façade by the architect Fernando Fuga, better known for his work in Rome. Inside, you can see more frescoes by the ill-starred Corenzio, as well as some by Luca Giordano—and also, in the left aisle, the modest tomb of one of the most subversive thinkers ever born, Giambattista Vico. Since his death in 1744, Vico's philosophy of historical cycles and the poetic origins of each new civilization has been a dark undercurrent in Western thought and literature; Joyce's *Finnegan's Wake* is based on it. Vico lived all his life in this neighbourhood, and had a wonderfully Neapolitan funeral; at the procession, members of his confraternity got into an argument with his University colleagues over who would carry the coffin. This somehow degenerated into a general neighbourhood brawl, and the corpse, abandoned and forgotten, spent the day and night in the middle of the Via dei Tribunali.

Naples' **University**, incidentally, is one of Europe's oldest and most distinguished. The Emperor Frederick founded it in 1224, as a 'Ghibelline' university to counter the pope's 'Guelph' university at Bologna, as well as to provide scholars and trained officials for the new state he was trying to build. It still occupies its ancient quarters in old Naples, around Via Mezzocannone.

Northwest of the Girolamini, around Via dell'Anticaglia, you'll find a few crooked streets, the only ones in old Naples that do not stick to the rectilinear Roman plan. These follow the outline of the Roman theatre, much of which still survives, hidden among the tenements. A few arches are all that is visible from the street.

The Cathedral of San Gennaro

The wide **Via del Duomo** is a breath of fresh air in this crowded district—exactly what the city intended, when they ploughed it through Old Naples after the cholera epidemic of 1884. The **Duomo** itself is another fine medieval building, though it is hidden behind an awful pseudo-Gothic façade pasted on in 1905—the original façade of 1323, and its replacement of 1407, both went down in earthquakes soon after they were completed.

The best things are inside: a hundred ancient columns from the temples of Jupiter and Apollo that once occupied this site; the Renaissance Capella Minùtolo; the tomb of Charles of Anjou, near the entrance; and the Capella San Gennaro, glittering with the gold and silver of the cathedral treasure. This huge chapel, behind an impressive gilded bronze grille by the mad Cosimo Fanzago, contains a series of turgid frescoes by Domenichino, and an equally tedious dome fresco, another vortex of writhing bodies, called the *Paradiso*. Domenichino's arch-enemy, Giovanni Lanfranco, got the commission for the dome in 1643, after he and his friends hounded Domenichino out of town. Take a minute to consider this trashy business—in the 18th century, Domenichino's vacuous classicism and his rival's pastel illusions were considered among the greatest works of all time.

Along the opposite aisle, the **Basilica Santa Restituta**, a sizeable church in its own right, is tacked on to the side of the cathedral. Begun in the 4th century over the old temple of Apollo, most of what you see is Baroque restorations, including ceiling frescoes by Luca Giordano. Just off the basilica, the 5th-century **baptistry** contains a good Byzantine-style mosaic by the 14th-century artist Lello di Roma; the baptismal font itself probably comes from an ancient temple of Dionysos. The last and most elaborate of the *guglie*, the **Guglia San Gennaro**, can be seen just outside the south transept.

If the sacristan is around, you may visit the **Crypt of San Gennaro**, a fine Renaissance interior built for the remains of the patron of Naples. Whoever is really buried here, San Gennaro (Januarius) is a rather doubtful character; most likely he is a Christian assimilation of the Roman god Janus. The saint's head is kept upstairs in the chapel named after him, along with two phials of his blood that miraculously liquefy and 'boil' three times each year—the first Sunday in May, 19th September, and 16th December—so as to prove that San Gennaro is still looking after the Napoletani. The only time the miracle has ever failed, during the Napoleonic occupation, the people of the city became enormously excited and seemed ready to revolt. At this the French commander, a true son of the Enlightenment, announced that San Gennaro had ten minutes to come through—or else he'd shoot the Archbishop. Somehow, just in time, the miracle occurred.

One block north of the Duomo, **Santa Maria Donnaregina** offers more overdone Baroque, but off to the side of this 17th-century work is the smaller, original church, built in 1307 by Queen Mary of Hungary (who was none other than the wife of Charles of Anjou; the title only reflects a claim to the throne). Her elaborate tomb, by Tino da Camaino (1326), and some good frescoes of the *Passion* and *Last Judgement* by Pietro Cavallini and his students, are the sights of the church. The **Filangieri Museum**, housed in the 15th-century Florentine-style Palazzo Cuomo, is a small collection of china, armour, and curiosities; its picture collection includes works by some of Naples' favourite artists: Luca Giordano, Mattia Preti, Ribera and others—the best of it was senselessly destroyed by the retreating Germans in 1943. (Via del Duomo, four blocks south of the cathedral; daily 9–2, Sun 9–1; closed Mon; adm). **San Giorgio Maggiore**, across Via Duomo, is one of Naples' oldest churches, but only the apse survives from the 5th century original.

Piazza Garibaldi

In Italian, the word for a market stand is *bancarella*. In Naples they are as much a part of everyday life as they must have been in the Middle Ages; the city probably has as many of them as all the rest of Italy put together. The greatest concentration can be found in the narrow streets east of the Via del Duomo, selling everything from phonographs to light bulbs. According to the government's economists, at least one-third of Naples' economy is underground—outright illegal, or at least not paying taxes or subject to any regulation.

Bootleg cassette tapes are one example; Naples is the world leader in this thriving industry, and you'll have your choice of thousands of titles along these streets. Hundreds of tired-looking folks sit in front of little tables, selling contraband American cigarettes. This is one of the easiest means for Naples' poor to make a living, and it is all controlled by the Camorra. As in New York, whenever it rains, shady characters crawl out of the woodwork selling umbrellas. You will see plenty of designer labels on the *bancarelle*—if they're real, don't ask where they came from.

Piazza Mercato, one of the nodes of the Neapolitan bazaar, has been a market square perhaps since Roman times. It has witnessed many events in the city's history. Masaniello's revolt began here in 1647, a brave but ultimately doomed attempt to throw off the tyranny of the Spaniards and the Inquisition. In 1269, Charles of Anjou had young Conradin beheaded here; the last of the Hohenstaufens (whose throne Charles had usurped) is buried nearby in S. Maria del Carmine, a much-remodelled church with more inevitable frescoes by Luca Giordano and his follower Francesco Solimena. Corso Umberto I, popularly known as the *Rettifilo*, does its best to lend a touch of respectability to this ragtag neighbourhood. Like Via del Duomo, this boulevard was chopped through primeval slums in the 1880s. It shows; elegant shops coexist peacefully with the *bancarelle* out on their pavements, while around any corner the ancient tenements and alleys moulder away.

The other main centre of the district is the incredible Piazza Garibaldi. For rail travellers, it is an unforgettable introduction to Naples; they walk out of the incongruously modern Stazione Centrale (successor to Italy's very first) into the vast square, paved with asphalt that melts in the hot sun and sticks to their shoes, and enter a world unlike anything else in Italy—bums, addicts and crazies draped picturesquely along the pavement, solid ranks of *bancarelle* wherever there's room, eternal crowds of odd characters from every nation of the world, Italy's worst hotels and its ugliest whores. Most of the piazza is really one gigantic parking lot; traffic whistles through it on lanes marked by yellow paint. Neapolitans don't mind the Piazza Garibaldi; tourists often come to like it. Sailors generally avoid it, as do the police.

The Capua Gate
Northwest of the Piazza Garibaldi, some of Naples' shabbiest streets lead towards the Piazza Enrico di Nicola, once the city's main entrance. The Porta Capuana, built into the walls in 1492, seems a smaller version of the Castel Nuovo's triumphal arch, crowded in by the same squat round towers. This celebration of Aragonese rule, like the Castel Nuovo's, was inspired by ancient Rome's triumphal arches (or perhaps Benevento's).

The Castel Capuano, next to it, began its life as a castle-residence for the Hohenstaufen kings. Since its construction in the 13th century it has been reshaped so many times it doesn't even look like a castle any more; for four centuries it has served as Naples' law courts. If anything makes wandering into this unlikely district worthwhile, though, it is Santa Caterina a Formiello, facing the Porta Capuana, an almost abandoned church by the obscure architect Romolo Balsimelli that is one of the forgotten masterpieces of 16th-century Italian architecture. Completed in 1517, the church's graceful façade and roofline were Renaissance eccentricities, but an important stepping-stone towards the Baroque. Today, Santa Caterina is hardly ever open, and its dome tilts at a more precarious angle with each passing year.

Another church nearby, the Santissima Annunziata on Via dell'Annunziata, is one of the first and best examples of the cool, restrained Neoclassical style introduced by court architect Luigi Vanvitelli in the 1760s—a reaction against a delerious century of Neapolitan Baroque. A few blocks north of Santa Caterina, towards Piazza Cavour, is S. Giovanni a Carbonara, on the street of the same name. This big church, begun in the 14th century, has a number of fine Renaissance sculptures and tombs, including works by Giovanni da Nola and another Tuscan visitor, Andrea da Firenze; he is responsible for the magnificent *tomb of King Ladislas* (1420) behind the high altar.

If you mean to continue through these unwholesome quarters, make your way eastwards, down Via Foria. The Baroque planning, with its wide boulevards, and the

210

contemporary squalor, make an unforgettable combination. Eventually you'll come to the small but pleasant **Botanical Gardens**, founded by Joseph Bonaparte in 1808. Just beyond it, facing the semicircular Piazza Carlo III, is the biggest, most preposterous building in all Naples—well over twice the size of the Royal Palace. In fact, the **Albergo dei Poveri** has a Baroque façade (by Fernando Fuga) some 1120 feet long. It's a poorhouse, built by that same well-meaning monarch, Carlo III, in 1751.

The Archaeological Museum

After passing Spaccanapoli, Via Roma continues northwards through the **Piazza Dante**, one of the most delightful and animated corners of the city, embracing its chaotic business in a semicircle of buildings by Vanvitelli. Pass under the 17th century **Porta Alba**, on the edge of the piazza, and in the back streets you will find the old Academy of Art and Conservatory of Music; next to the latter, **S. Pietro a Maiella** has two great series of paintings by Mattia Preti, of St Catherine and of the holy hermit Pope Celestine V (see below: Castel dell'Ovo).

North of Piazza Dante, in an area of oversized tenements and busy streets, Via Roma opens to display the crumbling red palazzo that contains the **Museo Archeologico Nazionale** (open winter 9–2; Sun 9–1; summer 9–7:30, Sun 9–9; adm, but free the 1st and 3rd Sat of each month, also the 2nd and 4th Sun).

Naples has the most important collection of Roman-era art and antiquities in the world, due partly to Vesuvius, for burying Pompeii and Herculaneum, and partly to the sharp eyes and deep pockets of the Farnese (the family of Pope Paul III). Many of the best works here come from the collection they built up over 200 years, eventually all inherited by the Bourbons of Naples. Unfortunately, the place is run by Neapolitans; at any given time, half of the collections will be closed for 'restorations' that never seem to happen, and what they condescend to let you see may well be the worst-exhibited and labelled major museum in Europe.

Ornamental with Nile scene, 1st century mosaic, Archaeological Museum

211

On the first floor, room after room is filled with ancient sculpture. Many are the best existing Roman-era copies of lost Greek statues, including some by Phidias and Praxiteles; some are masterpieces in their own right, such as the huge, dramatic ensemble called the *Farnese Bull*, the *Tyrannicides* (with other statues' heads stuck on them), and the truly heroic *Farnese Hercules* that once decorated the Baths of Caracalla. Several provocative Aphrodites compete for your attention, along with a platoon of formidable Athenes. Also the famous *Doryphorus* (spear-bearer), and enough Greek and Roman busts to populate a Colosseum.

Upstairs, most of the rooms are given to finds from Pompeii. The collection of **Roman mosaics**, mostly from Pompeii and Herculaneum, is one of the two best anywhere (the other is in Antakya, Turkey); the insight it provides into the life and thought of the ancients is priceless. One feature it betrays clearly is a certain fond silliness—plenty of chickens, ducks and grinning cats, the famous *Cave canem* (beware of dog) mosaic from the front of a house, comic scenes from the theatre, and especially one wonderful panel of crocodiles and hippopotami along the Nile. Some of the mosaics are very consciously 'art': a detailed scene of the Battle of Issus, where Alexander the Great defeated the Persian King Darius, and a view of the Academy of Athens that includes a portrait of Plato.

Besides the mosaics, nowhere in the world will you find a larger collection of **Roman mural painting**, and much of it is fascinatingly modern in theme and execution. Many of the walls of Pompeiian villas were decorated with architectural fantasias that seem strangely like those of the Renaissance. Other works show an almost Baroque lack of respect for the Gods—see the *Wedding of Zeus and Hera*. Scholars in fact do define a period of 'Roman Baroque', beginning about the 2nd century. From it come paintings graced by genuine winged putti; they called them *amoretti* in Roman days. Among the most famous pictures are *The Astragal Players*—young girls shooting dice—and the beautiful *Portrait of an Unknown Woman*, a thoughtful lady holding her pen to her lips who has become one of the best-known images from Roman art.

Other attractions of the museum include large collections of jewellery, coins, fancy gladiators' armour, a *sezione pornografico* that no one gets to see, Greek vases, decorative bronzes and a highly detailed, room-sized **scale model** of the entire city of Pompeii (lovingly restored since the memorable assault on it by the authors' baby boy, back in 1980). The Egyptian collection is not a large one, but it is fun, with a dog-headed Anubis in a Roman toga, some ancient feet under glass, and a mummified crocodile.

Capodimonte

North of the museum, the neighbourhoods along Via Roma begin to lose some of their Neapolitan intensity as they climb to the suburban heights. On the way, after changing its name to Corso Amedeo di Savoia, the street passes an area that was full of cemeteries in Roman times; three Christian underground burial vaults have been discovered here, and two may be visited: the **Catacombe di San Gennaro** (entrance off the northern end of the Corso; look for the yellow signs. Tours Sat and Sun only, at 9:30, 10:15, 11:00, and 11:45; adm) is the more interesting, with extensive early Christian mosaics and carvings, some as early as the 2nd century. The **Catacombe di San Gaudioso**, including the 5th-century tomb of the saint, a martyred African bishop, were discovered under the

Baroque church of Santa Maria della Sanità, on Via Sanità (tours Fri, Sat, and Sun 9:30, 10:15, 11, and 11:45; adm).

The **Parco di Capodimonte**, a well-kept and exotically tropical park, began as a hunting preserve of the Bourbons in the 18th century. Charles III built a Royal Palace here in 1738 that now houses Naples' picture gallery, the **Museo Nazionale di Capodimonte** (open daily, except Mon, 9–2, summer 9–7:30; Sun 9–1; adm). The collection is the best in the south of Italy, especially rich in works of the late Renaissance. Some of the works you shouldn't miss: an *Annunciation* by Filippino Lippi; a Botticelli *Madonna*; the mystical portrait of the mathematician *Fra Luca Pacioli*, by an unknown quattrocento artist; two wry homilies by the elder Brueghel, *The Misanthrope* and *The Blind*; works by Masaccio and Mantegna, and a hilarious picture of St Peter Martyr by Lotto, showing that famous anti-Semitic rabble-rouser conversing nonchalantly with the Virgin Mary—with a hatchet sticking out of his head.

Five big, beautifully restored Caravaggios take up one room; others are devoted to important works by Titian. One entire wing of the museum is filled with delightfully frivolous 18th-century **porcelain figurines**; the Bourbons maintained a royal factory for such things at Capodimonte that is still in operation today. In another hall, there are scores of 19th-century watercolour scenes of Naples and the Campanian countryside (the best of them by Giacinto Gigante). Here, for the first time, you will see the Naples that so struck the 18th-century travellers. Not much has changed, really; if only all the traffic could magically disappear, it would still be almost the same spectacular city today.

The museum's collections are mostly up on the second floor; the first, the old *piano nobile* (Royal apartments), is still much the way the Bourbons left it. Persevere through the score of overdecorated chambers; the **Salotto di Porcellana**, a little room entirely done in Capodimonte porcelain, makes the whole thing worth while.

The Certosa di San Martino

Up on the highest point overlooking Naples, the 17th-century **Castel Sant'Elmo** is an impressive enough Baroque fortification, though apparently abandoned; rumour has it the city now uses it to store the cars they tow away. Next to it, hogging the best view in Naples, the Carthusians built their modest, original monastery of **San Martino** some time in the early 14th century. By the 1500s, like most Carthusian branch offices, they were rolling embarrassingly in lucre; building the poshest monastery in all Italy was the only thing to do. The rebuilt *Certosa* (Charterhouse) is only marginally smaller than Fort St Elmo. Built on the slope of the mountain, it is supported by a gargantuan platform, visible for miles out to sea and containing enough stone to construct a small pyramid.

Nobody knows exactly what is in the **Museo Nazionale di San Martino**. Intended as a museum specifically of Naples, its history, art and traditions, San Martino suffers from the same mismanagement as the Archaeological Museum; only parts are ever open, and the Grand Cloister, at the time of writing, has become a wilderness of weeds and scaffolding. Not that this should discourage you from taking the long ride up the Montesanto Funicular. The views and the architecture are marvellous, and at least they always keep open the collection of *presepi*—what the Neapolitans come here to see.

Upon entering the complex, the first attraction is the **church**, another of the glories of Neapolitan Baroque, with an excess of lovely coloured inlaid marble to complement the superabundance of painting. The work over the altar, the *Descent from the Cross*, is one of the finest of José Ribera's works. This tormented artist, often called *Il Spagnuolo* in Italy, has paintings all over Naples. His popularity does not owe everything to his artistic talent; early in the 1600s he formed a little cartel with two local artists, and cornered the market by hiring a gang of thugs to harry all the other painters out of town. Among other artists of the decaying late Renaissance and Baroque represented are Cavaliere d'Arpino, Guido Reni, Lanfranco and Luca Giordano.

The **Chiostro Grande**, even in its present state, is a masterpiece of Baroque, elegantly proportioned and gloriously original in its decoration. Also, thanks to a sculptural scheme by the pious, tormented Cosimo Fanzago, it is the creepiest cloister east of Spain. Fanzago (who was also one of the architects of San Martino) gives us eight figures of saints that seem more like vampires in priestly robes and mitres, a perfect background for his little enclosed garden, its wall topped with rows of gleaming marble skulls. Most of the collections are in the halls surrounding the Chiostro Grande— costume, painting, ship models and every sort of curiosity; at the corners are **belvederes** from which to look over Naples. (Outside the complex, a series of lovely terraced gardens offer a view much the same.) The *presepi* take up a few large rooms near the entrance.

The Presepi

It would not be easy to explain why the genius of Naples should have chosen Christmas cribs as a subject to elevate to an art form. After philosophy, pizza, and music, it's what this city does best. Churches and private homes have always had a little competitive edge on when they begin their displays (some time in November, if not earlier). The most extreme cases have been assembled here. One is as big as a bus, and must have taken someone a lifetime; another is fitted inside an eggshell—with over a hundred figures in it. Best of all are the large, finely carved individual wooden or ceramic figures, some by noted local artists. Most are Neapolitans of two or three centuries ago, from every walk of life; with their painstakingly detailed and wonderfully expressive faces, each is a genuine portrait. To have them all here in one place is like old Bourbon Naples appearing before your eyes.

The curious fancy of the *presepi* certainly does not end with a Holy Family attended mostly by Neapolitans. Convention requires that certain things be present in every crib. Besides the usual angels, shepherds, and animals, a *Roman ruin* is absolutely necessary, as are several *Turks* in Ottoman Empire dress (these come in handy if one of the Three Kings gets lost). A *band of musicians* is also expected, and all the better if they too are Turks. *Beggars and dwarfs* earn envy for the crib-maker—there is a whole display of figures called the 'deformities'—but above all there must be *tons of food* everywhere there is room for it. The best cribs have the busiest cooks and the most bulging pantries, with tiny wooden roast pigs, sausages, eggs, plates of macaroni, cheeses and fancy cakes— even a pizza or two.

Castel dell'Ovo

The hill called Pizzofalcone rises directly behind the Piazza del Plebiscito; around it was the site of Parthenope, the Greek town that antedated Neapolis and was eventually swallowed up by it. (Neapolitans still like to refer to themselves as Parthenopeans.)

There is little reason to climb Pizzofalcone's steep streets, but any art detectives on the trail of the origins of Baroque should visit the little church of **S. Maria degli Angeli**, on Via Monte di Dio. Begun in 1600, designed by a Theatine monk named Francesco Grimaldi, it shows a style well in advance of its time.

Parthenope had a little harbour, formed by an island now almost completely covered by the ancient, strangely-shaped **Castel dell'Ovo**—the fortress Master Virgil is said to have built balanced on an egg, hence the name. Most of it was really built by Frederick II, and expanded by the Angevins.

There isn't much to see today—though once the chapel was covered with frescoes by Giotto, of which nothing remains—but the Egg Castle has been the scene of many unusual events in Italian history. Long before there was a castle, the island held the villa of the Roman general and philosopher Lucullus, victor over Mithridates in the Pontic Wars; in the 5th century the villa became a home in exile for Romulus Augustulus, last of the western Roman Emperors. The Goths spared him only for his youth and simple-mindedness, and pensioned him off here (Conradin, the last Hohenstaufen, was held prisoner in the Egg Castle by the Angevins, who were probably unaware of the connection). Columns from Lucullus' villa are still to be seen among the castle's famous dungeons.

In the castle's **Hall of the Barons**, one clever Norman king is said to have murdered dozens of his opponents after inviting them to a reconciliation banquet, Al Capone-style. Another simpleton, the Abruzzese hermit whom fortune cast on the throne as Pope Celestine V, was confined here in 1294, and tricked into abdicating by heavenly voices, whispered into his chamber through a hidden tube by the man who would soon take his job, the thoroughly vile Boniface VIII.

Modern Naples; the Villa Comunale

Once past the Egg Castle, a handsome sweep of coastline opens up the districts of **Chiaia and Mergellina**, the most pleasant parts of the new city. Here the long, pretty **Villa Comunale**, central Naples' only park, follows the shore. In it, there is an **Aquarium**, built by the German naturalist Dr Anton Dohrn in the 1870s, and perhaps the oldest in the world. All the wide variety of fish, octopuses and other marine delicacies here are from the Bay of Naples; depending on the hour of day, you will find them fascinating, or else overwhelmingly appetizing—when Naples was liberated, the Allied command was served a fabulous seafood feast from its tanks (daily, except Mon, 9–5; Sun and holidays 10–7; adm). Behind the park, on the Riviera di Chiaia, the **Museo Principe di Aragona Pignatelli Cortes** will show you more of the same kind of decorative porcelain as at Capodimonte, along with a score of 18th- and 19th-century noble carriages, furniture and art (daily, except Mon, 9–2; Sun and holidays 9–1; adm).

If you're still not tired of little smiling figurines, you can plunge deeper into Chiaia to see the greatest collection of all at the Museo Nazionale della Ceramica, also known as the Duca di Martina Museum, but familiar to the Neapolitans only as the **Villa Floridiana**, after the tasteful 18th-century estate it occupies. Here is one of the loveliest gardens in Naples (open 9 till one hour before sunset, closed Mon; free) and one of Italy's great hoards of bric-à-brac. (The museum is on Via Cimarosa, near the Funicolare di Chiaia; same hours as the Pignatelli Museum; adm.)

Virgil's Tomb
A few blocks beyond the western end of the Villa Comunale, **Mergellina** is one of the brightest and most popular quarters of Naples, a good place for dinner or a *passeggiata* around the busy Piazza Sannazaro. Its centre is the **Marina**, where besides small craft there are hydrofoils to Sorrento and the islands in the summer months. From May through to October, an excursion boat called the *Patrizia* starts from the Marina for daily tours of the shore between the Egg Castle and Point Posillipo (at 5:30, 6:30 and 7:30 pm; fare L2500). From the harbour, Mergellina rises steeply up the surrounding hills; there is a funicular up to the top. On the hillside, between the railway bridge and the tunnel that leads under the hill to Fuorigrotta, there is a Roman funerary monument that tradition has always held to be the **Tomb of Virgil**. The poet died in Brindisi in 19 BC, on his way back from a trip to Greece, but Neapolis was a city dear to him—he wrote most of the *Aeneid* here—and the legend may well be true.

Just below it lies the entrance to one of the little-known wonders of the ancient world. The **Crypta Neapolitana**, unfortunately closed at present, is a 606 m road tunnel built during the reign of Augustus, to connect Neapolis with Pozzuoli and Baiae, the longest such work the Romans ever attempted.

ACTIVITIES
Every Sunday the Naples' AAST organizes guided tours of the city; places of interest include the archaeological excavations of the Duomo, the ossuary of San Pietro ad Aram, and the ossuary of Le Fontanelle. For concerts, shows and other cultural events— Naples always has plenty—the best information will be found in the newspaper *Il Mattino*, or in the monthly guide *Qui Napoli*, in Italian and English, published by the AAST and available at their offices or in many hotels. By all means, catch the opera or anything else that's on at San Carlo. Whatever you think of the performance, an evening in Italy's grandest house will be a memorable affair. Dress up.

Naples isn't a big town for night-life, except the sort of amenities usually provided for sailors (though it is the capital of serious Italian rock). One neighbourhood where quite a few convivial bars can be found is around the Piazza Amedeo and Via Vittorio Colonna, and along Via Manzoni in Posillipo. Many of the city's permanent attractions are concentrated in the Fuorigrotta district. **Edenlandia** is a big amusement park there, on Viale Kennedy in the **Mostra d'Oltramare**, Naples' exhibition and entertainment complex. There is also a **dog-racing** track and a small but fun **zoo** in the grounds. Nearby, on Via Fuorigrotta just past the tunnel, there's **jai-alai** every night at 8 pm. Anything a Napoletano can bet on will flourish here; the **race-track**, running both thoroughbreds and trotters most of the year, is out west in Agnano. Of course there's always first division football, in Fuorigrotta's San Paolo Stadium. With the help of Diego Maradona, Naples won its first league title ever in 1987; these days every important victory calls forth a spontaneous celebration all over town that seems like Carnival in Rio.

WHERE TO STAY   (tel prefix 081)
Naples does have less than its share of top-quality hotels; the Germans, inexplicably, blew up a few of them before their retreat in 1943. Most of the best are along Via Partenope, near the Castel dell'Ovo, a location where the views over the bay more than compensate for the traffic noise below. Visiting sheikhs, kings and rock stars favour the

*****Excelsior**, Naples' finest, with beautiful suites and a tradition of perfect service since 1909 (Via Partenope 48, tel 417 111; doubles L230–450 000).

A dozen or so other expensive hotels cluster in the Excelsior's shadow on Via Partenope, but the consensus of travellers has long been that they are a dull lot, and that hasn't changed. You may have more fun—of all places—in a chain hotel, the ******Jolly Ambassador** off Piazza Municipi at Via Medina 70, tel 416 000. This is the tallest hotel in Italy, some 30 floors of priceless views around the bay and Vesuvius. Another advantage—it's always easy to find, no matter how lost you get on central Naples' crazy streets (L160–220 000 for a double; reserve in advance for a room with a good view). Both these hotels have their own garages, *importantissimo* if you bring a car. Another central choice, with views over the bay, nice rooms and a roof garden, is the ******Miramare**, Via Nazario Sauro 24, tel 427 388 (air-conditioned doubles L140–240 000).

A less expensive place in the centre with a garage is the ***Rex**, at Via Palepoli 12, tel 416 919 (doubles L86–150 000, and some cheaper without bath).

There are millions of hotel rooms around the Piazza Garibaldi, most of them horrible dives. If you do desire to stay close to the station, two respectable places are ***Cavour**, Piazza Garibaldi 32, tel 283 122 (L120–140 000 with bath) and **Eden**, Corso Novara 9, turn right from the station, one block up, tel 285 344; a garage, decent though not Edenic rooms, and a sleepy bar. Watch out for the cheaper places; the Polish-Italian *Fiore**, rumoured to have Naples' fattest cat, is barely acceptable but good for the area (Via Milano 109, tel 338 798; L24 000). A bit better, the *Zara**, Via Firenze 81, tel 287 125 (L24–32 000). One place to look for cheap accommodation is Via Mezzocannone, south of Spaccanapoli. This street borders the university, and many of the most pleasant cheap lodgings in Naples can be found here—though with so many students it may be hard to find a vacancy.

Around Mergellina and Chiaia
Even though a little removed from the sights of the city, perhaps this would be a more pleasant area in which to make your stay: less traffic and noise, fewer urban problems, and fewer Neapolitans per square yard. The only place of any pretensions here is the ****Majestic**, at Largo Vasta a Chiaia 68 near the Villa Pignatelli and the shorefront park, a quiet unremarkable hotel with air-conditioned rooms for L140–180 000 (tel 416 500). Less expensively, the **Bella Napoli** at Via Caracciolo 10, tel 663 811 (L28 000) is a modest walk-up that won't ruin your vacation.

EATING OUT
> 'Now, everyone thinks of China as a ponderous
> elephantine country; Naples, on the other hand we think of as
> something exciting, stimulating. Perhaps the Chinese invented
> slow, pacific fat macaronis, not the spaghetti that moves
> like the waves of the sea ...'
>
> *Domenico Rea*

This local savant, writing in the pages of *Qui Napoli*, is carrying on one of Naples' grand old causes. Forget those old legends about Marco Polo—just imagine anyone brazen enough to say spaghetti doesn't originally come from Naples! This capital of cooking, this citadel of Italianità, can already claim pizza, and probably many other Italian specialities as well. Neapolitans spend as much time worrying about what's for dinner as any people in the world, but like most other Italians they have a perfectly healthy attitude towards the subject. Neapolitan cuisine is simple—one of the most celebrated dishes is *spaghetti alle vongole*—and even in some of the more pretentious places you will see favourites of the Neapolitan *cucina povera* sneaking onto the menu, like *pasta fagiole*. There are very few bad restaurants or tourist restaurants in the city, but an infinity of tiny, family-run trattorie or pizzerie; you will depart from most of them serene and satisfied.

For famous Neapolitan pizza—the best east of Chicago—look for the genuine Neapolitan pizza oven, a built-in, bell-shaped affair made of stone with a broad, clean tile floor; the fire (only certain kinds of wood will do), is at the back, close to the pizza, not hidden underneath. That is what gives the crust its special taste. Watch out for the house wines; in cheaper places this is likely to be Gragnano from nearby Monte Faito—detestable rough stuff. On the other hand you can find some real surprises from Campania; a dry white called Greco di Tufo, and Taurasi, a distinguished red—also Falerno, the descendant of the far-famed ancient *Falernian* that Latin poets never tired of praising. Some restaurants you'll find in Naples are the cheapest in all Italy. They cheat on their taxes.

Restaurants in all price ranges are spread pretty evenly around central Naples. Near the Castel dell'Ovo at Via Nazario Sauro 23, **La Cantinella** is believed by many to be Naples' finest—also the place to be seen for the Parthenopeans, with a telephone on each table. Known for its four different kinds of risotto, and a dessert called *Millefoglie con Zuppa Inglese*, an average full dinner is L50 000—but you could easily drop twice that in other establishments nearby (tel 404 884). At **Ciro**, Via Santa Brigida 71 near the Castel Nuovo, go ahead and order *pasta fagiole* or any humble pasta dish; that's what the place is famous for, typical Naples cuisine at its best, and it has been a local favourite for decades (tel 324 072; L50 000, closed Sun).

More modestly, you can get many of those same Neapolitan dishes at **Da Peppino**, Vicolo I. Gravina 7, off Santa Lucia, tel 551 2854, at a more reasonable price—L15–20 000 on the average. Spaccanapoli's back streets seem to have a pizzeria on every corner. Pick any of them for an excellent L5 000 pizza lunch. For a more elegant pizza repast, try the **Pizzeria Lombardi a Santa Chiara** at Benedetto Croce 59 for that supreme Naples treat, the 'stuffed' pizza called a *calzone*, or L22 000 for a full dinner. The same prices obtain at **Pizzeria Mattozzi**, on Piazza Carità. A little more dear: the **Pizzeria Bellini** may set you back L30–40 000 for a complete dinner, but you can follow your pizza with second courses like stuffed kid or a memorable involtini with prosciutto (Via S. Maria di Constantinopoli 80, near the archaeological museum, tel 459 774).

Many of the cheapest and homeliest places in Naples are on or around **Via Speranzella**, a block west of Via Toledo in the *Tavoliere*, where few tourists ever penetrate. Finally, we offer you an honest breakfast—bacon and eggs, if you like—at the **Ristorante California**, Italy's greatest rendezvous for homesick Americans and a long a Naples landmark. For dinner, the menu is split between Italian and Gringo dishes; the roast turkey isn't bad (Via Santa Lucia 101, tel 421 752; dinners L18–25 000).

Around Piazza Garibaldi

More than elsewhere in Naples, restaurants around the railway station have succumbed to opportunity and necessity; Piazza Garibaldi isn't nearly as much fun as it was ten years ago, and its hundreds of restaurants are keeping neither standards up nor prices down. One exception is **Da Peppino Avellinese**, with typical dishes, and a cosy familiar clientele (Via Spaventa 35, off the south side of the piazza, tel 283 897; average dinner L17–22 000). This area, and also Piazza Mercato, is an open bazaar, and you can get fat and happy just snacking from the bars and stands—slices of pizza, heavy *arancini*, and the flaky pastries called *sfogliatelle*, another Naples speciality. There's another restaurant worth mentioning, from the station two blocks down the north side of Piazza Garibaldi, then 1½ blocks to the right. It doesn't have a name, but there's a big cardboard waiter standing out front with the daily menu. If the owner likes you, you can have a good full dinner here for L7000; you will probably be required to explain either Mrs Thatcher or Mr Bush to the fellows at your table, who come from the railway, the nearby power plant, or northern Nigeria.

Around Mergellina

Some of the most popular spots are in this area. Many bars and restaurants have outdoor tables in and around **Piazza Sannazaro** in the centre of Mergellina. At the **Pizzeria Pasqualino**, on the square, tel 248 062, you can get two pizzas and lots of wine for L15 000; if you need cigarettes, shout 'Gennaro!' to the balconies above and they will appear. Near Via Mergellina, another popular pizzeria is the **Port'Alba**, Via Port'Alba 18, tel 459 713, where in addition you can get full dinners including the house speciality, baked *linguine all'cartoccio*, for about L30 000. For a bundle of notes more, one of Naples' rarest dining experiences can be had at **La Sacrestia**, Via Orazio 116 on the hill above Mergellina, tel 664 185. The surroundings are more Hollywood than Naples, tricky frescoes, Murano glass and a terrace with a classic view of the city, but the cuisine is world renowned: exceptional fish, original dishes with truffles, pasta dishes raised to Baroque heights of excess—not bad at all for an average L60 000, closed Wed.

SHOPPING AROUND THE BAY OF NAPLES

Surprisingly, no one ever thinks of Naples as one of the prime shopping destinations of Italy; this is a mistake, as there are as many pretty and unusual things to be bought here as anywhere else, and usually at lower prices. The back streets around Spaccanapoli and other old sections are still full of artisan workshops of all kinds. The Royal Factory at Capodimonte, founded by the Bourbons, still makes what may be the most beautiful porcelain and ceramic figures in Europe, sold at the fancier shops in the city centre. Another old Naples tradition is the making of cameos in various materials; you'll see them everywhere, but the shops outside the San Martino monastery have a good selection at relatively low prices.

Via San Biagio dei Librai, the middle of the Spaccanapoli, is as its name implies a street of booksellers—some of the best old book dealers in Italy, conveniently near the University—but beyond these the street is full of odd surprises for shoppers. Many of the religious goods shops have surprisingly good works in terracotta; the *Doll Hospital* at No 81 is one of the most charming shops in Naples. All around the back streets there are antique and junk shops that won't overcharge you unless you let them. The city has a twice-monthly antiques market, the *Fiera dell' Antiquariato*; ask the AAST for details. Finally, for the once in a lifetime souvenir, the 150-year-old Fonderia Chiurazzi makes artistic bronzes, specializing in reproductions of works in the Museo Archeologico; if you have billions of lire to spare, they'll do them life-sized, or even bigger (on Via Ponti Rossi 271).

Around the bay, the town of Torre del Greco has for centuries been making fine jewellery out of the coral its fishermen bring home from the bay. You'll see it everywhere in Naples, but at the shops around the harbour in Torre del Greco itself it is much cheaper. Amalfi's specialities are fine stationery (papermaking was an art and an important industry here in the Middle Ages), and ceramics—mostly tourist bric-à-brac, but some of it very well done. You can tour one of the workshops: Giovanni Fusco, on Via della Cantiere behind the cliffs at the edge of town. Every conceivable luxury item Italy makes is sold in the shops of Sorrento—but make sure you come in the off season (December or January are best) when you'll find some outstanding bargains in fashions, Murano glass and other trinkets. Sorrento's own speciality is *intarsia*, inlaid wood scenes on tables or trays, or simply framed for hanging. These are exquisite things, and the price is right: from L25 000 in the off season. *Da Nicola* on Strada Tasso has some of the best work with *Ferdinando Corcione* on Piazza Gargiulo not far behind.

Around the Bay: From Baia to Sorrento

Naples' hinterlands share fully in the peculiarities and sharp contrasts of the big city. Creation left nothing half-done or poorly done; against any other part of the monotonous Italian coastline, the Campanian shore seems almost indecently blessed, possessing the kind of irresistibly distracting beauty that seduces history off the path of duty and virtue. Today, for all the troubles that come seeping out of Naples, this coast is still one of the capitals of Mediterranean languor.

In Roman days, it was nothing less than the California of the ancient world: fantastically prosperous, lined with glittering resort towns full of refugees from the Roman rat-race, as favoured by artists and poets as it was by rich patricians. Like California, though, the perfume was mixed with a little whiff of insecurity. Vesuvius would be enough, but even apart from the regularly scheduled eruptions and earthquakes, the region is Vulcan's own curiosity shop. West of Naples especially, there are eternally rising and sinking landscapes, sulphurous pools, thermal springs and even a baby volcano—altogether the most unstable corner of the broad earth's crust.

GETTING AROUND THE BAY OF NAPLES
Naples, of course, is the hub for transportation throughout the area; buses, ferries and local commuter railroads lead out from the city to all points.

By Rail
Regular FS trains aren't much help here, except for a fast trip between Naples and Salerno. Fortunately, there are other lines, of which the most important is the refreshingly clean and efficient **Circumvesuviana**, the best way to reach Pompeii, Herculaneum and Sorrento. This line has its own ultramodern station, on Corso Garibaldi just south of the Piazza Garibaldi (tel 779 2444), but all of its trains stop at the Stazione

Centrale itself before proceeding east. Here their station is in the basement, sharing space with that of the Naples Metropolitana; it can be confusing, since there are no timetables posted and the ticket windows aren't marked—you'll have to ask someone to make sure you are heading for the right train. The main lines run east through Ercolano (the stop very close to the ruins at Herculaneum) and Torre del Greco. Near Torre Annunziata they diverge, one line heading for Sarno out in the farming country east of Vesuvius, the other for Sorrento. Both pass Pompeii, though on opposite sides. The Sorrento train leaves you near the main entrance; on the other line the stop at Villa dei Misteri is closest. The Circumvesuviana terminal in Sorrento is two blocks east of Piazza Tasso, the town centre. Circumvesuviana trains usually run every half-hour from 5 am to 10:45 pm. If you wait for a *direttissimo*, of which there are several daily, the Naples–Sorrento trip takes an hour—locals are considerably slower. An additional Circumvesuviana line has infrequent trains north of Vesuvius to Nola and Baiano.

For the west bay, Naples' **Metropolitana** goes as far as Pozzuoli-Solfatara; there are two other lines, both of which leave every half-hour from Naples Montesanto Station, near the Piazza Dante. The **Ferrovia Cumana** (tel 313 328) takes the shore route, through Fuorigrotta, Bagnoli, Pozzuoli, and Baia to Torregaveta. The remarkable **Circumflegrea** (no phone) also finishes at Torregaveta, after passing plenty of places you don't want to visit; there is a stop at the archaeological site of Cumae. The Circumflegrea is easily the most macabre railway in the western world; the trip begins by passing a neon shrine to the Virgin Mary in the middle of the Montesanto Tunnel, then passing stations that are metal sheds or bombed-out ruins, with smashed and derailed cars lying alongside the tracks to give passengers something to think about. There are no timetables printed or even imagined, but the line usually closes down for a long lunch break. The station at Cumae is gutted and abandoned; head right, up towards the acropolis, through the thorn bushes and dense, viper-haunted forests, and eventually you'll sneak in at the back and see the ruins of Cumae for free. (There's a bus from Baia to the front gate for sissies.)

By Bus

Naples city bus No 152, from Piazza Garibaldi and Via Mergellina, travels to Solfatara and Pozzuoli. Other buses, run by the towns of Baia and Bacoli, run regular services from those towns along the coast road to Naples; all these stop every few blocks along the way. From the bus stop in the centre of Baia, there are connecting buses to Cuma, Bacoli, and Cape Misenum.

The Circumvesuviana makes buses for most of the east bay unnecessary. The express bus from Naples to Salerno, usually running every half hour, starts from the SITA office on Via Pisanelli, just off the Piazza Municipio (tel 322 176), and ends in Salerno at the terminal at Corso Garibaldi 117 (226 604). For the Amalfi coast, SITA also runs the buses, departing regularly for Sorrento (Piazza Tasso), or stopping short at Amalfi, Ravello or other towns along the route; buses are usually so frequent that it is easy to see all the main coast towns on a day trip, hopping from one to the next. Buses are definitely the best way to do it; driving yourself can be a hair-raising experience when it's busy. For some idea of the difficulties of this road, consider that it takes the express bus almost three hours to navigate the 66 km from Salerno to Sorrento.

From Salerno, there is a boat called the *Faraglione* that offers a different way of seeing the Amalfi coast, a daily ferry (7:30 pm from Molo Manfredi, at the western end of town)

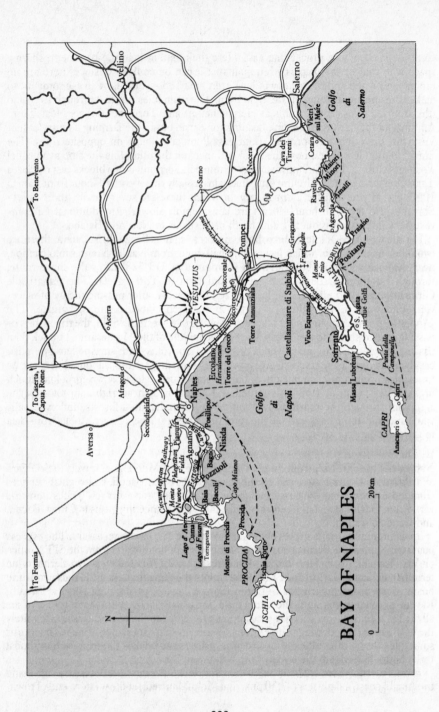

BAY OF NAPLES

that hugs the shore to Capri, stopping at Amalfi and Positano along the way. It doesn't run between 15th October and 6th January.

TOURIST INFORMATION
Pompeii: Via Sacra 1, tel (081) 863 1041
Vico Equense: Corso Umberto 1, tel (081) 879 8343
Sorrento: Via de Maio 21, tel (081) 878 2104
Positano: Via Saraceno, tel (089) 875 067
Amalfi: Corso Roma 19 (089) 871 107
Ravello: Piazza Arcivescovado (089) 857 096
Maiori: Viale Capone, (089) 877 452
Cava de' Tirreni: Piazza Duomo, tel (089) 341 605

Salerno's helpful EPT is just outside the railway station (tel 231 432). Their *Annuario Alberghi* has, besides a list of hotels in the province (which includes the Amalfi coast) a map and everything else you would need to know.

West from Naples: Pozzuoli and the Phlegraean Fields

The very pretty coastal road leaving the city, with views of Vesuvius all through the suburb of Posillipo, passes **Marechiaro**, a charming fishing village swallowed up by the conurbation, and then the little islet of **Nisida**; this was a favoured spot in ancient times, and legend has it that Brutus and Cassius planned Caesar's murder here in the villa of one of their fellow conspirators. Naples' suburbs are continuous through **Agnano**, a town of spas and hot springs set around a mile-wide extinct crater, and stretch as far as **Pozzuoli**.

Pozzuoli today is a modest little city, with only its ruins to remind it of the time when Roman *Puteoli*, and not Naples, was the metropolis of the bay. The **Amphitheatre**, on Via Domiziana, near the railway station, was the third-largest in the Roman world (behind Rome's and Capua's), with 60 gates for letting the beasts in, and pipes to flood it for mock naval battles. Pozzuoli's other important ruin is a little embarrassment to the town; for centuries people here were showing off the ancient **Serapeum**—temple to the popular Egyptian god Serapis—until some killjoy archaeologist proved the thing to be an unusually lavish *macellum*, or market. Only the foundations remain, in a park near Pozzuoli's small harbour, and they are usually under water, but it was an important tourist sight in the days of the Grand Tour, before the Bourbons stole all the columns for their dreary palace at Caserta.

For all ancient *Puteoli*'s size and wealth, little else remains. There is a reason, and Pozzuoli would like to introduce a new word to your vocabulary to explain it: *bradyseism* is a rare seismic phenomenon that afflicts this town and other spots around the bay. It manifests itself in the form of 'slow' earthquakes; no one notices them, but the level of the land can rise or fall several feet in a few months. Mostly, it has been falling, and all of Puteoli that hasn't been gently shaken to pieces over the centuries is now under water. Roman moles and docks can still sometimes be made out beneath the surface.

223

Solfatara

What's troubling Pozzuoli can be seen more clearly just outside the town at **Solfatara**, the storm centre of what the Greeks called the **Phlegraean** (fiery) **Fields**. To the Romans, it was the *Forum Vulcani*, and a major attraction of the Campanian coast. It hasn't changed much since. Solfatara (daily, 9–sunset; adm) is another crater of a collapsed volcano, but one that just can't be still; sulphur gas vents, bubbling mud pits and whistling superheated steam fumaroles decorate the eerie landscape. Guides are around to keep you away from the dangerous spots. Their favourite trick is to hold a flame to one of the gas vents—making a dozen others nearby go off at the same time. Solfatara is perfectly safe, even though the ground underneath feels hot and sounds strangely hollow. It is; scientists keep a close watch on the huge plug of cooled lava that underlies all the area about Pozzuoli, and they say the pressure on it from below is only one-third as much as it was under Vesuvius in AD 79.

We promised you a baby volcano, and you'll see it near the coast west of Pozzuoli. **Monte Nuovo** has been quiet for some time (inexplicably passing up the opportunity to celebrate its 450th birthday, back on 29th September 1988). The same earthquake in 1538 that wrecked much of Pozzuoli gave birth to this little cone. It's only about 140 m tall, and an easy climb up to the crater. Its percolation from the bowels of Campania filled up half of the **Lago di Lucrino**, separated from the sea by a narrow strip of land; since antiquity it has been synonymous with oysters.

Cape Misenum

Baia, the next town along the coast, was nothing less than the greatest pleasure dome of classical antiquity. Anybody who was anybody in the Roman world had a villa here, with a view of the sea, beach access, and a few hundred slaves to dust the statues and clean up after the orgies. You'll find little hint of that today; Goths, malaria and earthquakes have done a thorough job of wrecking the place. Most of ancient *Baiae* is now under water, a victim of the same bradyseism that afflicts Pozzuoli. Modern Baia is a pleasant small town, but its lovely bay has been consigned to use as a graveyard for dead freighters. Nevertheless, the humble remains of the imperial villa can be visited at the **Parco Archeologico** (daily, except Mon, 9–sunset; adm).

At Baia, the coast curves southwards towards Bacoli and **Cape Misenum** (Capo Miseno in Italian), a beautiful spot that for centuries was the greatest naval base of the Roman Empire. As at Baia, foundations and bits of columns and cornices are everywhere, though nothing of any real interest has survived intact. Nearby Lake Miseno, also called the 'Dead Sea', was a part of the base, joined to the sea by a canal.

Two other lakes, both created as a by-product of volcanic action, lie north of Cape Misenum; one, the **Lago di Fusaro**, is a large, shallow oyster farm, cut off from the sea by a sand bar near the woebegone fishing village of Torregaveta, the terminus of the Circumflegraean and Cumaean Railways. The decaying Rococo palace on an island in the centre is the Casino, built in 1782 by the Bourbon kings' favourite architect, Luigi Vanvitelli. **Lago d'Averno**—Lake Avernus—may ring a bell from your school days; it's the mouth of Hell, according to the ancient Greeks, who believed any passing bird would be suffocated by the infernal fumes rising from it. Agrippa, Augustus' great general, hadn't much respect for mythology, and turned the lake into a part of the naval base by cutting another canal. Among the ruins that surround it are the remains of a domed building, perhaps a sort of spa, originally as big as the Pantheon in Rome.

Cumae

As the story has it, King Tarquin of Rome came here, to the most venerable and respected oracle in all the western Mediterranean, with the intention of purchasing nine prophetic books from the Cumaean Sibyl. Unwisely, he said they were too dear, whereupon the Sibyl threw three of the books into the fire and offered him the remaining six at the same price. Again he complained, and the Sibyl put three more in the flames; finally Tarquin gave up, and took the last three at the original price. It was a good bargain. The Sibylline Books guided Rome's destiny until they too were burned up in the great fire of 82 BC.

Cumae had other distinctions. As the first Greek foundation in Italy, the city was the mother colony for Naples and many other cities of Magna Graecia. In 421 BC, Cumae lost its independence to the Samnites, and declined steadily from then on; Arab raiders, who did so much damage everywhere else around Campania, wiped the city off the map in the 9th century. They made a good job of it, and there is little to see at the site (open daily except Mon, 9–sunset; adm), only a few foundations of temples on the high **acropolis**, worth the climb for the views around Cape Misenum.

Just below the summit, you may visit the **Cave of the Cumaean Sibyl** itself, discovered by accident in 1932. This is a place of mystery, a long series of strange, trapezoidal galleries cut out of solid rock—impressive enough, even stripped of the sumptuous decoration they must once have had (all ancient oracles were marvellously profitable). We have no clear idea how old it is; Cumae may well have been a religious centre long before the Greek colonists arrived. By classical times, it took the form of an oracle quite like the one at Delphi. At the far end of the cave, a plain alcove with two benches marks the spot where the Sibyls would inhale fumes over the sacred tripod, chew laurel leaves, and go into their trances.

WHERE TO STAY AND EATING OUT   (tel prefix 081)
Nobody has made the western side of the bay a base for their vacation since the 4th century AD. But if you're out looking over the ruins at Pozzuoli, Baia and Cumae, there are a few good places to have lunch. In Pozzuoli's harbour, on Via Emporio, the **Martusciello**, Via Emporio 24, tel 526 1702, is one of the best places for fish you'll find anywhere—*zuppa di pesce, risotto al pescatore*, broiled sea bass, and any other dish you have ever seen in Italy goes well here, and it will seem a bargain when you get the bill for L45 000 (closed Tues). **Del Capitano**, Via Lungomare C. Colombo 10, tel 526 2283, is another good rendezvous for seafood lovers (L35 000); **Il Capriccio**, Trav. Italia 1, tel 866 5529, has a fish menu in the L35–40 000 range, or you can keep prices down with a pizza and beer for L10 000. At Baia's, **L'Altro Cucchiaro**, Via Lucullo 13, tel 868 7196, you can dine on divine concoctions of seafood and pasta, and superb, 'very noble' fish (L70 000 for the works, closed Mon and 3 weeks in Aug). Another member of the family runs the nearby **Franco Cucchiaro**, Via Lucullo 6, tel 868 7673, where you can dine on a fabulous *linguine alle zucchine* and not only fish, but lamb, rabbit and veal dishes as well (L40 000). At **La Ninfea**, Via Lago Lucrino, tel 866 5308, you can bask on the lakeside terrace and dine on fish and grilled meats (L30 000).

East of Naples: Mount Vesuvius

Despite its fearsome reputation, and its formidable appearance looming over Naples, **Mount Vesuvius** is a midget as volcanoes go—only 1281 m. No one suspected it even was a volcano, in fact, until it surprised the people of Pompeii, Herculaneum, and Stabiae on 24th August, AD 79. That titanic eruption did not include much lava, but it buried Herculaneum under mud and the other two cities under cinders and ash, while coating most of Italy with a thin layer of dust. Over a hundred eruptions since have destroyed various towns and villages, some more than once. But just as at Mount Etna in Sicily, people just can't stay away from Vesuvius' slopes. Volcanic soil grows grapes and olives most abundantly, though the novelty of it often makes the Italians exaggerate their quality. The AD 79 explosion hasn't been equalled since; it blew the top of the mountain clean off, leaving two peaks, with the main fissure in between. The lower one is called Monte Somma, or *nasone*—'big nose'—by the Neapolitans; the higher, symmetrical peak is Vesuvius proper.

Vesuvius was last heard from in 1944. The final eruption left the lava flows you'll see on the upper slopes; it also sealed the main fissure, putting an end to the permanent plume of smoke that once was such a familiar landmark. You can bet the scientists are watching Vesuvius. Despite the long hiatus, they say there is no reason to expect another eruption soon. To visit the main crater (between the two peaks), take the Vesuvius bus from the Circumvesuviana stop in Ercolano; then you have a choice of a stiff, one-hour climb over rough stones and ash, or a ride on the cable car (L7600 for round trip and guide at the top; it runs 10–5:30, April–Sept; 10–4 in Oct; closed all Nov; Dec–March, 10:30–3:30).

Herculaneum

Naples' discouraging sprawl spreads eastwards as far as Torre del Greco without a break, surrounding old towns and once-fashionable villas. The drab suburb of **Ercolano** is a part of it, built over the mass of rock that imprisons ancient **Herculaneum**, a smaller and less famous sight than Pompeii but just as much worth visiting (daily, except Mon, 9–one hour before sunset; adm expensive; free the first and third Sat, second and third Sun of each month).

Unlike Pompeii, an important commercial centre, Herculaneum seems to have been a wealthy resort, only about one-third the size. Vesuvius destroyed them in different ways. Pompeii was buried under layers of ash while Herculaneum, much closer to the volcano, drowned under a sea of mud. Over time the mud hardened to a soft stone, preserving the city and nearly everything in it as a sort of fossil—furniture, clothing and even some of the goods in the shops have survived.

Like Pompeii, Herculaneum was discovered by accident. In the early 1700s, a Bourbon officer named Prince Elbeuf had a well dug here; not too far down, the workmen struck a stone pavement—the stage of the city's theatre. The Bourbon government began some old-fashioned destructive excavation, but serious archaeological work began only under Mussolini. Only about eight blocks of shops and villas, some quite fashionable, have been excavated. The rest is covered not only by dozens of feet of rock, but above that a dense modern neighbourhood; bringing more of Herculaneum to

226

light is a fantastically slow and expensive operation, but new digs are still going on. Among many other things, the excavations uncovered some exquisite jewellery. You won't get to see it; thieves carted off the entire load in January 1990, the latest episode in a continuing problem that plagues the discoveries of both Herculaneum and Pompeii.

At any given time, most of the buildings will be locked; the guards wandering about have all the keys and will show you almost any of them upon request (they are not supposed to accept tips, though you'll find they often seem to expect them). Many of the most interesting houses can be found along Cardo IV, the street in the centre of the excavated area; on the corner of the Decumanus Inferior, the **House of the Wooden Partition** may be the best example we have of the façade of a Roman house. Next door, the **Trellis House** was a much more modest dwelling, with a built-in workshop; the **House of the Mosaic Atrium**, down the street, is another luxurious villa, built with a mind to the sea view from the bedrooms upstairs. On the other side of the Decumanus, Cardo IV passes the **Samnite House** (so named because of its architectural style), and further up a column with police notices painted on it stands near the **House of the Neptune**, with a lovely mythological mosaic in the atrium.

Other buildings worth a visit are the **House of the Deer**, with its infamous statue of a drunken Hercules relieving himself picturesquely; the well-preserved **Baths**; and the **Palaestra**, or gym, with its unusual serpent fountain and elegant, cross-shaped swimming-pool.

Beyond Ercolano, the coastal road passes through three sorry towns. The men of **Torre del Greco** have long been famous for gathering and working coral, a business now threatened by pollution. In **Torre Annunziata** they make lots of pasta, and in **Castellamare di Stabia**, under a 12th-century Hohenstaufen castle are the modern shipyards of the Italian Navy. Roman *Stabiae* was the port of Pompeii, and the other big town destroyed by Vesuvius, but it has never been excavated. From Castellamare, you can take a short ride on the funicular railway up to **Monte Faito**, a broad, heavily forested mountain that may well be the last really tranquil spot on the Bay—though a few hotels have already appeared.

Pompeii

Herculaneum may have been better preserved, but to see an entire ancient city come to life, the only place on earth you can go is this magic time capsule, left to us by the good graces of Mount Vesuvius. Pompeii is no mere ruin; walking down the old Roman high street, you can peek into the shops, read the graffiti on the walls, then wander off down the back streets to explore the homes of the inhabitants and appraise their taste in painting—they won't mind a bit if you do. Almost everything we know for sure concerning the daily life of the ancients was learned here, and the huge mass of artefacts and art dug up over 200 years is still helping scholars re-evaluate the Roman world.

Though a fair-sized city by Roman standards, with a population of some 20,000, Pompeii was probably only the third or fourth city of Campania, a trading and manufacturing centre of no special distinction. Founded perhaps in the 7th century BC, the city was occupied by Etruscans and Samnites for long periods before falling into the Roman sphere of influence around 200; by the fateful year of AD 79, it was still a cosmopolitan

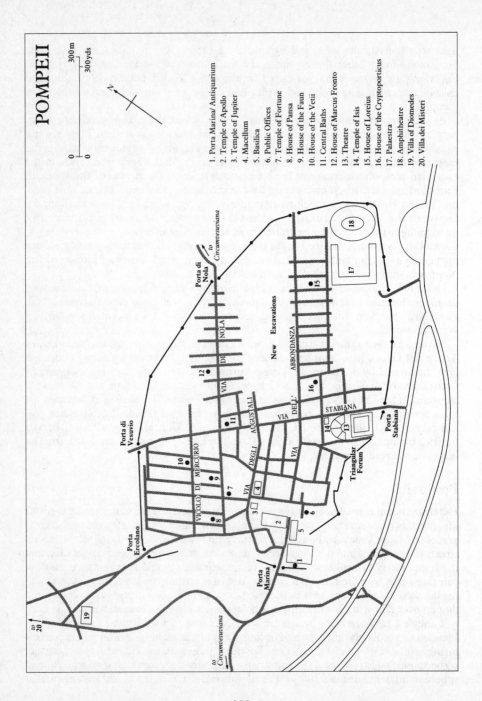

POMPEII

1. Porta Marina/ Antiquarium
2. Temple of Apollo
3. Temple of Jupiter
4. Macellum
5. Basilica
6. Public Offices
7. Temple of Fortune
8. House of Pansa
9. House of the Faun
10. House of the Vetii
11. Central Baths
12. House of Marcus Fronto
13. Theatre
14. Temple of Isis
15. House of Lorcius
16. House of the Cryptoporticus
17. Palaestra
18. Amphitheatre
19. Villa of Diomedes
20. Villa dei Misteri

place, culturally more Greek than Roman—also, incidentally, still trying to clean itself up from a bad earthquake seventeen years earlier. Vesuvius' rumblings, and the tall, sinister-looking cloud that began to form above it, gave those Pompeiians with any presence of mind a chance to leave. Only about 10 per cent of the population perished.

After the city was buried under the stones and ash of the eruption, the upper floors still stuck out; these were looted, and gradually cleared by farmers, and eventually the city was forgotten altogether. Engineers found it while digging an aqueduct in 1600, and the first excavations began in 1748—a four-star attraction for northern Europeans on the Grand Tour. The early digs were far from scientific; archaeologists today sniff that they did more damage than Vesuvius. Resurrected Pompeii has had other problems: theft of works of art, a good dose of bombs in the last War, and most recently the earthquake of 1980. The damage from that is still being repaired today, though almost all the buildings are once more open to visitors.

There are two ways to see Pompeii; spend two or three hours on the main sights, or the day on scrutinizing details for a total immersion in the ancient world you won't get anywhere else. (The detailed guidebooks sold in the stands outside will help you with this.) The arrangement is the same as at Herculaneum, and you'll need to ask the guards (or follow a tour group) to get into most of the buildings. Guards will discreetly extort large or small sums from you; this is Naples, after all. They can also be induced to show you the parts of the city that are technically closed to visitors. (The site is open daily, except Mon, 9–one hour before sunset; adm expensive.) Note that two-i Pompeii means the ruins; one-i **Pompei** is the sizeable modern town that has grown up around them, and around the popular pilgrimage church of Santa Maria del Rosario, begun only in the 1870s.

Pompeii isn't quite a perfect time capsule; a little background will help to complete the picture. The site today is all too serene, with a small-town air. Remember that almost every building was two or three storeys, and that most streets of a Roman town were permanent market-places. As long as daylight lasted, Pompeii's would have been crowded with improvised *bancarelle*; any chariot or wagon driver who wished to pass would need all manner of creative cursing. At least the streets are well-paved—better than Rome itself, in fact; Campania's cities, the richest in western Europe, could well afford such luxuries. All the pavements were much more smooth and even than you see them now. The purpose of the flat stones laid across the streets should not be hard to guess. They were places to cross when it rained—streets here were also drains—and the slots in them allow wagon wheels to pass through.

The shops, open to the street in the day, would be sealed up behind shutters at night, just as they are in the old parts of Mediterranean cities today. Houses, on the other hand, turn a completely blank wall to the street; they got their light and air from skylights in the *atrium*, the roofed court around which the rooms were arranged. Later, fancier villas will have a second, open court directly behind the first, modelled on the Greek *peristyle*. As in Rome, no part of town was necessarily the fashionable district; elegant villas will be found anywhere, often between two simple workmen's flats. And don't take the street names too seriously. They were often bestowed by the archaeologists, as with the Via di Mercurio (Mercury Street), after mythological subjects depicted on the street fountains.

Around the Forum

After the throng of hawkers and refreshment stands, the main entrance to the site takes you through the walls at the **Porta Marina**. Just inside the gate, the **Antiquarium** displays some of the art treasures that haven't been spirited off to the Naples museum, as well as some truly gruesome casts of fossilized victims of the eruption, caught in their death poses. Two blocks beyond the Antiquarium and you're in the **Forum**, oriented towards a view of Vesuvius. Unfortunately this is the worst-preserved part of town. Here you can see the tribune from which orators addressed public meetings (next to the Apollo temple), and the pedestals that held statues of heroes and civic benefactors, as well as the once-imposing **Basilica** (the law courts), temples to Apollo and Jupiter, and among other buildings a public latrine and a **Macellum**, or market, decorated with frescoes. One front near the market has the standard measures cut into it. It is hard to tell from the remains, but the temples were in the Etruscan style; that of Jupiter had three shrines, to the trinity of Jupiter, Juno and Minerva—common to the chief temple of any Etruscan town.

The buildings on the eastern side of the Forum include, to the right of the *macellum*, the *Sacrarium of the lares*, a shrine to the particular genii or deities of the town; a **Temple of Vespasian**, still under construction when Vesuvius erupted; and the 'Building of Eumachia'—a sort of showroom for locally produced fabrics.

Down Mercury Street

Heading for Pompeii's old North End, there are several interesting houses along the Via di Mercurio, including a **Temple of Fortune** on the corner of Via di Nola. The real attractions in this part of town, though, are a few lavish villas off on the side streets: the enormous **House of Pansa**; the **House of the Faun**, with the oldest known welcome mat (set in the pavement, really); and the wonderful **House of the Vetii**. Here are several rooms of excellent, well-preserved paintings of mythological scenes, but the guards will be whispering in your ear to show you the little niche off the entrance with the picture of Priapus. This over-endowed sport, in legend the son of Venus and Adonis, has single-handedly (if that is the word) made Pompeii something more than a respectable tourist trap. There are quite a few paintings of him showing it off in the houses of Pompeii, besides the phallic images that adorn bakers' ovens, wine shops, and almost every other establishment in town. The Pompeiians would be terribly embarrassed, however, if they knew what you are thinking. They were a libidinous lot, like anyone else fortunate enough to live on the Campanian coast during recorded history, but the omnipresent phalluses were never meant as mere decoration. Almost always they are found close to the entrances, where their job is to ward off the evil eye. They were probably doing it from the earliest times in southern Italy; the horn-shaped amulets that millions of people wear around their necks today are their direct descendants.

The nearby Via di Nola, one of Pompeii's main streets, leads to the north. It passes the **Central Baths**, a new construction that was not yet completed in AD 79, and the **House of Marcus Fronto**, with more good paintings and a reconstructed roof.

The 'New Excavations'

Beginning in 1911, the archaeologists cleared a vast area of western Pompeii, around what was probably the most important thoroughfare of the city, now called the Via dell'Abbondanza. Three blocks from the Forum, this street leads to the Via dei Teatri and the **Triangular Forum** bordering the southern walls. Two **Theatres** here are worth a visit, a large open one seating 5000, and a smaller, covered one that was used for concerts. The big quadrangle, originally a lobby for the theatres, seems to have been converted at one point into a gladiators' barracks. This is only one of the disconcerting things you will find on the streets of Pompeii. The ruined temple in the Triangular Forum was already long ruined in AD 79, and scholars who study the art of the city find the last (fourth) period to betray a growing lack of skill and coarseness of spirit—altogether there are plenty of clues that 1st-century Pompeii had its share of urban problems and cultural malaise.

The Via dell'Abbondanza

Next to the theatres, a small **Temple of Isis** testifies to the religious diversity of Pompeii; elsewhere around town there are graffiti satirizing that new and troublesome cult, the Christians. Three blocks north, there is a stretch of Via dell'Abbondanza that is one of the most fascinating corners of Pompeii. Among its shops are a smith's, a grocers, a weaver's, a laundry, and a typical Roman tavern with its modest walk-up brothel. The most common are those with built-in tubs facing the street—shops that sold wine, and oil for cooking and for the lamps. Notices painted on the walls announce coming games at the amphitheatre, or recommend candidates for public office.

Some of the best-decorated villas in this neighbourhood are to be found along the side streets: the **House of Loreius**, the **House of Amandus**, and an odd underground chamber called the **Cryptoporticus**. Pompeii's two most impressive structures occupy a corner just within the walls: the **Palaestra**, a big colonnaded exercise yard, and the **Amphitheatre**, the best-preserved in Italy, with seats for two-thirds of Pompeii's population.

Not all of Pompeii's attractions are within the walls. If you have the time, it would be worth visiting the tombs and suburban villas around the **Via delle Tombe**. One, the famous **Villa dei Misteri**, is thought to have been used as a place of initiation in the forbidden Bacchic (or Dionysiac) Mysteries, one of the cults most feared by the Roman Senate, and later by the Emperors. Scenes from the myth of Dionysos and of the rituals themselves are painted on the walls.

Sorrento and Its Peninsula

After Pompeii, the coastline swings outwards to meet Capri. At first, there is little intimation that you are entering one of the most beautiful corners of all Italy. The first clue comes when the coast road begins to climb into a corniche at **Vico Equense**, a pretty village that is becoming a small resort, absorbing some of the overflow from Sorrento; there is a nice beach under the cliffs at the back of the town.

Sorrento began its career as a resort in the early 1800s, when Naples began to grow too piquant for foreign tastes. The English, especially, have never forsaken it; Sorrento's secret is a certain perfect cosiness, comfortable like old shoes. Visitors get the reassuring sense that nothing distressing is going to happen to them, and sure enough, nothing ever does. It helps that Sorrento is a lovely, civilized old town. Not many resorts can trace their ancestry back to the Etruscans, or claim a native son like the poet Torquato Tasso.

(Today, the Sorrentines are more proud of a songwriter named De Curtio, whose *Come Back to Sorrento*, according to a local brochure, ranks with *O Sole Mio* as one of the 'two most familiar songs in the world'. There is a bust of him in front of the Circumvesuviana station.)

Sorrento doesn't flagrantly chase after your money, like many places in Italy, and it lacks the high-density garishness of, say, Rimini. If Sorrento has one big drawback, it is lack of a decent beach—though at some of the fancier hotels you may enjoy taking an elevator down to the sea. Sorrento is built on a long cliff that follows the shore. A narrow ravine cuts the town in half, between a suburban area of quiet, mostly expensive hotels around Via Correale, and the old town itself, which still preserves its grid of narrow Roman streets. There isn't much of artistic or historical interest; Sorrento was never a large town, and even today the population is only 15,000. It's pleasant to walk the old streets; half the shop windows seem to be displaying *intarsia*—surprisingly fine pictures done in inlaid woods that have been a local craft for centuries. If you are stuck on a rainy day, you can visit the **Correale Museum,** on Via Correale, a grab-bag of Neapolitan bric-à-brac, art and curiosities (daily, except Tues, 9:30–12:30; weekday afternoons 3–5 pm; adm).

Around Sorrento, as far as the mountains permit, stretches one of the great garden spots of Campania, a lush plain full of vines and orange groves. Some of the excursions that can be made from Sorrento: scanty ruins of the Roman **Villa di Pollio**, in a beautiful setting on the cape west of the town; **Massa Lubrense**, an uncrowded fishing village with more fine views as far as Point Campanella, the tip of the peninsula opposite the rugged outline of Capri.

WHERE TO STAY (tel prefix 081)

In addition to the ruins, Pompei has an important religious pilgrimage, and the town is well supplied with hotels, mostly inexpensive pensiones on or around Via Roma. A little fancier: the ******Rosario**, also on Via Roma, a serene, older hotel with a garage and pleasant rooms (tel 863 1002; doubles L135 000 with bath, some cheaper without). One chancy place for you to base yourself would be the ****Eremo**, above Ercolano on the very slopes of Vesuvius—an isolated spot, but there is a bar and restaurant on the premises (tel 739 0504; doubles L52–70 000 depending on plumbing). Out of reach of possible lava flows, the best resort hotel up on Monte Faito is the ******Grand Hotel Monte Faito**, with gardens and a pool in a lovely setting close to the funicular; not really Grand but still a relative bargain at L45–65 000 (tel 879 3134). In Vico Equense, the best places are a little outside the town centre, notably the ******Capo La Gala** on the beach at nearby Scrajo (where there are sulphur springs), a beautiful modern resort hotel where every room has a private terrace overlooking the beach. There's plenty of sea, and a pool too (tel 879 8278; L150 000, though full board—L180 000—is usually required).

In Sorrento, some 90 hotels compete for your attention, the best of which are converted villas by the sea—almost indecently elegant, even when they're a bit frayed about the edges. Sorrento isn't the status resort it once was, but it still has more four-star places than anywhere in the south; most of them are good bargains, too, compared with comparable spots in the north. At the top of the list is the ******Grand Hotel Ambasciatori**, a bit removed from the centre at Via Califano 18, with a palatial interior and gardens overlooking the sea (tel 878 2025; L110–200 000). In the same area is the beautifully remodelled ****Royal (tel 878 1922; pool and beach access; L150 000 depending on room and season). In a more central location, set in incredible tropical gardens on Via Vittorio Veneto, the ****Imperial Tramontana is one of the places long favoured by British travellers, as is evident from the club-like decor. There is an elevator down to the private beach, and also a pool (tel 878 1940; L170 000). Another villa-hotel, just around the corner on Via Marina Grande, is the ***Bellevue-Syrene. This one, though, despite its lush gardens, beautifully restored rooms, and lift to the beach, is a real bargain—L55–80 000 for spacious double rooms, some with a sea view (tel 878 1024).

Not all the hotels in Sorrento are luxury villas; one of the charms of the place is that it caters for every budget. An even better bargain than the Bellevue, in a villa with a private beach and a good restaurant, is the **Pensione La Tonnarella, Via Capo 31, tel 878 1153 (L43–52 000; make reservations early for this one). There are plenty of simple hotels around the town centre, of which the *City is one of the nicest (Corso Italia 217, tel 877 2210; L32–38 000).

EATING OUT
Restaurants in Pompei have a captive market in visitors to the ruins, and it is true that some of them see the tourists as easy targets. You can choose for yourself among the ubiquitous multilingual menus, or try one of these if you're in the mood for a treat: Zi Caterina at Via Roma 16, with live lobsters in the tank and other noteworthy seafood dishes, also a good place to try *Lacrima Cristi* wine from the nearby slopes of Vesuvius (L35 000; tel 863 1263); or a little further out at Via Roma 109, the Anfiteatro. Here the seafood is more modest—it's one of the few places where you'll ever see *bacalà*, salt cod, on the menu, along with truly good *spaghetti alla vongole* (average L30 000; tel 863 1245). At Nerano, on the road from Vico Equense to Sorrento, Da Pappone, Via Marina del Cantore 49b, specializes in fish fresh out of the sea and elaborate (but expensive!) antipasto surprises (tel 808 1209; about L30 000).

Sorrento has every sort of restaurant, from the grand and gloriously decorated Parrucchiano, one of Italy's best (Corso Italia 71, tel 878 1321; a choice of anything you could imagine, averaging about L50 000) to The Red Lion, Via Marziale 25, tel 878 1795, with light dinners from L6000, English beer and music nightly. Also inexpensive, but a little less creative in the kitchen, the Pizzeria Zi'ntonio, Via de Maio 11, tel 878 1623, (pizzas about L8 000, full dinners from L20 000). Ristorante Gioiello, nearby on Via Casarlano 19, tel 807 2200, is an inexpensive place very popular with the Sorrentini (about L13 000, less with the limited daily menu).

The Amalfi Drive

When confronted with something generally acclaimed to be the most beautiful stretch of scenery in the entire Mediterranean, the honest writer is at a loss. Few who have been there would argue the point, but describing it properly is another matter. Along this coast, where one mountain after another plunges sheer into the sea, there is a string of towns that not long ago were accessible only by boat. Today, a spectacular corniche road of 'a thousand bends' covers the route, climbing in places to a thousand feet above the sea; necessity makes it so narrow that every oncoming vehicle is an adventure, but everyone except the driver will have the treat of a lifetime. Nature here has created an amazing vertical landscape, a mix of sharp crags and deep green forests; in doing so she inspired the Italians to add three of their most beautiful towns.

The coast has always attracted foreigners, but only lately is it becoming a major resort area. Places like Positano have become reserves for the wealthy, and swarms of day trippers are likely to descend at any moment. They'll never spoil it; all the engineers in Italy couldn't widen the Amalfi road, and the impossible terrain leaves no room at all for new development.

Positano

To complement the vertical landscape, here is Italy's most nearly vertical town. **Positano** spills down from the corniche like a waterfall of pink, cream and yellow villas. The day trippers may walk down to the sea; only the alpinists among them make it back up. (Fortunately there is a regular bus service along the one main street.) After the War Positano became a well-known hideaway for artists and writers—mainly American, following the lead of John Steinbeck—and fashion was not slow to follow. Now, even though infested with boutiques, Positano reverts to the Positanesi in the off season and quietens down considerably. When you get to the bottom, there is a soft, grey beach and the town's church, decorated with a pretty tiled dome like so many others along this coast.

The next town along the drive, **Praiano**, could be Positano's little sister: with a similar beach and church, but not quite as scenic and perpendicular, and not quite as beleaguered by tourism, though this last feature is changing fast. After Praiano, keep an eye open for the most impressive natural feature along the drive, the steep, impenetrable **Furore Gorge**. On either side are tiny isolated villages along the shore with beaches—if only you can find a way to get to them. Further down the road you'll notice the elevator leading down to the **Grotta Smeralda** (open daily, 9:30–5; 10–6 pm in winter; adm); the strange green light that diffuses this sea-level cavern gives it its name. Beyond this, **Conca dei Marini** is another vertical village, with a beach and a Norman lookout tower to climb.

Amalfi

Sometimes history seems to be kidding us. Can it be true, can this miniscule village once have had a population of 80,000? There is no room among these jagged rocks for even a fraction of that—but then we remember that in Campania anything is possible, and we read how most of the old town simply slid into the sea during a storm and earthquake in 1343. The history is a glorious one. Amalfi was the first Italian city to regain its balance after the Dark Ages, the first to re-create its civic pride and its mercantile daring. As such, she showed the way to Venice, Pisa and Genoa, though she would manage to keep few of the prizes for herself.

There is a legend that Amalfi was founded by a party of Roman noblemen, fleeing the barbarians after the fall of the Empire, and carrying on the old Roman spirit and culture in this safe and hidden enclave. The Amalfitano Republic first appears in the 6th century; by the 9th it was probably the most important trading port of Italy, with a large colony of merchants at Constantinople and connections with all the Muslim lands. All of

Cathedral bell tower, Amalfi

this came at a time for which historical records are scarce, but Amalfi's merchant adventurers must have had as romantically exciting a time as those of Venice. Their luck turned sour in the 1130s, with one brief occupation by the Normans, and a sacking at the hands of their mortal enemies, the Pisans, after a fatal sea battle that broke Amalfi's power forever.

The disaster of 1343 ensured that Amalfi's decline would be complete, but what's left of the place today—with its 5000 or so people—is beautiful almost to excess. Over the little square around the harbour, a conspicuous inscription brags: 'The Judgement Day, when the Amalfitani go to heaven, will be a day like any other day'. The square is called **Piazza Flavio Gioia**, after Amalfi's most famous merchant adventurer—they claim he invented the compass in the 12th century.

From here, an arch under the buildings leads to the centre of the town, the Piazza del Duomo, with a long flight of steps up to what may be the loveliest **cathedral** in all the south of Italy (9th–12th centuries). Not even in Sicily was the Arab-Norman style ever carried to such a flight of fancy as in this delicate façade, with four levels of interlaced arches in stripes of different-coloured stone. The lace-like open arches on the porch are unique in Italy, though common enough in Muslim Spain, one of the countries with which Amalfi had regular trade relations. The cathedral's greatest treasure is its set of **bronze doors**, cast with scenes from scripture; they were made in Constantinople in 1066, commissioned by the leader of the Amalfitano colony there. The interior, unfortunately, was restored in the 18th century Baroque à la Napoletana, with plenty of frills in inlaid coloured marble. Down in the crypt you can see the head of St Andrew, patron of the city; this relic was a part of Amalfi's share of the loot in the sack of Constantinople in 1204.

One of the oldest parts of the cathedral to survive is the **Chiostro del Paradiso**, a whitewashed quadrangle of interlaced arches with a decidedly African air. Many of the bits and pieces of old Amalfi that have survived its calamities have been assembled here: there are classical sarcophagi, medieval sculpture and coats-of-arms. Best of all are the fragments of Cosmatesque work, brightly-coloured geometric mosaics that once were parts of pulpits and pillars, a speciality of this part of Campania.

From the centre of Amalfi, you can walk in a few minutes out to the northern edge of the city, the narrow 'Valley of the Mills', set along the bed of a stream between steep cliffs; none of the mills that made medieval Amalfi famous for paper-making is still in operation, but there is a small **Paper Museum**.

WHERE TO STAY   (tel prefix 089)

With Positano's new-found status has come some of the highest hotel prices in Italy. While the fad lasts, you can have the privilege of spending over L100 000 here for places that really have little to offer but the same marvellous views available to any day-tripper. If you're fixed, though, you can go all the way and spend L320–450 000 on a place many believe to be the finest resort hotel in Italy. The *****San Pietro, Via Laurito 2, is an intimate paradise, 46 rooms with individual terraces, strung down the cliffs next to Positano and connected to the coast road on top by a long elevator. The entrance is hidden behind an old chapel; there are no signs, all a part of the management's plan to maintain the privacy and tranquillity of its celebrity clientele (tel 875 455, 1.5 km from Positano on the Amalfi drive; private beach, tennis, and the hotel has its own excursion boat).

On a more modest level, the ***Casa Albertina is done in a lovely, understated manner, the better to accentuate the views over town and sea; it's a family-run place with a nice restaurant on the rooftop terrace, a few minutes from the beach, but in the busy season the quiet can be an advantage (Via Tavolozza 3; tel 875 143; L65–90 000). A little closer to the water, on Via C. Colombo 36, is the ***L'Ancora, a peaceful and professionally run place though it too is family owned (tel 875 318; L80–100 000). A few very inexpensive pensiones can be found on the streets leading down to the beach.

In Praiano, new hotels seem to be opening at least once a month; for now, the preferred choices are just outside the village at Vettica Maggiore, along the Amalfi drive. One exceptional bargain here is the ***Tramonto d'Oro, Via G. Capri (tennis, pool, beach access, and great views; the restaurant isn't exceptional but it will do; tel 874 008; L60–78 000). As at Positano, there are some cheaper old pensiones by the port, but they are usually full to bursting in the summer. If you have a car, you can expand your horizons to include some of the more secluded spots along the coast. At Conca dei Marini, another nearly vertical town on the outskirts of Amalfi, ****Belvedere on Via Nazionale is an airy and modern resort hotel in a delightful setting, with a nice beach and an old Norman tower in the grounds (tel 831 282; L90–140 000).

Unlike Positano, Amalfi has been a resort for a long time, and some of its older establishments are among the most distinctive on the Mediterranean. St Francis himself is said to have founded the ****Luna, Via P. Comite 19, though the elevators and Hollywood-style pool are a little more recent. This former monastery, above the drive on Amalfi's eastern edge, was already a hotel in the waning days of the Grand Tour—Wagner stayed here while searching for his Garden of Klingsor, and they can show you the room where Ibsen wrote *A Doll's House*. Among other famous guests, the owners claim the Luna to have been a favourite of Mussolini and Otto von Bismarck;

modern-day authoritarians will enjoy the comfortable rooms and attentive service (tel 871 1002; L140 000). If Franciscan accommodation isn't to your taste, see what the 12th-century Capuchins could come up with at the ****Cappuccini Convento, set on a mountainside over the town, with an elevator running down through the cliffs to the beach. The monks would have enjoyed seeing the Persian rugs and elegant furnishings in their old digs, though perhaps they might have been dismayed to see their cloister converted into a conference centre (Via Annunziatella; tel 871 008; L135 000; the restaurant is among the best around). One more modern, but equally luxurious place in the same area: the *****Santa Caterina, Via Nazionale 9, tel 871 012 with perhaps the loveliest gardens of all, a converted villa where most rooms have a sea view (L280–350 000).

Not all of Amalfi's accommodation offers such heights of luxury. Two pleasant hotels convenient to both the town and beach: the ***Miramalfi, Via Quasimodo 3, tel 871 588 (L75–95 000), and **La Conchiglia, at the end of the Lungomare by Amalfi's little harbour, at Piazzale de Protontini, tel 871 856 (L52–65 000). There is also a collection of inexpensive places around the cathedral, of which the well-kept **Amalfi on Via Truglio, tel 872 440, and the **Sole on Largo della Zecca, tel 871 147, stand out; both will cost L45–60 000.

EATING OUT

In the high-season at least, most of the resort hotels along the coast will coerce you into dining with them. Not that that's always bad—some of the better hotels have well-known gourmet restaurants—but there are some equally good places to enjoy if you can escape. Down on Positano's beach, the centre of the action in the summer is Chez Black, a slick and sophisticated spot that fortunately turns out to be a good deal cosier—and less expensive—than it looks. Good Neapolitan favourites like *spaghetti alle vongole* are done well here, leading up to a vast choice of seafood, and maybe a banana split with *Liquore Strega* for dessert (Via Brigantino 19, tel 875 036; average L40 000). O'Capurale, near the water on Via del Saraceno offers much of the same (and who needs anything fancier?); the swordfish and *zuppa di pesce* are particularly good (tel 875 374; average L35 000).

Seafood, not surprisingly, is on the menu at most of the places along the drive. Amalfi and Ravello have some fine restaurants, including those in the luxury hotels mentioned above. In Amalfi, almost directly under the cathedral, the Taverna degli Apostoli, Via S. Anna Piccola, tel 872 991, has a good *risotto marinaio* and other fish dishes for L30 000 and up. North of the centre, on Via Chiarito 1, in the Valley of the Mills, the Lemon Garden has lemons on the trees all around and as many in the kitchen—*spaghetti alla limone*, lemon chicken and more... (tel 872 295; average L20 000). There's a pretty old-fashioned trattoria wine shop a little way north of the cathedral on Via Pietro Capuana called La Vinicola, with a limited menu for L16 000.

Inland Villages: Ravello and Scala

As important as it was in its day, the Amalfitano Republic never grew very big. At its greatest extent, it could only claim a small part of this coast, including these two towns up in the mountains; like Amalfi these once were much larger and more prosperous than you see them today. **Ravello** is another beauty, a balcony overlooking the Amalfi coast and a treasure-house of exotic medieval art. As the second city of the Amalfi Republic, medieval Ravello is said to have had a population of 30,000; now it provides an example of that typically Italian phenomenon—a village of 2000 with its own bishop, and a first-rate cathedral to put him in.

Ravello's chief glories are two wonderful gardens: that of the **Villa Cimbrone**, laid out by an Englishman in the 1900s, with a priceless view over the Amalfi coast, and that of the **Villa Rùfolo**—which, as fans of Wagner will be interested to know, is none other than Klingsor's magic garden. Wagner says so himself, in a note scribbled in the villa's guest book. He really had come here looking for it, for the proper setting in which to imagine the worldly, Faustian enchanter of *Parsifal*. The villa itself is a remarkable 11th-century pleasure palace, a temporary abode of Charles of Anjou, various Norman kings, and Adrian IV, the only English pope (1154–59), who was fleeing Arnold of Brescia's rebellion in Rome. Even in its present, half-ruined state, it is worth a visit; inside is a small collection of architectural fragments. The garden, with more fine views, is a small semi-tropical paradise, full of fountains and flowers in every imaginable colour.

The **cathedral** is named for Ravello's patron San Pantaleone, an obscure early martyr; they have a phial of his blood in one of the side chapels, and it 'boils' like the blood of San Gennaro in Naples whenever the saint is in the mood. Lately he hasn't been, which makes the Ravellans worry. The cathedral has two particular treasures: a pair of bronze doors by the 12th century Apulian artist Barisano da Trani, inspired by the Greek ones at Amalfi, and an exquisite pair of marble *ambones*, or pulpits, that rank among the outstanding examples of 12th-century Cosmatesque work. Two other Ravello churches where you can see more of this are **Santa Maria a Gradillo** and **San Giovanni del Toro**. From Ravello, it is only a lovely 1.5 km walk to **Scala**, smallest and oldest of the three Amalfitano towns, with another interesting old cathedral.

Back on the Amalfi drive, just after Amalfi the road passes over **Atrani**, an old village whose cathedral has another tiled dome and yet another set of bronze doors from Constantinople. Next come **Minori** and **Maiori**, villages with pleasantly shady but absolutely indistinguishable lidos. **Erchie**, a tiny hamlet on the shore far below the road, seems a lovely spot—if you can figure out a way to get down to it. Then, near the end of the drive, **Cetara**, on the outskirts of Salerno, has a fine beach behind the mole of the fishing port.

Salerno

Anywhere else in the south of Italy, a city like Salerno would be an attraction in itself; here it gets lost among the wonders of the Campanian coast—just the big town at the end of the Amalfi drive—and few people ever stop for more than a very brief visit. Nevertheless, Salerno has its modest charms, not least of which is that it is a clean and orderly place; that should endear it to people who hate Naples. Its setting under a backdrop of mountains is memorable. The Italian highway engineers, showing off as usual, have brought a highway to the city on a chain of viaducts, one lofty span after another, an unusual and pleasing ornament for the city; at night the road lights hang on the mountain slopes like strings of fairy lights on a Christmas tree.

Salerno began in ancient times; its name may refer to salt pans on the shore long ago.

In medieval times the city gained distinction from its medical school, first and finest in Europe. Traditionally founded by the legendary 'Four Doctors'—an Italian, a Greek, a Jew and an Arab—the school was of the greatest importance in the transmission of Greek and Muslim science into Europe. Most of us, however, recognize Salerno better as site of the Allied invasion in September 1943, one of the biggest and most successful operations of World War II.

Salerno's port is on the outskirts of town, and the shore all through the city centre is graced with a pretty park, the Lungomare Trieste. Parallel to it, and two blocks back, the Corso Vittorio Emanuele leads into the old town. Here it changes its name to Via dei Mercanti, most colourful of Salerno's old streets. The **cathedral**, a block to the north on Via del Duomo, is set with its façade behind a courtyard with a fountain at the centre, and a detached campanile—as if it were not a church at all, but a mosque. The Corinthian columns around it come from the ancient city of Paestum, not far down the coast. Robert Guiscard, who built it, spent a lot of time in this city; his wife was a fearsome warrior-princess of Salerno named Sichelgaita. The cathedral was begun in 1086, the year after Guiscard sacked Rome. He brought Pope Gregory VII, ostensibly his ally, to Salerno for safe-keeping, and Gregory, the monk Hildebrand who laid the foundations of the powerful medieval papacy before himself becoming one of the greatest popes, is buried in one of the side chapels. The cathedral's treasures are of the same order as those of the Amalfi coast: another pair of bronze doors from Constantinople, and another beautiful pair of Cosmatesque pulpits. The Cathedral has been much restored, and many of the best original details have been preserved in the adjacent **Museo del Duomo** (daily, 9:30–12:30, 4–6 pm; adm).

From Salerno, you can make an easy excursion up into the mountains to the town of **Cava de' Tirreni**; near it, perched precariously on the slopes of the Val di Bonea, is a little-visited Benedictine monastery called **La Trinità di Cava**—rebuilt, as usual, in tiresome Baroque, but preserving a wealth of 12th–14th-century frescoes, stone-carving and Cosmati work.

WHERE TO STAY AND EATING OUT   (tel prefix 089)
Ravello has its share of dream hotels: no beach, but unforgettable gardens and views down over the coast. The finest, with an incredible guest book full of the names of the famous over the last 115 years, is the *******Palumbo**, Via del Toro 28, tel 857 244. The service is perfect, the rooms individually decorated with antiques, the restaurant renowned for seafood, local and international dishes (try the chicken Kiev; the excellent house wine is really house wine—made on the premises. If you aren't staying at the hotel, dinners average L45 000). Still, there are no recreational facilities or really special features, and the room prices may be a bit hard to justify L250–380 000; there is also a simpler *residenza* with rooms for L130–148 000). On the same street, the 12th-century palazzo of the grand duke, *****Gran Caruso**, Via Toro 52, tel 857 111, has charming rooms for L220–300 000, equally stupendous views, and Ravello's best restaurant, with fantastic pasta with seafood (L40–50 000). With the lushest gardens on the coast, the *****Villa Cimbrone**, tel 857 138, is a viable alternative: another elegant old villa, once the property of an English duke. The rooms are fine, though in refitting the old villa it was not possible to provide each one with its own bath (L70–100 000; has Ravello's only swimming pool). A delightful budget choice: the ****Villa Maria**, tel 857 170, near the

Villa Cimbrone: only seven rooms, but gardens and a terrace restaurant with a view over the hills (L48–65 000). If you make the trip up to Scala, near Ravello, try the wide range of delicious antipasto dishes and desserts at **La Margherita** in the village centre (about L22 000).

Hotels in Minori and Maiori are as hard to tell apart as the two towns themselves—no insult intended, but in the shadow of Amalfi and Ravello, these two thoroughly pleasant lidos seem a little dull. *****San Pietro** in Maiori, tel 877 220, with a pool and tennis, is typical of the modern, middle-range resort hotels you'll find in either town (L65–80 000). Also in Maiori, there are simple hotels near the beaches, like the ***Baia Verde**, tel 877 276, (L38–45 000) and the ***Vittoria**, tel 877 652, (L38–45 000), that offer some of the most convenient inexpensive accommodation on the Amalfi coast.

On the way to Salerno at Cetara, the *****Cetus**, tel 261 388, is a lovely newer hotel built into the cliffs, with steps down to a secluded beach (L56–85 000). Salerno's hotels are a modest and utilitarian lot; more than acceptable for an overnight stay is the *****Plaza**, right across from the station on Piazza Ferrovia, tel 224 477, (L78–90 000). Less expensive places can be found west of the station along Corso Vittorio Emanuele. Salerno has its share of good restaurants, many of them along the shore on Lungomare Trieste. **Rugantino**, at No 178, tel 229 768, is a local favourite for seafood; they have a special way with other dishes too—try the *scaloppine cordon bleu* (L35 000). Another good place for fish is **Il Gambero**, Via Cuomo 9, tel 225 039, three blocks east of the cathedral (average for fish L35–40 000, closed Sun). **Da Sasa** on Via Diaz is a good inexpensive trattoria, with full dinners for L16 000.

Islands in the Bay of Naples

Without a doubt, the islands in the Bay of Naples—Capri, Ischia, and to a far lesser extent Procida—are the holiday queens of the Italian islands. Every schoolchild has heard of Capri, made so notorious by the antics of Emperor Tiberius and Norman Douglas' 'gentlemanly freaks'. Ischia, fifty years ago, was the favourite island of jet-setters jaded by Capri. Renowned in ancient times for its mud baths, it has become a home-from-home for the German bourgeoisie. Procida, on the other hand, has hardly been developed at all, though not through any lack of charm.

By Boat to the Islands

Ferries leave from the docks at Naples' **Stazione Marittima** (usually the dock to the right, called Molo Beverello), just behind the Castel Nuovo, for Capri, Ischia, and Procida. In the summer, there can be as many as six ferries and 20 hydrofoils a day to Capri, and as many to Ischia. The CAREMAR company (tel 551 3882) runs all the ferries, and the hydrofoils that use the Stazione Marittimo; summer hydrofoils to all three islands from **Mergellina Marina** are operated by two companies, SNAV, Via Caracciolo 10, tel 761 2348, and Alilauro, Via Caracciolo 15, tel 761 1004. The hydrofoils are certainly faster—but note that the fares can be double that of the slower and much pleasanter steamers, which make the trip in about an hour.

In addition, CAREMAR runs a few daily ferries from Sorrento to Capri, from Pozzuoli to Procida and Ischia, and between Ischia and Procida, all very short rides.

Alilauro operates frequent hydrofoil runs from Sorrento to Naples as long as seas permit. All these schedules change from time to time, and the best up-to-date listings can be found in the city Tourist Board's publication *Qui Napoli*.

Capri

Capri can lay fair claim to being the most beautiful island in the Mediterranean. It is also the most overrun and exploited; recently so many tourists tried to jam on it that there was danger of some falling off, and the government moved to restrict the number of sailings. With more than 800 species of plant, it is very much a garden paradise perched on a rugged chunk of limestone. Unlike Ischia and other, more recent, tourist haunts, Capri has the relaxed air of having seen it all. Though between June and September you begin to understand why the word 'trash' is inscribed on the bins in 30 different languages, try going in November or February, when you may be lucky enough to arrive for a few brilliant days between the rains, and have this Garden of Eden practically to yourself. It's worth the risk of a soaking or two.

Of Capri (pronounced CAPri, not CapRI, like the Ford) little is known before Augustus made the island one of his retreats, calling it *Apragopolis*, the 'land of lay-abouts'. It was Augustus' stepson Tiberius whose dirty old man exploits, reported by that ancient scandal-monger Suetonius, gave Capri much of its early notoriety. After 1371 Capri went through a holy interlude, dominated by a Carthusian monastery (La Certosa). Capri's latest chapter began with the discovery of the Blue Grotto in 1826; the magic of the name has proved irresistible to the Grand and not so grand tourists ever since.

GETTING AROUND

Arriving in Marina Grande, you can ascend to either Capri or Anacapri by bus; after 10 pm they run every half-hour. The funicular ascends to Capri town every 15 minutes from 6.35 am until 10 pm; the chairlift from Anacapri to Monte Solaro (a 12-minute trip) runs continuously from 9 am to sunset. There are also buses from Anacapri to the Blue Grotto, Faro and Marina Piccola; and buses from Capri town to Damecuta and Marina Piccola. From June until September, there are daily tours of Capri by motor launch starting at 9am from Marina Grande.

TOURIST INFORMATION

AAST Main office: Piazza I. Cerio 11, Capri, tel (081) 837 0424, with information offices on the quay at Marina Grande tel 837 0634; Piazza Umberto I, Capri, tel 837 0686, and Via G. Orlandi 19/A, Anacapri, tel 837 1524.

Marina Grande and the Grotta Azzurra

All the ferries and hydrofoils from the mainland call at **Marina Grande**, where you can catch a bus or taxi up the cliffs, or a boat for the **Grotta Azzurra**. The Blue Grotto is well named if nothing else—its shimmering, iridescent blueness is caused by the reflection of light on the water in the morning. From June–September, boats for the Blue Grotto leave at 9 am—when the sea is calm. The **sea excursion around the island** is a rare experience, but again possible only in good weather. Besides visiting other lovely grottoes, such as the **Grotta Bianca** and the **Grotta Verde** (the White Cave and the Green Cave), there are breathtaking views of the cliffs and Capri's uncanny rock formations.

Capri Town
Haunted by the smiling shade of Gracie Fields, the charming white town of Capri is daily worn down by the tread of thousands of her less ectoplasmic followers. The **megalithic walls** supporting some of the houses have seen at least 3000 years of similar comings and goings, while the architecture of the older quarters complements the island's natural beauty: the moulded whitewashed arches and domes, the narrow streets and stairways crossed by buttresses supporting the buildings, and sudden little squares, just large enough for a few children to improvise a game of football. If you go up to Capri by funivia, you'll surface right next to the Piazza Umberto and the much photographed **cathedral**, with its joyful campanile and clock. Built in the 17th century in the local Baroque style, the cathedral has a charming buttressed roof. The little square in the church's shadow known as **La Piazzetta** is the centre of Capri café society.

Some of the prettiest walks around Capri begin on Via Vittorio Emanuele, heading towards Via Camerelle and Via Tragara. The latter street eventually leads to the **Faraglioni**, the three enormous sheer-sided limestone pinnacles towering straight up in the ever blue-green sea. Nearby is the **Tragara Terrace**, with magnificent views, and the tall skinny rock called **Pizzolungo**. Still following the main track along the coast and up the stairway, you'll come upon the **Grotta di Matromania**, where the Romans worshipped the fertility goddess Cybele, or Mater Magna; part of Capri's reputation as an island of orgies may derive from this ancient eastern cult's noisy rituals, which culminated abruptly in the self-castration of the priest-for-a-day. From the Grotta di Matromania a stepped path leads down to yet another famous eroded rock: the **Arco Naturale**, where dark pines—as everywhere else on Capri—cling to every tiny ledge they can sink their roots into. On the way back to town you'll pass some of the island's vineyards that produce the rare and famous *Lacrimae Tiberii*, the tears of Tiberius.

La Certosa and Gardens of Augustus
A shorter walk starting from Via Vittorio Emanuele, Via F. Serena, and Via Matteotti leads to **La Certosa**, the Carthusian charterhouse founded in 1371 and suppressed in 1808. Built over one of Tiberius' villas, the golden-hued church and cloisters are topped by a Baroque tower added in the 17th century (open 9 until 2, closed Mon).

A few minutes away from La Certosa are the **Gardens of Augustus**, planted on the fertile terraces and belvederes overlooking one of the most striking views in the world. Narrow Via Krupp leads down the cliffs in a hundred hairpin turns to the **Marina Piccola**, the charming little port with most of Capri's bathing establishments, near the **Scoglio delle Sirene** (Sirens' Rock); there is a bus, fortunately, that makes the steep climb back up the cliffs to Capri town.

A much longer but equally rewarding walk or drive is to the **Villa Jovis** (Via Botteghe to Via Tiberio) passing the church of **Monte San Michele**, a fine example of local architecture, built in the 14th century. The Villa Jovis on Punta Il Capo (1028 ft) was the most important of the twelve villas on Capri: from here Tiberius governed the Roman

Empire for his last ten years. Although much has been sacked through the centuries, the extent of the remaining walls and foundations gives a fair idea of the grandeur of the former Imperial Palace. Near here, the **Faro**, or lighthouse, was believed to have been part of a system of semaphores through which messages were sent to Rome. The great sheer cliff beside the villa, the **Salto di Tiberio**, is always pointed out as the precipice from which the emperor hurled the girls and boys who bored him.

Anacapri

Carved into the escarpment of Anacapri, the 800 steps of the **Scala Fenicia** (not really Phoenician, but Greco-Roman) was for thousands of years the only way to reach the upper part of the island. It is impassable today, you have to take the road; along the stretch from Marina Grande is the 11th-century church of Capri's patron, **San Costanzo**, where ancient columns support the Byzantine dome. On top, **Anacapri**, the island's second city, retains a rustic air, with its many olive trees and vineyards surrounding it on all sides, and its simple style of architecture, Moorish in style with cubic, flat-roofed houses.

In Anacapri's Piazza San Nicola, the 18th-century church of **San Michele** (open 10–6, April–Oct, 10–2 Sun; adm) contains a magnificent mosaic floor of majolica tiles by the Abruzzese artist Leonardo Chiaiese. From Piazza Vittoria a chair lift travels to the summit of **Monte Solaro**, the highest point on the island at 1920 ft. Also from Piazza Vittoria, take Via Orlandi to Via Capodimonte and the **Villa San Michele** of Axel Munthe (1857–1949), one of the greatest physicians of his day, who donated his services to the victims of plagues, earthquakes and World War I; he still had time to be visited by a Roman ghost which advised him to restore and live in this villa. Munthe describes it all in his 1929 *The Story of San Michele*; Roman artefacts discovered on Capri add to its fascination (open daily, 9 until sunset; adm).

From Piazza Vittoria, Via Caposcuro and Via Migliara skirt Monte Solaro and its vineyards for the **Belvedere della Migliara**, from where you can see the Faraglioni and the entrance of the **Green Grotto**. A bus leaves from here for the Grotta Azzurra and the bathing area adjacent to it, passing by way of the old windmill and the **Villa Imperiale**, another of the summer residences built by Augustus, known also as the 'Damecuta' because of the tower next to it. After the Villa Jovis, this villa is the best preserved, and has recently been further excavated (open from 9 am until one hour before sunset; closed Mon).

WHERE TO STAY (tel prefix 081)
Reserve as early as possible to stay on Capri after the trippers have gone. If you have the money, the smart place to stay on Capri is the sumptuous *******Quisisana**, set in lush gardens in the middle of town on Via Camerelle, tel 837 0788; open April–1 Jan, where a room in the high season will set you back L390 000. Open all year round, *****La Floridana**, Via Campo di Teste, tel 837 0101, also has fine panoramas of the sea and rooms from L110–150 000. ****Villa Krupp**, Via Matteotti, tel 837 0362, is also open all year round (L65–75 000 with bath). For the record, the **Faraglioni**, Via Camerelle, tel 837 0320, opens from April to Oct, and is the cheapest place to stay on Capri, at L25 000, without bath.

In Anacapri, ***San Michele**, Via G. Orlandi, tel 837 1427, is in an elegant villa with wonderful views. Open all year round, rates are L75–110 000, all rooms with bath. The **Bellavista**, Via G. Orlandi, tel 837 1463, has a fine view as well, and many facilities for L60 000 without bath, L80 000 with; open all year.

EATING OUT
Capri's best restaurant has long been **La Capannina**, Via delle Botteghe 14, tel 837 0732, set in a secluded garden, with delicately prepared shellfish, pasta, and fish, and desserts (L50 000). **I Faraglioni** on pretty Via Camerelle 75, tel 837 0320, has delectable house specialities like *crêpes al formaggio, risotto ai frutti di mare* (L60 000). **Bagni Tiberio**, near the Marina Piccola and its bathing establishments (Palazzo a Mare 41, tel 837 7688) is more moderately priced but excellent, with dinners (try the tagliatelle with prawns) for around L35 000. If you have your heart set on tasting Capri's famous wine, try **Da Paolino** on Via Palazzo a Mare 11, tel 837 6102, which has some unusual offerings like peppers stuffed with spaghetti, rabbit from the oven and some very good desserts (L45 000 at least).

In Anacapri, **Da Gelsomina la Migliara**, on Via Migliara 6, offers not only home-made wine, but true homecooked island specialities, including mushrooms collected on Monte Solaro, for around L40 000 a person (closed Tuesdays). For something less costly, **Materita**, on Via G. Orlandi 140, has pizza and other trattoria specialities for about L25 000.

Ischia

Ischia is a remarkably lovely island, able to hold its own even with Capri. The sea of vineyards encircling the island's highest peak, volcanic Monte Epomeo (2,600 ft) produces the excellent wine named after the mountain, and the villages high on its slopes remain untouched by the international onslaught of tourists at the resorts of Casamicciola, Forio, Lacco Ameno and Ischia town. Unlike Capri, Ischia has many long, first-class beaches, on one of which, Maronti, the volcanic nature of the island is very evident. The hot mineral springs that gush all year round have attracted cure-seekers since Roman times, and are still recommended today for people suffering from rheumatism, arthritis, neuralgia and obesity. The hottest spring on the island is Terme Rita, at Casamicciola, which belches from the earth at around 180°F. For a lark try the Terme Comunali at the port, or the unique baths at Cavascura above Sant'Angelo.

GETTING AROUND
Buses to the various towns on the island depart from the square next to Santa Maria di Portosalvo, near the beginning of SS260 which encircles Ischia. The service (SEPSA) is very good to all parts, but be prepared to put up with crowded buses from June onwards.

TOURIST INFORMATION
Via Iasolino, tel (081) 991146

Porto and Ponte
The first hint you receive of Ischia's volcanic origins comes when you enter the almost perfectly round harbour of Ischia Porto, formed by a sister crater of Monte Epomeo.

Now the prime tourist centre of the island, the sprawl has since gobbled up **Ischia Ponte**, once a separate fishing village. 'Ponte' refers to the causeway built by Alfonso (il Magnifico) of Aragon in 1438 to the **Castello d'Ischia** (or Aragonese) on its offshore rock. With the large dome of its abandoned church in the centre, the fortress where Vittoria Colonna spent so many years looks like a fairytale illustration from the distance; the views from its narrow streets and walls are superb. Even better views taking in Procida and the Phlegraean Fields can be had from the summit of the extinct volcano, **Montagnone** (835 ft); a cable car goes from Via Baldassarre Cossa at Ischia Porto.

WHERE TO STAY   (tel prefix 081)
The finest hotel in Ischia Porto is the ******Excelsior Belvedere** on Via E. Gianturco 19, tel 991 522, open from April until October. Not only is it quieter than most, but guests can enjoy the fine pool and garden; rates are L170–250 000. You can also indulge in luxury at the ******Mare Blu**, Via Pontano 40, tel 982 555, (L105–145 000) which sits in a charming position on the waterfront with a view of the Aragonese castle and the isle of Vivara. The least expensive place to stay is near the Castello Aragonese and is open all year: ***Il Monasterio**, tel 992 435; L23–25 000; and the showers are usually hot.

EATING OUT
Ischians, like Elmer Fudd, are very fond of rabbit stew, but on the whole the island is better known for its *vino* than its *cucina*; at least once treat yourself to a bottle of Epomeo (red or white), Ischia (red or white) and Biancolella. For fish the best place to look is along the port: at Via Porto 66, **Gennaro**, tel 992 917, open from April until Oct, has the biggest and most succulent shrimp, and much more (L50 000). **La Cantina**, Via Nitrodi 6, tel 99 071, serves typical Ischian dishes, local wine and home-made bread (L25 000, closed Oct–Mar). Near the Aragonese Castle stands the lovely and tranquil **Giardini Eden**, Via Nuova Cartaromana 50, tel 993 909. You couldn't find fresher fish or lobster, as they pluck it out of the water in front of you (L40–60 000, closed evenings and Oct–Apr). There are also many snack bars and pizzerias that save the pocket of budget travellers: try **Pizzeria Romana** at Via Alfredo da Luca 6.

Around Ischia: Casamicciola and Lacco Ameno

A few miles west of Ischia Porto (bus every half-hour) is the popular resort of **Casamicciola Terme**, the oldest spa on the island and the probable location of the first Greek settlement in Western Europe (756 BC), though an eruption from Montagnone's volcano persuaded them to move the colony to Cumae. Henrik Ibsen spent a summer in a nearby villa (a medallion minted in his honour can be seen in Piazza Marina). A half-hour's walk along the coast from Casamicciola leads to the more fashionable **Lacco Ameno**, another large resort, where the local landmark is the **Fungo**, a mushroom-shaped rock that dominates the beach. In the centre of town you can pay your respects at the bright pink **Sanctuary of Santa Restituta**, patron saint of Ischia. The oldest part of the Sanctuary dates from 1036, and was constructed on the site of an early Christian basilica and an even earlier Roman bath. Greek and Roman finds are in the local **Museum** (open mornings only) near the church and the neo-Pompeian **Terme Regina Isabella**.

Forio and Sant'Angelo

Forio, the wine-producing and art centre of Ischia, is one of the prettiest towns on the island. Forio has three outstanding landmarks, the first of which is the huge tower known as the **Torrione**, built by King Ferrante in 1480 on the site of an even older tower; later converted to a prison, it is now a gallery of local art. Near it rises the dome of **Santa Maria di Loreto**, a fine Baroque church begun in the 14th century; the two towers are decorated with majolica tiles. On the point furthest west stands the white church of the **Soccorso**, where the local fishermen pray for help, as can be seen from the numerous votive offerings inside. Near Citara beach are the **Gardens of Poseidon**, a complex of swimming-pools set in a Mediterranean garden.

From Forio, SS270 passes the hill villages of **Panza** and **Serrara Fontana**, both of which have roads leading down to **Sant'Angelo**. The walk down at the edge of the cliff takes in numerous views of **Punta Sant'Angelo**, a small islet with a stump of a tower connected to Ischia by a narrow isthmus of sand. East of the village stretches the lovely beach of **Maronti**, reached by way of a path passing numerous fumaroles, hissing and steaming; the beach itself has patches of scalding hot sand where you can warm a picnic lunch. Above the beach are the hot springs of **Cavascura**, at the mouth of an old river canyon, with sheer sides, little wooden bridges and the individual baths carved in the rock—each named after a mythological deity.

From Serrara Fontana the road towards Barano is most picturesque, winding its way around the inner valleys of Monte Epomeo (2,600 ft). From Fontana, you can start your climb up to the old volcano itself, fast asleep since 1302. There's a hermitage where you can spend the night, located in the very crater itself. Watching the sun rise or set from such vantage points is always memorable, but with the entire Bay of Naples spread out below you, it is sublime. **Barano**, a hill village up among the trees, is another place to escape the international bustle of Ischia.

WHERE TO STAY AND EAT   (tel prefix 081)

Many hotels in Forio are connected to thermal establishments, like the modern ***Punta del Sole** on Piazza Maltese, tel 998 208, with a pool and garden (L65 000). For something less expensive, **San Francesco** on Via T. Cigliano 9, tel 987 397, in nearby San Francesco, has similar facilities but no thermal baths (L45 000, all with shower). **La Giara** at Via Marina 40, has good fish meals for around L35 000. In Lacco Ameno, ****San Montano** on Via Monte Vico, tel 994 033, is a hotel that offers—in addition to thermal baths—a pool, tennis courts and many other comforts (L180–200 000). A bargain, by Ischia standards, is the **Bristol**, at Via Fundera 72, tel 994 566, with a small garden and swimming-pool (L45 000 with shower). Lacco Ameno's **Padrone d'o Mare**, open all year round, specializes in various fish dishes for around L30 000.

In Casamicciola: prices tend to be a little lower. There's the ***Ibsen** with a pool and thermal bath on the Corso V. Emanuele 35, tel 994 588 (L46–65 000) with special facilities for the handicapped. Less expensive *Delle Rose**, Via Casa Mennella 9, tel 994 082, has charm, a swimming-pool and rooms with bath for L45 000. Most of the hotels in Barano are down on Maronti beach, like the moderately priced ***Helios**, Via Maronti, tel 990 001 (L50 000). **La Luna**, Via Testaccio 2 is about the least expensive, tel 990 299 (L35 000 with bath). One of the prettiest spots to dine is **Franceshino**, at Belvedere di Barano, tel 990 396, with lovely views, delicious meat dishes and excellent fish (L30–35 000, closed Oct–Mar).

Procida

Lovely, uncomplicated, and tiny, Procida is scented by lemon groves, and embellished with colourful houses as original as they are beautiful. Procida is an island where most people still earn a living from the sea, as fishermen or sailors. Its very proximity to the glamour, chaos and more celebrated charms of Naples, Capri, and Ischia has saved it from the worst ravages of touristic excess. Two love stories are linked to the island: Alphonse Lamartine's *Graziella* and the Sixth Tale of the Fifth Day of Boccaccio's *Decameron*; perhaps the most striking thing about them is that both are true.

TOURIST INFORMATION
Via Rodia, tel (081) 896 9624

The Port, Corricella, and the Terra Murata
Ships and hydrofoils call at the port, the **Marina Grande**, also called Sancio Cattolico, or locally simply as Sent'Co. The church near the landing, **Santa Maria della Pietà** (1760) immediately gives you a taste of Procida's delightful architecture—wide arches in random rhythms and exterior rampant stairs crisscrossing the façades, all in softly moulded lines, their colours either faded pastel or more racy deep pinks, blues, and yellows. The style reaches its epiphany over the hill at **Corricella**, the oldest village on the island, built on a protected cove by fishermen, under the citadel of the Terra Murata. Some houses have been so remodelled over the centuries according to the needs of their inhabitants as to give immediate proof to an old island saying, that 'a house isn't only a house. A house is a story.'

Via Madonna delle Grazie leads up to the **Terra Murata**, Procida's highest point and citadel, passing the roofless ruins of **Santa Margherita Nuova**, built in 1586 at the edge of the Punta dei Monaci. The fortifications of the citadel belong to different dates, the latest portions from 1521; the oldest section of the medieval walls can be seen near the **Porta Mezz'Olmo**, at the beginning of the Via San Michele. Rising above the walls, houses and prison of the Terra Murata are the three domes of **San Michele Arcangelo**, which, despite its exotic, almost Saracen appearance from a distance wears a simple unadorned façade, rebuilt after the various pirates' depredations. Of the original pre-16th-century structure, only part of the ceiling in the Sala del Capitolo remains. Many rich works of art attest to the former splendour of the monastery; the ceiling frescoes date from the 17th century, as do the apse paintings by Nicola Rosso, the most interesting of which shows God's aide-de-camp Michael and his troop of putti swooping down to save Procida from the Turks. Pride of place goes to a splashy canvas by Luca Giordano.

In Piazza d'Armi is the Cardinal of Aragon's 1563 **Castello d'Aragona**, a fancy name for the clink (pop. 90, who wish they could catch the next boat to Naples); here, too, you can see parts of the walls, in which are crammed tortuous alleyways and steep narrow houses.

Across Procida

The rest of the island has many rural beauty spots, shaded lanes, old farmhouses and crumbling small palazzi. The area around **Centane**, especially Punta Solchiaro is most typical, and has the most striking belvedere, with views over the entire east coast of the island. On the west end of the island, the long stretch of sand between Punta Serra and the peninsula of Santa Margherita Vecchia has been divided into three beaches— **Spiaggia Ciraccio**, where two Roman tombs were discovered; **Spiaggia Ciraciello**, on the other side of the pyramid-shaped rock, Il Faraglione di Procida; and towards the peninsula, the **Lido**. To the south lies the small fishing port and beach **Marina di Chiaiolella**, on a rounded cove that was once a volcanic crater.

From here you can cross the new pedestrian-only bridge to the islet of **Vivara**, a Neopolitan natural park, where the birds are protected these days but the rabbits are fair game. A narrow road leads towards the summit of Vivara, through the crumbling arch of an old hunting lodge to the Belvedere, from which you can gaze on the fine panoramas of Procida and Pozzuoli on the mainland.

WHERE TO STAY AND EATING OUT   (tel prefix 081)

The only hotel open all year round on Procida is ****L'Oasi** at Via Elleri 16, tel 896 7499 (L70–75 000), a villa with a restaurant and garden. Others include ****Arcate**, Via Marcello Scotti 10 (open April–Oct) on the beach in Chiaia (tel 896 7120; L69–79 000) and the ****Riviera**, in Chiaiolella, which has fine views (tel 896 7197; L47 000 with bath, L38 000 without).

There are several fairly inexpensive restaurants along the port at Marina Grande, like **La Medusa**, tel 896 7481, with seafood and landfood, for around L40 000). **Il Cantino** serves a very good *pesce fritto* for around L25–35 000 (Via Nitrodi 6, tel 99 071). **Crescenzo** at Via Marina in Chiaiolella 28, tel 896 7255, does a mean *spaghetti ai frutti di mare* (L30–50 000; it also has a few rooms to let) and the **Lido Conchiglia** on the beach at Chiaia also specializes in seafood for around L35 000.

Campania Inland: Capua and Caserta

There's more to the region than just the Bay of Naples. The coast and its endless attractions draw off most of the tourists, and it's a rare soul indeed who ever makes it up to old Capua, or the distinguished little city of Benevento.

GETTING AROUND

This is a rather large piece of territory—the three main towns are all provincial capitals. None is on the main railway lines, however, and you will have to scrutinize the timetables in Rome or Naples carefully to find your way around. Some Rome-Naples trains pass through Caserta and Capua. Be careful about Naples-Benevento trains; some but not all of them are operated by a private railway, and you will need to to find out which—ask at the information booth in Naples Stazione Centrale—to buy the right ticket.

Buses for Avellino and Benevento, and other points in their two provinces, leave Naples from in front of the Stazione Centrale. Do not expect any signs or timetables—

just make the tour of the grey sheds in the big bus parking area and see if you can find the right company. It's the only way. In Benevento, buses to Naples and a surprising variety of other places (including one daily to Rome) leave from Piazza Pacca, on Corso Dante just west of the Cathedral. There are several companies; check at the Benevento EPT for timetables.

Buses to Caserta leave every 20 minutes from in front of the Capua Gate in Naples (tel 261 333).

TOURIST INFORMATION
Benevento: EPT is east of the city centre at Via Nicola Sala 31,tel (0824) 310 662.
Information office at Via N. Giustiniani, tel 25 424
Avellino: Via Due Principati 5, tel (0825) 35 169
Caserta: right in the Royal Palace, tel (0823) 322 233; also in Corso Trieste, tel 321 137

Capua

This is a double city, consisting of the modern town, founded in the 9th century, and the ancient one, once the second city of Italy, deserted in the Dark Ages and now modestly reborn as **Santa Maria Capua Vetere**.

Capua can trace its founding to the Oscans, blithe folk of ancient Italy who introduced farce to the theatre, and who probably give us the word *obscene*. It is believed that the Oscan farces, banned by all decent Roman emperors, created the prototypes of the *commedia dell'arte* stock characters, including Naples' favourite Pulcinello—Punch. All that should give you some idea of the spirit of old Capua, a city best known for beautiful women and the manufacture of perfume, and as renowned for loose morals in its day as Sybaris. Everyone but the jealous Roman historians liked to give Capua credit for defeating the great Hannibal. The Capuans had always hated those dreary dour Romans, and they eagerly took the Carthaginians' part. Hannibal's men enjoyed Capuan hospitality in the winter of 216 BC; they came out in the spring so dreamy-eyed and dissipated that they never beat the Romans again.

Of course there was hell to pay when the Romans came back, but Capua survived, even flourished for centuries more as the greatest city of the region (*Campania* takes its name from Capua). The city was the original destination of Rome's famous Appian Way, later extended out to Benevento and Brindisi. Finally though, some even worse drudges than the Romans arrived—the Arabs, who utterly destroyed the city *c.* 830; the survivors refounded Capua on a new site a few kilometres to the north. Of old Capua, at Santa Maria Capua Vetere, you can see the remains of the second-largest **amphitheatre** in Italy—largest of all before Rome built its Colosseum. Here Spartacus began his gladiators' revolt in 73 BC. Few sections of the stands are still intact, but there is an underground network of tunnels and trap-doors much like Rome's.

While there, ask the attendant to show you something much more interesting—a short walk away is perhaps the best example of a **mithraeum** discovered anywhere in the Mediterranean. The cult of the god Mithras, imported from Persia by the legionaries, was for a while the most widespread of the cults that tried to fill the religious vacuum of the Imperial centuries. Some scholars see in it much in common with Christianity. The resemblance isn't readily apparent; Mithraism was an archaic, gut-level cult, with

249

mystery initiations and lots of bull's blood splashing about. Though it originally took hold in the army, and always remained a men-only affair, as late as the 3rd century AD it could probably claim more adherents than Christianity. The upper classes were never too impressed with it; that is why it lost out to the Christians, and why such well executed frescoes as these are rare. The *mithraeum* is an underground hall, used in the initiations, and dominated by a large scene of Mithras, a typical Mediterranean solar hero, slaying a white bull with a serpent under its feet; the complementary fresco representing the moon on the opposite wall is less well-preserved.

Also around Santa Maria, there is a crumbling triumphal arch, and some elaborate Roman tombs off the road to Caserta. The new Capua has all the most interesting finds from the old one at the **Museo Provinciale Campano** (daily, except Mon, 9–1, 2–5 pm; adm). Just north of the town, on the slopes of Mount Tifata, a site once occupied by a temple of Diana is now the 11th-century basilica of **Sant'Angelo in Formis**. The 12th-century frescoes here are some of the best in the south, oddly archaic figures that would seem much more at home in Constantinople than in Italy. And more than mere artistry, there is an intense spiritual vision about these paintings—note especially the unearthly, unforgettable face of the enthroned St Michael above the portal.

North of Capua, near the border with Lazio, is **Sessa Aurunca**, set under an extinct volcano called Roccamonfina. There is a Roman bridge, the Ponte degli Aurunci, and some other scanty ruins; all the good surviving fragments seem to have been incorporated into the **cathedral**, begun in 1113. Inside, there is some good early medieval sculpture, and a wealth of Cosmatesque work, including a fine pulpit similar to the one at Salerno. Nearby **Teano** is just as old, and offers ruins of a Roman amphitheatre to prove it, along with a restored 13th-century cathedral.

The northernmost corner of Campania, along the roads leading over the mountains to Campobasso, is a lovely, little-known region called the **Matese**; half of it is in the Molise, and we have covered it all there for convenience's sake (see Molise, p. 309).

St Michael, Sant'Angelo in Formis

Caserta

In one shot, you can see the biggest palace in Italy, and also the most wearisome; both distinctions belong incontestably to the **Reggia**, or Royal Palace, built here by the Bourbon King of Naples, Charles III. His architect, Luigi Vanvitelli (really a Dutchman named Van Wittel) spared no expense; like the Spanish Bourbons, those of Naples were greenly jealous over Versailles, and wanted to show the big Louises back home that they, too, deserved a little respect. The Reggia has some 1200 rooms, not much compared with the 2800 of the Bourbon palace in Madrid, but larger than its Spanish cousin just the same; the façade is 245 m across. Inside, as in Madrid, everything is tasteful, ornate and soberingly expensive; the only good touches from Vanvitelli's heavy hand are the elegant grand staircases. Only the gardens make the trip worth while, an amazingly long axis of pools and cascades climbing up to the famous **Diana fountain**, with a lifelike sculptural group of the goddess and her attendants catching Actaeon in the act. There is also an **English Garden**, of the sort fashionable in the 18th century. The Reggia was commandeered for use as Allied military headquarters in 1943, and it was here that the final surrender of the German armies in Italy was accepted two years later.

Two miles north of Caserta, the village of **San Leucio** was founded by the Bourbon kings as a paternalistic utopian experiment, and also an establishment for the manufacture of silk. Ferdinand IV, for most of his life, personally saw to every detail of its operation, even christening the children of the workers. The successor of his *Real Fabbrica* is still a centre for silk. Some 9 km to the east, there is the half-deserted town of **Caserta Vecchia**. The building of the Reggia drew most of the population down to modern Caserta, but the old town still has the 12th-century **cathedral**, with a great octagonal cupola that is one of the glories of Arab-Norman architecture.

Benevento

Ever since the Middle Ages, the land around Caserta and Capua has been called the *Terra del Lavoro*—cultivated land—a broad garden plain that is one of the most fertile corners of Italy. Its lush landscapes have suffered a bit from creeping industrialism, and if you continue south towards Naples, you'll get even worse. The Napoletani call the towns around Afragola, Acerra and Secondigliano the 'Triangle of Death', an industrial wasteland of shanties and power lines ruled by the Camorra that has Italy's worst unemployment and some of its worst social problems.

Go east instead, up into the foothills of the Apennines towards **Benevento**, yet another smallish city that has often played a big role in Italian history. On an old tower in the centre of town, the city fathers have put up maps of southern Italy, showing the boundaries of the two important states of which Benevento was the capital.

At first, as *Malies* or *Maloenton*, it was the leading town of the Samnites, the warlike mountain people who resisted Roman imperialism for so long. The Romans were later to make a big city of it, an important stop along the Appian Way. They Latinized the name to *Maleventum*—ill wind—but after a lucky defeat of Pyrrhus of Epirus here in 275 BC, they thought it might just be a *Beneventum* after all. In 571, the city was captured by the bloodthirsty Lombards, becoming their southern capital. After the Lombards of the north fell to Charlemagne, the Duchy of Benevento carried on as an independent state;

at its greatest extent, under relatively enlightened princes like Arechi II (*c.* 800), it ruled almost all of southern Italy. The Normans put an end to it in the 1060s. For the medieval Ghibellines, it became an ill wind once again. The great Battle of Benevento, in February 1266, was one of the turning points in Italian history; the defeat and death of King Manfred at the hands of Charles of Anjou marked the end of the brilliant rule of the Hohenstaufen, and the beginning of many troubles for the south.

Coming to Benevento in the winter, you're bound to think the Romans were crazy to change the name. When people in Salerno are ready to hit the beaches, you'll find the Beneventani shivering on street corners like Muscovites in their fur caps, victims of traditionally the worst weather in southern Italy. It is often claimed that this makes them more serious and introspective than people on the coast—certainly coming here from Naples seems sentimentally like a journey of a thousand miles. Benevento has often been the scene of earthquakes, and the city took plenty of hard shots during the battles of 1943, but there are still enough attractions around to make a stop worth while.

Benevento's **cathedral** is in the lower town, the part that suffered most in the bombings, and which was rebuilt rather shabbily after the war. The cathedral itself was almost a total loss; only the odd 13th-century façade remains, built of miscellaneous bits of Roman buildings—inscriptions, reliefs, friezes and pillars—arranged every which way. In the old streets behind the cathedral, you can see a well-preserved **Roman Theatre**—not an amphitheatre, but a place for classical drama, something rare this far north. By the time the Romans conquered them, the culture of the Samnites was almost completely Hellenized. This theatre, built under Hadrian, originally seated 20,000 (open daily, 9–sunset). All through this quarter, called the Triggio, you will see bits of Roman brick and medieval masonry—something ancient built into the walls of every house. There is half a Roman bridge over the Sabato (one of Benevento's two rivers) that once carried the Appian Way, ruins of the baths, remains of a triumphal arch, and plenty of gates and stretches of wall from the fortifications built by the Lombards. On Via Posillipo, a Baroque monument houses the **Bue Apis**, a sacred Egyptian bull sculpture found in Benevento's Temple of Isis.

Trajan's Arch

With the triumphal arches in Rome itself usually covered in scaffolding, you'll have to come to Benevento to see a good example. This one, in fact, may be the best of them all; built in AD 117, it is a serious piece of work—over 15 m of expensive Parian marble from Greece—and better preserved than those in Rome. It marks the spot where the Appian Way entered Beneventum (now Via Traiana on the northern edge of the old town), and the skilfully carved reliefs on both faces record significant events in the career of the emperor. Trajan (AD 98–117), the conqueror of Dacia and Mesopotamia, ranks among the greatest of the emperors, and a little commemoration would not seem out of place; nevertheless, cynics will enjoy the transparent and sometimes heavy-handed political propaganda of ornaments like this. In one of the panels, Trajan (the handsome fellow with the curly beard) is shown distributing gifts to children; in others he opens new roads and presides over the *institutio alimentaria*—the dole. Most of the scenes are about victory: Trajan announcing military reforms, Trajan celebrating a triumph, Jove handing Trajan one of his thunderbolts; finally comes the Apotheosis, where the late emperor is received among the gods while the goddess Roma escorts Hadrian to coronation as his divinely ordained successor.

Museo Sannio

Corso Garibaldi is Benevento's main street, just south of Trajan's Arch. Near its eastern end stands the city's oldest church, **Santa Sofia**, built in the late 8th century. It is unusual for its plan, an irregular six-pointed star, built for the Lombard Duke Gisulfo by an architect thoroughly grounded in the mystic geometry of the early Middle Ages. The vaulting is supported by recycled Roman columns, and other columns are hollowed out for use as holy water fonts.

The church cloister contains one of the south's more interesting provincial museums, the **Museo Sannio**. (Sannio means Samnium, as Benevento's province is still officially called.) The 12th-century cloister itself is well worth a look, with a variety of strange, twisted columns under pulvins carved with even stranger scenes: monster-hunting, dancing, fantastical animals, bunnies, and a camel or two. The best things in the museum are in the archaeological section. Almost all the classic vases are Campanian copies of Greek ware—the production of ceramics was the engine that pulled *Campania Felix*'s economy in its glory days.

SOME SAMNITE CURIOSITIES

Two rooms in the museum are filled with objects from the Temple of Isis. Anyone who has read Apuleius' *The Golden Ass* will remember just how important the cult of the transcendent goddess Isis was throughout the Roman world. This Egyptian import certainly seems to have found a home in Beneventum; nowhere else in Europe has so much fine Egyptian statuary been retrieved. The temple had imperial backing. One of the statues is of the founder, Emperor Domitian himself, in Egyptian dress. Other works portray priestesses, sacred boats and sphinxes, another Apis bull, and a porphyry 'cista mistica', carved with a snake. The image of Isis is also there, formidably impressive even without a head.

Somehow this leads naturally to Benevento's more famous piece of exotica—the witches. In the days of the Lombards, women by the hundreds would dance around a sacred walnut tree on the banks of the River Sabato ('sabbath'). Even after the official conversion to Christianity in 663, the older religion persisted, and Benevento is full of every sort of witch story as a result. The best piece of modern sculpture in the Museo Sannio is a representation of the witches' dance. Of course, the city has found ways to put the legend to use. In any bar in Italy, you can pick up a bottle of 'Liquore Strega' (*strega* means witch) and read on the label the proud device: 'Made next to the train station in Benevento, Italy'.

Just a few blocks west of the museum on Corso Garibaldi, the dedicatory **obelisk** from the Isis temple stands in front of the town hall. East of the museum, the Corso takes you to the **Rocca de' Rettori**, a fortress built by the popes in the 14th century; for centuries Benevento was a papal enclave surrounded by the Kingdom of Naples. The fortress is now a part of the Museo Sannio. Behind it is a lovely park, the Villa Comunale.

Samnium

Samnium is one of Italy's smallest provinces, but there are a few towns and villages of interest; the countryside, full of oak and walnut forests, is often reminiscent of some corner of Umbria. **Morcone**, to the north, has a memorable setting, draped on the curving slope of a hill like a Roman theatre. **Telese**, to the west, lies near a small but pretty lake of the same name, with a popular spa establishment. The nearby ruins of the Samnite-Roman town of *Telesia* are remarkable for the perfectly octagonal walls, with gates at the cardinal points. **Cerreto Sannita**, up in the mountains north of Telese, has been making painted ceramics for centuries and it is still a flourishing craft today. You can see earlier examples in the colourful cupolas and pavement of the village's church.

Best of all, perhaps, is the town of **Sant'Agata de' Goti**, with its long line of buildings like a manmade cliff overhanging a little ravine. Sant'Agata takes its name from the Goths who founded it in the 6th century; it was badly damaged in the 1980 earthquake, and its modest monuments, the **Castello** and the 12th-century church of **Santa Menna**, are still undergoing restoration. A narrow ravine in the mountains just south of town is believed to be the site of the Battle of the Caudine Forks (321 BC, during the second Samnite War), one of the worst defeats ever suffered by Rome. The invading Romans had to pay a big ransom to get back their captured army, though unfortunately they regained control of the situation within seven years, ensuring their dominance of Samnium and the south. Heavily forested **Monte Taburno**, east of Sant'Agata, is one of the beauty spots of the region. The 17th-century Bourbons built an aqueduct from here to fill the great fountains of their palace at Caserta; it's still working today.

WHERE TO STAY AND EATING OUT

Capua and Caserta are not the most encouraging places to stay in, but Caserta does have some good restaurants; at **La Castellana**, in Caserta Vecchia, you can feast on wild boar or venison, when available, as well as a wonderfully innovative selection of soup and pasta openers (Via Torre 5, tel (0823) 371 230; expect to pay at least L35 000). **La Massa**, on Via Mazzini 55, tel (0823) 321 268, is a simple and convenient place for lunch near the Reggia (from L20 000).

Benevento sees few tourists, and accommodation is limited. The *****Gran Hotel Italiano** is a pleasant, simple place a block from the train station at Viale Principe di Napoli 137, tel (0824) 24 923—hardly grand, now or ever, but it will do fine (L60–72 000 with bath, some less without). The ***Genova** down the street at No 103, tel (0824) 42 926, has rooms without bath for L27 000. Dining in Benevento can be interesting; it's another world from the Campania coast, with seafood replaced on the menu by rabbit, duck, lamb and veal. Samnium makes some good but little-known wines; you might ask for a bottle of stout-hearted *Solopaca* red with your Samnite repast. Benevento's favourite restaurant is probably the **Antica Taverna**, Via Annunziata 41, not far from the Museo Sannio, tel 21 212, where roast kid is one of the more unusual items on the menu (average about L30 000). Two good, traditional restaurants where you can dine for about L20 000 can be found in the back streets around Trajan's Arch: **D'Arienzo** on Via Mutarelli, and **Ristorante Palmieri** at the end of Via Manciotti. Some of the best food, however, and most of the Beneventani, can be found in the stand-up tavola calda on the corner of Corso Dante and Corso Vitt. Emanuele, a block west of the Cathedral—really fine pizza there.

The Mountains of Irpinia

Continuing this broad arc around Naples, south and west of Benevento there are few attractions, but some attractive mountain scenery in a region called **Irpinia**, consisting of most of the province of Avellino. In places, the mountains bear fine forests of oaks and chestnuts, as well as plantations of hazelnut trees; other parts are grim and bare, an introduction to the 19th-century deforestation that ruined so much of southern Italy. Irpinia was the region worst affected by the 1980 earthquake.

The main highway south from Caserta, around the back side of Vesuvius, isn't that much more promising. **Nola**, the biggest town on the route, began as another Oscan foundation. It had a famous early bishop, St Paulinus, a friend of St Augustine and also, it is claimed, the inventor of the bell (bells are *campanelli* in Italian, from their Campanian origin). To celebrate the anniversary of St Paulinus' return from imprisonment at the hands of the Vandals, every 22nd June the people of Nola put on one of the more spectacular festivals of the south, the 'Dance of the Lilies', a procession of 15 m wooden steeples, elaborately decorated and carried by the men of the town. Further south, in the hills above the city of **Nocera Inferiore**, an ancient hamlet called **Nocera Superiore** has somehow kept intact its 5th-century church, an unusual round building with a cupola that may have been converted from a pagan sanctuary.

The road into the mountains of Irpinia begins at Nola, leading towards **Avellino**. This little provincial capital, important in Norman times, has been wrecked so many times by invaders and earthquakes that little remains to be seen. In the centre, the 17th-century Palazzo della Dogana has a façade of ancient statues and a big clock tower; nearby stands a Baroque fountain with Bellerophon dispatching the Chimaera. Archaeological finds, ancient and medieval, from around Irpinia are kept in the modern Museo Irpino on Corso Europa.

Northwest of Avellino, **Montevergine** has been the most important pilgrimage site of this region since the arrival of a miraculous 'Black Madonna' in 1310—a Byzantine icon of the Virgin, stolen from Constantinople by the Crusaders in the sack of 1204; like the others across Europe, the oxidation of its yellow paint has turned it black over the centuries. Montevergine can be reached either by a long and tortuous road, or by a cable railway from the village of Mercogliano. The 12th-century church, built over a sanctuary of Ceres and many times reconstructed, has two fine tombs of the 1300s.

North of Avellino, separate roads lead to Taurasi, the centre of a wine region, and **Prata di Principato Ultra**, a tiny village with the one of the oldest Christian monuments in the south. The Basilica dell'Annunziata was probably begun in the 3rd century; there are fragments of paintings and two small catacombs. Eastern Irpinia is a wild and mountainous area where villages are few and far between. **Monte Terminio**, lately become a modest skiing area, has extensive woods and rushing mountain streams, along with plenty of pheasants, stags and boars, wild mushrooms and chestnuts—and a few truffles, perhaps the southernmost truffles found anywhere. **Sant'Angelo dei Lombardi**, further east, was an important medieval monastic centre; the earthquakes have spared bits of two simple churches (12th and 13th centuries).

Southern Campania: Paestum and the Cilento

After the Bay and the Amalfi Drive—two heavy courses for a holiday banquet—we can offer the Cilento peninsula as a light, refreshing dessert. The Cilento is a squarish low massif jutting out from the coast between the Gulf of Salerno and the Gulf of Policastro. Its mountain scenery may not be quite as breathtaking as the Amalfi drive, but the Cilento makes up for it by being delightfully wild and unspoilt, altogether one of the most beguiling out-of-the-way places to spend your time in southern Italy. The interior of the Cilento is not traversed by any easy roads, and the traveller heading south from Salerno will have a choice of two routes: a long, leisurely drive along the coast, past the remarkable ruins of ancient Paestum and a number of small, very casual resorts, or along the main road, the *Autostrada del Sole*, over the mountains and skirting the eastern edge of the Cilento, a route of often beautiful, wild scenery down the valley of the Tanagro River.

GETTING AROUND
Paestum has a station on the main rail line between Naples and Règgio Calabria, but only local trains stop there. More conveniently, there are frequent buses from the Piazza Concordia in Salerno (on the shore at the Porto Turistico). These are run by several companies; some follow the coast route, while others go through Battipaglia. Some of these continue on to various resort towns on the Cilento coast.

All the Cilento towns are connected by bus to Salerno's Piazza Concordia; there is a bewildering list of companies, towns and timetables, but fortunately the EPT in Salerno publishes a full list of them in the front of their annual hotel book. The rail line only touches the Cilento coast at two points—Ascea and Pisciotta—and, as at Paestum, not too many trains stop.

TOURIST INFORMATION
Salerno: EPT, at Via Velia 15, tel (089) 224 322; AAST in the central Piazza Amendola, tel 320 793, for the most complete information on transportation and lodging in Paestum and the Cilento.
Paestum: Via Nazionale, tel (0828) 843 056
Cava de' Tirreni: Corso Umberto 208, tel (089) 341 605.

Paestum: A Lost City

Along the coast, the route begins in a fertile plain that meets the Cilento near the ruins of **Paestum**, site of the only well-preserved Greek temples north of Sicily. And now that we are in the real Mediterranean, there is a new player on the stage who needs to be introduced. The anopheles mosquito, as fate would have it, gets the credit for preserving Paestum's ruins so well. By the 9th century or so, this once-great city was breathing its last, a victim of economic decline and Arab raiders. As its people gradually abandoned it for safer settlements in the hills, Paestum was swallowed up by the thick forests of this subtropical corner of Italy.

As usual on a Mediterranean coastal plain, when the people leave, the malaria mosquitoes take over. By the Middle Ages, the site of Paestum has become utterly uninhabitable—certain death to stay there overnight—and after a while the city's very existence was forgotten. After being hidden away, like the Mayan temples in the Mexican jungle, for almost a thousand years, the city was rediscovered in the 18th century; a crew of Charles III's road builders stumbled onto the huge temples in the midst of the forest.

Originally *Poseidonia*, the city was founded in the 6th century BC by the Sybarites, as a station on the all-important trade route up Italy's west coast. The Romans took over in

273 BC, and the name became Latinized to Paestum. As a steadfast supporter of the Roman cause throughout the Punic Wars, Paestum was a favoured city. Famous around the Mediterranean for its flowers, especially roses, it prospered until the end of the Roman era. Today the forests have been cleared, and the ruins of the city stand in the open on the green and quiet plain. Not only the celebrated temples have survived; much of the 4-km circuit of **walls** still stands to some height, along with some of the towers and gates.

Most of Paestum's important buildings were grouped along an axis between the Porta Aurea and the Porta Giustizia, with the forum at its centre. The two grand temples that everyone comes to see are at the southern end: the **Basilica** and the **Temple of Neptune**, two Doric edifices in the finest classical style. The names were just guesses on the part of the early archaeologists; both temples in fact were dedicated to Hera, the tutelary goddess of the city. The 'Neptune' temple, the best preserved, was built about 450 BC. It is about 60 m long and all of the structure survives except the roof and the internal walls. The second temple, the 'Basilica', is a century older and a little smaller.

The aesthetic may not be quite what you expected—dimensions squat and strong rather than graceful and tall. Still, this is the classic austerity of Greek architecture at its best. There is more to it than meets the eye. If you look closely along the rows of columns, or the lines of the base, you may notice that nothing in either of them is perfectly straight. The edges bulge outwards, as they do in the Parthenon and every other Greek building; this is an architectural trick called *entasis*; it creates an optical illusion, making the lines seem straight at a distance. Greek temples like this are the most sober and serious buildings in western architecture, based on a simple system of perfect proportion. The form may seem academic, but with some imagination you can picture them in their original beauty—covered in a sort of enamel made of gleaming ground marble, setting off the brilliant colours of the polychrome sculptural reliefs on the pediments and frieze.

To the west, some of the streets of the city have been excavated, though there is very little left to see. To the north, around the broad Forum—really a simple rectangular space in the manner of a Greek *agora*—are the remains of a theatre, a round *bouleterion*, or council house, and other buildings. Still further north is the third and smallest of the surviving temples, the **Temple of Ceres**. Paestum's **Museum** holds most of the sculptural fragments and finds from the town. Some of the best reliefs are not from Paestum at all, but from the recently discovered sanctuary of Hera , a few kilometres north at the mouth of the river Sele. This temple, mentioned by many ancient writers, is said to have been founded by Jason and the Argonauts during their wanderings. From tombs excavated just outside the city come some examples of Greek fresco painting—nothing special in themselves, but probably the only ones in existence. Even though the Greeks took painting as seriously as they did sculpture, you will not find any surviving examples in Greece, or anywhere else.

While you are exploring Paestum, keep an eye open for the wild flowers. More than one 19th-century traveller claimed to have found descendants of Paestum's famous roses growing wild, and some may still be around. (Paestum is open daily except Mon, 9–two hours before sunset; the museum closes at 2 pm; joint adm for both.)

WHERE TO STAY AND EATING OUT (tel prefix 0828)
Most people think of Paestum as a day trip, but there are enough hotels around, and on the nearby beaches, to make an overnight stay possible—and very convenient if you have a car. Some of the best accommodation is at Laura beach, about 5 km north of Paestum: the ***Le Palme, tel 851 025, is a modern place with plenty of facilities for sports and recreation as well as its own stretch of beach (L56–68 000). The *Laura, tel 851 068, is a good budget choice, also with a private beach (L40–48 000). Near the ruins, close to the Porta Giustizia entrance, the ***Martini, tel 811 020, is a set of small bungalows set in a wooded area close to the beaches; (L46–55 000). Two good and typical restaurants specializing in seafood are in the archaeological zone itself: the Nettuno, near Porta Giustizia, tel 811 028 and the Museo, tel 811 135, at the centre of the zone—both well worth the average price of L25–35 000.

The Cilento Coast

For many, one of the best attractions of Paestum will be the fine, long beaches that line this part of the coast. South of the ruins, the shore becomes jagged and mountainous, passing groves of pines alternating with rugged cliffs and pocket-sized beaches. Most of the villages along it have become quiet, cosy resorts that cater mostly to Italians. One is usually close to the next, and if you care to stay over, you can keep going until you find one that suits your fancy.

Agropoli comes first, then Santa Maria di Castellabate, San Marco, and Punta Licosa on the westernmost point of the Cilento. From here, you can take a small boat out to an uninhabited islet, also called Licosa, where there are some unidentified ancient ruins. Further down the coast, Acciaroli and Pioppi are among the nicer resort towns of the Cilento. South of the latter, and just inland from the village of Ascea Marina, you may visit the ruins of another Greek city, Velia.

Don't expect any spectacular ruins of the order of Paestum. Velia disappeared gradually, and most of its buildings were carried off for building stone long ago. *Elea*, as it was known back then, was a colony of the Ionian city of Phocaea, and a sister city of another important Phocaean foundation—Marseilles, in France. Elea was never large or important, but its name lives on gloriously in philosophy; the Elean school of philosophers produced some of the most brilliant minds of the ancient world: logical grinds like Parmenides, who proposed the first theory of atoms, and wiseacres like Zeno with his pesty paradoxes denying the possibility of motion. Some of the fortifications survive, including one well-preserved gate and a tower, and just enough of the *agora*, baths, and streets are left for you to guess how the city may have looked. A small theatre has been excavated, in the shadow of a medieval fortress built over the foundations of a temple.

Both Ascea Marina and its neighbouring locality of Casalvelino have pretty beaches, but the best ones of all, perhaps, can be found in the rugged terrain around Palinuro. This town, which has a small museum of archaeological finds, takes its name from Aeneas' pilot Palinurus, who is supposedly buried here—Virgil made the whole story up for the *Aeneid*, but that hasn't stopped it from sticking fast in local legend. Beyond Palinuro, the coast curves back north into the Gulf of Policastro; here two more pleasant beach villages, Scario and Sapri, mark the southern boundary of Campania. (To continue this route, see Maratea, p. 263.)

The Inland Route: Around the Cilento

South from Salerno, the Autostrada skirts the back edge of the Cilento on its way to Calabria. Christ may have stopped at **Eboli**, but there's no reason why you should—and that goes for **Battipaglia** and **Polla** too. In the swampy zone between Battipaglia and Paestum you may see some of Italy's last water buffaloes. Introduced from South Asia by the Byzantines in the 6th century, this supremely ugly but useful beast supplies a gallon and a half of milk a day. Most of it is turned into that Italian staple, *mozzarella* cheese; with the shortage of buffaloes, real mozzarella becomes increasingly hard to find. The true delights of this region are subterranean, two first-rate caves on opposite slopes of Monte Alburno. **Pertosa**, near the highway, is the easier and probably the better choice (open daily, except Mon, until 5:30; adm); the pot-holers (spelunkers) suspect it is connected to the other one, at **Castelcivita**, near the village of Controne.

At **Teggiano**, there is a 13th-century castle and cathedral, as well as a little museum. **Padula**, just off the highway, is the unlikely location of the **Certosa di San Lorenzo**; after San Martino in Naples it is probably the biggest and richest monastery of the south. The Certosa has been closed for over a century, but in its heyday it could hold hundreds of Carthusians in a complex laid out in the form of a gridiron (supposedly recalling the martyrdom of St Lawrence; the same plan was used in El Escorial in Spain, also dedicated to the saint). Though it was continuously expanded and rebuilt over 400 years, the best parts are Baroque: an enormous, elegant cloister, some wonderfully garish frescoes and stucco figures in and around the chapel, and eccentric but well-executed decorative details throughout. A small archaeological museum is part of the complex.

WHERE TO STAY AND EATING OUT (tel prefix 0974)

Hotels on the Cilento are on the whole modern and unremarkable, modest resorts in the L30–70 000 range, though there are less expensive places almost everywhere along the coast. Most of the restaurants are in the hotels, and in the summer, chances are you'll be stuck on full board in the fancier places. In Castellabate, at San Marco, there is one special resort hotel, the attractive *******Castelsandra**, tel 966 021, with a pretty setting, pool and tennis, a fine restaurant and TV in many rooms to help your insomnia (L120–240 000, depending on the season). A less expensive choice is the ******L'Approdo**, also at San Marco, tel 966 001 (L60–75 000). Even less expensive spots are found mostly in the Santa Maria and Ogliastro areas—***Da Carmine** at the Ogliastro Marina, tel 963 023, has pleasant doubles with bath for L24–40 000. Acciaroli's hotels are similarly modest, and good bargains too; the best is *****Il Faro**, tel 904 030 (L45–55 000). Ascea has a small collection of hotels around its marina, but Palinuro and Camerota have developed into fully-fledged holiday towns. In Palinuro, try the *****Gabbiano** with pool and private beach, tel 931 155 (L48–60 000). ***Il Pinguino**, tel 932 115 in Marina di Camerota, is typical of the no fuss no frills accommodation in the region (L34 000 with bath). But Camerota also has a first-class restaurant: **Da Valentore**, Via Nazionale 48, tel 936 014, with freshly caught seafood, and first courses including such local specialities as *fusilli* and spaghetti with anchovies (L30 000 and up).

Part VI

CALABRIA AND THE BASILICATA

La Cattolica at Stilo

Italy may be a country unusually blessed, but by no means are her favours spread out evenly. To balance regions like Campania, with its manifold delights, nature has given Italy its own empty quarter, the adjacent regions of Calabria and the Basilicata.

Calabria is the toe of the Italian boot, a gnarled, knobby toe, amply endowed with corns and bunions and pointed accusingly at innocent Sicily. Almost all of it is ruggedly mountainous, leaving just enough room at the edges for the longest, broadest, emptiest beaches in Italy. It can claim two natural attractions: a scenic western coast, and the beautifully forested highlands region called the Sila, just east of Cosenza. The Basilicata, still better known to many people under its old name of *Lucania*, takes on all comers for the title of Italy's most obscure region.

Anyone coming to Italy for the first time, and wishing to see the best the country has to offer, would not come here. The more experienced traveller, a little jaded with the rest of Italy, may come hoping to find something new and different in these little-known spaces, but great expectations will likely go unrewarded.

Magna Graecia
It was not always this way. Starting about 750 BC, the Greeks began to colonize Southern Italy. *Rhegium*, today's Règgio Calabria, came first, followed in short order by Sybaris, Croton, and Locri among others. These towns, happily situated along the major trade route of the Mediterranean, rapidly became as cultured as those of Greece itself—and far wealthier. It was a brilliant hour, and a brief one. At first, blessed with a lack of

external enemies, the cities of 'greater Greece' took to fighting among themselves, in a series of ghastly, cruel wars over the most trivial of causes, often resulting in the total destruction of a city and the massacre of its inhabitants. Utterly weakened by their own barbarous behaviour, the Greek cities became pawns between Rome and Hannibal in the Punic Wars; the victorious Romans took a terrible vengeance on those such as Taras (Tàranto, in modern Apulia) that supported the wrong side. Roman rule meant a slow decline for the survivors, and by the 6th century, the beautiful cities of Magna Graecia were abandoned to the mosquitoes.

Don't come to Calabria looking for classical ruins. The great museum at Règgio gives a hint of what these cities were, but at the sites themselves almost nothing remains. Golden Sybaris has only just been found by the archaeologists, and only at Metapontum will you see so much as a few standing columns. Some may call the emptiness a monument to Greek *hubris*; perhaps somehow these cities were doomed from the start. Considering Magna Graecia can be profoundly disconcerting; even in the ancient Mediterranean it is strange and rare for so many big cities to disappear so completely.

Nor has this corner of Italy been any more hospitable to civilization in the centuries since. Calabria in particular has suffered more at the hands of history than any region deserves. After the Romans and the malaria mosquito put an end to the brilliant, short-lived civilization of Magna Graecia, Calabria has endured one wrenching earthquake after another, not to mention Arab raiders and Norman bully-boys, Spaniards and Bourbons, the most vicious of feudal landlords and the most backward and ignorant of monks and priests. By the 18th century, these had combined to effect one of the most complete social breakdowns ever seen in modern Europe. Calabria staggered into anarchy, its mountains given over to bands of cut-throats while the country people endured almost subhuman poverty and oppression. Not surprisingly, everyone who was able chose to emigrate; today there are several times as many Calabrese living in the Americas as in Calabria itself.

A New Land

While famine, disease and misgovernment were putting an end to old Calabria, natural disasters like the terrible earthquake of 1783, and the even worse one in 1908 that destroyed the city of Règgio, were erasing the last traces of it. Calabria's stage was cleared for a modest rebirth, and the opportunity for it came after World War II, when Mr Rockefeller's DDT made the coasts habitable for the first time in over a millennium. Within a few years, a government land reform improved the lives of thousands in both regions, and the *Cassa per il Mezzogiorno*'s roads and industrial projects helped pull their economies into the 20th century.

Today, despite the many problems that remain, you can witness the beginnings of an entirely new Calabria. A thousand years or more ago, the Calabrians deserted their once-great port cities for wretched, though defensible villages in the mountains. Now they are finally moving back, and everywhere around Calabria's long and fertile coasts you will see new towns and cities; some, like Locri or Metaponto, are built near the ruins of the Greek cities that are their direct ancestors. Most of this new Calabria isn't much to look at just yet; the bigger towns, in fact, can be determinedly ugly (like Crotone). Calabria these days, for all its history, has an unmistakable frontier air about it. The people are simple, straightforward, and a little rough. Unlike other Italians, they seem to

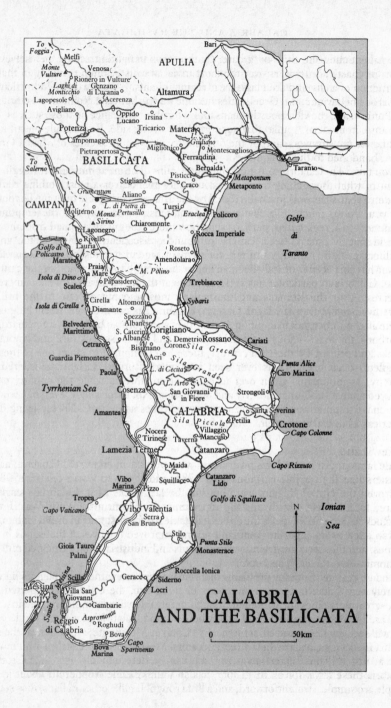

To Foggia
Melfi
Monte Vulture
Venosa
Rionero in Vulture
Laghi di Monticchio
Genzano di Lucania
Acerenza
Lagopesole
Avigliano
Potenza
Campomaggiore
Pietrapertosa
BASILICATA
To Salerno
CAMPANIA
Grumentum
Aliano
Stigliano
L. di Pietra di Pertusillo
Moliterno
Monte Sirino
Lagonegro
Rivello
Lauria
Golfo di Policastro
Maratea
Praia a Mare
Isola di Dino
Scalea
Isola di Cirella
Cirella
Diamante
Belvedere Marittimo
Cetraro
Guardia Piemontese
Paola
Tyrrhenian Sea
Cosenza
Amantea
Nocera Tirinese
Lamezia Terme
Maida
Vibo Marina
Pizzo
Tropea
Capo Vaticano
Vibo Valentia
Serra San Bruno
Stilo
Gioia Tauro
Palmi
Scilla
Messina
Villa San Giovanni
SICILY
Straits of Messina
Gambarie
Aspromonte
Reggio di Calabria
Roghudi
Bova
Bova Marina
Capo Spartivento

Bari
APULIA
Altamura
Oppido Lucano
Irsina
Tricarico
Matera
Miglionico
L. San Giuliano
Montescaglioso
Ferrandina
Bernalda
Pistico
Craco
Metapontum
Metaponto
Taranto
Tursi
Eraclea
Policoro
Rocca Imperiale
Roseto
Amendolara
M. Polino
Trebisacce
Sybaris
Altomonte
Spezzano Albanese
S. Caterina Albanese
Bisignano
Corigliano
S. Demetrio Corone
Rossano
Cariati
Sila Greca
Acri
L. di Cecita
Sila Grande
L. Arvo
San Giovanni in Fiore
Strongoli
Punta Alice
Ciro Marina
CALABRIA
Sila Piccola
Villaggio Mancuso
Taverna
Santa Severina
Petilia
Catanzaro
Crotone
Capo Colonne
Catanzaro Lido
Capo Rizzuto
Squillace
Golfo di Squillace
Punta Stilo
Monasterace
Roccella Ionica
Gerace
Siderno
Locri

Golfo di Taranto

Ionian Sea

N

CALABRIA
AND THE BASILICATA

0   50km

have lots of children; they work hard, fix their own cars and tractors, and lay cement everywhere. So far, the changes have amounted to such a humble revolution that few people have even noticed. But both these regions are, if anything, a land of survivors, and who is to say they aren't now taking their first baby steps on the road to reclaiming their ancient prosperity and distinction?

Calabrian Itineraries

If you're passing through on your way to Sicily, take the old coastal road south through Maratea and Paola; it branches off the Autostrada del Sole at Lagonegro-Nord, near Maratea, and it is much more scenic a route than the Autostrada, and though it takes a little longer it is a good smooth road, and actually shorter. Take as long as you like: Maratea, Praia a Mare, Vibo Valentia, or Gioia Tauro make good stopovers along the way. One possible detour is from Cosenza into the Sila—no little journey, some 89 km from the turn-off at Paola to San Giovanni in Fiore in the heart of the Sila. Another, shorter digression would be from Vibo Valentia, around the peninsula to Tropea and Cape Vaticano. This adds an extra 45 km to the trip, through some difficult corniche roads, but it includes some of the south's best coastal scenery. Before you make the crossing over to Messina, take an hour or two for the Museum in Règgio; even if you have no particular interest in archaeology, the collection contains some of the most beautiful art you'll see in southern Italy.

The West Coast: from Maratea to Règgio Calabria

GETTING AROUND

Two major railroad lines pass through these regions: the Rome–Naples–Règgio Calabria route along the west coast, and its branch from Battaglia in Campania through Potenza and Metaponto on its way to Tàranto. A third line follows the long shore of the Ionian Sea from Règgio to Tàranto. Connections to anywhere in the interior are chancy at best: a few trains go through to Cosenza, but you'll probably have to change at Paola or Sibari. There are also regular buses from Paola to Cosenza. At Catanzaro it is the same; most trains stop only at Catanzaro Lido, 9 km away (there is a regular city bus to the city centre). Règgio has two railway stations: the Stazione Marittima, from which crossings are made to Messina in Sicily, and the Stazione Centrale; if you're just making a quick stop to see the museum, the Marittima is closer.

In Cosenza, buses leave from Piazza L. Fera at the northern end of Corso Mazzini for Catanzaro (several daily) and points around the province including towns in the Sila. A pleasant way to see the Sila itself is the old FCL narrow-gauge railway that runs between Camigliatello and San Giovanni in Fiore.

TOURIST INFORMATION

Maratea: Piazza del Gesù 40, tel (0973) 876 908
Castrovillari: Via Calabria 45, tel (0981) 27 067
Vibo Valentia: Piazza Diaz 8, tel (0933) 42 008
Cosenza: Via P. Rossi, tel (0984) 30 595; also Via Tagliamento 15, tel 27 821
Villa S. Giovanni: Piazza Stazione, tel (0965) 751 160

Règgio Calabria: Via D. Tripepi 72, tel (0965) 98 496; also offices at the Stazione Centrale and the airport, tel 643 291

Just south of Campania's Cilento Peninsula, a little corner of the Basilicata stretches out to touch the Tyrrhenian Sea. The scenery here differs little from the dramatic coastline of the Cilento. After Sapri, in Campania, the coastal route 18 becomes a lovely corniche road, passing over cliffs covered with scrubby *macchia*, and soft grey beaches on hidden coves—not so hidden any more, since a few hotels have been springing up on the best of them, such as **Acquafredda**, just over the border. The centre of the Basilicata's coast is **Maratea**, a pretty old town of tiny alleys and steps. Maratea has some hazy ambition to become a big resort; until its ship comes in, however, the atmosphere is decidedly laid-back; besides some of the best coastal scenery in the deep south, you can enjoy relatively uncrowded beaches and modest hotels at Acquafredda, Fiumicello (the closest to Maratea) and Maratea Marina, among other places.

Maratea itself is up in the hills a little, under what must be the queerest hilltop Jesus in Italy; all marble and 20 m tall; from a distance it appears to be a perfume bottle with wings. There is little reason to leave the coast at this point. Some of the twistiest roads in the Basilicata will take you up to the A3 Autostrada, or to the sleepy medieval villages of **Lagronegro**, with its Baroque churches, and **Lauria**. The most interesting of them is **Rivello**, a charming, isolated hilltop village with some distinguished buildings and townscapes; well worth exploring, though on its steep alleys you'll be doing more climbing than walking.

Some 10 km further down the coast and you're in Calabria, on the outskirts of another, similar resort on a similarly lovely stretch of coast: **Praia a Mare**, where there is a 14th-century castle; from the beach you can rent a boat to visit the 'blue grotto' on the **Isola di Dino**, an uninhabited islet just off the shore. Further down, **Scalea** is a small beach resort under a pretty old village of narrow alleys, with a good early Renaissance tomb in its church of San Nicola and bits of Byzantine frescoes in another, the Spedale.

Alleys in city centre, Maratea

Up in the hills above Scalea is an area called the *Mercurion*, once a centre of Greek monasticism; only the ruins of a church remain. Further into the mountains, near **Papasidero**, is a cave decorated with Paleolithic bulls; all of Calabria seems to have been a busy place in the stone age, but this is the best of the art yet discovered.

Cirella and Diamante are the next two quiet towns along the coast. From Cirella, you may take a boat trip over to another coastal islet, the Isola di Cirella, or climb up to visit the overgrown remains of **Cirella Vecchia**, a village founded by the Greeks that survived until a battle and French bombardment in the Napoleonic wars; there are bits of a Greek mausoleum, and streets of half-ruined homes and churches. **Guardia Piemontese**, a small thermal spa on a balcony over the coast, is still partially inhabited by Waldenses, religious dissenters from 13th-century Piedmont and Liguria; Frederick II granted them refuge here from Church pogroms, but most of their descendants were massacred by the Spaniards in 1561. **Paola**, where the road from Cosenza meets the coast, is a large and somewhat dishevelled resort, a fitting introduction to the towns of the 'Calabrian Riviera' to the south.

Cosenza

So far, there hasn't been much reason to leave the coast. **Cosenza** may not be a stellar attraction, but it's the best Calabria can do. It has been one of Calabria's leading cities through most of recorded history; it began as the chief town of the Bruttians, the aboriginal nation from whom today's Calabrians are descended. Medieval Cosenza was a busy place: the Arabs took it twice, Norman freebooters fought over it, and at least one king of France passed through on his way to the Crusades.

The river Busento divides Cosenza neatly, between the flat modern town and the old citadel on the hill. The river is famous, if only because buried somewhere beneath it is no less a personage than Alaric the Goth. Alaric—no drooling barbarian, but just another scheming Roman general with a Teutonic accent—came to Cosenza in 410, fresh from his sacking of Rome and on his way to conquer Africa. He died of a fever here, and his men temporarily diverted the Busento and buried him under it, probably along with a fair share of the Roman loot. Archaeologists are still looking for it.

Cosenza gained some unexpected notoriety in the 16th century, as one of Counter-Reformation Italy's last bastions of tolerance and free thought, under the influence of the Waldenses and of an important humanist philosopher named Bernardino Telesio (1509–88), one of the first theorists of science. One of his students, a radical monk named Tommaso Campanella, turned into a fully-fledged utopian mystic, writing a splendidly crazy book called *The City of the Sun*, and leading an astrologically ordained revolt against the Spanish in 1599. He helped defend Galileo in his Inquisition trial—by letter, since he himself was in their gaols for 27 years.

For all its history, Cosenza has little left to show; even in Calabria, no place is more prone to earthquakes—four big ones in the last 200 years, with some help from the Allied air forces in 1943. The **cathedral** has survived, a simple Gothic structure built in 1222, during the reign of Frederick II. You'll have to make a special request to see the Cathedral Treasure—but here, for once, it's worth it. The real treasure is a little-known masterpiece of medieval art, a Byzantine-style gold and enamel crucifix, made in Sicily in the 12th century and given by Frederick himself on the occasion of the cathedral's founding. A few blocks south of the cathedral on Piazza XV Marzo, there is a small **Museo Civico**, with paintings and archaeological finds (daily, except Sun, 9–1 pm; adm), and from there you can climb to the well-preserved **castle** overlooking the city; most of that was built by Frederick too.

North of Cosenza, the valley of the Crati flows towards the Ionian sea; with it runs the A3 motorway, the route most people take travelling through Calabria. If you are passing this way, there are a few chances for detours. A stretch of Albanian villages occupies the hills west of the highway, all connected by a tortuous mountain road, from San Benedetto Ullano north to Santa Caterina Albanese. Further north are the roads that give easiest access to the Sila Greca (see below), and beyond them **Spezzano Albanese**, a small spa, and to the west of it, **Altomonte**. This unpromising little village, remote even by Calabrian standards before the building of the motorway, has one of the most unusual churches in the south; **Santa Maria della Consolazione** is genuine 14th-century Gothic, with a big rose window. Most likely it is the work of architects from Siena. Inside, contemporary works of art include a painting by the Tuscan master Simone Martini, and the fine *tomb of Duke Filippo Sangineto*, by a follower of Tino di Camaino. Sangineto was a local boy who made good fighting for Charles of Anjou. Besides being a duke down here, Sangineto also became Seneschal of Provence; his descendants, travelling in a cultural sphere a bit wider than most Calabrians, financed this church.

Further north, near the border with the Basilicata, **Castrovillari** has an Aragonese castle, a small archaeological museum, and the church of Santa Maria del Castello, interesting for the odd bits of art from many centuries inside (there is a small museum in the sacristy), and for the view over the mountains. From Castrovillari, you have the choice of either retreating eastwards to the seacoast, near Sybaris (see below), or west with the motorway for Naples. You can't go any further north, for in your way stands **Monte Pollino**, a huge patch of mountains, largely forested, that is one of the most unspoiled natural areas of the south—the difficult terrain and lack of roads see to that.

The Sila

Cosenza is the best base from which to see this region, a lovely, peaceful plateau between the mountains that offers an unusual experience of alpine scenery near the southern tip of Italy. Much of the Sila is still covered with trees—beeches, oaks and pines. In summer you can find wild strawberries, and in winter, well, maybe wolves. Some of Italy's last specimens make their stand in the Sila's wilder corners. Artificial lakes, built since the War as part of Calabria's hydroelectric schemes, add to the scenery, notably **Lake Arvo** and **Lake Cecita**, between Cosenza and the town of San Giovanni in Fiore. The Sila is the best place in Calabria for motoring, hiking or canoeing—from Cosenza you can float down the river Crati all the way to the Ionian Sea. Most likely you will see only the largest and prettiest section, the **Sila Grande** in the middle, though more adventurous souls can press on to the barely accessible **Sila Greca** to the north, or south to the **Sila Piccola**, Despite the name , the Sila Greca is inhabited not by Greeks, but Albanians of the Greek Orthodox faith—the Calabrians couldn't tell them from the real Greeks. These came to Calabria and Sicily as refugees from the Turks in the 1500s, and today constitute Italy's biggest ethnic minority. Albanians can be found all over Calabria, especially here and in the north around Castrovillari; you'll know you've stumbled on one of their villages if you see a Byzantine-domed church or a statue of Scanderbeg, the Albanian national hero.

East from Cosenza, route 846 heads into the centre of the Sila Grande, passing within a few kilometres of the region's biggest lakes: Lago di Cecita to the north, Lago di Arvo to the south. Both are more attractive than the average artificial lake, especially Arvo, and both are stocked with fish. **San Giovanni in Fiore**, the biggest village of the Sila, owes its founding and its fame to another celebrated Calabrian mystic, the 12th-century monk and devotional writer Joachim of Fiore. Emperor Henry IV granted the privileges of Joachim's new abbey in 1195, and throughout the Middle Ages it was one of the most important communities in the south.

The austere abbey complex has been restored, and now contains a deadly serious endeavour with the bizarre title of **Demographic Museum of the Economy, Labour and Social History of the Sila** (not yet complete, but open daily, July–Sept, 9–1, 3–7). Much of that economy and labour in this town has to do with handmade carpets and fabrics, still the speciality of the town. On the eastern edge of the Sila, the forests give way in many places to *calanchi*, strange rock formations caused by erosion and defor-estation. **Santa Severina**, population now about 2500, used to be a much more important place. You can walk through what used to be the old Greek quarter and Jewish quarter, both partially abandoned. There is a Norman castle, and two cathedrals (11th and 13th centuries); the original has been swallowed up into a Baroque church, while the later one has a unique circular baptistry, built by the Byzantines in the 800s. Another Byzantine survival is the charming 11th-century church of Santa Filomena, with a dainty cupola on sixteen little columns.

The Sila Piccola, to the south, is even wilder and more remote. **Villaggio Mancuso**, one of the few villages, is lately becoming a mountain resort; around it are some of the thickest and most extensive forests in the south. On the southern edge of the Sila, on the road for Catanzaro, **Taverna** was the birthplace of the only noteworthy artist ever to come out of Calabria, Mattia Preti. The best work of this 17th-century follower of Caravaggio can be seen in Naples and on Malta, but he left a number of paintings here; recently a large number of these works have been restored, and hung in the churches of San Domenico and Santa Barbara.

The Sila Greca

This northernmost section of the Sila consists of a number of parallel valleys, sloping down to the Ionian sea. Coming from Cosenza, the first towns you'll encounter are **Bisignano**, famous in bygone times for the manufacture of musical instruments (you can still order a handmade lute here), and **Acri**. **San Demetrio Corone**, north of Acri is the cultural centre for Calabria's Albanians, with an **Albanian College** founded in 1791. The church of **Sant'Adriano** had its beginnings in the 10th century, when the territory was still occupied by Byzantine Greeks, but most of the present structure is 11th- or 12th-century Romanesque—including the outlandish carvings and mosaics, with every sort of snake, dragon, bird and monster. The other important Albanian villages are all nearby, strung along the twisting mountain road to the east: Mácchia, San Cosmo, Vaccarizzo and San Giorgio.

The Calabrian Riviera

Back on the coast, south of Cosenza the road passes **Amantea**, a typical modern resort of concrete and good intentions, under an ancient village with a 15th-century church. Beyond it yawns a dull stretch through the Plain of Sant'Eufemia, one of the new agricultural areas reclaimed from the mosquito. The town of **Maida**, site of one of the first French defeats during the Napoleonic Wars, gave its name to London's Maida Vale. **Pizzo**, the largest town in the region, also has its Napoleonic association; the great French general Murat, whom Bonaparte made King of Naples, tried after Waterloo to begin a new revolution in Calabria. When his boat landed here, instead of the welcome he expected the crowd almost tore him to pieces. The Bourbons executed him a few days later.

The best part of Calabria's coast begins near Cape Vaticano. **Vibo Valentia**, the largest town in the district, has views overlooking the coast, a 12th-century castle, remains of its ancient Greek fortifications, and a number of overwrought Baroque churches. From here the main road cuts inland, but the railway and some back roads head around Cape Vaticano; this is a district of fine beaches and difficult mountains. **Tropea** is a lovely town on the coast; next to it, on a rocky peninsula that was once an island, you can climb up to the romantically ruined Benedictine monastery of **Santa Maria dell'Isola**. Around the cape itself, the road rises to some spectacular views, taking in on a clear day the volcano island of Stromboli and Sicily's northern coast.

Further south, the towns along the coast are more accessible, and some of them have grown into fair-sized holiday spots, such as **Gioia Tauro** and **Palmi**; the former is also a grim industrial town that squeezes out most of Calabria's olive oil. Palmi has a large collection on Calabrian folklore and traditional life in its Museo Civico.

Scilla, at the entrance to the Straits of Messina, is a fishing town that owes its fortunes to the Straits' greatest delight, the swordfish. Swordfish may be tasty but they are nobody's fools. To nab them, the Calabrians have invented one of the most peculiar styles of fishing boats you'll ever see. These small craft have metal towers, up to a hundred feet tall, precariously swaying above them, secured by wires. These are for the lookout; another metal contraption, equally as long, projects from the prow for the spearman.

Scilla marks the spot where the mythological Scylla, a daughter of Hecate who was changed by the gods into a dog-like sea monster, seized some of Odysseus' crewmen near the end of the *Odyssey*. In classical times, Scylla meant the dangerous rocks of the Calabrian side of the straits, a counterpart to the whirlpool Charybdis towards the Sicilian shore. So many earthquakes have rearranged the topography since that nothing remains of either. Still, the narrow straits are one of the most dramatic sights in Italy, with Messina and the Monti Peloritani visible over in Sicily, neatly balancing Règgio and the jumbled peaks of Aspromonte in Calabria.

Règgio di Calabria

The last big earthquake came in 1908, and over 100,000 people died here and in Messina across the straits. Both these cities have a remarkable will to survive, considering all the havoc earthquakes have played on them in the last 2000 years. Perhaps the setting is irresistible. Fortune has favoured them unequally in the rebuilding; though both are about the same size, Messina has made of itself a slick, almost beautiful town, while Règgio has chosen to remain swaddled in Calabrian humility. Its plain grid of dusty streets and low buildings, where anyone from a small town in Kansas might feel perfectly at home, was laid out only after the earthquake of 1783, when the destruction was even greater than in 1908 and the city had to be rebuilt from scratch. Before the earthquakes, travellers described Règgio as one of the most beautiful cities of Italy. No one has voiced any such opinions lately.

The Allies did a pretty thorough job of bombing Règgio in the last War; after all that, not surprisingly there is little left to see of the city that began its life as Greek *Rhegium* in the 8th century BC. Some bits of Greek wall and Roman baths along the waterfront promenade are almost the only things in the city older than 1908. Règgio does have one special attraction—its **Museo Nazionale della Magna Graecia** is the finest collection of Greek art between Naples and Sicily.

The Warriors of Riace

The museum, a dozen blocks north of the city centre on Corso Garibaldi, is a classic of Mussolini architecture built in chunky travertine. Even if there were nothing else—and on the contrary this is a hoard almost as precious as anything in Greece itself—the museum would make a trip to Règgio worth while just for the **Warriors of Riace**, two bronze masterpieces that rank among the greatest productions of antiquity to come down to us. If you haven't heard of them, it is because they were only found in 1972, by divers exploring an ancient shipwreck off Riace on Calabria's Ionic coast. They keep them down in the basement, in a room of their own next to a big exhibition detailing the tremendously complex—and excellently done—restoration job. These fellows, both about 6¹/₂ ft and quite indecently virile, may perhaps have come from a temple at Delphi; no one really knows why they were being shipped to Magna Graecia. One of them has been attributed to the great sculptor Phidias.

The Warriors share the basement with a few other rare works of Greek sculpture, notably the unknown subject called the *Philosopher*, as well as anchors and ship fittings, and amphorae that once held wine or oil—all recovered from the shipwreck, in mud well over a metre deep. The divers are convinced that the dangerous waters around Calabria may hold dozens of such treasures; don't be surprised if something new has found its way to the Règgio museum by the time you arrive. And don't neglect the rest of the museum collections. The most beautiful things in it are the terracotta **ex-voto plaques**, re-covered from the temples of Magna Graecia. Most of these offerings show goddesses in the magical Archaic style—usually Persephone, who has influence with Death because she was abducted by Hades—receiving propitiatory gifts, or accepting souls into the underworld. Chickens are a recurring motif, not too surprisingly, since to the ancient Greeks a soul rises out of its burial urn the same way a chicken hatches from an egg. Other works help complete the picture of life and art in Magna Graecia: Greek painted ceramics from Locri and from Attica, bits of architectural decoration from various temples, some still with bits of their original paint, records of city finances on bronze tablets, and a rare early Hellenistic mosaic of a dragon, made in Calabria (open daily, except Mon, 9–1:30, 3:30–7 pm; Sun 9–12:30; adm).

Around Aspromonte

All around the toe of Italy, from Palmi as far as Locri, the interior of the peninsula seems utterly impenetrable, a wall of rough peaks tantalizingly close to the narrow coastal plain. In fact all of the toe is one great round massif, the mountain called **Aspromonte**. Here, the tortuous mountain roads allow few opportunities for climbing inland, but from the north end of Règgio a 30-kilometre route will take you up to **Gambàrie**, with forests of pine, oak and chestnut, and views over the straits and Sicily. In winter Gambàrie is Calabria's only ski resort, with just enough snow to get by in an average year. Aspromonte, with its 22 summits and Greek-speaking villages, was the haunt of the chivalrous 19th-century bandit Musolino, a sort of Calabrian Robin Hood still well remembered in these parts.

Like the Albanians, Greeks are a Calabrian cultural minority. Scholars who have studied their language speculate that they are descendants of the original Greek population of Magna Graecia, holding on to their cultural identity this long thanks only to the barely accessible locations of their mountain villages. Going to look for them may prove a disappointment. Like most of the villages of the Aspromonte, the Greek ones are in various stages of abandonment. After generations of emigration—first to the Americas, now merely down to the coasts—only a few old folks are left behind. All the Greek villages require detours of at least 14 km from the coast: Roghudi and Roccaforte from Mélito di Porto Salvo; Condofuri from Condofuri Marina, and **Bova**, the largest, and once seat of a Greek archbishop, from Bova Marina.

On the coastal plain, snow is hardly ever seen. This is one of Italy's gardens, a panorama of lemon and orange groves; two more exotic crops have given some fame to the region: jasmine, which grows so well nowhere else in Italy, and bergamot, which refuses to grow anywhere else at all (outside of its native Antilles, that is). The bergamot is a small, hard, green orange, discovered and first cultivated only some 200 years ago. Now it is an indispensable ingredient in the making of the finest perfumes, and a surprisingly important source of income in this area. It's also the stuff used to flavour Earl Grey tea. If it is a clear day, the straits south of Règgio can treat you to the most unforgettable views in the south; much of the Sicilian coast is visible, and perhaps even Mount Etna will peek out from behind its usual entourage of clouds.

If you are especially lucky, you may be treated to an appearance of the famous *Fata Morgana*, the mirages of islands or many-towered cities that often appear over the straits. The name comes from the enchantress Morgan le Fay. Arthurian romance came to southern Italy with the Normans, and rooted itself deeply in these parts; old Sicilian legends have a lot to say about King Arthur. In one of the tales, Arthur sleeps and awaits his return not up in chilly England, but deep in the smoky bowels of Etna. Roger de Hauteville himself, a close relation of William the Conqueror, is said to have seen the Fata Morgana, and his learned men interpreted the vision as a divine invitation to invade Sicily. Roger demurred, thinking it would be better to wait and take Sicily on his own than do it with the aid of sorcery. Dawn is the best time to see the mirage; it often takes the form of the city of Messina, either distorted or turned upside-down.

Messina

If you are tempted to cross over, ferries leaave regularly from the railroad's *Stazione Marittima* in Règgio; the trip takes a little under an hour. Messina is an attractive modern city full of fountains, twice Règgio's size. The earthquakes did much more damage here (84,000 died in 1908), but the rebuilding was done much more gracefully. Still, there is little of art and monuments to trouble you; just make sure you're in Piazza del Duomo at exactly noon, to see the daily eruption of the great **astronomical clock**, built in Strasbourg in 1933 and set in the campanile of the 12th-century Norman cathedral. All the bells ring while a huge golden lion waves a banner and roars, a golden cock crows, Jesus resurrects himself, the four ages of man pass by in procession, and golden dignitaries in procession salute the Virgin Mary. After the dust settles, you can examine the various dials to check the location of the moon and planets.

From Messina, it's not far down the coast to **Taormina**, the famous resort with its Greek theatre. Excursions up to the summit of **Mt. Etna** begin from the big and exasperating city of **Catania**. To tackle a smaller volcano, take the coast west from Messina to Milazzo, ferry port for the exquisite **Aeolian Islands**. One of these is Stromboli, an easy climb to a crater that pops off mildly every eight minutes. Sicily is a continent unto itself, and we have covered it in the *Cadogan Guide to the Italian Islands*.

WHERE TO STAY

Nowhere in Calabria will you see a hotel older than the 1950s—a comment both on how much the region has changed since the War, and how little it has ever had to do with tourism. After the War, there were thoughts of a tourist boom—Calabria as the new Riviera—but problems with government bureaucracy and a lack of good sites for hotels has kept this from happening. Still, you will find acceptable hotels almost everywhere, whether you are just passing through or planning a week on the beach.

Maratea has become a mature enough resort to have some excellent accommodation. The *****Santavenere**, 1¹/₂ km north of Maratea's port at Fiumicello-Santa Venere, is a modern building, though furnished with unusual elegance; it has a fine setting on cliffs above the sea, a pool and tennis, and all the rooms are air-conditioned (tel (0973) 876 910; L130–175 000). Less expensive choices are many; some of the best are a little up the coast at Acquafredda: the ****Villa del Mare**, up on the cliffs with a lift down to the private beach (L52–75 000; tel (0973) 878 007, on the SS18 coastal highway).

Praia a Mare is a lovely spot, but the beach hotels are generally simple places; the **Astor**, Piazza Italia 5, tel (0981) 72 041, is one of the better ones, a small and personal establishment with private beach (L50–70 000). The same could be said about Scalea, though here the prices tend to be a little higher. The best part of the beach is occupied by the ****De Rose**, Viale Mediterraneo, a typical modern resort with air conditioning and TV (both considerations around these parts, where it's always hot and there's little to do; tel (0985) 20 273; L78–120 000). You can get many of the same amenities at ***Talao**, on Corso Mediterraneo 66, near the beaches; tel (0985) 20 444; L75–100 000). In Cetraro, you'll find an exception to the no pre-1950s rule—a pretty old villa, converted into a hotel to provide a rare island of elegance in homespun Calabria—the ****Grand Hotel San Michele**, Contrada Bosco 8–9, is in a location called Bosco—no lie, since there are plenty of trees around for shade, as well as a golf course, a beach, and a good restaurant that turns simple local specialities into gourmet treats. The house wine is made in the hotel's own vineyards (tel (0982) 91 013; L130–180 000).

If you are staying over in Cosenza, there is one really well-run and comfortable place, even though it only rates two stars, the **Alexander, Via Monte San Michele 3, tel (0984) 24 982 (L68 000 with bath, L50 000 without). If you want to see the Sila, San Giovanni in Fiore will make the best base; ***Dino's, Viale Repubblica 166, is a comfortable enough overnighter just outside the town at Pirainella (tel (0984) 992 090; L62 000 with bath, L48 000 without). Elsewhere around the Sila, there is very modest accommodation at Lorica, Bocchigliero, Longobucco, and Taverna-Villaggio Mancuso in the Sila Piccola. On Cape Vaticano, the best places are around Tropea and Parghelia, 3 km to the north. Here, on one of the prettiest parts of the coast, is ****Baia Paraelios, Località Fornaci, a group of well-furnished cottages set on a terraced hill overlooking a beautiful beach (reserve in advance for this one; tel (0963) 600 300 or 600 004; L160 000).

The most intense stretch of the 'Calabrian Riviera' begins as you round Capo Vaticano, through resort areas such as Ricadi, Nicotera, Gioia Tauro and Palmi as far as Règgio—nothing special here, but very simple family resorts. In Règgio itself, most of the hotels are uptown, clustered around the archaeological museum. The poshest is the modern ****Excelsior, on Via Vittorio Veneto 66, tel (0965) 25 801 (L130–180 000, all air-conditioned) but you can get by just as well at the unpretentious ***Lido, just around the corner at Via III Settembre 6, tel 25 001 (L76 000), or at the **Diana, at Via Vitrioli 12, tel 91 522 (L46 000).

EATING OUT

In ancient Sybaris, the gourmet centre of the Greek Mediterranean, and in the other towns of Magna Graecia, public gastronomical revues rivalled the athletic contests in popularity; good recipes for fish sauces were treated as state secrets, and slaves who happened to be good cooks were worth enormous sums in the open market. Forget all that—Calabrian cooking today is not at all distinctive, except perhaps in a certain fondness for really hot peppers, but with the simple, fresh local ingredients they use, it won't often be disappointing either. The biggest treat may be the best swordfish anywhere, caught fresh from the Straits of Messina. Some good wines come from Calabria, though nothing especially distinguished. You're most likely to encounter *Ciro* from the Ionian coast, a strong red wine best drunk in large quantities, or very good golden-coloured varieties from the same area like *Greco di Gerace* or *Kalipea*.

In Maratea Porto, at Via Grotte 2, Za Mariuccia is a practically perfect seafood trattoria, with tables overlooking the sea, excellent risottos and pasta dishes that use scampi, lobster and other delights, and the very best of whatever Maratea's fishermen have come up with on that particular day (tel (0973) 876 163; L40 000 and up). In Scalea, I Faraglioni, part of the Hotel de Rose, tel (0985) 20 273 serves a mix of fish and meat dishes to please any taste (L30 000, closed Mon). In Règgio, for lunch after the museum, Bonaccorso, Via C. Battisti 8, tel (0965) 96 048 is both elegant and locally popular. Fish dishes include crab, shrimp, smoked salmon and swordfish, and *filetto di pesce 'alla fiorentina'*—meaning big and expensive (L45 000, closed Mon and mid-Aug). Just outside town with a view of the Straits there, first class swordfish and *aragoste* await at Collina dello Scioattolo on the Via Provinciale at Gallina, tel (0965) 382 047

(L40 000). Or maybe something less elegant—the post-War black-and-white ambience of the **Trattoria Praticò Elvira** on Piazza Garibaldi next to the train station—a surprisingly good lunch for L16 000.

The Ionian Sea

From Règgio as far as Tàranto, the coasts of Calabria and later, the Basilicata, are one long beach—about 500 km of beach, broken in only a few places by mountains or patches of industry. All along this route, the pattern will be the same: sleepy new concrete settlements on the shore, within sight of their mother towns, just a few kilometres up in the mountains. If you come in summer, you will see great rivers, like the Amendolara, filled not with water but with pebbles; the terrible deforestation of Calabria in the 19th century (committed mostly by northern Europeans with the assistance of corrupt Italian governments) denuded most of Aspromonte and the mountains to the north, and made its rivers raging torrents in the spring. Recent governments have worked sincerely to reforest vast tracts, but wherever you see bare rock on the mountains, there is land that can never be redeemed. Incidentally, you are now properly in **Italy**. When the first Greek traders came to this coast, the natives told them their land was called *Vitellia*, which may mean simply 'grazing land'. The Greeks corrupted this to something like 'Italy', and over the centuries it came to be the name for the entire peninsula.

Many of the new villages and towns have become little resorts—two pensiones and a pizzeria, on the average; none is worth special mention, but you'll never have trouble finding clean water and a kilometre or so of empty beach uncomfortably close to the railway line.

TOURIST INFORMATION
Locri: Via Via Fiume 1, tel (0964) 29 600
Crotone: Via Firenze 43, tel (0962) 23 185
Catanzaro: Piazza Rossi, tel (0961) 45 530

Locri, Stilo, and Catanzaro

About 3 km south of **Locri** there are fragmentary ruins of the Greek city of the same name, a few bits of wall and bases of temples. Most of the art excavated from Locri has been taken to the Règgio museum, but enough was left behind to make the **Antiquarium** near the sea worth a visit (daily, except Mon, 9–1, 3:30–7:30, Sun 9–1; adm). When pirates and malaria forced the Locrians to abandon their city in the 8th century, they fled to the nearby mountains and founded **Gerace**. Though its population today is only about 2000, Gerace was an important centre in the Middle Ages; it still has Calabria's biggest **cathedral**, an 11th-century Romanesque work supported by columns dragged up from the ruins of Locri. The 13th-century **San Francesco** is the best of a few other Gerace churches that show a strong Arab-Norman influence in their architecture. Further inland, **Cittanova** is one of Italy's strange 'radial cities', a Baroque fancy of geometric planning. Begun as a new town after the earthquake of 1616, it never really prospered.

Roccella Ionica is an up-and-coming little town. Its hilltop setting and its half-ruined castle provide one of the few breaks in the monotony of beach. Up in the hills above Monasterace Marina, the Greek village of **Stilo** is famous for its simple 10th-century Byzantine church, **La Cattolica**, the best preserved and most characteristic of all Calabria's Greek churches, with five small domes and remains of medieval frescoes. The Cattolica has a beautiful site above the village. Its name, from the Greek *katholikon*, means that this was the central church of a monastic community; ruins of other buildings can be seen in the surrounding countryside.

Inland from Stilo, almost in the centre of the peninsula, is **Serra San Bruno**, an unexpectedly pretty and refined village surrounded by forests. It grew up around the 11th-century Charterhouse, the second one founded (after Grenoble's). The founder of the Carthusians himself, Bruno of Cologne, lived and died here. The **monastery**, 2 km outside the village (women not admitted), has the remains of the lavish Baroque complex destroyed in the earthquake of 1783, including one exotic church façade, now free-standing like a stage prop. In the village itself, the Rococo **San Biagio**, or *Chiesa Matrice*, has reliefs with scenes from Bruno's life, and one very unusual altarpiece of the Virgin.

Further north, there is little to detain you as far as **Catanzaro**, the Calabrian capital. Catanzaro, really an overgrown village that has straggled gradually down to the sea since the War, is a piquant little city, the kind of place where the young men call you *capo* and ask for a light while they look you over. The Byzantines founded the city in the 9th century, and if the records can be believed it attained great prosperity in the Middle Ages on the manufacture of silk. The city park, called the Villa Trieste, has nice views and a small **museum**, but as usual, thanks to the earthquakes, there is little else to see in Catanzaro.

Crotone—The City of Pythagoras

Heading into the gulf of Tàranto, the ghost cities of Magna Graecia make the only distractions along a lonely coast. **Crotone**, the Greek Croton, is an exception: no ghost, but a dismal middle-sized industrial city. All those dams up in the Sila were built to provide electricity for Crotone's chemical plants, in a big scheme started by Mussolini in 1925.

The old Croton was often the most powerful of the Calabrian cities, though more famous in the ancient world as the home of the philosopher Pythagoras. With his scientific discoveries, mathematical mysticism and belief in the transmigration of souls, Pythagoras cast a spell over the Greek world, and particularly over Magna Graecia. He was hardly a disinterested scholar in an ivory tower; around the middle of the 6th century BC, he seems to have led, or merely inspired, a mystic-aristocratic government in Croton based on his teachings. When a democratic revolution threw him out, he took refuge in Metapontum. Croton had a reputation, too, for other things: its medical school, the success of its athletes at the Olympic games, and especially its aggressive and unyielding attitude towards its neighbours. From all this, nothing is left but the **Museo Archeologico** (daily, except Mon, 9–1, 3:30–6:30), with a large collection of terracotta ex-votos like those at Règgio. On a promontory south of Crotone, a single standing column from a temple of Hera makes a romantic ruin on **Cape Colonna**. Travellers in the 1600s reported about 50 columns on the site; they must have been carted off for building stone since.

North of Crotone, the dry climate around **Cirò** makes it Calabria's biggest and best wine-growing region. From Lido S. Angelo, further up the coast, you can dip into the mountains at **Rossano**, one of the better-kept Calabrian hill towns. Rossano claims to have invented licorice candy; they've been making it since 1731. Like Cosenza's, Rossano's **cathedral** has one particular treasure, a beautiful 6th-century book called the Purple Codex, made in Syria and believed to be the oldest illuminated gospel anywhere. Rossano also has a small Byzantine church almost as good as Stilo's: five-domed **San Marco**, at the highest point of the town.

Past Rossano, the mountains recede into the plain of **Sibari** (ancient Sybaris), named after the Greek city so renowned for luxurious decadence that even today it is echoed in the word *sybarite*. Sybaris' only misfortune was to have jealous Croton for a neighbour. Croton besieged Sybaris and took it in 510 BC. After razing the city to the ground, the Crotonites diverted the river Crati over the ruins so that it could never be rebuilt. Until a few years ago modern archaeologists could not even find the site; some scholars became convinced the whole story of Sybaris was just a myth. Now that they've found it, excavations are under way, and it is hoped that the richest city of Magna Graecia may finally yield archaeologists something worth the trouble it has caused them. So far, they have learned that the Crotonians did not do as thorough a job of destruction as had been thought. Above Sybaris proper, levels of excavation reveal ruins of *Thurii*, an Athenian colony and base in the Peloponnesian Wars, and a Roman town above that called *Copia*.

Policoro and Metapontum

Nearing the northern boundaries of Calabria, there are castles frowning down over the sea at **Roseto** and at **Rocca Imperiale**, the latter built by Frederick II. The Basilicata's share of the Ionian coast offers little change from Calabria. The town of **Policoro** stands near the ancient city of Heracleia, and its **Museo Nazionale della Siritide** has a small but choice collection of Greek vases—some of them exquisite pieces from the height of classical Greek art—along with some bronzes and terracotta ex-votos; in the archaeological zone itself there is very little of anything to see. **Metapontum**, near the modern border with Apulia, was another rich city. It based its prosperity on growing and shipping grain; today its famous silver coins, always decorated with an ear of wheat, are especially prized by collectors. Even by the standards of Magna Graecia, Metapontum suffered bad luck. Among numerous sackings was one by Spartacus and his rebel army. In the Punic Wars the city sided with Hannibal, who upon his retreat courteously evacuated the entire population, saving them from a bloody Roman vengeance.

Metapontum has more ruins to show than any of the other Calabrian sites, but do not expect anything like Paestum. On the banks of the river Bradano, just north of the main road, there is a small **Museum**, with Greek ceramics and local Lucanian imitations, along with relics of the Oenotrians, a Lucanian people who inhabited the area before the Greeks arrived. Across from it stands a temple to Hera called the *Tavola Palatine* by locals (the 'Table of the Knights', the Round Table—another unexpected survival of Arthurian legends). Fifteen of its columns remain. The rest of the city's scanty remains, including the outlines of a horseshoe-shaped classical theatre, are a couple of kilometres walk to the south.

WHERE TO STAY AND EATING OUT

None of the various tiny 'lidos' on Calabria's Ionian shore is very inviting for a vacation; if you are passing through, there are simple hotels in Catanzaro: the modern and attractive ***Grand Hotel**, in the centre of town on Piazza Matteotti (tel (0961) 25 605; L125 000) or the ***Bellamena Residence Casalbergo** on Via Plutino 14 (tel (0961) 42 928; L40 000), or ***Mauro**, Via M. D'Amato 51, tel (0961) 41 259, where rooms are L30–40 000. One of the more pleasant spots is Gioiosa Marina, where the ***San Giorgio** on Via I Maggio has a nice garden, beach and pool, and rooms for L52–76 000 (tel (0964) 55 064).

Up the Ionian coast, dining is simple—perhaps a little seafood shack that is only open in the summer, or a small but lively pizzeria like **Da Bruno** at Palizzi Marina, with a little terrace and dinners in the L20 000 range, or try **La Vela**, Via Nazionale 197, L25 000. There are some exceptions, such as **La Fontanella** at Locri, Piazza C. Moschetta, tel (0964) 20 384, with fish as usual, but also lamb, kid, and sometimes boar (L20–25 000). Up in old Catanzaro, there is little choice and little seafood; the bar **Uno Piu Uno** has a restaurant section, where you can eat well and hobnob with the local politicos (L25 000). In Crotone, where you would least expect it, there is one very good restaurant: **Il Girarrosto**, which specializes in roast lamb and kid but also knows what to do with swordfish and other seafood; there is a nice terrace (Via Veneto 30; tel (0962) 22 043; average L35 000).

The Basilicata

The interior of the Basilicata has never been one of the more welcoming regions of Italy. Divided about equally between mountains and rolling hills, the relative isolation of this land has usually allowed it to ignore the major events of Italian history. The territory may be familiar if you have read Carlo Levi's *Christ Stopped at Eboli*, a novel written when the Basilicata was a national scandal, the poorest and most backward corner of all Italy. None of the famous 18th- and 19th-century travellers ever penetrated deeply into the region, and even today it is a part of the country few foreigners ever visit.

GETTING AROUND

Matera is served only by a private line, the FCL, which runs 12 trains a day from Bari in Apulia—in fact, a day trip from Bari, only 46 km, may be the most convenient way to see Matera. The station there is on Via Nazionale on the western edge of town. FCL and other companies operate daily bus services from Matera's Piazza Matteotti to Ferrandina, Potenza, Naples and Metaponto.

TOURIST INFORMATION

Potenza: Via Alianelli 4, tel (0971) 21 812
Matera: Via De Marco 9, tel (0835) 221 758

Matera and the *Sassi*

Of all the towns of the Basilicata, the only one that offers a real reason for stopping is **Matera**, and that only because it is a sort of freak. Matera is the provincial capital for the eastern Basilicata, and it has been an inhabited town since before recorded history in these parts began. Until recently, it had a certain notoriety as the most desperately poor provincial capital in Italy—as recalled in Carlo Levi's chilling book. Times are better now, but Matera has chosen to preserve rather than obliterate its terrible past by turning its poorest sections, the **Sassi**, into a sort of open-air museum, surely one of the most peculiar tourist attractions of southern Italy. *Sassi* are the cave neighbourhoods that line the two ravines between which Matera is built. Visitors as little as forty years ago reported people living in their cave homes in almost inconceivable poverty, sharing space with pigs and chickens, their children imploring outsiders not for money, but quinine.

Almost all of the Sassi are abandoned today—Matera and its province have benefited from post-War prosperity and the good works of the *Cassa per il Mezzogiorno* as has any part of the south. You may think it somewhat macabre, visiting the scenes of past misery, but the Sassi are indeed fascinating in their own way. Don't be surprised to see a group tour of bewildered foreigners being dragged through the cave neighbourhoods' steps and winding lanes.

There are two Sassi, the Sasso Barisano, north of the town centre, and the Sasso Caveoso, to the east. If you visit, before long a child or old man of the neighbourhood will come up and approach you with the offer of guide service—worth the trouble and slight expense if you have the time and find the Sassi interesting. They know where the old churches with the Byzantine frescoes are (some as old as the 9th century), and if you can pick out enough of their southern dialect, they have plenty of stories to tell. Don't get the idea that the Sassi are just plain caves. They started that way, but over the centuries they evolved into real neighbourhoods, with quite normal-looking façades, like the cave houses of southern Spain. The predominant stone of the area is tufa, a light volcanic rock that is easier to cut and shape than wood; in Matera it was always easier to dig out a house or church than build one. Opposite the Sassi, along the other side of the Gravina ravine, you will see the real caves, many of them with traces of habitation from prehistoric times.

Festa della Bruna, Matera

Not all of Matera's sights are in the Sassi. The 13th-century **cathedral** is a fine Romanesque building on the edge of the Sassi with a rose window and interesting carved portals. Inside, there are fine carved wood choir stalls from the 1450s, a famous and elaborate 16th-century wooden *presepio*, and the *Capella dell'Annunziata*, lavishly decorated by a Matera artist named Giulio Persio (late 16th century). Some 14th–15th-century frescoes have recently been uncovered near the baptistry, including part of a very Byzantine *Last Judgement*. Two other churches, **San Francesco** and **San Giovanni Battista**, both have good façades; in addition, there is a 15th-century castle called the **Castello Tramontano** above the city; an eccentric 18th-century church called the **Purgatorio**, with a leering skull over the main portal; and a first-class local archaeological museum, the **Museo Ridola**, set in the Baroque former convent of Santa Chiara (daily, except Mon, 9–2; Sun 9–1; adm).

The dry, austere countryside around Matera is full of tufa quarries. Across the Gravina ravine from the city, it holds a number of interesting **cave churches**, often with elaborate fronts, even domes, cut out of the tufa, and medieval frescoes. The majority of them date from the 10th–13th centuries, the height of this little-documented urge for troglodytic monasticism. But decorations in the churches can be as early as the 6th century or as late as the 1700s; some of the caves are actually adapted from Neolithic times, when an unknown people with a talent for digging inhabited these parts. Their 'trench villages', deep cuts in the earth that held the entrances to boths dwellings and tombs, can be seen around Matera.

There are over a hundred cave churches in and around Matera. Some are marked (the 'Strada panoramica dei Sassi'), but you'll need a map and some help from the tourist office to find them. Among the most interesting are those of **Santa Maria della Palomba**, **Santa Lucia alla Malve**, the **Madonna della Croce**, and **Santa Barbara**. These last three have some of the best Byzantine frescoes. Another good one, and one of the earliest, is the **Cripta del Pecccato Originale**, with a 10th-century fresco cycle that includes a lovely enthroned Virgin and scenes from the Book of Genesis. There are more of these half-forgotten churches in parts of neighbouring Apulia, but none anywhere else in Italy; indeed, they can only be compared to the similar Greek rock churches of Cappadocia in Turkey—except that these eerie, spoilt landscapes, in places on the verge of becoming desert, are emptier and stranger than anything Cappadocia has to offer.

Southern Basilicata

South of Matera, route 175 descends to the coast and Metaponto, a scenic route of pines and wild flowers that passes the attractive whitewashed village of **Montescaglioso**; at the top of this town is an impressive medieval monastery, the Abbazia di Sant'Angelo. To the southwest, route 7 passes an artificial lake, Lago di San Giuliano, and **Miglionico**, where there is a grim mouldering castle and perhaps the best painting in the Basilicata: a glorious 18-section altarpiece by the Venetian Renaissance artist Cima del Conigliano.

The valley of the Basento is one of the Basilicata's more modern and prosperous regions, due largely to a government industrial scheme—and the discovery of some modest gas reserves. **Ferrandina** is one of the prettier towns; its sun-bleached white terraces, similar to many places in Apulia, offer an example of the Basilicata's native style of building. Near Ferrandina is a picturesquely ruined castle on a round hill, the

Castello di Uggiano. Pisticci, down river, is the largest town south of Matera, though by no means the most pleasant; the weirdly eroded gullies around the town make a fitting introduction to the sad landscapes you will see throughout much of the southern Basilicata.

Craco, overlooking a steep cliff west of Pisticci, is a rarity in Italy—a ghost town, today almost completely abandoned after landslides, a recurring problem in the region thanks to deforestation, made the site unsafe. **Tursi** and **Stigliano**, otherwise unremarkable villages, both have remarkable churches; Tursi's is the sanctuary of S. Maria D'Anglona, out in the country on the road towards Policoro and the coast, a 13th-century work in an offshoot of the Pisan Romanesque style, with fragments of frescoes and carvings. Anglona, now almost completely disappeared, was once the seat of a bishopric. In Tursi itself, the **Chiesa della Rabatana** suffered a Baroque restoration, but the church and its crypt retain some 14th–16th-century frescoes, along with an unusual stone carved *presepio*. Tursi may have been founded by the Arabs; like Matera it had some cave homes in the surrounding ravines, though these are now used for wine cellars.

In Stigliano, it is the 17th-century church of San Antonio, with an odd waffle-iron façade even better than the one on the Gesù Nuovo in Naples. South of Stigliano, the countryside around **Aliano** offers some of the most outlandish scenery in southern Italy. Deforestation and consequent erosion have turned parts of it into a lunar landscape, exposing weirdly twisted rock formations called *calanchi*. Aliano itself is the village that inspired *Christ Stopped at Eboli*; Carlo Levi is buried there. Parts of the village stand on the very edge of the *calanchi*, which some day will swallow it up.

Aliano lies on the Agri river, like most of the Basilicata's rivers a raging torrent in the spring and a flat swath of pebbles the rest of the year. If you follow this discouraging valley westwards, you will come to a large artificial lake, Lago di Pietra del Pertusillo. Near its shores, saved from flooding only by good luck, are the ruins of ancient **Grumentum**—don't go out of your way; the best finds here are now in the British Museum. Some of the streets can be made out, along with remains of a theatre and an amphitheatre. The landscape in these parts is certainly greener than around Aliano; nearby **Moliterno**, under its ruined castle, is one of the prettier villages in the Basilicata.

Mount Vùlture and the Castles of Emperor Frederick

Eastern Basilicata is a province to itself, with a capital at **Potenza**, a plain modern city regularly rattled to pieces by earthquakes. Although present on this site since it was Roman *Potentia*, Potenza consequently has little to show: a few medieval churches and a small Archaeological Museum, on Via Cicotto. There are mountains on all sides, with some humble skiing areas to the south.

To the east, you'll find some startling landscapes in the mountains dubbed (by some clever tourist official, most likely) the **'Basilicatan Dolomites'**, a patch of jagged and sinister limestone peaks around the sombre villages of Pietrapertosa and Castelmezzano; the former has a ruined castle built by the Arabs, who were a power in this region back in the heyday of the Emirate of Bari. **Campomaggiore**, nearby, is entirely new; the original, higher up in the mountains on a dirt track, became a ghost town like Craco after a landslide in 1885. Its ruins are still visible.

Route 7, passing through Potenza, follows the course of the Appian Way. There's little point in taking it east, towards Benevento and Avellino in Campania; this area too suffered badly from the 1980 earthquake. In the other direction, the road passes through **Tricárico**, a pleasant village under the round donjon of a Norman castle. Further north, near the Apulian border, **Acerenza** was the Basilicata's capital when Potenza was still an insignificant mountain village. Acerenza's quite impressive 10th–13th century **cathedral** contains, along with some good Romanesque sculptural work, the drollest fraud in the Basilicata, a venerable bust believed for centuries to be the town's patron, San Canio; instead, the little icon has been identified as none other than that devout pagan, Emperor Julian the Apostate. **Genzano di Lucania** and **Irsina**, to the east, both retain bits of castles begun by Frederick II; next door to Irsina's, the church of San Francesco has a crypt full of good medieval frescoes.

The northern end of Potenza's province, astride the important routes between Naples and Apulia, was a very busy place in the Middle Ages, full of castles and fought over by Normans, Angevins and Holy Roman Emperors. Frederick II, in particular, haunted these bleak hills; he spent the last year of his life at the well-preserved castle of **Lagopésole** , halfway between Potenza and Melfi. Although this castle had a military role as a strong redoubt against the frequent rebellions of the Basilicatan barons, it was largely intended as a residence. Its austere rectangularity is strangely abstract and sophisticated, along the lines of the beautiful castle Frederick built in Prato, near Florence. Some good capitals and other sculptural details survive inside, including an image believed to be the emperor's grandfather, Frederick I Barbarossa—wearing ass's ears.

Earlier in his reign, the great Hohenstaufen had spent some time at the castle at **Melfi**, a stronghold rebuilt from an earlier one that had been, two centuries before, the first headquarters of the de Hautevilles in Italy; here Robert Guiscard had been crowned Duke of Apulia and Calabria. The castle, recently restored, is well up to cinematic standards, a romantic, asymmetrical mass of towers—none of Frederick's geometrical mysticism here; unlike Castel del Monte this one was built strictly for defence. Little remains of the original furnishings, but there is a small **archaeological museum** (daily, except Mon, 9–2; Sun 9–1; adm). Melfi itself is a sleepy town, with little but the castle and its 11th-century **cathedral** to remind it of the days when it was often occupying the centre stage of European politics. Several minor Church councils were held here, and here Frederick promulgated his famous *Costitutiones Melfitanes*, the first proper constitution in history. In the environs of Melfi there are two well-preserved Roman bridges, and the villages of **Barile** and **Ginestra**, largely populated by Albanians. Between Melfi and Rapolla are a number of small cave-churches cut in the rock, some with frescoes.

Looking out from Melfi's castle, the horizon to the south is dominated by the ragged, faintly menacing outline of **Monte Vùlture**, a long-extinct volcano with a forest where once it had a smoking crater. Around the back of the mountain, the Basilicata keeps one of its few beauty spots, the little **Lakes of Monticchio**, with lovely woods and a funicular to the top of the mountain. East of Melfi, there is another old castle at **Venosa**, an important town in Roman times and the birthplace of the poet Horace (also of King Manfred). Venosa was *Venusia* back in the days when it was republican Rome's most important base in the south. The name comes from the goddess Venus, who must have had a sanctuary here—and you can still find churches in the region dedicated to *Santa*

Venere. Venosa's Roman past shows itself only in scanty ruins of baths and an amphitheatre, and in the relief fragments built into the walls of the **cathedral**, last rebuilt in the 1600s.

The amphitheatre stands just outside town, on the road to Apulia, near the remains of one of the most ambitious church building projects ever undertaken in the south. The Benedictine **Abbazia della Trinità**, begun in the 1050s under the influence of the Cluniac revival, was never completed, but it became the resting-place of four of the five famous Norman brothers: William, Drogo, Robert (Guiscard), and Humphrey de Hauteville. Their tombs are in the older, completed church, along with some very fine surviving frescoes and carved capitals; among the heaps of stones tumbled about you may notice some Hebrew inscriptions; ancient and medieval Venosa had important Jewish communities, and some Jewish catacombs have been discovered nearby.

WHERE TO STAY AND EATING OUT
Despite the relative isolation of the area, you will find simple but good accommodation in all the larger towns, but nothing special. In Matera, the *****President** is a comfortable, air-conditioned hotel in the city centre, at Via Roma 13, with a fair restaurant (tel (0835) 214 075; L65–75 000). Down the street at No 62, there is a clean and welcoming budget choice: the ***Roma** (tel (0835) 212 701; L24 000 without bath, L28 000 with). Matera has some good restaurants; at **Casino del Diavolo**, Via La Martella 48 (tel (0835) 261 986; average L25 000) they lay on lots of *peperoncini* if you let them; fearfully hot dishes, one called 'souvenir of Lucania', explains the restaurant's name. **Lucana**, at Via Lucana 48, tel (0835) 216 779 offers some excellent home cooking, and you'll probably spend less than L25 000. In Ferrandina, there is only one tiny locanda, but the *****Degli Ulivi** outside of town on SS407 makes a comfortable stopover if you are passing through on the way to Tàranto (tel (0835) 757 020; L58 000). In Stigliano, where no one ever goes, you can have the modest charms of the *****Turistico** all to yourself—a nice place, and a steal at L27 000 (Via Principe di Napoli, tel (0835) 661 027).

Potenza is the kind of place where you will share a quiet hotel with a small group of government inspectors and travelling salami salesmen. If you are stuck there, try the ****Miramonti**, on Via Caserma Lucana 30 (tel (0971) 22 987; L38–45 000, all with bath). Console yourself with dinner at the singular, employee-owned **Fuori le Mura** on Via IV Novembre 34, famous for an enormous choice of antipasto treats and good roast pork and lamb (tel (0971) 25 409; L30 000 at the most). The people who run the *****Due Pini** in Melfi work hard to give you a pleasant stay (outside town at the railway station; tel (0972) 21 031; L42–55 000; some rooms with TV). For dinner in Melfi, try **Il Castagneto**, on the SS401, tel (0972) 23 531, with simple home cooking that fits in lots of mushrooms; also lamb *alla cacciatore* (L20–25 000).

Part VII
ABRUZZO AND MOLISE

Abuzzo Bear

In Italy's long and narrow peninsula, dense with cities and great monuments, art and ruins, autostradas and pizzerias, sultry sun-glassed signorinas and Vespa-wrangling dudes, Abruzzo and Molise come as a breath of fresh air. Sparsely populated, historically marginal to the great affairs of state, these two regions (made administratively independent of each other in 1963) stand out for their majestic natural beauty and vast tracts of unspoiled wilderness that encompass the highest peaks of the Apennines and the habitat of Italy's unique species of bear. Because of the harsh and rugged terrain, with only small pockets suitable for agriculture, the region's economy has been traditionally pastoral, but with a strong emphasis on crafts like pottery and ceramics, gold-, wood-, and iron-working, and weaving and lace-making. And although many Abruzzo towns wear the proud badges of progress and modernity, the Abruzzesi have little care to compete with Milan and Rome; like Candide, they tend their own garden, and hone their traditional skills—even if they use them to tailor suits as well as to embroider tablecloths. From this mountain-bound land of country tradition came two of of Italy's most urbane, sophisticated, and passionate poets, Ovid and Gabriele d'Annunzio, and its greatest modern philosopher, Benedetto Croce. It is also, for some reason, the most passionately enthusiastic about rugby—L'Aquila is usually Italy's national champion.

In prehistoric times, the coast of Abruzzo formed part of a little-known Bronze Age culture, sometimes known as the Middle Adriatic, that produced the enigmatic Warrior of Capestrano in Chieti's archaeology museum. Culture was less advanced up in the hills, but the different Italic tribes who gathered here—the Praetuttii, the Vestini, the Peligni, and others, of whom almost nothing is known beyond their names—formed a formidable challenge to Roman expansion before being overwhelmed by the legions in the Social Wars of 91–82 BC.

In the early Middle Ages, almost all of the Abruzzo was conquered by the Lombards. Lombard rule, as much a misfortune here as anywhere else in Italy, explains the Abruzzo's unusually large number of Roman ruins—eerie amphitheatres standing in open country, memorials of cities that simply withered and died. The Lombards apportioned what is now Abruzzo to the Duchy of Spoleto and the Molise to the Duchy of Benevento. The Normans, under King William, picked up the region from English Pope Adrian IV; the fine Romanesque churches found in unlikely places all over the Abruzzo testify to its prosperity and sophistication under their rule. Emperor Frederick II made the Abruzzo an independent province. Frederick had grand plans for the region, which died with him as the Abruzzo was then swallowed up by the Angevins, then kings of Naples. Like Umbria, Lazio, and most of the Marches, Abruzzo and Molise then began to stagnate, with a few exceptions—the only difference being that these regions stagnated under the Aragonese, Spaniards, and Bourbons on the throne of Naples instead of under the popes. It was the Bourbons who divided the Abruzzo into four administrative territories—Abruzzo Citeriore, Ulteriore Primo, Ulteriore Secondo, and Molise—which is why you'll often see the region's name in the plural (the *Abruzzi*). But if Abruzzo was neglected and sucked dry by the Neapolitans, its lot under the kings of Italy saw no improvement, and thousands of people migrated to North America and England, among them the father of Dante Gabriele Rossetti. Only after World War II, with the small boom of its small seaside resorts, the construction of small industries and new roads financed by the *Cassa per il Mezzogiorno*, and the growing interest in its unsullied environmental charms, has the tide of emigration been stemmed.

Almost entirely mountainous, the Molise is an atavistic and introspective *banlieue*, designated its own region in the '60s at the request of its inhabitants (though it formed its own county back in the 13th century, when its name, of unknown derivation, was first used). This rather dolorous patch of the Abruzzi that got away has its own customs and dialect—a direct result of its impossible geography, and the large settlements in the 15th and 16th century by Slavs and Albanians. Molise is one of the last regions in Italy where women still don their traditional costumes to please themselves and not the shutter-happy hordes.

Abruzzo Itineraries

The coast, like most of the Adriatic, is flat and dull, though there are some fine sandy beaches and pretty hills here and there; **Pescara**, the region's biggest resort, is ready to take on the international charter market with its newly expanded airport. Since opening the new tunnel through the Gran Sasso, you can drive to the north coast or Pescara on the autostrada from Rome in an hour and a half. **Termoli** in Molise is another big resort. Inland, mountains and magnificent scenery provide the main attractions, in the famous **Gran Sasso** and lesser-known **Maiella** and **Matese** ranges, and in the **National Park of the Abruzzo**—all paradises for hiking and climbing, and boasting the best downhill and cross-country skiing in Central Italy.

. Of the towns, there is pretty, old **L'Aquila**, the regional capital (and best base for visiting the Gran Sasso) and the ceramics town of **Castelli** just under the Gran Sasso; medieval **Sulmona** and **Scanno** near the National Park; **Penne** and **Arti** near the coast,

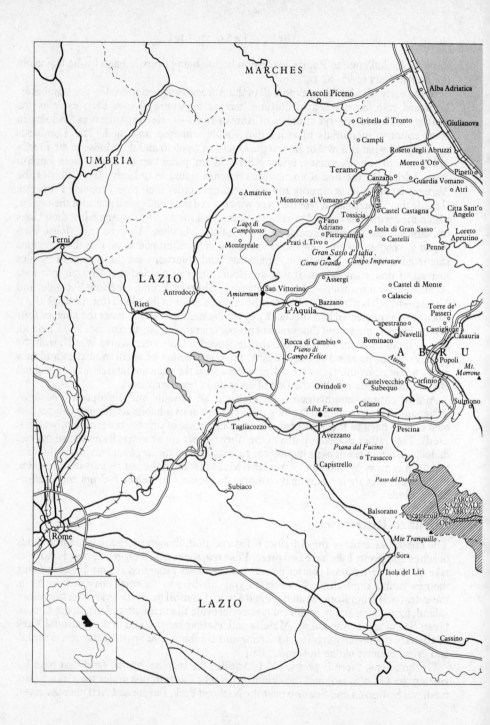

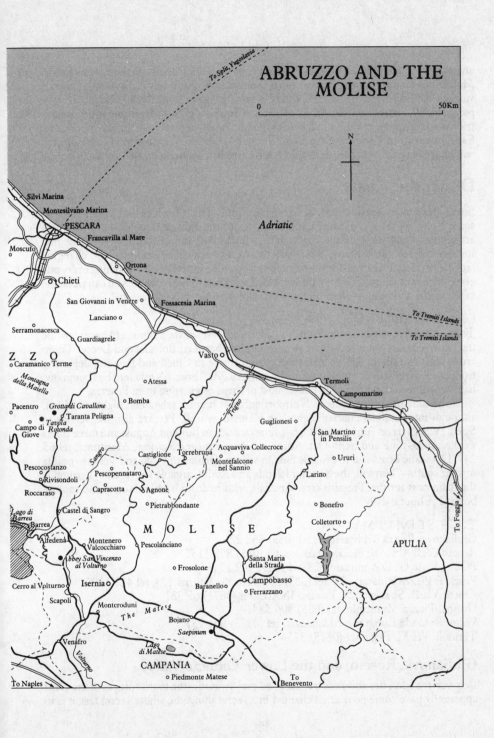

ABRUZZO AND THE MOLISE

0   50Km

N

Adriatic

To Split, Yugoslavia

Silvi Marina
Montesilvano Marina
PESCARA
Francavilla al Mare
Moscufo
Ortona
Chieti
San Giovanni in Venere
Fossacesia Marina
Lanciano
Serramonacesca
Guardiagrele
To Tremiti Islands
To Tremiti Islands
Z Z O
Caramanico Terme
Vasto
Montagna
della Maiella
Atessa
Termoli
Campomarino
Pacentro
Grotta di Cavallone
Bomba
Taranta Peligna
Guglionesi
Campo di
Giove
Tavola
Rotonda
San Martino
in Pensilis
Castiglione
Torrebruna
Acquaviva Collecroce
Pescocostanzo
Montefalcone
nel Sannio
Ururi
Sangro
Rivisondoli
Pescopennataro
Larino
Roccaraso
Capracotta
Agnone
Lago di
Barrea
Pietrabbondante
Bonefro
Barrea
Castel di Sangro
Colletorto
M O L I S E
Alfedena
APULIA
Montenero
Valcocchiaro
Pescolanciano
Abbey San Vincenzo
al Volturno
Frosolone
Santa Maria
della Strada
To Foggia
Cerro al Volturno
Isernia
Baranello
Campobasso
Scapoli
Ferrazzano
Venafro
Monteroduni
Matese
The
Bojano
Saepinum
Volturno
Lago
di Matese
CAMPANIA
To Naples
Piedmonte Matese
To
Benevento

Trigno

and medieval **Tagliacozzo** and the Roman ruins of **Alba Fucens** on the road to Rome. Molise has an exceptional Roman town, **Saepinum**, and lovely, unspoiled mountain villages like **Boiano** in the Matese, and bell-casting **Agnone** and the highest town on the peninsula, **Capracotta**. Artistically, Abruzzo preserves enough **Romanesque monuments** to warm the cockles of any anachronistic heart; several of them are superlative: **San Giovanni in Venere** on the coast, **Santa Maria di Collemaggio** in L'Aquila, the two churches of **Bominaco**, and **San Clemente in Casauria** on the Via Valeria.

Down the Coast

Small inexpensive seaside resorts, jam-packed with Italian families in the summer, and some beautiful artistic treasures and churches of the Romanesque era, are the main attractions along the Adriatic coast and its immediate hinterland. If you're not into Italian-style seaside holidays, where you pay for a beach chair, umbrella, and changing facilities in neat little rows, for the privilege of watching everyone else watching every one else do the same thing, there are undeveloped stretches of beach where you can sit on the sands under the pines—often on the fringes of even the busiest resorts.

GETTING AROUND
There is a direct rail line from Rome to Chieti and Pescara via Sulmona (4 hours), while the entire coast is covered by the north-south line between Bologna and Lecce. There are at least two direct ARPA buses a day from Rome to Chieti and Pescara, departing from the Piazza della Repubblica (2½ hours); ARPA, Abruzzo's efficient bus company, has many lines inland from the coast, most of them originating from Pescara.

At the time of writing, Pescara's airport only has regular scheduled flights to Milan, although international charter flights are planned as well. Pescara also has ferries to Split, Yugoslavia on Adriatic Lines, five times weekly in July and August and three times weekly April–June and Sept–Oct. Adriatic's office is at the Stazione Marittima, tel 65 247. Domestic boats and hydrofoils link, in season, Ortona to Vasto and Vasto to points further south—Termoli, the Tremiti Islands and Rodi Garganico in Apulia. Termoli is the main port for the Tremitis (see 'Apulia'), with hydrofoils (40 minutes) and motor-boats (1½ hours) daily.

TOURIST INFORMATION
Giulianova: Piazza del Stazione, tel (085) 862 226
Roseto degli Abruzzi: Piazza Stazione, tel (085) 899 1157
Pineto: Viale G. D'Annunzio 123, tel (085) 949 1745
Pescara: Piazza Rinascita 22, tel (085) 378 110; Via Fabrizi 173, tel 421 1707.
Chieti: Via B. Spaventa 29, Palazzo INAIL, tel (0871) 65 321
Ortona: Piazza Municipio, tel (085) 906 3841
Vasto: Rotonda Lungomare Dalmazia, tel (0873) 801 751
Termoli: Via M. Bega, tel (0875) 3754

Giulianova, Roseto, and the Lower Vomano Valley

Between the Marches and Pescara, the good grey Adriatic (the tourist offices of the coast apparently have some poor artist chained in a secret dungeon, whose secret task it is to tint it blue for their brochures) is lined with the same kind of small, Italian family resorts that form an unbroken line from Rimini to Apulia; places like Alba Adriatica, Giulianova, Roseto degli Abruzzi, Silvi, and Pineto all offer big beaches, modern hotels, amusement arcades, and playgrounds. The most interesting of the resorts is **Giulianova**, with its old town set back up behind the beach sprawl. Known in Roman times as *Castrum Novum*; within its old walls you can see the town's best monument, the Romanesque **Santa Maria a Mare**, with unusual bas-reliefs on its façade. From here Highway 80 turns inland for Teramo (see below).

Roseto degli Abruzzi, another resort out of the same mould, lies near the mouth of the Vomano River, one of the streams flowing down from the Gran Sasso, with fine views up the valley to its naked limestone peaks. From Roseto you can head up the valley to see two Romanesque gems: the 11th-century **San Clemente a Guardia Vomano** near Notaresco, whose builders made good use of Roman ruins lying about, fitting them in here and there like a jigsaw; the church houses an unusual and lovely 12th-century ciborium. In the church and abbey of **Santa Maria di Propezzano**, near Morro d'Oro, the Abruzzese fondness for simple forms has created a handsome asymmetrical façade and a charming two-storey cloister. The church walls are embellished with 12th- and 13th-century frescoes, the cloister with scriptural scenes by the 17th-century Polish artist Sebastiano Majewski. A side road to the north leads to **Canzano**, locally known as the 'Castle of King Turkey' after a popular Abruzzese dish.

Atri

Pineto, another little resort, with a pretty pine-lined beach, has for its landmark the **Torre di Cerrano**, built by Charles V against the Ottoman threat, and now a merchant marine research station. Pineto is also an easy starting point for visiting **Atri** (10 km), by car or bus. Atri stands on the site of the ancient Sabine city and Roman colony of *Hatriaticum*, founded under the sign of the woodpecker, the bird of Mars. Atri disputes with Adria in the Veneto the honour of having lent its name to the Adriatic sea, a controversy that raged among ancient scholars like Pliny, Livy and Strabo; Atri tried to boost its claim by engraving the fact on its singular coins—the heaviest ever minted in western Europe, guaranteed to put a hole in the pocket of any toga. Roman remains have recently been excavated in the piazza and in the crypt of Atri's majestic 13th-century **cathedral**. This has an elegant, tidily rectangular façade and matching campanile. In the choir are excellent quattrocento frescoes by Andrea Delitio, the Piero della Francesca of the Abruzzo; his series of *The Life of the Virgin* includes surreal landscapes of knobby hills and imaginary towers, and gentlefolk in the latest fashions from Florence. Other fine works include a 1503 tabernacle, and in the cathedral museum (open 9–1; adm) ivories, polyptychs and statues, majolicas by Grue of Castelli (see below), and some interesting mosaics and architectural fragments from the 9th-century church that preceded the cathedral. Atri was controlled, off and on in the Middle Ages and Renaissance, by the Acquaviva dukes; their frowning 14th-century **Palazzo Ducale** (now the municipio and post office), contains a cheerful courtyard. The outskirts of Atri boast some strange geology: once-inhabited caves, eroded rock formations (*calanchi*), and 'Dantesque pits'.

From Città Sant' Angelo Marina, a satellite resort of Silvi, route 16/bis heads inland to a clutch of interesting villages. In **Loreto Aprutino**, the church of **Santa Maria in Piano** contains 14th–15th-century frescoes—the *Life of St Thomas Aquinas* and one called *The Particular Judgement*, portraying Heaven's elect marching to the pearly gates on a bridge as wide as a hair (a striking and perhaps unique example of borrowed religious imagery; in the Koran that bridge is called *al-Sirat*). Loreto also has the **Galleria delle Antiche Ceramiche Abruzzesi** (closed Tues), with some charming pieces from around the region. The pale-pink town of **Penne**, further west, was an important town of the Vestini and today preserves a rare if eclectic urban harmony, its narrow winding streets dotted with Renaissance mansions; sights include the ancient crypt of the **cathedral**, itself destroyed in World War II and rebuilt, and the church of **Santa Maria in Colleromano**, a 15-minute walk from the centre, with good 14th–15th-century statues. In **Moscufo**, further south, **Santa Maria del Lago** merits a visit for its unique 12th-century pulpit adorned with painted reliefs.

Pescara

Pescara is both Abruzzo's biggest resort and most prosperous town, a fishing port and provincial capital. In ancient times it was an important port, shared by several Italic tribes and later by the Romans, who made it the terminus of their Via Tiburtina-Via Valeria (modern Highway 5). In 1864 Gabriele D'Annunzio was born in Pescara to a small merchant, and his birthplace, or **Casa Natale**, with its charming little courtyard on Corso Manthonè has been carefully preserved (9–2, summer 9–1 and 6–8 pm)—all well enough, but some people have such kitsch magnetism that when Pescara decided to build an outdoor theatre in D'Annunzio's honour, it just had to have a huge concrete obelisk cast with '60s designs, which rather nicely complement the rows of cheap plastic moulded chairs. Still, it's worth dropping by in July for the Pescara Jazz Festival.

Pescara's golden egg is a 16-km long sandy beach, almost solid with hotels between the Pescara River and Montesilvano; whatever old buildings it had were decimated in the fierce fighting that took place along the coast in World War II. Still, this is no Rimini; families bake together in the day, and stroll about eating ice cream in the evening. If you need some excitement, there are riding stables, go-kart tracks, tennis, sport fishing, and for some real thrills, the **Fish museum** in Pescaro's bustling Fish Market on Lungo-fiume Paolucci (open 8–2 and summer 3–9, closed Sun).

WHERE TO STAY AND EATING OUT   (tel prefix 085)
The hotels mostly date from the past two decades, but on the whole they're a bargain compared with the rest of Italy. On the coast, the seafood is as tempting as the beach, and to wash it down Abruzzo produces a good dry white Trebbiano wine as well as the smooth, dry red Montepulciano d'Abruzzo: look for the Valentini and Pepe labels.

In Giulianova, the ******Gran Hotel Don Juan**, Lungomare Zara 97, tel 867 341, is one of the smartest hotels on the coast, with contemporary Mediterranean styling. Located right on its own beach, it has a pool, tennis, and garden, and comfortable air-conditioned rooms (open May–Sept; L80–95 000). The smaller *****Promenade**, Lungomare Zara 119, tel 862 338, has the same amenities without the style or air conditioning (mid-May–Sept; L38–70 000, depending on the period). For a seaside bargain, ***Rouge et Noir**, Lungomare Zara, tel 864 434 has six rooms all with bath for

L35 000. Giulianova's—and indeed, all of Abruzzo's—most celebrated seafood restaurant is **Beccaceci**, Via Zola 18, tel 862 550, featuring its own long-established seafood and pasta inventions that are so good they've been copied elsewhere—try the stewed *sole alla giuliese* with black olives or the *marinara giuliese*, an exquisite local seafood stew (three menus available: L30 000, L50 000, or L65 000; closed Mon eve and Tues). For traditional regional cuisine, **Il Gabbiano**, Via Marsala 20, tel 863 413, serves the best in town; the pasta and seafood are outstanding too (L40 000, closed Tues except in summer). Penne has one of Abruzzo's best restaurants, **Tatobbe**, Corso Italia 41, tel 827 9512, where excellent dishes are prepared rigorously according to regional recipes, making use of the freshest ingredients—meats, vegetables, olive oil, and excellent wine—produced by the owner of the restaurant (L30 000).

Pescara has by far the most hotels and restaurants on the coast, but be aware that tranquillity is one of the rarest commodities in the summer, and full board is bound to be required in July and August. The top hotel, the ******Carlton**, Viale Riviera 35, tel 26 373, is a very comfortable resort palace on the sea, with gardens that almost absorb the racket—shut the window and bask in the quiet air conditioning. It has private beach facilities and is open all year (L78–100 000). *****Bellariva**, Viale Riviera 213, tel 70 641, is a moderate-sized, pleasant, and unpretentious place, good for families. All rooms have private bath; L55–70 000. In Pescara's resort suburb, Montesilvano Marina, there's the modern and comfortable ******Serena Majestic**, Viale Kennedy, tel 835 142, on the beach with gardens and tennis and a pool; open May–Sept (L55–95 000, all rooms with bath). Also in Montesilvano, ****Piccolo Mondo**, Via Marinelli 86, tel 838 647, is one of the best-value hotels on the coast. With only 20 rooms, a garden, and its own beach facilities, it is a pleasant choice for a family holiday, open all year (L20–25 000 without bath, L25–35 000 with).

Because Pescara is a working town as well as a resort, it has good restaurants unattached to hotels. **Guerino**, Viale Riviera 4, tel 421 2065, is the city's best seafood choice, elegant and serving the tasty Adriatic speciality of fillets of John Dory with prosciutto, which taste especially good in fine weather out on Guerino's seaside terrace (L35–40 000, closed Tues, but not in summer). **Duilio**, Via Regina Margherita 11, tel 378 278, features seafood in nearly every delicately prepared dish (closed Sun eve, Mon, and all of Aug; L35 000). One of Pescara's best restaurants, **La Terrazza Verde**, doesn't serve fish at all (except on Fridays). Located in a panoramic setting, with a beautiful garden terrace up in the hills behind the city, meals here feature delicious gnocchi, and duck, a popular dish in Abruzzo, prepared in a variety of ways, as well as meat dishes *alla brace* (Largo Madonna 6, tel 413 239; L30 000).

Chieti

For something a bit heavier than gills and beachballs, head up to **Chieti**, about 13 km up the Pescara river. Another provincial capital, Chieti was the Roman *Theate Marrucinorum*, a name that its bishop, Pietro Carafa, made use of when founding the Theatine Order, in 1524. Bishop Carafa went on to become Paul IV, the most vicious and reactionary of popes, but it's no reflection on Chieti.

The **Museo Nazionale Archeologico di Antichità** in the Villa Comunale is Chieti's star attraction (open 9–2, Sun 9–1, closed Mon; adm). The main building is the chief repository of pre-Roman and Roman art unearthed in Abruzzo, including the shapely 'Warrior of Capestrano' from the 6th century BC, dressed like a Mexican bandito and accompanied by an as yet untranslated inscription—the language of the mysterious Middle Adriatic Bronze Age culture. There is a room of other items from the Bronze Age, and others containing good Hellenistic and Roman sculptures, tombs, portraits, coins, jewellery, bronze figurines, vases and votive offerings, many of them discovered in Alba Fucens. A neighbouring building concentrates on the documentation of material from Abruzzo's many Upper Palaeolithic caves, ancient ceramics, and artefacts from Italic necropolises, all more or less in chronological order.

Out of doors, Chieti retains a couple of traces of *Theate Marrucinorum*—the remains of three little temples near the post office, while in the eastern residential quarters, you can visit the **Terme Romane**, or baths, of which a mighty cistern is the most impressive feature. Best of all are the lovely views, stretching from the sea to the Gran Sasso and Maiella mountains. From Chieti the Via Valeria (or Via Tiburtina, or Highway 5), the autostrada, and the railroad cross the peninsula to Rome.

Ortona and Lanciano

South of Pescara, beyond the pleasant resort of **Francavilla al Mare**, lies Abruzzo's largest port, **Ortona**, a town which took more than its share of bumps, earthquakes and major battle wounds in the Second World War; in the autumn of 1943, the Germans were well entrenched along a line north of the river Sangro, and to root them out, the six-week Battle of the Sangro and Moro Rivers cost thousands of lives before Ortona was entered at the end of December. There are two large British military cemeteries in the vicinity, one on the river Moro and one on the Sangro.

From Ortona, you can take the narrow-gauge train for an inland loop (although admittedly the bus is much faster), taking in Guardiagrele and Lanciano on the way. **Guardiagrele** was a famous goldsmiths' centre in the Renaissance, the birthplace of the renowned Nicola da Guardiagrele, who produced some of the 15th century's finest works, including the silver altar in Teramo Cathedral and a silver crucifix in the treasure of Guardiagrele's **Santa Maria Maggiore**. This church has a huge exterior fresco of St Christopher by Andrea Delitio, which brings good luck to any traveller who sees it. Guardiagrele still has a craft tradition in copper work and wrought iron—as you are bound to notice should you travel there.

Lanciano, with its unusual skyline of crumbling old towers, was a medieval market town that attracted merchants from all over the Mediterranean to its wool and cloth fairs; it retains several grey stone monuments from its golden days: **Porta San Biagio**, the only medieval gate to survive; **Santa Maria Maggiore**, with a refined Gothic portal with stone stitches like an embroidery sampler and Lanciano's chief treasure within, a crucifix by Nicola da Guardiagrele; and the **cathedral**, uniquely sited on a Roman bridge, which was restored in the 11th century to support the church. Lanciano is also the starting point for one of the most spectacular drives in Abruzzo—SS 84 to Roccaraso, near Abruzzo National Park.

San Giovanni in Venere

Back on the coast, above the railway station of the small resort of **Fossacésia Marina**, stands one of Abruzzo's most remarkable monuments: **San Giovanni in Venere**—Venere referring to the goddess Venus, over whose temple this church was erected, perhaps in the 8th century, though it was rebuilt in 1015 and converted into a Cistercian abbey in 1165. Temples to Venus were very often erected in similar spots, high over the sea, and there are several Apulian and Sicilian touches in the church—in the decoration of the narrow windows, in the robust figures of the bas-reliefs, in the name and design of the magnificent *Portale della Luna*, the marble 'Portal of the Moon' (1230)—that suggest the not-always-orthodox influence of Emperor Frederick II. Be sure to walk around the church to see the beautiful apses, in the Siculo-Norman style of Monreale; inside, the ceiling is supported by cruciform piers, and there are some old, if not very interesting, frescoes dating back to the 12th century. The large crypt, entered from the aisles, contains ancient columns from the temple of Venus.

Further south, salty old **Vasto** stands on a low natural terrace over its beach and port, the former attracting large numbers of French tourists. Its narrow streets end at the weathered but very distinctive 13th-century **castle** with a cylindrical tower. Vasto is proud of its local painter, Filippo Palizzi (1818–99), whose works hang in the **Museo Civico** and in the church of **San Pietro**.

Termoli

Crossing over the river Trigno, you enter Molise, which is, in the main, even more rural and unspoiled than Abruzzo, although it may not be immediately apparent from the busy beaches along the coast. **Termoli** gets top billing here, a bright little fishing port with a long sandy beach, palms and oleanders; its austerity and pale stone buildings are akin to Apulia, if not the sunny shores of North Africa. The diva of the old town, or at least what part of the old town survived the Turkish raid in 1566, is the 13th-century **cathedral**, its façade undulating with blind Apulian-style arcades. Frederick II built the **castle**, and most of the walls; after enjoying the view there's nothing more demanding to do than relax on the beach and try to decide which seafood restaurant to try in the evening. If Termoli's too crowded, there's another modest resort in Molise, **Campomarino**; further south the road enters Apulia (see p. 313).

WHERE TO STAY AND EATING OUT
In Chieti, the best place to stay and eat is *****Dangio'**, Via Solferino 20, tel (0871) 347 356, with good, comfortable rooms, all with bath (L75–80 000); its gourmet restaurant, **La Regine**, serves a famous *zuppa di cozze* (mussels) and other dishes prepared with refinement (L40 000). Alternatively, try the more modest ***Garibaldi**, Piazza Garibaldi 25, tel (0871) 345 318 (L30–35 000 without bath, L36–45 000 with). In Lanciano, the **Taverna Ranieri**, Via Luigi de Crecchio 42, tel (0872) 32 102, serves some unusual dishes, and rich Abruzzese desserts (L35 000).

Next to the abbey of San Giovanni in Venere, **Dei Priori**, Via S. Giovanni 41, tel (0872) 608 171, is located in a well-restored 18th-century villa, and serves lovely seafood, including lobster (L35 000 and up, depending on the type of fish you order). Vasto is a bit of a gastronomic capital on the coast: for the best *risotto di pesce* around, head up to the old town to **Jeannot**, Loggia Amblingh, tel (0873) 55 000, an elegant place that also specializes in seafood for *secondi* (L40 000; closed Wed, but never in summer). Both excellent sea and land food are served at Vasto's **Lo Scudo**, Via Garibaldi 39, tel (0873) 2782, followed by delicious dessert (L35–40 000, closed Tues).

In Termoli, the ******Corona**, Via M. Milano 2, tel (0875) 84 041, is a medium-sized traditional hotel located in the centre of town; all rooms have private baths, frigo-bar, and TVs, and there's a good Liberty-style restaurant (L115 000). The nine-room *****Cian**, Lungomare Colombo 48, tel (0875) 43 236, is located on a rock over the coast, with pleasant views; all rooms have showers (L48 000). Termoli is endowed with an excellent restaurant, **Lo Squalo Blu**, Via De Gasperi 49, tel (0875) 83 203, where the fare includes exquisitely cooked (and many raw) molluscs and crustaceans as well as duck, followed by a delicious variety of cheese from Molise (L35–45 000). Five kilometres north from the centre, on the Adriatica Highway, **Torre Saracena**, tel (0875) 3318, is located in an ancient watchtower on the beach, featuring the freshest of fish, prepared in some surprising ways (L40 000, depending on the fish).

Teramo, L'Aquila, and the Gran Sasso

Two provincial capitals—metropolises by Abruzzo standards—Teramo and L'Aquila, stand on either side of the Gran Sasso range, each providing access to the peaks' trails and ski slopes. L'Aquila, which also reigns as regional capital, is an intriguing town in its own right, and for many visitors makes an ideal base for travelling through the rest of Abruzzo.

GETTING AROUND
Teramo is easily reached by train, on a spur from the coastal line at Giulianova. The autostrada (and ARPA buses) link it quickly to the coast, to Ascoli Piceno, and to L'Aquila. L'Aquila itself is easily reached by bus from Rome, on either the ARPA or OGNIVIA lines, with 16 departures on weekdays (a 2-hour trip), and Pescara (7 times a day, 2 hours by autostrada, otherwise 3 hours). Trains connect L'Aquila (with no great speed or frequency) to Rieti in Lazio and Terni in Umbria, as well as to Pescara, by way of Sulmona.

TOURIST INFORMATION
Teramo: Via del Castello 10, tel (0861) 54 243
L'Aquila: Piazza Santa Maria di Paganica 5, tel (0862) 410 808

Teramo

From Giulianova, Highway 80 heads 20 km inland to **Teramo**, another sleepy Abruzzo provincial capital, set midway between the coast and Gran Sasso. Originally a Roman city, Teramo knew its happiest days in the 14th century under the Angevins, and even though it wears mostly 20th-century fashions now, it retains several fine monuments. The **cathedral** stands out, with its remarkable Cosmati portal and Romanesque statues of saints; around them a miscellany of lions, collected from here and there, lend feline elegance to the façade, which is simple, square and ungabled as is typical of Abruzzo. The cathedral's roofline has swallowtail Ghibelline crenellations (you can usually tell the state of local politics when any Italian medieval building was built by these; plain square crenellations are 'Guelph'); in spite of its imperial sentiments, though, Teramo was long the fief of its bishops. Today they still possess the title of 'Prince of Teramo', though they don't make much use of the special papal dispensation from more rough and ready days, that allowed them to wear armour under their robes and keep their swords handy on the altar. The pretty campanile is from the 15th century; inside there's a silver altar frontal with 30 scenes from the Bible, a masterpiece by Nicola da Guardiagrele (1448), and a rich golden polyptych by the 15th-century Venetian Jacobello del Fiore.

Near the cathedral lie scanty ruins of the **Roman Theatre** and, a block from this, the original cathedral, **Sant' Maria Aprutiensis** (6th–12th century) which has recently been restored—its name reminds us of the Italic tribe of the Praetuttii who once lived here, and gave their name to *Aprutium* (and hence to Abruzzo). Santa Maria (also called Sant'Anna), built over a Roman building, is Teramo's attic of odds and ends— Lombard carvings, a 6th-century triforium, and ancient angelic frescoes. Another block or so east is a well-preserved house built during the Angevin era, the **Casa dei Melatini**. In the Franciscan church of **Maria Santissima delle Grazie**, to the east by the Piazza della Libertà, is a painted wooden statue of the Madonna and child by one of Abruzzo's best sculptors, Silvestro dall'Aquila (15th century). More 15th-century Abruzzese works of art are on display in the **Museo Civico**, located in the Villa Comunale. If you're driving, take the road to the **Osservatorio Astrofisico** for good views of the Gran Sasso.

Around Teramo

Heading north from Teramo towards Ascoli Piceno on SS81, the road passes by **Campli**, a town that was bigger than Teramo in the Middle Ages; though there are no special monuments, Campli has the genuine, not too romantic, look of a medieval market town. In the centre are the **Palazzo del Comune** and the Romanesque church of **San Francesco**, a fine embodiment of the Abruzzese ideal that less is more; inside are some good 14th-century frescoes. Its former convent now houses an **Archaeology Museum**, containing artefacts from the 6th–3rd century BC Italic necropolis at Campovalano, a kilometre away. In Campovalano, the excavations aren't much to look at, but there's the interesting ancient abbey and church of **San Pietro**, founded in the 8th century and rebuilt in the 13th century; figures of saints are frescoed on the piers inside, pretending to be part of the congregation. Part of an early Christian sarcophagus may be seen along the wall.

A few kilometres north of Campli rises the superbly positioned town of **Civitella del Tronto**, crowned by an impregnable castle that the last Bourbon loyalists managed to hold to the bitter end in 1861. First built around the year 1000, the castle as you see it was completed by the Spaniards, a fine example of the daring (and expensive) military architecture of the day. Currently under restoration, the castle has a travertine walled terrace a half-kilometre in length, lending Civitella its distinctive crew-cut skyline.

Neither of these towns is a compelling attraction, but if you are travelling this way persevere for **Ascoli Piceno**, just over the border in the region of the Marches. Ascoli is famous for stuffed olives, and beyond that it is an exceptionally beautiful and sophisticated place, a sort of Tuscan art town transplanted to the southern Apennines. Its glistening travertine Piazza del Popolo is one of the most stunning spaces in Italy, and in addition there are some fine churches, Roman ruins and a clutch of skyscraping medieval tower-fortresses.

Eastern Approaches to the Gran Sasso

Some 15 km south of Teramo, Highway 150 follows the Val Vomano westwards and splits near the autostrada entrance into two arms embracing the Gran Sasso, one following the increasingly narrow Val Vomano on the north side, and the other the higher **Valle di Mavone** to the south. The latter (Route 491) is an excellent approach to the mountains, with the highest peak of the Apennines, the Corno Grande (2912 m) looming ahead. Several curiosities along the way offer tempting detours—near Castel Castagna there's **Santa Maria di Ronzano**, an ancient three-nave church embellished with frescoes dated 1181, strange and colourful works in a completely Byzantine style; another attraction is panoramic views of the Corno Grande. The scenery is stunning as the road reaches **Isola del Gran Sasso**, a fine stone village and good base for hikes up to the **Campo Imperatore** (see 'L'Aquila', below); it has another Romanesque church, **San Giovanni ad Insulam**, with good frescoes in the crypt (get the key in Isola before setting out), as well as a new shrine of the new patron saint of Abruzzo-Molise, San Gabriele dell'Addolorata, a young Franciscan monk from Assisi who died in the monastery here in 1862. His relics draw pilgrims by the bus-load, who are processed through a huge, disconcerting steel and concrete basilica designed in shopping-mall moderne.

To the southeast, dramatically positioned at the foot of the great wall of Monte Camicia, is **Castelli**, another good mountain base and a village worth visiting in its own right. Castelli is the ceramics centre of Abruzzo, a local industry that achieved art and glory in the 17th-century workshops of the Grue and Gentili families. The ceramic tradition is continued in the **Istituto Statale d'Arte Ceramica** (where you can see a remarkable 100-figure ceramic *presepio*), in the various workshops in town, and in the August ceramics fair, where part of the fun is tossing reject plates over the river. Castelli's artisans still do excellent work, perhaps the best in the Mezzogiorno, though the town makes more money on bathroom tiles and the little figurines Italians give as presents for their children's first communions. The **Chiesa Madre** contains an unusual majolica *pala* by Francesco Grue as well as 12th-century wooden statues; more of his work may be seen in the **Museo delle Ceramiche Abruzzesi**. Most splendiferous of all, however, is the rural church of **San Donato**, which Carlo Levi has rightfully dubbed 'The Sistine Chapel of Italian Majolica' for its ceiling of a thousand ceramic tiles—the only ceiling like it in Italy, an impressive 33.4 square metres covered by a colourful patchwork of different folk motifs—plenty of rabbits, skulls, portraits, notices of various kinds, geometric patterns and some mystic alchemical symbolism, made between 1615 and 1617. Also on the outskirts is the derelict Romanesque church of **San Salvatore**, with the charming remains of a medieval pulpit.

Upper Vomano Valley Towards L'Aquila

At **Montorio al Vomano** Highway 150 meets highway 80, the scenic road which, like the more efficient but less panoramic autostrada, links Teramo with L'Aquila. Montorio, topped by its grand but never completed Spanish castle, has an eclectic church, the **Collegiata di San Rocco**, with a façade that has been added to whenever funds were handy; within, the carved wooden Baroque altar and tapestries are the main attraction. South of Montorio on SS491 to Isola del Gran Sasso, you can take in the village of **Tossicia**, with some fairytale houses in a pretty medieval nucleus lying between two mountain streams; the tiny church of **Sant'Antonio Abate** has a grand 1471 portal by the Venetian Antonio Lombardo, a little Renaissance masterpiece in the most unlikely of places. Works by one of Italy's best known naif painters, Annunziata Scipione, may be seen in nearby **Azzinano**.

Further up the valley, the twin, blunt, snow-shrouded peaks of the Due Corni del Gran Sasso look over the shoulder of **Fano Adriano**, an old town now a small winter/summer resort, with skiing and hiking at **Pratoselva**. The village's name translates as 'Hadrian's Temple', although none of this remains; the 12th-century **San Pietro** is modern Fano's finest church. **Pietracamela**, even higher up in the lap of the Gran Sasso (1005 metres), is a base for hikes over the Sella dei Due Corni to the Campo Imperatore, and for skiing at the Gran Sasso's biggest resort, the **Prati di Tivo**, a fine lofty meadow among beech forests; on Sundays and holidays a helicopter takes expert skiers up to otherwise inaccessible runs.

Highway 80 continues towards L'Aquila, by-passing the **Lago di Campotosto**, an irregular, manmade lake richly stocked with fish, with the Gran Sasso for a striking backdrop. The road now winds around the western flank of the Gran Sasso; about 10 km before L'Aquila, it comes to **Amiternum**, the ruins of a Sabine city mentioned in the Aeneid, and later a Roman colony that was the birthplace of the Roman historian Sallust. A small theatre, amphitheatre, houses with mosaics and frescoes, etc. were brought to light in 1978. Nearby medieval **San Vittorino** has, under its 12th–16th century church of **San Michele**, something out of the ordinary in this part of the world—catacombs, although unlike the great ones in Rome, these have been embellished with 15th-century frescoes. The church itself is singularly split into two sections by a wall.

L'Aquila

L'Aquila in Italian means 'the eagle', the symbol of empire, and it's not surprising to learn that the city was founded by Emperor Frederick II in 1240 as a bulwark against the popes. L'Aquila is one of the few cities in Italy of any importance not to have ancient precedents; instead, to populate his new town, Frederick relocated the inhabitants of surrounding castles and hamlets—99 of them in all, according to tradition. But what made L'Aquila especially prosperous was its loyalty in 1423 to Queen Joan II when the city was besieged for over a year by the Aragonese. The queen thanked the city for its steadfastness by granting it numerous privileges that helped it to become, for several centuries, the second city in the Kingdom of Naples, minting its own coins, a chief wool and livestock market town, and a producer of silk and saffron. Its success attracted Adamo di Rottweil, a student of Gutenberg, who founded a printing press here in 1482, one of the first in the south.

L'Aquila's good fortune made it cocky, and in 1529 it rose up against its rulers in Naples. The Spanish viceroy quickly put an end to its pretensions and punished the Aquilani by forcing them to pay for a huge new citadel to discourage any further revolts. Much of what the Spaniards didn't destroy in their reprisal fell in the horrific earthquake of 1703. And yet, despite its various vicissitudes, L'Aquila has managed to keep a considerable portion of its labyrinthine old quarter, its walls, and even some of its exceptional 13th-century monuments.

A 99-headed Fountain

L'Aquila's most famous monument, the venerable **Fontana delle 99 Cannelle**, lies in a corner of the city walls near the Porta Rivera, a couple of blocks from the railway station at the bottom of the city. Built in 1272, the fountain's water flows through the mouths of 93 mouldering grotesque heads (and six unadorned spouts), each said to symbolize one of the hamlets that were joined to form the city of L'Aquila. The fountain has three sides (the one to the left is a more recent one, built in the 16th century), and the whole is sheltered in a pretty pink-and-white chequered courtyard. While you're there, try to figure out how the two sundials work on the façade of the little church opposite.

From the fountain the street ascends to join Via XX Settembre, the main entry-point into the city if you're coming from Rome. Follow Via XX Settembre straight into the municipal park and turn left a block for Viale di Collemaggio and L'Aquila's greatest Romanesque church, **Santa Maria di Collemaggio**, founded in 1270 by the hermit Pietro da Morrone. The church has one of the most sumptuous and attractive façades of any in Abruzzo, its three rounded portals decorated with spiral mouldings and niches for saints who have mostly vanished. Above the portals runs a pretty ribbon-like frieze, and above that are three rose windows of different patterns, the large centre one in particular a masterpiece of the stonecarver's art. The elegant interior has been stripped of centuries' accumulation of art and debris, leaving the fancy Renaissance tomb of Celestine V as its chief decoration. The hermit Pietro da Morrone, who founded the

Santa Maria di Collemaggio, L'Aquila

church, was an utterly holy man though rather naive, and in 1294, to his surprise, was crowned pope here by cardinals hoping to use him as their tool. After a few months it became evident to the powers in the Church that the new Pope Celestine V wasn't quite turning out the way they had hoped, and he was subtly 'encouraged' in Naples' Egg Castle (see p. 215) to resign St Peter's throne—the only pope ever to do so voluntarily. Soon after his death, however, one of his successors canonized him, and here he rests as St Peter Celestine. A privilege Celestine V granted the church during his brief office is a Holy Door, an uncommon feature, which is opened annually on 28 August for the faithful to pass through and receive the still distributed Papal Indulgence.

Around Piazza Duomo

From the park, Corso Federico II leads into the Piazza Duomo. L'Aquila is one town where the cathedral is the least interesting building, frequently shattered by earthquakes and now dressed in a dull Neoclassical façade. The large piazza itself is much livelier, having been L'Aquila's main market square ever since 1304, when Charles of Anjou granted the city the right to hold one—you'll find produce and vegetables, and a variety of handicrafts on sale here daily from dawn to 1 pm. The neighbourhood around the Piazza del Duomo is one of L'Aquila's most attractive. On Via Santa Giusta, the portal and rose window of the 13th-century church of **Santa Giusta** are worth a look, the rose window embellished with 12 droll figures. On Via Sassa, the church of **San Giuseppe** contains a 15th-century equestrian tomb by Ludovico d'Alemagna, while the **Palazzo Franchi**, at No 56, contains a lovely Renaissance courtyard with a double loggia.

From the Piazza Duomo, Corso Vittorio Emanuele leads to the **Quattro Cantoni**, the 'Four Corners', one of the city's main crossroads. To the left, on Corso Umberto, lies the Piazza del Palazzo, the palazzo in question being the **Palazzo di Giustizia**, from where Margherita of Austria, a daughter of Charles V born on the wrong side of the blanket, ruled as Governess of Abruzzo. The bell in the palace's tower sounds 99 strokes every day at dusk, in memory of the city's origins.

San Bernardino

In the opposite direction from the Quattro Cantoni, Via San Bernardino leads to the masterpiece of Abruzzese Renaissance art, the **Church of San Bernardino**. The great Franciscan revivalist preacher, San Bernardino da Siena, spent several years in the Franciscan convent in L'Aquila before he died, whereupon one of his chief disciples in Abruzzo, St John of Capestrano, founded this church as his memorial. The perfectly balanced, elegant façade was finished by Cola d'Amatrice in 1542, and is best seen from the bottom of the stair in front of the church; we are in Abruzzo so the roof is gable-less. The 1703 earthquake smashed the vast interior, which was rebuilt à la Grand Baroque; the magnificent gilt wood ceiling is by Ferdinando Mosca. San Bernardino's mausoleum and the *Tomb of Maria Pereira* are both works by Silvestro dell'Aquila, the master of Abruzzo sculpture and pupil of Donatello. The second chapel on the right contains a pala by Andrea della Robbia.

The Castello

At the end of the Corso Vittorio Emanuele opens the shady Parco del Castello and the grand, moated **Castello**, built in 1535 by Pier Luigi Scrivà, a veritable showpiece of military architecture unwillingly financed by the citizens of L'Aquila. Within its grand doorway, crowned by Charles V's two-headed eagle, it no longer contains Neapolitans and Spaniards, but the **Museo Nazionale d'Abruzzo**, the region's finest, with a well-arranged collection of archaeological and art treasures salvaged from abandoned churches (open 9–2, closed Mon; adm). The biggest exhibit is on the ground floor, near the entrance: the *Elephas Meridonalis*, a mighty reconstructed prehistoric pachyderm, discovered by accident near L'Aquila in 1954. The ground floor also contains an archaeological section, with Roman portraits, statues, tombs, several fine tympana, reliefs, tools, etc.; up on the first floor there are some beautifully carved wooden doors illustrating Biblical scenes, works in ivory and silver, polychrome wooden statues, including a *St Sebastian* and a *Madonna and Child* by Silvestro dell'Aquila, the latter sharing the same room with a fine 15th-century panel painting of *St John of Capestrano*. There are many other fine triptychs, one by Sano di Pietro and others showing Sienese-Umbrian influence, and later works by Neapolitan painters Mattia Preti and Andrea Vaccaro. One of the best things about the museum's long, long corridors are the lovely views they offer of the Gran Sasso. Concerts are frequently held in the castle's audi-torium—in August you can listen to classical guitar recitals.

Gran Sasso d'Italia

'The Big Rock of Italy' offers alpine grandeur only an hour by motorway from Rome, and as such is an immensely popular ski and hiking resort. There are plans to designate the Gran Sasso a natural park, but until it becomes official, environmentalists and de-velopers will continue to disagree on its future. If you plan to do any hiking, pick up a map, either from the tourist office or Italian Alpine Club in L'Aquila, Via XX Settembre 15, tel 24 342 (open 7 am–8 pm).

To reach the Gran Sasso from L'Aquila, catch the bus from Corso Vittorio Emanuele to the new (1987) funivia at Fonte Cerreto, near **Assergi**, the village at the mouth of the Gran Sasso Tunnel—or alternatively, if the roads are clear, drive up Highway 17bis by way of **Bazzano** (site of an interesting 12th-century church **Santa Giusta**). Both funivia and highway will take you to the **Campo Imperatore** (2126 m), the beautiful, gentle upland basin, filled with flowers in the late spring and ski bunnies in the winter. Near the upper funivia station stands the Albergo di Campo Imperatore, which once sheltered a real would-be emperor. After the Italians captured Mussolini in Rome in 1943, there remained the delicate question of what to do with him. After being shuttled off to a Tyrrhenian island, he was brought here, to this hotel, at the time inaccessible by road—setting the stage for pilot Otto Skorzeny's daredevil rescue on 12 September 1943. Skorzeny slipped in under the guards' noses by flying a Fiesler-Storch 103—an aeroplane the size of the average bedroom—into which he somehow managed to squeeze the portly Mussolini before escaping. Hitler then set up a new headquarters for Mussolini at Salò on Lake Garda, the capital of the puppet Italian Social Republic.

Many of the trails through the Gran Sasso begin at the hotel, including one up past the Duca d'Abruzzi refuge to the **Corno Grande** (2912 m)—a spectacular eight hour walk. There are also three ski lifts in the Campo Imperatore and above at Monte Cristo, with runs suitable for both novice and expert. On the west side of L'Aquila there is more good skiing as well as bob-sledding at **Campo Felice**, above the picturesque village of **Rocca di Cambio**, the highest in Abruzzo at 1434 m.

From L'Aquila to Popoli

Descending from the eastern side of Campo Imperatore, you will pass **Calascio**, with its impressive ruined citadel 1500 m up, or further up, **Castel del Monte**, with an interesting medieval core. The entire village is illuminated at night; isolated in its bare hills it is one of the most striking sights in the south. The mountains finally give way at the Plain of Novelli. The scrubby, seemingly empty fields all around are really saffron farms; you'll need to look closely to see the tiny purple flowers with their precious yellow pollen. Route 17, the main road of the central Abruzzo, follows the plain. South of it, **Bominaco** (near Caporciano), is the site of the most celebrated monuments in this corner of Abruzzo, the two churches formerly belonging to a fortified Benedictine abbey. The monastery dates from some shadowy three-digit year; the lower church, **San Pellegrino**, is said to have been founded by Charlemagne, though it was rebuilt in 1263. The interior, rectangular in shape, with an ogival vault, is covered with an excellent example of the colourful, stylized frescoes of the period; some of the upper pictures represent a calendar of the months and the major feast days, while others represent scenes from the New Testament, saints, and geometrical patterns. The sanctuary is set apart from the nave by marble transennae, one carved with a griffon with a cup, and the other with a fearsome dragon—not ordinary subject-matter for a Christian temple. The saint is buried under the sanctuary, and it is said that you can hear his heart beating through a hole next to the altar. The upper church, **Santa Maria Assunta**, has none of the ancient strangeness of San Pellegrino, but is a 12th-century gem, beautifully endowed with carved doors, windows, capitals, and a pulpit. From Navelli the road makes a dramatic writhing descent to Popoli (see below), on the Via Valeria and the Rome-Pescara autostrada, or you can continue on eastwards to **Capestrano**, birthplace of San Bernardino's saintly follower, St John Capestran (1386–1456); unlike its namesake in California, however, it has to get by without any swallows.

WHERE TO STAY AND EATING OUT

Teramo (tel prefix 0861) has a handful of hotels, the most attractive of which is the *****Sporting** because of its pool and garden, although it's located on the outskirts of town (Via De Gasperi 41, tel 414 723). All rooms have private bath (L65–75 000). Eating can be more adventurous, especially if you come in May when the locals are cooking up pots of *virtù*, a stew of seven vegetables, seven kinds of pasta, and seven pulses: peas, lentils, favas, garbanzos and other beans, cooked with pigs' ears and feet, sausage and lard; perhaps it's only eaten in May because you can go outside afterwards. More civilized Teramo specialities are served at **Il Duomo**, Via Stazio 9, tel 321 274, like *macaroni alla chitarra* (so named because it is cut with an instrument shaped like a guitar), also good meat dishes (L35 000; closed Mon and Aug). Up in the Prati di Tivo, above Pietracamela, the ******Miramonti**, tel 95 621, is a comfortable, modern, resort hotel, with a garden, pool, and tennis courts (open 20 Dec–10 April, 20 June–5 Sept; rooms, all with bath, L78–95 000). ****Europa**, also in Prati di Tivo, tel 95 630, is the largest and best-endowed hotel of its category (L35 000 without bath, L42–55 000 with).

In L'Aquila (tel prefix 0862), there are more choices: the ***Castello**, opposite the castle in Piazza Battaglione Alpini, tel 29 147, is an attractive, classy hotel; all rooms with bath, L70–80 000. Down at the foot of town, near the fountain and train station, ***Le Cannelle**, Borgo Rivera, tel 6981, has 115 modern furnished rooms, as well as a pool and tennis court (all with bath, L78–90 000). **Italia**, Corso Vittorio Emanuele 79, tel 20 566, has good centrally located rooms (L34 000 without bath, L42 000 with bath). Traditional Abruzzese cuisine is the speciality at **Tre Marie**, Via Tre Marie 3, tel 20 191; tasty regional *salumeria*, and dishes featuring truffles or saffron, and roast lamb and kid go down easily in a charming ambience of panelling and paintings (L45 000; closed Sun eve and Mon). **Aquila da Remo**, Via San Flaviano 9, tel 22 010, has good solid cooking in a simple setting (L25 000). Even cheaper, **Trattoria del Giaguaro**, Piazza Santa Maria Paganica 4, tel 24 001, is convenient, good and inexpensive (L15 000).

Mussolini's hotel, the old **Albergo Campo Imperatore**, has been closed for years, with no reopening in sight; the little **La Villetta**, at the lower funivia station at Fonte Cerreto, tel 606 134, is a pretty and friendly option as well as a base for visiting the Gran Sasso (L42 000, with bath).

Southern Abruzzo and the National Park

For many people the highlight of Abruzzo is its National Park, the second-largest in Italy and one of special interest for its rare fauna and flora. For mountain-lovers, there's also the Montagna della Maiella, a range nearly as impressive as the Gran Sasso and considerably less touristed. Manmade sights there are, too: Alba Fucens, Abruzzo's best archaeological site, intriguing old towns like Sulmona, Scanno, Pescocostanzo and Tagliacozzo.

GETTING AROUND

With trains big and small, and bus routes to most of the area, Sulmona, located near Abruzzo's main east-west and north-south arteries, makes an excellent base for exploring the works of nature and man. There are several spectacular drives in the region: Highway 5bis from L'Aquila to Celano, Highway 84 from Lanciano to Roccaraso, Highway 83 from Pescina through the National Park. Frequent buses run from L'Aquila to Avezzano, and from there to Pescassèroli, the administrative centre of the park. In the summer months you can find direct buses between Pescassèroli and Rome.

TOURIST INFORMATION

Sulmona: Via Papa Innocenzo VII 4, tel (0864) 53 276
Tagliacozzo: Piazza Andrea Argoli, tel (0864) 6348
Pescassèroli: Via Principe di Napoli, tel (0863) 91 461
Scanno: Piazza Santa Maria della Valle, tel (0864) 74 317

The Via Valeria: Pescara to Rome

Beyond Pescara and Chieti, the old Roman Via Valeria/Via Tiburtina (route 5) accompanies Autostrada 25 up the Pescara valley. This was also an important route in the

Middle Ages, and quite a few monuments from that time survive along it and in the surrounding hills. At Manoppello Scalo, just above route 5, **Santa Maria d'Arabona** is a Cistercian church of about 1200. Its asymmetrical façade has a big rose window, and inside is some lovely Gothic vaulting and sculpted details. Further west, on a long twisting road above the village of Manoppello, the stern and impressive **San Liberatore a Maiella** was also an abbey church; the rest of its buildings disappeared long ago in an earthquake. Completed in 1080, it marks a transition between the Lombard architecture from the north and the emerging Apulian Romanesque. The broad blank façade is covered in shallow blind arcades; two relief lions guard its simple portal. Inside, the best features are the pulpit and the Cosmatesque pavement, completely intact.

Near the village of **Torre dei Passeri**, just off the highway, the best of the Abruzzese Romanesque awaits at **San Clemente in Casauria**, founded by Emperor Louis II, Charlemagne's great-grandson, in 871. The Cistercians took over San Clemente and rebuilt the church in the 12th century, endowing it with a magnificent three-arched porch and intricately carved capitals, and a stunning portal with well-executed reliefs that form a fitting frame for the bronze doors, with their ornate panels of geometric patterns; these also date from the 12th century. The same sculptors, influenced by French Romanesque sculpture by way of Apulia, may also have carved the baldacchino, paschal candlestick and pulpit in the Romanesque interior; Louis II's original crypt was preserved in the reconstruction of the church, and may be reached by steps in the aisles.

From the nearby village of Tocco del Casauria, another back road heads up into the mountains, for **Caramánico Terme**, an ancient hill town with a modern spa attached. Caramánico stands on the edge of the **Maiella**, a group of mountains that is a fitting bookend to the Gran Sasso, nearly as tall and topped with snow for much of the year. The most scenic road along the fringes of the Maiella starts from Caramánico, eventually finding its way to Sulmona.

Popoli stands at the confluence of the Aterno and Sagittario rivers, where they meet to form the Pescara river. Popoli's largest church, **San Francesco**, boasting an elegant Romanesque façade topped with statues, has an unusual rose window. The 14th-century **Taverna Ducale**, decorated with a row of escutcheons, was not where Popoli's Cantelmi dukes drank, but where they stored the tithes from their subjects. It has survived in better shape than their ruined castle, looming over Popoli. **Corfinio**, next to the west, was renamed in Mussolini's campaign to restore geographical names of antiquity, for here stood the Peligni town of *Corfinium*, famous in history as the united headquarters of the rebellious Italic tribes in the Social Wars; they renamed the city *Italica* (the first time the name was used in history as a union of the peninsula's peoples) and hoped it would soon take over from Rome as capital. Its ruins are not much; there's a small archaeology museum in the convent of **Sant'Alessandro**. The most important monument in Corfinio is the large 13th-century **Basilica di San Pelino**, with its fine architectural details.

From Corfinio, Highway 17 continues to Sulmona (see below) while the autostrada veers south to avoid the scenic gorges of the Aterno river and the lofty pass at Forca Caruso. **Celano** is a pretty hilltown spread out under the skirts of its huge four-square **Piccolomini Castle**. Celano is best known as the birthplace of the Blessed Tomaso da Celano, a disciple of St Francis and his first biographer; he also composed the 'Dies

Irae', the eerie medieval hymn of the dead most often heard these days in the finale of Berlioz's *Symphonie Fantastique*. Nearby you can visit the stunning steep and narrow gorge, the **Gole di Celano**, or head north on the scenic Highway 5bis towards L'Aquila, by way of the mountain resort town of **Ovindoli** and Rocca di Cambio (see 'L'Aquila').

Avezzano and Alba Fucens

The region south of Celano is known as the Marsica, after its ancient inhabitants, the Marsi, who lived on the shores of Lake Fucino. The modern capital of the Marsica, **Avezzano**, has little to commend it, having been toppled by an earthquake in 1915 and bombed during World War II. Its one surviving monument, the **Castello Orsini** has a portal with a relief celebrating the Victory of Lepanto; inside there's a small museum of inscriptions and architectural fragments from the cities of the Marsica.

If the ancient Marsi were to return to their homeland today, they would be amazed to find their lake—once the largest in Central Italy—replaced by the fertile basin called the **Piana del Fucino**. But they would be the first to tell you that their *Lacus Fucinus* had an inadequate outlet and was prone to disastrous flooding. To drain it, Emperor Claudius in the year 54 ordered what became the greatest underground engineering work of antiquity—the 6-km-long tunnel intended to spill the lake's waters into the River Liri. Yet for all the amazing skill that went into the work, the tunnel didn't work very well and was eventually blocked up. In 1240 Frederick II tried to have it unblocked, but the project was not brought to a successful conclusion until 1875, when English, Italian, French and Swiss engineers finally drained the lake, reclaiming thousands of hectares. It's hard to imagine what the Marsi would make of the huge satellite dishes of Italy's biggest telecommunications centre, looming out of the west end of the basin.

Of all the ancient cities of the Marsica, the only one to leave behind considerable traces is *Alba Fucens*, near the modern village of **Albe**, 8 km from Avezzano. Alba was founded as a Roman colony in 300 BC, to keep an eye on the area's tribes—as evinced by its mighty walls. Ancient Alba occupies three hills, and its ruins intermingle with the ruins of medieval Alba. Much has been excavated, including the amphitheatre, the forum, the basilica, the weedy theatre, the baths, and a long section of the original Via Valeria. Near the amphitheatre is the well-preserved Romanesque church of San Pietro, adorned with pretty Cosmati work.

Avezzano is a main departure point for Abruzzo National Park (see below).

Tagliacozzo

Tagliacozzo, which discretion forbids us to translate, is actually named after Thalia, the Muse of Theatre. A pretty town on the slopes of Monte Bove, it is best known for the battle that took place nearby on 12 August 1268, which ended the reign of the Swabians and heirs of Frederick II; as Dante described it, the Swabians under Conradin were caught unawares and unarmed by the clever plans of the Angevins, led by William di Villehardouin. The site of the battle is marked by the ruined church of **Santa Maria della Vittoria**, at Scúrcola Marsicana, east of Tagliacozzo. The simple church of **San Francesco**, with its good rose window and portal, contains the relics of Tomaso da

Celano, but here the secular architecture is more interesting, beginning with the 14th-century **Palazzo Ducale**, a grand building on a grand piazza; the loggia on the first floor shelters fine though damaged frescoes by Lorenzo da Viterbo. The quarter around the genteel old **Piazza dell'Obelisco**, with its Renaissance obelisk, has many picturesque houses and peeling palaces from the 14th and 15th centuries. Buses from here continue to Tivoli and Rome, only a 40-minute drive away on the autostrada.

Sulmona

Sulmona, beautifully located in a green basin surrounded by mountains, was the ancient capital of another obscure Italic tribe, the Peligni. But it is best remembered as the birthplace of Ovid (43 BC–AD 17), and later as the capital of its own province created by Frederick II. As such Sulmona became a minor centre of learning and religion, home of the main abbey of the Celestine Order, and of Pietro Angeleri, who lived in the hermitage of Monte Morrone, before being brought down to L'Aquila to be crowned Celestine V. In the early Renaissance its craftsmen were celebrated for their gold-work, although since then they have learned a sweeter skill—what the Italians call *confetti*—colourful candy-coated almonds used as wedding favours. Sulmona's shop windows display them with an artistic pastel pageantry that is part of this little city's charm.

The main street, Corso Ovidio, holds Sulmona's loveliest monument, the church and palace of **Santa Maria Annunziata**, a Gothic and Renaissance ensemble, begun in 1320. Although the three portals on the palace's façade were done at different periods, the result is as harmonically sweet as *confetti*: here is a finely carved, floridly Gothic left portal, crowned by a statue of St Michael, while the middle portal is pure symmetrical Renaissance in form; the comparatively plain portal on the right was the last built, in 1522. Figures of Doctors of the Church and saints stand sentry along the façade, and above them runs an intricate ribbon frieze, and above that are three lacy Gothic windows. The first floor contains a small **Museum** where you can see some of Renaissance Sulmona's goldsmiths' work (open 10–12:30 and 4:30–7, Sun 9–12:30). The church's sombre Baroque façade was rebuilt after the 1703 earthquake, yet it is complementary to the adjacent palace.

Running through the centre of Sulmona is an unusual Gothic **aqueduct**, built in 1256, which supplied water to the towns and its mills; a good place to see it is the huge Piazza Garibaldi, site of the 1474 **Fontana del Vecchio**, so-called because of the bust of a jovial old man on top. Across from this stands the lovely carved Romanesque portal of **San Francesco della Scarpa** ('with shoes' because here the Franciscans wore shoes instead of sandals), but it's a portal and nothing more, the rest having tumbled in one of Sulmona's earthquakes. Outside town, towards Monte Morrone, are the ruins (steps, platform, and road) of a **Temple of Hercules**, which the locals are fond of calling 'Ovid's villa'.

Around Sulmona

There are several picturesque hill towns in the vicinity of Sulmona, like **Pacentro**, 9 km to the east, its lanes winding about the battlemented towers of the ruined Cantelmo

Castle. Beyond Pacentro the road heads up in a serious way into the rugged Maiella mountains, turning north towards **Caramánico Terme** (a pretty hill town and sulphur-water spa) and the Via Valeria, and turning south past the **Campo di Giove**, a winter sports centre with a funivia up the slopes of a mountain called the Round Table (2404 m) on its way to scenic Highway 84. This area is well endowed with summer/winter sports facilities, in **Pescocostanzo**, **Rivisondoli**, and especially **Roccaraso**, further south on Highway 17 (all stations on the Sulmona-Isernia railway). Pescocostanzo, which once owed allegiance to Vittoria Colonna, poet and friend of Michelangelo, is a charming little town, famous for its lace, and ornamented with the lovely **Collegiata di Santa Maria del Colle**, its interior adorned with excellent wood carvings, the oldest ones dating back to the 15th century.

On scenic Highway 84, between Roccaraso and Lanciano (bus), **Taranta Peligna** has a new funivia rising up to what must be the most spectacular cave in Central Italy, the **Grotta del Cavallone** (1425 m), used as a setting in D'Annunzio's play *La figlia di Jorio*. Its name, the 'Big Horse', comes from the profile carved by nature on the wall at the grandiose entrance of the grotto: other rooms are adorned with stone flowers and lace, alabaster streaks that remind the Italians of ham (in the 'Sala del Prosciutto'); there is a chamber of fairies and the 'Sala del Pantheon', full of curious stalagmite monsters and deities (guided visits last an hour and a half; open April–Sept; to make sure it's open, ring first (0872) 910 236).

South of Roccaraso, near the eastern entrance into Abruzzo National Park is **Castel di Sangro**, badly damaged in World War II, though still preserving its ruined citadel, reached by a steep mule path. The modern municipio contains a collection of ancient statues and bronzes found in the vicinity, and in the upper part of the town stands the fine Baroque church of **Santa Maria Assunta**, retaining its Renaissance plan and paintings by De Matteis and Vaccaro. Highway 17 continues south through Isernia towards Naples; for centuries this was the kingdom's busy 'Via degli Abruzzi'.

To the west of Sulmona lies **Cocullo**, famous for its 'Procession of Serpents' held on the first Thursday of every May. Live snakes are draped over a statue of Cocullo's patron, San Domenico, as well as over the more inspired locals, who thus form a procession through the streets, uncannily coiling and writhing. There is a story that St Dominic rid the area of poisonous snakes, but scholars have a sneaking suspicion that the festival is a living folk memory of the cult of the goddess Angizia, the enchantress of snakes.

Scanno

From Cocullo (or Anversa degli Abruzzi) SS479 ascends the lovely **Valle del Sagittario**, passing through the steep Gorge of the Sagittario and by the pretty trout-filled Lago di Scanno. Perched high over the lake, the village of **Scanno** is one of the most popular destinations in Abruzzo, a picturesque place that fascinated 18th-century travellers who wondered at its customs and costumes, more reminiscent of Asia Minor than Italy. Even today the women of Scanno still commonly wear their traditional dress, with their turban-like head-dresses, as much an attraction as the beautiful old village itself. For magnificent views of the sunset over the lake and mountains, drive up the zigzagging road to **Frattura**, or take the chair lift up Monte Rotondo, Scanno's small winter resort.

Abruzzo National Park

West of Cocullo lies **Pescina**, the birthplace of Cardinal Mazarin, and the road for the **Abruzzo National Park**. Founded in 1923 and enlarged in 1976, the park is Italy's second largest, covering 400 square kilometres of some of the loveliest scenery in the Apennine range, a little paradise of flowery meadows, forests of beech, pine, oak, ash, maple, and yew, that are the last home of *ursus arctos marsicanus*, the brown Abruzzo bear, and the Abruzzo chamois; here too are Apennine lynxes, boars, wolves, badgers, red squirrels, eagles, falcons, woodpeckers, owls, and many unusual species of songbirds, all protected by law from the enthusiastic Italian hunter. After passing through the scenic **Passo del Diavolo**, the road reaches **Pescassèroli**, the largest village within the confines of the park. The Park Visitors' Centre is here, where you can pick up trail maps and information on where to find the flora and fauna, although some of the fauna are most easily seen near the centre, in the small zoo. If you want to camp in the park, apply to the Ufficio di Zona del Parco, Piazza Sant'Antonio, tel 91 955. Pescassèroli was the birthplace of Benedetto Croce, the greatest Italian philosopher of this century, and is a pleasant town in its own right, and the base for the not very difficult two-hour walk up to the **Valico di Monte Tranquillo**. In the height of summer and in the winter you can ride Pescassèroli's funivia up to the summit of Monte Vitelle. **Opi** and **Barrea** are other pretty villages in the park, near the Lago di Barrea and the Camosciara, where most of the park's graceful chamois live.

Just outside of the park the fine scenery continues around the village of **Alfedena**, built on the site of the ancient Samnite town of *Aufidena*. Across the river you can browse through the ancient walls and necropolis (10–1 and 4–7, closed Mon); a 3-km dirt track leads up to Lago Montagna Spaccata. From here Highway 83 follows the river Sangro to main Route 17, the crossroads for Sulmona and Molise (see below).

WHERE TO STAY AND EATING OUT

This area is well served with hotels, but many are seasonal, open only in the summer and winter. Although not very attractive in itself, Avezzano has quite a few hotels and motels on Highway 5, and a good, reasonably priced restaurant: **Umberto**, Via Monte Grappa 56, tel (0863) 552 188, where meat specialities are the main attraction, especially the tender *bistecca alla fiorentina*; for primo try ravioli di ricotta with porcini mushroom sauce (L25 000). In Tagliacozzo, one nice hotel that stays open all year is the *****Miramonti**, tel (0863) 6581, with 23 comfortable rooms, garden and tennis (L49 000, all with bath).

Sulmona's most comfortable and largest hotel is the *****Europa Park**, on SS17 just north of town, tel (0864) 34 641. All rooms have private baths, and there's a tennis court, bar, and a good restaurant on the premises (L68–76 000). In town, the ****Italia**, Piazza XX Settembre, tel (0864) 52 308, has pleasant rooms (L33 000 without bath, L40 000 with). Here, too, is Sulmona's finest restaurant, **Da Nicola**, tel 33 070, with delicious homemade pasta and lamb with rosemary (L25–30 000).

Up in Scanno, you can stay in a lovely setting on the lake at *****Del Lago**, tel (0864) 74 343, a small, tranquil hotel with a garden and fine views (L65 000, with bath, open Mar–Oct and mid-Dec–mid-Jan). In town, ****Margherita**, tel (0864) 74 353, has simple rooms, all with bath, for L50 000. **Agli Archetti**, Via Silla 8, tel (0864) 74 645, is Scanno's top restaurant, serving dishes made from homegrown ingredients; try the grilled lamb with pears if it's on the menu. The ambience is all refined old elegance, the bill around L30 000; closed Tues. Further up from Scanno, at Passo Godi, is the **Paradiso**, tel (0864) 74 602, with simple rooms at L42 000 with bath, and a restaurant attached.

In Rivisondoli, ***Cinquemiglia**, up at Piano Cinquemiglia, tel (0864) 69 151, is a largish, cosy resort hotel, open all year, with a pool and tennis (L58 000, all rooms with bath). In nearby Roccaraso, the most developed resort in the area, the ***Excelsior**, tel (0864) 62 479, is one of the classier choices, all rooms with bath (L60 000); the ***Motel AGIP**, SS17, tel (0864) 62 443, is even more comfortable, though convenient only for motorists. It has an excellent restaurant as well (L60 000).

In the National Park at Pescasséroli, ****Grand Hotel del Parco**, tel (0863) 91 356 is indeed the grandest hotel in the area, enjoying a beautiful setting, with a garden and heated pool to keep its guests contented (open Christmas–March, and 15 June–Sept; L65–95 000). Another good choice is 'the penguin', ***Il Pinguino**, tel (0863) 91 482, with rooms far too snug for a real Antarctican (L48–52 000, all with shower).

Molise

Isolated, mountainous, and even more sparsely populated than Abruzzo, Molise is one of the least known regions of Italy. It belonged to the tenacious Samnites of old, and the Italians still sometimes call this part of the country (including parts of neighbouring Campania) Sannio; at some point in the murky early Middle Ages it became the county of Molise and then, like the other *Abruzzi*, it was joined to the Kingdom of Naples. In the 14th and 15th centuries Slav and Albanian refugees from the Turkish invasion found new homes in Molise; their languages contributed to the great variety of regional dialects, and there are still cases today of neighbouring villages unable to understand one another. Although an improved network of roads and even a superstrada have ended most of Molise's isolation, the rugged, mountainous terrain makes the going slow no matter how you travel. For the visitor, it is certainly one of Italy's last frontiers, and not without reason.

Somehow, in the tortuous machinations of Italian politics, the 350,000 or so Molisani acquired the right to have their own region in 1963. Do not let this mislead you into thinking this was warranted by something distinctive about the area's history or culture. In traversing this vale of humility, you may find the only distinctive thing to be humility itself. On these mountain roads you will pass towns with names like Stain, Little Whistle, Cooked Goat and Plenty of Rocks. Any of these would be a better bet than Isernia, the most thoroughly dismal provincial capital in Italy. The biggest event in Molise is a village rodeo, and the most famous attraction is a fossil (Stone Age man in his wisdom made Isernia the first inhabited place in Europe, as far as we know). Ask the Molisani for their culinary specialities, and you'll likely get beans and polenta, or stuffed lamb's brain—but lately they have discovered white truffles (the best kind) under their oak trees. But beyond these posh fungi, the Pope's bells, a well-preserved Roman town in the middle of nowhere, and the scenic border region of the Matese, the Molise is pure hillbilly—*all'italiana*.

(*Note:* for the short Molise coast, see above, p. 291)

GETTING AROUND

Isernia is linked by train with Naples, Rome, Sulmona, Pescara, and Campobasso; other trains from Naples to Isernia and Campobasso pass through Benevento, then continue on to the coast at Termoli. Buses—from Naples, Rome, Cassino, and Vasto to Campobasso and Isernia—are on the whole much quicker and less aggravating. Bus service for outlying villages is fair and invariably departs from the provincial capitals of Isernia or Campobasso.

TOURIST INFORMATION

Isernia: Via Farinacci, tel 3992

Isernia

Heading down Highway 17 from Sulmona and Castel di Sangro, you enter Italy's newest province, Pentria (or Isernia), created in 1970. The little capital **Isernia** was the Samnite town of *Aesernia*, where the Italic tribes either first united against Rome, or where they fled after the Romans captured their capital of Corfinium in the Social Wars—at any rate Isernia modestly puts forth a claim to be 'the first capital of Italy', although even that boast pales before the fame of its onions (fêted every 28–29 June) and its lace. Isernia has a sort of Old Town, the highlight of which is the 14th-century **Fontana Fraterna**, rebuilt of Roman bits on which an inscription reads 'AE PONT'—which led to a popular belief that Aesernia gave the world Pontius Pilate. This was Isernia's great sight until 1979 when, during the construction of the new superstrada, a Palaeolithic village was accidentally uncovered, bringing to light the million-year-old relics of a human genus dubbed *Homo Aeserniensis*, the most ancient remains of man yet discovered in Europe. His understandably scanty relics, along with those of the huge ancestors of the elephant, deer, rhinoceros, bison, bears, and hippopotami he ate for dinner, are given the red-carpet treatment in the slick new **Museo Nazionale della Pentria ed Isernia** (9–1, closed Mon).

North of Isernia

The *comuni* in the high altitudes north of Isernia have been compared to the isolated villages of Tibet, each perched on its lonely hilltop. Highest in all the Apennines is **Capracotta**, a village immersed in woods and mountain pastures, often buried under banks of snow in the winter. There are tales of the residents having to use their upper-floor windows as exits—a fitting place for the first Italian ski club, founded in 1914. Nearby **Agnone**, the 'Athens of the Samnites', has been known for the past thousand years for its bells; one factory, the **Marinelli Pontifical Foundry**, still survives, the oldest in Italy, supplier to the Vatican and to nearly every country in the world. They claim to have been in business since about 1000 though the current owners, the Marinelli family, have only owned it for a mere 650 years. Bells in the foundry are still made according to the ancient formula; while the molten bronze is being poured into the mould a priest is on hand to chant the medieval litanies that have always guaranteed a successful clear-toned bell. You can see the foundry in action and visit its small museum any weekday, at Via D'Onofrio 14 (but no photos; the Marinellis don't want the place to become 'another Disneyland'). Besides bells, Agnone is known for its sugared almonds (*confetti*) and its coppersmiths, whose workshops line the main streets of town, selling every imaginable utensil; also be sure to note the Romanesque portal on the cathedral of San Emidio.

South of Agnone, **Pietrabbondante** has some of the most extensive Samnite ruins yet discovered; the site excavated in the 19th century, was a religious sanctuary, and includes foundations of temples and a well-preserved Greek theatre. The ruins, attractively located in a green, flower-filled field bear witness to how strongly the Samnites were influenced by Hellenic culture both before and after their conquest by Rome. **Pesco-lanciano**, nearer to Isernia, is dominated by its picturesque **Castello D'Alessandro**, founded in the 13th century and topped in later years by a pretty arcade. Even closer to Isernia (8 km) is the old village and 14th-century castle of **Carpinone**.

West of Isernia

Spaghetti Western fans in Molise during the first part of August can whoop it up at an Italian 'rodeo' at **Montenero Valcocchiara**, northwest of Isernia; as usual in Italy, food is as much of an attraction as the events, and in this case it's barbecues. In the pre-cowboy days of the Lombards, the Benedictines had an abbey to the south at **Castel San Vincenzo**, near a small lake of the same name. Often restored and rebuilt, it was last restored in the 1950s; the nearby **Crypt of San Lorenzo** managed to escape the assorted disasters that befell the abbey, and preserves some interesting 11th-century frescoes.

The most impressive castle in Molise, **Cerro al Volturno** was originally built by the Benedictines in the 10th century, though rebuilt at the end of the 15th century. Appearing to grow organically out of a massive rock over the town, the castle is inaccessible except by a narrow path; in the 1920s the supporting cement bulwarks on the hill were added, all impressive enough to star on the L200 stamp. There aren't many souvenirs to buy in Cerro, but south, in **Scapoli**, you can visit the summertime bagpipe (*zampogna*) display-market, and choose your goat-bellied instrument among the olive- and cherry-wood models on display. In both the Molise and Abruzzo, shepherds often play the bagpipes; traditionally they take them down to Naples or Rome at Christmas-time to play in the streets, still a common sight.

Venafro to the south is famous for its olive oil. It is also one of the oldest towns in Molise; Cyclopean walls run along the road leading into town, and in the Middle Ages the Roman **Amphitheatre** was turned into an oval piazza, in which the arcades have been incorporated into the front doors of the houses. Portable remains of Roman *Venafrum* are now in the **Museo Nazionale** in the former convent of Santa Chiara (9–2, Sun 9–1, closed Mon). Of the churches, the most interesting are the 15th-century **cathedral** and the **Annunziata**, a church that has preserved its Romanesque interior if not exterior, and contains in one of its chapels a series of 15th-century English alabasters. Venafro's derelict **castle** (14th–16th centuries) hides some remarkable frescoes of horses, and is waiting for funds to be restored and opened to the public.

The Matese

South of Isernia and Campobasso is a lovely curve of snow-swept peaks and forests called the Matese, of which the southern half lies in Campania. Few Italians, much less foreigners, penetrate its quiet villages, where women in traditional dress sit out in the streets over their round *tomboli* making delicate lace. The lakes of the Matese are full of waterfowl, its streams brim with fish, its forests are home to squirrels, wildcats, and wolves, and other creatures seldom seen in the rest of Italy; its glens produce porcini mushrooms by the ton.

From Isernia, the way into the Matese leads through **Monteroduni**, a smiling village built around the Molise's best-preserved castle; the ancestors of its current occupants, the Pignatelli family, have lived here since 1668. Past Monteroduni you are over the border, on the Campanian side of the Matese. **Gallo**, the first town, has a pretty lake. The scenery is spectacular, continuing eastwards to the largest of the district's several lakes, the **Lago del Matese** and the resort of **Piedimonte Matese**. Return to the Molise by Passo del Prete Morto ('dead priest pass'); the northern slopes of the Matese are equally lovely, with a wonderful quality of light that gives **Campochiaro** its name. This medieval village retains its walls and tower; recently a huge Samnite temple complex was unearthed in the vicinity.

Just to the west is the lofty town of **Boiano**, the former Samnite stronghold of *Bovianum*. The upper part of town, called *Città*, retains Megalithic-era walls and the ruins of a Lombard castle. The views are great, but become fabulous if you're up to a rather stiff, two-hour climb to the summit of **Monte la Gallinola** (1923 m)—on a clear day you can see to the Bay of Naples. In winter, there's skiing at **Campitello Matese**, southwest of Boiano in the very centre of the Matese mountains.

Saepinum

In 295 BC, the Samnite city of Saipins was laid waste by the Romans. The few inhabitants who were neither killed nor taken into slavery went on to found a new town for themselves, a Roman colony called *Saepinum*. As a quiet provincial town, it managed to avoid most of history until the 9th century, when the Saracens destroyed it. Later in the Middle Ages, when times were surer, the site was resettled, only higher up (now modern **Sepino**), and Saepinum was slowly covered by the dust of the ages, quarried here and there for its stone. Dilettantes began excavating the ancient town in the 18th century, and now a few archaeologists come to uncover more of it every summer.

The charm of Saepinum comes partly from its remote and lovely setting in the Matese; its isolation has preserved it well, making it one of the most evocative Roman sites in all Italy—the most extant example of a small provincial city. In Saepinum there is very little marble, no plush villas as in Pompeii and Herculaneum, but neither are there any modern intrusions beyond a few farmhouses, making use of a column here, an architrave there; it is an ancient Anytown in the empire, in its layout and amenities a miniature version of nearly every colony founded by Rome.

The defensive **walls** encompassing Saepinum, built in the diamond patterns of *opus reticulatum*, are over 1 km long and defended by 27 bastions—the best-preserved, over 11 m high, stands near the theatre. Four gates lead into the central axes of the city; from the car park at Porta di Terravecchia you enter the walls on the *cardus maximus*. This preserves its original paving stones as you approach the central crossroads with the *decumanus*, the main street of every Roman town, and here, as usual, you'll find the **Forum** and civic buildings. The slender Ionic columns on the corner belonged to the **Basilica**, the main meeting place and courts of a Roman city, with its podium for orators and lawyers. Just off it is an octagonal atrium, surrounded by the foundations of shop counters—Saepinum's central market. Across from the forum itself, on the *decumanus*, are, first, on the corner, the elections office (*Comitium*), the *Curia* (town hall), a temple, believed to have been dedicated to the cult of the emperor, then the *Terme* (baths), and the well-preseved Griffon fountain. The *decumanus* continues past a house called the **Casa dell'Impluvio Sannitico**, its atrium holding a fountain and Samnite-style *impluvium* (container to collect rain water) with an inscription in Oscan, the pre-Roman language of the region, to the Porta di Benevento, marked by a figure of Mars; beyond the gate stands the funeral monument, with its inscriptions lauding the virtues of the deceased Caius Ennio Marso, one of the leading citizens. A **museum** near here documents the excavations of the site (9–2, Sun 9–1, closed Mon).

The *decumanus*, in the other direction, passes through Saepinum's main commercial district, lined with shops, taverns, and private residences. It ends at the most extant gate, the impressive **Porta di Boiano**, with steps to the top which you can ascend for an excellent view of the excavations. Figures of prisoners (or slaves?) stand on plinths on either side, and its inscription informs us that Tiberius and his brother Drusus paid for the fortifications. Beyond this gate is a monumental **mausoleum** of Numisio Ligure. Along the walls there are remains of a private bath complex; beyond is the well-preserved **Theatre**, with a crescent of medieval farmhouses that were built into the upper cavea; in the old days the theatre could seat 3,000 spectators. The stage is now occupied by another farmhouse, which contains an interesting museum of items found during the digs: funerary sculpture, plans and maps (same hours as above).

Campobasso

The regional capital from the days of the County of Molise, Campobasso was once best known for its engraved cutlery and its early June procession, the *Sagra dei Misteri di Corpus Domini*, but is now better known as the site of the National School for Carabinieri. In the 17th century, Campobasso's old Corpus Domini processions were banned by the bishop for making spectators laugh instead of increasing their faith; and they stayed banned until 1740, when a local sculptor named Di Zinno came up with the idea of building metal contraptions to support real people in the soaring Baroque postures of the angels and saints he carved for churches. The bishop accepted these as faith-increasers, and indeed they are, for it seems as if faith alone is holding up the bevy of six-year-old angels and saints on the 13 floats, the 'Mysteries' solemnly paraded through the streets to the accompaniment of three local bands.

Apart from the festival Campobasso doesn't have much to offer except Carabinieri cadets—the older, upper part of town has a couple of Romanesque churches, **San Giorgio** and **San Leonardo**, and the **Castello Monforte** on top. Ask at the tourist office to see if the planned museum of Samnite antiquities has been opened. From Campobasso, however, buses head out to some of the scenic villages nearby, like

Ferrazzano with a castle and belvedere, and **Baranello**, an ancient town, the heir of the Samnite *Vairanum*. Baranello has a little **Museo Civico**, containing Samnite artefacts, 17th- and 18th-century Neapolitan kitsch paintings, Chinese porcelains, and other *objets d'art* donated by a collector. Nearby, on the river Biferno, you can watch a still-functioning water-wheel grind some of the grains that go into Molise's folksy cuisine. The most striking church in the area is the hilltop Romanesque **Santa Maria della Strada**, off the road to Larino.

Larino

Midway between Campobasso and Termoli on the coast, the main attraction is the small town of **Larino**, the Samnite *Larinum*, pleasingly located amid hills and olive groves. The most important monument here is the **cathedral**, built in 1319 and embellished with an ornate portal in its Apulian-style façade; the nearby church of **San Francesco** has some good 18th-century frescoes. Take a look inside the **Palazzo Comunale** near the cathedral, which serves as the local repository of art and artefacts—a Romanesque statue of the Madonna, Bronze Age implements, coins from the 3rd century BC and Roman mosaics keep company with the books. The ancient Samnite town stood in the area around the station; along the road to the station there is an ancient cylindrical altar, the **Ara Frentana**, and further on, an amphitheatre and ruins of villas and walls. At the end of May Larino celebrates the Sagra di San Pardo with a procession of finely decorated Roman-style ox carts.

Albanian and Slavic villages

In the district around Larino there are several diehard communities of Albanians and Slavs, who have still maintained their language, traditions, and festivals. **Ururi**, east of Larino, is an Albanian town, as is **Portocannone**, which conserves in its Romanesque parish church an icon of the *Madonna of Constantinople*, brought over by settlers, as well as a baronial palace. The most interesting of the Slavic villages is **Acquaviva Collecroce**, where a dialect called 'Stokavo' is spoken. In the campanile of the church of Santa Maria Esther, there is a medieval curiosity: a stone carved with the palindromic magic square of the words SATOR TENET AREPO, an ancient charm.

WHERE TO STAY AND EATING OUT
The few hotels that grace Molise seem to be either recently built and sterile or old and rather worn-in at the heels. In Isernia there's the new ****La Tequila, just outside the centre at San Lazzaro 85, tel (0865) 51 356. All rooms have bath and TV, and there's a pool surrounded by young trees (L58 000). But if their hotels tend to be new and bland, the Molisani at the table are a stolidly old-fashioned and often spicy crew, favouring dishes like stuffed lamb heads (*testine d'agnello*), kid tripe, a kind of hillbilly pizza topped with greens and boiled pork (*pizza con le foglie*), smelly mountain cheese, and polenta with red beans, olive oil, hot peppers, and garlic *polenta maritata*. In Isernia you can dip your fork into these and tamer dishes at the **Taverna Maresca**, Corso Marcelli 186, tel (0865) 3976, a fine old restaurant in the old quarter (L30 000). If you get up in the mountains at Capracotta, the chilly and austere *Montecampo is the one and only place

to go, in Corso S. Lucia, tel (0865) 949 128, (L22 000 without bath, L33 000 with). In Agnone, ***Sammartino**, Via Pietro Micca 44, tel (0865) 78 239 is a medium-sized hotel in an attractive old building (rooms, all with bath, L42 000) and an excellent restaurant, where you can dine on the succulent lamb of Molise, prepared in traditional and innovative styles (L30 000; closed Mon and Oct). Another solid choice, both for sleeping and eating, is **Dei Buoni Amici**, Corso Vittorio Emanuele 39, tel (0865) 77 882, where like good friends you must use the shower in the hall (L36 000), but where you can dine on the best traditional food in the region, including wild mushrooms, strawberries, and hearty meat dishes, according to season (L25–35 000). Down in Venafro there are no places to stay, but there is a good restaurant: Il **Quadrifoglio**, Via Strepparo 6, tel (0865) 909 886, with a surprise—the freshest of seafood (Venafro is a stop for the seafood truck from the Adriatic to Rome), as well as lamb and other Molise dishes (L35 000, for fish, less for other dishes; closed Tues). Boiano has a few hotels, among them ***Mary**, Via Barcellona 7, tel (0874) 778 375, with good, unpretentious rooms, all with bath for L42 000. **Alla Letizia**, in Fraz. Sant'Eusanio, in Monteroduni (on the borders of the Matese), tel (0865) 564 277, is worth seeking out for its pretty location on the banks of the Volturno; lots of sea and fresh-water fish, boar and partridge to match the rustic setting (L30 000, closed Nov and April). Also in the Matese, at Campochiaro, little *La Stella del Matese**, Via Roma 16, tel (0874) 789 122, has good clean, simple rooms, all with bath (L40 000). There are no hotels in Sepino, but a good restaurant, **La Ninfa**, Via Tre Fontane, tel (0874) 790 144, with delicious Molise specialities, and an emphasis on mushrooms (L25–30 000).

In Campobasso there are more choices: the ****Hotel Roxy**, Piazza Savoia 7, tel (0874) 91 741, is a plush, newly modernized place. Rooms are air-conditioned, and fitted out with frigo-bars, private baths and TVs—there's even a discotheque for wild Campobassani nights (L56–82 000). ***Hotel Skanderbeg**, Via Novelli, tel (0874) 93 341, named after the national hero of Albania, offers modern comforts with touches of Molise tradition (all rooms with bath, L76 000). **Eden**, Via Colle delle Api 91, tel (0874) 698 441 has rooms for L55 000 without bath, L74 000 with. There are several good restaurants in town, beginning with **Aciniello**, Via Torino 4, tel (0874) 94 001, simple but genuine in its atmosphere and cuisine, with dishes like pizza rustiche and rabbit (L25 000). Il **Podestà**, Via Persichillo 3, tel (0874) 311 101, serves good traditional dishes and some bizarre ones, like *penne alla vodka* which sane people should avoid. The good wine list includes some of the finest from Molise (L40 000, closed Sun and Aug). One of the best restaurants is outside Campobasso in the pretty village of Ferrazzano: **Da Emilio**, Piazza Spensieri 19, tel (0874) 978 376, where you can dine out on the terrace on meals with a delightful Emilia-Romagna touch. Try the tasty kid cooked over embers, and especially the pasta and desserts (L30 000).

In Larino there isn't much, but the ***Campitelli**, Via Mazzini 16 (near the amphitheatre), tel (0874) 822 666, is modern and functional, with a good restaurant (L48 000).

Part VIII

APULIA

Poseidon, 5th Century BC, Tàranto Museum

In many ways, this region may well be the best of Italy's south. From the forests and shining limestone cliffs of the beautiful Gargano Peninsula in the north to the southern-most tip of Italy's heel, Apulia (Puglia) offers the most variety of any of the southern regions. Not only physically, but in its towns and in its art: in Apulia you can see Greek remains at Tàranto, a score or so of Norman Romanesque cathedrals, Santa Claus' tomb, the end of the Appian Way, the finest Baroque city in the Mediterranean, and a town of buildings with roofs shaped like oilcans. Here also are gleaming white villages of houses like tidily stacked cubes, salt pans, grapevines raised high on arbours, *trulli*, dolmens and palm trees. Along the coast is an incredible string of huge, salty boisterous fishing towns. Behind them stretches the long, long *Tavoliere* plain. Looking down at all this from any of the hills to the south makes another splendid sight—especially at night, when the lights follow the web of die-straight Roman roads from one neatly circular town to another. In brief, a world unto itself, pointed eastwards, towards Greece and the Levant, very hot and very dry, and fuelled on seafood and strong wine.

Ancient Apulia was home to a number of quiet, modestly cultured and prosperous nations—the Dauni around Fóggia, the Oscans, the Messapii and others. Under Roman rule it was a favoured province, Rome's gateway to the east, and one of the parts of Italy most heavily influenced by the proximity of Greek culture. In the Middle Ages, Apulia was the home of a unique culture influenced by Normans, Arabs and Greeks, fully the equal of the cities of the north in wealth and artistic talent. History, disguised as a Spaniard or a Bourbon or a priest, has wreaked havoc with the place in the end—the same old story, but compared with the rest of the south Apulia had farther to fall. Its

313

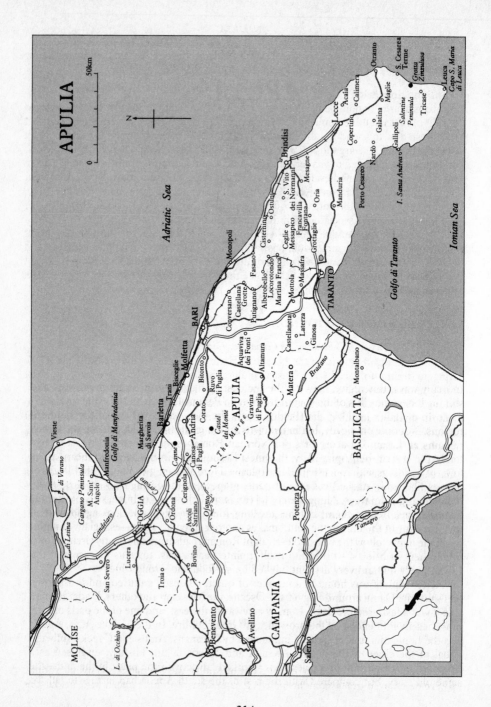

APULIA

Adriatic Sea

Ionian Sea

Golfo di Taranto

Golfo di Manfredonia

BARI

TARANTO

FOGGIA

BASILICATA

CAMPANIA

MOLISE

APULIA

The Murge

Gargano Peninsula

Salentine Peninsula

50km

Z

N

Vieste

M. Sant' Angelo

Manfredonia

Margherita di Savoia

Barletta

Trani

Bisceglie

Molfetta

Lucera

San Severo

Troia

Bovino

Benevento

Avellino

Salerno

Ascoli Satriano

Cerignola

Ordona

Canosa di Puglia

Andria

Corato

Castel del Monte

Ruvo di Puglia

Bitonto

Gravina di Puglia

Altamura

Aquaviva dei Fonti

Matera

Montalbano

Montescaglioso

Castellaneta

Laterza

Ginosa

Potenza

Monopoli

Coversano

Castellana Grotte

Putignano

Fasano

Cisternino

Alberobello

Locorotondo

Martina Franca

Mottola

Massafra

Ostuni

Ceglie Messapico

Francavilla Fontana

Grottaglie

Oria

Manduria

Porto Cesareo

Gallipoli

Nardò

Galatina

Copertino

Lecce

Acaia

Calimera

Maglie

Tricase

Leuca
Capo S. Maria di Leuca

Grotta Zinzulusa

S. Cesarea Terme

Otranto

S. Vito dei Normanni

Mesagne

Brindisi

Candelaro

Ofanto

Cannae

Carapelle

Ojanto

Bradano

Basentello

Tanagro

L. di Varano

L. di Lesina

I. Santa Andrea

314

ancient distinctions are forgotten, even by the Italians, despite the fact that Apulia is now the wealthiest and most forward-looking region of the Mezzogiorno.

Apulian Itineraries

Apulia is a large region—and a long one, all of 405 km from the northwestern corner to the tip of the Salentine peninsula. If you have more time for Apulia, it might be difficult to choose how to spend it—the region's attractions are many and varied, and spread all over the map. The Gargano and Salentine peninsulas have the best beaches and scenery, and the most engaging towns for a stay are Lecce and Tàranto. Apulia's greatest artistic productions are the medieval cathedrals and churches of Trani, Bari, Ruvo, Altamura, Molfetta, Bisceglie, Bitonto and Barletta, all close together in Bari province. The fascinating Castel del Monte west of Bari, and the great castle at Lucera, are only two of the important sites associated with the reign of Frederick II.

To get to know Apulia better, keep an eye open for some of the less important sights—pre-classical ruins, dolmens, relics of Greek Italy, religious centres, and especially the unique rural civilization of the *trullo* country. Apulia's landscapes cannot often be spectacular, but the depth and meaning of its culture will come as a surprise; it is one of the regions most worth knowing.

Fóggia and its *Tavoliere*

GETTING AROUND

Fóggia's railway station is on the Piazza Stazione, at the end of the central Viale XXIV Maggio (train info: tel 21 015). Buses for all points around the province leave from the bus station across the square (SITA line, tel 73 117): several a day to Manfredonia, Monte Sant'Angelo and Vieste, and also to Troia and Lucera. Some trains also run to Manfredonia, though it is a branch off the main east coast line. Fóggia is an important junction for north–south trains, and there will not usually be a long wait for trains to Bari, Naples or Rome.

Up in the Gargano peninsula, there is a little private railway called the Ferrovia del Gargano that clacks amiably from San Severo (30 km north of Fóggia) up the western edge of the peninsula to Rodi Garganico and Péschici; connecting buses from there take you to Vieste (6 trains a day; info: tel 214 15). Seeing the Foresta Umbra and the interior of the Gargano will be hard without a car; there is only one bus early in the morning from Monte Sant'Angelo.

TOURIST INFORMATION

Fóggia: Via Sen. Emilio Perroni 17, tel (0881) 23 650 (hard to find, on the second floor of an apartment block)
Manfredonia: Corso Manfredi 26, tel (0884) 21 998
Vieste: Piazza Kennedy, tel (0884) 708 806
San Giovanni Rotondo: Piazza Europa 104, tel (0882) 856 240

Fóggia

Fóggia, after Bari and Tàranto the third city of Apulia, was Frederick's erstwhile capital, where he enjoyed quiet moments between campaigns with his English wife, his falcons and his Muslim sorcerers. It must have been quite a place, but old Fóggia has since been obliterated by two of the usual southern plagues: earthquakes have levelled it on several occasions, and the French sacked it in 1528. Allied bombers finished off the remains, and the Fóggia you see today is a newborn—homely and awkward as newborns are, but still somehow endearing if you come in the right frame of mind. Its citizens haven't forgotten Frederick, but these days they seem more proud of a composer of operas named Umberto Giordano, born here in 1867. The municipal theatre is named after him, and he has a big statue in the city park, among a wonderfully eccentric set of statues representing characters from his works. Giordano's big hit was an opera called *Andrea Chénier*; another, with the intriguing title of *Fedora*, is claimed to be the only opera that calls for bicycles on stage. You'll be able to see one or the other when Fóggia runs its opera season in the autumn.

Modern Fóggia shows you broad, planned boulevards and low, earthquake-proof buildings. There's a little left of old Fóggia to see, a charming **cathedral** divided neatly in half, like a layer cake, 12th-century Romanesque on the bottom and Baroque on top. The early medieval door on the north side was rediscovered only during the last War, when bombs knocked down the adjacent building that was hiding it. A few twisting blocks to the north, on Piazza Nigri, a single portal with an inscription that is the last remnant of Frederick's palace has been incorporated into Fóggia's **Museo Civico**, with a collection devoted to archaeological finds and exhibits of folk life and crafts from around Apulia (daily, except Mon, 9–1; also Wed and Fri afternoons 5–7 pm; adm). Near the museum, on Piazza Sant'Egidio, the **Chiesa della Croce** (1693–1742), is one of Apulia's more unusual: an elegant Baroque gate leads to a long avenue, passing under five domed chapels that represent stages in the passion of Christ before arriving at the church itself.

Lucera and Troia

Why does Lucera have a cathedral from the 14th century, while almost all the other Apulian towns built theirs back in the 12th or earlier? Well, sir, there's a story for you. In the 1230s, Emperor Frederick II was hard pressed. Excommunicated by his devious rival, Pope Gregory IX, and at war with all the Guelph towns of Italy, Frederick needed some allies he could trust. At the same time, he had a problem with brigandage in some of the predominantly Muslim mountain areas of Sicily. His solution: induce 20,000 Sicilian Arabs to move to Apulia, with land grants and promises of imperial employment and favours. The almost abandoned town of *Luceria*, once an important Roman colony, was the spot chosen, and before anybody knew it, Frederick had conjured up an entirely Muslim metropolis 290 km from Rome. The emperor felt right at home in Lucera, and the new city became one of his favourite residences; later it would be the last stronghold of his son Manfred, in the dark days that followed Frederick's death. Charles of Anjou took the city in 1267; attempts at forced Christianization, and the introduction of settlers from Provence, caused a series of revolts among the population, which the Angevins finally solved in 1300 by butchering the lot.

Little remains of Muslim Lucera, or even of the Lucera of the French; most of the Provençals could not take the summer heat, but their descendants still live in the hills to the south. Charles II began the simple, Gothic **cathedral** in 1300, directly after the massacre of the Saracens. This and the equally plain **San Francesco**, a typical barn-like Franciscan church built from recycled Roman ruins, are Lucera's monuments, as well as parts of a gate and an amphitheatre from Roman *Luceria* on the edge of town; the smaller bits reside at the **Museo Civico**, just behind the cathedral (open Tues–Fri 9–2; Sat, Sun 9–1).

Frederick's **castle**, one of the largest ever built in Italy, was begun in 1233, the same year as the importation of the Saracens. It is still an impressive sight, with its score of towers and walls nearly a kilometre in circumference, set on a hill looking out over Lucera and the Fóggia plain. Inside, only ruins of Frederick's palace are left.

Fóggia's province is commonly known by its old Byzantine name, the *Capitanata*. The flatter parts of it, the *tavoliere*, were until this century too dry to be of much use. Another Mussolini project, as important as the reclaiming of the Pontine Marshes, has made it one of the Mezzogiorno's most productive corners; the **Apulian Aqueduct**, carrying water from the Apennines in northern Campania, is the longest and most capacious in the world. South and west of Fóggia, in the foothills of the Apennines bordering the Molise and the Basilicata, you may consider a side trip to the little village of **Troia** for its famous **cathedral**, one of the oldest and most beautiful in Apulia, and a good introduction to the glories of the Apulian Romanesque. Troia, once the Roman town of *Aecae*, was refounded in 1017, and prospered from the start. Popes held two small church councils here in the 11th and 12th centuries. The cathedral was begun in 1093, though not finished until the time of Frederick.

Much of the inspiration for the Apulian style came from Pisa, and the Pisan trademark—blind arcades decorated with circle and diamond shapes—is in evidence here. This eclectic building has some surprises, most especially a set of Byzantine-style bronze doors, and also perhaps the most beautiful **rose window** in Italy, a small, Arab-inspired fantasy from Frederick's time; the circle is divided into 11 sections, each with a carved screen in a different geometric design. Inside, the cathedral is austere, but strangely asymmetrical, with everything on the right side just slightly out of alignment. If you should be doing any more travelling through the pretty hills south of Fóggia, two places of interest are **Bovino**, a resolutely medieval-looking village with a 13th-century cathedral, and **Ascoli Satriano**, where a very well-preserved triple-arched Roman bridge still spans the river Carapelle. There are substantial remains of an abandoned Roman town near **Ordona**.

WHERE TO STAY
(tel prefix 0881)

In Fóggia, expect nothing special; the best is the ******Cicolella** at Viale XXIV Maggio 60 near the station. This old establishment is Victorian on the outside, but completely remodelled within; the restaurant is also the best in town (tel 38 90; L125–220 000). Two well-run and pleasant inexpensive places near the station are the ***Venezia**, Via Piave 40 (tel 70 903; L34–45 000) and the ***Bologna**, Via Monfalcone 53 (tel 21 341; L32–38 000). The only hotel in Lucera is a good one: the ****Al Passetto**, Piazza del Popolo 26–30, (tel 941 124; L38–45 000).

EATING OUT

The same family that runs the **Cicolella Hotel** in Fóggia also operates three fine restaurants; the one in the hotel itself is a rare find, and a good place to introduce yourself

317

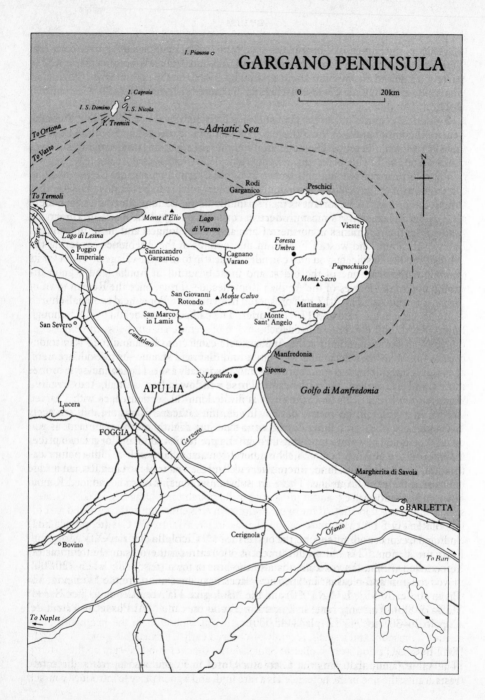

GARGANO PENINSULA

I. Pianosa

0   20km

I. Capraia

I. S. Domino   *I. S. Nicola*

I. Tremiti

To Ortona

To Vasto

~ *Adriatic Sea* ~

To Termoli

Rodi Garganico

Peschici

N

Monte d'Elio

Lago di Varano

Vieste

Lago di Lesina

Fortore

Poggio Imperiale

Sannicandro Garganico

Cagnano Varano

Foresta Umbra

Pugnochiuso

Monte Sacro

San Giovanni Rotondo

Monte Calvo

Mattinata

San Severo

San Marco in Lamis

Monte Sant' Angelo

Candelaro

Manfredonia

APULIA

S. Leonardo

Siponto

Golfo di Manfredonia

Lucera

FOGGIA

Cervaro

Margherita di Savoia

BARLETTA

Bovino

Cerignola

Ofanto

To Bari

To Naples

to Apulian specialities like *orecchiette*, little 'ears' of pasta that lately are becoming fashionable around Italy. The fish here is very good, and also the roast lamb (Viale XXIV Maggio 60, tel 38 90; average about L45 000). **Giordano,** by the theatre at Vicolo al Piano 14, tel 24 640 is where the Foggian theatre crowds go to satisfy more earthy appetites. Good home cooking, and lots of pasta straight from the oven (L30 000). For fewer lire, you won't do better than the anachronistically good, cheap and friendly **Trattoria Santa Lucia**, at Via Trieste 57; there is a fixed price of L15 000. In Lucera, the **Al Passetto**, Piazza del Popolo 28, tel 941 124, has a fine restaurant, with average prices of L25 000.

Fóggia province, like all of Apulia, produces some interesting wines, notably a full-bodied red called *Cacc'e mmitte* from around Lucera and Troia. During the summer, the Fóggia EPT and restaurants around the province conduct a 'gastronomic revue' called *A tavola con i Dauni*, where each establishment offers a special menu of Apulian specialities to visitors at special prices. Details are available from the Fóggia EPT.

The Gargano Peninsula

It looks a little out of place, being the only stretch of scenic coastline between Venice and the tip of Calabria. The 'spur' of the Italian boot is, in fact, a lost chip of Yugoslavia, left behind when two geological plates separated to form the Adriatic several million years ago. For a long time, before silt washed down by the rivers gradually joined it to the mainland, the Gargano was an island. It might as well have remained so, for the Gargano is as different from the adjacent lands in attitude as it is in its landscapes.

If you are coming from the north, you will enter the Gargano by way of Lésina and the Gargano's two lakes: the **Lago di Lésina** and the **Lago di Varano**, two large lagoons cut off from the sea by broad sand spits. From Fóggia, the logical base for attacking the Gargano would be **Manfredonia**, a dusty port town at the southern end of the peninsula that is the base for ferries to the Tremiti Islands and the towns of the Gargano, as well as being a small resort in its own right. As its name implies, this town was founded by Frederick's son Manfred, and it prospered well enough until Dragut's Turkish pirates sacked and razed it in 1620. (One of the home town girls ended up as the favoured wife of the Sultan.) Of old Manfredonia, all that is left is Manfred's **Castle**, rebuilt and extended by Charles of Anjou; it now contains a small archaeological museum. Along the Fóggia road, about 2 km south of the centre of Manfredonia, you can see the ruins of **Sipontum**, a Roman town finally abandoned to the malaria mosquitoes when Manfred moved the population to his healthier new city. As evidence of how important Sipontum was in the early Middle Ages, there is the impressive 11th-century church of **Santa Maria di Siponto**, in the same style of decoration as the cathedral at Troia, only built on a square, Byzantine Greek plan. Other remains of Sipontum in the neighbourhood include a museum and a small, recently discovered early Christian catacomb. A church from the same period, very similar to Santa Maria, survives another 9 km up the road to Fóggia: **San Leonardo**, an even better work, with finely sculpted portals and a small dome.

Monte Sant'Angelo

The tourists who come to the Gargano for the beaches probably never notice, but the peninsula is holy ground, and has been perhaps since the time of the ancient Daunians. Sanctuaries, ancient and modern, are scattered all over it; there are many stories of the apparitions of saints and angels, and even twenty years ago, a holy man who received the stigmata, and who is now well on his way towards canonization, lived at S. Giovanni Rotondo.

The centre of all this, for the last thousand years at least, has been **Monte Sant' Angelo**, one of the most important pilgrimage towns in Italy. Before Christianity, the cavern that now belongs to Saint Michael was the well-known site of a dream oracle; a 5th-century bishop of Sipontum had a vision of the archangel, who left his red cloak as a token and commanded that the sanctuary be converted to Christian worship. Soon the new Monte Sant'Angelo was attracting pilgrims from all over Europe—continuing a tradition that had begun long before the site was Christianized. Among the pilgrims were the first Normans, in the 9th century. They returned home with tales of a rich and fascinatingly civilized Apulia—a place they suspected just might be a pushover for mounted, heavily armoured knights. The first Norman adventurers were not slow in taking up the challenge. All the other sites dedicated to St Michael around the coasts of Europe—including, of course, Mont St Michel in Normandy—are the spiritual descendants of this one, founded as the cult of St Michael spread across Christendom in the early Middle Ages.

That Monte Sant'Angelo is a special place becomes evident even before you arrive. The trip up from Manfredonia passes through an uncanny landscape: chalky cliffs dotted with caves, ancient agricultural terraces, and a strange clarity in the light and air. The road climbs so quickly that you seem to be looking straight down into Manfredonia, even though it is 14 km away. After much twisting and grinding of gears, you arrive at a quiet, whitewashed city, a maze of steps and tunnels. The medieval centre of town, the **Junno**, is one of the most beautiful old quarters in southern Italy, a nonchalant harmony of colour and form that only a few coastal towns in Apulia can achieve. Here you will find the **Sanctuary of St Michael**, behind an eight-sided tower built by Charles of Anjou that reproduces the proportions (on one level) and much of the decoration of Frederick's Castel del Monte. The exterior of the sanctuary seems to be a normal church, with a Gothic porch and portals (mostly built in the 19th century ; see if you can guess which of the two identical portals is the original 12th-century work). Over the doors is a Latin inscription: 'Terrible is this place; this is the house of God and the Gate of Heaven'.

Inside, instead of the expected church, there is a long series of steps leading down to the cavern, passing a beautiful pair of bronze doors made in Constantinople in 1076, perhaps by the same artists who did the ones at Amalfi Cathedral. In the darkness most of the scenes are difficult to make out, but Jacob's ladder and the expulsion from Eden stand out clearly. Down in the cave, it is chilly and dark; in the old days pilgrims would come down on their knees, shuffling through the puddles to kiss the image of the archangel. The grotto is laid out like a small chapel. There are plenty of bits of medieval sculptural work around, but the best is a wonderful crazy-medieval bishop's chair from the 12th century.

The town records give us an almost endless list of celebrity pilgrims: a dozen popes,

King Ferdinand of Spain, four Holy Roman Emperors, Saints Bernard, Thomas Aquinas, Catherine of Siena, and so on; even St Francis came and they can show you the mark he made on the cavern wall. Behind the altar, you can see the little well that made this a holy site in the first place. Long before there was a St Michael, indigenous religions of Europe had a great interest in springs and underground streams; many scholars believe the idea of dragons began with a primeval fascination with buried streams and accompanying lines of telluric forces beneath the earth's surface; the sleepless 'eye' of the dragon is the fountain, where these forces come to the surface. In the icons of Monte Sant'Angelo, and in the innumerable souvenir figurines hawked outside the sanctuary, Michael is shown dispatching Lucifer in the form of a dragon.

Tomb of Rotari

A block or so downhill from the sanctuary, adjacent to the half-ruined church of San Pietro, stands the 12th-century work called the **Tomb of Rotari**. The idea that this was the tomb of 'Rotarus', a Lombard chief, stems from a misreading of one of the inscriptions. Some now believe it was intended to be a baptistry—a very large and unusual baptistry, if it was. It is hard to make out the original intention, since much of it has been swallowed up into the surrounding buildings, but the architecture is surpassing strange. Above the tall chamber hangs one of the three elliptical domes built in medieval Italy (the others are on the cathedrals in Molfetta, down the coast, and Pisa); below you will see some pointed arches, built before anyone in Italy had heard of Gothic. Some of the sculpted detail is extremely odd, including some imagery from the Apocalypse and the figure of a woman suckling a serpent—or dragon, lamely explained as representing one of the seven deadly sins.

More intimate scenes of ladies and dragons await next door, in an incredible relief over the entrance to **Santa Maria Maggiore**, completed in 1198. Inside this lovely church are two odd domes, very like the *trulli* of Alberobello (see below), a dignified fresco of St Michael in full Byzantine court dress, and tantalizing bits of other finely drafted Byzantine paintings from the 13th–14th centuries.

Also in the Junno disrict, the town has opened a small museum of the folk arts and culture of the Gargano, the **Museo Tancredi** (daily, except Sun, 9–12 and maybe 2:30–7 if anyone is around; adm). At the top of the town, there is a romantically ruined Norman **castle**, rebuilt by the Aragonese kings but left quite alone since.

Padre Pio

From the back of Monte Sant'Angelo, a narrow road leads into the heart of the Gargano, eventually branching off to the Forest of Shadows (see below) or **San Giovanni Rotondo**, a little town on the slopes of Monte Calvo. Here, besides the strange round temple that gives the town its name (believed, like the Tomb of Rotari, to have been intended as a baptistry), there is a 16th-century monastery that for over fifty years was the home of Padre Pio de Pietralcina, a simple priest who not only received the stigmata, the bleeding wounds of Christ, on his hands, feet and side, but also had the ability to appear before cardinals in Rome while his body was sleeping back in the Gargano. The Church always has its suspicions about phenomena like these, and it did its best, while acknowledging the honesty of Padre Pio's miracles, to keep him under wraps lest popular devotion get out of hand. Nevertheless, the town has become a pilgrimage destination in its own right, with 20 hotels at the last count. And before he died in 1968, Padre Pio was able to attract enough donations to build a large modern hospital, the first in the Gargano. West of San Giovanni and, like it, an old stop on the pilgrimage route to Monte Sant'Angelo, the town of **San Marco in Lamis** has always been a monastic centre; the present, huge Franciscan house dates from the 16th century.

Vieste

Enough of the holy Gargano. Once past Monte Sacro, on the coast north of Monte Sant'Angelo, you are in the holiday Gargano, on a gorgeous coastline of limestone cliffs, clean blue sea, and good beaches decorated with old watchtowers, or stumps and columns of rock and other curious formations. **Vieste**, at the tip of the peninsula, is in the middle of it, a lively and beautiful white town on white cliffs, surrounded by beaches. Within the last ten years, Vieste has become the major resort of the southern Adriatic, and boutiques and restaurants are crowding the town centre.

The best parts of the coast lie to the south of Vieste: beautiful coves like **Cala di San Felice**, with a small beach and a natural stone arch, and **Cala Sanguinaria**. A bit further south, at **Acqua della Rosa**, when conditions are just right, the reflection from the limestone cliffs gives the water near the shore a rosy tint. Near the road inland for Monte Sant'Angelo, **Mattinata** is one of the more eccentric examples of Apulian vernacular architecture, a gleaming white village of rectangular houses stacked in tidy rows like sugar cubes.

Most of the tourist sprawl, with miles of beaches and campsites, extends to the north of Vieste; here also are the **Grotta Sfondata** ('bottomless lagoon') one of a few marine grottoes and lagoons accessible by boat tours from Vieste; and a peculiar early Christian hypogeum (cave for burials) on the coast at the site of a long-disappeared town called *Merinum*.

On the Gargano's northern coast, **Péschici** and **Rodi Garganico** are two other pretty fishing villages that have become small resorts—rather like Vieste was ten years ago. Rodi is exceptional, a steep terraced village on the edge of a small promontory. From either of them, or from Vieste, it is an easy excursion up in the mountains to the **Foresta Umbra**, the 'forest of shadows' a thick, primeval forest of beeches, oaks, and pines, similar to those that covered most of Apulia in the Middle Ages. A visitors' centre run by the *Corpo Forestale* along SS528 will help you learn more about it.

WHERE TO STAY   (tel prefix 0884)
Manfredonia, a small resort in its own right, is full of hotels; the comfortable , modern ***Svevo** makes a convenient overnight stop for motorists (on Via Vittoria, tel 23 854; L45–70 000). In the town centre, the ***Gargano** has balconies by the sea in a quiet district, and sharp modern Italian design inside (Viale Beccarini 2, tel 27 261; L75 000).

Other places are much simpler; the *San Michele**, Via degli Orti 10, will do while waiting for a boat (tel 21 953; L28 000 without bath, L38 000 with). Outside Manfredonia, the **Posta del Falco** is a new complex in a restored post-house and *masseria* (enclosed manor-village typical of old Apulian agriculture). The restaurant on the premises is excellent (on the SS89, near the church of San Leonardo; tel 33 634; L48–72 000).

In Vieste, the best beach hotels are slightly garish places, a little bit of Rimini on the Gargano: ***Pizzomunno** is a luxurious place that keeps holiday-makers busy with sailing, sports, an enormous pool, a beautiful beach and a noisy disco, then fills them up in an exceptional, highly rated restaurant (about 1 km south of the town centre; tel 78 741; L190–240 000; less expensive rooms sometimes available in the *Pizzomunno Residence*). Second choice would be the ***Falcone**, Lungomare Enrico Mattei, with a private beach, slightly removed, and all the resort amenities at a much better rate (tel 708 251; L50–75 000). Right by the sea, ***Merinum**, Via Lungomare Enrico Mattei 32, tel 76 721, has rooms for L65–100 000. In the centre of Vieste, on Via Madonna della Libertà, there is the *Pensione San Giorgio** (tel 708 618; L40–65 000; good restaurant, too). Some good hotels can be found along the coasts around Vieste—usually in lovely spots, but convenient only if you have a car. *Gabbiano Beach**, 7 km north on the road to Péschici at Santa Maria di Merino, is one of the less expensive, though it has its own beach, pool and sailing (tel 707 038; L55–75 000). A large selection of hotels similar to those of Vieste—and more of them all the time—will be found in Péschici and Rodi Garganico. In Rodi, two reasonable resort hotels are ***La Scogliera**, Via Scalo Marittimo 13–15, tel 95 422 (L45–55 000 with bath), and ***Riviera**, Via Trieste 35, tel 95 057, on the beach, with private parking, for L48–60 000, with bath.

EATING OUT
Manfredonia's restaurants are mostly around the port, and most specialize in seafood; **Da Michele al Porto** is justifiably proud of its seafood risotto, and the linguine with clam sauce or lobster is also a treat (Piazza Libertà, tel 21 800; can be L30–40 000). In Monte Sant'Angelo, there is a place where you can get a L40 000 dinner for about half that—**Al Grottino**, on the Corso Vittorio Emanuele 179—roast lamb and kid, truly elegant antipasti, sweets and cheeses, and one memorable dish called *orecchiette in carozza* (tel 61 132). A good choice for lunch is the **Garden Paradise** on Via Basilica, with seafood and good *involtini* for about L19 000; there is an interior garden.

Not all the restaurants in Vieste are in hotels; on Via Barbicane, in the town centre, the award-winning **La Pentola** has every imaginable salt water treat on an extensive menu; the cooking is superb, and a tremendous bargain at L30–35 000 (tel 707 539). The **Vecchia Vieste** at Via Mafrolla 32 offers seafood and specialities like *involtini alla Viestiana* (tel 707 083; L25–30 000). Many in Vieste think their finest restaurant is the **San Michele**, for fish grilled or *alla pizzaiola* (Viale XXIV Maggio 72, tel 708 143; L25–35 000, closed Thurs, Nov and Dec).

The Tremiti Islands

Some 20 miles east of the Gargano peninsula are the four Tremiti Islands, where the population of 40 rises to 400 natives in the summer, to cater for an influx of 100,000 visitors on the busiest summer days. The striking beauty of this tiny archipelago is its main attraction—the bluest waters in the Adriatic and pale calcareous cliffs, much like the mainland.

For centuries the islands were ruled by abbots; beginning in 1010, Benedictines from Montecassino founded an abbey on San Nicola. They became wealthy with treasures deposited by mainlanders fearful of the Normans, and in 1236 the Inquisition dissolved the licentious abbey. The Cistercians who followed lasted until the 1350s, when pirates tricked them into believing their captain was dead and desired a Christian burial. The Cistercians complied, and during the night the captain rose from the grave and let his men in the gate to massacre the monks. In 1412 yet another order, the Lateranesi, was sent by Pope Gregory XII to restore the monastery of San Nicola Tremiti. The Bourbons of Naples claimed the islands in 1737, ending monastic rule to create another penal colony.

GETTING AROUND

From Manfredonia, the main port, the steamer departs several times a week (5 hours); other connections from Rodi Garganico take only 1½ hours. In the summer departures are daily, and there are additional ones from Vieste (3 hours), Pugnochiuso (4 hours) and Péschici (2 hours). Summer hydrofoils run from Ortona (2 hours), Vasto (1 hour) and Termoli (45 minutes).

San Nicola and San Domino

San Nicola is dominated by its fortress-monastery. Boats call just under its main gate, where an inscription reads *Conteret et Confringet* ('Crush and Kill')—referring to the rights granted to the Abbot by Pope Paul III to torture and kill heretics. Principal sights in the walls include the ancient church of **Santa Maria a Mare** (1045), with mosaic fragments and a large celebrated icon of Christ, the old cloisters, a fine cistern, and the grand **Dormitorio Nuovo**, built by the Lateranesi.

Nearby **San Domino**, the largest and most luxuriant of the Tremiti, was indefensible and thus uninhabited throughout most of history. Its marvellous coastline of cliffs and jutting rocks, penetrated by grottoes, is easy to explore in a day either by boat or on foot. Tourist facilities are concentrated around its beach, **Cala delle Arene**. From here you can walk to the **Cappella del Romito**, the highest point of the island—at all of 280 ft.

Along the coast are the violet-coloured **Grotta delle Ciole**, the **Grotto delle Murene** where sea eels are said to breed, and the Punta del Diavolo. The most spectacular feature on the island, the 250-ft crag known as the **Ripa dei Falconi** where falcons were bred in the days of chivalry, and the **Grotta del Bue Marino** beneath it, may seem vaguely familiar if you've seen *The Guns of Navarone*. Over 150 ft long, the cave is the largest on San Domino; if you go by boat, take a torch to see the rock formations.

The other two Tremiti Islands are uninhabited: **Pianosa**, low and flat, used by Italian and Yugoslav fishermen on overnight trips, and **Caprara**, island of rabbits, with an enormous natural arch and the lovely cave, the **Grottone**, almost 100 ft high at its mouth.

WHERE TO STAY AND EATING OUT   (tel prefix 0882)

All accommodation is on San Domino: ***Kyrie** at Vuccolo, tel 603 055, with a pool, tennis, and sailing (L120–170 000). Less well endowed, the ***San Domino** at Cameroni, tel 663 027, has 25 rooms (L65–100 000). *Gabbiano**, at Belvedere, tel 663 044, has pleasant rooms L38–50 000, and a good restaurant to boot.

San Nicola has some restaurants for the trippers from San Domino: **La Conchiglia** on Via Roma and **Al Torrione** at Via Marconi 74 have meals for around L25 000.

On San Domino, two places that specialize in local fish dishes are **Trattoria del Pesce** on Via Diomede (L30 000) and **Il Pirata**, on the beach at Cala delle Arene, tel 663 042 (L40 000).

Down the Coast to Bari

If you take the main route, a little bit inland, you will pass through the *Tavoliere*, the long, dull plain that stretches the length of Apulia. Tavoliere means a chessboard; 2000 years ago, when the Romans first sent in surveyors to apportion the land among their Punic War veterans, this flat plain—the only one south of the Po—gave the methodical rectangularity of the Roman mind a chance to express itself. They turned the plain into a grid of neatly squared roads and farms; many of their arrow-straight roads survive, and the many centuries have only succeeded in throwing a few kinks into the rest. But for the olive groves and vineyards, you might think you were in Iowa.

GETTING AROUND
Three different railways serve this area, and unlike most of Apulia you're more likely to find a train than a bus to all the out-of-the-way destinations. All the coastal towns from Barletta to Monópoli are on the main FS east coast route. A small line, the FCL, connects Altamura to Bari 12 times a day; another line, the Ferrovia Bari-Nord, is a kind of commuter train with frequent service to all the inland towns north of Bari—Bitonto, Ruvo, Andria and then Fóggia. The hardest place to reach is Castel del Monte: the Bari-Andria train at 7 am will connect you with the only bus to there.

TOURIST INFORMATION
Barletta: Via Gabbiani 4, tel (0883) 31 373
Trani: Via Cavour 140, tel (0883) 588 830; also Piazza Repubblica, tel (0883) 43 295

Barletta's Colossus

The coastal road, though just as flat, is much more interesting, passing through a string of attractive medieval port towns. Most of these can show their contribution to the Apulian Romanesque in a grand old cathedral; one that cannot is **Margherita di Savoia**, the first town south of the Gargano, a funky urban smudge surrounded by salt pans. No one seems to remember what the old name was, but they changed it in the last century to honour the formidable wife of King Umberto I. This is the best place to inspect a brand new style in folk architecture—the Apulian fancy for entirely covering buildings in patterned bathroom tiles. **Barletta**, the next town, is also one of the largest. Though quite a prosperous place these days, Barletta entered a long period of decadence with the coming of the Spaniards, and still sadly neglects its historical centre. If you pass it by, however, you will miss a unique and astounding sight. On Corso Vittorio Emanuele, beside the Church of San Sepolcro, stands the largest bronze statue of antiquity in existence, locally known as the **Colosso**.

To come upon this 20-foot figure in the middle of a busy city street, wearing an imperial scowl and a pose of conquest, with a cross and a sphere in his hands, is like lapsing into a dream. Scholars have debated for centuries who it might be: obviously a late Roman emperor, and the guesses have mentioned Valentinian, Heraclius and Marcian; the last is most probable, and especially intriguing, since the triumphal column of Marcian (a rather useless emperor with no real successes to commemorate) still stands in Istanbul, and the statue of the emperor that once stood on top of it was probably carried away by the Crusaders in the sack of Constantinople in 1204. A ship full of booty from that sack foundered off Barletta's coast, and the Colosso washed up on a nearby beach; the superstitious citizens let it stay there for decades before they got up enough nerve to bring it into the city. The figure is surpassing strange, a monument to the onset of the Dark Ages; the costume the emperor wears is only a pale memory of the dress of Marcus Aurelius or Hadrian, with a pair of barbaric-looking leather boots instead of imperial buskins.

San Sepolcro, finished in the 13th century, is interesting in its own right. Above the plain French Gothic vaulting, there is an octagonal dome, recalling the Holy Sepulchre in Jerusalem. Corso Garibaldi leads from here into the heart of old Barletta, passing the Museo Comunale (daily except Mon, 9–1; adm), which has in its collection the only surviving statue of Frederick II—a little the worse for wear, poor fellow. Barletta's 12th-century cathedral, near the end of Corso Garibaldi, is currently undergoing a fitful restoration, which it badly needs. Look on the left-hand wall, between the façade and the campanile, and you will see a cornice supported by thirteen strange figures. If you have a good eye, you may make out the letters on them that make an acrostic of *Richardus Rex I*—Richard the Lionheart, who contributed to the embellishment of the cathedral on his way to the Crusades.

Nearby is the 13th-century church of Sant' Andrea, with another fine façade, though the building is in almost as bad shape as the cathedral. The third Crusade was launched from Barletta's often-rebuilt castle, with a great council of Frederick and his knights. The polygonal bastions you see were added in the 1530s.

Trani

Trani, the next town along the coast, is as attractive as Barletta isn't, a sun- and sea-washed old port that still has a large and prosperous fishing fleet. Trani was an important merchant town in the early Middle Ages—it once fought a war with Venice, and its merchant captains created perhaps the first code of laws of the sea since ancient times (Trani disputes with Amalfi for the distinction). Trani's famous cathedral stands in an open piazza on the edge of the sea, another excellent work of the Apulian Romanesque, and a monument to the age of the Crusades. At the centre of the façade is another pair of 12th-century bronze doors, very much like those in Amalfi and other cities of the south. These are special, though, since the artist who did them and so many others is a native, Barisano of Trani. Inside, the most remarkable things are underground. This cathedral is really three buildings stacked on the same site; the lower church, called Santa Maria della Scala, is really the earlier, Byzantine cathedral. And below that is the Crypt of San Leucio, an unusual early Christian church or catacomb with solid marble columns and bits of medieval frescoes. Some of Trani's other notable buildings are the Ognissanti, a typical church of the 12th-century Knights Templar;

the **Palazzo Cacetta**, a rare (for southern Italy) example of late Gothic architecture from the 1450s; and two small churches that once were synagogues, Santa Maria Scuolanove and Sant'Anna, converted after the Spaniards chased out Trani's long-established Jewish community in the 1500s.

From Trani, **Bisceglie** is the next town, with another good Romanesque cathedral. South of town, on the edge of the modern superhighway, the **dolmen of Chianca** is one of the largest in Italy. Next comes **Molfetta**, with a Cathedral like Trani's on the picturesque harbour's edge, the **Duomo Vecchio**, or San Corrado. This may be the most peculiar of them all. Its plan, subtly asymmetrical like that of Troia, has a wide nave covered by three domes; each is different, and the central one is elliptical. The west front is almost blank, while the back has elaborate carved decoration, and a door that leads into the apse.

Castel del Monte

In Enna, the 'navel of Sicily', Emperor Frederick built a mysterious octagonal tower at the summit of the town. In Apulia, this most esoteric of emperors erected one of the most puzzling palaces of all time. It, too, is a perfect octagon, and if you have been travelling through the region with us, you will have noticed that nearly every town has at least one eight-sided tower, bastion or campanile, and that often enough Frederick is behind it. **Castel di Santa Maria del Monte**, to give it its original title, was begun by Frederick in the 1240s on a high hill overlooking the Apulian *tavoliere* south of the town of Andria.

At each of the eight corners of Castel del Monte is a slender tower, also octagonal. The building, though 24 m tall, has only two storeys; each has eight rooms, almost all interconnected, and each facing the octagonal courtyard. The historians sometimes try to explain the castle as one of Frederick's hunting lodges. This won't do; the rooms each have only one relatively small window, and in spite of the wealth of sculpted stone the castle once had, it would have seemed more like a prison than a forest retreat—though it does have remains of a bath with some sophisticated plumbing. Even Frederick really never spent much time here. Neither is it a fortification; there are no ramparts, no slits for archers, and not even a defensible gate. The entrances are raised on stairs, so it would be impossible to bring in horses. Some writers have suggested that Frederick had an artistic monument in mind. The entrance to the castle, the so-called 'triumphal arch', is a work unique for the 1200s, an elegant classical portal that prefigures the Renaissance. Inside, every room was decorated with columns, friezes and reliefs in Greek marble, porphyry and other precious stones. Almost all of these have disappeared, vandalized by the Angevins and the noblemen who owned the castle over the last five centuries. The delicately carved Gothic windows survive, one to each room, along with a few other bits of the original decoration: grotesques at the points of the vaults in some rooms, elegant conical fireplaces, capitals (some Corinthian, some Egyptian) and in two of the corner towers, corbels under the arches carved into peculiar faces and figures.

At Castel del Monte, however, it is the things you can't see that are the most interesting. This is nothing less than the Great Pyramid of Italy, and the secrets Frederick built into it have for centuries attracted the attention of cranks and serious scholars alike. Perhaps the best guess as to the castle's purpose is the idea that it was meant for meetings of a secret society, practising the sort of neo-Pythagorean mysticism current at Frederick's court. Books have been written about the measurements and proportions of the castle, finding endless repetitions of the Golden Section, its square and cubic roots, relations to the movements of the planets and the stars, the angles and proportions of the five-pointed star, and so on. The idiosyncrasies are just as interesting. For all its octagonal rigour, the castle is full of teasing quirks. Facing the courtyard (where there are some surviving fragments of reliefs), along the eight walls there are two large windows, two doors and two balconies, studiously arranged to avoid any sort of pattern or symmetry; some of the windows, facing the courtyard or between chambers, seem centrally placed from one side, but several feet off centre from the other—intentional, but unexplainable.

The relation of the castle to the ancient surveying of the Apulian plain is a fascinating possibility. Frederick's tower in Sicily has been found to be the centre of an enormous rectilinear network of alignments, uniting scores of ancient temples, towers, and cities in straight lines that run the length and breadth of the island. The tower is believed to be built on the site of some forgotten holy place; the alignments and the vast geometrical temple they form probably predate even the Greeks. No one has yet suggested that Castel del Monte replaced any ancient site, but the particular care of Apulia's ancient surveyors, and the arrangement of the region's holy places, sanctuaries and Frederick's castles suggests that something similarly strange may be hidden here. The wildest theory so far claims that the castle marks the intersection of the two greatest alignments of them all: lying exactly halfway between the Great Pyramid and Stonehenge, and halfway between Jerusalem and Mont-Sant-Michel.

Around the *Tavoliere*

The nearest town to Castel del Monte is **Andria**, a large and thriving centre with a street plan of spokes and concentric rings. Another of the cities associated with Frederick, Andria has an inscription from the Emperor on its Sant' Andrea's Gate, honouring it for its loyalty. Two of Frederick's wives, Yolande of Jerusalem and Isabella of England, daughter of King John, are buried in the crypt of Andria's cathedral. Two other churches worth a visit: 13th-century **Sant'Agostino**, built by, of all people, the Teutonic Order; and 16th-century **Santa Maria dei Miracoli**, restored in the Baroque.

Heading back towards Fóggia, on the banks of the river Ofanto you can visit the site of the Battle of **Cannae**; here, in 216 BC Hannibal trapped and annihilated four Roman legions in one of the most famous battles of history. Military strategists still study the Carthaginians' brilliant ambush, the only serious defeat Rome was to suffer for centuries. At the time, Hannibal and his elephants had already been in Italy two years. Cannae was the chance they were waiting for, and historians are puzzled as to why he didn't immediately follow it up with a march on Rome—probably it was due to a lack of siege equipment. The chance was missed; Hannibal spent another eight years campaigning fruitlessly in Italy, while the Romans were out conquering Spain and North Africa. Cannae also taught the Romans to be careful, and it could be said that Hannibal's great victory meant the defeat not of Rome, but of Carthage. A small **museum** on the site gives a blow-by-blow account, along with archaeological finds.

In Roman times, **Canosa di Puglia** was one of the most important towns in the region. It isn't much today, but its five-domed **cathedral** has in its courtyard the **Tomb of**

Bohemond, a striking marble chapel with a small cupola (octagonal, of course) that holds the remains of the doughty Crusader. Bohemund, who died in 1111, was the son of Robert Guiscard; renowned for valour and chivalry, he seized the main chance when the First Crusade was being proclaimed and ended up Prince of Antioch. The most remarkable feature of his tomb is the pair of bronze doors, signed by an artist named Roger of Melfi. The one on the left, inscribed with geometrical arabesques, is a single slab of bronze. Inside the cathedral, you may notice the early medieval pulpit and the bishop's chair, resting on two weary-looking stone elephants.

South of Andria, a country road follows the Via Appia Traiana between Canosa di Puglia and Corato, a branch of the famous Appian Way completed by Emperor Trajan. The busier route today, no. 98 for Corato, passes a monument to an episode drummed into the head of every Italian schoolboy, the *Disfida di Barletta*. In 1503, a noble French prisoner insulted the valour of an Italian company fighting with *El Gran Capitan*, Gonsalvo di Córdoba. A medieval-style tournament was arranged on this spot, in which thirteen Italians under Ettore Fieramosca individually defeated thirteen Frenchmen. Italian honour was saved—though with typically delicious Italian irony it must be noted that the victors were fighting for the very foreign invaders, the Spaniards, who would soon completely destroy Italian liberty.

Four Towns, Four More Cathedrals

In this corner of Bari province, there are altogether eight noteworthy cathedrals on a narrow strip of land only some 64 km long. They are the only real monuments—nothing has been built ambitiously and well around here since the 1300s—and they stand as the best evidence of Apulia's greatest period of culture and prosperity.

One of the best cathedrals in Apulia is at **Ruvo di Puglia**, an ancient settlement that was famous in classical times for pottery—reproducing Greek urns at a lower price. A large collection of these, and some Greek imports too, can be seen at the **Museo Jatta** (daily, except Sun, 10–12; adm). The **cathedral** is a tall, early Gothic work, with a richly decorated façade incorporating a fine rose window tucked almost under the roofline; above it is a seated figure believed to be Emperor Frederick. The little arches along the sides of the building are decorated with figures of pagan gods, copied from surviving pieces of ancient Ruvo's pottery.

Bitonto has a similar cathedral; here the best features of the exterior are the side galleries and the carvings of fantastical animals and scriptural scenes over the three front portals. Inside, there is a famous pulpit of 1226 displaying a fierce-looking eagle; on one side a curious, primitive relief shows Emperor Frederick, Isabella of England, and their family. Over the portal of the **Purgatorio** church, there is a charming relief of leering skeletons. On the left side of the road for Modugno, towards Bari, stands a lonely **menhir**.

Apulia's southern borders make up a distinct region, a slightly elevated jumble of dry plain and rolling hills called the **Murge**, very similar to much of the Basilicata. Here the important town is **Altamura**, founded by Frederick on the site of an abandoned ancient city. For centuries Altamura was a town of some distinction, even having its own university. Its rather advanced outlook led Altamura to support the French, and their short-lived Parthenopean Republic, during the Napoleonic Wars. As a result, a mob led by a cardinal and egged on by monks, called the Army of the Holy Faith, sacked and burned the city in 1799. The university never recovered, but Altamura still has a beautiful **cathedral**, begun by Frederick in 1232; heavy damage from an earthquake in 1316 accounts for the departures from the Apulian norm. The building retains its exceptional rose window and portal, but the twin towers above were added during the Renaissance. For some reason, in the course of doing so, they turned the cathedral backwards—the old portal and rose window were carefully taken apart, and placed where the apse used to be. For whatever reason they did it, the result is an outstanding and unique façade, completely unlike any other in Italy.

Gravina in Puglia has the fourth cathedral, but it is only a dull 15th-century replacement for the Norman original. Gravina does have other charms. The town is set above a steep ravine, lined with caves where the inhabitants took refuge from pirates and barbarians during the Dark Ages. One of the town's churches, **San Michele dei Grotti**, is a cave too, with a heap of human bones attributed to victims of the Arab pirates during the 8th century. Other churches show somewhat eccentric versions of Renaissance styles, notably the **Madonna delle Grazie** near the railway station.

WHERE TO STAY

Barletta is a discouraging place to spend a night, but if you insist, the ******Artù** on Piazza Castello between the castle and the cathedral will do (tel (0883) 32 778; L100 000). Trani would be a better bet: the ******Royal**, Via de Robertis 29, tel (0883) 588 777, has rooms with bath for L68–75 000, while between Bari and Trani, at Molfetta, ******Garden**, on the Via Provinciale per Terlizzi, tel (080) 941 772, has rooms for L70 000 with bath.

EATING OUT

Every town in the province has at least one restaurant worth staying for. In Barletta, it is **Bacco**, with all kinds of *orecchiette*, seafood antipasti and some exceptional marine concoctions for the second course (Via Sipontina 10, tel (0883) 517 460; L60 000 and up; closed Sun eve, Mon and Aug). In Trani, the place for shellfish is **Cristoforo Colombo**, on the Lungomare Colombo, tel (0883) 41 146 (L30 000) or else **Il Passetto** down the boulevard at Lungomare Colombo 110, tel (0883) 401 051; here, with dishes like smoked salmon in pastry, or lobster you should not be surprised by a bill of L55 000 or more . There's a similar place, though a little cheaper, in Molfetta, the **Alga Marina**, on the coastal highway SS16; fish dinners for about L45 000 (tel (080) 948 091). Andria offers a surprise, a restaurant inside an old Apulian farmhouse run by the *Agriturismo* programme: **Al Murgiano**, on SS170 near Castel del Monte, is a place where you can try the real traditional Apulian fare—many combinations of pasta, chick peas and fava beans, and simple dishes with lamb or kid. As on the farmer's table, the menu changes with the seasons (tel (0883) 82 849; L20 000).

Bari

Somehow Bari should be a more interesting place. The second city of the Mezzogiorno is a bustling town full of sailors and fishermen, but also boasting a university and a long heritage of cultural distinction. Bari nonetheless will be a disappointment if you come here expecting Mediterranean charm and medieval romance. If, on the other hand, you would be happy to see a southern city that has come close to catching up with the rest of Italy economically, Bari will be just the place. It has oil refineries, a busy port, and a new suburban business centre of glass skyscrapers called the *Baricentro*. The newer parts of town, with their smart shops and numb boulevards jammed with noisy traffic, exhibit a thoroughly northern glitter, and the good burghers who stroll down the Corso Cavour for their evening *passeggiata* are among the most overdressed in Italy.

History
Bari can trace its history back even before the Romans, to a colony founded by Illyrians from across the Adriatic. For centuries after the fall of Rome it was a Byzantine outpost. A strange interlude came in 847, with the founding here of the only Muslim state ever established on mainland Italy; the 'Emirate of Bari' lasted only thirty years before a Frankish army and Byzantine fleet chased the Arabs out of Apulia. By the early Middle Ages Bari had become the most important port on the Adriatic after Venice. As the seat of the nominally independent Byzantine governor, Bari was sometimes a rival of Venice, though more often its ally. Robert Guiscard and his Normans, who took the city in 1071, favoured Bari and helped it become the leading town of Apulia.

Since then Bari has been no stranger to adversity, though after each blow the city has managed to come back stronger than before. A later Norman ruler, William I, has gone down in the books as William the Bad for other indiscretions, but the Baresi would not argue. He razed the city to the ground after a revolt in 1156. Exactly 500 years later, a plague carried off nearly 80 per cent of the population. The most recent troubles came in 1943, when, like Naples, Bari had the honour of being thoroughly bombed by both the Allies and the Germans.

GETTING AROUND
Bari itself is not a large city, and though not a pleasant city for walking it doesn't take long to get from one side to the other. The airport, 11 km out, has regular connections to Rome, Milan and Pisa; the terminal for the airport bus is at Via Califati 43.
By Train: Besides the coastal trains (see p. 325), there is a busy FS branch from Bari to Tàranto. (Bari FS information: tel (080) 216 505.) Another line, the Ferrovia Sud-Est (FSE) runs a line from Bari's central FS station to Lecce, Tàranto (in competition with the FS) and to towns in the *trullo* country (tel 369 388). Just outside the FS station, in Piazza Aldo Moro on the southern end of town, there is another station serving yet two more lines: the FCL runs 12 trains a day to Altamura, and Matera in the Basilicata (tel (080) 216 980), and on the adjacent track Ferrovia Bari-Nord (tel (080) 213 577), runs a very frequent service to all the inland towns north of Bari.
By Ferry: for anyone discovering a sudden desire to bolt, Bari will be pleased to accommodate you. The port is the most important for connections to Yugoslavia; there are at least three a day to Dubrovnik, that incandescently lovely town, and three a month to Split, another fascinating destination with a city centre that has grown up inside the gigantic palace of the Roman emperor Diocletian (both run by Adriatica lines: Via Roberto di Bari 135, tel (080) 212 071). In addition, there is at least a weekly connection with the southern port of Bar (Traghetto Lines, Corso Tullio 36, tel (080) 235 323). For

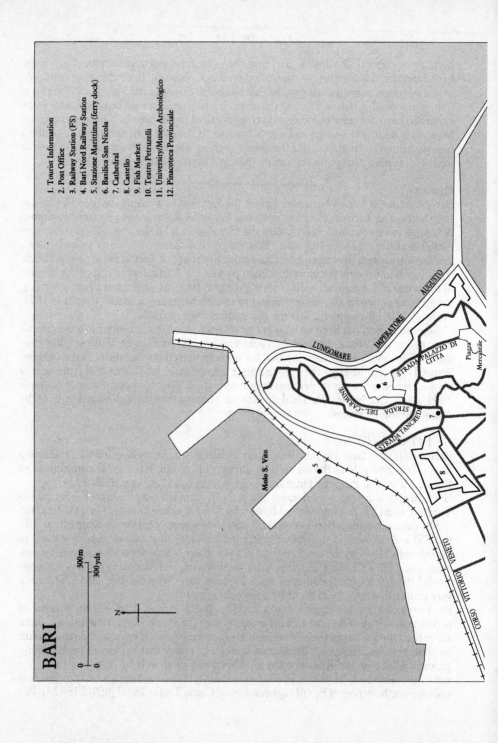

BARI

0   300m
0   300yds

1. Tourist Information
2. Post Office
3. Railway Station (FS)
4. Bari Nord Railway Station
5. Stazione Marittima (ferry dock)
6. Basilica San Nicola
7. Cathedral
8. Castello
9. Fish Market
10. Teatro Petruzzelli
11. University/Museo Archeologico
12. Pinacoteca Provinciale

Molo S. Vito

LUNGOMARE

IMPERATORE

AUGUSTO

STRADA PALAZZO DI CITTA

Piazza Mercantile

STRADA DEL CARMINE

STRADA TANCREDI

CORSO VITTORIO VENETO

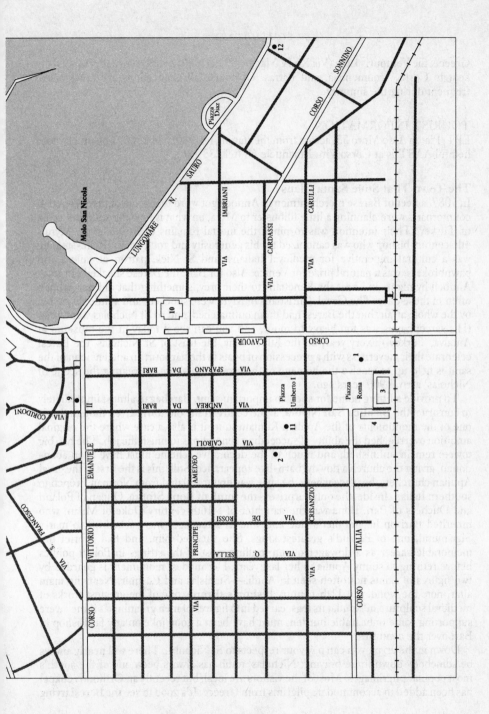

Greece, the Ventouris Line (Via XXIV Maggio 40, tel (080) 210 504) usually runs a daily boat to Corfu, Igoumenitsa, and Patras. Of course all connections are much more frequent during the summer.

TOURIST INFORMATION
EPT, Piazza Aldo Moro 33, across from the station, tel (080) 524 2361. The much more helpful AAST is at Corso Vitt. Emanuele 68 (tel 235 186).

The Town That Stole Santa Claus
In 1087, a fleet of Barese merchantmen in Antioch got word that some of their Venetian counterparts were planning a little filibuster to Myra, on what is now the southern coast of Turkey. Their intention was to pinch the mortal remains of St Nicholas, Myra's 4th-century bishop who was canonized for his generosity and good deeds. Relic-stealing was a cultural imperative for medieval Italians, and St Nick, patron of sailors and pawnbrokers, was a natural prize for Venice. Also for Bari; the Barese sneaked out from Antioch by night, and beat the Venetians to their prey, something that did not happen often in those days. The Greek Christians of Myra were shocked, and a little disgusted by the whole affair, but the Baresi had them outmatched, and so St Nicholas went west. (His sarcophagus was too heavy to move, and you can see it today in the museum at Antalya, Turkey.) Every year, on the 8th of May, the feast of St Nicholas, the Baresi celebrate their cleverness with a procession of boats in the harbour; an ancient icon of the saint is held up to receive the homage of the crowds on shore, recreating the scene of Nicholas' arrival 900 years ago.

To provide a fitting home for such an important saint, Bari began almost immediately to construct the **Basilica San Nicola**, at the centre of the old town. Even though this is one of the monuments of the Apulian Romanesque, it is also a case where the original ambition overreached the ability of succeeding generations to finish the job. The two big towers remain unfinished, and much of the decorative scheme must have been abandoned, giving the church a dowdy, barn-like appearance. Still, this is the first of the great Apulian churches, the place where the style was first translated from Norman French to southern Italian. Inside, the only surprise is the **tomb of Bona Sforza**, Queen of Poland and Duchess of Bari. Bona was the daughter of a 16th-century Duke of Milan, who inherited Bari on her mother's side and who as a teenager was packed off to marry Sigismund, one of Poland's greatest kings. She survived him, and had a brief but memorable career as a dowager queen, pulling most of the strings in Polish politics before retiring to sunny Apulia in her last years. Her modest monument is guarded by two figures of saints not often seen in Apulia—Stanislas and Casimir. Near the main altar, note the wonderful 11th-century **bishop's throne**, one of the greatest works of medieval sculpture in Apulia; its legs, carved into figures of men groaning as if they were supporting some unbearable burden, must have been a good joke on any fat Bishop of Bari over the centuries.

Down in the crypt, you can pay your respects to St Nicholas. There will nearly always be somebody down there praying; Nicholas' tomb has always been one of the south's most popular pilgrimages. Most of the visitors are local, but recently an Orthodox chapel has been added to accommodate pilgrims from Greece. It's good to see the Baresi trying

The Bishop's Throne, S. Nicola

to make amends after nine centuries; today this church is home to a centre for ecumenical studies. One of Nicholas' tricks is to exude gallons of a brownish liquid the faithful call *manna*, to which all sorts of miracles are attributed; half the families in this part of Apulia have a phial of it for good luck. The saint's reputation for helpfulness is certainly still current. The walls of the crypt are literally covered with supplications, written in ball-point pen. Most are from teenagers: 'Dear San Nicola, please let me be married to Alfredo...'

Around Old Bari

South of San Nicola, you will find the **cathedral**, difficult to distinguish from San Nicola though it was begun almost a century later. The plan is the same, as is the general feeling of austerity broken by small areas of richly detailed carving around some of the doors and windows. Unlike San Nicola, the cathedral still has its original beam ceiling, interrupted only by an octagonal cupola, and much more suited to its Romanesque plainness. Two unusual features are the stone baldachin over the main altar, and the *trullo*, the large round building adjacent to the north wall that once served as the baptistry.

Old Bari, as we have said, is a bit drab for a medieval historic centre. As a result of William the Bad, the plagues and the bombings, old Bari in some parts has the air of a new town. The buildings in the old centre may be all rebuilt or restored, but at least the old street plan survives—it's famous, in fact, for being one of the easiest places in all Italy to get lost. There will be no trouble finding the **castle**, however, just two blocks from the cathedral. The Normans began it, Frederick II completed it, and later centuries added the polygonal bastions to deflect cannonballs. Inside, some sculpted reliefs and window frames survive from Frederick's time, along with bits of sculpture and architectural fragments from all over Apulia. Excavations are currently under way on the castle grounds; apparently the centre of Roman Bari lies directly underneath.

Modern Bari

On your way back to the railway station, you'll be crossing the Corso Vittorio Emanuele—site of both the city hall and Bari's famous fish market, and also the boundary between the old city and the new. When the city's fortunes began to revive, in the early 1800s, Joachim Murat's Napoleonic government laid out this broad rectilinear extension. It is the plan of an old Greek or Roman town, but with wider streets, and it fits Bari well; many of the streets have a view open to the sea. Via Sparano di Bari and Corso Cavour are the choicest shopping streets. Bari's two museums are in the new town: the **Pinacoteca Provinciale**, in the Palazzo della Provincia on Lungomare Nazario Saura (Tues–Sat, 10–1, 4–7 pm; Sun 8:30–12:30) with a good selection of south Italian art through the ages—few Neapolitans are represented, though there is a genuine Neapolitan *presepio*. The **Museo Archeologico** occupies a corner of Bari University's sprawling, crowded old palace on the Piazza Umberto I, near the railway station. As is usual in southern museums, the star exhibits are classical ceramics: painted vases from Attica, including one very beautiful figure of the *Birth of Helen* (from Leda's egg), also Apulian copies, some of which are as good as the best of the Greeks. Much of the rest of the collection is devoted to the pre-Greek Neolithic cultures of Apulia (open Mon–Sat 9–2; adm).

WHERE TO STAY
(tel prefix 080)

Hotels of all kinds are surprisingly sparse in this region. Bari makes the most convenient base for seeing it, but be careful; the city is a major business centre, and full of bad hotels at outrageous prices for commercial travellers who don't care. Two unremarkable places that can provide a pleasant night's accommodation are the *****Grand Hotel Moderno** at Via Crisanzio 60, tel 213 313 (L65–95 000) and the *****Costa**, down the block at Via Crisanzio 12, tel 210 006 (L52 000 without bath, L72 000); both are within a few blocks of the railway stations.

EATING OUT

The province does better at restaurants than hotels, and especially at Bari, a city famous for fish. Like all the smaller towns around it, Bari still sends its own fishing fleet out each morning. **La Pignata** is considered by many to be the best restaurant in Apulia, with remarkable seafood risotto, and a different kind of risotto with chicken livers called a *sartù*; the chef likes to innovate, and you shouldn't be dismayed to find your fish done up in saffron or mint sauce; it is sure to be a treat (Via Melo 9, tel (080) 232 481; L60 000 average). Another local institution is **Vecchia Bari**, in the centre of the new town at Via Dante 47, where all the Apulian favourites are taken very seriously, and seafood shares top billing with roast meats and *terrine* of sausage and mushrooms (tel (080) 521 6496; L40 000 and up). **Ai Due Ghiottoni**—the 'two gluttons'—is a little more formal than the name might imply, but the food is good and the wine list extensive (Via Putignani 11, tel (080) 232 240; about L35–40 000). For less expensive places worth the trouble, you'll need to go out along the shore a bit; the **Taverna Verde**, Largo Adua 19, tel (080) 540 309 near the Molo San Nicola, is a popular place where fish and beer goes down well for about L20 000; **Da Tommaso**, outside town on the Lungomare Massaro (at Palese Marina) is another good place for seafood (tel (080) 320 038; about L25 000).

The Love of *Trulli*

It takes you by surprise. Turning a corner of the road or passing the crest of one of the low hills of the Murge, all at once you meet a kind of landscape you have never seen before. Low stone walls neatly partition the countryside, around acres of vines propped up on arbours, covering the ground like low flat roofs. The houses are the strange part, smooth whitewashed structures in a bewildering variety of shapes and forms, each crowned with one or more tall conical stone roofs. These are the **trulli,** and when there are enough of them in one place, they make a picture that might be at home in Africa, or in a fairy-tale, but certainly nowhere else in Italy.

The *trulli* are still built these days; the dome is easier to raise than it looks, and the form is adaptable to everything from tool sheds to petrol stations. It is anybody's guess as to their origins; some scholars have mentioned the Saracens, others, less probably, the Mycenaean Greeks. None of the *trulli* you see today are more than a century or two old. They are exotically beautiful, but if the form has any other advantage, it would be that the domes give warmer air a chance to rise, making the houses cooler in the broiling Apulian summers. Beyond that one modest tangible contribution, there is no real reason for building *trulli*—only that they are an inseparable part of the lives of the people who live in this part of Apulia. There is no special name for the area around Alberobello where most of the *trulli* are concentrated; people simply call it the '*trullo* district'.

Trulli are built of limestone, with thick, whitewashed walls and only a few tiny windows. The domes are limestone too, a single row of narrow slates wound in a gradually decreasing spiral up to the top. Most have some sort of decoration at the point, and a few of the older ones are embellished with some traditional but obscure symbols. *Trulli* seem to come only in one size; when a *trulli*-dweller needs more room, he simply has another unit added on. In this way, some of the fancier *trullo* palaces come to resemble small castles—Loire chateaux built for hobbits. Grandest of all is the one on

Trulli

Piazza Sacramento in Alberobello, the only specimen with a second floor; they call it the *Sovrano*, or Supreme Trullo.

TOURIST INFORMATION
Ostuni: Piazza della Libertà 63, tel (0831) 301 268 or 971 268.
Fasano: Piazza Ciaia 10, tel (080) 799 245
Martina Franca: Piazza Roma 37, tel (080) 705 702

Alberobello, Locorotondo and Ostuni

The **Valle d'Itria**, between the towns of Putignano and Martina Franca, is the best place for *trullo*-hunting. Alberobello, the *trullo* capital, has over a thousand of them (and perhaps as many souvenir stands) in two neighbourhoods called the Rione Monti and the Aia Piccola. The *trulli* look prettier out in the countryside, however, and particularly so around **Locorotondo**, a town on a hill with views all around the Itria valley. Locorotondo itself is stunning, a gleaming white town topped not with *trulli*, but with tidy rows of equally distinctive gables. The street plan, from which the town takes its name, is neatly circular, built around an ancient well dedicated to St George.

Not only Locorotondo, but many of the towns and villages in this district must be counted among the most beautiful in southern Italy. In each of them, white arches and steps climb the hillsides, sometimes punctuated by *trulli* and topped with surprisingly grand Baroque churches. You can spend as much time exploring these little towns as you care to. **Ostuni** is perhaps the loveliest, with an ornate 16th-century cathedral and a handful of other Renaissance and Baroque confections standing out among its white streets—including even a Neapolitan-style *guglia*. Ostuni also has the advantage of being near the sea, at the centre of the long strip of very modest but peaceful beach resorts that line the coast between Monópoli and Brindisi. **Martina Franca**, the highest town in Apulia, is a town quite similar to Ostuni, with a garland of Baroque monuments, including the old Ducal Palace and a cathedral at the top that towers over the city like a castle.

Caves, *Laure*, and a Dolmen

Nor are the attractions of this area limited to *trulli* and white towns. The people around **Castellana Grotte** never tire of bragging that their famous grotto is the most beautiful in Italy. They may be right; the deepest section of the grotto tour, called the Caverna Bianca, is a glistening wonderland hung with thousands of bright glassy stalactites (open daily, 8:30–12:30, 3–6:30 pm; tours given every hour; *very* expensive adm). Like much of Apulia, this region is what the geologists would call karst topography. Built mostly of easily-dissolving limestone, the territory is laced with every sort of cave, accompanied by such phenomena as streams and rivers that disappear into the ground, only to pop back up to the surface a few miles away. In the Middle Ages, the more inviting of the caves filled up with Greek Basilian monks. Here, following their burrowing instinct just as they did in Matera, and in Asia Minor, the Greek hermits turned literally dozens of caves into hidden sanctuaries and chapels. The best are around Tàranto, but quite a few can be seen around **San Vito dei Normanni**, and along the ravines near the town of **Fasano**, where they are called *laure*; some preserve faded bits of often surprisingly artistic medieval frescoes.

Also near Fasano, just off the Ostuni road at the village of Montalbano, you can visit what may be the most impressive **dolmen** in the south. Apulia's earliest cultures were not often great builders, but they nevertheless could be counted among the most sophisticated of all the Mediterranean Neolithic peoples. Much of their geometric pottery, which you can see scattered among Apulia's museums, is distinctively beautiful. This dolmen, a chamber formed by one huge slab of rock propped horizontally over two others, has acquired the same odd nickname as the Greek temple at Metaponto. Locals call it the **Tavole Palatine**, or Table of the Knights—the Round Table of King Arthur.

WHERE TO STAY

Because the *trullo* towns are easily accessible by rail from Bari or Tàranto, not many people stay over. If that is what you plan to do, however, the obviously perfect place to stay would be Alberobello's *****Hotel dei Trulli**; this is a group of *trulli* cottages set in a garden and beautifully furnished, each with its own terrace. There is a pool and a fair restaurant (Via Cadore 18, tel (080) 721 130; L105–120 000). A good bargain choice would be the ***Valle d'Itria**, the only hotel in Locorotondo (tel (080) 711 576; L38 000; some cheaper without bath). Ostuni and its stretch of coast are well equipped with hotels; the pleasant **Tre Torri**, Corso Vittorio Emanuele 298, tel (0831) 331 114, is fine for a short stay (L52 000); its excellent restaurant specializes in grilled lamb and fish, with dinners from L25 000. On the shore, the sharp modern design of the ***Grand Hotel Rosa Marina** and its surrounding holiday village stands out; it's a comfortable place too, with a pool, private beach and all the amenities (SS379 north of Ostuni; tel (0831) 970 411; L84 000). In Martina Franca, ***Dell'Erba**, Via dei Cedri 1, tel (080) 901 055, has a swimming pool and rooms with bath for L78 000. All across this area, there are dozens of privately owned *trulli* whose owners rent them out to visitors as part of the local *Agriturismo* programme; you can get more information and a list from the tourist information offices or from the Associazione Nazionale per l'Agriturismo, Palazzo Ducale, Martina Franca (tel (080) 701 096).

EATING OUT

For dinner, Alberobello logically follows the trullo hotel with a trullo restaurant—too much, you say, but the **Cucina dei Trulli**, in the hotel Lanzillotta has good home cooking and lets you go for only about L25 000 (Piazza San Fernando 31, tel (080) 721 511). A little fancier cuisine obtains at the **Trullo D'Oro** on Via Cavallotti 29, tel (080) 721 820; try the *spiedini* Apulian style (average L30 000). For dinner in Locorotondo, a bottle of *Locorotondo* wine is mandatory: a pale, dry white made by the local cooperative, much more delicate than most of the strong wines of Apulia. They'll be glad to slip you a bottle with the stuffed peppers or *coniglio al forno* at **Casa Mia**, a fine establishment on Via Cisternino, tel (080) 711 218 (about L30 000). At Castellana Grotte, the place to go is the friendly **Taverna degli Artisti** on Via Matarrese 27, where you might try the *cannelloni* or the lamb *spiedini* (tel (080) 896 8234; L25 000).

Tàranto

According to legend, Tàranto was founded by Taras, a son of Poseidon who came riding into the harbour on the back of a dolphin. According to the historians, however, it was only a band of Spartans, shipped here in 708 BC to found a colony. They chose a good spot: probably the best harbour in the south, and the only good one at all on the Ionian sea. Not surprisingly, their new town of Taras did well. Until the Romans cut it down to size, Taras was the metropolis of Magna Graecia, a town feared in war but more renowned in philosophy. Taras, now Tàranto, is still an interesting place, with an exotic old quarter, a good museum, and maybe the best seafood in southern Italy. Nevertheless, the best part of the story is all in the past.

History: Rotten Shellfish, Sheep With Overcoats

With its harbour, and with the help of a little Spartan know-how on the battlefield, Taras had little trouble acquiring both wealth and political power. By the 4th century BC, the population had reached 300,000. In its palmiest days, Taras' prosperity depended on an unusual variety of luxury goods. Its oysters were a highly prized delicacy that the Tarantines sent as far as Rome. Another shellfish, the murex, provided the purple dye—really a deep scarlet—used for the robes of Roman emperors and every other style-conscious ruler across the Mediterranean. This Imperial purple, the most expensive stuff of the ancient world, was obtained by allowing masses of the murex to rot in the sun; an enormous heap of the shells, with perhaps the mollusc who coloured Caesar's cloak somewhere near the bottom, was mentioned by travellers only a century ago. For a similarly high price, the Tarantines would have been happy to provide you with the cloth, too. Their sheep were known for the softest and best wool available, and the Tarantine shepherds actually put coats on their flocks to keep it nice.

If contemporary historians are to be believed, Taras managed to avoid most of the terrible inter-city conflicts of Magna Graecia simply by being much larger and more powerful than its neighbours. And it was spared civil troubles by a sound constitution, planned with a balanced mix of aristocratic and democratic elements. Pythagoras spent part of his life in Taras, an exile from his native Croton, and he helped to set a philosophic tone for the city's conduct of its affairs. The height of Taras' glory was perhaps the long period of rule under a Pythagorean mathematician and philosopher named Archytas (c. 400 BC), a paragon of wisdom and virtue in the ancient world. Plato himself came to visit Archytas, though he never mentions Taras in his writings.

When Taras and Rome went to war in 282 BC, they went as equals. Taras called in Pyrrhus of Epirus as an ally, but after ten years of inconclusive Pyrrhic victories, the Romans gained the upper hand and put an end to Taras' independence. Rome graciously refrained from razing the city to the ground after Taras helped Hannibal in the second Punic War; just the same the Tarantines felt the iron grip of the victors, and their city quickly dwindled both in wealth and importance. Of all the Greek cities of the south, Taras (along with Règgio) proved to be the best survivor. Throughout the Dark Ages the city never quite disappeared, and by the time of the Crusades it was an important port once more.

The modern city, Italianized to Tàranto, has known little of philosophers or well-dressed sheep, but still manages to send its fame around the world in other ways. The city gives its name to the fast country dance called the *tarantella*, and also to the *tarantula*. Before you change your travel plans, be advised there really are no large hairy spiders dripping poison in Apulia, just a few innocent little brown ones. Their bite isn't much, but a little bit of notoriety still clings to them thanks to the native religious pathology of the south Italian. Throughout antiquity and the Middle Ages, various cults of dancing were current around the Mediterranean. Everything from the worship of Dionysos to the medieval Dance of Death touched this region, and when the Catholic church began to frown on such carrying on, the urge took strange forms. People bitten by spiders became convinced they would die, and that the only thing that could save them was to dance the venom out of their system—dance until they dropped, in fact. Sometimes they would dance for four days or more, while their friends found musicians to play for them, and sought to discover the magic colour—the 'colour' of that particular spider—that would calm the stricken dancer. *Tarantism*, as 19th-century psychologists came to call it, is rarely seen anywhere in the south these days, and for that matter neither is the Tarantella, a popular style of music that took its name from this bit of folklore, and was in vogue a century ago.

GETTING AROUND
There are two railway lines, but both use the central station in Tàranto, on the far western end of town—between the old town and the steel mills—on Piazzale Duca d'Aosta. Regular FS trains leave for Bari, Brindisi and Lecce, as well as the horrible endless trip around the Ionian sea to Règgio Calabria (FS info tel 411 801). One or the other of these can drop you off in Massafra, Castellaneta, Grottaglie or Manduria. FSE trains (Ferrovia Sud-Est, operating from the last track) will take you to Locorotondo, Martina Franca, and Alberobello (tel 404 463). The FSE also operates much of the province's bus services; several a day for Alberobello, Bari or Lecce leave from Piazza Castello (tel 28 072). Their buses for Ostuni and Manduria leave from Via Magnaghi. Daily buses to Naples are run by Miccolis from the Corso Umberto (tel 36 623), and SITA buses go to Matera from Piazza Castello (tel 340 883).

TOURIST INFORMATION
Corso Umberto 113, tel (099) 21 233.

The Città Vecchia

Perhaps unique among cities, Tàranto has two 'seas' all to itself. Its harbour consists of two large lagoons, the **Mare Grande** and the **Mare Piccolo**. The city is on a narrow strip of land between them, broken into three pieces by a pair of narrow channels. Today, the westernmost section, around the railway station, is almost entirely filled up with Italy's biggest steel plant, begun as the showpiece project of the *Cassa per il Mezzogiorno* in the early '50s. The gargantuan complex has everything to do with Tàranto's current size and prosperity, and it provides an unexpected and memorable sight if you enter the city by night.

A few blocks from the station, a bridge takes you over to the old town, a nearly rectangular island that is only four blocks wide, but still does its best to make you lose your way. The ancient Tarantines, lacking any sort of hill, made the island their acropolis. Most of the temples were here, along with a famous gold-plated bronze statue of Zeus that was the second largest piece of sculpture in the world, surpassed only by the Colossus of Rhodes. Travellers of a century ago found nothing left of ancient Taras, but recent excavations have unearthed a collapsed **Temple of Poseidon**. At present its

341

columns are being re-erected in the square next to Tàranto's **Castello**, built in the 1480s by King Ferdinand of Spain. From the square, a **swing bridge**, something rare in Italy, connects the old town with the new. The Mare Piccolo, besides being an enormous oyster and mussel farm for the fishermen of Tàranto, also is the home of one of Italy's two important naval bases. If you come by very early in the morning when the bridge is open, you may see big warships, their missiles covered in canvas, waiting their turn with little fishing boats to squeeze their way through the narrow channel.

Follow the fishermen home, and you'll end up in the fish market on Via Cariati, near the docks on the opposite end of the Città Vecchia. In slick and up-to-date Italy this is one of the few places where you can truly believe you are on the Mediterranean, a wet and mildly grubby quay awash with the sounds and smells of the sea, where tired fishermen appear each morning at dawn to have a coffee, sort out the catch, and bang the life out of octopuses on the stones. Many of Tàranto's best restaurants are here too, hidden behind the most unpretentious of façades, and you can come back in the evening for an exceptional dinner. Of course there are plenty of cats around; true 'aristocats' they are, the descendants of the first cats of Europe. Ancient historians record how the ancient Tarantines imported them from Egypt.

From the fish market, pick your way a few blocks across the Città Vecchia to the **cathedral**, built and rebuilt in a hotch-potch of different styles beginning in the 11th century. Most of the last, florid Baroque remodelling has been cleared away, saving only a curious coffered ceiling, with two golden statues suspended from it. Roman columns and capitals support the arches, and there is a good medieval baptismal font under a baldachin. Some bits of mosaic survive on the floor; mosaics in the Byzantine manner were an important part of all Apulia's medieval churches. Tàranto's cathedral is dedicated to St Cataldus (nothing to do with the cats), a Munster Irishman who did good works here on his way to the Crusades, and you can see his tomb down in the crypt. The rest of the Città Vecchia's back streets hold few surprises. The area was down at the heels and half forgotten for a long time, but with Tàranto's new-found prosperity the city is putting a good deal of money into restoring old palaces and other monuments, a process that is already beginning to make a difference.

The Museum of Magna Graecia
As in Bari, crossing over from the sleepy old town into the hyperactive new centre is a startling contrast. Tàranto has nothing to envy Bari these days; its new town is surprisingly bright, busy and sprawling, with as many grey-suited businessmen as blue-clad sailors. There aren't many modern sights here, but the best of Magna Graecia is on display at the **Museo Nazionale** on Piazza Archita, just two blocks west of the swing bridge (Mon–Sat 9–2; Sun 9–1; adm).

With building activity going full blast around Tàranto, new discoveries are being made all the time; already the collection rivals Règgio's and Naples', and there is always the possibility that some new discovery, like that of the warriors of Riace, will turn up to broaden our appreciation of the ancient world. There are some fine pieces of sculpture from temples and funeral sites, including a head of Aphrodite and several other works attributed to the school of Praxiteles, and also a wonderful large bronze of the god Poseidon, in the angular, half-oriental Archaic style.

The museum has what is believed to be the largest collection of Greek terracotta figures in the world. These are fascinating in their thousands, the middle-class *objets d'art* of antiquity. The older ones are more consciously religious, images of Dionysos, Demeter or Persephone that served the same purpose as the crucifix on the wall of a modern Italian family. Later examples give every evidence of creeping secularism; the subjects range from ladies at their toilette to grotesque theatre masks, comic dancers, and figures from mythological stories. A few are copies of famous monuments; one figurine reproduces a statue of *Nike*, or Victory, erected in Taras after one of Pyrrhus' defeats of the Romans—and later moved to the Roman forum after the war went the other way.

Among the fragments from Taras' buildings, there is an entire wall of leering Medusas, protection against the evil eye—as much a preoccupation among the ancient Greeks as it is with the south Italians today. Besides a large collection of delicate jewellery and coins, many minted with the city's own symbol of Taras riding his dolphin, there is also an important selection of Greek ceramics, including fine examples of the earlier, less common black figure-work. In one room, a rare evocation of Magna Graecia at play is provided by scenes on vases of Athene and contending athletes, near a case full of such odd finds as javelin points, and a genuine ancient discus.

Towns Around Tàranto

The tradition of making fine pottery in Apulia never died out entirely. In **Grottaglie**, just outside the city, they have been working in ceramics at least since the Middle Ages; the thousands of plates and vases stacked on the pavements and rooftops make an arresting sight. Right now Grottaglie's potters are on an antique kick, turning out kraters, amphorae and every sort of copy of painted ancient Greek ware. They do it so well— better than any of the other places around the Mediterranean that specialize in such souvenir trinkets—that it's hard to quibble. Further down the road towards Brindisi, **Francavilla Fontana** takes its title of 'free town' from a favour granted by King Ferdinand IV; the town conserves several 14th–18th-century palaces, including a small palace of the 18th-century Bourbon kings, as a reminder of its days as a feudal stronghold. Nearby **Oria** has a history much the same. Frederick II built a strong **castle** here with three tall round towers. It's one of the few such you can visit; the city has assembled a collection of antiquities and bric-à-brac inside (daily, except Mon, 9–12, 2–7 pm; adm). In the Middle Ages, Oria had an important Jewish community; the ghetto and its buildings are still intact.

Oria is believed to have been the capital of the ancient Messapii, a quietly civilized people who suffered many indignities at the hands of the Greek colonists, and finallly succumbed to the allure of classical culture. **Cèglie Messapico**, south of Ostuni, was another of their cities, and it is here you can see the most noteworthy surviving Messapian monuments. The *specchie* are tall conical stepped towers; they get their name intriguingly from the Latin *speculum*, a mirror, but no one has the faintest idea what they are or what purpose they served. One is in Cèglie itself, and the other two out in the country. The most impressive, the 11-m **Specchia Miano**, is 7 km down the road from Cèglie to Francavilla, under a kilometre off the road to the right.

Manduria was another Messapian city, mentioned in the histories as fighting con- tinuous wars with Taras. Ruins of its fortifications can still be seen—three concentric

343

circuits of which the outermost is three miles round—along with caves, necropolises, and a famous well mentioned in Pliny's *Natural History*. The new city has an interesting **cathedral**, with a beautifully carved rose window and portals in the Baroque style of Lecce.

Massafra

West of Tàranto, heading back toward the Murge of Apulia and Matera, you can visit one of the most unusual cities of Apulia. **Massafra**, even more than Matera, was a city of troglodytes and monks. A steep ravine, the **Gravina di San Marco**, cuts the city in two. The ravine and surrounding valleys are lined with caves, and many of these were expanded into cave-chapels, or *laure* by Greek monks in the early Middle Ages. Between the caves and the old church crypts, it has been estimated that there are over a hundred medieval frescoes in, around, and under Massafra—some of considerable artistic merit. One of the best is a beautiful Byzantine Virgin called *La Vergine della Scala*, in a sanctuary of the same name, reached from Via del Santuario in the old town of Massafra by a long naif-Baroque set of stairs. The Madonna is shown receiving the homage of two kneeling deer, the subject of an old legend. Adjacent to the sanctuary, more paintings can be seen in the **Cripta della Bona Nova**.

Beyond these, you will have to rely on the locals' considerable goodwill towards strangers to find the rest of the caves, crypts and frescoes. None of the sites is well marked. Ask for the **Crypt of San Marco**, the **Crypt of the Candelora**, the **Crypt of San Antonio Abate**, and the **Crypt of San Lorenzo**, the four most interesting of the *laure*, all near the centre of town. Other cave churches and frescoes can be seen at **Mottola**, and in **Ginosa**, built like Massafra over a ravine full of caves. **Castellaneta** also has a ravine, the steepest and wildest of them all, and some cave-churches, but this town cares more to be known as the birthplace, in 1895, of Rudolph Valentino. There's a monument, with a life-size ceramic statue of the old matinée idol dressed as the Sheikh of Araby.

WHERE TO STAY AND EATING OUT   (tel prefix 099)
In Tàranto, most of the better hotels are inconveniently located on the far eastern edge of town; one luxurious, well-run spot in the centre is the *****Plaza**, facing Piazza Archita at Via D'Aquino 46. All of the rooms are air-conditioned, and most have a balcony over the square (tel 91 925; L125 000). Less expensive, and in a nice location overlooking the channel and the Mare Piccolo, is the ****Miramare**, Via Roma 4, tel 22 854 (L50 000 without bath, L75 000 with). The bargain places are in the old town, in the picturesque environs of the fish market. The ***Ariston** is a clean and shipshape establishment, and the views over the Mare Piccolo are priceless (Piazza Fontana 15, tel 407 563; L34 000 with bath, L27 000 without).

The fish market of course is also the place to go for dinner; right across the street there are a number of popular places where you can feast on the fruits of the sea and rub elbows with half Tàranto: **Posìllipo a Mare**, Via Cariati 38, tel 411 519 and the **Gambrinus**, Via Cariati 24, tel 407 603. The latter is a little more adventurous in its dishes, but you can leave either of them with a bill of L25 000. For something a little more elegant, there's **Al Gambero**, just across the channel on Vico del Ponte 4, a place that has earned its reputation for having the best *zuppa di pesce* in Apulia, as well as creative dishes involving nearly all the fantastic array of marine delicacies the Ionian sea has to offer (tel 411 190; L45–55 000, closed Mon and Nov). One item that figures prominently on the menus of all these places is mussels; here, the word for them is *mitili*, not *cozze*, and they are in truth a larger and tastier variety, farmed by the fishermen in the Mare Grande. One place to try them is **Le Rendez-Vous**, Viale Virgilio 66, tel 339 981, along with other fish and shellfish in all shapes and sizes, also grilled meats if you need some land food (L25–30 000, closed Fri). There are many good inexpensive places in the new city: the **Ristorante-Pizzeria Mario** at Via Acclaio 68, tel 26 009, besides good pizza, has seafood dinners for about L18 000; even better, the **Ristorante Basile** on Via Pitagora 76, tel 26 240, across from the city park, cooks fine dinners at rock-bottom prices; pass up the menu turistico and spring for a good fish dinner for L20 000 or so.

Tàranto is a comfortable city in which to spend a few days, and there is little reason to try and find accommodation out in the hinterlands. West of the city, at Castellaneta Marina–Riva dei Tessali, the ****Golf Hotel** is a resort complex of cottages in a grove near the links—not much of a course, really, but a full 18 holes, and a genuine novelty in these parts (tel 643 9251; L140–175 000). Also at Castellaneta Marina, there's the **Lisea**, on the beach at Lungomare Eroi del Mare, tel 643 495 (L40–48 000). There are no hotels in Massafra—only a locanda or two, and only one in Manduria, the *Nuovo Marinelli, Via Pacelli 19, tel 807 680 (L25 000 without bath).

The Salentine Peninsula

It has lovely Lecce and dowdy Brindisi, some flat but unusual countryside, the sun-bleached and sea-washed old towns of Gallipoli and Otranto, lots of caves and Neolithic remains. Its coastline, while not as ruggedly beautiful as that of the Gargano, does have its charms, not least of which is that it is relatively uncrowded. Not many tourists, even among the Italians, make their way to this distant Land's End. If you are beachcombing or backpacking, and can resist the temptation presented by the ferries to Greece, this might be a good place to spend a lazy week or so.

GETTING AROUND

Lecce, despite its location, is well served by rail; the city is a terminus for long sleeper runs across Italy to Rome and Milano. All of these also pass through Brindisi, and both towns have trains all the time heading for Bari or Tàranto. In addition, there is always the tired but game FSE, which has services from Lecce to Otranto, Gallipoli and Nardò, as well as some to Bari and Tàranto (FS info in Lecce 21 016, in Brindisi 21 975; FSE info in Lecce 41 931). In Brindisi, buses to all provincial towns and nearby cities leave from the Viale Porta Pia. In Lecce, most buses to towns in the Salentine, run by the Sud-Est Company, leave from Via Adua near the old western walls. Marozzi (Via U. Foscolo, tel 23 016) runs a daily service to Rome.

By Ferry: Brindisi, the most important Italian port for ferries to Greece, has daily connections almost the year round to Corfu, Patras and Igoumenitsa, with several a day in the busy summer season. Schedules, prices, and even the names of the lines change all the time, but the EPT office will probably have up-to-date information. That may not be much help in summer—frequently as the boats run, it is a good idea in July and August to book a passage before you get to Brindisi. At present, there are nine companies competing for your trade; any travel agent you talk to may only deal with one or a few of them, and you may wish to shop around if you have the time. The two biggest companies, and their main agents in Brindisi are: Adriatica, Stazione Marittimo (tel 23 825) and Hellenic Mediterranean, Corso Garibaldi 10 (tel 28 531).

TOURIST INFORMATION
Brindisi: Piazza A. Dionisi, tel (0831) 21 944; AAST at Via Rubini 19, tel (0831) 21 091
Lecce: Via Visconti 14, tel (0832) 24 443; also Via Francesco Rubini 19, tel (0832) 54 117
Otranto: Via Rondachi 8, tel (0836) 814 36
Santa Cesarea Terme: Via Roma 209, tel (0836) 944 043

Brindisi

The word *brindisi* in Italian means a toast. It's just a coincidence; the name comes from the original Greek colony of *Brentesion*, and it isn't likely that anyone has ever proposed a toast to this grey and dusty port. Brindisi today is what it was in Roman times: the gangplank to the boat for Greece. On the Viale Regina Margherita, to the right of the port, a small piazza at the top of a formal stairway holds a magnificent **Roman column**, once topped by the statue of an emperor, that marked the end of the Appian Way. For six centuries, all of Rome's trade with the East, all its legions heading toward new conquests, and all its trains of triumphant or beaten Emperors and generals passed through *Brundisium*. From the 11th century on, the city resumed its old role when it became one of the most important Crusader ports. A memory of this survives too; if you enter the city from the north or west, you will pass the **Tancredi Fountain**, an Arab-inspired work built by the Norman chief Tancred. Here the Christian knights watered their horses for the last time before setting out for the Holy Land.

As a city where people have always been more concerned with coming and going than settling down, Brindisi has not saved up a great store of monuments and art. Travel agents and steamship offices are more in evidence than anything else, helping expedite the hordes of tourists flowing to and from Patras, Corfu, and Igoumenitsa. If you're staying, there are a few things to look at: on the square facing the 12th-century cathedral, rebuilt in warmed-over Baroque, there is a small exotic-looking portico with striped pointed arches; this is all that remains of the **Temple**, a headquarters church of the Knights Templar, and closely related somehow to The Temple in London. Nearby, a small collection of ancient Apulian relics has been assembled at the **Museo Archeologico**. Down Via San Giovanni, a few blocks south, another curious souvenir of the Templars has survived, the round church of **San Giovanni al Sepolcro**, built in the late 11th century, with fanciful carvings of dancers and lions on the portal.

Santa Maria del Casale
The greatest of Brindisi's attractions, however, lies just north of the city, near the sports complex on the way to the airport. **Santa Maria del Casale** is a church unlike any other in Italy; built in the 1320s, in an austere, almost modern economy of vertical lines and

arches, the façade is done in two shades of sandstone not striped, as in so many other Italian churches, but shaped into a variety of simple, exquisite patterns. The church makes use of many of the features of Apulian Romanesque, but defies classification into any period or style; neither is any foreign influence, from the Saracens or Greeks, readily apparent. Santa Maria is a work of pure imagination.

The interior, a simple, barn-like space, is painted with equally noteworthy frescoes in the Byzantine manner. The wall over the entrance is covered with a remarkable visionary **Last Judgement** by an artist named Rinaldo of Tàranto, full of brightly coloured angels and apostles, saints and sinners; a river of fire washes The Damned into the Inferno while above, the fish of the sea disgorge their human prey for the Judgement. Many of the other frescoes, in the nave and transepts, have become badly faded, though they are still of interest.

Lecce

Unfortunately for the traveller, you will have to come a long way, to the furthest corner of Apulia and the last city in this book, to find the most beautiful town in southern Italy. Lecce is worth the trip if you have the time. Its history, and its tastes, have given it a fate and a look different from any other Italian town. First and foremost, Lecce is a Baroque city—not the chilly, pompous Baroque of Rome, but a sunny, almost frivolous style Lecce created on its own.

Lecce started as a Messapian town, and flourished as the Roman *Lupiae*, but really only came into its own during the Middle Ages, as centre of a semi-independent county comprising most of the Salentine peninsula. Few buildings are left from this period, only because Lecce, uniquely among Apulian cities, was prosperous enough to replace them in later centuries when styles changed. Lecce enjoyed royal favour under the Spaniards in the 16th century; with its location near the front lines of the continual wars between Habsburg and Turk, Lecce often found itself the centre of attention even though it is not a port. Somehow during the Spanish centuries, while every other southern city except the royal seat of Naples was in serious decline, Lecce was enjoying a golden age. In these centuries, the city attained distinction in literature and the arts, giving rise to such unfortunate nicknames as 'The Athens of Apulia'. Lecce also found the wealth to virtually rebuild itself, and took the form we see today with the construction of dozens of palaces, churches and public buildings in the city's own distinctive style.

Even though Lecce was doing well under the Spaniards and Bourbons, it was hardly enjoying the privilege of being ruled by them. On the contrary, perhaps more than any other city in Italy, Lecce's resistance to the new order manifested itself in four serious revolts. First, in 1648, came a popular revolution coinciding with Masaniello's revolt in Naples, and like it bloodily repressed by Spanish troops. A second rebellion, in 1734, almost succeeded; the rebels were tricked into submitting by the Bourbons, who offered them reforms that were later withdrawn. In the wake of the French Revolution, another revolt occurred, and the last came in 1848; the Leccesi also worked hard for the unification of Italy, and contributed to the fight both men and ideas.

Leccese Baroque
One critic has called Baroque the 'most expensive style of architecture ever invented'.

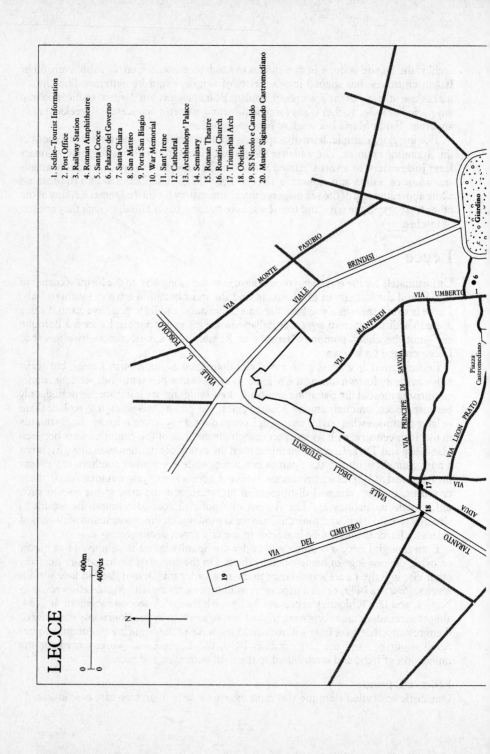

LECCE

0 — **400m**
0 — **400yds**

N

1. Sedile–Tourist Information
2. Post Office
3. Railway Station
4. Roman Amphitheatre
5. Santa Croce
6. Palazzo del Governo
7. Santa Chiara
8. San Matteo
9. Porta San Biagio
10. War Memorial
11. Sant' Irene
12. Cathedral
13. Archbishops' Palace
14. Seminary
15. Roman Theatre
16. Rosario Church
17. Triumphal Arch
18. Obelisk
19. SS Nicolo e Cataldo
20. Museo Sigismundo Castromediano

Giardino

VIA MONTE

PASUBIO

VIALE BRINDISI

VIA UMBERTO I

6

VIA MANFREDI

VIALE U. FOSCOLO

VIA PRINCIPE DI SAVOIA

Piazza Castromediano

VIALE DEGLI STUDENTI

VIA LEON PRATO

17

VIA

18

ADUA

TARANTO

VIA DEL CIMITERO

19

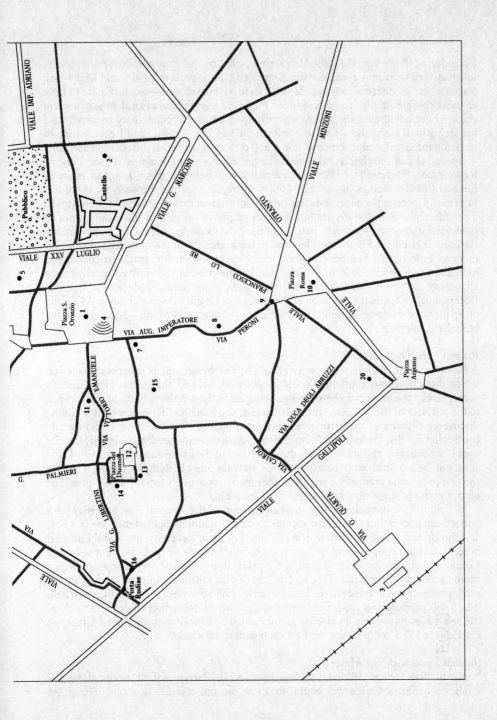

Considering all the hours of skilled labour it took to carve all those curlicues and rosettes, this may well be true. Lecce, like southern Sicily, some parts of Spain, and Malta—all places where southern Baroque styles also were well developed—was fortunate to have an inexhaustible supply of a perfect stone. *Pietra di Lecce* is a kind of sandstone of a warm golden hue, possessing the additional virtues of being extremely easy to carve, and becoming hard as granite after a few years in the weather. Almost all of Lecce is built of it, giving the city the appearance of one great, delicately crafted architectural ensemble.

The artists and architects who made Lecce's Baroque were almost all local talent, most notably Antonio and Giuseppe Zimbalo, who between them designed many of Lecce's finest buildings in the mid-16th century, and carried the style to its wildest extremes. Leccese Baroque does not involve any new forms or structural innovations. The difference is in the decoration, with an emphasis on vertical lines and planes of rusticated stonework, broken by patches of the most intricate and fanciful stone-carving Baroque ever knew. These churches and palaces, along with the hundreds of complementary little details that adorn almost every street—fountains, gates, balconies and monuments—combine to form an elegant and refined cityscape that paradoxically seems all gravity and restraint. Leccese Baroque owes more than a little to the Spanish Plateresque style, and the city itself still has an air of Spanish reserve about it. As a King of Spain once described a similar Baroque city—Valletta, in Malta—Lecce is a 'town built for gentlemen'.

Piazza Sant'Oronzo

A Baroque city, of course, was conceived as a sort of theatre set, its squares as stages on which these decorous gentlemen could promenade. An odd chance has given Lecce's main piazza something even better—a genuine arena right in the middle. In 1901, much to the surprise of the Leccesi, workmen digging the basement for a new bank building discovered a **Roman Amphitheatre**, with seats for some 15,000, directly under the city centre. In the '30s, the half that lay under the piazza was excavated; occasionally the city uses it for concerts and shows. Only the lower half of the grandstands has survived; the stones of the top levels were probably carted away for other buildings long ago, allowing the rest to become gradually buried and forgotten. Some badly faded reliefs can still be seen, but the best are now kept in the city's museum.

In Brindisi, by the column that marked the end of the Appian Way, you may have noticed the pedestal of a vanished second column. Lightning toppled that one in 1528, and the Brindisians let it lie until 1661, when the city of Lecce bought it and moved it here, attaching a copper statue of their patron, Sant'Oronzo, or Orontius, first bishop of Lecce, and supposedly a martyr during the persecutions of Nero. What appears to be a small pavilion in the middle of the square, overlooking the amphitheatre, is the **Sedile**, an elegant early masterpiece of the Leccese style (1596) that once served as the town hall. The lovely portico, now glassed in, serves as the tourist information office. The clock on the second level is run by an electric motor, added by a local inventor named Giuseppe Candido in 1868 and perhaps the first such gadget anywhere.

Santa Croce and San Matteo

North of Piazza Sant'Oronzo, the most outrageous Baroque of all awaits along Via Umberto I. **Santa Croce** was begun in 1549, but not completed until 1680, giving

Lecce's Baroque berserkers a chance at the façade. The lower half of it is original, done mainly in a sober Renaissance style. The portal, however, and everything above it, is a fond fancy of Zimbalo and his colleague Cesare Penna. Among the florid cake-icing decoration the rose window stands out, made of concentric choirs of tiny angels. Look carefully at the figures on the corbels supporting the second level: among the various cartoon monsters can be made out Romulus' and Remus' she-wolf, a few dragons, a Turk, an African, and a German. Always have a look inside Lecce's churches if they are open; Santa Croce is one of the best, with beautiful altars in the transept chapels by Penna and Antonio Zimbalo. Giuseppe Zimbalo also designed the **Palazzo del Governo** next door, originally built as a monastery.

Behind Santa Croce, Lecce's pretty **Giardino Pubblico** and a **castle** built by Emperor Charles V mark old Lecce's eastern edge. For another interesting walk through the old town, start from the Piazza Sant'Oronzo down Via Augusto Imperatore (Augustus was in Lecce when he got the news of Caesar's assassination). This street passes another Baroque church, **Santa Chiara**, and a Salesian convent with a skull and crossbones over the portal—the ultimate Spanish touch. Even better, in a small garden there is the most preposterous statue of Vittorio Emanuele in all Italy, surpassing even the bronze colossus on the Altar of the Nation in Rome. This Vittorio is smaller, but in his epaulettes and ponderous moustaches he comes off looking half a pirate, half the leader of the firemen's band.

The next Baroque church is **San Matteo** (1700), architecturally the most adventurous of the lot, with an elliptical nave and a complex façade that is convex on the lower level, and concave above. Continue straight down Via Perroni and you will come to one of Lecce's fine Baroque town gates, the **Porta San Biagio**. To prove that this city's curiosities are not all Baroque, we offer the Neoclassical **War Memorial**, across Piazza Roma near the gate, and off to the right a block of mansions, built around the turn of the century in a style that perfectly imitates the Alhambra in Spain, complete with pointed arches, minarets and Koranic inscriptions.

Piazza del Duomo

Leaving Piazza Sant'Oronzo by Via Vittorio Emanuele, you pass the church of **Sant' Irene**, a relatively modest Baroque church of the 1720s. If you're not careful you may entirely miss the little alley off to the left that leads to the **Piazza del Duomo**, one of the finest Baroque architectural groups anywhere. It was the plan of the designers to keep this square cut off from the life of the city, making it a sort of tranquil stone park; the alley off Via Vittorio Emanuele is the only entrance. The boys of the neighbourhood take advantage of the lack of traffic to use it as a football ground, and the piazza does the best it can to maintain its dignity in the circumstances.

The **cathedral**, presently undergoing restoration, is one of the finest works of Giuseppe Zimbalo (1659–70). To make the building stand out in the L-shaped medieval piazza, Zimbalo gave it two façades: one on the west front and a second, more gloriously ornate one facing the open end of the piazza. The angular, unusually tall campanile (68 m), with its simple lines and baby obelisks, echoes the Herreran style of Imperial Spain. If you can find someone to let you in, the long climb is worth the trouble, with an exceptional view over the city and most of the Salentine peninsula; on a clear day you can see Albania. Adjoining the Cathedral are the complementary façades of the **Archbish-**

ops' Palace and the Seminary, the latter the work of Giuseppe Cino, a pupil of Zimbalo.

Behind the cathedral, in the back streets off Via Paladini, there is a small but well-preserved Roman Theatre. In the opposite direction, Via Libertini passes several good churches, including the unique Rosario (1691–1728), last and most unusual work of Giuseppe Zimbalo. Further down, the street leaves the city through the Porta Rudiae, the most elaborate of the city's gates, bearing yet another statue of Sant' Oronzo. From here, the broad Viale Tàranto follows the northwestern face of this diamond-shaped city, passing the remains of the walls Charles V rebuilt to keep out Turkish corsairs; further up, you don't need to read Latin to recognize another relic of Charles' in the Triumphal Arch, erected in 1548. Most destructive and least modest of monarchs, Charles erected monuments like this around the Mediterranean, usually after unsuccessful revolts, to remind the people who was boss. This one, featuring crowned screaming eagles and a huge Spanish coat-of-arms, is a chilling reminder of the militaristic, almost totalitarian government with which the Habsburgs tried to conquer Europe.

In a little park in front of the Arch, there is an attractive monument to the less grisly, though thoroughly useless King Ferdinand I, called the Obelisk. From here, a road off to the right leads to the city cemetery, behind a quite elegant 19th-century Neoclassical gate; next to it stands the church of SS. Nicola e Cataldo. The façade is typical Baroque, but if you look carefully you will notice that the portal and rose window are much older. Behind the 18th-century front hides one of the best Apulian Romanesque churches, and one of the only medieval monuments to survive in Lecce. The nave and the dome are unusually lofty, and the carvings on the portal and elsewhere are especially good.

The Museo Sigismundo Castromediano

The founder of this collection, now Lecce's city museum, was a Duke, and also a famous local patriot who fought against the Bourbons and earned long spells in the Neapolitan dungeons. His prison memoirs shocked Europe in the 1880s, and moved William Gladstone to a few rousing anti-Bourbon speeches. Duke Sigismundo would be happy if he could see his little collection, now become one of the best arranged and most modern museums in Italy. The most prized works are several excellent Apulian and Greek vases, found all over the Salentine Peninsula, though there is also a good collection of medieval art and architectural fragments, and a small picture gallery. (The museum is on Viale Gallipoli, at the southern end of the old town; daily 9–1:30, 3:30–6:30 pm; Sun 9:30–1; adm.)

The Tip of the Salentine

Italy's furthest southeastern corner is one of the quieter parts of the country. It offers a low, rocky coastline, rather like that of the Gargano but without the mountains, a number of towns embellished in the Leccese Baroque style, and a lonely beach or two. One of the most noticeable features of the countryside—and this is true for all of the Salentine Peninsula—is the eccentricity of the rural architecture. There aren't many modern *trulli* here, but a few of their ancient predecessors, low-domed houses of unknown age. Besides these, there are little houses with flat roofs curled up at the corners, some recent artistic do-it-yourself experiments in cinder block, and many tiny pink Baroque palaces, sitting like jewel-boxes in a prairie landscape of olive trees, tobacco, and wild flowers even in December.

The towns here show an almost African austerity, except perhaps **Nardò**, decorated with a lovely square called the **Piazza Salandra**, in which there is a *guglia* as frilly as those in Naples. Nardò's much-rebuilt 11th-century **cathedral** retains some medieval frescoes. Near the town walls, on Via Giuseppe Galliano, is a strange, unexplained circular temple called the **Osanna**, built in 1603. Other towns around Lecce: **Acàia**, with a romantically ruined Aragonese castle; **Galatina**, with a wonderful set of Renaissance frescoes in the 1392 church of Santa Caterina; and **Calimera**, one of the centres of Apulia's Greek community—oddly enough the town's name means 'good morning' in Greek. Very few people anywhere in Apulia actually still speak Greek, though their thick dialect has led many writers into thinking so; the Greeks that are left are more likely to be descendants of refugees from Albania than of the ancient Greek colonists.

Nearby **Copertino**, in the early 17th century, was the home of the original flying monk. St Joseph of Copertino, a carpenter's son born in a stable, was a simple fellow if his many biographers are to be believed, but he got himself canonized for his nearly effortless talent for levitating. Thousands saw him do it, including the pope's emissaries, a king of Poland, and a Protestant German duke, who immediately converted. Joseph's heart is buried under the altar of the little church named after him. Copertino also has a large Angevin **castle**.

Along the Ionian coast, **Porto Cesareo** is a peculiar little resort, facing two islets inhabited entirely by rabbits. **Gallipoli**, like its namesake on the Hellespont, was once thought of highly by somebody; the name comes from the Greek *kalli poli*, or 'beautiful city'. The old quarter still has a Greek air about it, with whitewashed houses scoured by the sea air and fishermen folding their nets in the little port. The oldest part was once an island, now bound to the mainland and dominated by a huge **castle** with squat rounded bastions; parts of it date back to the Byzantines. There is a Baroque **cathedral** that would look right at home in Lecce, but the unexpected attraction is a Greek **nymphaion**, a trough-like fountain decorated with caryatids and badly faded mythological reliefs. In itself it isn't much, but for such a thing to survive the Christians and the barbarians is rare; there are few in Greece itself, and this is the only one in Italy.

Gallipoli has the best sort of **museum**—nothing pretentious, nothing even labelled, but good fun in a big atrium lined with dusty bookshelves, and full of cutlasses, whale bones, old cannonballs, coins and amphorae, even a crocodile skeleton (on Via De Pace; in summer daily 8:30–12:30, 5:30–8:30; Sun 10–12:30; in winter, daily 8:30–1, 4:30–6:30, Sun 10–12).

Down the coast, the Salentine's southern tip, not surprisingly, is called Land's End—*Finibus Terrae*. The spot is marked by the church of **Santa Maria di Leuca**, built over the ruins of a Temple of Minerva that must have been a familiar landmark to all ancient mariners. The church's altar stone served the same purpose in the original temple. As in the Land's Ends of Celtic Europe, this corner of the Salentine has quite a few standing stones and dolmens, left from the days of the Messapians or perhaps even earlier. The most important Neolithic monument is called the **Centopietre**—'hundred stones'—near the village of Patù; it is a small temple of two aisles divided by columns, with flat stone slabs for a roof.

Coming back up the Adriatic side towards Otranto, the coast is lined with caves, many showing evidence of Stone-Age habitation or later religious uses. The **Grotte Zin-zulusa**, hung with stalactites, may be one worth visiting. Just to the north is a thermal spa, **Santa Cesarea**, built around a charming neo-Moorish bathhouse.

Otranto

Readers of Gothic novels might choose to leave **Otranto** out of their itineraries, but there's no reason to be afraid. Horace Walpole, when he was writing his *Castle of Otranto*, had never heard of the place; he merely picked the name off a map. There really is a **castle**, built by the Aragonese in the 1490s, but it is largely in ruins. Otranto today, (stress on the first syllable, as in most Apulian towns) despite a long and proud history, is best known as a departure point for car ferries to Greece.

Although originally a Messapian settlement, the city first entered the Mediterranean consciousness as Greek *Hydruntion*, conquered and probably resettled by Taras; its proud citizens still refer to themselves as *Idruntini*. The city rivalled Brindisi as Rome's window on the east, and later reappeared in the 11th century as one of the leading Crusader ports. Otranto's finest hour came in 1480, during Naples' wars with the Turks and their Venetian allies; according to a delicately embroidered old legend, Turkish pirates sacked the city, killing some 12,000 or so, and massacred the 800 survivors when they refused, to a man, to forsake Christianity. The place hasn't been the same since; only recently, and thanks to the ferry business, Otranto is beginning to regain the size and importance it had in the Middle Ages.

If you're not bound for Greece, the best reason for visiting will be the **cathedral**, begun in the 11th century by the Normans, and the only one in the south to have conserved an entire medieval **mosaic pavement**. H. V. Morton wrote that coming here felt like 'walking on the Bayeux tapestry'. The vigorous, primitive early medieval figures are the work of a priest named Pantaleone, from about 1165. Three great trees stand at the centre of his composition, supporting small encircled images that encompass all creation: scriptural scenes, animals, heroes, symbols of the months and seasons. If you look carefully, you can find Alexander the Great, and even King Arthur.

WHERE TO STAY

Brindisi's hotel-keepers, accustomed to folks staying just overnight while waiting for the boat to Greece, have not been inspired to exert themselves, and there are no really outstanding places in the city. The best is the ******Internazionale**, at Lungomare Regina Margherita 26, very convenient for the ferry docks. This is an older hotel, though very well kept; you're likely to encounter grandmotherly furnishings, and maybe you'll get one of the rooms with a marble fireplace (tel (0831) 23 473; L110 000). The *****Barsotti** is a plain, but acceptable place, near the train station at Via Cavour 1, tel (0831) 21 997 (L60–75 000).

Lecce's hotels are like the town itself: quiet, tasteful and restrained. The best of them is an attractive, gracious, older establishment, the *****Risorgimento**, in the centre at Via Imperatore Augusto 19, tel (0832) 42 125 (L100 000). Near the station, the *****Grand Hotel** offers a bit of faded elegance for L54 000 without bath, L78 000 with (Viale Quarta 28, tel (0832) 29 405). In Gallipoli, most of the accommodation is on the outlying beaches; there are some fine modern resort hotels at Baia Verde: *******Grand Hotel Costa Brada**, Via Litoranea, tel (0833) 22 551 (L125–175 000) and the *****Le Sireneuse**, Via Litoranea, tel (0833) 22 536 (L95–120 000)—both typical white Mediterranean palaces, and both have good restaurants. Otranto, and all the inland towns, all have only the most basic accommodation.

EATING OUT

Right behind the Appian Way column in Brindisi, you can enjoy excellent seafood in a beautifully restored old palazzo at the **L'Antica Trattoria**, Via Colonne 49, tel (0831) 26 005; with some dishes the bill can go as high as L40 000. For something a little simpler, but still good, **Il Gabbiano** on Via Lungomare, tel (0831) 529 769—a fine seafood mixed grill, or roast lamb and other specialities if you're getting tired of fish (about L25 000). Vegetarians and fish lovers will find contentment at **La Botte**, Corso Garibaldi 72, tel (0831) 28 400; chicory and artichoke starters, simple but tasty pasta dishes, shellfish soups and lobster salad (L25–30 000, closed Tues and Nov).

Lecce is an inland city, but the sea isn't far, and most of the city's restaurants have always specialized in fish. One new and popular place, on Via Idomeneo in the northern part of the old town, is **I Tarocchi**, tel (0832) 29 925, known for *zuppa di pesce* and seafood crêpes (L35 000). Another winner, though a little bit distant from the centre, is **Gino e Gianni**, with a long list of seafood dishes prepared according to the local traditions (Via IV Finite 2, tel (0832) 45 888; L30–36 000). Also in Lecce, **Carlo V**, Via Palmieri 46, tel (0832) 54 151, has more fish, but also a few unusual dishes—risotto with truffles, duck with orange, pepper steak, all served in the pleasant surroundings of one of the older palazzi (L30–40 000). Less expensively, **Gala**, Via U. Foscolo 53, tel (0832) 28 432, has a varied menu with a touch of Sardinia, as well as Scottish smoked salmon *crostini*, pappardelle with prosciutto and mushrooms, mixed meats, roast Sard cheeses and Tiramisù at the end, all for around L25 000; closed Sun eve and Mon. In Gallipoli, **Marechiaro**, Lungomare Marconi, tel (0833) 476 143 offers traditional fish and grilled meats. It attracts the occasional celebrity, though not because of its prices (L25–30 000; closed Tues in winter).

ARCHITECTURAL, ARTISTIC
AND HISTORICAL TERMS

Acroterion: decorative protrusion on the rooftop of an Etruscan, Greek, or Roman temple. At the corners of the roof they are called *antefixes*.

Aedicule: a decorative niche, often a free-standing shrine dedicated to a god.

Ambones: twin pulpits in some southern churches (singular: *ambo*), often elaborately decorated.

Atrium: entrance court of a Roman house or early church.

Badia: *abbazia*, an abbey or abbey church.

Baldacchino: baldachin, a columned stone canopy above the altar of a church.

Basilica: a rectangular building, usually divided into three aisles by rows of columns. In Rome this was the common form for lawcourts and other public buildings, and Roman Christians adapted it for their early churches.

Calvary chapels: a series of outdoor chapels, usually on a hillside, that commemorate the stages of the Passion of Christ.

Campanile: a bell tower.

Campanilismo: local patriotism; the Italians' own word for their historic tendency to be more faithful to their home towns than to the abstract idea of 'Italy'.

Camposanto: a cemetery.

Cardo: transverse street of a Roman *castrum*-shaped city.

Carroccio: a wagon carrying the banners of a medieval city and an altar; it served as the rallying point in battles.

Cartoon: the preliminary sketch for a fresco or tapestry.

Caryatid: supporting pillar or column carved into a standing female form; male versions are called *telamones*.

Castrum: a Roman military camp, always neatly rectangular, with straight streets and gates at the cardinal points. Later the Romans founded or refounded cities in this form, hundreds of which survive today (Ostia is a clear example).

Cavea: the semicircle of seats in a classical theatre.

Ciborium: a tabernacle; the word is often used for large, freestanding tabernacles, or in the sense of a baldacchino.

Comune: commune, or commonwealth, referring to the governments of the free cities of the Middle Ages. Today it denotes any local government, from the Comune di Roma down to the smallest village.

Condottiere: the leader of a band of mercenaries in late medieval and Renaissance times.

Confraternity: a religious lay brotherhood, often serving as a neighbourhood mutual-aid and burial society, or following some specific charitable work (Michelangelo, for example, belonged to one that cared for condemned prisoners in Rome).

Cosmati work, or *Cosmatesque*: referring to a distinctive style of inlaid marble or enamel chips used in architectural decoration (pavements, pulpits, paschal candlesticks, etc.); the Cosmati school of Rome were its greatest practitioners.

Cryptoporticus: any vaulted or colonnaded underground room or passage.

Cupola: a dome.

Cyclopean walls: fortifications built of enormous, irregularly-shaped polygonal blocks, as in the pre-Roman cities of Latium.

Decumanus: street of a Roman *castrum*-shaped city parallel to the longer axis, the central, main avenue called the Decumanus Major or Maximus.

Duomo: cathedral.

Ex-voto: an offering (a terracotta figurine, painting, silver bauble, medallion or whatever) made in thanksgiving to a god or Christian saint; the practice has always been present in Italy.

Forum: the central square of a Roman town, with its most important temples and public buildings. The word means 'outside', as the original Roman Forum was outside the first city walls.

Fresco: wall painting, the most important Italian medium of art since Etruscan times. It isn't easy; first the artist draws the *sinopia* (q.v.) on the wall. This is covered with plaster, but only a little at a time, as the paint must be on the plaster before it dries. Leonardo da Vinci's endless attempts to find clever shortcuts ensured that little of his work would survive.

Ghibellines: one of the two great medieval parties, the supporters of the Holy Roman Emperors.

Grotesques: carved or painted faces used in Etruscan and later Roman decoration; Raphael and other artists rediscovered them in the 'grotto' of Nero's Golden House in Rome.

Guelphs: (see *Ghibellines*). The other great political faction of medieval Italy, supporters of the Pope.

Hypogeum: an underground burial cavern.

Intarsia: work in inlaid wood or marble.

Laura: a Greek cave-chapel or monastic cell of southern Apulia, often with frescoes.

Lozenge: the diamond shape—along with stripes, one of the trademarks of Pisan architecture.

Naumachia: a mock naval battle, like those staged in the Colosseum.

Narthex: the enclosed porch of a church.

Nymphaeum: originally a temple of the nymphs, later any decorative pavilion, well house or fountain, often with statues of nymphs or marine deities.

Opus reticulatum: common Roman masonry consisting of small diamond-shaped blocks.

Palazzo: not just a palace, but any large, important building (though the word comes from the Imperial *palatium* on Rome's Palatine Hill).

Pantocrator: Christ 'ruler of all', a common subject for apse paintings and mosaics in areas influenced by Byzantine art.

Polyptych: an altarpiece composed of more than three panels.

Predella: smaller paintings on panels below the main subject of a painted altarpiece.

Presepio: a Christmas crib.

Pulvin: stone, often trapezoidal, that supports or replaces the capital of a column; decoratively carved examples can be seen in many medieval cloisters.

Putti: flocks of plaster cherubs with rosy cheeks and bums that infested much of Italy in the Baroque era.

Quadriga: chariot pulled by four horses.

Quattrocento: the 1400s—the Italian way of referring to centuries (*duecento*, *trecento*, *quattrocento*, *cinquecento*, etc.).

Sinopia: the layout of a fresco (q.v.), etched by the artist on the wall before the plaster is applied. Often these are works of art in their own right.

Stele: a vertical funeral stone.

Stigmata: a miraculous simulation of the bleeding wounds of Christ, appearing in holy men like St Francis in the 12th century.

Telamone: see *caryatid*.

Thermae: Roman baths.

Tondo: round relief, painting or terracotta.

Transenna: marble screen separating the altar area from the rest of an early Christian church.

Travertine: hard, light-coloured stone, sometimes flecked or pitted with black, sometimes perfect, the most widely used material in ancient and modern Rome.

Triclinium: the main hall of a Roman house, used for dining and entertaining.

Triptych: a painting, especially an altarpiece, in three sections.

Trompe l'oeil: art that uses perspective effects to deceive the eye—for example, to create the illusion of depth on a flat surface, or to make columns and arches painted on a wall seem real.

Tympanum: the semicircular space, often bearing a painting or relief, above the portal of a church.

CHRONOLOGY

* = Traditional Date

c.7000 BC	Beginnings of the Neolithic Age
c.3000	Arrival of Indo-Europeans
c.2000	Bronze Age technology reaches Italy
c.900	Arrival of Etruscans in Italy
*753	Legendary founding of Rome by Romulus
c.775	Greek colonization of S. Italy begins (Pithecusa)
*750	Rape of the Sabine women; Greeks found Cumae
*747	Tarpeia betrays capital to Sabines
c.723	Founding of Rhegium (Règgio Calabria)
*715	Numa Pompilius, First Pontifex Maximus
*616	Etruscan king Tarquinius Priscus lays out the Forum and Circus Maximus
*579	King Servius Tullius develops Roman class system
*535	Pythagoras visits Magna Graecia
525	Greek victory over Etruscans at Cumae
*510	Tarquin the Proud consecrates Temple of Capitoline Jupiter Destruction of Sybaris by Croton
*509	Rape of Lucretia; Roman Republic established
*501	Latins, egged on by Tarquins, declare war on Rome
*499	Roman victory of Lake Regillus over Latins
*494	Tribunate established to defend plebeian interests; Rome founds Latin League of Cities
*491	Roman war with Volscians and Aequians
450	Aventine Succession/Twelve Tables codified
434	Rome fights the Etruscans
c.430–365	Archytas of Taras
423	Samnites take Capua, expand to coast
396	Romans defeat and destroy Veii
390	Gauls sack Rome
388	Plato visits Taras
351	Rome annexes southern Etruria
343	First Samnite War; Rome annexes Campania
327–304	Second Samnite War
326	Rome captures Naples
321	Roman defeat at the Caudine Forks
312	Appian Way begun by censor Appius Claudius
298–290	Third Samnite War
281	Pyrrhus leads Tarantines against Rome
275	Rome finally defeats Pyrrhus at Beneventum

272	Rome annexes Tarantum
264–41	First Punic War
238	Rome annexes Sardinia and Corsica
236–22	Romans conquer Po Valley from Gauls
219	Second Punic War; Hannibal crosses the Alps
216	Battle of Cannae, Rome's worst defeat, by Hannibal
212	Rome captures Sicily
202	Battle of Zama, Scipio Africanus takes Carthage
200–168	Rome conquers Greece
149–46	Third Punic War; salt sown on site of Carthage
133–121	Agrarian reforms; murders of Tiberius and Caius Gracchus
112	North African war against Jugurtha
106	Birth of Cicero
100	Julius Caesar born, 12 July
92–89	Social Wars, factions led by Marius and Sulla; Sulla becomes dictator
73	Rebellion of Spartacus
70	Birth of Virgil
60–50	First Triumvirate: Caesar, Pompey, and Crassus
51	Caesar conquers Gaul
50	Caesar crosses the Rubicon and seizes Rome
48	Caesar defeats Pompey at Pharsalia and dallies with Cleopatra
45	Caesar declared 'imperator', the greatest of generals
44	Caesar done in by friends
43–32	Second Triumvirate: Octavian, Mark Antony, and Lepidus
42	Battle of Philippi; Brutus and Cassius defeated
34	Agrippa constructs Aqua Julia
31	Battle of Actium leaves Octavian sole rule of Empire
27	Octavian proclaimed Princeps, changes name to Augustus
19	Death of Virgil
AD	
14	Tiberius emperor
17	Deaths of Livy and Ovid
27	Tiberius moves to Capri
37	Caligula emperor
41	Claudius emperor
42	St Peter comes to Rome
54	Nero emperor
64	Great Fire destroys much of Rome
67	Martyrdom of SS. Peter and Paul
69	Vespasian emperor
79	Pompeii and Herculaneum buried in ashes and lava; Titus emperor
81	Colosseum completed; Domitian emperor
96	Nerva, the first of the 'five good emperors'
98	Trajan emperor
117	Hadrian emperor
138	Antoninus Pius emperor

161	Marcus Aurelius emperor
164–180	Great plague decimates Roman Empire
180	Commodus emperor
193	Septimius Severus emperor
211	Caracalla emperor
217	Elagabalus emperor
222	Alexander Severus
235	Roman military machine runs down into anarchy; Maximin emperor
247	Wild celebrations of Rome's millennium
250–270	Roman military disasters in Germany
269	Claudius II soundly defeats Goths
270	Dacia ceded to Goths; Aurelian emperor
275	Aurelian builds Rome's walls
305	Diocletian's reforms turn the Empire into a bureaucratized despotism
296	Severe persecutions of Christians
306	Constantine emperor
312	Constantine wins Battle of Milvian Bridge with Christian cross on banner
313	Edict of Milan stating tolerance of Christianity
323	Empire reunited
326	First basilica of St Peter built
330	Constantine orders pagan temples closed; capital moved to Constantinople
379	Theodosius emperor
382	Severe persecutions of pagans
402–5	Vandal general Stilicho defends Italy from Goths
408	Stilicho murdered on Emperor Honorius' orders
410	Alaric the Goth sacks Rome
455	Genseric the Vandal sacks Rome
475	Western Empire ends as last emperor Romulus Augustulus pensioned off to Naples; Byzantium becomes seat of empire
476	Goths rule Rome; Odoacer King of Italy
493	Ostrogoths defeat Odoacer; Theodoric King of Italy in Ravenna
496	Anastasius II, first pope to take title of Pontifex Maximus
498	Rival popes fight street battles in Rome
527	Justinian emperor in east
536–53	Greek-Gothic Wars; Rome falls to Belisarius
547	Totila the Goth sacks Rome; city is abandoned; Totila holds last games in Circus Maximus
547	Belisarius comes back
549	Totila does it again
553	Byzantine Narses abolishes Roman Senate, founds Exarchate in Ravenna to rule West
567	Lombards overrun much of Italy
571	Lombard Duchy of Benevento founded
590	Plague and famine in Rome; Gregory the Great pope

361

c. 603	Lombards convert to Christianity
664	Eastern Emperor Constans visits Rome, campaigns against Lombards of Benevento
717	Iconoclasm in East; Leo III (the Isaurian) emperor in East
750s	Campaigns of Pepin the Short increase temporal power of popes
751	Lombards capture Ravenna; end of Exarchate
763	Naples becomes an independent city
778	Charlemagne defeats the last Lombard king
786	Amalfi becomes an independent city
800	Leo III crowns Charlemagne Holy Roman Emperor
814	Forged 'Donations of Constantine and Pepin' spur temporal ambitions of popes
817	Carolingian Renaissance in Rome; Pope Paschal I
827	First Saracen raids
846	Saracens attack Rome, sack the Vatican; end of Lombard Duchy of Benevento
871	End of Saracen Emirate of Bari
877	Paestum destroyed by Saracen raiders
880–96	Theodora Senatrix and her daughter Marozia rule Rome
896	Germans under Arnulf capture Rome
932	Alberic revolts against mother, Marozia
955	Alberic's son becomes Princeps as Octavian and pope as John XII
962	Pope John XII crowns Saxon king Otto I, re-establishing the Holy Roman Empire
999	Pope Sylvester II (Gerbert)
1015	First Normans arrive in south Italy
1033–48	One of the worst popes, Benedict IX, elected and deposed three times
1061	Normans invade Sicily
1063	Merchants of Trani create first maritime code
1071	Normans capture Bari from Byzantines
1073	One of the best popes, Gregory VII (Hildebrand)
1077	Normans unsuccessfully besiege Naples
1084	Henry IV takes Rome; Robert Guiscard's Normans sack Rome while supposedly allied with the Pope
1080s	Revival of the arts at Montecassino under Desiderius
1087	Basilica of S. Nicola begun at Bari
1097	First Crusade begins
1105–54	King Roger II of Sicily
1135	Sack of Amalfi by Pisa
1145	Revolution of Arnold of Brescia; Roman Republic temporarily re-established
1152	Frederick I (Barbarossa), Holy Roman Emperor
1154–66	William I, the Bad, of Naples
1155	Adrian IV (Nicholas Breakspear), only English pope, executes Arnold of Brescia
1156	William the Bad destroys Bari

1166–89	William II, the Good, of Naples
1194	Emperor Henry IV conquers the south
1197–1250	Frederick II (Stupor Mundi) Holy Roman Emperor and King of Sicily
1198	Innocent III; high-water mark of medieval papacy
1224	Frederick founds University of Naples
1231	Constitutions of Melfi
c.1240	Castel del Monte built; L'Aquila founded
1250–54	Conrad IV, of Sicily
1254–66	Manfred, of Sicily
1260	Charles of Anjou invades Italy at behest of the Pope
1266	Charles defeats Manfred at Benevento
1266–68	Conradin, of Sicily
1268	Charles wins again at Tagliacozzo, executes last Hohenstaufen, Conradin
1278	Papal states chartered in deal with Emperor Rudolph
1282	Revolt of the 'Sicilian Vespers'
1294	Pope Celestine V tricked into abdicating
1300	First Holy Year brings Rome big profits
1302	'Slap of Anagni'; humiliation of Boniface VIII
1309	Clement V moves papacy to Avignon, the 'Babylonian Captivity'
1309–43	Robert the Wise, of Sicily
1343–81	Joan I, of Sicily
1347	Cola di Rienzo's May–December Roman republic
1354	Cola di Rienzo returns, assassinated in October
1364	Cardinal Albornoz conquers central Italy for Pope Urban V
1377	Gregory XI returns papacy to Rome
1386–1414	Ladislas, of Naples
1435	Alfonso the Magnanimous takes Naples, rules to 1458
1447–55	Renaissance patron, Pope Nicholas IV
1458–94	Ferdinand I ('Ferrante'), of Naples
1462	Pro-Angevin revolt defeated in Apulia
1480	Turks temporarily seize Otranto
1492	Election of Alexander VI (Borgia)
1494	Charles VIII of France invades Italy
1503	The 'Challenge of Barletta'
1503	Gonsalvo di Córdoba defeats French; South Italy passes under direct Spanish rule
1508	Michelangelo begins Sistine Chapel ceiling for Julius II
1519–56	Emperor Charles V
1522	Adrian VI, last foreign pope before John Paul II
1527	Troops of Charles V sack Rome (6 May)
1532	Don Pedro de Toledo viceroy at Naples
1534	Michelangelo paints *Last Judgement* for Paul III; founding of the Jesuits by Spaniard, St Ignatius
1538	New volcano appears near Naples: Monte Nuovo
1540	Pope Paul IV unleashes Inquisition on Italy

1559	Treaty of Cateau-Cambresis confirms Spanish control of Italy
1563	Council of Trent initiates Counter-Reformation
1564	Death of Michelangelo
1571	Battle of Lepanto
1572	Gregory XIII introduces reforms of Julian calendar
1585	Sixtus V plans monumental Rome
1600	Giordano Bruno burned at the stake for heresy
1606	Caravaggio murders man over tennis match, has to flee Rome
1626	Consecration of St Peter's Basilica
1647	Masaniello's Revolt in Naples
1656	Great plague in Apulia; Bari loses 80 per cent of its population
1668	Birth of Giambattista Vico
1700–13	War of the Spanish Succession
1713	South passes to Austrian rule
1734–59	Charles III, of Naples, first Bourbon king
1783	Great earthquake at Règgio Calabria
1798	French abduct Pope, declare Rome a republic
1805–6	Napoleon subdues Kingdom of Naples
1806	British victory at Maida
1808	Napoleon annexes Rome as free city in French Empire
1808–15	Joachim Murat king
1818–25	Ferdinand IV, of the 'Two Sicilies'
1820	Constitutionalist revolts in Naples
1849–66	French troops rule Rome
1859–60	Garibaldi's Thousand conquers Sicily and Naples
1870	Italian army enters Rome, 20 September; 9 October, Rome made capital of united Italy under King Vittorio Emanuele II
1908	Second great earthquake at Règgio Calabria, city destroyed
1922	Mussolini marches on Rome
1929	Lateran Treaty creates Vatican City
1943	Allied invasion of Italy, Neapolitan revolt of the 'Quattro Giornate'
1944	Landings at Anzio; liberation of Rome; last eruption of Vesuvius
1945	Vittorio Emanuele III abdicates
1946	National referendum makes Italy a republic
1957	Treaty creating European Common Market signed in Rome
1960	Olympic Games in Rome
1962	John XXIII's Second Vatican Council initiates major church reforms
1978	Assassination of Aldo Moro
1980	Major earthquake causes severe damage in Campania

LANGUAGE

The fathers of modern Italian were Dante, Manzoni, and television. Each did his part in creating a national language from an infinity of regional and local dialects; the Florentine Dante, the first 'immortal' to write in the vernacular, did much to put the Tuscan dialect in the foreground of Italian literature. Manzoni's revolutionary novel, *I promessi sposi* (The Betrothed), heightened national consciousness by using an everyday language all could understand in the 19th century. Television in the last few decades is performing an even more spectacular linguistic unification; although the majority of Italians still speak a dialect at home, school, and work, their TV idols insist on proper Italian.

Perhaps because they are so busy learning their own beautiful but grammatically complex language, Italians are not especially apt at learning others. English lessons, however, have been the rage for years, and at most hotels and restaurants there will be someone who speaks some English. In small towns and out of the way places, finding an Anglophone may prove more difficult. The words and phrases below should help you out in most situations, but the ideal way to come to Italy is with some Italian under your belt; your visit will be richer, and you're much more likely to make some Italian friends.

Italian words are pronounced phonetically. Every vowel and consonant (except 'h') is sounded. Consonants are the same as in English, except the *c* which, when followed by an 'e' or 'i', is pronounced like the English 'ch' (*cinque* thus becomes cheenquay). Italian *g* is also soft before 'i' or 'e' as in *gira*, pronounced jee-ra. *H* is never sounded; *z* is pronounced like 'ts'. The consonants *sc* before the vowels 'i' or 'e' become like the English 'sh' as in *sci*, pronounced shee; *ch* is pronouced like a 'k' as in *Chianti*, kee-an-tee; *gn* as 'ny' in English (*bagno*, pronounced ban-yo; while *gli* is pronounced like the middle of the word million (*Castiglione*, pronounced Ca-steely-oh-nay).

Vowel pronunciation is: *a* as in English father; *e* when unstressed is pronounced like 'a' in fate as in *mele*, when stressed can be the same or like the 'e' in pet (*bello*); *i* is like the i in machine; *o* like 'e', has two sounds, 'o' as in hope when unstressed (*tacchino*), and usually 'o' as in rock when stressed (*morte*); *u* is pronounced like the 'u' in June.

The accent usually (but not always!) falls on the penultimate syllable. Also note that in the big northern cities, the informal way of addressing someone as you, *tu*, is widely used; the more formal *lei* or *voi* is commonly used in provincial districts.

Useful words and phrases

yes/no/maybe	si/no/forse
I don't know	Non lo so
I don't understand (Italian)	Non capisco (italiano)
Does someone here	C'è qualcuno qui
speak English?	chi parla inglese?
Speak slowly	Parla lentamente
Could you assist me?	Potrebbe aiutarmi?

Help!	Aiuto!
Please	Per favore
Thank you (very much)	(Molto) grazie
You're welcome	Prego
It doesn't matter	Non importa
All right	Va bene
Excuse me	Scusi
Be careful!	Attenzione!
Nothing	Niente
It is urgent!	E urgente!
How are you?	Come sta?
Well, and you?	Bene, e lei?
What is your name?	Come si chiama?
Hello	Salve *or* ciao (both informal)
Good morning	Buongiorno (formal hello)
Good afternoon, evening	Buona sera (also formal hello)
Good night	Buona notte
Goodbye	Arrivederla (formal), arrivederci, ciao (informal)
What do you call this in Italian	Come si chiama questo in italiano?
What	Che
Who	Chi
Where	Dove
When	Quando
Why	Perchè
How	Come
How much	Quanto
I am lost	Mi sono smarrito
I am hungry	Ho fame
I am thirsty	Ho sede
I am sorry	Mi dispiace
I am tired	Sono stanco
I am sleepy	Ho sonno
I am ill	Mi sento male
Leave me alone	Lasciami in pace
good	buono/bravo
bad	male/cattivo
It's all the same	Fa lo stesso
slow	piano
fast	rapido
big	grande
small	piccolo
hot	caldo
cold	freddo
up	su

down	giù
here	qui
there	lì

Shopping, service, sightseeing

I would like...	Vorrei...
Where is/are...	Dov'è/Dove sono...
How much is it?	Quanto viene questo?/Quante'è/Quanto costa questo?
open	aperto
closed	chiuso
cheap/expensive	a buon prezzo/caro
bank	banca
beach	spiaggia
bed	letto
church	chiesa
entrance	entrata
exit	uscita
hospital	ospedale
money	soldi
museum	museo
newspaper (foreign)	giornale (straniero)
pharmacy	farmacia
police station	commissariato
policeman	poliziotto
post office	ufficio postale
sea	mare
shop	negozio
room	camera
telephone	telefono
tobacco shop	tabaccaio
WC	toilette/bagno
men	Signori/Uomini
women	Signore/Donne

TIME	
What time is it?	Che ore sono?
month	mese
week	settimana
day	giorno
morning	mattina
afternoon	pomeriggio
evening	sera
today	oggi
yesterday	ieri

367

tomorrow	domani
soon	presto
later	dopo/più tarde
It is too early	E troppo presto
It is too late	E troppo tarde

DAYS

Monday	lunedì
Tuesday	martedì
Wednesday	mercoledì
Thursday	giovedì
Friday	venerdì
Saturday	sabato
Sunday	domenica

NUMBERS

one	uno/una
two	due
three	tre
four	quattro
five	cinque
six	sei
seven	sette
eight	otto
nine	nove
ten	dieci
eleven	undici
twelve	dodici
thirteen	tredici
fourteen	quattordici
fifteen	quindici
sixteen	sedici
seventeen	diciassette
eighteen	diciotto
nineteen	diciannove
twenty	venti
twenty-one	ventuno
twenty-two	ventidue
thirty	trenta
thirty-one	trentuno
forty	quaranta
fifty	cinquanta
sixty	sessanta
seventy	settanta
eighty	ottanta
ninety	novanta

hundred	cento
one hundred and one	cento uno
two hundred	duecento
thousand	mille
two thousand	due mila
million	milione
a thousand million	miliardo

TRANSPORT

airport	aeroporto
bus stop	fermata
bus/coach	auto/pulmino
railway station	stazione ferroviaria
train	treno
platform	binario
port	porto
port station	stazione marittima
ship	nave
automobile	macchina
taxi	tassi
ticket	biglietto
customs	dogana
seat (reserved)	posto (prenotato)

TRAVEL DIRECTIONS

I want to go to...	Desidero andare a...
How can I get to...?	Come posso andare a...?
Do you stop at...?	Ferma a...?
Where is...?	Dov'è...?
How far is it to...?	Quanto siamo lontani da...?
When does the... leave?	A che ora parte ...?
What is the name of this station?	Come si chiama questa stazione?
When does the next ... leave?	Quando parte il prossimo...?
From where does it leave?	Da dove parte?
How long does the trip take...?	Quanto tempo dura il viaggio?
How much is the fare?	Quant'è il biglietto?
Good trip!	Buon viaggio!
near	vicino
far	lontano
left	sinistra
right	destra
straight ahead	sempre diritto
forward	avanti
backward	in dietro
north	nord/settentrionale
south	sud/mezzogiorno

east	est/oriente
west	ovest/occidente
around the corner	dietro l'angolo
crossroads	bivio
street/road	strada
square	piazza

DRIVING

car hire	noleggio macchina
motorbike/scooter	motocicletta/Vespa
bicycle	bicicletta
petrol/diesel	benzina/gasolio
garage	garage
This doesn't work	Questo non funziona
mechanic	meccanico
map/town plan	carta/pianta
Where is the road to...?	Dov'è la strada per...?
breakdown	guasto *or* panna
driving licence	patente di guida
driver	guidatore
speed	velocità
danger	pericolo
parking	parcheggio
no parking	sosta vietato
narrow	stretto
bridge	ponte
toll	pedaggio
slow down	rallentare

Italian menu vocabulary

Antipasti
These before-meal treats can include almost anything; among the most common are:

Antipasto misto	mixed antipasto
Bruschetto	garlic toast
Carciofi (sott'olio)	artichokes (in oil)
Crostini	liver pâté on toast
Frutta di mare	seafood
Funghi (trifolati)	mushrooms (with anchovies, garlic, and lemon)
Gamberi al fagioli	prawns (shrimps) with white beans
Mozzarella (in carrozza)	buffalo cheese (fried with bread in batter)
Olive	olives
Prosciutto (con melone)	raw ham (with melon)
Salame	cured pork
Salsicce	dry sausage

Minestre e Pasta

These dishes are the principal typical first courses (*primo*) served throughout Italy.

Agnolotti	ravioli with meat
Cacciucco	spiced fish soup
Cannelloni	meat and cheese rolled in pasta tubes
Cappelletti	small ravioli, often in broth
Crespelle	crepes
Fettuccine	long strips of pasta
Frittata	omelette
Gnocchi	potato dumplings
Lasagne	sheets of pasta baked with meat and cheese sauce
Minestra di verdura	thick vegetable soup
Minestrone	soup with meat, vegetables, and pasta
Orecchiette	ear-shaped pasta, usually served with turnip greens
Panzerotti	ravioli filled with mozzarella, anchovies, and egg
Pappardelle alla lepre	pasta with hare sauce
Pasta e fagioli	soup with beans, bacon, and tomatoes
Pastina in brodo	tiny pasta in broth
Penne all'arrabbiata	quill shaped pasta in hot spicy sauce
Polenta	cake or pudding of corn semolina, prepared with meat or tomato sauce
Risotto (alla Milanese)	Italian rice (with saffron and wine)
Spaghetti all'Amatriciana	with spicy sauce of salt pork, tomatoes, onions, and chilli pepper
Spaghetti alla Bolognese	with ground meat, ham, mushrooms, etc.
Spaghetti alla carbonara	with bacon, eggs, and black pepper
Spaghetti al pomodoro	with tomato sauce
Spaghetti al sugo/ragu	with meat sauce
Spaghetti alle vongole	with clam sauce
Stracciatella	broth with eggs and cheese
Tagliatelle	flat egg noodles
Tortellini al pomodoro/panna/ in brodo	pasta caps filled with meat and cheese, served with tomato sauce/with cream/in broth
Vermicelli	very thin spaghetti

Second courses–Carne (Meat)

Abbacchio	milk-fed lamb
Agnello	lamb
Animelle	sweetbreads
Anatra	duck
Arista	pork loin

371

Arrosto misto	mixed roast meats
Bistecca alla fiorentina	Florentine beef steak
Bocconcini	veal mixed with ham and cheese and fried
Bollito misto	stew of boiled meats
Braciola	pork chop
Brasato di manzo	braised meat with vegetables
Bresaola	dried raw meat similar to ham
Capretto	kid
Capriolo	roe deer
Carne di castrato/suino	mutton/pork
Carpaccio	thin slices of raw beef in piquant sauce
Cassoeula	winter stew with pork and cabbage
Cervello (al burro nero)	brains (in black butter sauce)
Cervo	venison
Cinghiale	boar
Coniglio	rabbit
Cotoletta (alla Milanese/alla Bolognese)	veal cutlet (fried in breadcrumbs/with ham and cheese)
Fagiano	pheasant
Faraono (alla creta)	guinea fowl (in earthenware pot)
Fegato alla veneziana	liver and onions
Involtini	rolls (usually of veal) with filling
Lepre (in salmi)	hare (marinated in wine)
Lombo di maiale	pork loin
Lumache	snails
Maiale (al latte)	pork (cooked in milk)
Manzo	beef
Osso buco	braised veal knuckle with herbs
Pancetta	rolled pork
Pernice	partridge
Petto di pollo (alla fiorentina/bolognese/sorpresa)	boned chicken breast (fried in butter/with ham and cheese/stuffed and deep fried)
Piccione	pigeon
Pizzaiola	beef steak with tomato and oregano sauce
Pollo (alla cacciatora/alla diavola/alla Marengo)	chicken (with tomatoes and mushrooms cooked in wine/grilled/fried with tomatoes, garlic and wine)
Polpette	meatballs
Quaglie	quails
Rane	frogs
Rognoni	kidneys
Saltimbocca	veal scallop with prosciutto and sage, cooked in wine and butter
Scaloppine	thin slices of veal sautéed in butter
Spezzatino	pieces of beef or veal, usually stewed
Spiedino	meat on a skewer or stick

372

Stufato	beef braised in white wine with vegetables
Tacchino	turkey
Trippa	tripe
Uccelletti	small birds on a skewer
Vitello	veal

Pesce (Fish)

Acciughe or Alici	anchovies
Anguilla	eel
Aragosta	lobster
Aringa	herring
Baccalà	dried cod
Bonito	small tuna
Branzino	sea bass
Calamari	squid
Cappe sante	scallops
Cefalo	grey mullet
Coda di rospo	angler fish
Cozze	mussels
Datteri di mare	razor (or date) mussels
Dentice	dentex (perch-like fish)
Dorato	gilt head
Fritto misto	mixed fried delicacies, usually fish
Gamberetto	shrimp
Gamberi (di fiume)	prawns (crayfish)
Granchio	crab
Insalata di mare	seafood salad
Lampreda	lamprey
Merluzzo	cod
Nasello	hake
Orata	bream
Ostriche	oysters
Pesce spada	swordfish
Polipi/polpi	octopus
Pesce azzurro	various types of small fish
Pesce di San Pietro	John Dory
Rombo	turbot
Sarde	sardines
Seppie	cuttlefish
Sgombro	mackerel
Sogliola	sole
Squadro	monkfish
Tonno	tuna
Triglia	red mullet (rouget)
Trota	trout
Trota salmonata	salmon trout

Vongole	small clams
Zuppa di pesce	mixed fish in sauce or stew

Contorni (side dishes, vegetables)

Asparagi (alla fiorentina)	asparagus (with fried eggs)
Broccoli (calabrese, romana)	broccoli (green, spiral)
Carciofi (alla giudia)	artichokes (deep fried)
Cardi	cardoons, thistles
Carote	carrots
Cavolfiore	cauliflower
Cavolo	cabbage
Ceci	chickpeas
Cetriolo	cucumber
Cipolla	onion
Fagioli	white beans
Fagiolini	French (green) beans
Fave	broad beans
Finocchio	fennel
Funghi (porcini)	mushroom (boletus)
Insalata (mista, verde)	salad (mixed, green)
Lattuga	lettuce
Lenticchie	lentils
Melanzana (al forno)	aubergine/eggplant (filled and baked)
Mirtilli	bilberries
Patate (fritte)	potatoes (fried)
Peperoni	sweet peppers
Peperonata	stewed peppers, onions, etc. similar to ratatouille
Piselli (al prosciutto)	peas (with ham)
Pomodoro	tomato(es)
Porri	leeks
Radicchio	red chicory
Radice	radishes
Rapa	turnip
Sedano	celery
Spinaci	spinach
Verdure	greens
Zucca	pumpkin
Zucchini	zucchini (courgettes)

Formaggio (Cheese)

Bel Paese	a soft white cow's cheese
Cascio/Casciocavallo	pale yellow, often sharp cheese
Fontina	rich cow's milk cheese
Groviera	mild cheese (gruyère)
Gorgonzola	soft blue cheese
Parmigiano	Parmesan cheese

Pecorino	sharp sheep's cheese
Provalone	sharp, tangy cheese; *dolce* is more mild
Stracchino	soft white cheese

Frutta (Fruit, nuts)

Albicocche	apricots
Ananas	pineapple
Arance	oranges
Banane	banana
Cachi	persimmon
Ciliege	cherries
Cocomero	watermelon
Composta di frutta	stewed fruit
Dattero	date
Fichi	figs
Fragole (con panna)	strawberries (with cream)
Frutta di stagione	fruit in season
Lamponi	raspberries
Macedonia di frutta	fruit salad
Mandarino	tangerine
Melagrana	pomegranate
Mele	apples
Melone	melon
More	blackberries
Nespola	medlar fruit
Pera	pear
Pesca	peach
Pesca noce	nectarine
Pompelmo	grapefruit
Prugna/susina	plum
Uve	grapes

Dolci (Desserts)

Amaretti	macaroons
Cannoli	crisp pastry tubes filled with ricotta, cream, chocolate or fruit
Coppa gelato	assorted ice cream
Crema caramella	caramel topped custard
Crostata	fruit flan
Gelato (produzione propria)	ice cream (homemade)
Granita	flavoured ice, usually lemon or coffee
Monte Bianco	chestnut pudding with whipped cream
Panettone	sponge cake with candied fruit and raisins
Panforte	dense cake of chocolate, almonds, and preserved fruit
Saint Honoré	meringue cake

375

Semifreddo	refrigerated cake
Sorbetto	sorbet/sherbet
Spumone	a soft ice cream
Tiramisù	cream, coffee, and chocolate dessert
Torrone	nougat
Torta	cake, tart
Torta millefoglie	layered pastry with custard cream
Zabaglione	whipped eggs and Marsala wine, served hot
Zuppa inglese	trifle

Bevande/beverages

Acqua minerale con/senza gas	mineral water with/without fizz
Aranciata	orange soda
Birra (alla spina)	beer (draught)
Caffè (freddo)	coffee (iced)
Cioccolata (con panna)	chocolate (with cream)
Gassosa	lemon flavoured soda
Latte	milk
Limonata	lemon soda
Succo di frutta	fruit juice
Tè	tea
Vino (red, white, rosé)	wine (rosso, bianco, rosato)

Cooking terms, miscellaneous

Aceto (balsamico)	vinegar (balsamic)
Affumicato	smoked
Aglio	garlic
Alla brace	on embers
Bicchiere	glass
Burro	butter
Caccia	game
Conto	bill
Costoletta/Cotoletta	chop
Coltello	knife
Cotto adagio	braised
Cucchiaio	spoon
Filetto	fillet
Forchetta	fork
Forno	oven
Fritto	fried
Ghiaccio	ice
Griglia	grill
Limone	lemon
Magro	lean meat/or pasta without meat
Mandorle	almonds
Marmellata	jam

Menta	mint
Miele	honey
Mostarda	candied mustard sauce
Nocciole	hazelnuts
Noce	walnut
Olio	oil
Pane (tostato)	bread (toasted)
Panini	sandwiches
Panna	fresh cream
Pepe	pepper
Peperoncini	hot chilli peppers
Piatto	plate
Pignoli/pinoli	pine nuts
Prezzemolo	parsley
Ripieno	stuffed
Rosmarino	rosemary
Sale	salt
Salmi	wine marinade
Salsa	sauce
Salvia	sage
Senape	mustard
Tartufi	truffles
Tazza	cup
Tavola	table
Tovagliolo	napkin
Tramezzini	finger sandwiches
Umido	cooked in sauce
Uovo	egg
Zucchero	sugar

FURTHER READING

General and Travel

Barzini, Luigi, *The Italians* (Hamish Hamilton, 1964). A perhaps too clever account of the Italians by an Italian journalist living in London, but one of the classics.
Douglas, Norman, *Old Calabria* (Century, 1983). Reprint of a rascally travel classic.
Goethe, J. W., *Italian Journey* (Penguin Classics, 1982). An excellent example of a genius turned to mush by Italy; brilliant insights and big, big mistakes.
Guido, Margaret, *Southern Italy—An Archaeological Guide* (Faber & Faber, 1978).
Haycraft, John, *Italian Labyrinth* (Penguin, 1987). One of the latest attempts to unravel the Italian mess.
Hutton, Edward, *Rome* and *Naples and Campania Revisited* (Hollis & Carter, 1972).
Lewis, Norman, *Naples '44* (Eland, 1983). A riveting account of anarchy squared—full of insight into what makes Naples Naples.
Morton, H. V., *A Traveller in Rome, A Traveller in Southern Italy* (Methuen, 1957, 1969). Among the most readable and delightful accounts of the region in print. Morton is a sincere scholar, and a true gentleman. Also a good friend to cats.
Nichols, Peter, *Italia, Italia* (Macmillan, 1973). An account of modern Italy by an old Italy hand.
Revel, Jean-François, *As For Italy* (Weidenfeld and Nicolson, 1959). A devastating critique of modern Italy.

History

Acton, Harold, *The Bourbons of Naples* (Methuen, 1956).
Carcopino, Jérôme, *Daily Life in Ancient Rome* (Penguin, 1981). A thorough and lively account of Rome at the height of Empire—guaranteed to evoke empathy from modern city dwellers.
Bloch, Raymond, *The Etruscans* and *The Origins of Rome* (Thames and Hudson, 1958, 1960). Light cast on mysterious subjects.
Clark, Martin, *Modern Italy: 1871 to the Present Day* (Longman, 1983).
Grant, Michael, *History of Rome* (Faber & Faber, 1979). A good modern account of events up to the fall of Rome.
Hale, J. R., (ed.), *A Concise Encyclopaedia of the Italian Renaissance* (Thames and Hudson, 1981). An excellent reference guide, with many concise, well-written essays.
Herder, Harry, *Italy in the Age of the Risorgimento 1790–1870* (Longman, 1983). Light shed on a very confusing period.
Hibbert, Christopher, *Benito Mussolini* and *Rome: The Biography of a City* (Penguin, 1965, 1987).
Masson, Georgina, *Frederick II of Hohenstaufen* (London, 1957).

Procacci, Giuliano, *History of the Italian People* (Penguin, 1973). An in-depth view from the year 1000 to the present—also an introduction to the wit and subtlety of the best Italian scholarship

Art and Literature

Cellini, *Autobiography of Benvenuto Cellini* (Penguin, trans. by George Bull). Fun reading by a swashbuckling braggart and world-class liar.

Dante Alighieri, *The Divine Comedy* (plenty of equally good translations). Few poems have ever had such a mythical significance for a nation. Anyone serious about understanding Italy and the Italian world view will need more than a passing acquaintance with Dante.

Gilbert/Linscott, *Complete Poems and Selected Letters of Michelangelo* (Princeton Press, 1984).

Hamilton, Edith, *The Roman Way* (Norton, 1984). A charming look at the ancient Romans through the eyes of their own writers.

Henig, Martin, (ed.), *A Handbook of Roman Art* (Phaidon, 1983). A beautifully illustrated survey of visual arts produced by Rome and its empire.

Lawrence, D.H., *Etruscan Places* (Olive Press).

Levi, Carlo, *Christ Stopped at Eboli* (Penguin, 1982). Disturbing post-war realism.

Levy, Michael, *Early Renaissance* (1967) and *High Renaissance* (1975), both by Penguin. Old-fashioned accounts of the period, with a breathless reverence for the 1500s—but still full of intriguing interpretations.

Murray, Linda, *The High Renaissance* and *The Late Renaissance and Mannerism* (Thames and Hudson, 1977). Excellent introduction to the period; also Peter and Linda Murray, *The Art of the Renaissance* (Thames and Hudson, 1963).

Suetonius, Gaius, *The Twelve Caesars* (Penguin, 1957, trans. by Robert Graves). The sourcebook of scandal in the original Caesar's Palace.

Vasari, Giorgio, *Lives of the Artists* (Penguin, 1985). Readable, anecdotal accounts of the Renaissance greats by the father of art history, also the first professional Philistine.

Wittkower, Rudolf, *Art and Architecture in Italy 1600–1750* (Pelican, 1986). The classic on Italian Baroque, but fun to read, too, with plenty on Rome and Naples.

GENERAL INDEX

Note: Page references in *italics* indicate illustrations; references in **bold** indicate maps.

INDEX OF ARTISTS AND ARCHITECTS

Other Cadogan Guides available from your local bookshop or from the UK or the USA direct:

From the UK: Cadogan Books, 16 Lower Marsh, London SE1.
From the US: The Globe Pequot Press, 138 West Main Street, Chester, Connecticut 06412.

Title

Australia .... ☐
Bali .... ☐
The Caribbean (available November 1990) ...... ☐
Greek Islands (Update) .... ☐
India (Update) .... ☐
Ireland (Update available January 1991) .... ☐
Italian Islands (Update) .... ☐
Italy .... ☐
Morocco .... ☐
New York .... ☐
Northeast Italy .... ☐
Northwest Italy .... ☐
Portugal .... ☐
Rome .... ☐
Scotland (Update) .... ☐
South Italy .... ☐
Spain (Update) .... ☐
Thailand & Burma .... ☐
Turkey (Update) .... ☐
Tuscany & Umbria .... ☐
Venice (available September 1990) .... ☐
                                                                    ☐

Name ....

Address ....

.... Post Code ....

Date .... Order Number ....

Special Instructions ....

....

Please use these forms to tell us about the hotels or restaurants you consider to be special and worthy of inclusion in our next edition, as well as to give any general comments on existing entries. Please include your name and address on the order form on the reverse of this page.

Hotels

Name ....

Address ....

Tel.. Price of double room ....

Description/Comments ....

....

....

Name ....

Address ....

Tel.. Price of double room ....

Description/Comments ....

....

....

Name ....

Address ....

Tel.. Price of double room ....

Description/Comments ....

....

....

Name ....

Address ....

Tel.. Price of double room ....

Description/Comments ....

....

....

Restaurants

Name ....

Address ....

Tel... Price per person ....

Description/Comments ....

....

....

Name ....

Address ....

Tel... Price per person ....

Description/Comments ....

....

....

Name ....

Address ....

Tel... Price per person ....

Description/Comments ....

....

....

Name ....

Address ....

Tel... Price per person ....

Description/Comments ....

....

....

General Comments